Developments in Financial Reporting by Multinationals

The New Library of International Accounting

Series Editor: Christopher W. Nobes

PricewaterhouseCoopers Professor of Accounting, University of Reading, UK

Wherever possible, the articles in these volumes have been reproduced as originally published using facsimile reproduction, inclusive of footnotes and pagination to facilitate ease of reference.

For a list of all Edward Elgar published titles visit our site on the World Wide Web at
www.e-elgar.com

Developments in Financial Reporting by Multinationals

Edited by

Clare B. Roberts

Head
University of Aberdeen Business School, UK

THE NEW LIBRARY OF INTERNATIONAL ACCOUNTING

An Elgar Reference Collection
Cheltenham, UK • Northampton, MA, USA

Published by
Edward Elgar Publishing Limited
Glensanda House
Montpellier Parade
Cheltenham
Glos GL50 1UA
UK

Edward Elgar Publishing, Inc.
136 West Street
Suite 202
Northampton
Massachusetts 01060
USA

A catalogue record for this book is available from the British Library.

ISBN   1 84376 209 9

Printed and bound in Great Britain by MPG Books Ltd, Bodmin, Cornwall

Contents

Acknowledgements

The editor and publishers wish to thank the authors and the following publishers who have kindly given permission for the use of copyright material.

American Accounting Association for articles: Stephen R. Goldberg, Charles A. Tritschler and Joseph H. Godwin (1995), 'Financial Reporting for Foreign Exchange Derivatives', *Accounting Horizons*, **9** (2), June, 1–15; Carol A. Frost and Grace Pownall (1996), 'Interdependencies in the Global Markets for Capital and Information: The Case of Smithkline Beecham plc', *Accounting Horizons*, **10** (1), March, 38–57; Don Herrmann and Wayne B. Thomas (1997), 'Reporting Disaggregated Information: A Critique Based on Concepts Statement No. 2', *Accounting Horizons*, **11** (3), September, 35–44.

Blackwell Publishing Ltd for articles: Carol A. Frost and William R. Kinney, Jr (1996), 'Disclosure Choices of Foreign Registrants in the United States', *Journal of Accounting Research*, **34** (1), Spring, 67–84; Wayne B. Thomas (2000), 'The Value-relevance of Geographic Segment Earnings Disclosures Under SFAS 14', *Journal of International Financial Management and Accounting*, **11** (3), 133–55; Hollis Ashbaugh and Morton Pincus (2001), 'Domestic Accounting Standards, International Accounting Standards, and the Predictability of Earnings', *Journal of Accounting Research*, **39** (3), December, 417–34.

Canadian Academic Accounting Association for article: Eli Bartov (1997), 'Foreign Currency Exposure of Multinational Firms: Accounting Measures and Market Valuation', *Contemporary Accounting Research*, **14** (4), Winter, 623–52.

Elsevier Science for articles: Nandu J. Nagarajan and Sri S. Sridhar (1996), 'Corporate Responses to Segment Disclosure Requirements', *Journal of Accounting and Economics*, **21** (2), April, 253–75; Ajay Adhikari and Emmanuel N. Emenyonu (1997), 'Accounting for Business Combinations and Foreign Currency Translation: An Empirical Comparison of Listed Companies from Developed Countries', *Advances in International Accounting*, **10**, 45–62; Norvald Monsen and Wanda A. Wallace (1997), 'Norsk Hydro's Communication to International Capital Markets: A Blend of Accounting Principles', *Scandinavian Journal of Management*, **13** (1), March, 95–112; Gordon M. Bodnar and Joseph Weintrop (1997), 'The Valuation of the Foreign Income of US Multinational Firms: A Growth Opportunities Perspective', *Journal of Accounting and Economics*, **24** (1), December, 69–97; Catherine Craycraft, Stanley Sedo and David Gotlob (1998), 'Foreign Operations and the Choice of Inventory Accounting Methods', *Journal of International Accounting, Auditing and Taxation*, **7** (1), 81–93; Edwin R. Etter (1998), 'The Information Content of U.S. Versus Japanese GAAP Annual and Quarterly Earnings Announcements and their Relative Informativeness to Japanese Investors: A Small Sample Case Study', *Journal of International Accounting, Auditing and Taxation*, **7** (2), 233–49;

David A. Ziebart and Jong-Hag Choi (1998), 'The Difficulty of Achieving Economic Reality Through Foreign Currency Translation', *International Journal of Accounting*, **33** (4), 403–14; Donna L. Street, Sidney J. Gray and Stephanie M. Bryant (1999), 'Acceptance and Observance of International Accounting Standards: An Empirical Study of Companies Claiming to Comply with IASs', *International Journal of Accounting*, **34** (1), 11–48; Wayne B. Thomas (2000), 'A Test of the Market's Mispricing of Domestic and Foreign Earnings', *Journal of Accounting and Economics*, **28**, 243–67; Donna L. Street and Stephanie M. Bryant (2000), 'Disclosure Level and Compliance with IASs: A Comparison of Companies With and Without U.S. Listings and Filings', *International Journal of Accounting*, **35** (3), 305–29; Mark Whittington (2000), 'Problems in Comparing Financial Performance Across International Boundaries: A Case Study Approach', *International Journal of Accounting*, **35** (3), 399–413; Timothy S. Doupnik and Larry P. Seese (2001), 'Geographic Area Disclosures Under SFAS 131: Materiality and Fineness', *Journal of International Accounting, Auditing and Taxation*, **10** (2), 117–38; Hollis Ashbaugh (2001), 'Non-US Firms' Accounting Standard Choices', *Journal of Accounting and Public Policy*, **20**, 129–53; Vivek Mande and Richard Ortman (2002), 'The Effect of Japanese Business Segment Reporting on Analysts' Forecasts: Implications for US Investors and the SEC', *Journal of Accounting and Public Policy*, **21**, 31–70.

Emerald MCB University Press Ltd for articles: David Bailey, George Harte and Roger Sugden (2000), 'Corporate Disclosure and the Deregulation of International Investment', *Accounting, Auditing and Accountability Journal*, **13** (2), 197–218; Craig Deegan, Michaela Rankin and John Tobin (2002), 'An Examination of the Corporate Social and Environmental Disclosures of BHP from 1983–1997: A Test of Legitimacy Theory', *Accounting, Auditing and Accountability Journal*, **15** (3), 312–43.

Taylor and Francis Ltd (http://www.tandf.co.uk/journals) for articles: Kurt V. Auer (1996), 'Capital Market Reactions to Earnings Announcements: Empirical Evidence on the Difference in the Information Content of IAS-based Earnings and EC-Directives-based Earnings', *European Accounting Review*, **5** (4), 587–623; Juha Kinnunen, Jyrki Niskanen and Eero Kasanen (2000), 'To Whom are IAS Earnings Informative? Domestic versus Foreign Shareholders' Perspectives', *European Accounting Review*, **9** (4), 499–517.

Every effort has been made to trace all the copyright holders but if any have been inadvertently overlooked the publishers will be pleased to make the necessary arrangement at the first opportunity.

In addition the publishers wish to thank the Marshall Library of Economics, Cambridge University, the Library of the University of Warwick and the Library of Indiana University at Bloomington, USA for their assistance in obtaining these articles.

Introduction

Clare B. Roberts

One of the more important recent changes in accounting regulations was, for many multinational corporations, the introduction of a new standard on segment reporting, either SFAS #131 in the USA or the revised IAS #14 internationally. SFAS #131 in particular marked a fundamental move away from the earlier standards that it replaced (i.e. SFAS #14, 18, 24 and 30). Segments are no longer based upon external criteria, or the 'risks and rewards' approach, instead, it takes a managerial approach. Thus, the main or primary basis of segmentation is determined by the internal operating structure. The introduction of this standard has led to renewed interest in segment reporting by researchers. The first part of this book of readings is therefore devoted to the issue of segment reporting.

Chapter 1, by Herrmann and Thomas, looks at the extent to which the standard (or more specifically, the earlier exposure draft) meets the desirable qualitative characteristics of accounting information, as described by the FASB Conceptual Framework. This is an interesting, but unusual, approach to questions of the appropriateness of accounting standards. More common, especially in the USA, is work that considers the relevance of information in terms of whether or not it affects stock market behaviour. As this paper amply illustrates, there are also many other desirable qualitative characteristics. As Herrmann and Thomas conclude, the extent to which segment disclosures will meet the required qualitative characteristics depends crucially upon the specific information disclosed and, in particular, what the primary basis of segmentation is. A number of papers have sought to answer this question. For example, surveys by Herrmann and Thomas (2000) and Nichols *et al.* (2000) both conclude that, while the new standard has meant that some companies now report finer geographical segments (i.e. country level segments), the amount of geographical segment information has actually declined, as most companies do not organise their internal structures on a geographical basis. Street *et al.* (2000) instead conclude that a significant number of US companies still use geographical segment definitions that conflict with the narrative disclosures made elsewhere in the annual report and accounts. A similar study by Doupnik and Seese is reproduced in Chapter 2. This study concentrates upon geographic disclosures and looks in particular at the question of whether or not the disclosures made under SFAS #131 are finer than those that were made under SFAS #14.

While the first two chapters look at the position in the USA, obviously it is not only US companies that report segment information. Research in other countries is less common, probably because segment reporting has been less of an issue, but there have been a number of important research studies. For example, the introduction of segment reporting in Japan has been described by Ozu and Gray (2001) while Mande and Ortman (2002) have carried out empirical work. Their study on the impact of disclosures upon financial analysts' forecasts is reproduced in Chapter 3. They found that analysts' forecasts of sales improved following segmental reporting requirements, but earnings forecasts did not improve.

In the UK there have been similar studies of financial analysts' forecasts (Hussain, 1997) as well as some interesting work reporting the views of companies (Edwards and Smith, 1996). The findings of Edwards and Smith, that companies are often worried about the competitive disadvantage of segment disclosures, supports the theoretical work of Nagarajan and Sridhar in Chapter 4, this volume. They show that increased disclosure requirements may actually result in decreased disclosures. Using a two company model they demonstrate that this can happen when new requirements to disclose proprietary information mean that previously disclosed non-proprietary information becomes value-relevant when used in conjunction with the new information.

Chapter 5 is an empirical study by Thomas, who looks at the value relevance of segment earnings disclosures. He concludes that the information is useful. In addition, he finds that the market tends to value earnings from Europe and the UK more highly than it values earnings from domestic (i.e. USA) and South American segments.

While segment reporting involves a number of measurement issues, the segment standards are disclosure standards. The group of papers in Part II instead looks at a number of measurement issues. As explored in subsequent sections, international differences in measurement will affect the comparability of the figures reported by companies from different countries and they may also mean that a single company will report alternative figures complying with different sets of rules or GAAP. However, differences in rules internationally may affect companies in other ways as well. Chapter 6, by Craycraft *et al.*, looks at a major area where the USA is different from most other countries, namely inventory, or stock, valuation, where the USA allows companies to use last in, first out (LIFO). This paper uses this example to look at the question of whether or not accounting rules in foreign countries affect the accounting policies chosen in the domestic country. Specifically, it looks at the question of why some US companies choose to use first in, first out (FIFO) even though LIFO offered significant cash advantages during the period examined due to its impact upon taxable earnings. Using probit analysis, the authors find that the use of LIFO decreases as the importance of foreign operations increases. This suggests that there are other advantages to using FIFO for these companies. Two are suggested – either that there are significant accounting costs incurred when using different rules in different countries, or that the use of an unusual or unfamiliar accounting method decreases a company's competitiveness in international capital markets.

An obvious issue of accounting that is of prime importance to multinational corporations is foreign currency translation and this is the next issue covered in Part II. Most recent interest in this area has not focused upon economic consequences of the various alternative methods, but instead upon the value relevance of the information provided. In other words, does the disclosure of foreign currency translation information affect stock behaviour and is it therefore used in the market? One example of such study, by Bartov, is reproduced as Chapter 7. This builds upon earlier work by Bartov and Bodnar (1994, 1995) exploring the relationship between currency exchange rate changes and a firm's abnormal stock returns. The study reproduced here examines the value relevance of the US standards. It asks whether SFAS #8 (which called for the use of the temporal method) produced value relevant information and whether SFAS #52 (under which most companies use the closing rate method) is more value relevant. These two questions are explored by examining the association between foreign currency translation adjustments and changes in share prices. The paper shows that, as expected, stock market participants found the figures produced under SFAS #8 difficult to interpret. In contrast, where SFAS #52 led to the use of the closing rate method, the market was much better able to use the figures reported to evaluate equity in companies.

Chapter 8 by Bodnar and Weintrop looks at a related issue that is also relevant with respect to segmental disclosures – are domestic and foreign income both value relevant? They find that, for a sample of US multinationals, foreign income appears to be more closely associated with annual abnormal stock performance. This suggests that not only are there different growth opportunities between domestic and foreign operations but that foreign operations are perceived as having the better growth prospects at least as regards the USA. The evidence in the UK, for example, does not appear to support this conclusion (see Garrod and Rees, 1998). Chapter 9, by Thomas, also looks at the issue of the market's reactions to foreign operations. Using data for the period from 1988 when SFAS #131 became operative, to 1995, he found that foreign earnings tend to be more persistent or less transitory than domestic earnings. However, the market underestimates this persistence. As such it is possible, using information on foreign and domestic earnings, to construct a portfolio that generally earns abnormal returns.

Chapter 10, by Ziebart and Choi, offers a rather different insight into the usefulness of foreign currency translation information. It explores the issue of the extent to which this information is economically interpretable and so, at least potentially, of use to readers of accounts. They argue that, only if the figures reported in the group's financial statement are based upon current costs translated at a current exchange rate, are they potentially economically interpretable. However, even here the figures reported will misrepresent the underlying economic value if purchasing power parity does not hold. Using empirical evidence, they argue that the extent of misstatement can be very large, at least for some countries and some time periods.

Chapter 11 by Adhikari and Emenyonu, looks at the issues of foreign currency transactions and translation, and consolidation and goodwill. Using measures of harmonisation (similar to those used in several papers in Part 2 of Volume 1) the paper looks at the policies adopted by multinationals from France, Germany, Japan, UK and USA. The authors find substantial differences across the sample companies, especially with regard to goodwill amortisation periods and foreign currency transactions. The final chapter in this part by Goldberg *et al.* explores instead the issue of foreign exchange derivatives and their treatment in the USA. While most companies comply with the accounting requirements, these requirements are found to be deficient. In particular, there is too little information disclosed about market risk.

Part III moves on to look at the issue of financial reporting and stock markets. When looking at multinational companies, two issues are particularly interesting. Firstly, there is the issue of what information these companies disclose and how either dual listings or IAS rules affect their disclosures. Secondly, there is the related issue of whether stock market participants find the extra information contained in reconciliation statements or IAS-based statements useful.

Chapter 13 by Frost and Kinney looks at disclosure practices of US companies compared to foreign registrants in the USA. They find evidence that foreign companies are generally not as informative as US companies, in that they tend to file later and also often do not comply with all the US disclosure requirements. One reason for this may be that relatively little interest is shown in these companies in the USA, as evidenced by their smaller US analyst following, although, in contrast, they have a larger non-US analyst following than do the comparator US group of companies. Ashbaugh in Chapter 14 explores a rather different disclosure issue, namely, why companies choose to report foreign GAAP financial statements. Her sample is made up of non-US companies that report on the London exchange using either US or

International Accounting Standard (IAS) GAAP. The results suggest that companies will be more likely to do this as the number of exchanges they report on increases, and as they issue more new equity. In addition, they will only do so if they can provide more standardised financial statements relative to domestic GAAP statements. In addition, the evidence presented suggests that companies will choose IAS rather than US GAAP when they want some of the benefits of standardised information but do not want to incur the costs of implementing US GAAP.

Chapter 15 by Street and Bryant looks at the level of disclosures made by those companies that claim to follow IAS GAAP. They find that the level of disclosure and the extent of compliance with IAS disclosure rules are higher if companies also have a US listing. It also appears essential that, if we want high levels of compliance and disclosure, we should ensure that companies have audits that comment upon whether the statements meet IAS GAAP and that use International Auditing Standards when conducting the audit. Street *et al.* (Chapter 16, this volume) look at the accounting policies used by these same companies. They find a significant level of non-compliance with some of the IASs amongst those companies that claim to follow IAS. Areas where particular problems occur include the use of the lower of cost or market for valuing inventories, extraordinary items, capitalisation of development costs and goodwill and the disclosure of both pension costs and asset revaluation information.

The second strand of research in this part looks at the uses made of the information disclosed. Two main user groups have been examined – analysts and the stock market. In the first category are papers such as Fulkerson and Meek (1998), who add to the prior literature on the value relevance of reconciliation statements by exploring the confounding impact of analysts' forecasts, which often appear to pre-empt the information provided in reconciliation statements, so reducing their usefulness to the market. Chapter 17, by Ashbaugh and Pincus, instead looks at the accuracy of analysts' forecasts to see if these are affected by IASs. They find that IAS statements appear to be useful to analysts in that the greater the difference between IAS and domestic standards, the greater the forecast errors made, while forecast accuracy improves after companies adopt IAS.

There is also a growing strand of research looking at the value relevance of figures produced using different GAAP. Papers in Volume 3 – *Country Studies in International Accounting – Americas and the Far East* – explore the value relevance of the information provided in 20-F statements (US SEC filing requirements by non-US companies). Rees and Elgers (1997) build upon prior research suggesting that 20-Fs are value relevant. They instead look at initial registration documents and retrospective reconciliation statements and conclude that the value relevant information is actually fully impounded in share prices before the reconciliation statements are disclosed. Harris and Muller (1999) instead investigate the market valuation of IAS statements and US GAAP reconciliation statements. Although the reconciliation statement amounts are generally less when companies use IAS instead of domestic GAAP, they find that the US reconciliation statements are still value relevant. They also find that IAS and US GAAP earnings are valued differently by the market.

Three papers in this part look at the value relevance of various GAAP. Chapter 18 by Auer compares Swiss companies using domestic, IAS and EC based GAAP. He finds that IAS GAAP earnings have significantly higher information content than Swiss GAAP earnings, but they are not significantly more information relevant than EC GAAP based earnings. Chapter 19 by Kinnunen *et al.* looks instead at Finnish and IAS GAAP and their relevance to domestic and foreign investors. They similarly find that IAS GAAP information is more value relevant than domestic GAAP, at least for foreign investors and that this group also find IAS GAAP statements more useful than do the domestic investors. Turning instead to Japan, Etter in Chapter 20 finds that US GAAP based consolidated earnings are at least as value relevant as Japanese GAAP unconsolidated earnings to Japanese investors.

Having looked in Part III at the question of differences in reporting across jurisdictions using a cross-sectional approach, the final part looks at the reporting practices of individual companies over time. One interesting question is that of the extent to which companies cope with different sets of accounting rules and how, if at all, they change their reporting practices as they become more international. This is the issue explored in Chapter 24, by Monsen and Wallace (1997), who look at the reporting practices of Norsk Hydro, the largest company on the Oslo stock market. It is also listed on another eight exchanges, including New York. The paper documents the company's changing disclosure practices and the ways in which the US GAAP figures have been given greater prominence in the annual report over the 1980s and 1990s. While Norsk Hydro uses two sets of GAAP, this paper is not concerned with the issue of the impact of GAAP differences in the reported figures. However, this is of concern to Whittington (2000) in Chapter 25, who explores the reporting practices of one UK and one French steel company (British Steel and Usinor) over a period of up to 11 years. This study supports earlier work on Daimler Benz by Radebaugh *et al.* (1995), namely, that the magnitude and indeed direction of differences between local and foreign GAAP can change greatly from one year to the next. This appears to be especially the case for cyclical industries, suggesting that studies of GAAP differences which explore differences over only one or a very few years may reach misleading conclusions.

Rather than exploring the differences between the figures reported under various GAAP by individual companies, Chapter 23 by Frost and Pownall (1996) looks instead at differences in stock prices and returns in different stock markets using the example of the UK based company SmithKline Beecham. This company had large price and return differences between its equity which is traded in the USA and the UK and the paper discusses two sets of possible reasons for these differences – namely accounting differences (GAAP differences, disclosure differences or differences in investors' reactions to accounting information) and non-accounting differences (differences in the cash flows from dividends, share liquidity or interest in the company). The authors conclude that there is no evidence that accounting differences offer an explanation for equity performance differences (i.e. there is no evidence of market inefficiencies). Instead, they find significant differences between the two tax regimes, in share liquidity and in the interest shown by market participants in the company.

Chapter 22 by Deegan *et al.* (2002) looks at a rather different area of disclosure, namely social and environmental reporting. This is a study of an Australian multinational company, BHP, and provides an update to an earlier study of the same company by Guthrie and Parker (1989). It looks at whether the disclosures made reflect media interest and, in particular, negative media interest. This is of concern as the earlier study of BHP failed to find evidence to support legitimacy theory and so conflicts with many other studies of social or environmental reporting practices (see for example, Brown and Deegan (1998); Deegan and Gordon (1996) and Grolin (1998)). This study seems not to support Guthrie and Parker, instead it finds evidence to support legitimacy theory. Continuing with the general theme of expanding the set of disclosures made by multinational (or transnational) companies the first paper, Chapter 21 by Bailey *et al.*, takes as its starting point the general deregulation of multinationals and international investment as evidenced by such agreements as the General Agreement on Tariffs and Trade, North Atlantic Free Trade Agreement, Multilateral Agreement on Investment and the work of the World Trade Organisation. They argue that the size and geographical mobility of large multinationals creates problems for nation states who cannot assume that the current free trade philosophy results in optimal relationships between the nation state and the multinational. They argue that this means that there is a need for the better monitoring and, by extension, reporting, of the activities of these companies rather than simply an increase in the harmonisation of current accounting rules. While this type of argument is generally noticeable only by its absence in the accounting literature, it obviously has important implications for accountants and accounting regulators. While these are not explored in this paper, any monitoring and reporting would involve many of the issues already familiar to accountants from the financial reporting debates.

References

Bartov, E. and G.M. Bodnar (1994), 'Firm valuation, earnings expectations and the exchange rate exposure effect', *Journal of Finance*, **49** (5), 1755–85.

Bartov, E. and G.M. Bodnar (1995), 'Foreign currency translation reporting and the exchange rate exposure effect', *Journal of International Financial Management and Accounting*, **6** (2), 93–114.

Brown, N. and C.M. Deegan (1998), 'The public disclosure of environmental performance information – a dual test of media agenda setting theory and legitimacy theory', *Accounting and Business Research*, **29** (1), 21–41.

Deegan, C.M. and B. Gordon (1996), 'A study of the environmental disclosure practices of Australian corporations', *Accounting and Business Research*, **26** (3), 187–99.

Edwards, P. and R.A. Smith (1996), 'Competitive disadvantage and voluntary disclosures: the case of segmental reporting', *British Accounting Review*, **28** (2), June, 155–72.

Fulkerson, C.L. and G.K. Meek (1998), 'Analysts' earnings forecasts and the value relevance of 20-F reconciliations from non-US to US GAAP', *Journal of International Financial Management and Accounting*, **9** (1), 1–15.

Garrod. N. and W. Rees (1998), 'International diversification and firm value', *Journal of Business Finance and Accounting*, **25** (9/10), 1255–81.

Grolin, J. (1998), 'Corporate legitimacy in risk society: the case of Brent Spar', *Business Strategy and the Environment*, **7**, 213–22.

Guthrie, J. and L. Parker (1989), 'Corporate social reporting: a rebuttal of legitimacy theory', *Accounting and Business Research*, **19** (76), 343–52.

Harris, M.S. and K.A. Muller (1999), 'The market valuation of IAS versus US-GAAP accounting measures using Form 20-F reconciliations', *Journal of Accounting and Economics*, **26**, 285–312.

Herrmann, D. and W.B. Thomas (2000), 'A model of forecast precision using segment disclosures: Implications for SFAS131', *Journal of International Accounting, Auditing and Taxation*, **9** (1), 1–18.

Hussain, S. (1997), 'The impact of segment definition on the accuracy of analysts' earnings forecasts', *Accounting and Business Research*, **27** (2), 145–56.

Mande, V. and R. Ortman (2002), 'Are recent segment disclosures of Japanese firms useful? Views of Japanese financial analysts', *The International Journal of Accounting*, **37**, 1–36.

Nichols, N.B., D.L. Street and S.J. Gray (2000), 'Geographic segment disclosures in the United States: reporting practices enter a new era', *Journal of International Accounting, Auditing and Taxation*, **9** (1), 59–82.

Ozu, C. and S.J. Gray (2001), 'The development of segment reporting in Japan: Achieving international harmonisation through a process of national consensus', *Advances in International Accounting*, **14**, 1–13.

Radebaugh, L.H., G. Gebhardt and S.J. Gray (1995), 'Foreign stock exchange listings: A case study of Daimler-Benz', *Journal of International Financial Management andAccounting*, **6** (2), Summer, 158–92.

Rees, L. and P. Elgers (1997), 'The market's valuation of nonreported accounting measures: Retrospective reconciliations of non-US and US GAAP', *Journal of Accounting Research*, **35** (1), 115–27.

Street, D.L, N.B. Nichols and S.J. Gray (2000), 'Segment reporting under SFAS 131: Has business segment reporting improved?', *Accounting Horizons*, **14** (3), September, 259–85.

Part I
Segmental Reporting

[1]

© 1997 American Accounting Association
Accounting Horizons
Vol. 11 No. 3
September 1997
pp. 35–44

Reporting Disaggregated Information:
A Critique Based on Concepts Statement No. 2

Don Herrmann and Wayne B. Thomas

*Don Herrmann is Assistant Professor at Oregon State University and
Wayne B. Thomas is Assistant Professor at University of Utah.*

INTRODUCTION

In January 1996, the Financial Accounting Standards Board (FASB) in cooperation with the Accounting Standards Board (AcSB) of the Canadian Institute of Chartered Accountants issued an exposure draft, *Reporting Disaggregated Information About a Business Enterprise,* that dramatically changes the segment disclosures to be provided by U.S. and Canadian companies. The proposed statement adopts a management perspective whereby public companies are required to report financial information on the basis that it is used internally for evaluating segment performance and allocating resources to segments. An operating segment is defined as a component of an enterprise that earns revenues and incurs expenses, whose operating results are regularly reviewed by the chief operating decision maker, and for which discrete financial information is available from the internal financial reporting system (FASB 1996, para. 11).

The FASB is reconsidering segment reporting due primarily to the criticisms expressed by financial analysts, creditors, portfolio managers and other users as to the shortcomings found in SFAS No. 14, *Financial Reporting for Segments of a Business Enterprise* (see Pacter 1993, chap. 4). SFAS No. 14 (FASB 1976) requires firms to disclose industry and geographic information for segments exceeding 10 percent of specified consolidated amounts. Furthermore, the combined revenue of all separately disclosed segments must exceed 75 percent of consolidated firm revenues. Segment definitions under SFAS No. 14 are not specifically defined, allowing management great flexibility in defining industry and geographic segments, and leading to many of the complaints against segment reporting practices expressed by users of financial reporting information.

The exposure draft represents several "firsts" for the FASB. It is the first standard to be developed jointly with a standard setting body from another country. It is also the first standard to allow disclosures of accounting information that are not in conformity with generally accepted accounting principles (GAAP). Operating segments are disclosed based on a company's internal financial reporting system, even if the internal accounting policies are not in conformance with GAAP. Finally, it arguably represents the first real example in the FASB era whereby users of accounting information go head to head with corporate America on an accounting issue. The FASB has received more than 200 comment letters on the proposed standard. While users are generally supportive of the new approach, corporations criticize the management approach as requiring too detailed information, requiring too many items or items which are not important, and requiring disclosures that may put an enterprise at a competitive disadvantage (Beresford 1996).

Submitted September 1996
Accepted May 1997

Corresponding author: Don Herrmann
Email: herrmann@bus.orst.edu

The purpose of this article is to critique the proposed standard on segment reporting. Our critique is structured around Statement of Financial Accounting Concepts No. 2 (SFAC No. 2), *Qualitative Characteristics of Accounting Information* (FASB 1980). Figure 1 presents the qualitative characteristics, in a hierarchy format, as set forth in SFAC No. 2. Each of these qualitative characteristics are formally defined at the beginning of their respective discussions in the paper. The stated purpose of SFAC No. 2 is to examine the characteristics that make accounting information useful. Since SFAC No. 2 was issued in 1980, the FASB has used it as a guideline in the standard-setting process. The current exposure draft on reporting disaggregated information refers to SFAC No. 2 numerous times in the background information and basis for conclusions (FASB 1996,

paras. 70, 84, 103, 111). It seems appropriate, then, that an analysis of the proposed standard on segment reporting be structured around SFAC No. 2. The exposure draft is analyzed using the disclosure requirements under SFAS No. 14 as a benchmark. By observing the changes in the required disclosures under SFAS No. 14, it is possible to determine whether the proposed standard represents an increase in the qualitative characteristics of accounting information provided. Table 1 provides a summary of the effect of the FASB's Exposure Draft, relative to the requirements under SFAS No. 14, on the qualitative characteristics of segment information.

RELEVANCE

Relevance is defined as the capacity of information to make a difference in a decision

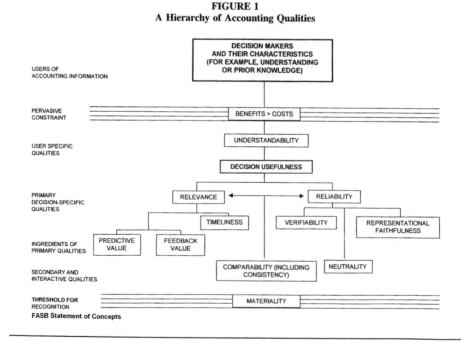

FIGURE 1
A Hierarchy of Accounting Qualities

TABLE 1

The Effect of the FASB's Exposure Draft for Reporting Disaggregated Information Relative to SFAS No. 14 on the Qualitative Characteristics of Accounting Information

| Qualitative Characteristics | Effect of the Exposure Draft Relative to SFAS No. 14 | |
	Increases	Decreases
Predictive/ Feedback Value	Increase in the number of items disclosed by segment.	
	Disclosures are consistent with managements' view.	
Timeliness	Interim segment information is required.	
Representational Faithfulness	Segments represent divisions used by management internally (i.e., management approach). Under SFAS No. 14, segments represent distinct industry and geographic segments.	In some cases, the management approach may not accurately represent companies' risks and returns.
		Potential asymmetry between income statement and balance sheet accounts.
Verifiability	Explanation of the measurement basis is required.	
	Reconciliation is required between segment and consolidated amounts.	
Neutrality		Justification is not required for omission of supplemental disclosures.
Comparability	Changes in segment definitions requires restatement of prior periods.	Internally reported segments may not be comparable across firms.
	Increased consistency between segment disclosures and other information provided by management.	The level of segment profits is not consistent.
Materiality	The lack of materiality guidelines may increase the number of primary segments disclosed.	The lack of materiality guidelines may reduce reporting of supplementary disclosures.
Costs/Benefits	Reporting data that are already generated internally should reduce preparation cost.	Reporting more items for a greater number of segments may increase competitive cost.
	Benefits (see increases above).	

by helping users to form predictions about the outcomes of past, present and future events or to confirm or correct prior expectations (FASB 1980, glossary). Relevance is discussed in the context of its primary characteristics: predictive/feedback value and timeliness.

Predictive/Feedback Value

Predictive value is defined as the quality of information that helps users to increase the likelihood of correctly forecasting the outcome of past or present events. In a similar manner, feedback value is defined as the quality of information that enables users to confirm or correct prior expectations (FASB 1980, glossary). These two qualitative characteristics lie at the heart of reporting disaggregated information. In fact, reporting of business results by segments was used as a specific example of both predictive value and feedback value in the development of SFAC No. 2 (FASB 1980, para. 52). Furthermore, SFAS No. 14 includes these two characteristics in its initial justification for segment disclosures: "The purpose of requiring segment disclosures is to assist financial statement users in assessing an enterprise's past performance and future prospects" (FASB 1976, para. 5).

A real strength of the proposed statement in comparison to SFAS No. 14 is the substantial increase in the amount of information to be disclosed for each operating segment. The proposed statement requires disclosure of the following items for each operating segment: revenues from internal and external transactions, interest revenue and expense, research and development costs, depreciation, depletion, amortization, unusual items, equity in the net income of investees, income taxes, extraordinary items, other non-cash items, assets, liabilities, amount of investment in equity-method investees, capital expenditures, and reconciliations of revenues, profits, assets and liabilities by operating segment to amounts reported in the consolidated financial statements. Under the proposed statement, enough information is provided to allow financial statement users to estimate cash flow information at the segment level. The disclosure of these items goes a long way in satisfying the need consistently expressed by users for more information about segments.

However, one item is notably missing—gross profit. The Association for Investment Management and Research (AIMR), representing professional analysts worldwide, specifically recommended the disclosure of gross profit in its list of necessary additional segment disclosures (AIMR Position Paper, 1992). In the FASB's Invitation to Comment (FASB 1993, 14), gross profit is

separately identified as valuable in assessing an enterprise's risks and prospective returns. Gross profit conveys information to users substantially different from that found in revenues or profits. Users desire information not only on revenues per segment, but on gross profit margins per segment, demonstrating the degree to which each segment generates revenues in excess of cost of goods sold. It would be especially insightful for users to observe gross profit margins per segment from a management perspective. In a comment letter to the FASB, the AIMR reaffirmed its request for gross profit information in the analysis of segment profitability, especially when the information is used internally to evaluate segment results.

Predictive/feedback value may be increased by allowing users to see through the eyes of management. The management approach determines operating segments based on the way that management disaggregates the enterprise for making operating decisions (FASB 1996, para. 6). A management perspective may increase users' ability to predict management actions that significantly impact company operations (FASB 1996, para. 67). Furthermore, a management perspective should align segment disclosures with other disclosures in the annual report, such as the management discussion and analysis and review of operations, as well as other information about the company including press releases, special reports and meetings with key executives. Under SFAS No. 14 segments were arbitrarily determined using the ten percent materiality rule resulting in rather broad inconsistent segments. Thus, segment definitions under SFAS No. 14 were, at times, inconsistent with other disclosures provided by management.

Timeliness

Timeliness is defined as having information available to a decision maker before it loses its capacity to influence decisions (FASB 1980, para. 56). Timeliness of segment information will be substantially increased under the proposed standard on disaggregated information. Interim disclosures are not required under SFAS No. 14, whereas the exposure draft requires selected information about operating segments for interim periods. The exposure draft requires interim disclosure of revenues and profits by operating segment, changes in the measure of segment profits, and a reconciliation of segment profits to total profits. Interim disclosure of assets by operating segment is also required if there has been a material change from the amount disclosed in the previous annual report.

The disclosure requirements for interim information are substantially less than that required in the annual financial statements. The FASB's decision to require disclosures of selected information by operating segment in interim reports represents a compromise between the needs of users who want the same segment information for interim periods as that required in annual financial statements and the costs to preparers who must report the information (FASB 1996, para. 100). The additional costs of interim segment information to preparers should be minimal since the disclosures are based on information that is already available internally.

RELIABILITY

Reliability is defined as the quality of information that assures that information is reasonably free from error and bias and faithfully represents what it purports to represent. Accounting information must be both relevant and reliable to be useful, although information may possess both characteristics to varying degrees (FASB 1980, para. 42). In the proposed standard on disaggregated information, the FASB acknowledges that the relative weight given to relevance may be greater than that given to reliability (FASB 1996, para. 86). This can be seen as a general trend during the FASB's tenure as standard setter. Reliability is discussed in terms of its three primary ingredients of representational faithfulness, verifiability, and neutrality.

Representational Faithfulness

Representational faithfulness is defined as a correspondence or agreement between a measure or description and the phenomenon it purports to represent (FASB 1980, para. 63). Operating segments under the proposed standard may obtain a greater degree of representational faithfulness than under SFAS No. 14. Under the proposed standard, operating segments need only represent divisions used by management internally, whereas under SFAS No. 14, segments were maintained to represent distinct industry segments and geographic areas, regardless of the internal structure of the firm. However, in some cases the proposed standard may actually decrease the representational faithfulness of segment information.

Strict adherence to the management approach may not, in all cases, accurately represent the differential risks and opportunities of companies' individual segments. For example, in the Financial Executives Institute's comment letter to the FASB an example is given of a well-regarded company in which each of several key executives has responsibility for a portfolio of diverse businesses as a test of their ability to manage an entire organization. For this company, reporting segment information according to the management approach would provide limited insight to users. In this case, reporting segment information by related products and services would more accurately reflect the risks and opportunities of the firm. In contrast to the proposed standard, SFAS No. 14 (FASB 1976, para. 100a) specifically explains that factors such as profitability, risk and growth should be used to determine whether products and services are related and, therefore, should be grouped into a single industry segment. Segmenting a business based on management talent or organizational philosophies may not provide the type of information needed to understand the company's financial position. The FASB may want to allow flexibility in applying the management approach. In situations where reporting along internal segments would not provide the necessary risk and return information to users, an exception could be made to the management approach, allowing companies to segment their operations on other factors such as products and services.

The exposure draft decreases the representational faithfulness of disaggregated information by maintaining a strict adherence to internal reporting practices even when this may result in inconsistent applications between income statement and balance sheet accounts. Due to the nature of double entry accounting, the accounting model assumes revenues and expenses correspond with assets and liabilities. This is why audit firms are able to place reliance on balance sheet tests when examining income statement accounts. Related to the reporting of disaggregated information, revenues and expenses for an operating segment are assumed to correspond with the assets and liabilities for that segment. However, the FASB's exposure draft takes a strict view of the management approach using internally reported measures of operating segment revenues, expenses, assets and liabilities without regard to symmetry. For example, depreciation expense may be allocated to segments, while the corresponding assets are not allocated to segments. This is acceptable, although supplemental disclosure of the lack of symmetry is required (FASB 1996, para. 31c). Allowing differences in allocations between segment revenues, expenses, assets and liabilities could misrepresent segment information, creating real difficulties for users attempting to combine income statement and balance sheet ratios.

Another difficulty related to representational faithfulness can be found in the additional information required about geographic areas. For each operating segment that has not been determined based on geography, disclosures of revenues by location of customer, and both assets and capital expenditures by location of assets, are required for each country in which segment operations are deemed material (FASB 1996, para. 35). In many cases revenues reported by location of customer will not match with assets and capital expenditures reported by location of

assets. If the two different bases of geographic segment disclosure are not clearly explained, users may misappropriately conclude that the country-level disclosures for revenues correspond with those for assets. Requiring disclosure of revenues by both source and destination, as in the United Kingdom (ASC 1990, SSAP No. 25), would improve the comparability of revenues with assets and capital expenditures.

Verifiability

Verifiability is the ability through consensus among measurers to ensure that information represents what it purports to represent or that the chosen method of measurement has been used without error or bias (FASB 1980, glossary). In the basis for conclusions, the FASB specifically states that verifiability may have been traded for greater relevance in allowing segment information to be prepared using accounting policies followed for internal management reporting purposes (FASB 1996, para. 84).

In comparison to SFAS No. 14, verifiability is increased in the proposed statement in two ways. First, companies are required to provide sufficient explanation to permit users to understand the basis on which the information was prepared (FASB 1996, paras. 26 and 31). Under SFAS 14, users complained that arbitrary cost allocations, transfer pricing policies, etc., hindered their ability to effectively utilize the segment information since many companies did not disclose the basis on which the information was prepared. Second, the proposed statement requires a reconciliation of profit or loss, revenues, assets and liabilities to the consolidated amounts prepared for external reporting in conformity with GAAP, increasing the verifiability of the information. A reconciliation was not required under SFAS No. 14 resulting in inconsistencies between segment information and consolidated totals.

The proposed standard allows reporting of segment information based on internal sources even when those policies differ from the methods used in the consolidated finan-cial statements. As pointed out in the basis for conclusions of the FASB's exposure draft, preparing segment disclosures in accordance with GAAP would be difficult since some ac-counting principles are not intended to apply at the segment level (FASB 1996, para. 82). Numerous convincing examples are given, including the allocation of assets and liabil-ities under purchase accounting, company-wide employee benefit plans, accounting for income taxes, pooled LIFO, allocation of joint costs, assets, liabilities, etc., and transfer pricing. By not requiring segment disclo-sures in accordance with GAAP, the FASB's approach will result in lower costs to prepar-ers and may increase the willingness of pre-parers to disclose additional information by operating segment. In some instances, vio-lations of GAAP could prove more beneficial to users than strict adherence to GAAP. For example, many companies track inventory on a FIFO basis for management purposes, but report inventory on a LIFO basis for ex-ternal financial reporting to obtain favorable tax benefits. The FIFO basis is more realistic and likely more informative to users.

Neutrality

Neutrality is defined as an absence of bias in reported information intended to at-tain a predetermined result or to induce a particular mode of behavior (FASB 1980, glossary). An omission can rob information of its claim to neutrality if the omission is in-tended to induce or inhibit some particular mode of behavior (FASB 1980, para. 108). The exposure draft requires supplemental disclosures of information about products and services and geographic areas (FASB 1996, paras. 32–35). However, an exclusion is allowed. Omission of the supplemental dis-closures is allowed if reporting of the infor-mation is deemed impracticable and the fact is disclosed. Justification is not required to be disclosed. Firms may be more likely to omit supplemental disclosures in situations where the information may be interpreted

negatively by the market, resulting in a vi-olation of neutrality. Omission by reason of impracticality may inhibit to a greater ex-tent the disclosure of negative information. While auditor involvement and/or potential market penalties should mitigate this bias, a requirement for specific justification may further reduce this potential bias toward the omission of negative information. The re-quirement of specific justification should in-crease auditor involvement, reduce the num-ber of firms avoiding disclosure for reasons of impracticality, and provide potentially useful information regarding the capabilities of the firm's internal financial reporting sys-tem. Care must be taken to require specific justifications and not a general statement, since justification is only informative if it is not boilerplate.

COMPARABILITY

Comparability is defined as the quality of information that enables users to identify similarities in and differences between two sets of economic phenomena (FASB 1980, glossary). Comparability of information has been credited as the principal reason for the development of accounting standards (FASB 1980, para. 112). Comparability has two di-mensions; interfirm comparability and inter-period comparability.

The management approach will likely de-crease interfirm comparability. Segments based on internal organizations may not be comparable among enterprises. If segment information is derived from internal finan-cial reporting systems, it is possible that two enterprises can account for the same eco-nomic phenomena differently. For example, two firms could be in the same industries and geographic locations yet have totally separate reporting schemes because of differ-ent organizational philosophies. As pointed out in SFAC No. 2, "there is a gain from the greater comparability and consistency that adherence to externally imposed standards brings with it. The public is naturally skep-tical about the reliability of financial report-ing if two enterprises account differently for the same economic phenomena" (FASB 1980, para. 16). Ernst & Young states in its comment letter to the FASB that "the industry segment approach under Statement 14 promotes more comparability than the management approach."

The FASB's proposed statement requires disclosure of profit or loss for each segment based on the internal financial reporting system. The level of earnings is to be consistent with that used for internal analysis. Thus, companies will report operating segment profit or loss at different levels, such as operating earnings, pre-tax earnings and net income. Reported information could differ even among operating segments within the same company. A standardized measure, or at the minimum a recommended measure, of segment earnings will improve comparability. Since the FASB already requires reconciliation of segment profit or loss to income from continuing operations before income taxes, why not at least recommend this level of segment earnings to improve interfirm comparability?

The management approach should increase interperiod comparability. Interperiod comparability is improved when companies report information in a consistent manner from year to year. Under SFAS No. 14, changes in segment definitions were common, but rarely did companies restate prior period segment information to be in conformity with current year changes. The proposed statement requires that if an enterprise changes its organization in a manner that causes the composition of its operating segments to change, the previously reported information for earlier periods must be restated to conform with the new format (FASB 1996, para. 39). The statement does not clearly define earlier periods, although it is likely to represent previous periods included in the audited financial statements. Companies are allowed to circumvent restating segment data for previous periods for reasons of impracticality, simply stating that it is not possible to gather such information or else the cost of gathering the information

is too great. However, the audit process should help counterbalance management's tendency to claim impracticality.

The management approach should increase the consistency of segment disclosures with other parts of an annual report such as the management discussion and analysis and the review of operating results. The agreement between segment disclosures in the footnotes and disclosures of information in other parts of the annual report should increase the overall usefulness of information available to users in comparing operations from period to period.

MATERIALITY

Materiality is defined as the magnitude of an omission or misstatement of accounting information that, in light of surrounding circumstances, makes it probable that the judgment of a reasonable person relying on the information would have been changed or influenced by the omission or misstatement (FASB 1980, glossary). Unlike SFAS No. 14's ten percent materiality rule, the proposed statement on disaggregated information does not include quantitative guidelines for materiality of operating segments. The Board concluded that quantitative criteria might interfere with the determination of operating segments and may reduce the number of segments disclosed (FASB 1996, para. 110).

For primary operating segments, we agree with the FASB's decision to exclude quantitative materiality guidelines. In order to provide users of financial statements insights into how management views the business, operating segments need to be defined consistent with management's internal operating system. Quantitative materiality guidelines may interfere with this process, potentially resulting in less relevant information. However, numerous companies indicated in their comment letters to the FASB that the lack of materiality guidelines may result in the reporting of too many segments, resulting in disclosure overload. Similar concerns were expressed by auditors and users.

In its comment letter to the FASB, the Financial Executives Institute expressed concern that the proposed standard would result in far too many segments and, when coupled with the increase in the required items per operating segment, disclosures would mushroom and "become unmanageable and too voluminous to be understandable." Rather than providing materiality guidelines, the FASB/AcSB might alleviate this problem by including a limit on the maximum number of segments required to be disclosed.

In contrast to the arguments for primary operating segments, quantitative materiality guidelines are necessary for supplemental disclosures of information about products or services and geographic areas (FASB 1996, paras. 32–35). Supplemental disclosures about products or services and geographic areas are required to be reported in a matrix format (i.e., by operating segment and products or services, or by operating segment and geographic area). An illustrative example of supplemental geographic disclosures in a matrix format is given in paragraph 117 of the exposure draft. Companies defining primary operating segments on a basis other than geography are required to report supplemental geographic disclosures of revenues, assets and capital expenditures for each country in which operations are deemed material. The operations of all other countries would be aggregated into a "total foreign" category (FASB 1996, para. 35). When faced with the choice of additional country-level disclosures in a matrix format or aggregating immaterial amounts into a total foreign category, managers are likely to favor the latter to avoid both additional administrative disclosure costs and potential competitive disadvantage costs.

Managers' interpretation of materiality will be critical to the quality of supplemental disclosures under the proposed statement. Under the proposed statement, supplemental disclosures by geographic area may greatly diminish. Supplemental disclosures by geographic area will likely be provided for only a minority of companies and then only

for a few of the United States' closest trading partners, such as Canada and Great Britain. Quantitative guidelines need to be provided to encourage disclosure of this valuable information. Quantitative guidelines could also encourage geographic information to be disclosed by region, when individual countries within a region are not separately material.

COSTS/BENEFITS

One of the precepts of the FASB's mission is to promulgate standards only if the expected benefits of the resulting information exceed the perceived costs (FASB 1996, para. 103). The overall costs of disclosing disaggregated information should be less under the proposed standard than under SFAS No. 14. In its comment letter to the FASB, KPMG Peat Marwick states that reduced preparation cost is the principal advantage of the proposed statement over SFAS No. 14. The proposed statement requires segment information to be provided on the same basis as it is used internally. Management does not have to incur reporting costs for both internal and external reporting purposes. Enterprises have incurred internal reporting costs for years to gather information about its operating segments. Now, they only have to disclose that information externally, resulting in limited additional administrative costs. SFAS No. 14 required industry and geographic segment disclosures that were often inconsistent with segment definitions used internally, resulting in duplicate reporting costs for disaggregated disclosures.

However, the proposed statement may result in increased competitive costs. If strictly applied, the proposed statement would result in more items being disclosed for a greater number of segments than under SFAS No. 14. Disclosing sensitive data, such as research and development and expenditures for long-lived assets, could give significant insight into the companies' investment strategies, causing competitors to revise their strategies accordingly. The National Association of Manufacturers reports in its comment letter that approximately ninety-two

44

Accounting Horizons / September 1997

percent (107 of 116) of its members who sent comment letters to the FASB opposed the proposed statement. The most often cited reason for opposition was competitive disadvantage.

The overall benefits of the proposed standard should exceed those under SFAS No. 14. Disclosing segments under the management approach should better link the reported segments and management discussions in the annual report, press releases, special reports and meetings with key executives, and should allow users to better see "through the eyes" of management. In addition, the proposed standard calls for more financial data to be disclosed by operating segment and for segment information to be disclosed in quarterly reports, both of which should increase the relevance of segment information. Reliability of segment information should be enhanced by a discussion of the basis on which segment information is prepared and by the reconciliation of segment and consolidated amounts. Interperiod comparability should also increase due to the requirement for prior period restatement when changes to current period segment definitions are made.

There are still many changes that could be made to the proposed standard which would further enhance the benefits of segment information. For example, gross profit should be disclosed by segment, flexibility in segmentation should be allowed when the management approach does not sufficiently reflect the risks and returns of the company, assets and liabilities should be allocated to segments only if their related revenues and expenses are also allocated, an explanation should be provided in cases where firms do not provide supplemental segment disclosure because of impracticality, a consistent level of operating results should be used across segments, and a materiality guideline for supplemental segment disclosures should be used. Note that these improvements could be made with very little additional cost to the company.

Despite the shortcomings of the proposed standard on segment reporting, the FASB's and AcSB's effort should not be understated. The proposed standard is an ambitious project which adopts a distinctly new approach for segment reporting to meet the information needs of users and, at the same time, attempt to lower the costs to preparers.

REFERENCES

Accounting Standards Committee. 1990. *Segmental Reporting.* Statement of Standard Accounting Practice No. 25. CCAB.

Association for Investment Management and Research, Financial Accounting Policy Committee (AIMR). 1992. *Financial Reporting in the 1990s and Beyond: A Position Paper of the Association for Investment Management and Research.* Prepared by Peter H. Knutson. Charlottesville, VA: AIMR.

Beresford, D. 1996. Presentation at the American Accounting Association Annual Meeting, August 16. Chicago, IL.

Financial Accounting Standards Board (FASB). 1976. *Financial Reporting for Segments of a Business Enterprise.* Statement of Financial Accounting Standards No. 14. Stamford, CT: FASB.

————. 1980. *Qualitative Characteristics of Accounting Information.* Statement of Financial Accounting Concepts No. 2. Stamford, CT: FASB.

————. 1993. *Reporting Disaggregated Information by Business Enterprises.* Invitation to Comment. Norwalk, CT: FASB.

————. 1996. *Reporting Disaggregated Information About a Business Enterprise.* Proposed Statement of Financial Accounting Standards. Norwalk, CT: FASB.

Pacter, P. 1993. *Reporting Disaggregated Information.* Norwalk, CT: FASB.

[2]

ELSEVIER

Journal of International Accounting,
Auditing & Taxation 10 (2001) 117–138

Journal of
**International
Accounting
Auditing &
Taxation**

Geographic area disclosures under SFAS 131: materiality and fineness

Timothy S. Doupnik[a,*], Larry P. Seese[b]

[a]*The Darla Moore School of Business, University of South Carolina, Columbia, SC 29208, USA*
[b]*School of Business, East Carolina University, Greenville, NC 27858, USA*

Abstract

This paper describes and evaluates certain aspects of the enterprise-wide geographic area disclosures provided by *Fortune* 500 companies in the implementation of SFAS 131, "Disclosures about Segments of an Enterprise and Related Information." The first objective of this study is to determine how companies are complying with the materiality criterion of SFAS 131 for determining when an individual country is reportable. The second objective is to evaluate whether foreign operation disclosures provided by companies in accordance with SFAS 131 result in a finer set of information than was provided under SFAS 14. The results suggest that there is considerable diversity among companies in the way that materiality is defined, with a majority of companies that provide country-level disclosures using quantitative thresholds less than 10%. For a large percentage of companies, the information provided under SFAS 131 appears to be finer than the information provided under SFAS 14. However, a significant minority of companies has taken a step backward in this regard. © 2001 Elsevier Science Inc. All rights reserved.

Keywords: Geographic areas; SFAS 131; Materiality; Fineness; *Fortune* 500; Segment reporting

1. Introduction

The FASB issued Statement of Financial Accounting Standards 131 (SFAS 131), "Disclosures about Segments of an Enterprise and Related Information" in June 1997, effective for fiscal years beginning after December 15, 1997 (FASB, 1997). In addition to disclosures by operating segment, SFAS 131 requires certain enterprise-wide disclosures to be made. For

---

* Corresponding author. Tel.: +803-777-7450; fax: +803-777-0712.
E-mail address: doupnik@darla.badm.sc.edu (T.S. Doupnik).

1061-9518/01/$ – see front matter © 2001 Elsevier Science Inc. All rights reserved.
PII: S 1061-9518(01)00040-4

118   *T.S. Doupnik, L.P. Seese / Journal of International Accounting, Auditing & Taxation 10 (2001) 117–138*

those companies that define operating segments on a basis other than geographic location, SFAS 131 requires two items of information to be disclosed by geographic area: revenues from external customers and long-lived assets. SFAS 131 supersedes SFAS 14 which required companies to provide information by line-of-business and geographic segments.

In reporting geographic segments, consolidated totals are disaggregated into subtotals based on geography. Unlike SFAS 14, which allowed geographic areas to be defined as groups of countries, SFAS 131 requires disclosures to be made by individual country. The FASB believes that finer, country-level disclosures will provide more useful information than disclosures provided at a more aggregated level (1997, para. 105). Several studies provide partial evidence that country level disclosures can be useful (Doupnik and Rolfe, 1989; Boatsman et al., 1993; Herrmann, 1996; Nichols et al., 1996; Thomas, 2000).

SFAS 14 established a 10% materiality criterion for determining when geographic segments must be reported separately. SFAS 131 requires separate reporting for those countries with a *material* amount of revenues or long-lived assets, but leaves the determination of materiality to management decision. Nichols and Street (1999) suggest that SFAS 131 will result in companies reporting more geographic segments. Herrmann and Thomas (2000a), on the other hand, argue that companies are likely to apply a relatively high level of materiality and thus avoid country-level disclosures.

SFAS 131 was first implemented by companies in their 1998 annual reports.[1] This study describes and evaluates the initial geographic area disclosures provided by U.S.-based companies through the implementation of SFAS 131. Specifically, this study focuses on two important issues related to geographic area disclosures: materiality and fineness. The first objective of this study is to investigate the cutoff points used by companies in determining the materiality of individual countries. The focus is on both the materiality levels used by individual companies as well as the range of materiality levels used across companies. The second objective of this study is to evaluate whether disclosures provided by companies in accordance with SFAS 131 are finer than the disclosures provided under SFAS 14. In the context of geographic area information, fineness can be defined in terms of the extent to which consolidated amounts are disaggregated into specifically defined geographic areas and the level of aggregation at which geographic areas are reported. Information provided at a less aggregated level should be at least as useful as more aggregated information, and potentially is more useful.

The results of this study should be of interest to the FASB and to financial analysts. Information about materiality thresholds should be of particular interest to the FASB which has decided to allow management judgment on this issue. If the results of this study indicate the use of unreasonably high or widely varying materiality cutoff points, the FASB may want to consider establishing a quantitative threshold similar to that used in determining when an operating segment must be separately reported. A comparison of the fineness of disclosures under SFAS 131 and under SFAS 14 should be of interest to the FASB and to financial analysts because fineness potentially affects the usefulness of the information being provided.

The next section describes the requirements of SFAS 131 with regard to foreign operations and summarizes research investigating the implementation of SFAS 131. The research questions then are explicitly stated, and the sample and research methodology described.

T.S. *Doupnik, L.P. Seese / Journal of International Accounting, Auditing & Taxation 10 (2001) 117–138* 119

This is followed by a description of the results. The last section provides a summary and conclusions.

2. SFAS 131 and related research

SFAS 131 requires companies to provide substantial information for each reportable *operating* segment. An operating segment is defined as a component of an enterprise: (1) that engages in business activities from which it may earn revenues and incur expenses, (2) whose operating results are regularly reviewed by the enterprise's chief operating decision maker, and (3) for which discrete financial information is available (SFAS 131, para 10). Under SFAS 131, companies can define operating segments by means of products or services, type of customer, geographic locations of the customer, shipping location, or by other methods (Coller and Pierce 1999). Operating segments are a function of the enterprise's organizational structure. An operating segment is *reportable* if it meets at least one of three explicitly defined quantitative tests. The quantitative threshold used in each of these tests is 10%.[2]

For companies that do not define operating segments on the basis of geographic location, SFAS 131 requires information about geographic areas to be provided as part of enterprise-wide disclosures. Two items of information must be disclosed by geographic area: (1) revenues from external customers and (2) long-lived assets. SFAS 131 requires these items of information to be disclosed (a) for the company's country of domicile and (b) for all foreign countries in total from which the company derives revenues or in which the company has long-lived assets. In addition, if revenues or long-lived assets attributed to an *individual foreign country are material,* those revenues and/or long-lived assets must be disclosed separately (SFAS 131, para. 38) (emphasis added).

Disclosures must be provided for each country in which a *material* amount of revenues or long-lived assets are located. Although SFAS 131 provides an explicit quantitative threshold for determining when an operating segment or major customer is reportable, it does not establish a threshold for determining when a country has a material amount of revenues or long-lived assets. The determination of materiality with regard to individual countries is left to management judgment.

Requiring disclosures to be provided by individual country is a major difference from SFAS 14 which allowed the grouping of countries into geographic areas.[3] Although an individual country could have been designated as a geographic area under SFAS 14, more commonly, countries were aggregated into broad geographic areas such as Asia-Pacific, Europe, and Latin America. Individual country disclosures creates a less aggregated, finer information set than disclosures by continent or region of the world.

SFAS 131 indicates that, because they are easier to interpret, disclosures by individual country should be more useful in assessing the impact of concentrations of risk than disclosures by aggregated geographic area. Moreover, disclosure by individual country will avoid the problem of countries of diverse risk being grouped together, the usefulness of which has been questioned by analysts (SFAS 131, para. 105). Herrmann and Thomas (2000a) argue that country-level disclosures under SFAS 131 should result in a significant improvement over the broader disclosures provided under SFAS No. 14 "as they better differentiate among potential risk, return, and growth prospects" (p. 10). Thus, the geographic segment disclosures provided under SFAS 131 have the potential of being more useful than those provided under SFAS 14.

The potential improvement in usefulness might not be realized in practice, however, due to two aspects of SFAS 131. First, whereas SFAS 14 required disclosure of profit or loss, in addition to revenues and assets, SFAS 131 only requires disclosure of revenues and assets. Unless companies voluntarily disclose profit in complying with SFAS 131, this item of information will be unavailable to analysts. Nichols et al. (2000) and Herrmann and Thomas (2000b) found that few companies voluntarily disclose profit by geographic area under SFAS 131.

Second, SFAS 131 requires country specific disclosures to be provided only when an individual country is material. However, the Statement does not establish a quantitative threshold for determining materiality, instead leaving the determination of materiality to management discretion. Nichols and Street (1999) suggest that SFAS 131 will result in companies reporting more geographic segments, and that "(s)ignificant operations in a single country, such as Germany or Japan, no longer can be concealed by including them in vague groupings such as Europe/Asia or Asia/Pacific" (p. 41). This will be true, however, only if companies establish quantitative materiality thresholds low enough that individual countries become reportable.

Herrmann and Thomas (2000a) suggest that "the potential benefits of country-level disclosures may never be realized because companies are likely to apply a relatively high level of materiality in defining 'material' individual foreign countries" (p. 10). Moreover, under SFAS 131, companies are not required to combine individually immaterial countries into broader country groupings for reporting purposes. In this situation, SFAS 131 only requires disclosure of revenues and long-lived assets for total foreign operations in aggregate.[4] Through the use of high materiality thresholds, companies might report fewer geographic segments than under SFAS 14. Thus, depending on the quantitative thresholds used by companies to determine whether an individual country is material, the application of SFAS 131 could result in less (or more) aggregated, and therefore potentially more (or less) useful, geographic area information being reported than under SFAS 14.

2.1. Previous research

Because SFAS 131 only became effective for periods beginning after December 1997, little research on enterprise-wide geographic area disclosures provided under the new standard has been conducted. In an examination of early adopters of SFAS 131, Nichols and Street (1999) discovered that eight of ten companies reported only the required items of revenues from external customers and long-lived assets, but two companies voluntarily reported operating income as well. They also cite anecdotal evidence from two companies that increased the number of geographic areas reported.

Nichols et al. (2000) conducted an analysis of the enterprise-wide geographic area disclosures provided by 123 U.S. multinationals included in *Business Week*'s Global 1000 list of companies. In comparing SFAS 131 disclosures provided in 1998 with SFAS 14 disclosures from 1997, they found one change that they believe would be welcomed by

T.S. Doupnik, L.P. Seese / Journal of International Accounting, Auditing & Taxation 10 (2001) 117–138   121

financial analysts. The percentage of companies in their sample providing country specific information increased from 4% in 1997 to 28% in 1998. Contrary to their expectations, they discovered no significant relationship between the reporting of country specific disclosures and the level of a company's international involvement (measured as % of foreign sales and dollar amount of foreign sales). Comparing the number of geographic areas reported in 1997 and 1998, there was no change for 43% of their sample companies, an increase for 35%, and a decrease for 22%.

Nichols et al. (2000) obtained several results that they expect will not be viewed positively by analysts. Specifically, they found (1) an increase in the number of companies providing information using a "U.S., Other" classification, with no disaggregation of "Other;" (2) few companies voluntarily disclosing operating income by geographic area; and (3) a large percentage of companies reporting geographic areas that exceed 25% of total sales and/or assets.

Herrmann and Thomas (2000b) compared geographic segment disclosures under SFAS 131 with those reported under SFAS 14 for a sample of 74 firms. They found a slight increase in the mean number of geographic areas reported under SFAS 131, with twice as many countries reported as under SFAS 14. They also found that 33 firms used "finer" (less aggregated) definitions of geographic segment under SFAS 131, 28 firms had no change, and 13 provided information under broader geographic segment definitions than under SFAS 14. Herrmann and Thomas (2000b) criticize the continued use of broad geographic regions, and express concern over the fact that few firms voluntarily disclose earnings by geographic area under SFAS 131.

Nichols et al. (2000) and Herrmann and Thomas (2000b) provide a great deal of information about how U.S. companies have implemented the geographic area disclosure requirements of SFAS 131. The current study adds to this body of knowledge by focusing on two important aspects of SFAS 131 geographic area disclosures: materiality and fineness. Neither Nichols et al. (2000) nor Herrmann and Thomas (2000b) attempted to determine the materiality thresholds adopted by companies in implementing SFAS 131's geographic area disclosure requirements. We examine the individual country-level disclosures provided by companies to gain insight into this management judgment issue. Herrmann and Thomas (2000b) introduce the notion that disclosure at the country-level provides finer information than disclosure by groups of countries, and they counted the number of firms in their sample using a finer definition of geographic segment under SFAS 131. We develop two additional measures of fineness and examine the change in fineness of the geographic area information set provided by companies as they implemented SFAS 131. The current study also differs from previous research in that a substantially larger sample of companies is used as the basis for analysis.

3. Research questions

The objective of this study is to describe and evaluate certain aspects of the initial enterprise-wide geographic area disclosure of revenues provided by U.S. companies in implementing SFAS 131. The two primary questions addressed by this study are:

122   *T.S. Doupnik, L.P. Seese / Journal of International Accounting, Auditing & Taxation 10 (2001) 117–138*

Table 1
Implementation of SFAS 131 Geographic Area Information Requirements by *Fortune* 500 Companies

Implementation	No. of Companies
Enterprise-wide geographic area disclosures	263*
Operating segments defined based on geography	34
No disclosures by geographic areas	178
Financial statements not available	25
Total	500

*254 companies disclosed revenues by geographic area

1. What quantitative thresholds are used to determine the materiality of revenues in individual countries?
2. Is the SFAS 131 information set with regard to revenues by geographic area finer than the information set provided under SFAS 14?

In the context of geographic area reporting, fineness can be viewed in terms of the level at which individual countries are aggregated to form geographic areas. A hierarchy of fineness can be developed as follows (from finest to least fine): individual country (e.g., France), subcontinent (e.g., Western Europe), continent (e.g., Europe), multicontinent (e.g., Europe, Middle East, and Africa), hemisphere (e.g., Eastern Hemisphere), and nondomestic (i.e., Foreign). The less aggregated the information provided, the easier it should be for financial analysts to incorporate factors related to foreign operations, such as country specific foreign exchange risk and economic growth, into their evaluation of a company's future potential. Materiality and fineness should be related. The fineness of the information set provided by companies should be a function of the cutoff point used to determine when revenues in an individual country are significant enough to warrant separate disclosure.

This study focuses on the disclosure of revenues only. Previous research investigating the usefulness of segment information has concentrated on revenues and profit, ignoring assets.

4. Sample and methodology

The 500 largest U.S.-based companies as measured by revenues reported in the April 26, 1999 issue of *Fortune* magazine comprised the sample examined in this study. As the largest U.S. companies, this sample is likely to contain a high percentage of multinationals that would be required to provide enterprise-wide geographic area disclosures under SFAS 131. Table 1 indicates the incidence of SFAS 131 implementation with regard to geographic area disclosures for the *Fortune* 500 companies.

Financial statements could not be located for 25 companies, primarily in the insurance industry or not-for-profit organizations. Thirty-four companies defined operating segments according to geography and did not provide additional enterprise-wide geographic area disclosures. A relatively large percentage of companies (n = 178 or 36%) did not provide

T.S. Doupnik, L.P. Seese / Journal of International Accounting, Auditing & Taxation 10 (2001) 117–138 123

any disclosures by geographic area, presumably because they do not have foreign operations. A total of 263 companies provided enterprise-wide disclosures by geographic area. Of these, 254 companies disclosed revenues by geographic area. Subsequent analysis focuses on the geographic area revenue disclosures of this subset of *Fortune* 500 companies.

4.1. Measurement of materiality threshold

Unless specifically disclosed, it is not possible to determine with certainty the materiality threshold used by companies in determining whether revenues located in a specific foreign country are material in amount.[5] However, by examining individual country disclosures made by companies providing such disclosures, it is possible to determine the upper bound to the quantitative threshold used by these companies in determining materiality. We assume that companies determine the materiality of revenues located in a specific country by comparing that amount with total revenues located in all countries, foreign and domestic.[6] Any country in which the percentage of total revenues exceeds the company's materiality cutoff point would be reported separately.

To measure the upper bound of the materiality cutoff point used by companies, the percentage of total revenues located in each individually disclosed country was calculated and the country with the smallest percentage of total revenues (hereafter referred to as "smallest" country) was identified. That percentage is evidence of the upper bound needed for an individual country to be deemed material. For example, if the percentage of total revenues in the "smallest" country is 7%, we infer that the company used a cutoff point with an upper bound of (no greater than) 7% of total revenues in determining materiality. However, it is not possible to determine whether the actual cutoff point is something less than 7%. For example, the cutoff point might be 5%, but the smallest country meeting this threshold happened to have 7% of total revenues.

4.2. Measurement of fineness

To evaluate whether SFAS 131 has led to the disclosure of finer geographic area information, revenue disclosures made in the year of adopting SFAS 131 (generally 1998) were compared with those made in the last year of applying SFAS 14 (generally 1997) for those companies providing geographic area disclosures under SFAS 131. Fineness was measured in two ways–as a count of the number of areas reported and through the calculation of a "fineness score."

Nichols and Street (1999) suggest that SFAS 131 should result in companies reporting more geographic segments, and Nichols et al. (2000) found that 35% of a sample of 123 companies had an increase in the number of areas reported. In the current study, the number of areas reported in 1997 and in 1998 was counted for each company in the sample and the difference was determined. An increase in the number of areas reported is one indication of an increase in fineness in the resulting information set.

Comparing the number of geographic areas reported under SFAS 131 and under SFAS 14 is an imperfect measure of the change in fineness, however, because the areas reported under SFAS 131 are often at the country-level whereas the areas reported under SFAS 14 are likely

124   *T.S. Doupnik, L.P. Seese / Journal of International Accounting, Auditing & Taxation 10 (2001) 117–138*

to be at a more aggregated level. As stated earlier, information reported on an individual country basis is likely to be more useful than information reported on a more aggregated basis. An information set in which disclosures are made on a country basis but for a small number of countries may be more useful than an information set in which data are provided for a greater number of areas but at a more aggregated level. In addition, the greater the percentage of total foreign revenues disclosed by geographic area, the more useful the information set is likely to be. The finest (and potentially most useful) information set would be one in which 100% of foreign revenues is disclosed by individual country. The coarsest (least useful) information set is one in which 100% of foreign revenues is disclosed simply as "foreign" with no indication of location.

In addition to a count of areas reported, a second measure of fineness was developed that combines the number of areas reported, the level of aggregation represented by each area, and the percentage of foreign operations in that area. The fineness score was calculated for each company in the following manner:

$$F = \sum_{i=1}^{n} (AREAREV_i/FORREV) \times weight_i \qquad (1)$$

where   AREAREV   =   revenue for geographic area i
        FORREV   =   total foreign revenues
        weight   =   0, for geographic areas described as "Foreign" or "Other"
                      1, for geographic areas defined as multicontinents
                      2, for geographic areas defined as continents
                      3, for geographic areas defined as countries

The larger the score, the finer the information set provided by a company.[7]

A weight of zero assigned to areas described as "foreign" or "other" is intended to indicate that this level of aggregation provides no useful information for assessing a company's specific exposure to international risk. Assigning weights of 1, 2, and 3, respectively, to multicontinent, continent, and country-level disclosures is intended to show that disclosures become potentially more useful as the level of aggregation in the reported area decreases. The ratio $AREAREV_i/FORREV$ reflects the portion of total foreign revenues disclosed within a particular geographic area. The F score increases as the percentage of total foreign revenues disclosed by geographic area increases. Also, by applying different weights, the F score increases as the geographic areas reported become less aggregated. Scores range from 0.0 for companies that disclose the amount of foreign revenues only with no disaggregation, to 3.0 for companies that disclose all of their foreign operations by individual country.

Other weighting schemes could be employed but the scheme adopted here serves the purpose of the current study. The objective is not to compare the score across companies but instead to evaluate the change in fineness of a company's disclosures in implementing SFAS 131. The most important attribute is whether the fineness score increased or decreased as companies implemented SFAS 131. However, to partially test the sensitivity of the score to the weights assigned, the fineness score was also calculated by assigning country-level disclosures a weight of 4 and a weight of 8, with other weights remaining the same. These weights were selected presupposing that country-level disclosures are two times and four times as useful, respectively, as continent-level disclosures in assessing a company's future potential.

5. Results

Before presenting the results related to materiality and fineness, a description of the aggregation levels used by *Fortune* 500 companies in their disclosures of revenues by geographic area is provided. For subsequent analysis of the fineness scores, companies are grouped according to the aggregation level used.

5.1. Level of aggregation in defining geographic areas for disclosure of revenues

SFAS 131 *requires* the disclosure of total foreign revenues as well as revenues attributed to an individual material country. SFAS 131 also *allows* companies to provide additional subtotals for groups of countries that are determined to be individually immaterial. As shown in Table 2, Panel A, of the 254 *Fortune* 500 companies reporting foreign revenues, 86 disclosed the amount of foreign revenues in total only, with no further disaggregation. Apparently, these companies have determined that they do not have a material amount of revenues in any individual foreign country. The companies in this group also elected not to voluntarily provide disclosures by groups of countries.

The companies reporting total foreign revenues only had an average 21.4% of total revenues attributed to foreign operations (Mean Foreign Revenue %); 25 of the 86 companies had less than 10% of their total revenues in foreign operations. Assuming the use of a 10% materiality cutoff point, these 25 companies could not have any material countries. On the other hand, 15 companies in this group had more than 40% of revenues from foreign operations. At the extreme, Gillette reported that 62% of its revenues was attributed to foreign countries in total but it did not disclose the amount of revenues in any single country (or region of the world).

Although SFAS 131 only requires disclosure to be made by material country, Panel A of Table 2 shows that 92 of the 168 companies that disaggregated total foreign revenues provided disclosures by "continent." Fifty-three companies provided disclosures by continent only.[8] It can be assumed that these companies do not have a material amount of operations in any individual country and therefore are voluntarily providing disclosures not required by SFAS 131.

A total of 115 of the 254 companies in the sample (45.3%) provided disclosures for one or more individual countries in 1998. Of the 229 companies in the sample that also provided geographic area disclosures in 1997, only 53 (23.1%) provided one or more country-level disclosures in that year. Thus, SFAS 131 appears to have caused a significant number of companies to begin disaggregating revenues at the individual country level.

Thirty-nine companies provided a mix of both country and continent-level disclosures. This group provided disclosures for a mean of 1.4 countries; 74% provided disclosures for

Table 2
Level of Aggregation Provided in Enterprise-Wide Geographic Area Disclosures of Revenues by *Fortune* 500
Companies in 1998

Panel A: Number of Companies Providing Disclosures at Different Levels of Aggregation

Level of Aggregation	No. of Companies	Mean Foreign Revenue %*
Total foreign revenues only	86	21.4%
Continent** only	53	37.3%
Mix of country and continent	39	35.3%
Country only	76	31.4%
Total	254	29.9%

* Calculated as: Total Foreign Revenues (Total Domestic Revenues + Total Foreign Revenues)
** "Continent" denotes sub-continent, continent, and multi-continent levels by Companies

Panel B: Number of Disclosures Provided at Different Levels of Aggregation by Companies Disaggregating
Total Foreign Revenues

Level of Aggregation	No. of Disclosures	% of Total Disclosures
Country	242	43.8%
Continent*	120	21.7%
Multi-continent**	73	13.2%
"Other" (undefined areas)	118	21.3%
Total	553	100.0%

* Includes areas such as Europe, Africa, Asia, and Latin America, and areas identified as portions of a
   continent such as Western Europe, Southeast Asia, and Other Latin America.
** Includes areas created by combining countries located on more than one contient such as Europe/Midddle
   East/Africa, Asia/Pacific, and Western Hemisphere.

one country only. By providing continent-level disclosures in addition to country disclosures, this group is providing more information than is required by SFAS 131. Seventy-six companies (45.2% of 168) disaggregated total foreign revenues by individual country only. This group disclosed an average of 2.5 countries each, but 35 companies (46.1% of 76) provided disclosures for only one foreign country. At the other extreme, eight companies provided disclosures for more than five countries (the maximum was 11 countries reported by DuPont).

The right hand column in Table 2, Panel A reports the Mean Foreign Revenue % for each of the four groups of companies. Nichols et al. (2000) found no significant relationship between the type of geographic area disclosed (i.e., country, continent, mixed, or foreign only) and companies' foreign revenue percentage. Results of a one-way ANOVA indicate that there is a significant difference (at 0.01 level) across the four groups in the current study. Posthoc comparison tests indicate that the foreign revenue only group is significantly different (at 0.05 level) from each of the other groups in terms of Foreign Revenue %, but there are no differences across the other groups. This suggests that the relative level of

T.S. Doupnik, L.P. Seese / Journal of International Accounting, Auditing & Taxation 10 (2001) 117–138   127

Table 3
Individual Countries and Groupings of Countries Reported in Enterprise-Wide Geographic Area Disclosures
of Revenues by *Fortune* 500 Companies in 1998

Individual Country	No. of Companies*	Grouping of Countries	No. of Companies**
Canada	53	Europe	56
U.K.	43	Latin America	28
Japan	24	Asia/Pacific	25
Germany	22	Asia	11
France	19	Pacific	11
Brazil	10	Europe/Middle East/Africa	10
Mexico	8	Other Europe	9
Italy	6	Western Hemisphere (excl. U.S.)	7
China	5	Other North America	4
Spain	5	Other Asia	4
Australia	5	Atlantic	3
Korea	4	Western Europe	3
Netherlands	4	Other groupings of countries	22
Argentina	3	Total	193
Chile	3		
Singapore	3		
Taiwan	3		
Other individual countries	22		
Total	242		

* Out of 115 companies providing disclosures for at least one individual country.
** Out of 92 companies providing disclosures for at least one geographic area defined as a grouping of
   countries.

international involvement affects whether a company disaggregates total foreign revenues or
not, but it does not affect a company's propensity to disclose by country, continent, or a mix
of the two.

The 168 companies that disaggregated total foreign revenues disclosed revenues for 553
geographic areas (countries, continents, "other"), an average of 3.3 areas per company. Panel
B in Table 2 indicates the level of aggregation provided in these disclosures. More than 40%
of geographic area disclosures were made at the individual country level. Although SFAS
131 only requires country-level disclosures, 34.9% of geographic area disclosures were
provided at the "continent" or "multicontinent" level.

Table 3 reports the individual countries and groupings of countries for which disclosures
are most commonly provided. As the countries with the greatest amount of U.S. foreign
direct investment, it is not surprising to find more companies reporting a material amount of
revenues in Canada and the United Kingdom than in any other countries. The top five
countries listed in Table 3 are five of the top seven countries in terms of U.S. foreign direct
investment (OECD 1997). Only five countries were reported by more than 10 of the 254
companies disclosing revenues by geographic area. By far the most common grouping of
countries (continent) for which disclosures are provided is Europe. A number of companies
continue to use vague geographic areas such as Pacific and highly aggregated areas like

128   *T.S. Doupnik, L.P. Seese / Journal of International Accounting, Auditing & Taxation 10 (2001) 117–138*

Table 4
Fortune 500 Companies Grouped on the Basis of the Percentage of Total Revenues Located in the Smallest Country Reported: Number of Companies by Group, Foreign Revenues as a Percentage of Total Revenues by Group, and Number of Countries Reported by Group

Panel A: Companies Grouped on the Basis of Smallest Country in 1998

Group	% of Total Revenues in Smallest Country	No. of Companies	Mean Foreign Revenue %	Number of Countries Reported		
				1	>1	mean
1	<5%	49	26.32%	17	32	3.00
2	5–10%	34	38.2%	20	14	1.71
3	>10%	32	37.9%	27	5	1.16
		115		64	51	

Panel B: Companies Grouped on the Basis of Smallest Country in 1997

Group	% of Total Revenues in Smallest Country	No. of Companies	Mean Foreign Revenue %	Number of Countries Reported		
				1	>1	mean
1	<5%	23	32.8%	15	8	1.50
2	5–10%	16	26.6%	15	1	1.10
3	>10%	14	30.7%	14	0	1.00
		53		44	9	

Europe/Middle East/Africa. These results are consistent with Herrmann and Thomas (2000b).

SFAS 131 provides companies flexibility in determining how to attribute revenues to individual countries, but the basis selected must be disclosed (para. 38a). Only 111 of the 254 sample companies disclosed their basis for attributing revenues to specific countries. Approximately half (49%) use the location of the customer or where services are performed for this purpose. Another 31% attribute revenues on the basis of the location of the seller or point of origin. The remaining companies use a variety of other bases such as location of operations (or assets) and where the transaction is recorded.

5.2. Thresholds used to determine materiality of revenues in individual countries

By examining the individual country disclosures that were made by the companies providing such disclosures, it is possible to determine the upper bound to the thresholds used by these companies in determining materiality. Table 4 provides summary information for the companies that provided disclosures by individual country only or in combination with continent-level disclosures. The companies were classified into three groups–those for which the "smallest" country had (1) less than 5% of total revenues, (2) between 5% and 10% of total revenues, and (3) greater than 10% of total revenues.

Table 4, Panel A, shows that 49 companies (42.6% of those providing country-level disclosures) are in Group 1. These companies apparently used a cutoff point smaller than 5% to determine the materiality of revenues in individual countries. In fact, 20 companies from this group provided disclosures for one or more countries that had less than 2% of total revenues, suggesting the use of a materiality cutoff point of less than 2%.

For another 34 companies (29.6%), the smallest country for which disclosures were provided had between 5% and 10% of total revenues. These companies either used a materiality threshold somewhere within this range or do not have revenues attributed to any single country less than 5–10%. Only 32 companies (27.8%) had more than 10% of total revenues in their smallest country. These companies either defined materiality at 10% or higher or did not have revenues in any single country below this level.

The middle column in Table 4 reports the Mean Foreign Revenue % for the three groups of companies. These numbers suggest that companies with a smaller Foreign Revenue % are more likely to use a quantitative threshold of less than 5% for determining material countries, whereas companies with a larger percentage of foreign revenues are more likely to use higher cutoff points. There is a positive correlation of 0.253 (significant at 0.01) between Foreign Revenue % and the percentage of revenues in the smallest country.

The three right-most columns in Table 4 show the number of companies within each materiality threshold group providing disclosures for one country or for more than one country, and the mean number of countries reported. Thirty-two (65%) companies in Group 1 determined that they have more than one material country but only five (16%) companies in Group 3 determined that they have more than one material country. To further explore the relationship between the quantitative threshold used to determine materiality and the number of countries reported, a correlation coefficient was calculated. There is a negative correlation of -0.477 (significant at 0.01) between the percentage of revenues in the smallest country and the number of countries reported. As would be expected, this indicates that the lower the cutoff point used, the greater is the number of countries reported.

These results suggest that there is a wide range of cutoff points being used by companies in determining the materiality of operations in individual countries (from 2% or less to 10% or greater). Approximately 72% (83 out of 115) of the companies reported a country that had less than 10% of total revenues. This is somewhat surprising given that SFAS 131 uses 10% as the quantitative threshold for determining reportable operating segments and SFAS 14 used 10% in determining when geographic areas were separately reportable. Perhaps even more surprising is the finding that 20 companies used a materiality threshold of less than 2%.

There are at least two reasons why management may wish to use low cutoff points in determining reportable individual countries, to signal potential diversification benefits and/or to signal low international risk. Adler and Dumas (1983) suggest that individual investors can obtain the benefits of international diversification indirectly by holding shares of multinational corporations, as these companies, in and of themselves, represent a portfolio of international investments. By disclosing even relatively small percentages of revenue by individual country, management may wish to signal that their company is multinational and therefore offers potential diversification benefits to investors. Doupnik and Rolfe (1989) demonstrated that analysts are able to distinguish between high risk and low risk countries in assessing a firm's international risk. Managers may have an incentive to disclose revenues in low risk countries even if the amounts are small to signal that the company's foreign operations are of low risk. Conversely, there may be an incentive for companies with operations in high risk countries to use high materiality cutoff points to avoid disclosing the individual country location of their foreign operations.

Fifty-three companies that provided individual country disclosures in 1998 also did so in 1997 under SFAS 14. These companies were grouped on the basis of the percentage of total revenues in the smallest country in 1997 (see Table 4, Panel B). Of the companies providing individual country disclosures, approximately the same percentage falls into Group 1 in 1997 as in 1998. Thus, whatever the incentive is to disclose relatively small percentages of total revenues by individual country, it seems to have affected approximately the same proportion of companies before and after the advent of SFAS 131.

Unless specifically disclosed, it is not possible to determine the cutoff points that were used by those companies that did not provide any country-level disclosures. As reported in Table 2, the group of companies reporting total foreign revenues only had the smallest mean Foreign Revenue % (21.4%). As a group, these companies are the least likely to have individual countries with a material amount of revenues. On the other hand, it is interesting to note (from Table 2) that the continent only group has the largest Foreign Revenue % (37.3%) of the three groups that disaggregated foreign revenues. Two possible explanations for the companies in this group not providing any country specific disclosures are that (1) they are relatively more diversified across countries than are the companies in the other two groups and therefore no single country is material, or (2) they used higher cutoff points in determining materiality.

5.3. Comparison of SFAS 131 disclosures with SFAS 14 disclosures–fineness

To address the research question whether the implementation of SFAS 131 has resulted in companies providing finer information, two measures of fineness were compared for 1997 and 1998.[9] Of the 254 companies reporting revenues by geographic area in 1998, 19 companies did not provide geographic area disclosures in 1997 presumably because they did not meet SFAS 14's threshold that required disclosure only when foreign revenues (or assets) exceeded 10% of total revenues (or assets). SFAS 131 requires companies to disclose total foreign revenues and long-lived assets without regard to a mandated quantitative threshold. Most of these newly reporting companies reported foreign revenues only in 1998 with no disaggregation. In addition, six companies were newly formed in 1998 (as the result of mergers) and comparable 1997 disclosures were not available. Thus, the comparison of 1998 and 1997 disclosures is made for 229 companies.

For purposes of analysis and presentation, companies are divided into four groups based upon the aggregation level used in their 1998 geographic area disclosures:

1. Companies providing disclosures by individual country only (n = 68).
2. Companies providing a mix of country and continent disclosures (n = 37).
3. Companies providing disclosures by continent only (n = 52).
4. Companies disclosing "foreign" revenues only (n = 72).

The number of areas reported and fineness scores (F) for these four groups are presented in Table 5. Fineness scores were calculated and are reported using three different weighting

T.S. Doupnik, L.P. Seese / Journal of International Accounting, Auditing & Taxation 10 (2001) 117–138   131

Table 5
Comparison of Number of Geographic Areas Reported and Fineness Scores Under SFAS 14 (1997) and SFAS 131 (1998) for *Fortune* 500 Companies Providing Geographic Area Disclosures in 1997 and 1998

All Companies (n=229)	Number of Areas		Fineness Scores					
			Weight=3		Weight=4		Weight=8	
	1997	1998	1997	1998	1997	1998	1997	1998
Mean	2.25	2.65	1.11	1.13	1.19	1.34	1.54	2.20
Increase (No. of co.'s)		66		94		98		113
Decrease		39		84		80		65
No change		124		51		51		51
Total companies		229		229		229		229
Companies Disclosing by Country Only in 1998 (n=68)	1997	1998	1997	1998	1997	1998	1997	1998
Mean	2.44	3.72	1.34	1.70	1.49	2.25	2.07	4.48
Increase		36		43		46		60
Decrease		11		24		21		7
No change		21		1		1		1
Total companies		68		68		68		68
Companies Disclosing Mix of Country and Continent in 1998 (n=37)	1997	1998	1997	1998	1997	1998	1997	1998
Mean	3.03	3.89	1.63	1.94	1.85	2.24	2.59	3.47
Increase		17		21		22		23
Decrease		0		16		15		14
No change		20		0		0		0
Total companies		37		37		37		37
Companies Disclosing by Continent Only in 1998 (n=52)	1997	1998	1997	1998	1997	1998	1997	1998
Mean	2.38	2.63	1.25	1.38	1.25	1.38	1.27	1.38
Increase		13		30		30		30
Decrease		5		20		20		20
No change		34		2		2		2
Total companies		52		52		52		52
Companies Disclosing Foreign Only in 1998 (n=72)	1997	1998	1997	1998	1997	1998	1997	1998
Mean	1.57	1.0	0.51	0.00	0.54	0.00	0.68	0.00
Increase		0		0		0		0
Decrease		24		24		24		24
No change		48		48		48		48
Total companies		72		72		73		72

schemes in which country specific disclosures were assigned a weight of 3, 4, and 8, respectively.

5.3.1. All companies

Table 5 first summarizes the results across all 229 companies. The mean number of areas disclosed increased significantly from 1997 to 1998 ($p = .001$). The number of areas reported increased for 28.8% of the sample companies and decreased for 17.0%; there was no change in number of areas for a majority of companies. The number of companies with an increase or decrease in number of areas reported is not as large as was found by Nichols et al. (2000) for their sample. They found an increase in number of areas for 35% and a decrease in number of areas for 22% of their sample.

Assigning country disclosures a weight $= 3$, there is no significant change in the mean F score from 1997 to 1998 ($p = .687$). The increase in F score from 1997 to 1998 is significant using weight $= 4$ ($p = .041$) and weight $= 8$ ($p = .000$). Thus, the conclusion regarding the increase (or no change) in fineness as measured by F for the entire sample depends upon the weight assigned to the country-level disclosures. Additional insight is gained by partitioning the complete sample into those companies with an increase in F score and those with a decrease.

With country weight $= 3$, the F score increased for 94 companies (41% of the sample), and decreased for 84 companies (37%). No change was registered for 22% of the sample. For the "increase" subsample, the F score rose significantly from 1.10 in 1997 to 1.80 in 1998 ($p = .000$). The F score for the "decrease" subsample fell significantly from 1.71 in 1997 to 0.99 in 1998 ($p = .000$). Note that the F score under SFAS 14 for the "decrease" subsample is almost as high as the F score under SFAS 131 for the "increase" subsample. The mean change in score for the decrease companies is larger than the mean change for the increase companies.

Similar results obtain with country weights $= 4$ and 8. Even with weight $= 8$ assigned to the country-level disclosures, there is a decrease in F score for 65 companies (28% of the sample). Given the weighting schemes used to calculate the fineness score, SFAS 131 appears to have led to finer information being provided by at least 40% of the *Fortune* 500 companies that reported foreign operations. However, for at least 28% of the sample, the fineness of the geographic information reported has deteriorated under SFAS 131.

5.3.2. Companies disclosing by country only in 1998

There is a significant increase in the mean number of areas reported by those companies disclosing by country only in 1998; 2.44 areas under SFAS 14 versus 3.72 areas under SFAS 131 ($p = .000$). There is an increase in the number of areas reported by 36 (52.9%) of the 68 companies in this group. Only 11 companies in this group reported fewer countries in 1998 than they reported geographic areas in 1997.

Of the 68 companies reporting countries only in 1998, only 19 provided any disclosures by country in 1997–10 reported countries only and 9 reported a mix of country and continent. Thus, implementation of SFAS 131 has caused 49 companies in this group to begin reporting country specific information.

The increase in number of areas reported in conjunction with reporting at a less aggregated

T.S. Doupnik, L.P. Seese / Journal of International Accounting, Auditing & Taxation 10 (2001) 117–138 133

country level results in a significant increase in the mean fineness score for this group ($p =$ .007, wt = 3). Assigning a weight = 3 to country-level disclosures, fineness increased for 63% of the companies in this group. Nine of the 11 companies with a decrease in number of areas also had a decrease in the F score.

Companies with substantial increases in fineness score include Federal Mogul which changed from disaggregating its foreign operations into Europe and Other in 1997 (F score of 1.10 with country weight = 3) to providing information on six specific countries in 1998 (F score of 2.61), and Airtouch Communications which reported aggregate foreign operations as International in 1997 (F score: 0.0) but disaggregated all of its foreign operations into two countries (Portugal and Sweden) in 1998 (F score: 3.0).

For some companies, the change from continent-level to country-level disclosures has led to a decrease in fineness score. The company in this group with the greatest decrease in F score is Merck (from 1.826 to 0.520). Merck disaggregated 100% of its foreign operations into Europe, Asia-Pacific, and Other in 1997, but disclosed only 17% of its foreign operations by country (Japan) in 1998. IBM made a similar change with a resulting decrease in F score.

To examine the impact the materiality threshold has on fineness, the percentage of revenues in the "smallest" country was correlated with the number of countries disclosed and the fineness score. As would be expected, there is a significant negative correlation between "smallest" country and number of countries reported (r = -0.56). The correlation between "smallest" country and the F score is also negative, but not significant (r = -0.10). Contrary to expectations, the materiality cutoff point does not appear to significantly influence fineness as measured by the F score.

5.3.3. Companies disclosing by country and continent in 1998

The number of areas reported by those companies providing a mix of country and continent disclosure in 1998 (3.89 areas) also increased significantly ($p =$ .000) over 1997 (3.03 areas), but the increase is not as great as for the country only disclosers. Almost half of this group had an increase in the number of areas reported, and none had a decrease. The majority of companies in this group (24 of 37) already reported a mix of countries and continents in 1997. SFAS 131 caused 13 companies in this group to begin providing country-level disclosures.

The mean fineness scores under the various weighting schemes also increased significantly for this group of companies ($p =$ .015, wt = 3). There is a direct relationship between the change in number of areas and the change in fineness score (r=0.795). Only three companies with an increase in areas had a lower F score in 1998 (regardless of weighting scheme). In each case, a geographic area at the continent level was added in 1998, possibly due to foreign expansion, causing the overall F score to decrease. Each of these three companies already provided country-level disclosures in 1997 under SFAS 14.

5.3.4. Companies disclosing by continent only in 1998

Fifty-two companies provided disclosures by continent only in 1998, doing so on a voluntary basis. The increase in mean number of areas reported by this group is significant ($p =$ .027). However, almost two-thirds of the companies in this group reported the same number of areas in 1998 as in 1997, and in most cases the areas are the same. These companies appear to be interested in continuing to provide financial statement readers with the same level of disclosure as was provided in the past. There were only two companies in this group that separately disclosed information for a country in 1997, but not in 1998. Revenues attributed to Canada represented 2.5% of total revenues for Allied Signal and 2.2% of total revenues for Comdisco in 1997.

There is a small and insignificant increase in mean fineness score for this group (p = .082). Regardless of weighting scheme, approximately 58% of the companies had an increase in F score and 39% had a decrease.[10] All but one of the 13 companies with an increase in number of areas also had an increase in F score. Almost all of the continent only disclosers had a change in F score even though a majority had no change in the number of areas reported. This is explained by a change from 1997 to 1998 in the percentage of total revenues disclosed as "other" that was assigned a weight = 0.

5.3.5. Companies disclosing foreign revenues only in 1998

There were 86 companies in the full sample of 254 companies that reported foreign revenues in total only in 1998. Fourteen of these companies provided no geographic disclosures in 1997, presumably because they did not meet any of SFAS 14's quantitative thresholds triggering the reporting of geographic segment information. Ten of these 14 companies had a Foreign Revenue % less than 10% in 1998 but disclosed foreign revenues because SFAS 131 requires disclosure of total foreign revenues without regard to meeting a minimum quantitative threshold.

Of the 72 companies in this group that provided geographic area information in both 1998 and 1997, 48 reported foreign revenues only in both years. There was no change in the number of areas reported or in F score for these 48 companies.

The remaining 24 companies disaggregated total foreign revenues into one or more geographic areas in 1997 but not in 1998. This result is consistent with Nichols et al. (2000), who also found an increase in the number of companies providing no disaggregation of foreign revenues under SFAS 131. Eight of these companies disclosed revenues for one or more countries in 1997. The greatest change in this regard was made by Pepsico which reported the following geographic areas in 1997–U.S, Europe, Canada, Mexico, U.K., and Other–but reported U.S. and Foreign only in 1998.

There is a significant decrease in the mean number of areas reported (p = .000) and the mean fineness score (p = .000) for this group of 24 companies. Some of the largest decreases in fineness score from 1997 to 1998 are found within this group. Several examples are reported in Table 6. There is an obvious decline from 1997 to 1998 in the fineness (and potential usefulness) of the geographic area information provided by these companies.

6. Summary and conclusions

This study investigated the implementation of SFAS 131's geographic area disclosure requirements especially with regard to the determination of individually material countries and the change in fineness of the resulting information set.

T.S. Doupnik, L.P. Seese / Journal of International Accounting, Auditing & Taxation 10 (2001) 117–138 135

Table 6
Examples of *Fortune* 500 Companies that Disaggregated Foreign Revenues in 1997 but not in 1998

	1997	% of Total Revenues	1998	% of Total Revenues
Honeywell	U.S.	60.3%	U.S.	61.7%
	Europe	26.6%	Foreign	38.3%
	Other	13.1%		
Number of areas:	2		1	
F score:*	1.342		0.0	
Caterpillar	U.S.	49.3%	U.S.	51.8%
	Europe	14.5%	Foreign	48.2%
	Asia/Pacific	13.7%		
	Latin America	9.4%		
	Canada	6.7%		
	Africa/Middle East	6.5%		
Number of areas:	5		1	
F score:	1.733		0.0	
Rohm & Haas	U.S.	56.7%	U.S.	47.2%
	Canada	3.1%	Foreign	52.8%
	Europe	24.0%		
	Asia/Pacific	11.1%		
	Latin America	5.1%		
Number of areas:	4		1	
F score:	1.813		0.0	
Pepsico	U.S.	66.3%	U.S.	68.8%
	Europe	11.1%	Foreign	31.2%
	Canada	4.5%		
	Mexico	7.4%		
	U.K.	4.1%		
	Other	6.6%		
Number of areas:	5		1	
F score:	2.085		0.0	
Ball	U.S.	79.1%	U.S.	84.6%
	Canada	11.2%	Foreign	15.4%
	Asia	9.7%		
Number of areas:	2		1	
F score:	2,536		0.0	

* F score based on country weight = 3.

Approximately one-half of *Fortune* 500 companies provided geographic area revenue disclosures in their 1998 annual report. A significant number of these companies (34%) provided no disaggregation of total foreign revenues. As a group these companies had the smallest foreign revenue percentage and therefore would be least likely to have a material amount of total revenues located in any individual foreign country. However, several companies in this group had 40% or more of their revenues attributed to foreign operations. These companies may be significantly exposed to risks associated with the generation of foreign revenues but, not knowing where those revenues are located and in what magnitude, financial analysts will find it difficult to incorporate information about those risks into their evaluation of these companies. Of particular concern in terms of the potential deterioration in usefulness of geographic area information caused by implementation of SFAS 131 is the subset of 24 companies within this group that provided disaggregated information in 1997 but discontinued doing so in 1998.

A significant number of companies (36%) voluntarily disclosed revenues by groupings of countries (continent) in 1998. To the extent that the continent disclosures under SFAS 14 were useful, this voluntary disclosure should enhance the information value of the individual country disclosures required by SFAS 131. This is especially true for those companies that otherwise would have provided no disaggregated information for foreign revenues (the continent only disclosure group).

There appears to be considerable diversity in the quantitative threshold used by companies to evaluate the materiality of revenues in individual countries. Both the FASB and financial analysts should welcome the fact that among the 44% of sample companies providing country specific disclosures, more than 70% disclosed individual countries attributed with less than 10% of total revenues and more than 40% disclosed individual countries with less than 5% of total revenues. By selecting their own quantitative threshold, these companies are providing finer information than they would have if SFAS 131 had mandated a 10% cutoff point and this threshold had been strictly followed. It is interesting to note that companies with a smaller percentage of foreign revenues provide disclosures for more individual countries than do companies with a larger percentage of foreign revenues. Future research investigating the incentives management has for using low (or high) materiality thresholds in determining reportable countries might prove interesting.

Implementation of SFAS 131 has resulted in a significantly greater percentage of companies providing country-level disclosures in 1998 (115 of 254 companies or 45.3%) than in 1997 (53 of 229 companies or 23.1%). Somewhat surprisingly, ten companies that provided country-level disclosures in 1997 discontinued doing so in 1998. Sixty-two companies (27% of 229) initiated country-level disclosures in 1998.

Although twice as many companies provided country-level disclosures in 1998 as in 1997, financial analysts should be concerned about the fact that more than one-half of the sample did not provide any country-level disclosures in 1998. A future study may want to focus on this group of companies to ascertain whether this lack of disclosure is the result of effective international diversification or the use of a high quantitative threshold to determine materiality.

Contrary to the prediction made by Nichols and Street (1999), only 29% of the sample companies increased the number of areas reported from 1997 to 1998 as they implemented SFAS 131. There is no change in the number of areas for more than 50% of the companies. In most cases, companies with no change in number of areas still had a change in fineness score because of a change in the aggregation level or the percentage of foreign revenues in the reported areas.

Regardless of the weighting scheme used, at least 40% of the sample companies have an increase in fineness score after implementing SFAS 131. To the extent that finer information is potentially more useful, financial analysts and the FASB should welcome this result. On the other hand, more than 25% of the sample posted a decrease in fineness score from 1997 to 1998. Fineness tends to increase for companies providing country specific disclosures (alone or in conjunction with continent disclosures). Mean fineness remains about the same for the group of companies disclosing by continent only, and deteriorates for the group reporting foreign revenues only. Future research might examine whether the change in fineness score is a function of company specific factors. Perhaps the most important question to be addressed by future research is whether the change in fineness of geographic area disclosures results in a change in the usefulness of those disclosures.

NOTES

1. Several companies adopted SFAS 131 early in 1997 (see Nichols and Street 1999).
2. An operating segment is separately reportable if (a) its revenues are 10% or more of the combined revenues of all reported operating segments, (b) its profit or loss is 10% or more of the combined amount of profit or combined amount of loss, whichever is greater, or (c) its assets are 10% or more of the combined assets of all operating segments. The existence of a major customer must be disclosed if revenues from transactions with a single customer amount to 10% or more of total revenues.
3. SFAS 14 required companies to report data on foreign operations by significant geographic segments if (1) revenues from foreign operations were at least 10% of consolidated revenues or (2) identifiable assets of foreign operations were at least 10% of consolidated assets. An individual geographic segment was significant and separately reportable if identifiable assets or revenues were 10% or more of consolidated assets or revenues. Geographic segments could be individual countries or groups of countries or regions of the world and the designation of geographic segment was left to management discretion.
4. However, SFAS 131 indicates that, in addition to providing information by individual material country, "an enterprise may wish to provide subtotals of geographic information about groupings of countries" (para. 38).
5. Of the *Fortune* 500, six companies disclosed the materiality threshold used to determine whether countries were individually material. Chase Manhattan, Dana, 3Com, and Parker Hannifin used 10%, and McGraw-Hill and Merck used 5% as the cutoff point.
6. This approach is consistent with the guidelines for determining reportable operating segments under SFAS 131 and reportable geographic segments under SFAS 14 as described in footnotes 2 and 3 above, respectively.
7. For purposes of calculating the F score, "multicontinent" denotes areas created by combining countries located on more than one continent such as Europe/MiddleEast/Africa, Asia/Pacific, and Western Hemisphere (excluding U.S.), and "continent" includes groupings of countries described as Europe, Africa, Asia, and Latin America, as well as portions of a continent such as Western Europe and Southeast Asia.
8. Note that most companies providing disaggregated disclosures (by country and/or continent) combine revenues not disclosed by separate geographic area in a line item labeled "other."

9. Although several companies initially implemented SFAS 131 either in their 1997 or 1999 annual reports, for simplicity sake, 1998 is used to connote the year of SFAS 131 implementation and 1997 as the final year of SFAS 14 application.

10. The mean fineness score in 1998 for this group is unaffected by the value used to weight country-level disclosures because no country specific disclosures were made by this group in 1998. The mean fineness score in 1997 is 1.25 using country weight = 3 and 4 and 1.27 using country weight = 8, the difference is due to the fact that several companies in this group provided country specific disclosures under SFAS 14. The different weightings did not affect the number of companies experiencing an increase or decrease in score from 1997 to 1998.

References

Adler, M., & Dumas, B. (1983). International portfolio choice and corporation finance: a synthesis. _Journal of Finance,_ (June), 925–984.

Boatsman, J. R., Behn, B. K., & Patz, D. H. (1993). A test of the use of geographical segment disclosures. _Journal of Accounting Research,_ (Supplement), 46–74.

Coller, M., & Pierce, B. (1999). The new segment information: is it any better?" _The Journal of Financial Statement Analysis,_ (Winter), 65–72.

Doupnik, T. S., & Rolfe, R. J. (1989). The relevance of level of aggregation of geographical area data in the assessment of foreign investment risk. _Advances in Accounting,_ 51–65.

Financial Accounting Standards Board (FASB). (1976). _Statement of financial accounting standards No. 14,_ Financial reporting for segments of a business enterprise. Stamford, CT.

_____. 1997. _Statement of financial accounting standards no. 131,_ Disclosures about segments of an enterprise and related information. Norwalk, CT.

Fortune. (1999). Fortune five hundred largest U.S. corporations. _Fortune_ (April 26), F1–F20.

Herrmann, D. (1996). The predictive ability of geographic segment information at the country, continent, and consolidated levels. _Journal of International Financial Management and Accounting,_ (Spring), 50–73.

_____ & Thomas, W. B. (2000a). A model of forecast precision using segment disclosures: implications for SFAS no. 131. _Journal of International Accounting, Auditing & Taxation,_ (No. 1), 1–18.

_____ & _____. 2000b. An analysis of segment disclosures under SFAS no. 131 and SFAS no. 14. _Accounting Horizons,_ (September), 287–302.

Nichols, D., Tunnell, L., & Waldrup, B. (1996). An exploratory study of the effect on forecast accuracy of using different geographic segment data sources. _Journal of International Financial Management and Accounting,_ (Summer), 125–136.

Nichols, N., Street, D., & Gray, S. (2000). Geographic segment disclosures in the United States: reporting practices enter a new era. _Journal of International Accounting, Auditing & Taxation,_ (No. 1), 59–82.

_____ & Street, D. 1999. Segment information: what early adopters reported. _Journal of Accountancy,_ (January), 37–41.

Organisation for Economic Cooperation and Development (OECD). (1997). _International Direct Investment Statistics Yearbook._ Paris: OECD.

Thomas, W. B. (2000). The value-relevance of geographic segment earnings disclosures under SFAS 14. _Journal of International Financial Management and Accounting,_ (Autumn), 133–155.

[3]

N·H

ELSEVIER   Journal of Accounting and Public Policy 21 (2002) 31–70

Journal of
Accounting
and
Public Policy

www.elsevier.com/locate/jaccpubpol

The effect of Japanese business segment reporting on analysts' forecasts: implications for US investors and the SEC

Vivek Mande *, Richard Ortman *

Department of Accounting, College of Business Administration, University of Nebraska, Omaha, NE 68182-0048, USA

Abstract

Japan has required that business segment data be disclosed in annual financial statements since 1990. This study examines the information content of business segment disclosures of multisegmented Japanese firms on the Nikkei 225 index. Specifically, we test whether Japanese analysts' forecast accuracy of consolidated sales and net income improves following the disclosure of segment data. Our study finds that the introduction of the segment reporting standard aids analysts in forecasting sales of well-diversified firms, but there is no improvement in the forecast accuracy of earnings. We conclude from our results that financial analysts do not generally find Japanese segment disclosures to be useful in their equity analysis. These results have implications for US investors and the US Securities and Exchange Commission which allows Japanese firms to list on US exchanges using Japanese segment reporting standards. © 2002 Elsevier Science Ltd. All rights reserved.

1. Introduction

Segment reporting became a controversial issue in the US during the 1960s with the rise of conglomerates. Because diverse industries and regions have varying rates of growth and risk, the Financial Accounting Standards Board

---

*Corresponding authors. Tel.: +1-402-554-2504 (V. Mande); fax: +1-402-554-3747 (V. Mande).
E-mail addresses: vivekmande@unomaha.edu (V. Mande), richard_ortman@unomaha.edu (R. Ortman).

0278-4254/02/$ - see front matter © 2002 Elsevier Science Ltd. All rights reserved.
PII: S0278-4254(02)00036-4

32   *V. Mande, R. Ortman / Journal of Accounting and Public Policy 21 (2002) 31–70*

(FASB) believed that the financial analyses of firms operating in diverse industries and/or geographic areas would be aided by the disclosure of segment information.

Because segment reporting standards allow managers great latitude in defining segments and in allocating common costs, there was concern that the reported segment data would be of no real value to users. However, during the past 30 years, numerous studies have found that segment reporting does, in fact, provide US financial markets with useful information. There is substantial evidence, for example, that US financial analysts' forecasts of consolidated performance improve when based on segment information.

In more recent years, US analysts' use of segment data has expanded to include such data disclosed in annual reports of foreign firms. There are two main reasons for the increased interest in segment data disclosed by foreign firms. First, there has been an explosion of trading on global markets by US financial institutions and individual investors. Second, the US Securities and Exchange Commission (SEC), under pressure from the New York Stock Exchange (NYSE), has removed certain barriers impeding foreign firms access to US markets. Under current regulations foreign firms are able to satisfy US listing requirements by disclosing segment data using their own country's GAAP instead of US GAAP which was previously required.

At issue is the responsibility of the SEC to US investors and firms. Specifically, allowing foreign firms, using foreign segment reporting standards, to list on US exchanges raises two questions: Are US investors harmed using segment data prepared under foreign GAAP? And, are US firms at a competitive disadvantage having to report more information regarding segment financial results than foreign·firms?

The study of Japanese segment reporting represents a unique environment to examine the above issues. There is a significant amount of US investment in Japanese stocks which requires that US investors have relevant and reliable data available regarding Japanese firms to make informed investment decisions. In contrast to the US, a significant proportion of a Japanese firm's capital is supplied by its creditors who have a close relationship with the firm and thus receive a significant amount of private information. Therefore, US and other investors cannot look to the largest contributor of capital in Japan to clamour for better financial reporting. An additional concern is that segment reporting represented a major reporting issue to the extent that Japanese firms refused listing on US stock exchanges for over a decade because they feared disclosing sensitive segment information to competitors. Therefore, it was not until 1986 that the Ministry of Finance (MOF) was able to take tentative steps towards requiring segment disclosures. However, before requiring segment disclosures, the MOF surveyed CEOs for their opinions on segment reporting. Not surprisingly, most of the CEOs responding to the MOF survey were opposed to disclosing segment information because they believed that segment

V. Mande, R. Ortman / Journal of Accounting and Public Policy 21 (2002) 31–70 33

reporting would place sensitive information in the public domain (Ozu and Gray, 2001). Despite overwhelming opposition, the MOF, under pressure from the SEC, mandated segment reporting for Japanese firms beginning April 1, 1990. However, when compared to the US standard, the MOF's standard requires fewer segment disclosures and given the history of resistance to reporting segment data, an interesting question for this study is whether financial reports of Japanese firms contain useful or coarse segment data.

In evaluating the usefulness of segment data, prior work has examined how financial analysts respond to the disclosures. Because of cultural differences affecting interpretation of financial data in evaluating a foreign country's standard, an important first step should be to determine how financial analysts of that country respond to the standard. If the foreign analysts find segment disclosures to be "garbled", then it is likely that US investors attempting to use that segment footnote will be misled to a greater degree in their equity analyses of the foreign firm.

The results of this study show that the introduction of segment reporting provided Japanese financial analysts with information to significantly improve their forecasts of sales, but only for the more diversified firms. However, forecasts of net income did not improve. These findings are based on an analysis of prominent (Nikkei 225) Japanese firms over the period 1989–1994. The results of this study should be of interest to investors in Japanese financial markets who have concerns about the quality of segment information disclosed by Japanese firms. For the SEC, important policy questions are whether allowing Japanese firms, reporting segment data under Japanese standards, to list on US exchanges places US firms at a competitive disadvantage and whether US investors are harmed using Japanese segment disclosures.

In the following section, we review the literature on segment disclosures as prelude to developing our hypotheses for Japanese segment disclosures. Section 3 describes the data and empirical test results, while Section 4 concludes the paper.

2. Literature review and development of hypotheses

In 1976 the FASB introduced SFAS 14 (replaced in June 1997 by SFAS 131) which mandated the disclosure of identifiable assets, revenues and net operating income or net income or other profitability measures by business and region. The stated objective of these disclosures is to provide investors with useful information for assessing the overall profitability and risk of firms composed of segments operating in diverse industries and/or regions. However, there have been concerns about the overall costs associated with segment reporting. In a survey mailed to US multinational firms, Radebaugh and Gray (1997) find that managers expressed concern that the standards place in the

34   *V. Mande, R. Ortman / Journal of Accounting and Public Policy 21 (2002) 31–70*

public domain sensitive information which could be used against by them by their competitors. On the other hand, because accounting standards allow discretion in defining segments, a frequent criticism of segment reporting has been that the "coarse" definitions of business and geographic segments used by many firms often make the resulting financial statements useless to investors. Another complaint has been that the allocation of common costs among segments can be arbitrary, making measurement of segment performance unreliable.

2.1. Empirical evidence on the usefulness of segment reporting

Numerous studies using US data conclude, however, that investors do find segment reporting useful. Collins (1976) finds that time-series forecasts of consolidated net income increase in accuracy with the use of business segment information. Similarly, Baldwin (1984) finds that Value-Line forecasts are more accurate following the SEC's business segment reporting requirements. [1] Fried et al. (1992) examine the effects of voluntary reporting of quarterly business segment data by US companies. The authors report that analysts' forecasts improve following disclosure of quarterly segment data. Supporting the idea that investors associate increased forecast accuracy with lower risk, Collins and Simonds (1979) showed that *beta* decreases following the introduction of business segment reporting. [2]

Despite empirical evidence to the contrary, several investment groups and associations (e.g., Association for Investment and Management Research (AIMR)) describe segment reporting in the US as being meaningless (Saudagaran, 1993; Afterman, 1995). The most frequent demand of users in recent years has been for rules to restrict managerial discretion in defining segments. In response, the FASB recently issued SFAS 131 mandating quarterly reporting and defining segments for external reporting that are consistent with the firm's internal organizational structure and reporting system.

International practices regarding segment reporting have also come under criticism. Saudagaran and Meek (1997) state that while five international organizations and 30 countries have strongly endorsed segment reporting, the quality of disclosures has been less than adequate. [3] With few exceptions, work on this topic has been confined to surveys of segment disclosure practices in different countries. There has been little empirical work on the usefulness of

---

[1] In 1969, the SEC required business segment reporting for US firms. These requirements were replaced by FASB's SFAS 14 requiring both business and geographic disclosures.

[2] There is also separate evidence that geographic segment disclosures by US firms have information content (e.g., Balakrishnan et al. (1990)).

[3] In response to criticism, the International Accounting Standards Committee (IASC) recently adopted a new standard on segment disclosures (IAS 14).

V. Mande, R. Ortman / Journal of Accounting and Public Policy 21 (2002) 31–70   35

segment disclosures in an international context. Exceptions include Emmanuel and Gray (1977), who find that segments are defined very "coarsely" by UK firms making segment performance comparisons across firms nearly impossible. However, Roberts (1989), Prodhan (1986), and Prodhan and Harris (1989) find that segment disclosures of UK firms contain useful information. Aitken et al. (1994) examine business segment disclosures of Australian firms and report that these disclosures have information content. Our study contributes to this literature by providing some of the first evidence on the usefulness of business segment disclosures of Japanese corporations.

2.2. Segment reporting in Japan

For Japanese firms segment reporting constituted a major hurdle when it came to listing on US exchanges, primarily because of concerns about segment disclosures that were required by the SEC (Balakrishnan et al., 1990). [4] The major complaint of Japanese firms was that disclosing segment information would place them at a competitive disadvantage (Balakrishnan et al., 1990; Choi and Stonehill, 1982). The issue was a source of conflict between the SEC and the NYSE which stood to gain substantial revenue from Japanese firms which would list their stocks on its exchange. In order to entice the Japanese firms to list, efforts were made to allay their fears about the information that would be required in segment disclosures. Balakrishnan et al., for example, state that a US law firm retained by the Japanese Chamber of Commerce advised the Chamber that segment reporting did not require sensitive disclosures about individual products and profits in different areas. [5]

Once the Chamber of Commerce was reassured that segment disclosures did not have to be "fine", the MOF in turn began to consider revising the Ministerial Ordinance On Business Disclosure in 1988 to include segment disclosures (Balakrishnan et al., 1990).

---

[4] In 1982, however, the SEC, under pressure from investors, adopted the Integrated Disclosure System (IDS) for foreign firms. Under IDS, several regulations with regard to listing were relaxed. Foreign firms wishing to list on US exchanges could, for example, satisfy listing requirements by disclosing segment data mandated under their own GAAP.

[5] The Japanese Chamber of Commerce retained a prominent US law firm (Sullivan and Cromwell) to examine whether listing and capital issue requirements in the US would be relaxed for Japanese firms. Balakrishnan et al. quote a 1985 report (Report to the Keidanren on Segment Reporting by Japanese Companies) to the Chamber from Mr. Grant of Sullivan and Cromwell who states that: Industry segment reporting does not require disclosing profits by individual products, and US companies have shown the way in combining different operations into broad segments which do not disclose sensitive information. Geographic segment reporting does not require showing profit in different areas that can be compared when products are manufactured in Japan and sold abroad.

36   *V. Mande, R. Ortman / Journal of Accounting and Public Policy 21 (2002) 31–70*

Pressure to require segment disclosures by Japanese firms was also brought on the MOF by the SEC at the 1987 MOF–SEC Round Table Conference. Additionally, in the late 1980s, the US demand for segment disclosures from Japanese firms was a key item that was included in the Japan–US Structural Impediments Initiative, whose objective was to search for ways in which the US trade deficit could be reduced. Ozu and Gray (2001) argue that the MOF was persuaded by the above developments to mandate segment reporting. Therefore, despite widespread opposition by Japanese firms, the MOF mandated reporting of business segment data beginning with April 1990.

2.3. Ministry of Finance surveys on segment reporting in Japan

In 1987, while developing segment reporting standards, the MOF sent a survey to 683 companies (preparers of financial statements) and 219 financial institutions (users of financial statements) requesting their opinions on segment reporting. Of the firms that responded, 76% were opposed to having a segment reporting standard because they believed that segment reporting would reveal sensitive information to their competitors putting them at a competitive disadvantage, especially with regard to overseas trading. Reporting geographical segment data was the most opposed provision because firms believed that it would lead to allegations of dumping and increased transfer pricing taxation. Also, firms believed that requiring simultaneous disclosures by both line of business and geographic area would be too costly.

Several areas of conflict between financial statement preparers and users were revealed by the MOF survey. For example, 96% of users stated that segment information should be mandated. In addition, users also had differences regarding such important issues as segment definition and allocations of common costs. On the issue of how segments should be defined, most firms (60%) responded that the judgement of directors should be the most important factor in defining reportable segments. However, if segment definition were based on management's discretion, users were concerned that segments may not be defined meaningfully and that comparability among firms would be lost. About half of the users wanted the MOF to require that the Japanese SIC (JSIC) code be used as a basis for defining business segments. Regarding geographic disclosures, half of the firms wanted the MOF to allow disclosure by just two broad geographic areas: Japan and Overseas. By contrast, over half of the users responding believed that geographic segment data should be provided by individual country and region. Users in the survey also expressed concern that arbitrary allocation of common costs could make segment information meaningless.

Ozu and Gray (2001) showed that, throughout this debate, the MOF had to confront the dramatically different views of users and preparers regarding very significant issues relating to segment reporting. While users were constantly concerned about consistency and comparability, the MOF realized that firms were very hesistant to disclose any segment information whatsoever. In the end, the MOF took the side of the firms on all three critical issues, namely: geographic segment reporting, how a segment is to be defined and how common costs are to be allocated. On the issue of reporting geographic segment data, the MOF adopted the firms' position that sales be reported in only two categories: those made in Japan and those overseas; hardly data rich in information content (disclosure of geographic segment data by region was required for fiscal years beginning on or after April 1, 1997). The MOF also concluded that the use of the JSIC code would make segment reporting too rigid and less meaningful when compared to the approach that took into account management's judgement. On the issue of allocating common costs, the MOF decided that common costs should be allocated among segments in a way that directors view most appropriate. Because of the strong opposition by Japanese firms and their success in influencing the MOF, it appears essential to test whether or not Japanese segment reports contain useful information for users of Japanese financial statements.

In defining a segment, the Japanese standard states that firms should consider the type of product, manufacturing process and marketing regions. [6] Disclosure of segment information is required if: (a) segment sales (including intergroup sales) exceeds 10% of total firm sales, or (b) if segment operating revenue (loss) is greater than 10% of total firm operating revenue (loss) from all segments having operating revenues (losses). [7] Once specific segments are identified, the firm must continue to report data on these segments for a while. Similar to the US accounting standard, the Japanese standard does not require separate disclosure of common costs subjectively allocated to each division.

The Japanese MOF began requiring that segment data be disclosed in 1990, with increasing disclosure requirements in 1995 and 1997. For fiscal years starting April 1, 1990, disclosure of sales and income by segments was required along with export sales (but not by country) if export sales exceeded 10% of total sales. Assets, depreciation and capital expenditures by business segment had to be disclosed for fiscal years beginning April 1, 1995. Most recently,

---

[6] The discussion summarizes segment reporting rules under the Securities and Exchange Law set by the MOF in consultation with Business Accounting Deliberation Council.

[7] Firms are allowed to combine outside sales with intragroup sales and transfers in applying these conditions. The firm may use a different measure of profit or loss instead of operating profit or loss in cases where the former is a better indicator of firm performance. The Japanese Institute of Certified Public Accountants (JICPA) has issued several guidelines for the preparation and audit of segment information. We thank Mr. Fumito Kogomori of the JICPA for his information.

38   *V. Mande, R. Ortman / Journal of Accounting and Public Policy 21 (2002) 31–70*

disclosure of sales, operating income and asset investment by geographic region was required for fiscal years starting April 1, 1997. [8] Because segment footnote data were available to us only for the years 1989–1994, we test whether the disclosure of only sales and income by business segment during that period aided users of Japanese financial statements.

A comparison of Japanese segment reporting standards and practice with US standards (SFAS 131) and practice reveals additional differences (Exhibit A (Table 1)). [9] First, Japanese firms are not required to disclose sales to major customers. Second, US standards require that at least 75% of total sales (or operating income etc.) be shown by reportable segments (the 75% test); Japanese standards only contain a 50% test. This difference allows Japanese firms to disclose fewer number of segments. [10] Third, Japanese firms only report annual segment data, unlike US firms, which are required to disclose segment data each quarter. Fourth, unlike US firms which report segments by internal management structure, Japanese firms generally disclose segment data by *major* industry grouping which can result in far greater aggregation of data and loss of information content. [11] Fifth, US firms are required to report financial results (where material) by country; Japanese standards only require reporting by geographic region. Finally, whether the quality of the audit function in Japan is as high as that in the US is another concern. [12] Low quality monitoring by auditors increases managerial opportunities to "garble" segment data.

US accounting standards on segment reporting are the most stringent standards in the world (Radebaugh and Gray, 1997) Under the IDS, annual reports and filings of Japanese firms with the SEC may contain segment data

---

[8] There was much stronger opposition by Japanese firms to disclosing geographical segment information (Ozu and Gray, 2001). Japanese firms, therefore, were not required to make geographical segment disclosures immediately. Most firms reported geographical segment data for the first time in their financial statements ending March 31, 1998.

[9] While SFAS 131 was not in effect for the sample period analyzed in our study, we use it to discuss differences because it is relevant to current SEC policy that allows foreign firms to list using host country segment reporting standards. However, Exhibit A (Table 1) shows a comparison of SFAS 14 and earlier US standards on segment reporting with the Japanese standard.

[10] The Japanese standards state that if the total sales or operating revenue of reportable segments are less than 50% of total sales or operating revenues, then the firm must explain the reason for this situation. No additional segment disclosures are required.

[11] Japanese financial analysts wanted the MOF to mandate segment disclosures according to the JSIC code. The MOF, however, took the side of the managers who were opposed to disclosing this data and mandated that managers could use their discretion in defining segments. As a result Japanese firms mostly disclose segment data using very broad industry classification (see Ozu and Gray (2001) for more discussion on this point).

[12] A survey of over 50 Japanese equity analysts (Mande and Ortman, 2000) found that Japanese analysts do not believe the audit of segment data by Japanese auditors to be "useful".

V. Mande, R. Ortman / Journal of Accounting and Public Policy 21 (2002) 31–70   39

Table 1
Exhibit A: a chronology of US and Japanese segment disclosure rules

Effective date	A description of US disclosure rules	Effective date	A description of Japanese disclosure rules
1967	The APB encouraged, but did not require that segment disclosures be reported in annual reports.	1990	The MOF required an unaudited, annual footnote disclosing: (a) sales and operating profit/loss by broad industry classification if a segment's sales or operating profit/loss exceeded 10% of consolidated sales or operating profit/loss. Only 50% of consolidated sales must be disclosed by individual segments even if a segment's sales is not 10% of consolidated sales. (b) Overseas sales if such exceed 10% of consolidated sales.
1969	The SEC required annual disclosure of line of business data, such as, sales, operating profit/loss and assets if segment sales, profit, or assets equal 10% of consolidated sales, profit/loss or assets.	1993	The MOF required that the segment footnote be subject to audit.
1974	The SEC required that line of business disclosures be audited and included in annual reports to the SEC.	1995	The MOF required that assets, depreciation expense and capital expenditures be reported annually by business segment.
1976	The FASB required four types of segment disclosures: (a) sales, operating profit/loss and assets, etc. by line of business, (b) sales, operating profit/loss and assets, etc. of foreign operations, (c) export sales, (d) sales by major customer. In addition, sales to unaffiliated customers and the profit therefrom were required. The reporting threshold for items (a)–(d) above was 10% of respective consolidated figures accept that at least 75% of consolidated sales must be disclosed by individual segments even if a segment's sales is not 10% of a consolidated sales.	1997	The MOF required that overseas sales, operating income/loss, assets, etc. be reported by geographic region.

(continued on next page)

40   *V. Mande, R. Ortman / Journal of Accounting and Public Policy 21 (2002) 31–70*

Table 1 (*continued*)

Effective date	A description of US disclosure rules	Effective date	A description of Japanese disclosure rules
1996	The FASB required that the definition of a segment must be consistent with the company's organizational structure and internal reporting system and segment disclosures must be reported quarterly. Also, geographic reporting of revenues and long-lived assets (non-profit) must be done by individual country, not geographic region, if such is material (no definition of material given); otherwise just an overseas vs. domestic reporting need to be disclosed).		

Summary of disclosure differences as of 12/31/99

	United States	Japan
• Frequency of required reporting of segment data	Quarterly	Annually
• Proportion of consolidated sales that must be reported by segments regardless of the 10% rule	75%	50%
• Disclosure of sales to major customers	Required	Not required
• How a segment must be defined	Must be consistent with firm's organizational structure and internal reporting system	Broadly by industry classification
• Definition of area by which geographic sales and long-lived assets must be reported	Individual country	Region

required of them by the Japanese MOF. An important policy issue for the SEC, therefore, is whether US firms are at a competitive disadvantage because Japanese firms are permitted to list their stocks on US exchanges with less informative segment disclosures. [13] Another group to consider is global investors who own significant amounts of Japanese stocks. According to the Securities Industry Association, purchases and sales of Japanese stocks by US investors, for example, amounted to $153 billion in 1997. The value of US

---

[13] See, for example, Saudagaran and Biddle (1994).

V. Mande, R. Ortman / Journal of Accounting and Public Policy 21 (2002) 31–70 41

direct investment (private enterprises owned or controlled by US investors) in Japan amounted to $35.6 billion as of December 31, 1997. [14] For these reasons, examining the quality of segment information disclosed in Japanese financial statements is important to US and global financial markets.

2.4. Hypothesis

This study tests whether segment information of Japanese firms contains useful information by examining whether disclosing such information increases financial analysts' ability to forecast consolidated performance. Specifically, if segment disclosures have information content, analysts' forecast errors of future consolidated performance should decrease. On the other hand, if Japanese annual reports contain coarse segment information, there should be no improvement in forecast accuracy. [15] There would also be no effect on analysts' forecast errors if, prior to 1991, analysts had access to reported segment information from other sources (e.g., insider information, trade journals) that was as rich in information content as segment disclosures. [16] To be consistent with prior work, we hypothesize that:

Hypothesis 1. Japanese analysts' forecasts of consolidated performance improve following business segment disclosures mandated by the Japanese MOF.

All else constant, the greater the degree of corporate diversification, the more relevant segment disclosures become for analysts (e.g., Dunn and Nathan (2000)). We, therefore, partition our sample into four groups according to extent of diversification: firms with a high degree of diversification (hereafter high diversification firms), firms with a medium degree of diversification (hereafter medium diversification firms), firms with a low degree of diversification (hereafter low diversification firms), and firms that were not diversified (hereafter non-diversified firms). We examine whether segment disclosures most benefited analysts following more diversified, multisegmented firms.

---

[14] See, The Statistical Abstract of the United States 1998 published by Hoover Business Press.

[15] The stiff resistance that Japanese firms put up for 13 years and the resulting staggered and possibly lax segment disclosure standards generated for them by the MOF would indicate that Japanese firms would define segments coarsely and allocate common costs to achieve their reporting objectives.

[16] Baldwin (1984), however, points out that even if firms were voluntarily disclosing information (e.g., in annual reports or to analysts), we should expect to find information content in segment disclosures. He argues that accounting standards require presentation of segment information under a different format. Analysts' reports, for example, are not likely to be homogeneous because each analyst is likely to follow a different firm (or group of firms). Under accounting rules, however, there is greater homogeneity in information that becomes publicly available which should lead to improvement in analysts' forecast accuracy.

42   V. Mande, R. Ortman / Journal of Accounting and Public Policy 21 (2002) 31–70

A number of measures have been used in the literature to proxy for the extent of diversification. These include number of business segments, proportion of employees in the largest two-digit SIC business, measures of dominant proportion (e.g., percentage of sales or assets of a single line of business) and Herfindahl ratio (e.g., Dunn and Nathan (2000) and Cardinal and Opler (1995)). Unlike the other proxies mentioned, the Herfindahl ratio takes into account the importance of *each* segment to total operations. Therefore, in our study to group firms according to extent of diversification we use the Herfindahl ratio, defined as $\sum_i (s_i/S)^2$, where s_i is the sales of business segment i and S is total firm sales.

This study differs from prior research in three important ways. First, prior research has mostly focused on the effects of segment reporting on UK and US analysts' forecast errors. Because Japanese financial reporting is less transparent and is oriented towards creditors, this study contributes by examining the relevance of segment reports in a different cultural context. Second, prior work has mostly examined analysts' forecast errors of consolidated income. However, there is no reason to expect that analysts will benefit from segment reporting only in their forecasts of net income. For years Japanese companies have focused on sales growth and market share believing profitability would follow. Therefore, our focus also includes analysts' forecasts of consolidated sales. Finally, our study differs from prior work in that we examine the usefulness of product segment disclosures by partitioning the sample according to extent of corporate diversification.

2.5. Tests of hypothesis

Our tests of Hypothesis 1 are operationalized as follows: for each group of diversified firms, we separately empirically examine whether there is a decrease in the forecast errors of sales and earnings following the introduction of segment reporting in Japan.

As a first test, we compute the change in absolute sales and earnings forecast errors (FE) from year $t-1$ to t ($t = 1990–1994$) for each firm i for sales and net income:

$$\Delta FE_{it} = |FE_{it}| - |FE_{it-1}|$$

For each group, we then compute the mean of the changes in absolute forecast errors across all N sampled firms for each year. That is:

$$\overline{\Delta FE}_t = \sum_{i=1}^{N} \Delta FE_{it}/N$$

We then examine whether the mean absolute change in 1992 statistically significantly decreased following business segment disclosures.

V. Mande, R. Ortman / Journal of Accounting and Public Policy 21 (2002) 31–70   43

By using consecutive changes in forecast errors of a given firm, each firm in these tests serves as its own control. However, a limitation of examining year-to-year changes is that, to test the effect of segment reporting, we only compare forecast errors of 1992 with 1991, i.e., the tests of Hypothesis 1 only use information relating to two years. Therefore, for our next test we compute the mean sales and earnings forecast errors for each diversified group during the pre-segment reporting period (1989–1991) and compare these with corresponding mean values during the post-segment period (1992–1994). That is, we test whether for each group:

$$\overline{FE_{i1}} - \overline{FE_{i0}} < 0$$

where $\overline{FE_{i1}}$ and $\overline{FE_{i0}}$ are the mean forecast errors over the period 1992–1994 and 1989–1991 respectively. A limitation of these tests, however, is that by expanding the test period we may be allowing other events affecting forecast errors to confound our results.

Because the tests above are univariate and do not control for factors shown in the literature affecting forecast accuracy, we now will discuss tests that do. For example, Brown et al. (1987) show that analysts' forecast accuracy is positively related to firm size and thus we include the log of the number of employees at the beginning of the fiscal year (SIZE) in our tests as a control for firm size. [17] Mande (1996) suggests that foreign owners of Japanese firms act as company monitors and demand more information about the firm from Japanese management. We, therefore, include the log of the percentage of stock owned by foreign investors (FOROWN) in our tests and predict that analysts' forecast accuracy will be positively related to foreign ownership. Baldwin (1984) argues that analysts have a more difficult time predicting company performance in a recession. Because our sample period covers a recession, we include the change in GNP (ΔGNP) as a control variable. As ΔGNP decreases we expect forecast accuracy to also decrease. Balakrishnan et al. (1990) argue that analysts have a more difficult time forecasting consolidated income for firms with significant foreign sales. Like Balakrishnan et al., we use the percentage of export sales (EXPT) and predict that forecast accuracy will be negatively related to EXPT. Several studies (Brown, 2001; Dowen, 1996; Hwang et al., 1996) find that analysts have difficulty forecasting even the occurrence of a loss, let alone its magnitude. Therefore, we include: (1) a loss dummy variable, LOSS – DUM, that equals 1 when a firm experiences a loss

---

[17] We do not use sales, market value or book value of owners' equity because these variables fell dramatically during the recession years, which might lead to a spurious negative association between these variables and forecast errors. Because Japanese firms during the period of our study generally had a policy of providing life-long employment, the number of employees is a more stable measure of firm size.

44   V. Mande, R. Ortman / Journal of Accounting and Public Policy 21 (2002) 31–70

and 0 otherwise, and (2) a variable, ABS – LOSS, which equals the absolute value of a loss divided by owners' equity when a firm experiences a loss and 0 otherwise. [18] Income manipulation will negatively affect forecast accuracy. Therefore, we include a variable for the absolute value of abnormal, discretionary accruals, ABS – DACC, which we computed using Jones (1991) as modified by Dechow et al. (1995). [19] Japanese analysts have more difficulty forecasting earnings for Japanese firms who adopt US GAAP versus Japanese companies that do not (Mande and Kwak, 1996). Therefore, we include a US GAAP variable that is 1 if a firm uses US GAAP and 0 otherwise. We included the standard deviations of sales divided by owners' equity (STDDEV – S) and net income divided by owners' equity (STDDEV – NI) as variables because past variability in sales and net income can negatively affect forecast accuracy (Kross et al., 1990; Dunn and Nathan, 2000). [20]

We control for these variables using a pooled cross-sectional regression model. As Fig. 2 shows, after 1992 there is a significant increase in earnings forecast errors of all groups. The early 1990s saw the beginning of a deep and prolonged recession in Japan. In order to deal with this situation our study includes a control group of firms that were not diversified. We expect this control group to mitigate the effects of unknown factors on forecast errors that are not a function of the degree of diversification. We accomplish this by subtracting the respective non-diversified firms' yearly mean absolute percentage sales (earnings) forecast error from the absolute percentage sales (earnings) forecast error of each firm for each year. These "adjusted" forecast errors for the three groups (high, medium and low) are used as dependent variables in the regressions below. Using intercept dummies for the periods 1989–1991 and 1992–1994 for each diversified group, we test if there is a decrease in forecast errors following the introduction of business segment disclosures.

---

[18] Hwang et al. argue that losses are transitory and, as such, analysts have difficulty predicting their occurrence.

[19] The model we used was: $TACC_{it}/TASS_{it-1} = \alpha_1(1/TASS_{it-1}) + \alpha_2(\Delta REV_{it} - \Delta REC_{it})/TASS_{it-1} + \alpha_3(PPE_{it}/TASS_{it-1}) + \epsilon_{it}$, where TACC is total accruals which is net income before extraordinary items less operating cash flow, TASS is total assets, ΔREV is the change in revenue, ΔREC is the change in accounts receivable and PPE is gross plant, property and equipment. Deflating by TASS controls for scale bias while ($\Delta REV - \Delta REC$) and PPE control for non-discretionary levels of working capital accruals related to revenues and depreciation expense, respectively. ϵ_{it} is the residual which is used to proxy for abnormal, discretionary accruals. The model is estimated using OLS for each sample year allowing for coefficients to vary with industry.

[20] We required 10 years of continuous historical data for computing the standard deviations (i.e., data starting from 1979).

V. Mande, R. Ortman / Journal of Accounting and Public Policy 21 (2002) 31–70   45

$$\text{ADJFES}_{it} \text{ or } \text{ADJFENI}_{it}$$
$$= \alpha_0 + \alpha_1 \text{SIZE}_{it} + \alpha_2 \text{FOROWN}_{it} + \alpha_3 \Delta\text{GNP}_{it} + \alpha_4 \text{EXPT}_{it}$$
$$+ \alpha_5 \text{LOSS} - \text{DUM}_{it} + \alpha_6 \text{ABS} - \text{LOSS}_{it} + \alpha_7 \text{ABS} - \text{DACC}_{it}$$
$$+ \alpha_8 \text{US GAAP}_{it} + \alpha_9 \text{STDDEV} - S_{it} + \alpha_{10} \text{STDDEV} - \text{NI}_{it}$$
$$+ \beta_1 \text{LD}_{1it} + \sum_{k=0}^{1} \gamma_k \text{MD}_{kit} + \sum_{k=0}^{1} \delta_k \text{HD}_{kit} + \epsilon_{it}$$

where ADJFES (ADJFENI) is the absolute percentage sales (earnings) forecast error of firm i at time t less the mean absolute percentage sales (earnings) forecast error of the non-diversified group of firms at time t; $k = 0$ ($k = 1$), used to denote the pre-segment (post-segment) period; α_0, the intercept that represents the mean forecast error of firms in the low diversified group during 1989–1991; LD_1, the dummy variable that takes a value of one for low diversified firms during post-segment reporting period and 0 otherwise; $\text{MD}_0(\text{MD}_1)$, the dummy variable that takes a value of one for medium diversified firms during the pre- (post-)segment reporting period and 0 otherwise; $\text{HD}_0(\text{HD}_1)$, the dummy variable that takes a value of one for high diversified firms during the pre- (post-)segment reporting period and 0 otherwise.

If segment reporting conveys useful information, we should find smaller forecast errors or significantly smaller coefficients on intercept dummies of the post-segment period ($k = 1$) for diversified firms reporting segment information. Further, we should also find that the decrease in forecast errors, measured by the difference between pre- and post-intercept dummies, to be most (least) significant for the high (low) diversified firms.

3. Test results

3.1. Data

Our sample is composed of firms that were included on the Nikkei 225 index every year from 1989 through 1994. [21] For these firms, we obtained consolidated sales and net income data and analysts' forecasts of these amounts from the Japan Company Handbook–First Section. [22] (JCH) published by Toyo

---

[21] The Nikkei 225 index, computed using stock prices of 225 leading Japanese issues, is Japan's benchmark stock average index.

[22] Stocks on the Tokyo Stock Exchange are traded on two sections. In order to be listed on the First Section, firms must meet certain standards set by the exchange. These standards relate to the minimum number of shares outstanding, trading volume and frequency, and minimum dividend payment. It is usual for new firms to be listed on the Second Section first, before they are transferred to the First Section. In 1987 there were 1100 (435) firms listed on the First (Second) Exchange with a total market value of 352 (11.4) trillion yen (see Hamao (1991)).

46   *V. Mande, R. Ortman / Journal of Accounting and Public Policy 21 (2002) 31–70*

Kezai, a Japanese brokerage house. [23] Beginning in 1988, the JCH was published four times a year (Winter, Spring, Summer and Autumn). The forecasts were collected for the period 1989–1994 for firms with fiscal years ending on March 31. [24] The March 31 year-end restriction is to ensure that the forecast horizon is the same for all sampled firms. [25] Analysts' forecasts were obtained from the Autumn issue of the JCH because the first forecasts made by analysts after consolidated financial statements of the preceding year were made public are reported in this issue. Baldwin (1984) finds that the impact of segment information is felt mostly on longer-term forecasts; fourth quarter analysts' forecasts were least affected by business segment disclosures in his study. For these firms we also obtained the following additional data. From the JCH: the number of employees, percentage of foreign ownership, percentage of export sales, whether a firm adopted US GAAP, and a breakdown of sales by business segment for each firm for each year during the sample period; from Pacific-Basin Capital Markets databases (PACAP): common shares outstanding, year-end stock price, variables employed in the modified Jones (1991) model and those used to compute the standard deviations of sales and earnings; from Worldscope/Disclosure (W/D) databases: segment information in Japanese annual financial statements. [26] Using the W/D databases we: (1) obtained the segment footnote information as reported by the sampled firms in their annual consolidated financial statements during the years 1991–1994, (2) verified that for these firms there were no voluntary disclosures of segment performance in the annual reports in the years prior to 1991, and (3) identified a control group of 98 firms on the First Section of the Tokyo Stock Exchange that did not disclose a segment footnote in any of the years in the sample period.

Finally, for all fiscal years ending March 31 during the sample period, we obtained gross national product (GNP) indices. These indices, measured in

---

[23] Toyo Keizai is a highly respected brokerage house in Japan. Forecasts provided by Toyo Keizai analysts are of high quality and Japanese investors place a high degree of trust and confidence in these forecasts (Mande, 1996).

[24] The most common year end for Japanese firms is March 31. Approximately two-thirds of all firms on the First Exchange have this fiscal year end.

[25] Brown et al. (1987) show that forecast horizon is an important determinant of forecast accuracy.

[26] W/D databases are organized by the Disclosure National Research Center, Maryland, USA. To our knowledge W/D is the only database which organizes segment footnote information reported by Japanese firms in their financial statements. Segment footnote information on Japanese firms is not available, for example, on Compustat-Global Vantage, the PACAP or the NEEDS/MICRO tapes. For a random sample of firms we checked the accuracy of the footnote reported on W/D with the actual financial statements in the National Diet Library in Tokyo, Japan and found the segment information on W/D to be reliable. We thank Mr. Mathew Menheneott from Disclosure National Research Center for his assistance in retrieving segment information from Japanese financial statements.

V. Mande, R. Ortman / Journal of Accounting and Public Policy 21 (2002) 31–70 47

terms of the base year 1985, were obtained from the monthly publications of the International Monetary Fund, titled *International Financial Statistics*. We use GNP indices to control for national economic conditions that can affect forecast accuracy. [27]

We then define analysts' percentage sales and net income forecast errors: [28]

- FE_{it}^{S} = *percentage sales forecast error*, which is defined as sales minus analysts' forecasted sales divided by forecasted sales.
- FE_{it}^{NI} = *percentage net income forecast error*, which is defined as net income minus analysts' forecasted net income, divided by absolute forecasted net income.

As discussed, we use the Herfindhal ratio (DIVINDX), defined as the sum of squares of sales of each product segment, s_i, divided by total sales, S (i.e., $DIVINDX = \sum_i (s_i/S)^2$), to divide our sample into three categories of diversification: high, medium and low. Smaller values of DIVINDX indicate greater degree of diversification. Using sales percentages reported each year in the JCH for each business segment of a firm, we compute DIVINDX for each firm and year beginning with 1989 and obtain the median DIVINDX for each firm over the sample period. [29] Firms with median DIVINDX that are in the lower (upper) quartile of all median DIVINDX values are classified in the high (low) category of diversification; the remainder are classified in the medium diversification category. We also compare changes in forecast errors for the three levels of diversified groups with a control sample consisting of firms which did not report segment data in their annual financial statements (i.e., non-diver-

---

[27] See O'Brien (1994) whose study examined the relation of macro-economic conditions and US analysts' forecasts.

[28] We use percentage forecast errors rather than forecast errors deflated by stock prices because stock prices of Japanese firms fell dramatically during the Japanese recession (1991–present). Using stock price as a deflator would, therefore, result in larger price-deflated forecast errors during the post-1991 years, confounding our tests which involve a comparison of forecast errors prior to 1991 with those after 1991. Literature that has used percentage sales and net income forecast errors include Ely and Mande (1996).

[29] Information on sales breakdown is provided by JCH to indicate the extent of a firm's diversification. This is obtained by JCH from annual reports in which management voluntarily provides supplementary information about their firm's business composition. The data is not part of the audited financial statements of the firm and does not follow Japanese segment reporting standards. This supplementary information consists only of sales by division and does not contain income data. This could imply that analysts will be better able to forecast sales than income. In a conversation, however, with Mr. T. Shibata, Editor of JCH, he stated that he believed that forecasting sales is just as difficult as forecasting earnings. We discuss the value of voluntary sales breakdown data in Section 3.3.

48   *V. Mande, R. Ortman / Journal of Accounting and Public Policy 21 (2002) 31–70*

sified firms). Including the non-diversified group of firms, we have 1593 (1458) firm/year observations of sales (net income) forecast errors. [30]

3.2. Results

3.2.1. Summary statistics for sampled firms

Table 2 summarizes the distribution of relevant variables according to diversification strategy of Japanese firms. [31] Because there are extreme observations affecting the mean, we discuss our results using median values of these variables.

The median sales and net incomes of firms in all three categories of diversification are similar in magnitude. For example, the median value of sales (net income) of firms with a medium or low degree of diversification is 106% (102%) and 109% (106%) of the median sales (net income) of firms with a high degree of diversification. There are also no large differences in the median number of employees and foreign owners among the three groups; the median number of employees (foreign ownership percentage) of medium and low groups is 84% (94%) and 122% (96%) of the median values of the highly diversified group. While the highly diversified firms export more than firms with a medium and low degree of diversification, export sales do not constitute a large percentage of sales for any of the three groups. All the groups, therefore, appear to have similar characteristics with regard to the variables examined—sales, net income, foreign ownership percentage and export sales. However, the highly diversified firms are, on the average, 2.5 (1.5) times more diversified than the low (medium) group of firms. Therefore, differences in forecast errors among the three groups most likely reflect differences in the degree of their diversification. [32] And, because we hypothesize that the impact of business segment disclosures will vary with extent of diversification, results showing significant changes in forecast errors partitioned according to extent of diversification, will most likely be due to informative segment disclosures rather than other confounding events.

---

[30] To ensure that our results are not being driven by a few observations we deleted "outliers" consisting of forecast errors that were larger than 200% in absolute value. Results were robust to their deletion at levels of 100, 150 and 250%. We also obtained similar regression results when we deleted forecast errors if the absolute *R*-Student statistic was larger than 2.

[31] There are marginally fewer observations (especially net income forecast errors) available in the group with a high degree of diversification because there were more firms with missing data in this group.

[32] Prior work has found that analysts' forecast errors are related to degree of diversification (e.g., Dunn and Nathan (2000)). Net income forecast errors show differences across the three groups more than sales forecast errors.

V. Mande, R. Ortman / Journal of Accounting and Public Policy 21 (2002) 31–70   49

Table 2
Summary statistics for the variables used in this study

Variables	N	Quartiles			Mean	Std. Dev.
		25th	50th	75th		
High diversification						
NEMPL	275	3261	5707	9214	8650	10,451
SALES	279	263,969	454,785	1,689,691	2,969,719	5,715,091
NETINC	279	2471	6180	21,743	17,977	32,897
FOROWN	279	3.3	5.1	8.6	6.7	4.9904
EXPT	282	0.04	0.14	0.30	0.20	0.1924
DIVINDX	282	0.2573	0.2320	0.2068	0.2349	0.0398
FES	276	0.0229	0.0441	0.0706	0.0533	0.0496
FENI	252	0.0882	0.1855	0.4303	0.3079	0.3358
Medium diversification						
NEMPL	531	2293	4789	9878	7996	10,817
SALES	549	224,862	482,444	1,074,515	1,022,698	1,686,070
NETINC	549	2148	6286	18,755	17,135	33,209
FOROWN	549	2.7	4.8	7.8	6.5	6.8273
EXPT	554	0.00	0.04	0.16	0.10	0.1470
DIVINDX	554	0.4202	0.3465	0.3058	0.3868	0.1476
FES	540	0.0215	0.0433	0.0712	0.0662	0.1122
FENI	499	0.0830	0.2019	0.4398	0.3279	0.3634
Low diversification						
NEMPL	276	1784	6971	12,642	15,148	36,518
SALES	280	195,075	499,255	1,210,492	1,042,823	1,398,766
NETINC	280	1603	6539	22,945	20,727	42,172
FOROWN	280	2.8	4.9	6.9	5.5	3.7561
EXPT	282	0.00	0.06	0.18	0.11	0.1441
DIVINDX	282	0.7014	0.5871	0.5330	0.6362	0.1503
FES	275	0.0209	0.0403	0.0715	0.0574	0.0756
FENI	259	0.0982	0.2219	0.4584	0.3444	0.3419
Non-diversified						
NEMPL	523	747	1648	3007	2509	3330
SALES	523	44,356	113,705	239,673	248,793	431,957
NETINC	523	545	1664	3917	21,573	5347
FOROWN	523	0.9	2.0	5.0	4.4	7.1645
EXPT	487	0.01	0.07	0.19	0.13	0.1679
DIVINDX	540	1	1	1	1	0
FES	502	0.0219	0.0490	0.0895	0.0643	0.0608
FENI	448	0.0933	0.2126	0.4526	0.3458	0.3883
Other variables						
% ΔGNP during the year	6	0.0131	0.0360	0.0464	0.0324	0.021

Notes: NEMPL: no. of employees; SALES: sales for the year in million yen; NETINC: net income for the year in million yen; FOROWN: percentage of common stock owned by foreign investors; EXPT: percentage of overseas sales; DIVINDX: Herfindahl ratio of diversification which is $\Sigma(s_i/S)^2$, where s_i is the percentage of sales of product i and S is total sales; FES: absolute percentage sales forecast error; FENI: absolute percentage net income error; % ΔGNP: percentage change in GNP during the fiscal year.

50   *V. Mande, R. Ortman / Journal of Accounting and Public Policy 21 (2002) 31–70*

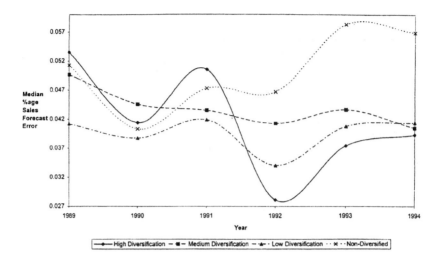

Fig. 1. Plot of median sales forecast errors for high, medium, low and non-diversified groups.

Interestingly, the non-diversified firms are more export oriented than the medium and low diversified firms. Non-diversified firms, however, are significantly smaller than firms reporting segment information, as measured by sales, net income and number of employees. The median values of these variables are about 25–30% of the median values of the highly diversified firms. Non-diversified firms also have a lower percentage of foreign owners (about 39% of the median value of the highly diversified group). Comparisons of forecast errors with those of the non-diversified firms must, therefore, be interpreted with caution. However, we use forecast errors of the non-diversified firms to gauge the effects of confounding events and environmental changes that cannot be completely controlled in an empirical research design.

3.2.2. Plots of sales and income forecast errors

Fig. 1 shows that prior to segment disclosures (1989–1991), median sales forecast errors of the highly diversified firms are generally larger and display more variation when compared to sales forecast errors of firms with medium or low degrees of diversification during the same period. [33] These results are consistent with prior work showing that analysts find financial results of more

---

[33] Again, we plot median rather than mean forecast errors.

V. Mande, R. Ortman / Journal of Accounting and Public Policy 21 (2002) 31–70 51

diversified firms to be more difficult to predict (e.g., Dunn and Nathan (2000)). Following segment disclosures (1992–1994), consistent with analysts' use of segment disclosures, the most pronounced decrease in variation occurs in sales forecast errors of highly diversified firms. For firms with medium diversification, forecast errors appear to display a slight downward trend during the post-segment reporting period, while for firms with low diversification, forecast errors return to their pre-segment period levels.

Fig. 2 plots median net income forecast errors and shows that income is more difficult to predict than sales. The worst median income forecast error is about six times larger in magnitude than the worst median sales forecast error. This is most likely because analysts attempting to predict income must forecast, in addition to sales, a myriad of expenses and discretionary allocations to reserves and provisions permitted under the Japanese Commercial Code. Interestingly, in contrast to sales, predictability of income is higher for more diversified firms. These findings contradict Dunn and Nathan (2000), who find that for US firms analysts' forecasts of earnings are less accurate for more diversified firms. However, these results are consistent with well-diversified Japanese firms being more successful at meeting analysts' expectations of net income (i.e., smoothing income). [34] Fig. 2 also shows that following the segment reporting mandate, median income forecasts errors of all groups increase. In contrast to sales forecast errors, our results, therefore, do not suggest that segment disclosures were useful for the prediction of net income for any classification of diversified firm.

Next, we compare the forecast errors of firms reporting segment information with those that do not. In Fig. 1, median sales forecast errors of the non-diversified firms closely follow those of the high, medium and low groups in the pre-segment period. However, in the post-segment reporting period sales errors of the non-diversified firms increase during the period 1992–1994, which is consistent with segment disclosures potentially conveying useful information to analysts following some or all of the diversified groups of firms. By contrast, Fig. 2 shows that income errors of non-diversified firms are generally increasing during the post-segment period similar to that of firms reporting segment information, supporting our earlier analyses that segment disclosures did not

---

[34] Managers of highly diversified firms have numerous segments to which they can apply alternative accounting techniques. This situation gives them more opportunities to manage net income to achieve analysts' income forecasts. The ability to manage sales, however, is far more limited because accounting rules provide far less latitude to do so. Consistent with income smoothing, Fig. 2 shows that compared to sales (Fig. 1), net income, for only the highly diversified firms, displayed lower variability over the entire sample period. Using 10 years of data, we also computed for each firm the variance of annual changes in sales (σ_S^2) and net income (σ_I^2). Ely and Mande (1996) argue that higher the ratio of σ_S^2 to σ_I^2 the greater the likelihood of income smoothing. We found that highly diversified firms had the highest ratio of σ_S^2 to σ_I^2.

52   *V. Mande, R. Ortman / Journal of Accounting and Public Policy 21 (2002) 31–70*

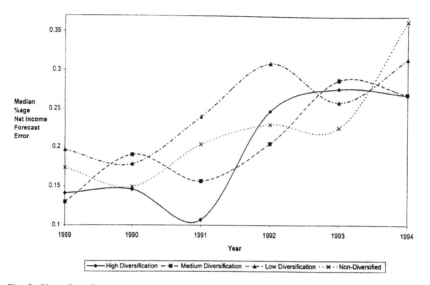

Fig. 2. Plot of median net income forecast errors for high, medium, low and non-diversified groups.

convey useful information to analysts for forecasting net income. Statistical test results in support of these analyses are discussed next.

3.2.3. Analyses of year-to-year changes in sales and income forecast errors before and after segment disclosures

Table 3 shows results associated with consecutive annual changes in sales and income forecast errors. For sales, in the years following 1992, there are two test results showing significant (10% level of testing) consecutive annual changes in forecast errors for firms reporting business segment information. By contrast, there are seven such test results showing significant consecutive changes in the pre-disclosure period which was prior to 1992. Consistent with the plot of sales forecast errors, this suggests that year-to-year variability in sales forecast errors decreased following the introduction of segment reporting. More significantly, in 1992, for the highly diversified firms, we find a statistically significant reduction in sales forecast errors using both parametric and non-parametric tests.

For net income, Table 3 shows that in the years prior to segment reporting there is one test result showing significant (10% level of testing) annual changes in forecast errors for firms reporting business segment information; in the years

Table 3
Consecutive annual changes in sales and net income forecast errors for high, medium, low and non-diversified groups

Group	Annual changes in % sales forecast errors					Annual changes in % net income forecast errors				
	Year	N	Mean	Median	Test statistic (T / Sign)	Year	N	Mean	Median	Test statistic (T / Sign)
High diversification	1990	44	0.0131	-0.0125	0.97 / -2.71***	1990	38	-0.1159	-0.0675	-2.82*** / -1.62
	1991	45	-0.0266	0.0011	-1.71* / -1.04	1991	44	-0.0062	-0.0105	-0.12 / -0.60
	1992	**46**	**-0.0192**	**-0.0217**	**-2.96*** / -3.83***	**1992**	**44**	**0.1275**	**0.0507**	**2.28** / 0.90**
	1993	47	0.0097	0.0148	1.50 / 0.15	1993	41	0.1391	0.0792	2.39** / 1.41
	1994	47	-0.0067	-0.0059	-1.13 / -2.19**	1994	34	0.0579	0.0455	1.14 / 1.37
Medium diversification	1990	85	-0.0672	-0.0092	-2.71*** / -1.19	1990	82	-0.0325	-0.0298	-0.88 / -1.33
	1991	90	-0.0174	-0.0011	-2.23** / -0.42	1991	84	0.0010	0.0051	0.03 / 0.44
	1992	**90**	**-0.0008**	**-0.0018**	**-0.13** / -0.42	**1992**	**84**	**0.0479**	**0.0292**	**1.22 / 1.96**
	1993	92	-0.0011	-0.0026	-0.20 / -0.42	1993	81	0.1814	0.0554	3.55*** /
	1994	91	-0.0034	-0.0061	-0.83 / -1.78*	1994	68	0.0317	0.0048	0.63 / 0.00
Low diversification	1990	42	-0.0301	-0.0119	-1.71* / -2.47**	1990	41	-0.0195	0.0124	-0.32 / 0.47
	1991	45	0.0164	0.0077	1.38 / 1.94*	1991	44	0.0265	0.0251	0.44 / 1.21
	1992	**47**	**-0.0092**	**0.0018**	**-0.91 / 1.02**	**1992**	**45**	**0.1346**	**0.0995**	**2.61*** / 2.24**
	1993	47	-0.0047	-0.0030	-0.77 / -0.15	1993	42	0.0634	0.0498	0.94 / 1.54
	1994	47	-0.0012	-0.0042	-0.14 / -0.73	1994	36	0.0331	0.0032	0.56 / 0.33
Non-diversified	1990	70	-0.0102	-0.0124	-0.99 / -1.91*	1990	65	-0.0486	-0.0114	-1.03 / -0.12
	1991	84	0.0043	0.0166	0.50 / 1.31	1991	78	0.0678	0.0378	1.83* / 2.04**
	1992	**87**	**0.0094**	**-0.0039**	**1.21 / -0.54**	**1992**	**77**	**0.1114**	**0.1166**	**2.10** / 2.17**
	1993	86	0.0024	0.0085	0.35 / 1.29	1993	66	0.1517	0.0645	2.92*** / 1.23
	1994	85	-0.0096	-0.0065	-1.34 / -0.98	1994	58	-0.0116	0.0116	-0.24 / 0.53

Notes: */**/*** denotes statistical significance at the 10%/5%/1% level of testing (two-tail); 1992 is the first year the new segment reporting requirements could affect analysts' forecasts.

54   *V. Mande, R. Ortman / Journal of Accounting and Public Policy 21 (2002) 31–70*

following 1992 there are three such significant test results. Therefore, in contrast to results on sales, it does not appear that there were any decreases in the year-to-year variability of income errors. Further, in 1992 all groups, including the control, show an increase in earnings forecast errors. These results confirm that segment reporting is viewed by analysts as being more useful for the prediction of sales than net income. [35]

3.2.4. Analyses of average sales and income forecast errors before and after segment disclosures

Table 4 shows results comparing average sales and net income forecast errors of the pre-segment period (1989–1991) with those of the post-segment period (1992–1994). Supportive of earlier findings, it shows a significant decrease in average sales forecast errors following segment disclosures for the highly diversified firms using the parametric *t*-test and the non-parametric Mann–Whitney Rank Sum (MW) test. As expected Table 4 also shows a decrease in sales forecast errors during 1992–1994 for firms with medium diversification, but not as significant a relationship. For the low and non-diversified groups, results do not show a statistically significant decrease. The bottom panel of Table 4 shows results that are also consistent with prior analyses. We find that income errors significantly increase for all firms, including non-diversified firms, during 1992–1994.

3.2.5. Regression test results

Table 5 presents summary statistics on control variables used in our tests, while Tables 6 and 7 show results obtained using regression models. [36] Consistent with prior work, the coefficients on SIZE and FOROWN are negative in Tables 6 and 7, suggesting that as firms get larger and as holdings of foreign owners increase, forecast errors decrease. A comparison of the tables shows, however, that the coefficients on firm size and foreign ownership are highly (0.01 level) statistically significant only in the regression using earnings forecast errors; the coefficient on SIZE is statistically significant at the 0.05 level, while the coefficient on FOROWN is not statistically significant in the regression using sales forecast errors. These findings are consistent with large firms and firms with a higher proportion of foreign owners being more successful at

---

[35] The total number of changes in forecast errors in Table 3 do not equal the total number of forecast errors in Tables 2 and 4 because we lose a year (1988) when we compute changes and because data were not continuously available for all firms for all years.

[36] Table 6 (Table 7) has 864 (783) observations which is 227 fewer than what we had in previous tests due to missing data on PACAP and JCH.

Table 4
Average percentage sales and net income forecast errors in the three-year periods before and after segment reporting disclosures

	Period	N	Mean	Median	t-Test	MW test
Sales forecast errors						
High diversification	1989–1991	135	0.0677	0.0503	−4.32***	−4.20***
	1992–1994	141	0.0397	0.0357		
Medium	1989–1991	265	0.0855	0.0446	−3.92***	−2.32**
diversification	1992–1994	275	0.0476	0.0413		
Low	1989–1991	134	0.0624	0.0415	−1.08	−0.91
diversification	1992–1994	141	0.0526	0.0397		
Non-diversified	1989–1991	243	0.0603	0.0463	1.45	1.04
	1992–1994	259	0.0681	0.0533		
Net income forecast errors						
High	1989–1991	129	0.2401	0.1298	3.25***	3.69***
diversification	1992–1994	123	0.3792	0.2630		
Medium	1989–1991	255	0.2766	0.1599	3.24***	4.01***
diversification	1992–1994	244	0.3815	0.2455		
Low	1989–1991	132	0.2647	0.1867	3.99***	3.56***
diversification	1992–1994	127	0.4272	0.2839		
Non-diversified	1989–1991	233	0.2787	0.1718	3.82***	3.95***
	1992–1994	215	0.4186	0.2632		

Note: */**/*** denotes statistical significance at the 10%/5%/1% level of testing (two-tail).

achieving analysts' earnings rather than sales forecasts. The coefficient on ΔGNP is not statistically significant in either table suggesting that our treatment of adjusting forecast errors by subtracting the mean forecast error of the control group mitigated the effects of unknown economic factors during the recession upon the diversified groups. The positive and statistically significant coefficient on EXPT supports the idea that analysts' forecast accuracy is inversely related to the magnitude of foreign sales. The coefficient on LOSS – DUM is significant for both sales and earnings forecast errors which suggests that analysts have difficulty in predicting the occurrence of a loss. Our results also show that the coefficients on ABS – LOSS, ABS – DACC, US GAAP, STDDEV – S are not significant in explaining sales and earnings forecast errors. Finally, our results show that the variability of net income, STDDEV – NI, is significantly related to earnings but not to sales forecast errors. The adjusted R^2 is nearly five times greater in the regression of earnings errors than sales errors which would be expected because earnings is more

56   *V. Mande, R. Ortman / Journal of Accounting and Public Policy 21 (2002) 31–70*

Table 5
Summary statistics on control variables used

Variables	N	Quartiles			Mean	Std. Dev.
		25th	50th	75th		
NEMPL	864	2171	4975	10,457	10,303	23,337
FOWN	864	2.6000	4.5000	7.0000	5.7745	5.4940
ΔGNP	864	0.0131	0.0360	0.0464	0.0307	0.0219
EXPT	864	0.0100	0.0800	0.1900	0.1331	0.1582
LOSS – DUM	864	0.0000	0.0000	0.0000	0.1123	0.3159
ABS – LOSS	864	0.0000	0.0000	0.0000	0.0086	0.0613
ABS – DACC	864	0.0113	0.0245	0.0450	0.0328	0.0308
US GAAP	863	0.0000	0.0000	0.0000	0.0881	0.2836
STDDEV – S	864	0.5400	0.9437	1.8611	3.0329	11.2489
STDDEV – NI	864	0.0249	0.0440	0.0707	0.0449	0.0790
FSUB	728	1.0000	7.0000	22.0000	15.8721	26.7230

Notes: NEMPL: no. of employees; FOWN: % of common stock owned by foreign investors; ΔAGNP: % change in GNP during the fiscal year; EXPT: % of overseas sales; LOSS – DUM: dummy variable which takes a value of 1 for firms that experience a loss and 0 otherwise; ABS – LOSS: the absolute value of a loss deflated by owners' equity for firms that experience a loss and 0 otherwise; ABS – DACC: the absolute value of discretionary accruals computed using the modified Jones (1991) model; US GAAP: dummy variable which takes a value of 1 for Japanese firms using US GAAP and 0 otherwise; STDDEV – S: the standard deviation of sales divided by owners' equity; STDDEV – NI: the standard deviation of net income divided by owners' equity; MARKETVAL: market value of the firm at the beginning of the fiscal year in million yen; FSUB: number of foreign subsidiaries.

predictable using financial data. Overall, these results are consistent with those documented by prior research.

The coefficients on the dummy intercepts, MD_0 and HD_0, are positive in Table 6 indicating that, all else constant, the means of sales forecast errors for these groups are higher than the mean of the low diversified group in the pre-segment period confirming that sales forecast accuracy is negatively related to a firm's degree of diversification, but not to a statistically significant extent. By contrast, during the period 1992–1994, the coefficients on LD_1, MD_1 and HD_1, in Table 6 are negative and statistically significant for the high and medium groups at the 1% and 10% levels, respectively, suggesting an improvement in sales forecast accuracy for firms that are well diversified. F-tests comparing coefficients on the dummy intercepts for the period 1989–1991 with those for the period 1992–1994 show that there is a statistically significant improvement in sales forecast accuracy following the segment reporting disclosures for the high and medium group (F-value = 13.11, Prob. $> F = 0.0003$

V. Mande, R. Ortman / Journal of Accounting and Public Policy 21 (2002) 31–70 57

Table 6
Regression relating diversification strategy and control variables to sales forecast errors

Independent variables	Parameter estimate	t-Value[@]
INTERCEPT	0.0157	0.88
SIZE	−0.0039	−2.29**
FOROWN	−0.0000	−0.01
ΔGNP	0.0349	0.23
EXPT	0.0373	2.85***
LOSS − DUM	0.0206	3.24***
ABS − LOSS	0.0055	0.16
ABS − DACC	0.0650	1.14
US GAAP	0.0063	0.81
STDDEV − S	0.0002	1.10
STDDEV − NI	−0.0061	−0.24
1989–1991		
MD_0 (Medium diversification)	0.0067	1.21
HD_0 (High diversification)	0.0104	1.56
1992–1994		
LD_1 (Low diversification)	−0.0136	−1.56
MD_1 (Medium diversification)	−0.0144	−1.78*
HD_1 (High diversification)	−0.0246	−2.59***
N	864	
Adjusted	0.0604	
Prob. $> F$	0.0001	

Notes: [@]: reported t-values are computed using White (1980) adjustment; */**/*** denotes statistical significance at the 10%/5%/1% level of testing (two-tail); ADJFES: absolute percentage sales forecast error of firm i at time t minus the absolute mean % sales forecast error of the control group at time t; SIZE: log of NEMPL, the no. of employees; FOROWN: log of FOWN, the % of common stock owned by foreign investors; ΔGNP: % change in GNP during the fiscal year; EXPT: % of overseas sales; LOSS − DUM: dummy variable which takes a value of 1 for firms that experience a loss and 0 otherwise; ABS − LOSS: the absolute value of a loss deflated by owners' equity for firms that experience a loss and 0 otherwise; ABS − DACC: the absolute value of discretionary accruals computed using the modified Jones (1991) model; US GAAP: dummy variable which takes a value of 1 for Japanese firms using US GAAP and 0 otherwise; STDDEV − S: the standard deviation of sales divided by owners' equity; STDDEV − NI: the standard deviation of net income divided by owners' equity; MD_0: dummy variable which takes a value of 1 in years 1989–1991 for the medium diversified group and 0 otherwise; HD_0: dummy variable which takes a value of 1 in years 1989–1991 for the highly diversified group and 0 otherwise; LD_1: dummy variable which takes a value of 1 in years 1992–1994 for the low diversified group and 0 otherwise; MD_1: dummy variable which takes a value of 1 in years 1992–1994 for the medium diversified group and 0 otherwise; HD_1: dummy variable which takes a value of 1 in years 1992–1994 for the highly diversified group and 0 otherwise.

Model: $ADJFES_{it} = \alpha_0 + \alpha_1 SIZE_{it} + \alpha_2 FOROWN_{it} + \alpha_3 \Delta GNP_{it} + \alpha_4 EXPT_{it} + \alpha_5 LOSS - DUM_{it} + \alpha_6 ABS - LOSS_{it} + \alpha_7 ABS - DACC_{it} + \alpha_8 USGAAP_{it} + \alpha_9 STDDEV - S_{it} + \alpha_{10} STDDEV - NI_{it} + \beta_1 LD_{1it} + \sum_{k=0}^{1} \gamma_k MD_{kit} + \sum_{k=0}^{1} \delta_k HD_{kit} + \varepsilon_{it}.$

Table 7
Regression relating diversification strategy and control variables to net income forecast errors

Independent variables	Parameter estimate	t-Value[@]
INTERCEPT	0.3131	2.74***
SIZE	−0.0367	−3.37***
FOROWN	−0.0622	−2.98***
ΔGNP	1.2355	1.28
EXPT	0.1909	2.31**
LOSS – DUM	0.9107	14.68***
ABS – LOSS	−0.5747	−1.28
ABS – DACC	0.1674	0.44
USGAAP	−0.0128	−0.27
STDDEV – S	−0.0007	−0.72
STDDEV – NI	0.1682	2.06**
1989–1991		
MD_0 (Medium diversification)	0.0108	0.32
HD_0 (High diversification)	0.0123	−0.30
1992–1994		
LD_1 (Low diversification)	−0.0092	−0.17
MD_1 (Medium diversification)	−0.0357	−0.69
HD_1 (High diversification)	−0.0174	−0.29
N	783	
Adjusted	0.2885	
Prob. $> F$	0.0001	

Notes: @: reported t-values are computed using White (1980) adjustment; */**/*** denotes statistical significance at the 10%/5%/1% level of testing (two-tail); ADJFENI: absolute percentage earnings forecast error of firm i at time t minus the absolute mean % earnings forecast error of the control group at time t; SIZE: log of NEMPL, the no. of employees; FOROWN: log of FOWN, the % of common stock owned by foreign investors; ΔGNP: % change in GNP during the fiscal year; EXPT: % of overseas sales; LOSS – DUM: dummy variable which takes a value of 1 for firms that experience a loss and 0 otherwise; ABS – LOSS: the absolute value of a loss deflated by owners' equity for firms that experience a loss and 0 otherwise; ABS – DACC: the absolute value of discretionary accruals computed using the modified Jones (1991) model; US GAAP: dummy variable which takes a value of 1 for Japanese firms using US GAAP and 0 otherwise; STDDEV – S: the standard deviation of sales divided by owners' equity; STDDEV – NI: the standard deviation of net income divided by owners' equity; MD_0: dummy variable which takes a value of 1 in years 1989–1991 for the medium diversified group and 0 otherwise; HD_0: dummy variable which takes a value of 1 in years 1989–1991 for the highly diversified group and 0 otherwise; LD_1: dummy variable which takes a value of 1 in years 1992–1994 for the low diversified group and 0 otherwise; MD_1: dummy variable which takes a value of 1 in years 1992–1994 for the medium diversified group and 0 otherwise; HD_1: dummy variable which takes a value of 1 in years 1992–1994 for the highly diversified group and 0 otherwise.

Model: $ADJFENI_{it} = \alpha_0 + \alpha_1 SIZE_{it} + \alpha_2 FOROWN_{it} + \alpha_3 \Delta GNP_{it} + \alpha_4 EXPT_{it} + \alpha_5 LOSS - DUM_{it} + \alpha_6 ABS - LOSS_{it} + \alpha_7 ABS - DACC_{it} + \alpha_8 US\ GAAP_{it} + \alpha_9 STDDEV - S_{it} + \alpha_{10} STDDEV - NI_{it} + \beta_1 LD_{1it} + \sum_{k=0}^{1} \gamma_k HD_{kit} + \varepsilon_{it}.$

V. Mande, R. Ortman / Journal of Accounting and Public Policy 21 (2002) 31–70 59

and F-value $= 8.08$, Prob. $> F = 0.00046$, respectively), but not for the low group (F-value $= 1.68$, Prob. $> F = 0.1947$). Consistent with our expectations, the greatest (smallest) increase in sales accuracy is for the high (low) group. [37]

Table 7 results also show that the coefficients on MD_0 and HD_0 are mostly statistically insignificant. However, in sharp contrast to Table 6 results, Table 7 shows that the coefficients on dummy intercepts, LD_1, MD_1 and HD_1 are all statistically insignificant. These results, therefore, do not support the hypotheses that segment reporting aided analysts' in forecasting net income.

As a check for sensitivity and robustness, we also ran regressions that did not "back-out" the mean absolute forecast error of the control group. These regressions include intercept dummy variables for the non-diversified group of firms. We obtained qualitatively similar results for sales forecasts errors. With regard to earnings forecast errors, the only significant difference was that the dummy intercepts increased similarly for all four groups in the post-1992 period. Specifically, we could not reject that the intercept dummies for the four groups in the post-1992 period were statistically different from each other (F-value $= 1.31$, Prob. $> F = 0.2684$). This implies that the increase in earnings forecast errors experienced by all four groups was possibly due to unknown factors.

An interesting question concerns why just earnings forecast errors increase for all groups during the early 1990s. Regardless of economic conditions, in our study earnings were more difficult to predict than sales. Furthermore, beginning in the early 1990s, Japan began experiencing a severe and prolonged recession which neither management nor analysts had dealt with previously. This economic climate must certainly have been troubling for both management and financial analysts. The result would be that predicting net income and management behavior must have been extremely difficult for financial analysts. One outcome of this turbulent economic environment was that many firms for the first time began experiencing losses which are difficult for analysts to predict, as

---

[37] We also deleted a few firm-year observations because of mergers and acquisitions involving our sampled firms, without a change in results. Because accounting changes can affect forecast accuracy (Baldwin, 1984), we also examined yearly number of voluntary changes in accounting methods for inventory, depreciation, and classification of marketable securities for a random subsample of 40 firms over the entire period. We did not find any differences in number of accounting method changes in the post-segment years when compared to the pre-segment years. We also examined if there were any mandated accounting changes during these years that may have affected analysts' forecast accuracy. Our examination showed that segment reporting was the most significant mandate affecting these firms in the years 1992–1994. Finally, we included slope dummies (1-DIVINDX), instead of intercept dummies in the regressions and obtained marginally weaker, but otherwise qualitatively similar results. The weaker relation suggests that the improvement in forecast accuracy is possibly not linearly related to the magnitude of the Herfindahl ratio.

60   *V. Mande, R. Ortman / Journal of Accounting and Public Policy 21 (2002) 31–70*

numerous studies have found. Because of the decreased profitability and increased incidence of losses, it is no surprise that, for all groups in our study, earnings forecast errors increased during the recession. Our regression results also give us some basis for an explanation as to why earnings forecast errors were affected to a greater extent during the recession. They show that analysts have much more difficult time predicting earnings than sales when firms experience losses; the coefficient on LOSS – DUM in the earnings forecast error regression is 45 times larger than that in the sales forecast error regression.

Because we use panel data, the same firm is repeated each year in the regressions in Tables 6 and 7. Only if we assume that Japanese analysts do not provide unbiased forecasts, could we expect that their forecast errors for each firm would be related over time. Because our data set does not have a sufficiently long time series of analysts' forecast errors, it was not econometrically feasible for us to completely correct for the serial correlation. However, we mitigate the problem by splitting the sample into "before" and "after" segment reporting sub-samples and then testing the equality of the coefficients across the sub-samples for firms with high, medium and low diversification. The results of these tests did not alter our prior conclusions.

3.3. Additional tests

A possible cause of the improvement in sales forecast accuracy observed in Fig. 1 in 1992 might be that management's voluntary disclosures of divisional sales data may have improved in 1992. Since such data is published in the JCH, it can be assumed that the analysts at Toyo Kezai could have used such divisional sales data to prepare their sales forecasts. To test whether the improved sales forecast accuracy observed in 1992 was due to the improved quality of management's voluntary divisional sales data, we computed the absolute yearly differences between management's percentage breakdown of divisional sales for every firm. By year, by firm, these absolute differences were summed and the mean and median were computed. These computations were done by the four groups of diversified firms. If this voluntary sales breakdown information was significant in reducing sales or earnings forecast errors, one would expect a significant change in the average percentage breakdown in years where there was a significant change in forecast errors, yet we found no such change in 1992 from 1991. In addition, a regression analyses of the absolute total differences in divisional sales on changes in sales forecast accuracy for each diversified group revealed a statistically insignificant relationship. Our study, therefore, does not indicate that voluntary disclosures of divisional sales data improved in 1992 and that the disclosures had an effect on sales forecast accuracy.

To this point we have only examined whether the informativeness of segment data increases with extent of diversification. In the tests below, we attempt to determine if the informativeness of segment data increases with the use of other criteria to partition our sample instead of extent of diversification. To identify what different criteria to use Mande and Ortman (2000) surveyed 53 Japanese Chartered Financial Analysts (CFAs) listed as members of the AIMR. The analysts were asked to describe "characteristics of Japanese firms that they believe report segment data reliably". Japanese analysts believe that firms with significant international investor following (34%) and significant overseas operations (34%) report segment data reliably. [38] We could have selected other criteria, such as, firm size and sales and earnings stability and profitability to partition the data, but we did not select these because they were not identified as significant by the analysts surveyed.

Therefore, to address "significant international investor following" we partition the data according to the degree of foreign ownership in Japanese firms and the number of listings on foreign exchanges. When we partition the data according to foreign ownership, we create three groups: (1) firms with high foreign ownership which are those in the upper quartile of all firms (firms with median foreign ownership exceeding 8.50%), (2) firms with low foreign ownership which are those in the lower quartile of all firms (firms with median foreign ownership less than 3.80%), and (3) firms with medium foreign ownership which are the remaining firms. When we partition the data according to number of listings on foreign exchanges, we only create two groups because the Japanese firms in our sample are mostly listed on only domestic exchanges. The two groups are: (1) firms with one or more foreign listings (about 30% of the sampled firms), and (2) the remainder of the firms.

Our results (not reported) show that while mean and median changes in sales forecast errors decreased in 1992 (and thereafter) for the high and medium foreign ownership groups, the decreases were not as large nor as significant as when the sample was partitioned according to the extent of diversification. Average changes in net income errors increased in all years for all groups following segment reporting, except during 1993–1994 for the low diversification group, but this decrease was not statistically significant at the 0.05 level. Earnings forecast accuracy statistically significantly declined in 1991–1992 for firms with medium and high foreign ownership, consistent with our prior findings, but the decrease in forecast accuracy was not statistically significant for firms with low foreign ownership during the same period. For the sample partitioned according to number of foreign exchange listings, results (not reported) showed that mean and median changes in earnings and sales forecast errors of the foreign listed firms, contrary to expectations, did not decrease in 1992.

---

[38] Of the remaining 32% of analysts responding, 18% said that these were firms with a concern for their stockholders' interests, while 14% of the analysts gave "other" reasons.

62   *V. Mande, R. Ortman / Journal of Accounting and Public Policy 21 (2002) 31–70*

With regard to the period 1989–1994, the question of whether "significant overseas operations" affects the usefulness of segment data was addressed in the preceding section using export sales as a proxy. We find that segment data did not have increased information content for firms with significant export sales during this period. For fiscal years beginning April 1, 1997, the MOF required segment disclosures by geographic region and, therefore, we examine the change in forecast errors from the fiscal year ended March 31, 1998 (before) to March 31, 1999 (after). [39] Our test results (not reported) do not show a statistically significant improvement in forecast accuracy in sales and net income errors for any of the three export groups. However, because PACAP data and the segment footnotes for this period were not available, we were not able to perform more rigorous tests regarding the usefulness of geographic segment data. This we leave for future work. [40]

3.4. The information relevance of Japanese consolidated financial statements

Before presenting the conclusion of our study an issue that should be addressed is whether the effect of the introduction of business segment disclosures on sales and earnings forecast accuracy can even be measured given Japanese consolidation practices in force during the period of our study. The most critical problem is that while Japan had adopted the rule of consolidating when more than 50% ownership exists, the fact is that effective control commonly exists where ownership is less than 50% (Lowe, 1990). [41] Thus, policy decisions concerning segment disclosure standards may also require policy decisions concerning consolidation standards. We will attempt to provide relevant research studies supporting and criticizing these consolidation practices.

Ely and Pownall (2001) study two matched groups of 23 Japanese firms: one group listed on US stock exchanges and one group not. Neither group showed any difference in correlation between stock price and consolidated net income as compared to the same firm's unconsolidated income. However, a sample of 23 might limit the generalizability of this study's results. In contrast to the above study, several studies have found information value in Japanese con-

---

[39] The first time the firms in our sample disclosed geographic segment data in their financial statements was in March 31, 1998. Therefore, we expect an improvement in forecast accuracy for the fiscal year ended March 31, 1999.

[40] We looked for additional partitions by analyzing every segment footnote. For example, we found firms who voluntarily disclosed geographic segment data beyond what was required ($N = 6$ firms) and we also found firms ($N = 10$ firms) that met the Japanese 50% rule but not the US 75% rule. The analyses of these partitions found no statistically significant results but this may be due to the use of small samples.

[41] Since April 1, 1999 the Japanese MOF requires consolidation of subsidiaries where effective control exists.

V. Mande, R. Ortman / Journal of Accounting and Public Policy 21 (2002) 31–70 63

solidated statements. Sakakibara et al. (1988) examine the market reaction to those Japanese firms whose announcement dates of consolidated and parent-only earnings differ by more than 31 trading days. In this strong test there was a significant change in stock price at each announcement date and thus the authors state it is "safe to conclude that the consolidated announcement also has significant information content (p. 89)". Beckman (1998) argues that Japanese companies often exclude a subsidiary's bad news from the parent-only financial statements. This bad news does, however, show up on the consolidated statements. Japanese firms can do this because most parent firms do not apply properly the equity method of accounting for investments in subsidiaries, resulting in a significant difference between parent-only and consolidated results. [42] Beckman's (1998) study found that non-operating losses experienced by subsidiaries during 1989–1991, averaging 6% of consolidated earnings, were excluded from parent-only income statements. She indicates how an analysis of the consolidated statements can disclose this treatment of excluding subsidiary's non-operating losses from parent-only statements. Therefore, Japanese consolidated principles, though not perfect, result in consolidated statements possessing significant information content.

As discussed above, a comparison of the parent-only and consolidated financial statements of a diversified firm could also disclose that the parent excluded a particular loss sustained by one of its subsidiaries. Analysis of the segment footnote in the consolidated report might disclose which segment experienced the loss. If the parent's industry segment on the consolidated statements had less net income than the parent-only statement, then one could conclude that the loss was experienced by a subsidiary in the same industry as the parent. If, however, the loss was experienced in another different industry/segment, this too would be exposed by an analysis of the segment footnote in the consolidated statement. Traditionally, the use of segment footnotes is in forecasting consolidated sales and earnings by applying diverse rates of growth and risk to each segment. Given the above described practice in Japan of a parent excluding a subsidiary's loss, the analyses of consolidated statements and the accompanying segment footnotes become even more essential.

3.4.1. Japanese consolidation of foreign subsidiaries

Consolidation practices are especially controversial with regard to Japanese firms with foreign subsidiaries. Japanese consolidation standards allow parent companies with foreign subsidiaries to consolidate these subsidiaries using each individual subsidiary's accounting techniques which may be different from

---

[42] When properly applied, the equity method should result in parent-only and consolidated net income being identical.

64   *V. Mande, R. Ortman / Journal of Accounting and Public Policy 21 (2002) 31–70*

accounting techniques used by the parent or other subsidiaries. While this is criticized by some, the MOF has reviewed this practice and believes allowing foreign subsidiaries to select accounting procedures which best reflect each subsidiary's unique financial realities is a better alternative than forcing all foreign subsidiaries to adopt the same accounting procedures whether such principles best apply to their unique economic situation or not. [43]

Relevant to our study, the above situation may have resulted in the decrease in earnings forecast accuracy after 1992 for highly diversified firms. These firms in particular may have more foreign subsidiaries than lesser diversified firms. To test this contention, we examined Moody's International Edition to determine the number of foreign subsidiaries each firm in our sample had. Our findings support the conjecture that highly diversified firms have more foreign subsidiaries than less diversified firms. In our study, the median number of foreign subsidiaries was 10 for firms in the highly diversified group; the median was five for firms in the least diversified group. Since the focus is on the highly diversified group of firms, we test whether the number of foreign subsidiaries affected sales and earnings forecast errors by dividing the highly diversified firms into two groups: those with no foreign subsidiaries (10% of sample) and those with. We then computed consecutive changes in forecast errors for the two subgroups. Our results did not show support for the contention that the existence of foreign subsidiaries for highly diversified firms negatively impacts either sales or earnings forecast errors. We also included the number of foreign subsidiaries, FSUB, and included these in our regressions in Tables 6 and 7. The coefficient on FSUB was statistically insignificant in both regressions. Due to a significant number of lost observations, we do not report our regression results with FSUB included. [44]

4. Conclusion

For Japanese firms, the disclosure of segment information constitutes a major reporting issue. For over 10 years, they refused to list their stocks on US stock exchanges because a condition of listing was reporting segment data. Despite opposition from Japanese management and after being advised that segment disclosures did not have to be fine, the MOF, under pressure from the US, mandated segment reporting for Japanese firms starting April, 1990. The

---

[43] See Opinions on Review of Reporting System of Consolidated Financial Statements issued by the Business Accounting Deliberation Council (BADC) on June 6, 1997.

[44] We lose an additional 136 observations when we include FSUB in the regressions. Our logic for not including FSUB was that results on all coefficients with and without FSUB included were virtually unchanged, and, the coefficient on FSUB was insignificant in both regressions.

V. Mande, R. Ortman / Journal of Accounting and Public Policy 21 (2002) 31–70 65

segment reporting standards adopted were less stringent in their disclosure requirements than US segment reporting standards. An interesting question for this study, therefore, is whether segment data reported by Japanese firms are too coarse to be of any use to investors.

Our study sheds light on this question by examining analysts' forecasts for Nikkei 225 firms over the period 1989–1994. To provide evidence on the usefulness of segment data, we examine whether Japanese analysts' forecast accuracy increased following segment disclosures. Because Japanese firms have for years focused on sales growth, we examine analysts' forecasts of consolidated sales, as well as, forecasts of consolidated net income. A further contribution of our study is that we examine if segment disclosures were more relevant for analysts following more diversified firms. By partitioning the sample by extent of diversification, our confidence increases that the test results are due to segment disclosures and not confounding events. The impact of confounding events was also evaluated by conducting several tests, which included a comparison with a control group consisting of single segment firms that did not need to disclose segment information throughout the period.

Our study found that the introduction of segment reporting in Japan improved analysts' forecasts of sales, but only for the more diversified firms. However, results showed that forecast accuracy of consolidated net income did not increase following segment disclosures. The results were robust to different econometric specifications and remained unchanged after considering events such as mergers and accounting changes. These results constitute some of the first evidence on the information content of segment disclosures of Japanese firms. The findings of this study are of importance to global investors and policy makers concerned about the quality of segment information disclosed in Japanese financial statements. For years, the SEC has been at the center of a controversy involving segment reporting by foreign firms wishing to list on US exchanges. Because of the enormous size of the Japanese market, the SEC has paid attention to segment reporting by Japanese firms. The SECs involvement in Japanese segment reporting was largely due to pressure from the NYSE which wanted the SEC to relax rules on segment reporting by Japanese firms. The SEC's role in Japanese segment accounting is evidenced by its participation in Round Table Conferences with the MOF. Ozu and Gray (2001) state that the SEC's participation was key to the MOF's adoption of the segment reporting standard. The findings of this study will undoubtedly be of interest to the SEC.

The SEC presently allows Japanese firms to list their stocks disclosing only segment data required by the standards of the MOF. Critics of this policy (e.g., Saudagaran and Biddle (1994)) argue that allowing foreign firms to list on US exchanges with fewer disclosures places US firms at a competitive disadvantage. An important policy question for the SEC is whether its rules are creating a double standard for domestic firms.

Table 8
US mutual funds investing in only Japanese equities

Fund name	Fund balance December 31, 1999 (in millions)
Fidelity: Japanese Small Co.	$2189
Japan: Japan	1151
Fidelity: Japan	1091
Warburg Pinus: Japanese Small Co.	1090
Warburg Pinus: Japanese Growth	689
Price: International Japan	574
Morgan Stanley/Dean Witter: Japan B&C	248
AIM: Japan Growth A&B	232
DFA: Japanese Small Co.	145
Dimensional: Japan Small Co.	145
Fidelity: Advisor 13, C&T Japan	107
TCW Galileo ICL: Japan Equities	84
GAM: Japan Capital	67
Morgan Stanley/Dean Witter Institutional: Japanese Equity A	65
Goldman Sachs: Japanese Equity A	40
Liberty-Newport 13: Japan Opportunities Growth	35
Mattews International: Japan	27
CIBC: Japan Equity	26
Warburg Pinus: Institutional Japan Growth	22
GMO: Japan Fund 111	15
Flag Investments: Japan Equity	10
Caspstone: Japan	6
Barr Rosen: Japan Institutional	2
Grand total	$8060

Another group concerned with the information content of Japanese segment reporting is the global investor body. Table 8 provides a breakdown of balances of US mutual funds invested in Japan. It shows that as of December 31, 1999 the value of mutual funds invested solely in Japanese stocks was $8.1 billion. Not included in this amount are funds that purchase only Pacific Rim, Global and/or International stocks. The balance of US mutual funds that specialize in Pacific Rim stocks as of December 31, 1999 was $12.4 billion. Undoubtedly, a high proportion of the Pacific Rim funds is invested in Japanese equities. Because of their large investments in Japanese stocks, examining the quality of Japanese segment disclosures is important to US fund managers and other US investors.

Our test results indicate to us that even highly reputed Japanese analysts, who should be able to interpret Japanese segment data better than US investors, do not find the reported segment information in Japanese financial statements to be generally useful for equity analysis. Our conclusion is underscored by the fact that the firms examined belong to the Nikkei 225 index, which consists of firms in which US investor interest is very high. While one can argue that the usefulness of Japanese segment reporting depends on the value investors place on sales, some of our tests show an improvement in sales forecast accuracy for only highly diversified firms. Further, there was no improvement in sales forecast accuracy for what we call low diversified firms, which, however, are firms that are also fairly diversified (median DIVINDX = 0.58) and for which one should ordinarily expect segment reporting to be useful. Finally, there was no improvement in earnings forecast accuracy for any group of firms.

Since generally the segment footnote data was of no help in improving Japanese analysts' forecasts, we can conclude that the information content of the segment footnote was equal to or less than the information content of the Japanese analysts' private information. Because Japanese analysts are likely to have private access to information of higher quality than do US analysts, we conclude that US investors that rely on the Japanese segment footnote disclosures are put at a distinct economic disadvantage. The only way that the US investor would not experience negative economic consequences is if we assume that the information content of the segment footnote was equal to that of the private information obtained by Japanese analysts. However, we believe this assumption is not likely. And, regardless, private information is usually more timely than published information. Therefore, we recommend that the SEC consider continuing to influence the Japanese MOF to adopt rigorous segment reporting rules. Further, while we do not conclusively prove that US firms have suffered negative economic consequences, because US GAAP standards regarding segment reporting are significantly more stringent than those of Japan, we believe that requiring all Japanese firms that list on US exchanges to adopt US GAAP segment reporting rules would aid in leveling the playing field for US firms.

The conclusions of this study should be viewed in light of the following. There could be several additional reasons why analysts' forecasts did not improve after the introduction of segment footnote data. First, there are confounding factors to consider which we attempt to control for by using a battery of tests that involve: (1) the partitioning of data according to factors we believe affect how useful segment footnotes should be, and (2) the controlling of variables that we believe would affect analysts' forecasts using multiple regression analyses. However, these tests may not guarantee that our results are uncontaminated by confounding events. Second, because of the way Japanese firms consolidate their financial statements as we discuss in Section 3.4, it has been contended that consolidated data, though they conform to US style standards, do not represent the economic entities because corporate control in Japan is exercised in different ways than in the US (e.g., Lowe (1990)). Third,

68   *V. Mande, R. Ortman / Journal of Accounting and Public Policy 21 (2002) 31–70*

because of their alleged close ties with management (Mande and Kwak, 1996), Japanese analysts' forecasts may not have improved because the analysts may have obtained segment information prior to the requirement of disclosing segment data from management or other sources. [45] However, even if analysts had been receiving this private information we would still expect analysts' forecasts to improve after the introduction of segment reporting since the footnote data was audited, as well as, presented in a standardized format which should allow for more valid comparisons among firms (see, for example, Baldwin (1984)). This suggests to us that the footnote segment data is potentially garbled. Indeed, a recent survey (Mande and Ortman, 2000) showed that Japanese financial analysts had serious concerns whether Japanese firms: (1) defined segments meaningfully, (2) were consistent in defining segments over time, (3) objectively traced data on sales, operating income etc., to various segments, and (4) were deliberately misallocating common costs. Their findings suggest that a more likely explanation for our findings is that Japanese firms were presenting coarse data in their segment footnotes. These results are also consistent with an early survey conducted by the Commercial Law Center in Japan in 1991 which found that a significant percentage (31% of the 548 Japanese firms sampled) did not disclose any data, indicating that many Japanese firms were hesistant to disclose segment data and were able to do so by inappropriately using the discretion given to management under Japanese standards. Further, the survey found that among the firms that did disclose segment data, 55% did not define their segments meaningfully. [46] With the explosion of on-line trading by US investors and with an increasing number of foreign firms beginning to list on US exchanges, there is a critical need at this time that foreign firms provide US investors with reliable financial information. While our study on Japanese segment disclosures made an initial effort at exploring the issue of whether the SEC's rules on segment reporting were creating a double standard, more research is needed on the informativeness of segment reporting disclosures of firms from other foreign countries seeking to list on US exchanges.

---

[45] Mr. T. Shibata, Editor of JCH, informed us that JCH analysts did not obtain private segment information from management. Instead, segment information was obtained solely from published annual reports. When asked why, after April 1, 1990, the JCH continued to publish an unaudited breakdown of sales rather than the information disclosed in the audited footnote, Mr. T. Shibata responded that there was not room to print both. He would not explain why the audited footnote was not substituted for unaudited data. We will leave it to the reader to infer how this decision reflects JCH analysts' view of the usefulness of the audited footnote.

[46] See, Ozu and Gray (2001) for more discussion on this issue. These findings are also consistent with statements made by Japanese financial analysts to the authors of this study expressing dissatisfaction with segment reporting in Japan, some of them noting that the quality of segment disclosures would improve if Japan adopted US or IASC standards.

Acknowledgements

We thank two anonymous reviewers and workshop participants at Southern Methodist University for their comments. We also thank Wenhong Wang and Yoshie Uchida for their research assistance.

References

Afterman, A., 1995. International Accounting, Financial Reporting and Analysis, first ed. Warren, Gorman and Lamont, Boston.

Aitken, M., Czernkowski, R., Hooper, C., 1994. The information content of segment disclosures: Australian evidence. Abacus 30 (1), 65–77.

Balakrishnan, R., Harris, T., Sen, P., 1990. The predictive ability of geographic segment disclosures. Journal of Accounting Research 28 (2), 305–325.

Baldwin, B., 1984. Segment earnings disclosure and the ability of security analysts to forecast earnings per share. The Accounting Review 59 (3), 376–389.

Beckman, J., 1998. A comparison of consolidated and parent-only earnings forecasts for Japanese firms. Journal of Financial Statement Analysis 3 (3), 17–28.

Brown, L., 2001. A temporal analysis of earnings surprises: profits versus losses. Journal of Accounting Research 39 (2), 221–241.

Brown, L., Hagerman, R., Griffin, P., Zmijewski, M., 1987. An evaluation of alternative proxies for the market's assessment of unexpected earnings. Journal of Accounting and Economics 9 (2), 159–193.

Cardinal, B., Opler, T., 1995. Corporate diversification and innovative efficiency: an empirical study. Journal of Accounting and Economics 19 (2/3), 365–381.

Choi, F., Stonehill, A., 1982. Foreign access to US securities markets: the theory, myth and reality of regulatory barriers. Investment Analyst 65, 17–26.

Collins, D., 1976. Predicting earnings: entity versus sub-entity data: some further evidence. Journal of Accounting Research 14 (1), 163–177.

Collins, D., Simonds, R., 1979. SEC line-of-business disclosure and market risk adjustments. Journal of Accounting Research 17 (2), 352–383.

Dechow, P., Sweeney, A., Sloan, R., 1995. Detecting earnings management. The Accounting Review 70 (2), 193–225.

Dowen, R., 1996. Analyst reaction to negative earnings for large well-known firms: systematic differences for negative and non-negative earnings firms. Journal of Portfolio Management 23 (1), 49–55.

Dunn, K., Nathan, S., 2000. The effect of industry diversification analysts' earnings forecasts. Working Paper, Georgia State University.

Ely, K., Mande, V., 1996. The interdependent use of earnings and dividends in financial analysts' earnings forecasts. Contemporary Accounting Research 13 (2), 435–456.

Ely, K., Pownall, G., 2001. The endogeneity of incentives, earnings and book value, and value relevance: evidence from US-listed Japanese firms. Working Paper, Emory University.

Emmanuel, C., Gray, S., 1977. Segmental disclosures and the segment identification problem. Accounting and Business Research 8 (1), 37–50.

Fried, D., Schiff, M., Sondhi, A., 1992. Quarterly segment reporting: impact on analysts' forecasts and variability of security price returns. Working Paper, New York University.

Hamao, Y., 1991. A standard data base for the analysis of Japanese securities markets. Journal of Business 64 (1), 87–102.

Hwang, L., Ching-Lih, J., Basu, S., 1996. Loss firms and analysts' earnings forecast errors. Journal of Financial Statement Analysis 1 (1), 18–30.

Jones, J., 1991. Earnings management during import relief investigations. Journal of Accounting Research 29 (2), 193–228.

Kross, W., Ro, B., Schroeder, D., 1990. Earnings expectations: the analysts' information advantage. The Accounting Review 65 (2), 461–476.

Lowe, H., 1990. Shortcomings of Japanese consolidated financial statements. Accounting Horizons 4 (3), 1–9.

Mande, V., 1996. A comparison of US and Japanese analysts' forecasts of earnings and sales. International Journal of Accounting 31 (2), 143–160.

Mande, V., Kwak, W., 1996. Do Japanese analysts overreact or underreact to earnings announcements? Abacus 32 (1), 81–101.

Mande, V., Ortman, R., 2000. Are recent segment disclosures of Japanese firms useful?: Views of Japanese financial analysts. Working Paper, University of Nebraska, Omaha.

O'Brien, P., 1994. Corporate Earnings Forecasts and the Macroeconomy. Working Paper, University of Michigan.

Ozu, C., Gray, S., 2001. The development of segment reporting in Japan: achieving international harmonization through a process of national consensus. Advances in International Accounting 14, 1–13.

Prodhan, B., 1986. Geographic segment disclosure and multinational risk profile. Journal of Business Finance and Accounting 13 (1), 15–37.

Prodhan, B., Harris, M., 1989. Systematic risk and the discretionary disclosure of geographical segments: an empirical investigation of US multinationals. Journal of Business Finance and Accounting 16 (4), 467–492.

Radebaugh, L., Gray, S., 1997. International Accounting and Multinational Enterprises, first ed. John Wiley, New York.

Roberts, C., 1989. Forecasting earnings using geographic segment data: some UK evidence. Journal of International Financial Management and Accounting 1 (3), 130–151.

Sakakibara, S., Yamaji, H., Sakurai, H., Shiroshita, K., Fukuda, S., 1988. The Japanese Stock Market, first ed. Praeger Publishers, New York.

Saudagaran, S., 1993. A discussion of a test of the use of geographical segment disclosures. Journal of Accounting Research 31 (Supplement), 65–74.

Saudagaran, S., Biddle, G., 1994. Financial disclosure levels and foreign stock exchange listing decisions. In: Choi, F., Levich, R. (Eds.), International Capital Markets, first ed. Irvin Publishing, London, pp. 159–201.

Saudagaran, S., Meek, G., 1997. A review of research on the relationship between international capital markets and financial reporting by multinational firms. The Journal of Accounting Literature 16, 127–159.

White, H., 1980. A heteroscedasticity-consistent covariance matrix estimator and a direct test for heteroscedasticity. Econometrica 48, 817–838

[4]

JOURNAL OF
Accounting
& Economics

ELSEVIER   Journal of Accounting and Economics 21 (1996) 253–275

Corporate responses to segment disclosure requirements

Nandu J. Nagarajan[a], Sri S. Sridhar[*,b]

[a]*Joseph M. Katz Graduate School of Business, University of Pittsburgh, Pittsburgh, PA 15260, USA*
[b]*J.L. Kellogg Graduate School of Management, Northwestern University, Evanston, IL 60208, USA*

(Received June 1992; final version received September 1995)

Abstract

This paper shows through increasing disclosure requirements may induce firms to reduce their value-relevant disclosures. In the absence of segment reporting requirements, an incumbent firm may voluntarily disclose value-relevant information because it can use other, value-irrelevant, information to jam proprietary disclosures. However, when required to disclose segment data, the incumbent may aggregate proprietary information with other value-relevant information to deter entry by a rival. Hence, the firm does not disclose value-relevant information it would have revealed voluntarily in the absence of segment disclosure requirements. In such situations, requiring more disaggregate disclosures can actually decrease price efficiency.

Key words: Capital markets; Disclosure requirements; Proprietary and nonproprietary information; Cost allocation; Price efficiency

JEL classification: M4

1. Introduction

Corporate responses to additional mandatory disclosure requirements are determined by diverse and complex forces such as product market competition, financial market valuation, political and contracting cost considerations, and

---

*Corresponding author.

We thank Stan Baiman, Ronald A. Dye, Harry Evans, Jerry Feltham, Yuhchang Hwang, Robert P. Magee, Ross L. Watts (the editor), workshop participants at the 1991 UBCOW conference, the University of Iowa, Northwestern University, and, especially, an anonymous referee for helpful comments. The authors acknowledge research support from the Katz Graduate School of Business, the University of Pittsburgh, and the Accounting Research Center at Northwestern University, respectively.

254   *N.J. Nagarajan, S.S. Sridhar / Journal of Accounting and Economics 21 (1996) 253–275*

internal control issues. The presence of such a multitude of factors that can influence disclosure decisions makes predictions about firms' reactions to a given accounting or disclosure standard difficult. Thus, firms might react to a proposed disclosure standard in ways that are unintended by the standard setter, thereby potentially defeating the purpose of the standard.

This paper predicts that firms will sometimes cut back on their voluntary disclosures in order to avoid proprietary costs entailed by more disaggregate disclosure requirements. As a result, an increase in disclosure requirements can actually lead to a strict reduction in the firms' value-relevant disclosures.

Consider a firm consisting of two divisions that operate in different industries. One of the two divisions faces potential entry. The rival's entry decision is based on its assessment of the vulnerable division's proprietary direct cost information. Absent mandatory segment disclosure requirements, the incumbent could withhold its proprietary disclosures by aggregating the direct costs of both divisions. This would permit the incumbent to maximize its market value by voluntarily disclosing its total indirect costs.

On the other hand, when the incumbent has to report segment data, the only way it can jam the vulnerable division's direct cost disclosures is by aggregating the allocated indirect costs and the vulnerable division's direct costs in such a fashion that disclosing one would reveal the other.[1] It follows that the incumbent may, in equilibrium, refrain from disclosing both its indirect costs and the vulnerable division's direct costs, thereby reducing the total value-relevant information available to the market.

The above result also implies that greater disclosure requirements can lead to less efficient prices, where price efficiency is defined as the expected absolute or squared difference between the full information price and the market price prevalent in any given disclosure requirement setting.

There exists a second potential inefficiency that a standard setter would like to avoid. Under certain conditions the incumbent will disclose *all* its value-relevant private information regardless of mandatory segment disclosure requirements. Thus, under the stated conditions, imposing greater disclosure requirements is superfluous.[2]

---

[1] See Dye (1985) for another example of the use of an accounting method to deter entry. However, the intuition in this paper for such strategic use is different: a cost allocation procedure enables the incumbent to jam the disclosure of proprietary direct cost information to the potential entrant, whereas in Dye (1985) the incumbent reveals greater information through its choice of a given accounting method.

[2] Dye (1990) compares the relative levels of disclosures by multiple firms in a mandatory versus a voluntary regime, when their cash flows are correlated. Under certain conditions of financial externalities, mandatory disclosures are found to be redundant in his setting. In contrast, in this paper, the disclosure disincentives induced by mandating segment disclosures are entirely internal to the firm. Verrecchia (1983) examines a firm's discretionary disclosures when it is not subject to any mandatory disclosure requirements.

N.J. Nagarajan, S.S. Sridhar / Journal of Accounting and Economics 21 (1996) 253–275   255

Further, this paper demonstrates that the friction between the informational demands of the product and financial markets enables the incumbent to avoid revealing proprietary information independent of its ability to commit to an accounting method. We also generate several testable hypotheses about the likelihood of the standard setter encountering the above-mentioned inefficiencies.

Grossman (1981) and Milgrom (1981) demonstrate that full disclosure will be obtained in equilibrium if the financial market adopts a skeptical posture about the firm's private value-relevant information. Wagenhofer (1990) and Darrough and Stoughton (1990) show that if both product and financial markets use an incumbent's disclosures, the friction between the informational demands of these two markets can sustain nondisclosure of the incumbent's proprietary information under certain conditions. Thus, the above papers examine a firm's voluntary disclosure strategies when the firm is not subject to any mandatory disclosure requirements. In contrast, this paper focuses on the impact of mandatory disclosure requirements on a firm's supplementary disclosures, and illustrates how a firm can cut back on its supplementary disclosures in response to increased disclosure requirements in order to protect its proprietary information.

The remainder of the paper proceeds as follows. Section 2 introduces the model. Section 3 presents the analysis and the results. Section 4 concludes the paper.

2. The model

There are two firms, an incumbent and a rival, and two periods. The incumbent is a two-division firm with one division operating as a natural monopoly and the other division as a monopoly facing potential entry by the rival in the second period.

Assume each division produces only one product and the inverse demand functions for the divisions' products are common knowledge. Assuming that the prices are publicly observable and the incumbent can carry no inventories, produced quantities for each division are public information. The incumbent decides its optimal production quantities for the vulnerable division, Q, and the natural monopoly division, Q^m, before observing its realized costs.[3]

The total cost for each of the incumbent's two divisions consists of two components, a direct cost and an indirect cost. The only element in each

---

[3]At the time of its production decision, the incumbent has no superior private information. Therefore, the incumbent does not gain anything by distorting the optimal production quantities.

256   *N.J. Nagarajan, S.S. Sridhar / Journal of Accounting and Economics 21 (1996) 253–275*

division's indirect cost is assumed to be the portion of common operating costs allocated to that division.[4] As the quantity produced by the divisions can be inferred by the external users of the incumbent's financial statements, it will be expositionally convenient to think of the direct costs for each division as unit costs.

The vulnerable division's direct cost per unit may be either C_L (low) or C_H (high), where $C_L < C_H$. The realization of the vulnerable division's direct cost is dependent on an underlying unobservable production parameter, $\theta \in \{\theta_G, \theta_B\}$ as follows:

$$1 > \Pr(C_L \mid \theta_G) > \Pr(C_H \mid \theta_G) > \Pr(C_L \mid \theta_B) = 0. \tag{A1}$$

Assume that the underlying production parameter, θ, interpretable as an industry specific factor, is perfectly correlated between the vulnerable division of the incumbent and the rival and across the two periods.[5] Given assumption (A1), this implies a positive correlation between the division's direct costs across the two periods, and also between the direct costs of the incumbent's vulnerable division and those of the rival.

The natural monopoly division's direct cost is assumed to be uniformly distributed over the region, $[\underline{C}^m, \bar{C}^m]$, where $\bar{C}^m > \underline{C}^m$.[6] Assume that the distribution of the direct costs of the natural monopoly division is independent of the vulnerable division's direct costs.

It is expositionally convenient to represent the total common operating cost (also referred to as indirect cost) as a cost per unit of the vulnerable division. Let this allocable common operating cost per unit, $\tilde{K}$, be stochastic and distributed uniformly over the interval $[0, \bar{K}]$, where $\bar{K}$ is strictly greater than $\partial C \equiv C_H - C_L$.[7] Assume that the common operating costs, K, follow a martingale process such that $E[K_2 \mid K_1] = K_1$, where the subscripts denote the periods.

The incumbent privately observes the realization of this common operating cost and then, if required to provide segment data, decides how to allocate it

---

[4]Such indirect costs could include factory rent, maintenance, property taxes, salaries of common sales personnel, etc.

[5]This assumption of perfect correlation of the productivity parameter between the vulnerable division and the rival and across the two periods simplifies the analysis considerably, but is not crucial to obtaining the results in this paper.

[6]Our model formulation permits the dependence of each division's direct costs, C and C^m, on the chosen quantity for that division, Q and Q^m, respectively, and the time period. The notational references to such dependencies are suppressed.

[7]Random variables are denoted by a tilde ($\sim$) on the top, while their realized values do not have a tilde. Thus, the realized total common operating cost is QK, where K is the realized unit common cost.

N.J. Nagarajan, S.S. Sridhar / Journal of Accounting and Economics 21 (1996) 253–275 257

between the two reportable segments, i.e., the two divisions.[8] Under GAAP, the basis for allocation of such common operating costs between the segments must be 'reasonable' and correspond to the underlying economics.[9] In this simple setting, each division's production volume, sales revenues, direct costs, or earnings are the only possible bases available for the incumbent to allocate the common operating costs to the two divisions. Therefore, the incumbent's choice of an allocation basis is assumed to be restricted to this feasible set.[10] Further, consistent with the SFAS 14 requirements, assume that the incumbent is not required to report the actual amount of the common operating cost that is allocated to either division.

The allocation decision is assumed to have no impact on the incumbent's payoffs other than through influencing the product market competition. Therefore, factors such as potential tax consequences of different allocation strategies are ignored.

The incumbent produces publicly observable financial statements at the end of the first period. It is assumed that the firm always reports truthfully whenever it makes any voluntary or mandatory disclosures.

In deciding on entry at the end of the first period, the rival firm has to rely on the incumbent's published financial statements and supplementary disclosures, if any, to infer the vulnerable division's direct cost, C, and hence, the underlying productivity parameter, θ.

The only costs that the rival faces in the event of an entry are the cost of entry, K_E, and its own expected direct cost determined by the productivity parameter, θ, that is common to both firms.

Let R_M^x and R_D^x denote the vulnerable division's second-period payoffs, where the subscript D (for duopoly) or M (for monopoly) indicates whether entry occurred or not, and the superscript denotes the state of production, $x \in \{G, B\}$. Assume that $R_M^x > R_D^x$ and $R_z^G > R_z^B$ for $z \in \{M, D\}$ and $x \in \{G, B\}$. Further, it is assumed that $R_D^B > 0$, implying that the incumbent never has to withdraw from the market in the second period.

---

[8] In a mandatory segment disclosure setting, each division is assumed to be treated as a reportable segment. SFAS 14 provides guidelines as to what may constitute a reportable segment. Generally speaking, if an industry segment produces 10% or more of the revenues or operating profits of the firm as a whole or employs 10% or more of the combined assets of the firm, it may be regarded as significant and, therefore, be treated as a reportable segment.

[9] See Nikolai and Bazley (1991, pp. 1283–1284).

[10] To simplify our analysis, these allocation bases are assumed to involve allocating the entire common operating costs between both divisions, so that no unallocated portion remains to be shown as a line item. Further, even if this feasible set of allocation bases were expanded to include the divisions' assets, all the analysis and the results of this paper would remain identical.

258   *N.J. Nagarajan, S.S. Sridhar / Journal of Accounting and Economics 21 (1996) 253–275*

	First Period			Second Period

The incumbent   The incumbent   The incumbent   The external users   Second-period
decides on the   privately observes allocates K infer the underlying   payoffs are
quantities to be   the direct costs   between the two   productivity   realized
produced by   for the divisions, divisions. Further, parameter for the   by all players.
each division, C and C^m,   the incumbent   division, θ, from
Q and Q^m,   and the common   makes mandatory   the incumbent's
based on prior   operating costs,   and supplementary   disclosures.
beliefs about its K.   disclosures, if any. The rival firm
costs.   decides on entry.

Fig. 1

On entry, the rival's second-period payoffs conditioned on the state, θ_x, are denoted by π_D^x, $x \in \{G, B\}$. It is assumed that

$$\pi_D^G > K_E > \Pr(\theta_G \mid C_H)\pi_D^G + \Pr(\theta_B \mid C_H)\,\pi_D^B. \tag{A2}$$

This assumption is essential to ensure that the incumbent's direct cost disclosures are material in the rival's entry decision.[11] If the rival does not enter, its payoffs are normalized to zero.

Finally, it is assumed that the entire structure of the game is common knowledge to all players. The sequence of events is captured by the following time line shown in Fig. 1.

3. The analysis

This section consists of three subsections. Sections 3.1 and 3.2 analyze the firm's disclosure strategies in the presence and absence of mandatory requirements, respectively. Section 3.3 examines the impact of introducing greater disaggregate disclosure requirements on the incumbent's disclosure strategies.

3.1. Disclosures in the presence of mandatory requirements

When segment disclosures are mandated, the incumbent's publicly observed financial statements are assumed to provide revenues and operating profits at the individual divisional level. In this setting, the incumbent has two choice variables: (a) the choice of an accounting method, i.e., the basis for allocating the common operating costs to each division, and (b) whether to make any

---

[11]For instance, if $K_E \leq \Pr(\theta_G \mid C_H)\pi_D^G + \Pr(\theta_B \mid C_H)\pi_D^B$, then regardless of the division's direct cost, entry will occur. On the other hand, if $\pi_D^G \leq K_E$, entry will never occur.

N.J. Nagarajan, S.S. Sridhar / Journal of Accounting and Economics 21 (1996) 253-275   259

supplementary disclosures. The incumbent's objective in its disclosure and accounting method decisions is to maximize the expected price for the firm at the end of the first period.[12]

For any given first period common operating costs, K_1, the price for the firm at the end of the first period is $P = V^m + V - K_1$, where $V^m(V)$ refers to the expected payoffs for the natural monopoly (vulnerable) division in the second period, excluding common operating costs, with the expectation conditioned on all the information available till that point in time. Assuming that the natural monopoly division's direct cost, C^m, is independently distributed across the two periods, we could normalize V^m to be equal to zero without loss of generality. Therefore, the firm value can be simplified as $P = V - K$, after dropping the indexing of K to the time period.

The sequential equilibrium concept (Kreps and Wilson, 1982) as refined by the 'perfectness' requirement of Grossman and Perry (1986) is used as a solution to this game. In this equilibrium, each firm decides its strategy in a sequentially rational way, based on its beliefs that are Bayesian updated using all observed variables.

The sequential equilibrium conditions themselves do not impose any 'reasonableness' requirements on out-of-equilibrium beliefs. By adopting the refinement of perfect sequential equilibrium, the following analysis eliminates unappealing equilibria created by implausible beliefs.[13] Under this equilibrium concept, no incumbent type wishes to deviate from its equilibrium disclosure strategy given that the external users of its disclosures would alter their beliefs correspondingly, contingent on such deviations. Appendix 1 contains a complete technical specification of the equilibrium.

The external users of the firm's financial statements can infer the vulnerable division's reported total cost per unit, C_T, by subtracting the vulnerable division's profits from its revenues, where C_T is equal to the sum of the vulnerable division's direct cost and the portion of the common operating costs allocated to that division. However, if the incumbent chooses not to allocate any common operating costs to the vulnerable division, the rival can infer the division's realized direct cost from the published financial statements.

If the observed total cost for the vulnerable division, C_T, is less than C_H, the rival will infer that the division's direct cost is low, i.e., C_L, and entry will occur. On the other hand, if C_T is greater than $C_L + \bar{K}$, then the rival infers that the division's direct cost is high, i.e., C_H, and no entry will occur. In both these instances, the full disclosure principle (Grossman, 1981; Milgrom, 1981) ensures

---

[12]This objective of the incumbent is equivalent to maximizing the net expected cash flows over both periods for the firm as a whole.

[13]The perfect sequential equilibrium concept is stronger than the Intuitive Criterion of Cho and Kreps (1987) because every perfect sequential equilibrium satisfies the Intuitive Criterion but not vice versa.

260   *N.J. Nagarajan, S.S. Sridhar / Journal of Accounting and Economics 21 (1996) 253–275*

that the incumbent will always disclose its realized indirect costs, K, to distinguish itself from firms with greater indirect costs.

However, if the division's observed total cost, C_T, is in the jamming region, $J \equiv [C_H, C_L + \bar{K}]$, the external users cannot unambiguously infer the vulnerable division's realized direct cost. In making their inferences about the value of the productivity parameter, θ, the external users of the firm's disclosures have access to the following information: the vulnerable and natural monopoly divisions' total costs, C_T and C_T^m, respectively, any unallocated common operating cost, and supplementary disclosures, if any.

Because both financial and product markets use the incumbent's disclosures, different incumbent types have different disclosure incentives. If the vulnerable division's direct cost is C_H, disclosing this information will deter entry by assumption (A2). However, such a disclosure would reduce the vulnerable division's value to

$$V_H = V(C = C_H) = \Pr(\theta_G \mid C = C_H)R_M^G + \Pr(\theta_B \mid C = C_H)R_M^B.$$

Conversely, after realizing a low direct cost for the vulnerable division, C_L, the incumbent would like to disclose its direct cost to obtain a higher value in the financial market for that division. However, in the presence of a rival, such a disclosure would entail a proprietary cost, reducing the prospective buyers' valuation of the division to R_D^G.

Let $\pi \equiv \Pr(\theta_G) \, \pi_M^G + \Pr(\theta_B) \, \pi_M^B$ refer to the rival's expected payoffs from entry, based on the prior beliefs about the state, $\Pr(\theta_x)$, $x = G,B$. Let $V_J \equiv \Pr(\theta_G) \, R_M^G + \Pr(\theta_B)R_M^B$ refer to the expected second-period payoffs for the vulnerable division based on the common priors about the division's productivity at the beginning of the game, and given that entry does not occur at the end of the first period. Assume without loss of generality that $V_H \geq R_D^G$.[14] After privately observing the realized direct and indirect costs, the incumbent chooses the fraction of common operating costs allocated to the vulnerable division, b_i, where i refers to the selected allocation basis, for $i \in$ {each division's production volume, sales revenue, direct costs, and earnings}. Let $b = \max_{b_i}\{b_i\}$. The need for this definition of b (as the largest possible fraction of the common operating costs that can be allocated to the vulnerable division under any of the four available allocation bases in this model) will become clear in the discussion following Lemma 1.

Lemma 1 characterizes sufficient conditions for the incumbent not to disclose value-relevant information when it is required to report segment data.

---

[14] The only role for this assumption is to simplify condition (C2) stated in Lemma 1 below. All the results of this paper would otherwise remain identical even if V_H were less than R_D^G.

N.J. Nagarajan, S.S. Sridhar / Journal of Accounting and Economics 21 (1996) 253–275 261

Lemma 1. The incumbent firm will, in equilibrium, disclose neither the vulnerable division's direct costs, C, nor the total common operating costs, K, if the following conditions are satisfied:

(i) *the cost of entry, K_E, is greater than the rival's expected payoffs from entry based on prior beliefs about the division's productivity, π.* (C1)

(ii) $V_J \geq V_H + Q\bar{K}/2.$ (C2)

(iii) *The realized common operating costs, K, fall in the region* $[(\delta C/b),$ $\bar{K} - \delta C/b].$ (C3)

All proofs are in Appendix 2. The intuition for this nondisclosure equilibrium follows. Whenever condition (C3) is met, the reported total cost for the vulnerable division, C_T, will fall in the jamming region, $J \equiv [C_H, C_L + \bar{K}]$. If $C_T \in J$, the incumbent makes no supplementary disclosures, and condition (C1) is satisfied, then entry does not occur because the rival's posterior beliefs about the vulnerable division's productivity parameter, θ, remain unchanged from its priors. The financial market will assign a price of V_J for the vulnerable division because its posterior beliefs also remain the same as its priors. Further, if $C_T \in J$ and conditions (C1) and (C2) are satisfied, the incumbent maximizes its financial market value by not disclosing the vulnerable division's direct or indirect costs, regardless of the realized value of the vulnerable division's direct cost, C.

Further, disclosing the realized common operating costs, K, would enable the external users to infer the vulnerable division's direct costs because the equilibrium choice of b can always be computed from the firm's segment disclosures. Therefore, the incumbent will not disclose its realized common operating costs, K, if conditions (C1)–(C3) are met.

Moreover, even though the natural monopoly division's direct costs are assumed to be distributed independently across periods, their realized values are of interest to the users of the incumbent's disclosures. In the above nondisclosure equilibrium, the incumbent discloses neither the direct costs of the natural monopoly division nor the amount of indirect costs allocated to either division because such disclosures would enable the markets to infer the vulnerable division's direct costs. Therefore, even though the natural monopoly's direct costs are neither value relevant nor proprietary in nature, the incumbent will not disclose them when conditions (C1)–(C3) are met.

The incumbent will choose the allocation basis that results in the largest fraction, b, of the common operating costs being allocated to the vulnerable division, because this basis maximizes the probability that the vulnerable division's reported total cost, C_T, lies in the jamming region, J. Thus, in equilibrium, the incumbent exercises its discretion over the choice of an appropriate allocation basis to guard its proprietary information. In this nondisclosure equilibrium, entry does not occur unless the observed total cost for the vulnerable division is strictly less than C_H.

Lemma 1 has several significant implications. First, in contrast to the traditional role of cost allocation as an internal incentive mechanism to mitigate agency problems (see, for example, Balachandran, Li, and Magee, 1987; Magee, 1988), it identifies an external, strategic role for cost allocation in the context of segment disclosures.[15]

Second, the tension between the financial and product market users of the incumbent's disclosures enables the incumbent firm to jam its proprietary disclosures regardless of its ability either to commit to an accounting method, b_i, before observing its realized costs or to make any supplementary disclosures.

Third, the earlier literature on disclosures (see Grossman, 1981; Milgrom, 1981) implies that the financial markets act as a catalyst for increased disclosures by firms. However, our analysis provides a contrasting result: that is, the financial markets can also discourage firms from disclosing their value-relevant information. If we started with the product market alone, for all practical purposes only a full disclosure equilibrium will prevail.[16] However, with the addition of the financial market, the level of disclosure decreases because the firm does not reveal the division's direct or indirect cost when conditions (C1)–(C3) are met.

Fourth, the results of this paper indicate that the level of disclosure decreases with interaction between multiple markets regardless of which benchmark we use. We know from the previous literature that considering the financial market alone, full disclosure is the only equilibrium.[17] With the addition of the product market, we know from Lemma 1 that the firm will disclose its direct cost less often. Thus, the addition of either market's informational demands to those of the other market reduces the firm's level of disclosures.

Finally, Lemma 1 identifies conditions under which it is in the interests of the shareholders of a publicly held corporation *not* to be informed of all the value-relevant information in the possession of the company. The reason for the optimality of such incomplete communication is that all communications by a publicly held corporation to its shareholders are public. Therefore, disclosure of any favorable information could lead to potential proprietary and political costs. This trade-off between the costs of disclosures and the benefits in the form

---

[15]This strategic role for internal cost allocation is consistent with the empirical findings of Givoly, Hayn, and D'Souza (1991) that allocation of joint costs reduces the quality of reported segment earnings.

[16]When only the product market user is present, two of the necessary conditions required to sustain any nondisclosure of the vulnerable division's direct cost are (1) the incumbent be unable to make any supplementary disclosures, and (2) the incumbent be able to commit to the fraction of the common operating costs to be allocated to both divisions. Considering the implausibility of these conditions, a nondisclosure equilibrium in the presence of the rival alone appears impractical.

[17]See Grossman (1981) and Milgrom (1981). This full disclosure equilibrium is supported by the skeptical posture of prospective investors.

N.J. Nagarajan, S.S. Sridhar / Journal of Accounting and Economics 21 (1996) 253–275   263

of higher prices for the company's stock, results in the optimality (from the shareholders' perspective) of the firm withholding significant value-relevant information from the financial markets.

Next, to understand the impact of increased disclosure requirements on corporate disclosure policies, it is essential that we compare the above results with the firm's disclosure strategy in the absence of such requirements.

3.2. Disclosures in the absence of mandatory requirements

Suppose the incumbent is not required to provide segment data as part of its published annual report. Now, also assume that the incumbent is required to provide only aggregate revenues and earnings for the two divisions put together. It follows that any external user can observe only the incumbent's aggregate cost, C_A, from the published financial statements, where $C_A = Q^m C^m + QC + QK$.[18]

Thus, in the absence of mandatory segment disclosures, the incumbent's choice variable is restricted to either making a supplementary disclosure or not. Because the incumbent provides only aggregate revenue and earnings information as part of its published financial statements, it is unable to use its choice of an accounting method, i.e., the fraction of total common operating cost allocated to each division, to manage its direct cost disclosures.

When the incumbent provides only aggregate information, an external user of the published financial statements will infer that the vulnerable division's direct cost is high if the reported aggregate cost, C_A, is greater than $Q^m \bar{C}^m + QC_L + Q\bar{K}$. On the other hand, if the firm's aggregate cost, C_A, is less than $Q^m C^m + QC_H$, an external user of the published financial statements will infer that the vulnerable division's direct cost is low. In both these situations the incumbent will disclose the realized indirect costs, K, to distinguish itself from firms with greater indirect costs.

The remaining possibility is that the observed aggregate cost, C_A, is in the jamming region, $J_A \equiv [Q^m C^m + QC_H, Q^m \bar{C}^m + QC_L + Q\bar{K}]$. When this happens, no external user can, in the absence of supplementary disclosures by the incumbent, unambiguously infer the vulnerable division's realized direct cost.

Absent segment reporting requirements, the following lemma characterizes sufficient conditions under which the incumbent will disclose the total common operating costs, and yet, not reveal its proprietary information, i.e., the vulnerable division's direct costs.

Lemma 2.   Assume that the incumbent is not required to report segment revenues and earnings information. The incumbent will disclose the total common operating

---

[18]For notational convenience, only the aggregate cost, C_A, is *not* expressed in unit terms. All other costs in this paper are denoted in unit terms.

264   *N.J. Nagarajan, S.S. Sridhar / Journal of Accounting and Economics 21 (1996) 253–275*

costs, K, but not the vulnerable division's direct costs, C, if conditions ($C1$) and ($C2$) in Lemma 1 and the following condition are satisfied:

The realized direct cost for the natural monopoly division,

$$C^m \in \left[\; \underline{C}^m + \frac{Q\,\delta C}{Q^m}, \quad \bar{C}^m - \frac{Q\,\delta C}{Q^m} \right]. \tag{C4}$$

The intuition for Lemma 2 follows. The external users of the incumbent's disclosures observe the aggregate cost, C_A. If the incumbent discloses the common operating costs, K, then the external users can deduce that the sum of the direct costs for the two divisions is equal to $C_A - QK = Q^m C^m + QC$. If the realized direct cost for the natural monopoly division, C^m, falls either below $\underline{C}^m + Q\,\delta C/Q^m$ or above $\bar{C}^m - Q\,\delta C/Q^m$, the external users will be able to infer from the observed $C_A - QK$ that the incumbent's realized direct cost for the vulnerable division is low or high, respectively. However, when the realized C^m falls in the region, $[\underline{C}^m + Q\,\delta C/Q^m, \; \bar{C}^m - Q\,\delta C/Q^m]$, the external users cannot unambiguously infer the vulnerable division's direct costs. Given the financial market's skeptical beliefs that $K = \bar{K}$, the incumbent maximizes its market value by disclosing its common operating costs, K, when condition (C4) is satisfied. Further, such disclosure of K does not induce entry because the realized value of the vulnerable division's direct cost cannot be inferred by the rival despite its knowledge of K. Finally, when conditions (C1) and (C2) are met, the markets' posterior beliefs about the vulnerable division's productive state remain the same as the priors only if the reported aggregate cost for the incumbent falls in the jamming region, J_A, and condition (C4) holds.[19]

Note that if the aggregate cost, C_A, falls in the jamming region, J_A, but the realized direct cost of the natural monopoly division is such that condition (C4) does not hold, then the incumbent will not disclose the realized common operating costs, K, as long as conditions (C1) and (C2) are met because doing so would reveal its proprietory information. Further, notice that when conditions (C1) and (C2) are not simultaneously satisfied, full disclosure is obtained regardless of segment disclosure requirements. Next, we compare the incumbent's disclosure strategies in the presence and absence of segment disclosure requirements.

3.3. Impact of mandatory disclosure requirements

When condition (C4) holds and the incumbent is required to disclose only aggregate cost information, the financial market's skeptical beliefs about the

---

[19] Letting $F(.)$ denote the cumulative distribution function of C^m, if $F(\bar{C}^m - Q\,\delta C/Q^m) - F(\underline{C}^m + Q\,\delta C/Q^m) \geq 0.5$, the prior probability of the incumbent revealing its common operating costs, K, is greater than not doing so.

N.J. Nagarajan, S.S. Sridhar / Journal of Accounting and Economics 21 (1996) 253–275   265

realized value of the common operating costs, K, result in the incumbent disclosing it fully. This is made possible because, in the absence of segment disclosure requirements, the incumbent is able to use the natural monopoly division's direct costs, instead of the common operating costs, to jam the inference of the vulnerable division's direct costs.

In contrast, when the incumbent is required to make segment disclosures. Lemma 1 states that when conditions (C1)–(C3) are met, the firm will not disclose the total common operating costs, K, because the common operating costs allocated to the vulnerable division are used to withhold proprietary information, C. This intuition leads to our main result.

Proposition 1. Imposing mandatory segment disclosure requirements results in a strict reduction in value-relevant disclosures by the incumbent firm if conditions (C1)–(C3) in Lemma 1 and (C4) in Lemma 2 are met.

The above proposition captures the incentives that fashion corporate responses to additional disclosure requirements. In the absence of mandatory segment disclosure requirements, the incumbent does not disclose the total costs of individual divisions and, therefore, has no need to rely on the common operating costs to jam proprietary disclosures. Instead, the incumbent relies on using the direct costs of the natural monopoly division to jam the vulnerable division's direct costs. Therefore, when condition (C4) is met, the incumbent discloses the realized common operating costs, K, to meet the informational demands of the financial market. The price for the incumbent, given that it discloses K but not C in the no disclosure requirements (NDR) setting, will be $P_{\text{NDR}} = V_J - QK$.

In contrast, when required to report segment data, the incumbent uses the common operating costs to jam its proprietary disclosures and, hence, does not disclose the total common operating costs, K. Therefore, the price for the firm in a disclosure requirements (DR) setting, given that it does not disclose its proprietary information, C, will be $P_{\text{DR}} = V_J - Q\bar{K}/2$, regardless of the value of its realized common operating costs, K.

One implication of Proposition 1 is that greater disclosure requirements can actually reduce price efficiency, where price efficiency is defined as the expected absolute or the squared difference between the full information price and the market price prevalent in any given disclosure requirement setting. When conditions (C1)–(C4) are met, the price in the no disclosure requirement setting, P_{NDR}, captures more of the underlying value-relevant information than the price in the disclosure requirement setting, P_{DR}, thus leading to greater price efficiency with fewer disclosure requirements.

Another implication of Proposition 1 is that sometimes the firm's market value can be greater when it reduces its value-relevant disclosures rather than increasing them. For any realized $K > \bar{K}/2$, we get $P_{\text{NDR}} < P_{\text{DR}}$. This implies that given $K > \bar{K}/2$, the incumbent's price is greater in the presence of disclosure requirements than in their absence.

Corollary 1 identifies circumstances under which conditions (C1)–(C4) are more likely to hold, resulting in a more frequent occurrence of the phenomenon identified in Proposition 1.

Corollary 1.   The probability that mandatory segment disclosure requirements will result in strictly less value-relevant disclosures increases weakly as:

(i)   *The natural monopoly division's production volume, Q^m, increases.*

(ii)   *The difference between the high and low direct costs of the vulnerable division, δC, decreases.*

(iii)   *The vulnerable division's volume of production, Q, decreases.*

(iv)   *The rival's cost of entry, K_E, increases.*

(v) $\Pr(C = C_H | \theta_G)$ *decreases.*

The rationale for these results is intuitive. For instance, in the absence of segment disclosure requirements, as the natural monopoly division's production volume, Q^m, increases, it is more likely that C^m will fall in the region $[C^m + Q \, \delta C/Q^m, \bar{C}^m - Q \, \delta C/Q^m]$; therefore, the incumbent will be able to disclose the common operating costs, K, more often. In contrast, in the presence of segment disclosure requirements, the incumbent's ability to jam its proprietary information is independent of the natural monopoly division's production volume because each division's total costs are disclosed separately. This yields part (i) of Corollary 1.

As the difference between the high and low direct costs of the vulnerable division (δC) or the volume of production by the vulnerable division (Q) decreases, the probability of C^m falling in the region specified by condition (C4) increases. This increases the likelihood of the incumbent disclosing the common operating costs, K, when it is not required to report segment data. On similar lines, condition (C3) is also met with greater probability as δC decreases. As K_E increases, the chances of condition (C1) being met increase. Finally, as $\Pr(C = C_H | \theta_G)$ decreases, the posterior $\Pr(\theta_G | C = C_H)$ also decreases, resulting in a decrease in V_H. This increases the probability that condition (C2) will be satisfied.

The above result that imposing mandatory segment disclosure requirements could result in a strict reduction in value-relevant disclosures arises under conditions that sustain a *nondisclosure* equilibrium. In contrast, we next identify conditions that result in *full disclosure* of the vulnerable division's direct costs even in the absence of segment reporting requirements, thereby establishing the redundancy of such greater disclosure requirements.

N.J. Nagarajan, S.S. Sridhar / Journal of Accounting and Economics 21 (1996) 253–275 267

*Proposition 2. The incumbent makes full disclosure of all value-relevant informa-
tion independent of mandatory segment disclosure requirements provided that*

$$K_E \leq \pi.$$

Condition (C1) is also a necessary condition for the equilibria characterized in
Lemmas 1 and 2 to hold. Therefore, when condition (C1) is not satisfied in
Lemma 1, the incumbent will disclose all value-relevant information when
required to report segment data. Similarly, when condition (C1) is not satisfied
in Lemma 2, full disclosure of all value-relevant information obtains even
without segment disclosure requirements. Further, whenever the incumbent
discloses the vulnerable division's direct costs, it will also disclose the common
operating costs, K, because otherwise the financial market's skeptical beliefs
would result in a lower market value for the firm. Thus, when condition (C1) is
not satisfied, imposing more disaggregate disclosure requirements is superfluous
because full disclosure is obtained regardless of such disclosure requirements.

Wagenhofer (1990) and Darrough and Stoughton (1990) examine the voluntary disclosure incentives of a single-product firm and show that nondisclosure
can be sustained in equilibrium because of the friction between the informational demands of the capital and product markets. In contrast, this paper shows
that mandatory disclosure requirements faced by a multi-product firm can
actually reduce the amount of supplementary disclosures that a firm makes
when multiple markets use such disclosures, thus strictly reducing the amount of
value-relevant information available to the markets.

4. Conclusion

This paper studies a multi-division incumbent firm's incentives to choose an
accounting method and make supplementary disclosures in the presence of
multiple users of the firm's disclosures. It is shown that imposing additional
disclosure requirements can result in the incumbent strictly reducing its value-
relevant disclosures. This arises because the incumbent responds to the additional disclosure requirements by choosing an accounting method that obfus-
cates proprietary information. This masking of proprietary information is ac-
complished by aggregating proprietary and nonproprietary, but value-relevant,
information in such a manner that disclosing one type of information reveals the
other.

Further, this paper identifies conditions under which a firm will disclose all its
value-relevant information regardless of whether it is subject to mandatory
disclosure requirements or not. Thus, by implication, mandating disclosures
under these circumstances is redundant. Overall, in contrast to past research
such as Wagenhofer (1990) and Darrough and Stoughton (1990), this paper
examines how mandatory disclosure requirements link a firm's disclosure

268　*N.J. Nagarajan, S.S. Sridhar / Journal of Accounting and Economics 21 (1996) 253–275*

decisions in one product market with its disclosures in other product markets even though not all the product markets are subject to competitive losses.

This paper's analysis is based on the assumption that the common operating costs are correlated across the two periods and, hence, their disclosures are value-relevant. Alternatively, even if the common operating costs were independently distributed across the two periods, all the results of this paper would still remain qualitatively the same. Define value-relevant information as any information whose disclosure or nondisclosure alters the market value of a firm. Then one could show that even if the realization of the current period's common operating costs were not informative of its future realization, the portion of common operating cost that is allocated to the vulnerable division would become value-relevant information. Further, the imposition of mandatory disclosure requirements once again results in a strict reduction in value-relevant (defined above) disclosures for reasons similar to the ones discussed in this paper.

In other words, introducing more disclosure requirements could convert otherwise value-irrelevant information into value-relevant information because it is used in conjunction with other data that are informative about the underlying economic value of the firm (e.g., the vulnerable division's direct cost). Another interpretation of this nondisclosure result is that, under these conditions, the firm will also refrain from disclosing some of its nonproprietary information (e.g., the amount of common operating costs allocated to the vulnerable division) because the disclosure of such nonproprietary information could reveal its proprietary information.

This model can be generalized by enlarging the set of direct costs for the vulnerable division from two outcomes to an interval. Another avenue for extending this model would be to let the second-period distribution of the natural monopoly division's direct costs depend on its first-period realization. This would make all cost information value-relevant. We expect our results to remain qualitatively the same although the specific forms of conditions, under which the incumbent refrains from disclosing its common operating costs when required to provide segment information, will be different. The financial market's pressures to disclose the natural monopoly division's information would increase as such information became value-relevant. The incumbent would, therefore, find it more difficult not to disclose its proprietary information when subject to segment disclosure requirements. Hence, we would expect the set of conditions that are required to sustain a nondisclosure equilibrium, such as the one described in this paper, to expand relative to what we need when the natural monopoly division's direct costs are not value-relevant.

Finally, our model can be adapted to capture a political cost story (see Watts and Zimmerman, 1986). The proprietary cost suffered by the incumbent consequent to entry may be interpreted as political costs. With such an adaptation, our analysis would examine a firm's trade-off between boosting its share price by

N.J. Nagarajan, S.S. Sridhar / Journal of Accounting and Economics 21 (1996) 253–275 269

revealing good news and minimizing its political costs by concealing its good news.

Appendix 1

Definition of an equilibrium

As an illustration, we provide the definition of an equilibrium only in a mandatory segment disclosure regime. A similar equilibrium definition follows for the other regime in which segment disclosures are not mandated.

Let $\mathscr{C} \equiv \{C_L, C_H\}$, $\mathscr{C}^m \equiv [\underline{C}^m, \bar{C}^m]$, $\mathscr{C}_T \equiv \{C_T: C_T = C + bK$, for any $C \in \mathscr{C}$ and $b \in [0, 1]\}$, and $\mathscr{C}_T^m \equiv \{C_T^m: C_T^m = C^m + (1 - b)K$, for any $C^m \in \mathscr{C}^m$ and $b \in [0, 1]\}$, where $b\,((1 - b))$ refers to the fraction of the common operating costs allocated to the vulnerable (natural monopoly) division. Further, let $\hat{d} \in \Delta \equiv \{D_C, D_K, D_{C,K}, ND\}$, where the elements of the set Δ represent supplementary disclosures of C only, K only, both C and K, and no supplementary disclosures, respectively. Also, let e denote the probability of entry. Let $R_2 \in R \equiv \{R_M^G, R_D^G, R_M^B, R_D^B, V_H, V_J, R_D\}$ denote the vulnerable division's second-period payoffs, where $R_D \equiv Pr(\theta_G)R_D^G + Pr(\theta_B)R_D^B$.

Define the incumbent firm's disclosure strategy as a correspondence, $d: \mathscr{C} \times \mathscr{C}^m \times [0, \bar{K}] \to [0, 1] \times \Delta$; the rival's entry strategy as a function, $e: \mathscr{C}_T \times \mathscr{C}_T^m \times \{b\} \times \Delta \to [0, 1]$; and the financial market's price for the incumbent, determined in a perfectly competitive fashion, as a mapping, $P: \mathscr{C}_T \times \mathscr{C}_T^m \times \{b\} \times \Delta \to \mathscr{R}$. Finally, let $\mu(.)$ denote the posterior beliefs of external users of the incumbent's disclosures about the vulnerable division's underlying productive state.

A sequential equilibrium in this game consists of an assessment $((d, e, P), \mu)$ (i.e., a vector of strategies and beliefs) such that:

(i) $d(C, C^m, K) \in \text{argmax } E[P \,|\, C]$.

(ii) $e(C_T, C_T^m, b, \hat{d}) \geq 0$,

$$\sum_{d} \int_{C_T^m} \int_{C_T^m} \sum_{a} e(C_T, C_T^m, b, \hat{d})\, dC_T\, dC_T^m = 1,$$

$$e(C_T, C_T^m, b, \hat{d}) \in \text{argmax } E[\pi \,|\, \mu(.)] - K_E.$$

(iii) $P = E[R_2 \,|\, C_T, C_T^m, b, \hat{d}] - E[K \,|\, C_T, C_T^m, b, \hat{d}]$.

(iv)   There exist a sequence of manager's disclosure strategies, $d_n(C, C^m, K)$, a sequence of rival's entry strategies, $e_n(C_T, C_T^m, b, \hat{d})$, and sequences of beliefs, $\mu_n(C_T, C_T^m, b, \hat{d})$:

270   N.J. Nagarajan, S.S. Sridhar / Journal of Accounting and Economics 21 (1996) 253–275

a) $1 > d_n(C, C^m, K) > 0, \qquad \forall(C, C^m, K), \quad \forall n,$
        $1 > e_n(C_T, C_T^m, b, \hat{d}) > 0, \quad \forall(C_T, C_T^m, b, \hat{d}), \forall n;$

b) $\mu^n(C_T, C_T^m, b, \hat{d})$ satisfies Bayes' rule, whenever possible;

c) $\lim_{n \to \infty} d_n(C, C^m, K) = d(C, C^m, K),$

        $\lim_{n \to \infty} e_n(C_T, C_T^m, b, \hat{d}) = e(C_T, C_T^m, b, \hat{d}),$

        $\lim_{n \to \infty} \mu^n(C_T, C_T^m, b, \hat{d}) = \mu(C_T, C_T^m, b, \hat{d}).$

Define $E^*[V(C)]$ as the expected market value for the vulnerable division that realizes a direct cost of C and adopts a candidate equilibrium disclosure strategy. Also, define $E[V(C, C', a^*)]$ as the expected market value for the division that realizes a direct cost of C and deviates from the candidate equilibrium disclosure strategy to C', where a^* refers to the vector of best responses by the product and financial markets when those markets believe that $\Pr(C \in X) = 0$, for some $X \subset \mathscr{C}$.

A *perfect sequential equilibrium* is an assessment $((d, e, P), \mu)$ such that:

(a) conditions (i)–(iv) are met, and

(b) for any message C' that is never sent in equilibrium, there exists no subset $X \subset \mathscr{C}$ such that $E^*[V(C)] < E[V(C, C', a^*)]$, if and only if $C \in \mathscr{C}\backslash X$.

Condition (b) is adapted from Grossman and Perry (1986) to ensure that the updating rule is 'credible'. Condition (b) implies that there exists no incumbent firm type that would like to deviate in equilibrium, where if deviation is taken as a signal that $C \in \mathscr{C}\backslash X$, then every $C \in \mathscr{C}\backslash X$ wants to deviate and no $C \in X$ does.

Appendix 2

Proof of Lemma 1

This lemma is proved in two steps. In the first step, the optimality of the players' strategies and the derivation of their beliefs are established. The second step demonstrates how the proposed equilibrium satisfies the perfectness requirements of Grossman and Perry.

Step 1

Consider the following equilibrium allocation strategies for the incumbent. Suppose the incumbent realizes $C = C_L$, and $K \in [\delta C/b, \bar{K} - \delta C/b]$. By choosing $b = \max_{b_i}\{b_i\}$ as the fraction of common operating costs allocated to the vulnerable division, the incumbent maximizes the $\Pr(C_T \in J)$. That is, the choice

N.J. Nagarajan, S.S. Sridhar / Journal of Accounting and Economics 21 (1996) 253-275   271

of b maximizes the probability that the rival is unable to deduce from the reported C_T that the incumbent has realized C_L.

Next, suppose the incumbent realizes $C = C_H$, and $K \in [\delta C/b, \bar{K} - \delta C/b]$. The incumbent will still choose $b = \max_{b_i}\{b_i\}$ as the fraction of common operating costs allocated to the vulnerable division, because the choice of b again maximizes the probability that the financial market is unable to deduce from the reported C_T that the incumbent has realized C_H.

Lemma A.1. $(C_T, C_T \in J, ND)$ *is a sufficient statistic for* $(C_T^m, C_T, C_T \in J, ND)$ *with respect to the vulnerable division's direct cost, where ND refers to no disclosure.*

With the uniform distribution assumption for C^m and K, and the assumption that C^m and C are independently distributed, the proof for this observation follows from regular Bayesian analysis, and is omitted here.[20] Using the result from Lemma A.1, the term C_T^m is omitted from the argument for the external users' posterior beliefs about the vulnerable division's direct costs, and therefore, for the expected payoffs for the rival and the division's value.

Lemma A.2. *For any arbitrary* $C_T \in J$ *and* $C_T' \in J$ *such that* $C_T \neq C_T'$, *if the incumbent makes no disclosure (ND) of the vulnerable division's direct or indirect costs, the posterior beliefs about the division's state are the same as the priors, i.e.,* $\Pr(\theta_x | C_T, C_T \in J, ND) = \Pr(\theta_x | C_T', C_T' \in J, ND) = \Pr(\theta_x)$ *for* $x \in \{G, B\}$.

This lemma can also be proved through simple Bayesian analysis, and a detailed proof is omitted here.

Given that $C_T \in J$, if the incumbent makes no disclosure of the vulnerable division's direct costs, the rival's expected payoffs from entry will be equal to $\Pr(\theta_G)\pi_M^G + \Pr(\theta_B)\pi_M^B$ (from Lemma A.2 above). Then, if condition (C1) holds, i.e., if $\pi \equiv \Pr(\theta_G)\pi_M^G + \Pr(\theta_B)\pi_M^B < K_E$, the incumbent will deter entry by not disclosing the vulnerable division's direct or indirect costs.

After realizing C_L and any given K, for the incumbent not to disclose its C and K it must be the case that firm's market price given no disclosure (ND) of its proprietary information, $P(ND) = V_J - Q\bar{K}/2$, must be greater than the firm's market price given disclosure, $P(D) = R_D^G - QK$. This is true by condition (C2) because $V_J \geq V_H + Q\bar{K}/2 > V_H \geq R_D^G \geq R_D^G - QK$. Therefore, when both conditions (C1) and (C2) hold, after realizing C_L and any K, the incumbent has no incentive to reveal C and K.

Similarly, after realizing C_H, for the firm not to disclose C and K it must be the case that firm's market price given no disclosure of its proprietary information,

---

[20] Detailed proofs of Lemmas A.1 and A.2 are available from the authors.

$P(ND) = V_J - Q\bar{K}/2$ must be greater than the firm's market price given disclosure, $P(D) = V_H - QK$. If $V_J - Q\bar{K}/2 \geq V_H$, then $V_J - Q\bar{K}/2 \geq V_H - QK$ for any K. This condition is also met by (C2).

Next, we show that in equilibrium the incumbent will also not disclose its total common operating costs, K. This occurs because the incumbent's chosen allocation basis can only be drawn from the set {each division's production volume, sales revenues, direct costs, earnings}. Regardless of the incumbent's choice of the allocation basis, the fraction of the common operating costs allocated under each of these bases, b_i, is either known or can be inferred by external users. If the incumbent chooses the total direct costs of the two divisions as the allocation basis, then the proportion of the total costs of each division to the sum of the total costs of both divisions will be the same as the proportion of the total direct costs of each division to the sum of the total direct costs of both divisions.[21] The fractions under the other three allocation bases are public information. Therefore, in equilibrium, the external users can always compute $b = \max\{b_i, QC_T/(QC_T + Q^m C_T^m)\}$ for $i =$ each division's production volume, sales revenues, and earnings. This implies that if the incumbent disclosed the common operating costs, K, the rival and the financial markets would always be able to infer the amount of indirect costs allocated to the vulnerable division, and hence, its direct costs from the reported total cost for the vulnerable division, C_T.[22] Hence, the incumbent will never disclose its realized common operating costs, K, if conditions (C1)–(C3) are met.

Step 2

First, it is shown how the perfectness requirement eliminates all the implausible equilibria. In addition to the proposed nondisclosure equilibrium, there exists another sequential equilibrium that involves full disclosure. Suppose the rival believes that the incumbent would not disclose the vulnerable division's direct cost only if it were C_L. With this belief, the rival would enter whenever it did not observe any disclosures, causing the incumbent with a low direct cost, C_L, to separate out because the division's value with disclosure of the low direct cost, $R_D^G > R_D \equiv \Pr(\theta_G)R_D^G + \Pr(\theta_B)R_D^B$. Thus, if the rival adopts a skeptical

---

[21] To see this, define $b_i \equiv QC/(QC + Q^m C^m)$. Then, $QC = b_i(QC + Q^m C^m)$. If the incumbent chooses the total direct costs as the allocation basis, the amount of indirect costs allocated to the vulnerable division will be $b_i QK$. This implies that $QC_T = b_i(QC + Q^m C^m) + b_i QK = b_i(QC + Q^m C^m + QK)$. Therefore, it is also true that $b_i = QC_T/(QC + Q^m C^m + QK)$.

[22] For some $b_i < b$, if the realized $K \in [\delta C/b_i, \bar{K} - \delta C/b_i]$ the incumbent could achieve jamming by choosing the allocation basis associated with such b_i. Still, the incumbent would not reveal its K because such a disclosure would, other than in certain pathological knife-edge cases, enable the external users to infer the amount of common operating costs allocated to the vulnerable division, and thereby, the vulnerable division's direct costs.

N.J. Nagarajan, S.S. Sridhar / Journal of Accounting and Economics 21 (1996) 253–275 273

posture, then regardless of the financial market's beliefs there exists a sequential equilibrium which involves full disclosure.[23]

Next, it is shown that with such sets of beliefs, the full disclosure sequential equilibrium fails to satisfy the perfectness requirements of Grossman and Perry. Consider the above full disclosure equilibrium. Fix message $C' = ND$, that is, the message that is never sent in equilibrium is a null signal (no disclosure). Let the set $X = \Phi$, i.e., a null set. Then, if the incumbent realizes C_L, $E^*[V(C_L)] = R_D^G < E[V(C_L, C' = ND, a^*)] = V_J$, because given the product market's belief that $\mathscr{C} \backslash X = \{C_H, C_L\}$ and condition (C1), the rival's best response is not to enter; similarly, given the financial market's revised belief that $\mathscr{C} \backslash X = \{C_H, C_L\}$, the competition in the financial market will ensure a price of V_J for the vulnerable division. Next, if the incumbent realizes C_H, $E^*[V(C_H)] = V_H < E[V(C_H, C' = ND, a^*)] = V_J$, for similar reasons as discussed in the earlier case. Thus, any full disclosure equilibrium fails the perfectness criterion of Grossman and Perry.

Finally, it remains to be shown that the proposed equilibrium satisfies the perfectness requirements of Grossman and Perry. This is done through checking that there exists no set $X \subset \mathscr{C}$ such that all incumbent types in X do not wish to deviate with all manager types in $\mathscr{C} \backslash X$ wishing to deviate, when the product and financial markets believe that any deviation comes only from types in $\mathscr{C} \backslash X$. First, let $X = \Phi$. Then, if the incumbent realizes C_L and discloses it, $E^*[V(C_L, ND)] = V_J > R_D^G = E[V(C_L, C' = C_L, a^*)]$ by virtue of condition (C2), implying that $C_L \in \mathscr{C} \backslash X$ does not wish to deviate. Hence, X cannot be a null set. Similarly, if $X = \{C_H\}$, then $E^*[V(C_L, ND)] = V_J > R_D^G = E[V(C_L, C' = C_L, a^*)]$, again implying that $C_L \in \mathscr{C} \backslash X$ does not wish to deviate. Hence, X cannot be $\{C_H\}$. Finally, if $X = \{C_L\}$, then $E^*[V(C_H, ND)] = V_J > V_H = E[V(C_H, C' = C_H, a^*)]$, implying that $C_H \in \mathscr{C} \backslash X$ does not wish to deviate. Hence, X cannot be $\{C_L\}$. Therefore, the proposed equilibrium is perfect in the sense of Grossman and Perry. ∎

Proof of Lemma 2 (sketch)

Consider a setting in which the incumbent is not subject to mandatory segment disclosure requirements. The markets observe $Q^m C_T^m + Q C_T$. Therefore, when the incumbent discloses K, the markets know that the sum of the two

---

[23] Note if the financial market believed that the incumbent would not disclose its direct cost only after realizing a high direct cost, C_H, it would not result in a full disclosure equilibrium. This is because such beliefs would cause the incumbent with a low direct cost, C_L to separate out only if $V_H = \Pr(\theta_G | C_H) R_M^G + \Pr(\theta_B | C_H) R_M^B < R_D^G$. However, this contradicts our assumption that $V_H \geq R_D^G$. Further, even if V_H were less than R_D^G a full disclosure equilibrium, supported by such implausible beliefs of the financial markets, would fail to satisfy the perfectness requirements of Grossman and Perry.

274   *N.J. Nagarajan, S.S. Sridhar / Journal of Accounting and Economics 21 (1996) 253–275*

divisions' direct costs is equal to $Q^m C_T^m + Q(C_T - K) = Q^m C^m + QC$. Let $z = Q^m C^m + QC$. First, we show that conditions (C1) and (C2) are sufficient for the incumbent not to disclose the vulnerable division's direct cost. This is achieved through demonstrating that the external users' posteriors about the vulnerable division's state after the incumbent discloses K, but not C, remain the same as its priors.

Lemma A.3. For any arbitrary $z \neq z'$, if the incumbent discloses K but makes no disclosure (ND) of either division's direct costs, the posterior beliefs about the vulnerable division's state are the same as the priors, i.e., $\Pr(\theta_x | z, K, ND) = \Pr(\theta_x | z', K, ND) = \Pr(\theta_x)$ for $x \in \{G, B\}$.

This lemma can be proved through simple Bayesian analysis and a detailed proof is omitted here. Using this result and following the lines of the proof of Lemma 1, it can be shown that conditions (C1) and (C2) are sufficient for the incumbent not to disclose the vulnerable division's direct costs, C.

Next, we establish the sufficient condition for the incumbent to disclose K. If the vulnerable division realizes $C = C_L$ and discloses K, the external users cannot infer the vulnerable division's direct cost from $Q^m C^m + QC$ only if $Q^m [C^m - C^m] \geq Q[C_H - C_L]$. Conversely, if the vulnerable division realizes $C = C_H$ and discloses K, the external users cannot infer the vulnerable division's direct cost only if $Q^m [\bar{C}^m - C^m] \geq Q[C_H - C_L]$. Hence, if $C^m \in [C^m + Q\delta C/Q^m, \bar{C}^m - Q\delta C/Q^m]$, the incumbent can disclose K and still not reveal the vulnerable division's direct cost. Therefore, given the skeptical beliefs of the financial market about K, the firm will always disclose K if $C^m \in [\underline{C}^m + Q\delta C/Q^m, \bar{C}^m - Q\delta C/Q^m]$, thus yielding the sufficient condition (C4). Finally, how this equilibrium satisfies the conditions of a perfect sequential equilibrium can be established following the lines of the proof for Lemma 1. ∎

Proof of Proposition 1

Follows directly from a comparison of Lemmas 1 and 2. ∎

Proof of Corollary 1

Signing the derivative of conditions (C4), (C1), and (C2), respectively with respect to the variables of interest yields the desired results. ∎

Proof of Proposition 2

It can be shown that condition (C1) is both necessary and sufficient in both Lemmas 1 and 2. Therefore, if (C1) is not met in Lemma 2, the incumbent will disclose the vulnerable division's direct costs, C, and also its common operating

N.J. Nagarajan, S.S. Sridhar / Journal of Accounting and Economics 21 (1996) 253–275 275

costs. K. Thus, in the absence of condition (C1), full disclosure is obtained even without requiring the firm to report segment information. Because the same condition (C1) is necessary to sustain the nondisclosure of the incumbent's proprietary information, C, even when it is required to report segment information. we get the redundancy of disclosure requirement result. ∎

References

Balachandran. B., L. Li. and R. Magee. 1987, On the allocation of fixed and variable costs from service departments, Contemporary Accounting Research. 164–185.

Darrough, M. and N. Stoughton, 1990. Financial disclosure policy in an entry game, Journal of Accounting and Economics, 219–243.

Cho. I. and D. Kreps, 1987, Signaling games and stable equilibria, Quarterly Journal of Economics, 179–221.

Dye. R., 1985, Strategic accounting choice and the effects of alternative financial reporting requirements, Journal of Accounting Research, 544–574.

Dye. R., 1990. Mandatory versus voluntary disclosures: The cases of financial and real externalities, The Accounting Review, 1–24.

Givoly, D., C. Hayn, and J. D'Souza, 1991, The segment disclosure requirement: An analysis of the quality of the reported data, Working paper (Northwestern University. Evanston, IL).

Grossman, S., 1981, The informational role of warranties and private disclosure about product quality, Journal of Law and Economics, 461–483.

Grossman and M. Perry, 1986, Perfect sequential equilibrium, Journal of Economic Theory, 97–119.

Kreps. D.M. and R. Wilson, 1982, Sequential equilibria, Econometrica, 863–894.

Magee. R.P., 1988, Variable cost allocation in a principal/agent setting, The Accounting Review, 42–54.

Milgrom, P.R., 1981, Good news and bad news: Representation theorems and applications, Bell Journal of Economics, 380–391.

Nikolai, L.A. and J.D. Bazley, 1991, Intermediate accounting (PWS–Kent Publishing Company, Boston, MA).

Verrecchia, R., 1983, Discretionary disclosure, Journal of Accounting and Economics, 179–194.

Wagenhofer, A., 1990, Voluntary disclosure with a strategic opponent, Journal of Accounting and Economics, 341–363.

Watts. R. and J. Zimmerman, 1986, Positive accounting theory (Prentice-Hall, Englewood Cliffs, NJ).

[5]

Journal of International Financial Management and Accounting 11:3 2000

The Value-relevance of Geographic Segment Earnings Disclosures Under SFAS 14

Wayne B. Thomas *

University of Oklahoma

Abstract

This study examines whether geographic segment earnings as reported under the requirements of SFAS 14 provide value-relevant information. The FASB recently issued SFAS
131, which drastically changes the segment reporting requirements for US firms. Firms
are required to disclose segment information by operating segment. For those firms that
define operating segments along industry lines, disclosure of geographic segment earnings
is no longer required. If geographic segment earnings provide value-relevant information,
a potentially valuable source of information may be lost.

In this study, geographic segment earnings coefficients are estimated by (1) regressing
unexpected security returns on unexpected geographic segment earnings and (2) regressing
leading-period returns on current geographic segment earnings. Leading period returns
involve extending the return interval to include the returns for prior years. The results show
that unexpected geographic segment earnings relate differentially to unexpected security
returns. For the leading-period returns model, little significant evidence is found for the
market's differential valuation of geographic segment earnings coefficients for one- and
two-year return intervals. When the return intervals extend to three years or more, significant evidence is found that the market values geographic segment earnings differently,
which suggests that such disclosures reflect information used by market participants in
setting security prices. The FASB may want to reconsider or amend its segment reporting
requirements.

I. Introduction

This study examines the value-relevance of geographic segment earnings
disclosures. Until recently, disclosure of segment information, including
geographic earnings, was required under Statement of Financial Accounting Standards No. 14 (SFAS 14). Some complained that geographic
segment earnings disclosures were not useful because of (1) the lack of
comparability and consistency in segment definition both across firms and
over time for the same firm, (2) insufficient disaggregation, (3) failure to

* I am grateful for comments received from my dissertation committee, Gary Meek (chair), Wade
Brorsen, Carol Johnson, and Dennis Patz. This paper is part of my dissertation which was awarded
the Outstanding Doctoral Dissertation Award in International Accounting in 1996 by the International
Accounting Section of the American Accounting Association. Helpful comments were also received
from Jeff Abarbanell, James Boatsman, Barry Cushing, Don Herrmann, Tatsuo Inoue, Glade Tew, Joseph
Weintrop, and an anonymous reviewer, as well as workshop participants at Oklahoma State University
and the University of Utah.

134   *Wayne B. Thomas*

group foreign operations according to similar risk and return characteristics, and (4) management manipulation through transfer pricing policies
and common cost allocations. This criticism came from both the financial
community (AIMR, 1992; AICPA, 1994) and the academic community
(Bavishi and Wyman, 1980; Arnold et al., 1980; Roberts, 1989; Balakrishnan
et al., 1990; Boatsman et al., 1993). As a result, many questioned whether
geographic segment earnings disclosures provided any value-relevant
information beyond that provided by consolidated earnings.[1]

In response to these criticisms and others, the Financial Accounting
Standards Board (FASB) recently issued SFAS 131, *Disclosures about
Segments of an Enterprise and Related Information* (FASB, 1997). This
statement became effective for periods beginning after December 15, 1997.
Unlike SFAS 14, SFAS 131 does not require firms to disclose earnings by
both line of business and geographic area. Instead, firms are required to
report earnings by operating segment only.[2] Possible ways of identifying
and separating an enterprise into operating segments include products
or services, geographic areas, legal entities, or types of customers (FASB,
1997, para. 4). Companies which define their operating segments along
industry lines or on any basis other than geography will be required to
report only limited supplemental geographic disclosures of revenues and
assets (and *not* earnings) for each country in which operations are deemed
material, and companies will do this only if it is not impractible (FASB,
1997, para. 38). Herrmann and Thomas (2000) sample US companies that
have adopted SFAS 131 and find that of the 74 companies that provide
enterprise-wide geographic disclosures, only 12 (16%) report geographic
earnings. Herrmann and Thomas (2000) further show that 74 (96%) of
77 firms that reported geographic information under SFAS 14 report geographic segment earnings. Thus, SFAS 131 appears to have reduced significantly the reporting of geographic segment earnings.

Boatsman et al. (1993) provide the only previous study to investigate
the market's valuation of geographic segment earnings and find that for a
16-day return window surrounding the filing of the Form 10-K,[3] unexpected geographic segment earnings are, in general, not differentially related
to unexpected security returns.[4] Only for extreme changes in geographic
segment earnings does the market appear to use geographic segment
earnings to value the firm. Boatsman et al. (1993) also investigate the
association between changes in geographic segment earnings and raw
returns for a fifteen-month window extending from the beginning of
the fiscal period. This test further indicated that there were no significant
differences in the market's valuation of geographic segment earnings (see

their table 4, p. 62). They conclude that "for the most part, however, we find little evidence that these disclosures affect equity values" (p. 46). Their results suggest that the loss of geographic segment earnings disclosures under SFAS 131 will have little impact on financial statement users' decisions (i.e., geographic segment earnings provide little, if any, value-relevant information beyond that provided by consolidated earnings).

This study examines whether disclosures of geographic segment earnings under SFAS 14 provide value-relevant information. Two approaches are used to address this question. First, this study re-examines the association between unexpected returns and unexpected geographic segment earnings using different measures of unexpected earnings and unexpected returns than those used by Boatsman et al. (1993). These measures and other improvements are discussed in more detail below. Second, this study addresses the market's valuation of geographic segment earnings using a leading-period returns model. Kothari and Sloan (1992) suggest that the earnings coefficients in returns/earnings studies are biased downward because of the mistiming between value-relevant events being incorporated into security prices and being reflected in reported earnings. They show that one way to mitigate this bias is to include leading-period returns in a regression of returns on current earnings. The leading-period returns model involves extending the return interval beyond one year which enhances the observed statistical relationship between returns and total earnings. The benefits of this method are also discussed in more detail below. Evidence of the value-relevance of (unexpected) geographic segment earnings is found if earnings coefficients differ across geographic segments.[5] If the coefficients do not differ, then total earnings is sufficient (relative to geographic segment earnings) for explaining security returns. If evidence is found which suggests that such disclosures provided value-relevant information, then this would indicate that a valuable source of information may no longer be available to market participants because of the changes required by SFAS 131.

The results of the unexpected returns/earnings model in this study show a significant difference in the valuation of unexpected earnings across geographic segments. These findings contrast with those of Boatsman et al. (1993) who found little evidence of the market's differential valuation of unexpected geographic segment earnings. For the leading-period returns model, little evidence is found for the market's differential valuation of geographic segment earnings for the one- and two-year return intervals. However, when the return intervals extend to three years or more, significant evidence is found that the market values geographic segment

136   *Wayne B. Thomas*

earnings differently, which suggests that such disclosures reflect information incorporated into security prices. Furthermore and as expected, the valuation of geographic segment earnings appears to be approximately in line with the growth and risk characteristics of those earnings.

Under the reporting guidelines of SFAS 131, most companies define their operating segments along industry lines (Herrmann and Thomas 2000) and are therefore not required to disclose earnings by geographic segment. The results of this study suggest that geographic segment earnings disclosures under SFAS 14 provide value-relevant information. Therefore, with respect to geographic segment earnings disclosures, SFAS 131 has resulted in a loss of value-relevant information for financial statement users.[6] The FASB may want to reconsider its guidelines for disclosures of geographic segment earnings.

II. Sample Selection

To estimate the geographic segment earnings coefficients, it is first necessary to identify the geographic segments that will be used as the regressors. Only geographic segments that are distinctly defined for a large number of companies can be used as regressors. Using only distinctly defined geographic segments helps to assign the estimated earnings coefficients to particular geographic areas. For example, if a company disclosed foreign operations in a Canada/Europe/Asia segment, then it would be difficult to determine to what extent the information in Canadian versus European versus Asian earnings reflects the information in the company's security price. If, however, the company disclosed the earnings of the three geographic segments separately, then it is possible to determine whether the information in the geographic segment disclosures reflects the differential impact that these earnings have on the value of the firm. Also, the more firms that disclose a particular geographic area, the more precise will be the estimated earnings coefficient for that geographic segment.

The *Compustat Business Information File* identifies firms' geographic segment disclosures with up to four two-digit area codes. Continents are identified by the tens digit and countries within the continent are identified by the ones digit (see Table 1). As an example, suppose a company discloses four geographic segments: Domestic, Canada, South America/Mexico, and Europe/Asia. The Domestic segment is coded as 70, the Canada segment is coded as 62, the South America/Mexico segment is coded as 50/63, and the Asia/Europe segment is coded as 20/30. The *Compustat Business Information File* also provides an additional segment, which is

Geographic Segment Earnings Disclosures   137

Table 1. *Composition of the Geographic Segment Regressors for the Final Sample of 1,912 Firm/year Observations for the Period 1984–95*

Regressor	Reported Geographic Segment	Code(s)[a]	Number
Canada	Canada	62	728
United Kingdom	Europe/United Kingdom	30/31	
	United Kingdom	31	197
			169
			366
Europe	Europe	30	
	France	32	701
	Germany	33	27
	Europe/France	30/32	39
	Europe/Germany	30/33	13
	France/Germany	32/33	26
	Europe/France/Germany	30/32/33	13
			21
			840
Asia/Pacific	Asia	20	
	Japan	21	114
	Middle East	23	21
	Asia/Japan/Philippines	20/21/22	7
	Pacific	40	12
	Australia	41	34
	Pacific/Australia	40/41	51
	Asia/Pacific	20/40	6
	Asia/Australia	20/41	85
	Japan/Australia	21/41	31
	Middle East/Australia	23/41	3
	Asia/Japan/Pacific	20/21/40	2
	Asia/Japan/Australia	20/21/41	7
	Asia/Japan/Pacific/Australia	20/21/40/41	30
			27
			430
South America/Mexico	South America	50	
	Brazil	51	54
	Mexico	63	33
	South America/Brazil	50/51	33
	Brazil/Mexico	50/63	3
	South America/Mexico	51/63	64
	S. America/Brazil/Mexico	50/51/63	1
			58
			246

[a]Geographic area codes as listed on the *Compustat Business Information File*. Compustat refers to the United Kingdom segment as Great Britain.

138   *Wayne. B. Thomas*

the total of all foreign operations. Continuing the example, the total earnings, sales, and assets of the Canada, South America/Mexico, and Asia/Europe segments would be combined into the Total Foreign segment and coded as 98.

To be included in the study, firms must meet the following criteria: (1) have geographic segment earnings available on the *Compustat Business Information File*, (2) have security price information available from the *Center for Research in Security Prices*, (3) be listed on the NYSE or AMEX, (4) be incorporated in the USA, and (5) have December year-ends. These criteria led to an initial sample of 3,068 firm/year observations for the 1984–95 test period. Only five general regions were deemed to be disclosed commonly enough to be included as regressors: Canada, United Kingdom,[7] Europe, Asia/Pacific, and South America/Mexico. Therefore, to be included in the study, a firm/year observation must also report earnings from one of the five foreign geographic segments. This criterion resulted in a final sample of 1,912 firm/year observations. Table 1 details the composition of the geographic segment regressors and the number of firm-year observations reporting earnings for each geographic segment. The total number of individual segments (2,610) exceeds the sample size because some firms disclose two or more of the five geographic segments.

The Canada segment and United Kingdom segment are country-specific segments. The Europe segment includes any geographic segment that is specific to Europe, excluding the United Kingdom. For example, a segment that is defined as Europe/Africa would not be included as a Europe segment. The Asia/Pacific segment includes any geographic segment that is specific to Asia or to the Pacific or that is a combination of Asia and the Pacific. Similarly, the South America/Mexico segment includes any geographic segment that is specific to South America or to Mexico or that is a combination of South America and Mexico. In addition to the five segments shown in Table 1, a Domestic segment and an Other Foreign segment are also included as regressors. The Other Foreign segment serves to capture the remainder of earnings of each firm not included in the Domestic segment or one of the five foreign geographic segments.

For each model, outliers are controlled for by eliminating observations that have absolute R-studentized residuals greater than two.[8] Elimination of influential observations resulted in approximately 3–4 per cent of the usable observations for each model being omitted. To help reduce the effects of cross-sectional correlation, yearly dummy variables are included in the models (Collins and Kothari, 1989).

III. Results

Unexpected Returns/Unexpected Earnings Model

The only previous study to investigate the market's valuation of geographic segment earnings is Boatsman et al. (1993) (hereafter BBP). In their study, unexpected security returns are regressed on unexpected geographic segment earnings for the period 1985–89. Unexpected returns are measured over a 16-day period surrounding the filing of the Form 10-K. Unexpected geographic segment earnings are measured as the annual change in earnings for that geographic segment, adjusted for exchange rate movements for the year unless it is not possible to identify the specific source of geographic segment earnings (e.g., the South America and Asia segments). BBP find that the use of geographic segment earnings by market participants is highly contextual and that, in general, the market does not appear to value geographic segment earnings differently.[9] This evidence suggests that either the market does not value geographic segment earnings differently (because risk and growth characteristics do not vary across geographical area) or firms do not disclose geographic segment earnings in such a way as to provide value-relevant information to the market, where the former is unlikely.

There are several methodological issues which may have caused the lack of significant results in BBP. First, BBP use a 16-day return window surrounding the filing of the Form 10-K to measure the association between unexpected returns and unexpected geographic segment earnings. The assumption is that this is the first time the information is made available to the market and could therefore be incorporated into security prices. However, some firms may have voluntarily released this information in quarterly reports or press releases so that the change in annual geographic earnings is largely known before the Form 10-K is filed. In addition, consolidated earnings have already been released before the 16-day window and the market may be able to reasonably infer the changes in current geographic segment earnings based on the change in total current earnings. In this case, geographic information may be impounded well before the filing of the Form 10-K. In contrast, this study uses a one-year return interval to avoid the problem of determining when unexpected geographic segment earnings were first impounded into security prices. However, if a significant association between returns and geographic segment earnings is found, a one-year return interval (in contrast to a 16-day window) makes it more difficult to conclude that this information is *used* by the market in setting security prices. Instead, it must be conceded that geographic

140   *Wayne B. Thomas*

segment earnings either are used in setting security prices or are consistent with underlying events and the information set reflected in security prices. This represents a common tradeoff between event studies and association studies.

Second, BBP use the previous year's geographic segment earnings times the change in the exchange rate for the year as expected geographic segment earnings. BBP determine precisely the exchange rate effects only for the United Kingdom and Canada segments. For the other segments, they must either estimate the exchange rate effects on earnings (e.g., Europe segment) or make no adjustment at all (e.g., South America and Asia segments). Therefore, unexpected geographic segment earnings will almost certainly be measured with error for these segments because of the difficulty in measuring the market's expectation with respect to exchange rates. As Lev (1989) notes, measuring unexpected earnings with error can lead to coefficients which are biased toward zero. In this study, there is no need to incorporate changes in exchange rates into the earnings expectation model since a one-year return interval is employed. Annual exchange rates approximately follow a random walk so the expected change in exchange rates for the following year is zero (Frankel and Rose, 1995) and the expectation for geographic segment earnings at time t is simply geographic segment earnings at time t − 1.[10]

Third, this study uses size-adjusted returns to measure unexpected geographic segment earnings instead of cumulative market model adjusted returns as in BBP. Fama and French (1992) show that beta is a poor predictor of returns and size is a much better predictor. Using size-adjusted returns instead of beta-adjusted returns should result in a superior measure of unexpected returns. Similar to Fama and French (1992), size portfolio returns are calculated by dividing all firms on the NYSE and AMEX into deciles based on their market value of equity at the beginning of year t. The portfolio return is then calculated as the average return for all firms in the portfolio from April of year t to March of year t + 1. Unexpected returns are then measured as a security's current raw return from April of year t to March of year t + 1 minus the return for the corresponding size-based portfolio. This study also has the advantage of using a longer time period, 1985–95.[11] The test period in BBP was 1985–89. Taken collectively, the improvements in this study should provide a stronger test of the market's valuation of unexpected geographic segment earnings.

The results are reported in Table 2. The first column of results reports the estimated coefficients and adjusted R^2 for a regression of unexpected returns on unexpected total earnings. The coefficient on unexpected total

Table 2. Estimated Coefficients (p-values) from Pooled Cross-sectional Regressions of Twelve-month Size-adjusted Returns on Changes in Geographic Segment Earnings Scaled by Beginning Price[a]

Regressor	Model 1[b]	Model 2[c]	Model 3[d]	Model 4[d]	Model 5[d]	Model 6[d]	Model 7[d]	Model 8[d]	Model 9[d]
Domestic		.056 (.017)	-.602 (.001)						
Canada		.689 (.006)		.114 (.719)					
United Kingdom		.762 (.009)			.819 (.008)				
Europe		.864 (.001)				.675 (.146)			
Asia/Pacific		.536 (.206)					.446 (.268)		
S. Amer/Mexico		-.328 (.682)						-1.745 (.046)	
Other Foreign		.329 (.101)							.432 (.062)
Total	.161 (.001)			.264 (.001)	.040 (.287)	.134 (.028)	.415 (.001)	.532 (.001)	.048 (.292)
Constant	-.057 (.004)	-.061 (.002)	-.061 (.002)	-.133 (.001)	-.115 (.008)	-.046 (.135)	-.046 (.250)	-.041 (.401)	-.015 (.552)
Adj. R^2	.044	.061	.061	.066	.056	.077	.069	.073	.035
N	1398	1398	1398	554	249	606	310	167	889
F-test[e] (p-value)		5.633 (.001)							
F-test[f] (p-value)		6.643 (.001)							

[a] All regressions models include annual dummy variables. Estimated coefficients and p-values are not reported for dummy variables and are available from the author upon request.

[b] Model 1 estimates the relation between unexpected returns and unexpected total earnings.

[c] Model 2 provides an overall test of incremental value-relevance by estimating the relation between unexpected returns and unexpected geographic segment earnings.

[d] Models 3–9 provide individual tests of incremental value-relevance by estimating the relation between unexpected returns and unexpected earnings for individual geographic segments while controlling for unexpected total earnings.

[e] The F-test is a test of the null hypothesis that the earnings coefficients are equal for the Domestic, Canada, United Kingdom, Europe, Asia/Pacific, South America/Mexico, and Other Foreign segments.

[f] The F-test is a test of the null hypothesis that the earnings coefficients are equal for the Domestic, Canada, United Kingdom, Europe, Asia/Pacific, and Other Foreign segments (South America/Mexico is excluded).

142   *Wayne B. Thomas*

earnings is highly significant (p-value = .001) and the adjusted R^2 is .044. These results are consistent with those reported in prior research (Lev, 1989). The second column of results reports the estimated coefficients of a regression of unexpected returns on all unexpected geographic segment earnings. As expected, the coefficients are positive with the exception of South America/Mexico, which is negative but insignificant from zero.[12] The adjusted R^2 is .061 and the F-test for equality of the seven geographic coefficients is easily significant (p-value = .001).[13] Since it may appear that the South America/Mexico coefficient may be largely responsible for the significance in differences, an F-test for equality of the other six geographic coefficients is presented. It is also easily significant (p-value = .001).

The remaining columns report results from regressions of unexpected returns on unexpected total earnings and individual unexpected geographic segment earnings. These tests determine whether the particular unexpected geographic segment earnings provides any incremental information content in explaining security returns once unexpected total earnings is controlled for. Significance of the coefficient for the individual geographic segment earnings provides evidence in favor of incremental information. A positive (negative) coefficient indicates that the earnings from the particular geographic segment are generally valued more (less) than the earnings from the remainder of the segments. The results suggest that unexpected earnings from the Domestic, United Kingdom, Europe, South America/Mexico, and Other Foreign segments provide incremental information in explaining security returns. The coefficients for unexpected Canada and Asia/Pacific earnings are not significant. Furthermore, earnings from the Domestic and South America/Mexico segments are generally valued less than the earnings from other areas, whereas earnings from the United Kingdom, Europe, and Other Foreign segments are generally valued more. These results provide significant evidence for the value-relevance of geographic segment earnings in explaining security returns. The market either uses geographic segment earnings in valuing the firm or geographic segment earnings disclosures correlate with the underlying information set used in valuing the firm. The next section investigates the association between security returns and geographic segment earnings without adjusting for market expectations.

Leading-period Returns

Kothari and Sloan (1992) show that a regression of current returns on current earnings biases estimated earnings coefficients toward zero and that including leading-period returns in the estimation of earnings coefficients mitigates this bias. Using leading-period returns, Kothari and Sloan (1992) estimate the average earnings coefficient to be 5.45, which is much closer to the theoretically-predicted value than that found by the traditional regression of current returns on current earnings. Properties of generally accepted accounting principles such as conservatism, objectivity, and verifiability limit the ability of earnings reported in period t to reflect the market's revision in expectation of future net cash flows in period t.[14] That is, value-relevant events may be captured in the current period's security return but not in the current period's earnings, or value-relevant events which occurred prior to the return interval are recognized in the current period's earnings. As the return interval extends backward, information reflected in security prices also reflects in earnings.

The leading-period returns model regresses the firm's buy and hold security return for period $t-\tau$ to t (where $\tau = 1, 2, 3, 4,$ or 5 years) on geographic segment earnings for period t. All geographic segment earnings are defined as current earnings per share of the respective geographic segment, deflated by price at the beginning of the return period. The model is estimated for return intervals varying from one to five years. Even though the leading-period returns model uses only current geographic segment earnings, a regressor will have a nonzero value only when the respective geographic segment is consistently defined over the entire return interval. This assures that geographic segment earnings, if value-relevant, are reflected in the leading-period security prices. The leading-period returns models are estimated over the 1984–95 period. The one-year return interval begins in April of year t and extends through March of year t + 1. The two-year return interval begins in April of year t − 1 and extends through March of t + 1, and so on.

For return intervals greater than one year (i.e., $\tau > 1$), observations will have overlapping return intervals causing autocorrelated error terms. Therefore, the multi-year models are estimated by modeling the residuals from the ordinary least squares regressions as a first-order autoregressive process and then the ordinary least squares parameters are re-estimated using a rho transformation of the variables. Rho is the estimated coefficient of regressing ordinary least squares residuals of the original model on the lag residuals. This method is similar to Cochrane and Orcutt (1949). The standard F-test is used to test whether the estimated earnings coefficients are equal across geographic segments. If the estimated earnings coefficients are significantly different across geographic segments, then this difference would suggest that geographic segment earnings are reflected in security prices and that such disclosures provide value-relevant information.

144   *Wayne B. Thomas*

First, the relation between current returns and current geographic segment earnings is estimated. This provides a benchmark for the longer return interval models. Results of the one-year model are shown in Table 3. The first column of results shows the relation between current returns and total current earnings. The estimated coefficient on total earnings is positive and highly significant (p-value = .001) and the adjusted R^2 is .168. These results are comparable to those in prior studies.[15]

The second column shows the results of a regression of current returns on all current geographic segment earnings. All coefficients are positive except for South America/Mexico, which is negative but insignificant from zero. An F-test for the equality of the coefficients is significant at approximately the .05 level. The F-test for the equality of the geographic segment earnings coefficients excluding South America/Mexico is not significant at usual levels. Therefore, most of the significance in the over-all F-test is due to one geographic segment, South America/Mexico. These results provide little evidence for the differential valuation of geographic segment earnings. The remaining columns show results from regressions of current returns on current total earnings and individual current geographic segment earnings. The only geographic segments shown to provide incremental information in explaining returns are the Domestic, United Kingdom, and South America/Mexico segments. Next, I investigate the relation between returns and geographic segment earnings when leading-period returns are included in the model.

Table 4 reports the results of the leading-period returns model for total earnings (panel A) and geographic segment earnings (panel B) for the two- to five-year return intervals. The earnings of all geographic segments are combined and the leading-period returns model is estimated to compare the results of the data in this study with the results found by Kothari and Sloan (1992). From the pooled cross-sectional regressions, Kothari and Sloan (1992) estimated the earnings coefficient to be 1.25 for the one-year return interval and 4.89 for the four-year return interval. As shown in panel A of Table 4, the estimated earnings coefficients are 1.283 for the one-year return interval and 3.430 for the five-year return interval. The estimated earnings coefficients monotonically increase as the return interval increases. The coefficients, however, are lower than those reported by Kothari and Sloan (1992) for longer return intervals. One explanation for the lower coefficients may be that Kothari and Sloan (1992) used firms' total earnings whereas the results reported in Table 4 are based on total geographic segment earnings, which are generally firms' total *operating* earnings. Since expenses such as taxes and interest are excluded from

Table 3. Estimated Coefficients (p-values) from Pooled Cross-sectional Regressions of Current Twelve-month Raw Returns on Current Geographic Segment Earnings Scaled by Beginning Price[a]

Regressor	Model 1[b]	Model 2[c]	Model 3[d]	Model 4[d]	Model 5[d]	Model 6[d]	Model 7[d]	Model 8[d]	Model 9[d]
Domestic		.332 (.001)	-.191 (.043)						
Canada		.576 (.044)		.020 (.952)					
United Kingdom		.477 (.058)			.784 (.013)				
Europe		.548 (.001)				.177 (.232)			
Asia/Pacific		.596 (.039)					0.30 (.929)		
S. Amer/Mexico		-.531 (.168)						-1.083 (.015)	
Other Foreign		.797 (.001)							.264 (.187)
Total	.373 (.001)		.524 (.001)	.531 (.001)	.171 (.023)	.338 (.001)	.610 (.001)	.250 (.025)	.258 (.001)
Constant	.184 (.001)	.181 (.001)	.180 (.001)	.095 (.005)	.180 (.001)	.206 (.001)	.151 (.001)	.296 (.001)	.230 (.001)
Adj. R²	.168	.171	.179	.201	.125	.190	.211	.195	.188
N	1858	1858	1858	716	356	799	420	240	1161
F-test[e] (p-value)		2.094 (.051)							
F-test[f] (p-value)		1.729 (.125)							

[a]All regressions models include annual dummy variables. Estimated coefficients and p-values are not reported for dummy variables and are available from the author upon request.

[b]Model 1 estimates the relation between returns and total earnings.

[c]Model 2 provides an overall test of incremental value-relevance by estimating the relation between returns and geographic segment earnings.

[d]Models 3-9 provide individual tests of incremental value-relevance by estimating the relation between returns and earnings for individual geographic segments while controlling for total earnings.

[e]The F-test is a test of the null hypothesis that the earnings coefficients are equal for the Domestic, Canada, United Kingdom, Europe, Asia/Pacific, South America/Mexico, and Other Foreign segments.

[f]The F-test is a test of the null hypothesis that the earnings coefficients are equal for the Domestic, Canada, United Kingdom, Europe, Asia/Pacific, and Other Foreign segments (South America/Mexico is excluded).

146   *Wayne B. Thomas*

Table 4. *Estimated Coefficients (p-values) from Pooled Cross-sectional Regressions of Leading-period Stock Returns on Current Geographic Segment Earnings Scaled by Beginning Price*[a]

Return Interval Regressor	2-year	3-year	4-year	5-year
Panel A: Total Earnings				
Total Earnings	1.283	1.963	2.436	3.430
	(.001)	(.001)	(.001)	(.001)
Constant	.178	.108	.127	.058
	(.001)	(.006)	(.005)	(.277)
Adj R^2	.278	.408	.430	.536
N	1442	1064	842	648
Panel B: Geographic Segment Earnings				
Domestic	1.169	1.969	1.992	2.529
	(.001)	(.001)	(.001)	(.001)
Canada	1.283	2.003	3.596	3.694
	(.024)	(.002)	(.001)	(.001)
United Kingdom	.830	1.147	4.496	5.997
	(.070)	(.227)	(.001)	(.001)
Europe	1.688	1.491	3.269	4.590
	(.001)	(.001)	(.001)	(.001)
Asia/Pacific	1.707	2.297	2.491	6.278
	(.007)	(.001)	(.001)	(.001)
South America/Mexico	−.033	.551	−.281	−.879
	(.977)	(.707)	(.864)	(.642)
Other Foreign	1.807	3.427	5.455	7.737
	(.001)	(.001)	(.001)	(.001)
Constant	.179	.099	.111	.046
	(.001)	(.001)	(.012)	(.360)
Adj. R^2	.280	.414	.454	.583
F-test[b]	1.665	2.152	6.410	12.980
(p-value)	(.126)	(.045)	(.001)	(.001)
F-test[c]	1.832	2.582	7.563	15.188
(p-value)	(.104)	(.025)	(.001)	(.001)

[a]All regressions models include annual dummy variables. Estimated coefficients and p-values are not reported for dummy variables and are available from the author upon request.
[b]The F-test is a test of the null hypothesis that the earnings coefficients for the Domestic, Canada, United Kingdom, Europe, Asia/Pacific, South America/Mexico and Other Foreign segments are equal.
[c]The F-test is a test of the null hypothesis that the earnings coefficients for the Domestic, Canada, United Kingdom, Europe, Asia/Pacific, and Other Foreign segments are equal (South America/Mexico is excluded).

operating earnings, total geographic segment earnings will generally exceed total earnings, which would cause lower earnings coefficients. Another reason for the lower coefficients may be the relatively high risk of the sample firms. The average beta for the sample firms is 1.13. Collins and Kothari (1989) show that the estimated earnings coefficient and beta are negatively related.

Panel B of Table 4 reports the estimated geographic segment earnings coefficients of the leading-period returns models for the two- to five-year return intervals.[16] For the two-year model, all estimated coefficients are positive and the F-test for the equality of geographic segment earnings coefficients is not significant (p-value = .126). Excluding the South America/Mexico segment, the differences in the coefficients remain insignificant (p-value = .104). Extending the return interval to three, four, or five years shows much stronger support for value-relevance of geographic segment earnings disclosures. The differences in geographic segment earnings coefficients are significant at the .05 level for the three-year model and significant at the .001 level for the four- and five-year models. Extending the return interval appears to reduce the measurement error in reported earnings and provides a more precise measure of the relationship between returns and geographic segment earnings. If only the one- or two- model is estimated, then we would conclude that geographic segment earnings disclosures weakly reflect the information in security prices. By using longer return intervals, evidence is found that geographic segment earnings do in fact reflect the information used in setting security prices.

Sample Selection Bias

The results of the previous section suggest that disclosures of geographic segment earnings reflect the information used in setting security prices. In general, as the return interval increases, this conclusion strengthens. The increase in significance as the return interval increases, however, may be attributable to a sample selection bias. Only firms which consistently define their geographic segments for at least two years are included in the two-year model, for at least three years in the three-year model, and so on. Thus, the five-year model includes a select group of firms that define their geographic segments consistently for at least five years. The increase in significance as the return interval increases may be the result of using firms which provide more consistent disclosures and/or which have more stable foreign operations and therefore self select into the longer return models rather than of longer return intervals providing a more precise measure of the relationship between returns and geographic segment earnings.

To test the effects of eliminating observations because of inconsistent geographic segment definitions, geographic segment earnings coefficients

148   *Wayne B. Thomas*

are estimated for the one-, two-, three-, and four-year return intervals using the observations that were used to estimate the five-year leading-period returns models. Such a test provides evidence as to whether the increase in significance as the return interval increases is attributable to eliminating firms that do not provide consistent disclosures or to longer return intervals providing a more precise measure of the relationship between returns and geographic segment earnings.

The results of these regressions, not shown in the tables, closely follow the pattern of the full sample. The geographic segment earnings coefficients are not statically different for the one- or two-year return interval (p-value = .932 and p-value = .291, receptively). For the three- and four-year return interval the coefficients are statistically different at the .001 level. The increase in significance as the return interval increases, while the sample composition remains the same, indicates that the increase in significance can be attributed to longer return intervals providing a more precise relation between security returns and geographic segment earnings rather than any sample selection bias.

Magnitude of the Estimated Geographic Segment Earnings Coefficients

One means of determining whether the models are truly capturing the market's differential pricing of geographic segment earnings or are merely statistical artifacts is to determine whether the magnitudes of the geographic segment earnings coefficients make economic sense. Since the coefficient for total earnings has been shown to be positively related to growth (e.g., Collins and Kothari, 1989; Biddle and Seow, 1991) and negatively related to risk (e.g., Easton and Zmijewski, 1989; Collins and Kothari, 1989; and Biddle and Seow, 1991), we should also expect geographic segments which have higher expected growth to have higher earnings coefficients and geographic segments which have higher risk to have lower earnings coefficients. However, traditional measures of risk (e.g., beta and leverage) and expected growth (e.g., market-to-book ratio) are not available on a geographic segment basis. Under SFAS 14, firms are required to report only sales, assets and earnings by geographic segment. Using these measures, proxies are developed for the market's expected growth and risk of each segment.

Expected growth is measured as geographic segment sales growth (i.e., the percentage change in geographic segment sales). Bodnar and Weintrop (1997) use domestic and foreign sales growth as measures of the expected growth in domestic and foreign earnings, respectively. They provide an extensive discussion for the use of this measure as an indicator of expected growth and find that the market's higher valuation of foreign earnings is likely attributable to higher expected growth in foreign earnings. Similarly, this study uses geographic segment sales growth as an indicator of which geographic areas are experiencing (or expected to experience) higher growth, which should directly impact the growth of earnings in these areas.

Geographic segment risk is measured as return on assets (i.e., geographic segment earnings divided by lagged geographic segment assets). Since firms themselves are rational economic agents, we would expect them to be compensated for risk in the same way market participants are. Firms will require a higher return on their assets when investing in riskier projects. For less risky segments, firms are willing to invest even though the return on assets may be lower. We should therefore expect, on average, a riskier segment to produce a higher return on assets. While geographic segment sales growth and return on assets are clearly imprecise measures of the market's expectation of geographic segment growth and risk, they should provide some reasonable indication of whether geographic segment earnings coefficients vary according to the risk and expected growth of the corresponding geographic segments.

Descriptive statistics for the geographic segment sales growth and return on assets are reported in Table 5. Medians, first quartiles, and third quartiles are shown in addition to mean values since much of the data are highly skewed. These measures are compared to the coefficients estimated for the five-year leading-period returns model (Table 4), since this model is expected to provide the most accurate measure of the market's valuation of geographic segment earnings.

Cursory inspection shows that, as expected, geographic segment earnings are valued approximately according to their risk and growth characteristics. The South America/Mexico segment has the highest measure of risk (according to median, first quartile and third quartile values) and only the fifth largest median measure of growth. Consequently, this segment has the lowest earnings coefficient. The United Kingdom segment has lower risk and higher growth than the Domestic and Canada segments and also has a higher earnings coefficient than these segments. The Other Foreign segment has the lowest mean measure of risk and the highest mean measure of growth and has the highest earnings coefficient.

It is possible to test statistically whether the geographic segment earnings coefficients are positively related to growth and negatively related to risk. For example, Biddle and Seow (1991) use a two-step procedure to determine

150 *Wayne B. Thomas*

Table 5. *Descriptive Statistics for Sales Growth and Return on Assets for Geographic Segments*

	Mean	Median	Q1	Q3
Panel A: Sales Growth[a]				
Domestic	.080	.055	−.014	.123
Canada	.159	.032	−.073	.142
United Kingdom	.181	.091	−.059	.273
Europe	.256	.120	−.001	.268
Asia/Pacific	.206	.133	.031	.236
S.America/Mexico	.129	.087	−.008	.198
Other Foreign	.300	.092	−.007	.207
Panel B: Return on Assets[b]				
Domestic	.120	.101	.039	.188
Canada	.117	.083	.023	.181
United Kingdom	.110	.075	.014	.165
Europe	.129	.106	.033	.188
Asia/Pacific	.222	.121	.045	.223
S. America/Mexico	.169	.163	.083	.279
Other Foreign	.077	.120	.041	.211

[a]Sales growth is measured as the change in geographic sales in period t divided by geographic sales in period t − 1.
[b]Return on assets is measured as geographic earnings in period t divided by geographic assets in t − 1.

whether earnings response coefficients vary according to certain industry characteristics. In step one, earnings coefficients are estimated for each of 39 industries. In step two, the estimated earnings coefficients are used as the dependent variable and regressed on the risk, growth, and persistence variables of each industry. Thus, there were 39 observations. In this study only seven geographic segment earnings coefficients are estimated because of data limitations, which creates statistical problems in determining whether these earnings coefficients vary according to risk and growth. Nevertheless, I proceed with a regression, which uses the estimated geographic segment earnings coefficients for the five-year model as the dependent variable and the median values of growth and risk as the independent variables. Since there are only seven observations in the regression, such a test should be viewed as descriptive statistics rather than a formal hypothesis test.

The results are shown in Table 6. As expected, the growth variable relates positively to geographic segment earnings coefficients and the risk variable relates negatively. Both are significant at the .05 level. These results, along with casual inspection, suggest that for the five-year return

Table 6. *Regression of Estimated Geographic Segment Earnings Coefficients from the Five-year Leading-period Returns Model (Table 4) on Median Measures of Geographic Segment Growth and Risk (Table 5) (n = 7)*

Regressor	Coefficient (p-value)
Constant	8.267
	(.080)
Growth[a]	55.755
	(.050)
Risk[b]	−77.932
	(.038)
Adj. R^2	.505

[a]Growth is measured as the percentage change in geographic segment sales (see Table 5).
[b]Risk is measured as the geographic segment earnings divided by geographic segment sales (see Table 5).

interval geographic segment earnings are valued approximately according to their risk and growth characteristics, which gives us additional confidence in the models' results.

IV. Summary and Conclusions

This study examines the value-relevance of geographic segment earnings disclosures. Differences in earnings coefficients across geographic segments provide evidence of the value-relevance of such disclosures. Failure to find differences in geographic earnings coefficients indicates that such disclosures either are not used or are unrelated to the underlying set of information used in setting security prices and, therefore, total earnings is sufficient (relative to geographic segment earnings) for explaining security returns.

Geographic segment earnings coefficients are estimated by regressing unexpected security returns on unexpected geographic segment earnings and by regressing leading-period security returns on current geographic segment earnings. The leading-period returns models are estimated using one- to five-year return intervals. The results show that unexpected geographic segment earnings are differentially related to unexpected security returns. For the one- and two-year leading-period returns models, little evidence is found that earnings coefficients are different across geographic segments. When return intervals of three years or more are used, significant differences are found across geographic segment earnings coefficients,

152   *Wayne B. Thomas*

which suggests that such disclosures reflect the information used in setting security prices and therefore provide useful information.

The geographic segment earnings data used in this study are reported under the guidelines of SFAS 14. The FASB recently issued SFAS 131, which drastically changes the segment reporting requirements for US firms. Firms are no longer required to provide disclosures of earnings along both industry lines and geographical location. Instead, firms are required to disclose earnings by operating segment only. Since most firms define operating segments along industry lines, geographic segment earnings are not a required disclosure for most firms. As a result, there has been a significant reduction in the number of firms reporting geographic segment earnings. The results of this study suggest that geographic segment earnings disclosures under SFAS 14 provide value-relevant information. Thus, a valuable source of information may no longer be available now that SFAS 131 is effective. The FASB may want to reconsider its reporting requirements for geographic segment earnings.

Notes

1. See Pacter (1993) for a thorough discussion of the alleged shortcomings of current segment reporting practices.
2. An operating segment is a component of an enterprise (a) that engages in business activities from which it may earn revenues and incur expenses, (b) whose operating results are regularly reviewed by the enterprise's chief operating decision maker to make decisions about resources to be allocated to the segment and assess its performance, and (c) for which discrete financial information is available (FASB, 1997, para. 10).
3. Or annual report if filed earlier than the Form 10-K.
4. Other research in this area has primarily focused on the association between geographic segment earnings and (1) earnings forecast models (e.g., Roberts, 1989; Balakrishnan et al., 1990; Ahadiat, 1993; Herrmann, 1996), (2) shifts in systematic risk (e.g., Prodhan, 1986; Prodhan and Harris, 1989; Chan et al., 1993), and (3) the ability of the market or analysts to predict consolidated earnings (e.g., Senteney and Bazaz, 1992; Nichols et al., 1995). For a more complete review of this literature, see Herrmann and Thomas (1998).
5. The results of several studies show that (total) earnings coefficients vary cross-sectionally according to risk and growth characteristics (e.g., Easton and Zmijewski, 1989; Collins and Kothari, 1989; Biddle and Seow, 1991; Ali and Zarowin, 1992; and others]. Furthermore, Bodnar and Weintrop (1997) show that total foreign earnings coefficients are valued higher than domestic earnings coefficients. They provide evidence that this result is attributable to the greater growth opportunities abroad. Consequently, there is reason to believe that geographic segment earnings should also be valued differently according to their risk and growth characteristics. Geographic segments that have greater growth opportunities should have higher earnings coefficients and geographic segments that have greater risks should have lower earnings coefficients.
6. This argument is, of course, one-sided. Even if geographic segment earnings disclosures under SFAS 14 provide value-relevant information, the new disclosure requirements under

SFAS 131 may provide more total information relevant for valuing the firm. Thus, this study does not claim to provide a direct comparison of the informational quality of SFAS 14 versus SFAS 131.

7. Compustat refers to the United Kingdom segment as Great Britain.

8. Since BBP found evidence of differential valuation of geographic segment earnings only in outlying cases, a check for outliers in this study was conducted. The significance of the results should not be attributable to a few extreme observations. Similar methods of detecting outliers have been employed in this type of research (Kothari and Sloan, 1992; Boatsman et al., 1993).

9. Specifically, BBP (1993) find that geographic segment earnings are used to value securities only when there is an unusually large change in the geographic segment's earnings. When outlying observations are eliminated, there is no evidence of differential valuation of geographic segment earnings.

10. This also assumes that the appropriate expectations model for geographic segment earnings is a random walk. While the random walk assumption will not be true for all observations, it should be approximately descriptive of market expectations. For earnings prediction, a random walk assumption for geographic segment earnings appears to work as well as segment-specific forecast (Balakrishnan et al., 1990; Herrmann, 1996). In addition, inherent data limitations prevent the estimation of more sophisticated time-series expectations and analysts' forecasts of geographic segment earnings are unavailable.

11. Since unexpected geographic segment earnings are measured as the change in earnings, 1985 becomes the first year of usable observations. For the levels models used in the next section, 1984 is the first year of usable observations.

12. It is difficult to explain why the South America/Mexico coefficient would be negative. BBP also found that their South America segment had a negative coefficient (see their Table 4, p. 62). The negative coefficient may be attributable to the high operating risk in these areas.

13. Dummy variables are used to control for yearly effects in size adjusted-returns. The coefficient on each dummy variable provides a measure of the difference in the average annual size-adjusted return not explained by the regressors. The difference is the average size-adjusted return for the year minus that of the base year. The base year (1995) size-adjusted return is captured by the intercept. The coefficients for 1985, 1986, 1987, 1989, 1990, and 1994 are positive and significant at the .05 level. All of the other coefficients on the yearly dummy variables are not significant. These results can be obtained from the author upon request.

14. Basu (1997) shows that because of the conservative nature of reported earnings, there is less timing difference between returns and earnings for firms that experience negative earnings changes.

15. The adjusted R^2 is somewhat larger than those found in previous studies. The increase is partly attributable to the significance of the dummy variables controlling for yearly effects. The coefficient on each dummy variable provides a measure of the difference in the average annual return not explained by the regressors. The difference is the average return for the year minus that of the base year. The base year (1995) return is captured by the intercept. The coefficients for 1985 and 1986 are positive and significant at the .001 level. The coefficients for the other years are negative and significant at the .001 level. These results can be obtained from the author upon request.

16. All of the leading-period returns models were tested for multicollinearity. Belsey et al. (1980) suggest that a condition index greater than 30 was evidence of severe multicollinearity. None of the leading-period returns models has a condition index greater than 15, which suggests that multicollinearity is not a problem.

154   *Wayne B. Thomas*

References

Ahadiat, N., "Geographic Segment Disclosure and the Predictive Ability of the Earnings Data," *Journal of International Business Studies* (Second Quarter 1993), pp. 357–371.

Ali, A. and P. Zarowin, "Permanent Versus Transitory Components of Annual Earnings and Estimation Error in Earnings Response Coefficients," *Journal of Accounting and Economics* (June/September 1992), pp. 249–264.

American Institute of Certified Public Accountants, *The Information Needs of Investors and Creditors* (New York: AICPA, 1994).

Association for Investment Management and Research, Financial Accounting Policy Committee, *Financial Reporting in the 1990's and Beyond: A Position Paper of the Association for Investment Management and Research* (prepared by Peter H. Knutson, Charlottesville, VA, October 1992).

Arnold, J., W. Holder and M. Mann, "International Reporting Aspects of Segment Disclosures," *International Journal of Accounting* (Fall 1980), pp. 125–135.

Bavishi, V. and H. Wyman, "Foreign Operations Disclosures by US-Based Multinational Corporations: Are They Adequate?" *International Journal of Accounting* (Fall 1980), pp. 153–168.

Balakrishnan, R., T. Harris and P. Sen, "The Predictive Ability of Geographic Segment Disclosures," *Journal of Accounting Research* (Autumn 1990), pp. 305–325.

Basu, S., "The Conservatism Principle and the Asymmetric Timeliness of Earnings," *Journal of Accounting and Economics* (December 1997), pp. 3–37.

Belsey, D., E. Kuh, and R. Welsch, *Regression Diagnostics: Identifying Influential Data and Sources of Collinearity* (New York: John Wiley, 1980).

Biddle, G. and G. Seow, "The Estimation and Determinants of Associations Between Returns and Earnings: Evidence from Cross-industry Comparisons," *Journal of Accounting, Auditing and Finance* (Spring 1991), pp. 183–232.

Boatsman, J., B. Behn and D. Patz, "A Test of the Use of Geographical Segment Disclosures," *Journal of Accounting Research* (Supplement 1993), pp. 46–64.

Bodnar, G. and J. Weintrop, "The Valuation of the Foreign Income of US Multinational Firms: A Growth Opportunities Perspective," *Journal of Accounting and Economics* (December 1997), pp. 69–97.

Chan, A., P. Chan, W. Chan, M. Leung and N. Won, "Segmental Reporting and Risk Reduction: The Hong Kong Experience," *International Journal of Accounting* (1993), pp. 232–247.

Cochrane, D. and G. Orcutt, "Application of Least Squares Regressions to Relationships Containing Autocorrelated Error Terms," *Journal of the American Statistical Association* (1949), pp. 32–61.

Collins, D. and S. Kothari, "An Analysis of the Intertemporal and Cross-Sectional Determinants of the Earnings Response Coefficients," *Journal of Accounting and Economics* (July 1989), pp. 143–181.

Easton, P. and M. Zmijewski, "Cross-Sectional Variation in the Stock Market Response to Accounting Earnings Announcements," *Journal of Accounting and Economics* (1989), pp. 117–141.

Fama, E. and K. French, "The Cross-section of Expected Stock Returns," *Journal of Finance* (June 1992), pp. 427–465.

Financial Accounting Standards Board. Statement of Financial Accounting Standards No. 131: *Disclosures about Segments of an Enterprise and Related Information* (Stamford CT: FASB, 1997).

Frankel, J. and A. Rose, "A survey of Empirical Research on Nominal Exchange Rates", in *Handbook of International Economics*, G. Grossman and K. Rogoff, eds. (New York: North-Holland, 1995).

Herrmann, D., "The Predictive Ability of Geographic Segment Information at the Country, Continent, and Consolidated Levels," *The Journal of International Financial Management and Accounting* (Spring 1996), pp. 50–73.

Herrmann, D. and W. Thomas, "Geographic Segment Disclosures: Theories, Findings, and Implications," *International Journal of Accounting* (No. 4 1998), pp. 487–501.

Herrmann, D. and W. Thomas, "An Analysis of Segment Disclosures Under SFAS No. 131 and SFAS No. 14," forthcoming in *Accounting Horizons* (2000).

Kothari, S. and R. Sloan, "Information in Prices about Future Earnings," *Journal of Accounting and Economics* (June/September 1992), pp. 143–171.

Lev, B., "On the Usefulness of Earnings: Lessons and Directions from Two Decades of Empirical Research," *Journal of Accounting Research* (Supplement 1989), pp. 153–192.

Nichols, D., L. Tunnell, and C. Seipel, "Earnings Forecast Accuracy and Geographic Segment Disclosures," *Journal of International Accounting, Auditing and Taxation* (1995), pp. 113–126.

Pacter, P., *Reporting Disaggregated Information* (Norwalk, CT: FASB, 1993).

Prodhan, B., "Geographical Segment Disclosure and Multinational Risk Profile," *Journal of Business Finance & Accounting* (Spring 1996), pp. 15–37.

Prodhan, B. and M. Harris, "Systematic Risk and the Discretionary Disclosure of Geographical Segments: An Empirical Investigation of U.S. Multinationals," *Journal of Business Finance and Accounting* (Autumn 1989), pp. 467–492.

Roberts, C., "Forecasting Earnings Using Geographical Segment Data: Some U.K. Evidence," *Journal of International Financial Management and Accounting* (Summer 1989), pp. 130–151.

Senteney, D. and M. Bazaz, "The Impact of SFAS 14 Geographic Segment Disclosures on the Information Content of U.S.-Based MNEs' Earnings Releases," *International Journal of Accounting* (Fall 1992), pp. 267–279.

Part II
Financial Accounting Measurement Rules

[6]

Foreign Operations and the Choice of Inventory Accounting Methods

Catherine Craycraft
Stanley Sedo
David Gotlob

Many companies continue to use the FIFO or other inventory cost flow assumption even though empirical research has shown that the LIFO assumption provides significant cash flow advantages over the other methods. One potential influence on the choice of inventory method that has not been investigated in prior empirical studies is the potential effect of a firm's foreign operations. Because LIFO is not commonly used and/or permitted in most foreign countries, high levels of foreign inventory may influence the choice of inventory method for the firm's domestic inventory. The purpose of this paper is to determine if a firm's level of foreign operations influences its choice of inventory cost flow assumptions for its U.S. inventory. A probit model of inventory choice is developed using variables that have been found to differentiate LIFO and non-LIFO firms in previous studies. The results indicate firms with higher relative levels of foreign operations are more likely to use a non-LIFO inventory method for their domestic inventory than firms that are less involved in foreign markets. The results suggest that the level of foreign operations should be considered in future models of inventory choice and possibly other accounting choice models when there are differences in accounting standards since firms with significant levels of foreign operations may be influenced by these differences.

Key Words: Inventory; Accounting Choice; International Accounting Standards

Catherine Craycraft • University of New Hampshire, 320 McConnell Hall, Durham, NH 03824. E-mail: cac6@christa.unh.edu. **Stanley Sedo** • University of Michigan, Dept. of Economics, Lorch Hall, Ann Arbor, MI 48109. E-mail: sasedo@umich.edu. **David Gotlob** • Indiana University/Purdue University, 2101 Coliseum Blvd., East, Fort Wayne, IN 46805-1499. E-mail: gotlob@cvax. ipfw.indiana.edu.

Journal of International Accounting, Auditing & Taxation, 7(1):81-93   ISSN: 1061-9518

82   INTERNATIONAL ACCOUNTING, AUDITING & TAXATION, 7(1)   1998

INTRODUCTION

During the past decade, international capital market activity has grown tremendously because of many factors including deregulation, political changes, and improved communications (Gray and Roberts 1991). Examples of this growth include the fact that foreign investments in U.S. equity securities exceeded $260 billion in 1989, which is an increase of more than 300% over 1980 (Wells, Thompson, and Phelps 1995) and that U.S. investors bought more than $91 billion of foreign equity securities in 1989, which is almost a 500% increase over the $19 billion purchased in 1980 (Peavy and Webster 1990). This rapid increase in international capital market activity has led to many calls for the harmonization of worldwide accounting practices.

Currently, accounting standards and practices vary worldwide exogenously because of differences in economic environments and endogenously because the purpose of accounting and the accounting standard setting process varies between countries (Meek and Saudagaran 1990). Many studies have established the lack of harmonization (Choi and Levich 1991; Moulin and Solomon 1989; Peavy and Webster 1990). Even though much effort is being spent examining the extent of accounting diversity between countries and considering ways to eliminate it, the important question of how harmonization affects companies still remains. Several studies have examined this issue in terms of the ability of firms to raise capital. Choi and Levich (1991) found accounting differences affect the capital marketing decisions of market participants. Wells et al. (1995) conclude that accounting differences affect the ability of U.S. firms to compete with foreign enterprises for capital. Since the market for capital is becoming more global, an important issue is whether U.S. firms make accounting choices that increase harmonization in order to better compete in the limited market for capital.

This paper examines whether or not differences in international accounting standards do, in fact, affect U.S. accounting choices. Although many differences exist between U.S. GAAP and other countries' GAAP, the choice of inventory method is an appropriate accounting principle to examine because U.S. firms have a choice of conforming to other countries' standards by choosing to use a non-LIFO method of inventory. Other accounting differences, for example the treatment of research and development costs, do not give U.S. companies the option of conforming. U.S. companies do not have the choice of capitalizing research and development as is common in other countries. Accordingly, this paper examines whether the lack of acceptance of a LIFO costing system by most countries influences U.S. firms to forgo the tax benefits of a LIFO system for their U.S. inventory. The LIFO inventory cost system has virtually no acceptance in any other country (Hampton 1980). "FIFO and the weighted average method are the most commonly used methods worldwide. The use of LIFO is essentially limited to companies in the United States" (White, Sondhi, and Fried 1994, 379). U.S. firms that operate in foreign countries may not have the choice of inventory systems for their foreign operations but they do have the option of using LIFO for their domestic inventory. Using LIFO for their U.S. inventories gives them tax advantages and a corresponding increase in cash flows.

Consequently, LIFO would seem to be the preferred choice. However, the choice of LIFO has a cost. U.S. firms that have inventory in foreign countries and choose to use the LIFO costing system for their U.S. inventories must bear the additional cost of maintaining dual inventory record keeping systems. For example, Hilke (1986) found LIFO bookkeeping costs for wholesalers varied from 0.7% to 7.9% of average profit. In addition, the use of an inventory method that is not accepted in other countries may put corporations at a competitive disadvantage in the international market for capital because of the difficulty in comparing firms that use different accounting standards (Wells et al. 1995). As the proportion of foreign inventory to total inventory increases, the costs relative to the tax savings that are realized by using LIFO for domestic inventories increase and the competitive disadvantage costs which could dominate any LIFO savings through significant increases in capital costs also increases. Companies facing higher costs and lower tax savings may allow the inventory methods used for foreign inventory to drive the inventory method choice for the company as a whole. The increase in costs, if high enough to offset the benefits of a LIFO system, should discourage U.S. firms with foreign operations from using a LIFO system. Therefore, this paper explores whether U.S. firms with higher levels of foreign operations are less likely to use LIFO for their domestic inventories than companies with relatively lower levels of foreign operations.

A large literature has explored the question of why some U.S. firms use the LIFO inventory cost flow assumption while others continue to use FIFO despite the cash flow advantages of LIFO (Cushing and LeClere 1992; Dopuch and Pincus 1988; Lee and Hsieh 1985). Lindahl (1989) also provides a comprehensive review. However, none of the models developed to explain choice of inventory method includes a measure of foreign operations. As global markets continue to grow and more research is done on the effects of diversity of accounting methods on investment decisions, lack of control for foreign operations may become more problematic. In this paper, a model of inventory choice is developed that specifically includes a variable designed to identify a firm's level of involvement in foreign operations.

The paper is organized in the following manner. A discussion of the sample and development of a probit model is included in the next section. The empirical results and a discussion of their implications are in the concluding section.

84 INTERNATIONAL ACCOUNTING, AUDITING & TAXATION, 7(1) 1998

RESEARCH DESIGN AND VARIABLE SELECTION

Research Model

Probit analysis is used to estimate the following model to determine whether foreign operations influence accounting choice for inventory valuation.

$$Y = a + b_1 SIZE + b_2 LEV + b_3 CAP + b_4 TAX + b_5 FOR + b_6 DUM + e$$

where

Y =dummy; 0 for non-LIFO, 1 for LIFO
$SIZE$ =total annual sales
LEV = long-term debt to equity
CAP = fixed assets to total assets
TAX = tax loss carryforwards to total assets
FOR = foreign assets to total assets
DUM = 55 dummy variables for SIC codes

Since the dependent variable is binary, a probit analysis is more appropriate than discriminant or regression analyses. When a model contains a limited dependent variable, regression analysis produces biased coefficients. Probit analysis, under the same circumstances, gives unbiased estimates of the coefficients. Probit, unlike discriminant analysis, does not require the independent variable to be normally distributed or the equality of covariance matrices. Probit analysis provides consistent estimates of the coefficients which can be tested individually, or in any combination, for significance. These reasons make probit the most suitable method for analyzing the results. In this model, a positive coefficient estimate indicates that the firm is more likely to choose LIFO while negative estimates reduce the probability of making this choice.

Specification of Variables

The following variables are included in the model to determine if firms with foreign operations are relatively more likely to use non-LIFO inventory methods than firms without foreign operations. These variables are the most commonly used in prior research and are most likely to control for possible differences between firms that choose LIFO and those that do not.

Foreign operations. As noted above, firms with significant levels of foreign operations are hypothesized to be more likely to use a non-LIFO inventory method. In order to test this hypothesis, a measure of the level of foreign operations is included in the inventory choice model. The appropriate measure to be used in examining inventory choice is the measure "foreign inventory to total inventory." However, data that separates inventory into foreign and domestic components are unavailable. Therefore, a proxy for this measure is used. The proxy used in this paper is foreign assets to total assets. This proxy assumes that the ratio of foreign inventory to foreign assets and total inventory to total assets is consistent across firms but not necessarily that the two ratios are consistent within firms. The variable foreign assets is obtained from the footnotes of the firm's annual reports. The rest of the variables are from Compustat.

Firm size. Size of the firm has been used in other studies of inventory choice for various reasons (Cushing and LeClere 1992; Dopuch and Pincus 1988; Morse and Richardson 1983). Size may be a proxy for political concerns or managerial complexities that can adversely affect large firms. For example, firms reporting large profits may attract the attention of antitrust authorities. These firms may choose to use the LIFO inventory method to reduce reported accounting income and thereby avoid the appearance of monopolistic behavior (Morse and Richardson 1983). In addition, larger firms may be in a better position to benefit from the use of LIFO and to bear any increased costs that this inventory accounting system requires (Cushing and LeClere 1992; Dopuch and Pincus 1988). As in all of the previously mentioned studies, total sales is used as a measure of firm size.

Leverage. Highly leveraged firms may be more concerned about access to international capital markets and, therefore, more likely to choose FIFO in an effort to harmonize their accounting methods. In addition, Dhaliwal (1980), Holthausen (1981), and Leftwich (1981) argue that firms with high debt to equity ratios experience more restrictive debt covenants than firms with lower ratios and hypothesize that this encourages managers to choose accounting alternatives that increase reported income. Managers seek to operate within the constraints imposed by debt covenants because violation of these covenants are costly to the firm and affect the wealth of the firm's managers (Beneish and Press 1993). Press and Weintrop (1990) show that leverage serves as a proxy for closeness to debt covenants and suggests that leverage is associated with accounting choices that increase income. These studies indicate that highly leveraged firms are more likely to choose FIFO.

However, Dopuch and Pincus (1988) suggest that all firms have incentives to add debt to their capital structure to take advantage of the tax deduction for interest. Therefore, LIFO firms may also be highly leveraged and a measure of leverage will not affect the choice of inventory method. Since both explanations appear equally likely, leverage is included in the model, but no sign is predicted. The ratio of long-term debt to equity is used to measure leverage because it is the most commonly used ratio and has been found to be a good proxy for closeness to debt covenant restrictions (Press and Weintrop 1990).

Capital intensity.   There are two different arguments as to why a measure of capital intensity should be included in a model of inventory choice. The first argument by Lee and Hsieh (1985) hypothesizes that the need for planning and control inherent in a LIFO system may be less burdensome for capital intensive firms. Capital intensive firms should have an effective information system already in place because of the increased control necessary when a high ratio of fixed to variable costs exists. Therefore, firms with high capital intensity will not find the planning and control needs of a LIFO system as costly as firms with lower capital intensity. A second argument for a positive relationship between LIFO and capital intensity is provided by Hagerman and Zmijewski (1979). They note that capital intensive firms do not include cost of capital in computing net income. A capital intensive firm, therefore, will report higher profits than a labor intensive firm even if the economic income of the two firms are the same. This reasoning suggests that capital intensive companies are more likely to use LIFO to reduce reported income, taxes, and the likelihood that political costs will be imposed on the firms. This study uses the ratio of fixed assets to total assets as a measure of capital intensity and predicts this variable to be positively related to the choice of LIFO.

Tax loss carryforwards.   Previous studies have found that tax loss carryforwards also influence inventory choice (Cushing and LeClere 1992; Lindahl 1989). Firms with loss carryforwards are less likely to use LIFO because they may derive no tax benefit from doing so yet would incur the additional bookkeeping costs associated with the LIFO method. As Lindahl (1989) notes, firms with loss carryforwards have less of an incentive to reduce future tax payments particularly if there is a risk the loss carryforwards will expire unused. Tax loss carryforwards scaled by total assets are used in the model and are predicted to be negatively associated with the choice of LIFO.

Industry classification.   The American Institute of Certified Public Accountants' *Accounting Trends and Techniques* (1990) has consistently found the adoption of LIFO to be strongly affected by industry classification. Firms within an industry tend to use the same accounting practices. As in previous studies, two digit SIC codes are included in the model to control for industry effects (Lee and Hsieh 1985; Morse and Richardson 1983). Although wide varia-

TABLE 1
Inventory Method by SIC Code

	LIFO		non-LIFO	
SIC Code	Number	Percent	Number	Percent
1000-1999				
Mining and Construction	5	11%	39	89%
2000-3000				
Manufacturing	257	39%	399	61%
4000-4999				
Transporation, Communication, Utilities	1	2%	50	98%
5000-5999				
Trade	59	38%	97	62%
6000-6999				
Finance, Insurance, Real Estate	2	50%	2	50%
7000-8999				
Services	3	6%	48	94%

tions may exist within the two digit classifications, further breakdown by industry is not feasible given the large number of dummy variables that would have to be included in the model.

Sample Selection

The sample consists of 962 U.S. corporations for which complete data are available on Compustat Annual Industrial File for the year 1990. These firms are classified as LIFO or non-LIFO depending on the cost flow assumption used to account for the largest share of their inventory. All firms without LIFO as the primary inventory method are classified as non-LIFO regardless of the methods used, resulting in 635 non-LIFO and 327 LIFO firms. Of the 962 firms in the sample, 445 firms reported foreign income. A cross sectional design is used for comparability with previous studies. Table 1 contains the breakdown of LIFO and non-LIFO firms by industry. One digit SIC codes are used in the table (as opposed to two digit SIC codes used in the analysis) for simplicity.

Descriptive statistics for the variables are contained in Tables 2 and 3. These statistics are divided into LIFO and FIFO firms and also into firms with and without foreign operations.

Table 4 contains a correlation matrix of the variables included in the model. When using probit analysis, multicollinearity does not bias the coefficient estimates. In addition, multicollinearity makes it more difficult to find significance in the results and therefore, should not pose a problem in the analysis.

88   INTERNATIONAL ACCOUNTING, AUDITING & TAXATION, 7(1)   1998

TABLE 2
Descriptive Statistics

Variable	Mean	Standard Deviation
Total Sample N = 962		
Foreign assets/total assets (FOR)	0.087	0.158
Total sales (SIZE) (in thousands)	2801.78	8678.87
Long term debt/equity (LEV)	0.237	0.188
Fixed assets/total assets (CAP)	0.632	0.423
Tax loss carryforwards/total assets (TAX)	0.066	0.278
LIFO FIRMS N = 327		
Foreign assets/total assets (FOR)	0.083	0.144
Total sales (SIZE) (in thousands)	4678.37	13009.65
Long term debt/equity (LEV)	0.217	0.169
Fixed assets/total assets (CAP)	0.672	0.329
Tax loss carryforwards/total assets (TAX)	0.022	0.089
Non-LIFO FIRMS N = 635		
Foreign assets/total assets (FOR)	0.088	0.165
Total sales (SIZE) (in thousands)	1835.41	4938.88
Long term debt/equity (LEV)	0.247	0.196
Fixed assets/total assets (CAP)	0.612	0.463
Tax loss carryforwards/total assets (TAX)	0.088	0.334

RESULTS, LIMITATIONS, AND CONCLUSIONS

Results

The results of the probit analysis are reported in Table 5.

The focus of this study is whether foreign operations affect the choice of inventory method. As hypothesized, the ratio of foreign assets to total assets is significant and negatively related to the use of LIFO. As a further means of testing this hypothesis, a log likelihood ratio is calculated where the model is estimated without the measure of foreign operations and then compared to the original model. The value of the likelihood ratio statistic is 5.917 with a p-value of .016 which indicates that the model fits significantly better with the inclusion of a measure of foreign operations.

The coefficients of all of the other variables are significant, and their signs are in the expected direction. Larger firms measured in terms of annual sales are more likely to use LIFO. In addition, capital intensive firms are more likely to use LIFO. These results are consistent with previous research as cited above. Firms that have a tax loss carryforward are more likely to use a non-LIFO method of inventory probably because the tax savings of LIFO are not an incentive to bear the additional costs of a LIFO system. Further research is needed to determine

TABLE 3
Descriptive Statistics by Foreign Operations

Variable	Mean	Standard Deviation
U.S. Firms with foreign operations N = 445		
Foreign assets/total assets (FOR)	0.282	0.163
Total sales (SIZE) (in thousands)	4016	10755
Long term debt/equity (LEV)	0.219	0.169
Fixed assets/total assets (CAP)	0.630	0.342
Tax loss carryforwards/total assets (TAX)	0.058	0.190
U.S. Firms without foreign operations N = 517		
Foreign assets/total assets (FOR)	0.0	0.0
Total sales (SIZE) (in thousands)	1756	6194
Long term debt/equity (LEV)	0.252	0.202
Fixed assets/total assets (CAP)	0.634	0.482
Tax loss carryforwards/total assets (TAX)	0.072	0.336

whether tax loss carry-forwards must persist over time to affect the choice of inventory method. The results find debt to equity significant which is consistent with the theory that managers are influenced by debt covenants rather than the Dopuch and Pincus theory (1988) that all firms have the same incentives to increase debt. To further test the results, univariate analysis is performed and the results are contained in Table 6. They are consistent with the results of the probit model.

Limitations

A limitation of this study is that the dependent variable should reflect the *choice* of inventory method. However, Compustat codes inventory method in the order of the percentage of inventory that uses a method. A firm with 40% of its inventory accounted for using FIFO and 39% using LIFO would be coded as a FIFO firm. This manner of coding does not necessarily reflect the portion of the inventory over which management has the option to choose LIFO. For example, a firm that has 90% of its inventories in a foreign country will be coded as non-LIFO even if it chooses LIFO for all of its domestic inventory because a majority of their inventory would be mandated to use a non-LIFO method. Coding this firm as non-LIFO would not accurately reflect the firm's choice.

The coding limitation described in the previous paragraph would have firms classified as non-LIFO simply because they have high levels of foreign inventory, not because they choose to use a non-LIFO method. To determine if this coding system imposes a major limitation on the results, additional analysis is done.

Firms with high levels of inventory in foreign countries are more likely to be coded as non-LIFO firms since a manager's choosing LIFO for a larger portion of

TABLE 4
Correlation Matrix
(p-values)

	FOREIGN	SIZE	LEVERAGE	CAPITAL	CARRYFORWARDS
FOREIGN	1.00	.155	−.074	.067	−.112
		(.000)	(.022)	(.037)	(.001)
SIZE		1.00	−.026	.052	−.064
			(.412)	(.109)	(.047)
LEVERAGE			1.00	.189	.088
				(.000)	(.006)
CAPITAL				1.00	−.060
					(.064)
CARRYFORWARDS					1.00

TABLE 5
Results of Probit Analysis
N = 962

Variable	Predicted* Sign	Estimate	Significance
INTERCEPT		−1.111	.013
FOREIGN	−	−.715	.016
SIZE	+	.0000	.000
LEVERAG		−.462	.069
CAPITAL	+	.507	.000
CARRYFORWARDS	−	−1.334	.001

Note: * Negative values are associated with non-LIFO inventory choice; positive values are associated with LIFO inventory choice.

TABLE 6
Univariate Analysis

Variable	Estimate	p-value
FOREIGN	−.407	.041
SIZE	.000	.000
LEVERAGE	−.187	.022
CAPITAL	.075	.037
CARRYFORWARDS	−.191	.001

their inventory is not an option. Therefore, to more closely examine the *choice* of inventory method, firms with high levels of foreign inventories are eliminated from the sample which should eliminate the firms that are coded as non-LIFO but do not reflect the choice of being non-LIFO. The model is recomputed eliminating all firms with a ratio of foreign assets to total assets over 10% leaving 741 firms in the sample. The results, reported in Table 7, are robust with those previously reported.

TABLE 7
Probit Analysis of Firms with Less than 10 percent Foreign Operations
N = 741

Variable	Predicted* Sign	Estimate	Significance
INTERCEPT		−.401	.000
FOREIGN	−	−1.55	.046
SIZE	+	.0000	.000
LEVERAGE		−.687	.007
CAPITAL	+	.231	.023
CARRYFORWARDS	−	−1.34	.001

Note: * Negative values are associated with non-LIFO inventory choice; positive values are associated with LIFO inventory choice.

Although the method of coding does preclude the testing of inventory choice per se, these results indicate that the dependent variable captures the choice of accounting method made by the firm for their domestic inventory. These results further support the conclusion that firms with higher relative levels of foreign operations are more likely to use a non-LIFO inventory method than firms with lower levels of foreign involvement. These results indicate that foreign operations influence the inventory accounting method selected for U.S. operations.

Conclusions

This study shows that the level of foreign operations influences the choice of inventory accounting methods for domestic inventories. Firms with foreign operations make different choices with regard to the inventory method used for their U.S. inventory than firms without foreign operations. One possible reason for this difference is that firms with foreign operations incur a relatively higher cost in reporting their domestic inventory on a LIFO basis than firms without foreign operations. These higher costs include additional bookkeeping costs but also possibly the higher costs of raising capital in international markets due to their lack of harmonization with international accounting standards. These costs must outweigh the benefits associated with the LIFO system since firms with foreign operations are more likely to adopt FIFO for their entire inventory system. These results show empirical support for the Wells et al. (1995) and the Choi and Levich (1991) studies that companies do feel there is a cost to not harmonizing with international accounting standards. The results suggest that U.S. firms, at least with respect to choice of inventory costing method, are influenced by the extent of their foreign operations and the accounting methods permitted in the international arena. More empirical research is needed to explore and quantify the costs incurred because of lack of harmonization of accounting standards.

There are two major implications from these results. The first implication suggests the level of involvement of U.S. firms in foreign markets should be considered in modeling the choice of inventory accounting methods and possibly other accounting choice models. The accounting choice models currently used may not reflect an important managerial consideration especially when accounting standards differ significantly between countries.

The results indicate that firms with higher levels of foreign operations are more likely to use non-LIFO for their domestic inventory. These results may suggest that as firms become more involved in foreign markets, they may have a higher propensity to harmonize their accounting methods to international standards.

This may have important implications to the international standard setting bodies and all others who are interested in harmonizing accounting standards. Determining how to motivate firms to adopt common standards is important to the future of harmonization.

REFERENCES

American Institute of Certified Public Accountants. 1990. *Accounting Trends and Techniques.*

Beneish, M., and E. Press. 1993. Cost of technical violation of accounting-based debt covenants. *The Accounting Review* 68 (April): 233-257.

Choi F., and R. Levich. 1991. Behavioral effects of international accounting diversity. *Accounting Horizons* (June): 1-13.

Cushing, B.E., and M.J. LeClere. 1992. Evidence on the determinants of inventory accounting policy choice. *The Accounting Review* 67 (April): 355-366.

Dhaliwal, D. 1980. The effect of the firm's capital structure on the choice of accounting methods. *The Accounting Review* 55 (January): 78-85.

Dopuch, N., and M. Pincus. 1988. Evidence on the choice of inventory accounting methods: LIFO vs. FIFO. *Journal of Accounting Research* 26 (Spring): 28-59.

Gray, S., and C. Roberts. 1991. East-West accounting issues: A new agenda. *Accounting Horizons* (March): 42-50.

Hagerman, R.L., and M.E. Zmijewski. 1979. Some economic determinants of accounting policy choice. *Journal of Accounting & Economics* 1(August): 141-61.

Hampton III, R. 1980. A world of differences in accounting and reporting. *Management Accounting* (September): 14-18.

Hilke, J.C. 1986. Regulatory compliance costs and LIFO: No wonder small companies haven't switched. *Journal of Accounting, Auditing, & Finance* 1 (Winter): 17-29.

Holthausen, R. 1981. Evidence on the effect of bond covenants and management compensation contracts on the choice of accounting techniques: The case of the depreciation switchback. *Journal of Accounting and Economics* 3 (March): 73-109.

Lee, C.J., and D.A. Hsieh. 1985. Choice of inventory accounting methods: Comparative analysis of alternative hypotheses. *Journal of Accounting Research* 23 (Autumn): 468-85.

Leftwich, R. 1981. Evidence on the impact of mandatory changes in accounting principles on corporate loan agreements. *Journal of Accounting and Economics* 3 (March): 3-36.

Lindahl, F.W. 1989. Dynamic analysis of inventory accounting choice. *Journal of Accounting Research* 27 (Autumn): 201-26.

Meek G., and S. Saudagaran. 1990. A survey of research financial reporting in a transnational context. *Journal of Accounting Literature* 9: 145-182.

Morse, D., and G. Richardson. 1983. The LIFO/FIFO decision. *Journal of Accounting Research* 21(Spring): 106-27.

Moulin, D., and M. Solomon. 1989. Practical means of promoting common international standards. *The CPA Journal* (December): 38-48.

Peavy, D., and S. Webster. 1990. Is GAAP the gap to international markets? *Management Accounting* (August): 31-35.

Press E., and J. Weintrop. 1990. Accounting-based constraints in public and private debt agreements: Their association with leverage and impact on accounting choice. *Journal of Accounting and Economics* 12 (January): 65-95.

Wells, C., J. Thompson and R. Phelps. 1995. Accounting differences: U.S. enterprises and international competition for capital. *Accounting Horizons* (June): 29-39.

White, G., A. Sondhi and D. Fried. 1994. *The Analysis and Use of Financial Statements.*

[7]

Foreign Currency Exposure of Multinational Firms: Accounting Measures and Market Valuation*

ELI BARTOV, *New York University*

Abstract. The accounting method in *Statement of Financial Accounting Standards* (*SFAS*) No. 8 for restatement of a foreign operation's financial statements denominated in a foreign currency into the parent's currency equivalents for inclusion in the parent company's financial statements was severely criticized by market participants and managers. Its replacement, *SFAS* No. 52, represented an attempt to improve on the methods of *SFAS* No. 8. This study examines two questions: did *SFAS* No. 8 produce relevant information for valuing US multinational firms, and are the results reported under *SFAS* No. 52 more valuation relevant than those reported under *SFAS* No. 8? Valuation relevance is studied because the Financial Accounting Standards Board (FASB) has stated that relevance is an important criterion for choosing among alternative accounting methods. Considered collectively, the results suggest that the rules in *SFAS* No. 8 produced a poor accounting measure for valuing US multinational firms, and that the introduction of *SFAS* No. 52 has resulted in a significant improvement in the valuation relevance of the accounting numbers associated with the restatement of a foreign operation's financial statements. However, this improvement applies only to the subset of firms that designated a foreign currency as their functional currency (i.e., switched to the current-rate method) and not to firms that designated the dollar as their functional currency (i.e., as if they still reported under *SFAS* No. 8).

Condensé
Réagissant à la modification du système monétaire international (c'est-à-dire au passage du taux de change fixe au taux de change flottant) et à la complexité croissante des établissements étrangers, le Financial Accounting Standards Board (FASB) publiait, en octobre 1975, le *Statement of Financial Accounting Standards (SFAS)* n° 8, Accounting for the Translation of Foreign Currency Transactions and Foreign Currency Financial Statements. Cette prise de position, en vertu de laquelle les sociétés devaient appliquer la méthode temporelle à la conversion en dollars US des états financiers établis en monnaie étrangère par leurs établissements étrangers, a suscité de vives critiques, qualifiée par les participants au marché et par les gestionnaires d'« inadéquate », voire de « trompeuse ». La prise de position qui l'a remplacée, le *SFAS* n° 52, Foreign Currency Translation, publiée en décembre 1981, visait à améliorer les méthodes du *SFAS* n° 8 en

---

*   I thank Michael Adler, Andrew Alford, Larry Brown, Steve Bryan, Jules Cassel, Fred Choi, Steve Goldberg, April Klein, Pat McQueen, Jerry Mueller, Diane Satin, Paul Zarowin, and workshop participants at City University of Hong Kong for their comments. I also acknowledge the editor, Lane Daley, and two anonymous reviewers for useful suggestions. This work has been presented at the Second (1995) International Conference on Contemporary Accounting Issues in Taipei, Taiwan, and at the Conference on International Accounting Related Issues, at the School of Business, Rutgers University, Camden.

permettant aux sociétés qui convertissaient les états financiers établis en monnaie étrangère de leurs établissements étrangers de choisir soit la méthode temporelle, soit la méthode du taux courant.

Les faits évoqués pour appuyer ce verdict à l'égard du *SFAS* n° 8 ou l'opinion selon laquelle le *SFAS* n° 52 a entraîné une amélioration de la qualité de l'information publiée ne sont que des observations anecdotiques et conflictuelles. Si Collins et Salatka (1993) concluent que le marché perçoit les bénéfices déclarés par les sociétés qui utilisent la méthode temporelle comme étant moins fidèles à la réalité, Gilbert (1989) et Soo et Soo (1994), pour leur part, ne relèvent aucune différence sensible entre les deux méthodes de conversion, résultats étonnants si l'on considère que la méthode temporelle et celle du taux courant abordent la conversion des états financiers établis en monnaie étrangère sous un angle fort différent. Ces deux méthodes de conversion produisent donc des mesures très différentes du gain ou de la perte de change, mesures qui ont une incidence importante sur les états financiers des sociétés multinationales. En outre, du fait que ni l'une ni l'autre de ces méthodes ne prévoit la réévaluation de l'actif et du passif de l'établissement étranger par rapport au marché avant la conversion, ni ne permet de saisir toutes les répercussions de la variation du taux de change au cours de la période sur la valeur de la société.

La présente étude porte donc directement sur l'examen de deux questions : le *SFAS* n° 8 a-t-il produit de l'information pertinente à l'évaluation des sociétés multinationales aux États-Unis, et les résultats publiés conformément au *SFAS* n° 52 sont-ils plus pertinents à l'évaluation que ceux qui ont été publiés selon le *SFAS* n° 8 ? La pertinence de l'évaluation est analysée en raison du fait que le FASB a déclaré qu'il s'agissait d'un critère important dans la formulation d'un choix parmi différentes méthodes comptables possibles. L'auteur vérifie empiriquement la réponse à ces questions en examinant le lien entre les gains ou pertes de change résultant de la conversion attribuables aux différentes méthodes de conversion et aux variations des cours des actions.

L'auteur procède au test empirique des questions énoncées en jaugeant le lien entre, d'une part, les différents gains ou pertes de change résultant de la conversion (associés aux différentes méthodes de conversion) indiqués dans les états financiers de sociétés multinationales des États-Unis et, d'autre part, les variations des cours des actions. Les gains ou pertes de change résultant de la conversion tiennent compte de l'incidence de la fluctuation du dollar par rapport à l'investissement net dans l'établissement étranger, et l'on peut donc supposer que ces gains ou pertes jouent un rôle important dans l'explication de la valeur de l'entreprise. Les résultats de la présente étude confirment cette supposition [voir le tableau 3 du texte integral anglais], puisqu'ils révèlent que les gains ou pertes de change résultant de la conversion sont significatifs sur le plan économique (c'est-à-dire qu'ils sont importants par rapport à la valeur de l'entreprise). Par conséquent, si les gains ou pertes de change résultant de la conversion fournissent de l'information pertinente au sujet de l'incidence de la fluctuation du dollar sur la valeur de l'entreprise, une corrélation positive entre ces variables et les rendements des actions devrait être observée. C'est pourquoi la pertinence des données produites par chacune des méthodes de conversion en ce qui a trait à l'évaluation est jaugée au moyen du modèle suivant :

$$CAR_i = a_0 + a_1 R\Delta EPS_i + a_2 RCURADJ1_i + a_3 RCURADJ2_i + \varepsilon_i \qquad (1)$$

où CAR_i est la somme des rendements quotidiens bêta de la New York Stock Exchange ou de l'American Stock Exchange, obtenus du Center for Research in Security Prices, excédant un intervalle de mesure, pour l'exercice-société i ; $R\Delta EPS_i$ est la variation dans le bénéfice premier par action avant postes extraordinaires et abandons d'activités, à l'exclusion des gains ou pertes de change, de l'exercice-société i, pondéré par le cours de l'action au début de l'exercice ; $RCURADJ1_i$ représente les gains ou pertes de change indiqués dans l'état des résultats de l'exercice-société i et $RCURADJ2_i$ représente la variation dans les gains ou pertes de change cumulatifs entre l'exercice $t - 1$ et l'exercice t inscrits dans le bilan de l'exercice- société i ; et ε_i est le résidu de CAR_i, tandis que les a_j ($j = 0, 1, 2, 3$) sont des paramètres qui doivent être estimés. L'autre hypothèse, selon laquelle les *SFAS* n° 8 et n° 52 avec le dollar comme monnaie d'exploitation (le *SFAS* n° 52 avec une monnaie étrangère comme monnaie d'exploitation) ont produit des gains ou pertes de change résultant de la conversion pertinents à l'évaluation, suppose $a_2 > 0$ ($a_3 > 0$).

Un choix important, dans le plan de recherche sous-jacent au modèle empirique, a trait à la mesure de la variable dépendante, CAR_i, sur un intervalle de douze mois par opposition à un intervalle de deux jours avant ou après la publication des bénéfices. En général, la relation entre une variable comptable qui présente un intérêt (par exemple, les bénéfices ou les flux de trésorerie imprévus) et les rendements peut être explorée grâce à une méthodologie basée sur l'étude d'« événement » ou l'étude d'« association ». Dans l'estimation du modèle (1), toutefois, il convient de recourir à la méthodologie d'association, compte tenu de l'impossibilité de déterminer quand, au cours de la période étudiée, l'information relative aux gains ou pertes de change résultant de la conversion a été incorporée dans le cours des actions. Cela tient au fait que les investisseurs observent, au terme de l'exercice, la fluctuation de la valeur du dollar au cours de la période, et qu'ils ont observé l'incidence des fluctuations passées du dollar sur les gains ou pertes de change résultant de la conversion. En s'appuyant sur cette information, les investisseurs devraient être en mesure de formuler des prévisions exemptes de distorsion en ce qui a trait aux gains ou pertes de change résultant de la conversion que déclare la société, et d'en tenir compte dans l'évaluation de cette dernière au moment de la décision. Ainsi donc, la plus grande partie de l'information contenue dans les gains ou pertes de change résultant de la conversion devrait être incorporée dans le cours des actions avant que cette information ne soit officiellement publiée. Bartov et Bodnar (1994) sont toutefois d'opinion que les investisseurs sous-estiment systématiquement l'incidence de la fluctuation de la valeur du dollar sur la valeur de la société et qu'ils ne rectifient cette erreur d'estimation que lorsqu'ils reçoivent de l'information supplémentaire au cours d'une période subséquente. Le problème que soulève la délimitation d'une courte période pendant laquelle l'information contenue dans les gains ou pertes de change résultant de la conversion est incorporée dans le cours des actions se complique davantage puisque ces gains ou pertes de change ne sont officiellement présentés que lorsque les états financiers sont intégralement publiés et non au moment de la déclaration préalable des bénéfices ; ainsi est-il difficile de déterminer la date à laquelle les investisseurs ont pour la première fois accès aux états financiers complets.

Étant donné que les états financiers annuels sont normalement mis à la disposition des investisseurs dans les trois mois qui suivent la clôture de l'exercice (voir, par exemple, Basu, 1983, et Ou et Penman, 1989), et que le marché est efficient en période de fermeté modérée (c'est-à-dire que le cours des actions incorpore immédiatement et sans distorsion l'information publiée), un intervalle de rendement de douze mois à compter du début du deuxième trimestre de l'exercice t jusqu'à la fin du premier trimestre de l'exercice $t + 1$ peut être utilisé pour tester la pertinence, en ce qui a trait à l'évaluation, des gains ou pertes de change résultant de la conversion, soit $RCURADJ1_i$ et $RCURADJ2_i$, qui figurent dans les états financiers. Il se peut toutefois que les sociétés publient leurs rapports annuels tardivement ou que les investisseurs éprouvent des difficultés à interpréter les gains ou pertes de change résultant de la conversion qui sont déclarés (voir, par exemple, Bartov et Bodnar, 1994). Dans un cas comme dans l'autre, la réaction du cours des actions à l'information concernant les gains ou pertes de change contenue dans les états financiers peut avoir lieu après l'intervalle de douze mois. Pour

tenir compte de cette possibilité, il faut donc prévoir un intervalle de rendement supplémentaire. Cet intervalle consiste dans une période de soixante jours de négociation,
à compter du début du deuxième trimestre de l'année $t + 1$.

L'auteur ne décèle aucune relation significative entre les gains ou pertes de change
résultant de la conversion qui sont déclarés et les variations des cours des actions dans
le cas de l'application du *SFAS* n° 8 (la méthode temporelle), mais une association positive significative dans le cas du *SFAS* n° 52. Cette association positive est toutefois trib-
utaire de la monnaie d'exploitation choisie : une association importante est observée
seulement chez les sociétés qui choisissent une monnaie étrangère comme monnaie
d'exploitation (c'est-à-dire qui optent pour la méthode du taux courant), et non chez les
sociétés qui choisissent le dollar comme monnaie d'exploitation (c'est-à-dire, qui
préfèrent continuer de présenter l'information conformément au *SFAS* n° 8).

Pris dans leur ensemble, ces résultats donnent à penser que les règles de conversion
des états financiers établis en monnaie étrangère dans le *SFAS* n° 8 (méthode temporelle)
livrent une piètre mesure comptable du risque économique de conversion qu'assument
les sociétés multinationales aux États-Unis, et que l'adoption du *SFAS* n° 52 a grande-
ment amélioré l'utilité de la conversion des états financiers établis en monnaie étrangère
dans l'évaluation des sociétés. Cette amélioration ne vaut cependant que pour le sous-
ensemble des sociétés qui ont choisi une monnaie étrangère comme monnaie d'exploitation (c'est-à-dire qui ont opté pour la méthode du taux courant). Donc, même si le
choix du dollar comme monnaie d'exploitation (conformément à la méthode temporelle), par ailleurs permis par le *SFAS* n° 52, se justifie parfois sur le plan conceptuel
dans certaines circonstances — lorsque, par exemple, les établissements étrangers font
partie intégrante de l'établissement de la société mère ou en sont le prolongement (voir
le *SFAS* n° 52, paragraphe 6) —, et même si le *SFAS* n° 52 (annexe A) aide à la déter-
mination de la monnaie d'exploitation, l'analyse empirique réalisée par l'auteur ne con-
firme pas la pertinence des données comptables issues de ce choix, en ce qui a trait à
l'évaluation. Ce résultat et les inconvénients que comporte la possibilité pour les
sociétés de choisir une méthode comptable (un choix qui a, par exemple, pour effet de
réduire les possibilités de comparaison des sociétés, ce qui constitue précisément l'un
des avantages de l'information comptable), peuvent servir de toile de fond à la réévaluation du caractère souhaitable de la perspective des monnaies multiples avalisée par le
SFAS n° 52.

Néanmoins, puisque les sociétés qui choisissent le dollar comme monnaie d'exploitation peuvent être économiquement différentes de celles qui optent pour une monnaie étrangère, et puisque le choix de la monnaie d'exploitation reflète (en partie) des
disparités économiques réelles entre les deux sous-ensembles de sociétés, les sociétés
qui choisissent le dollar comme monnaie d'exploitation ne font pas toutes nécessaire-
ment un moins bon choix. Quoi qu'il en soit, il ne serait pas opportun de trop insister
sur ce point, puisque, dans bon nombre de cas, on observe des choix de méthodes de
conversion qui diffèrent dans des contextes pourtant très similaires à l'intérieur d'un
secteur d'activité donné. Citons, par exemple, le cas de Texaco, Occidental et Unocal
qui ont opté pour le dollar comme monnaie d'exploitation, tandis qu'Exxon, Mobil et
Amoco ont choisi une monnaie étrangère (voir Helns, 1986, p. 139).

In response to changes in the international monetary system (i.e., the switch
from fixed to flexible exchange rates) and the increasing complexity of foreign
operations, the Financial Accounting Standards Board (FASB) issued
Statement of Financial Accounting Standards (*SFAS*) No. 8, in October 1975.
SFAS No. 8, which requires firms to use the temporal method in translating

financial statements of their foreign operations into US dollars, elicited severe criticism, ranging from "inadequate" to "misleading," from market participants and managers. Its replacement, *SFAS* No. 52, issued in December 1981, attempted to improve on the methods of *SFAS* No. 8 by allowing firms translating financial statements of their foreign operations to select either the temporal method or the current rate method.[1]

Extant evidence supporting the inadequacy of *SFAS* No. 8 or an improvement in the quality of the reporting associated with *SFAS* No. 52 consists only of anecdotal and conflicting empirical findings. Whereas Collins and Salatka (1993) conclude that the market perceives the earnings of firms using the temporal method to be of lower quality, Gilbert (1989) and Soo and Soo (1994) find no significant differences between the two translation methods. The latter results are surprising, because the temporal and currentrate methods have substantially different approaches to the translation of foreign financial statements.[2] Consequently, these two translation methods produce very different measures of the translation gain or loss, which have a material effect on the financial statements of multinational companies.[3] Furthermore, because neither method revaluates the foreign operation's assets and liabilities to market before translation, neither captures the full effects of the exchange rate change on firm value during the period.

This study thus directly examines two questions: did *SFAS* No. 8 produce relevant information for valuing US multinational firms, and are the results reported under *SFAS* No. 52 more valuation relevant than those reported under SFAS No. 8? Valuation relevance is studied because the FASB has stated that relevance is an important criterion for choosing among alternative accounting methods.[4] I test these research questions empirically by examining the association between foreign currency translation adjustments related to alternative foreign currency translation methods and changes in stock prices.

The results show no significant relation between reported currency translation adjustments and changes in stock prices for *SFAS* No. 8 (the temporal method), but a positive and significant association for *SFAS* No. 52. This positive association, however, is conditional on the functional currency chosen: a significant association is observed only for firms designating a foreign currency as the functional currency (i.e., switching to the current-rate method), not for firms designating the dollar as the functional currency (i.e., as if they still reported under *SFAS* No. 8).

Considered collectively, these results suggest that the foreign currency translation rules in *SFAS* No. 8 (the temporal method) produce a poor accounting measure of the foreign currency economic exposure of US multinational firms, and that the introduction of *SFAS* No. 52 has resulted in a significant improvement in the valuation relevance of foreign currency translation reporting. However, this improvement applies only to the subset of firms that have designated a foreign currency as their functional currency (i.e., switched to the current-rate method). Thus, although choice of the dollar as the functional currency (i.e., the temporal method), allowed by *SFAS* No. 52, can be conceptual-ly justified under certain circumstances — such as foreign operations that are an integral component or extension of the parent's operation (see *SFAS* No. 52, paragraph 6) — and although SFAS No. 52 (Appendix A) provides guidance for determination of the functional currency, the valuation relevance of the accounting numbers produced by this choice is not supported by this paper's empirical analysis. This result and the disadvantages inherent in allowing the use of alternative accounting methods (e.g., a reduction in comparability between firms, which is one of the characteristics that make accounting infor-mation useful)[5] might provide a backdrop for reassessing the desirability of the multiple currency perspective permitted by *SFAS* No. 52.

However, because firms selecting the dollar as the functional currency may be economically different from firms selecting the foreign currency as the func-tional currency, and because the selection of functional currency (partially) reflects real economic differences between the two subsamples of firms, it fol-lows that not all firms selecting the dollar as the functional currency are nec-essarily making an inferior choice. Still, this point should not be overempha-sized, because in many cases different choices of translation methods are observed even in substantially similar circumstances within a particular indus-try. For example, while Texaco, Occidental, and Unocal settled on the dollar as the functional currency, Exxon, Mobil, and Amoco chose the foreign currency as the functional currency (Helns 1986).

The remainder of this article is organized into five sections. Now the moti-vation and the research questions to be addressed are discussed. Next the arti-cle outlines the model used in the empirical tests and discusses econometric issues associated with these tests. The following section describes the sample selection procedure, and the next presents the empirical results and contrasts them with previous literature. The final section briefly summarizes the main findings and interpretations.

Motivation and research questions

The SFAS No. 8 question
As mentioned previously, under the temporal method monetary items are trans-lated at the current rate, whereas nonmonetary items are translated at rates that preserve their original measurement bases. Consequently, if exchange rate changes affect the value (in dollar terms) of the monetary assets and liabilities of the foreign operation, but have no effect on the value of its nonmenatary assets valued at cost, the translation gain or loss produced by the temporal method will capture the effects of exchange rate changes on the net investment in the foreign operation. If, however, nonmonetary assets and liabilities provide a (natural) hedge for each other, the reported translation gain or loss of the tem-poral method will be misleading, because it fails to account for the fact that translation gains (losses) on liabilities are hedged (i.e., offset) by correlated

translation losses (gains) on nonmonetary assets. Furthermore, because under the current rate method all assets and liabilities are translated at the current rate, it follows that the measure of the translation gain or loss produced by this method, although imperfect, will come much closer to capturing the valuation effect of the total exchange gain or loss than the temporal method.

It is hard to imagine a case where foreign operations' assets and liabilities do not provide a fairly effective hedge for each other. Therefore, it is not that surprising that the introduction of *SFAS* No. 8 elicited severe criticism from market participants, managers, and researchers. To begin, in May, 1978, the FASB invited comments from the public on *SFAS* Nos. 1–12, each of which had been in effect less than two years. *SFAS* No. 8 was the subject of most of the more than 200 responses received. Many respondents said that foreign currency economic exposure on foreign currency debt is effectively hedged by operating assets and foreign currency revenue potential, but that this natural hedge was ignored by *SFAS* No. 8's temporal method. This deficiency in *SFAS* No. 8 resulted in an artificial fluctuation in reported earnings, which obscured the operating performance of US multinational companies. Another adverse outcome was that the foreign currency accounting exposure and the associated currency translation adjustment under *SFAS* No. 8 were at odds with the foreign currency economic exposure of a firm (see FASB 1981, Appendix D). More evidence is provided by Massaro (1978), who surveyed 117 corporate executives familiar with *SFAS* No. 8 and found that 60 executives favored repeal of the statement and 24 executives favored substantial modification or amendment. This opposition arose chiefly because *SFAS* No. 8 made the income figure excessively vulnerable to changes in foreign exchange rates.[6]

These deficiencies have also been recognized by researchers. Selling and Sorter (1983, 65), for example, noted that "under this standard, economic gains often resulted in accounting losses. For example, the use of the temporal method meant that economically related items ... were translated at different rates ... , so that a translation gain or loss resulted even though these items, in a sense, serve as economic hedges for each other." Interestingly, in explaining the reasons for issuing *SFAS* No. 52, the FASB also recognized that *SFAS* No. 8 "produced results that the Board and many other constituents believe do not reflect the underlying economic reality of many foreign operations and thereby produces results that are not relevant" (FASB 1981, Appendix C, paragraph 63).

SFAS No. 8 thus seems to have been widely perceived as producing inadequate accounting measures of the foreign currency economic exposure of US multinational firms.[7] However, these perceptions are based primarily on anecdotal evidence and intuition rather than on convincing empirical findings. My first research question therefore directly investigates whether these perceptions can be supported empirically. More specifically, it asks whether *SFAS* No. 8 produced relevant information for valuing US multinational firms.

The SFAS No. 52 question
SFAS No. 52, in an effort to improve on the methods in *SFAS* No. 8, sought to
provide investors with "information that is generally compatible with the
expected economic effects of a rate change on an enterprise's cash flows and
equity" (FASB 1981, Paragraph 4). It recognized, however, that this task is a
formidable one because "foreign operations differ greatly in structure and substance. In some situations, only certain assets and liabilities are exposed to foreign exchange risk, whereas in others the entire foreign operation or net investment is exposed to foreign exchange risk. These differences can significantly
change the economic effect of exchange rate fluctuations" (FASB 1981,
Appendix C, paragraph 67). After extensive consideration, however, *SFAS* No.
52 concludes that the method associated with a foreign currency as the functional currency "has the most conceptual merit, particularly for foreign operations that are reasonably self-contained. It will result in reports of financial
condition and results of operations that, within the constraints of the historical
cost model, will most closely reflect economic effects" (FASB 1981, Appendix
C, paragraph 66).[8]
     The findings of recent empirical research seem to suggest that this effort
by the FASB to improve on the methods of *SFAS* No. 8 was not in vain. Griffin
and Castanias (1987) document that, relative to a set of control firms, the accuracy of analysts' earnings forecasts improved when the sample firms designated a foreign currency as the functional currency. Ziebart and Kim (1987)
demonstrate that the stock prices of US multinational firms reacted negatively
to the introduction of *SFAS* No. 8 and positively to *SFAS* No. 52. Collins and
Salatka (1993) study two-day abnormal stock returns around the quarterly earnings announcements of 27 multinational firms during the period 1976–87 and
report (weak) results suggesting an increase in the earnings response coefficients (ERCs) of firms that chose a foreign currency as the functional currency.[9] They interpret their findings as evidence that "the market perceives the
earnings of firms to be of lower quality if they use the US dollar as the functional currency and carry translation gain/losses to the income statement"(p.
122). These results, however, are clouded by findings in Gilbert (1989), who
uses a sample of 343 firms and annual data and finds no significant difference
in ERCs between the two accounting standards.
     SFAS No. 52 thus seems to have alleviated many of the problems arising
from *SFAS* No. 8. Still, its new method brought forth new criticism on both
conceptual and practical levels. For example, Selling and Sorter (1983) demonstrate by a numerical example that the balance sheet and income statement
numbers produced under *SFAS* No. 52 with a foreign currency as the functional currency may be difficult to interpret under certain circumstances, and E. I.
Du Pont de Nemours & Company point out that operations that seem profitable
under *SFAS* No. 52 with a foreign currency as the functional currency may actually be unprofitable from a US dollar perspective (see Wojciechowski 1982).
This discussion suggests that determining whether *SFAS* No. 52 did, in fact,

improve on the methods in *SFAS* No. 8 is largely an open empirical matter. Thus, my second research question reads as follows: is the information report- ed under *SFAS* No. 52 more relevant for valuing US multinational firms than the information under *SFAS* No. 8?[10]

Methodology

Empirical model

The research questions are empirically tested by estimating the association between alternative foreign currency translation adjustments (related to alter- native translation methods) reported on the financial statements of US multi- national companies and stock price changes. Foreign currency translation adjustments capture the impact of the change in the dollar on the net investment in the foreign operation, and thus they are expected to be important for explain- ing firm value. This expectation is confirmed by the findings of this study (reported later in Table 3), which demonstrate that foreign currency translation adjustments are economically significant (i.e., material relative to firm value). Thus, if currency translation adjustments provide relevant information about the impact of the change in the dollar on firm value, a positive correlation between these variables and stock returns should be observed. Therefore, the valuation relevance of the numbers produced by each translation method is assessed by the following model:

$$CAR_i = a_0 + a_1 R\Delta EPS_i + a_2 RCURADJ1_i + a_3 RCURADJ2_i + \varepsilon_i \qquad (1)$$

where CAR_i is the sum of the (Center for Research in Stock Prices (CRSP) New York Stock Exchange (NYSE)/American Stock Exchange (AMEX)'s) daily beta excess returns over a measurement interval (specified below) for firm year i. $R\Delta EPS_i$ is the change in primary earnings per share before extra- ordinary items and discontinued operations, exclusive of the foreign currency adjustment, of firm year i, scaled by the stock price at the beginning of the year.[11] $RCURADJ1_i$ is the foreign currency adjustment reported in the annual income statement of firm year i, and $RCURADJ2_i$ is the change from year $t - 1$ to year t in the cumulative translation adjustment entry reported on the balance sheet of firm year i.[12] ε_i is the CAR_i residual, and the a_j ($j = 0, 1, 2, 3$) are para- meters to be estimated. In the context of equation (1), the hypothesis that *SFAS* No. 8 and *SFAS* No. 52 with the dollar as the functional currency produced val- uation relevant currency translation adjustments implies $a_2 > 0$; the alternative hypothesis for *SFAS* No. 52 with a foreign currency as the functional currency implies $a_3 > 0$.

There are three important research design choices underlying the empirical model that differentiate this study from prior research (e.g., Collins and Salatka 1993).[13] First, the dependent variable, CAR_i, is measured over a twelve-month window as opposed to a two-day interval around the earnings announcement. In general, the relation between an accounting variable of interest (e.g., unexpected earnings or cash flows) and returns can be explored by using either an "event" study or an "association" study methodology.[14] In estimating model (1), however, the latter must be used, because it is impossible to determine when in the period the information in the currency translation adjustment was assimilated into stock prices. This reasoning follows because at the end of the year investors observe the change in the value of the dollar over this period and have observed the impact of past dollar changes on currency translation adjustments. Based on this information, investors should be able to form unbiased expectations about the reported foreign currency adjustments and incorporate this effect into firm value by this time. This approach suggests that most of the information in the currency translation adjustment should be incorporated into stock prices prior to its formal release. However, Bartov and Bodnar (1994) find that investors systematically underestimate the impact of the change in the value of the dollar on firm value and that this underestimation is corrected only when additional information is disclosed during a subsequent period. The problem of identifying a short period during which the information in the currency translation adjustment is assimilated into stock prices is further complicated because the currency translation adjustment is formally disclosed only when the full financial statements are released — not when the preliminary earnings announcements are made — and because it is difficult to determine the date when the full financial statements first become available to investors.

Because it is standard to assume that annual financial statements are available to investors within three months of the end of the fiscal year (see, e.g., Basu 1983, and Ou and Penman 1989),[15] and that the market is efficient in the semistrong form (i.e., stock prices immediately and unbiasedly incorporate public information), a twelve-month return interval from the beginning of the second quarter of year t through the end of the first quarter of year $t + 1$ can be used to test the valuation relevance of reported foreign currency adjustments $RCURADJ1_i$ and $RCURADJ2_i$. However, companies may issue their annual reports late,[16] and/or investors may have difficulties in interpreting reported foreign currency adjustments (see, e.g., Bartov and Bodnar 1994). In either case, the stock price response to information on foreign currency adjustments in the financial statement may occur beyond the twelve-month interval. To allow for this possibility, an additional return interval is used. This interval is measured over a sixty-trading-day window from the beginning of the second quarter of year $t + 1$.

The second research design choice concerns the separation of foreign currency translation adjustments from earnings when used as explanatory variables. Four reasons motivate this choice. First, drawing inferences from ERCs about the relative valuation relevance of foreign currency translation numbers produced by alternative accounting methods is problematic because the income from foreign currency translation of most companies is only a (small) part of their net earnings. As a result, even a small variation in the valuation relevance of earnings from domestic operations between the two samples confounds any effects of foreign currency translation on the ERCs. This problem may explain why Gilbert (1989) and Collins and Salatka (1993), who used similar methodologies and different samples, arrived at opposite conclusions. A second reason is that this separation allows inferences about the valuation relevance of each method by itself; the inference is not restricted only to the relative informativeness of the two methods. Furthermore, separating currency translation adjustments from earnings allows one to evaluate not only the valuation relevance of the foreign currency translation adjustment numbers reported on the income statement, but also that of the numbers reported directly on the balance sheet, bypassing the income statement.[17] A third reason is that, although annual earnings (without the currency translation adjustment component) are generated by a random walk process and thus annual earnings changes are appropriate proxies for earnings surprises (see, e.g., Ball and Watts 1972), as explained later in detail, levels, not changes, of the currency translation adjustments are the appropriate variables for the unexpected translation adjustment. Thus, separating the currency translation adjustments from earnings should have the desirable effect of reducing noise in the explanatory variables. Finally, Ohlson and Penman (1992) show an improvement in fit between returns and earnings when different components of earnings are considered separately, rather than combined into a "bottom line" number.

The third research design choice involves the form in which the currency translation adjustments enter the regression. Levels of the adjustments as opposed to first differences are the appropriate variables because the adjustments are (approximately) serially uncorrelated random variables with a mean of zero. This result follows because the translation adjustment is calculated as the product of the firm's exposed net asset position and the change in the value of the dollar for the accounting period, and because changes in the value of the dollar are (approximately) serially uncorrelated random variables with a mean of zero (see, e.g., Frenkel 1981, Jorion 1990, and Bartov and Bodnar 1994).[18]

An econometric issue
Equation (1) relies on the assumption (among others) of a linear relation between the dependent and explanatory variables. Evidence in recent empirical studies (see, e.g., Cheng, Hopwood, and McKeown 1992; Freeman and Tse 1992) suggests that this assumption may not hold for the return/earnings relation, nor is there a compelling reason to expect the relation between foreign currency adjustments and returns to be linear. One way to address this problem is to model first, and then estimate a nonlinear relation, as in Freeman and Tse (190). However, theory does not provide guidance on the nature of the nonlinear relation, and thus the estimates of the model parameters will be only as reliable as the ad hoc model in use. In addition, whereas Freeman and Tse's model has only one explanatory variable, the model used here has three, making it more difficult to identify an appropriate nonlinear model. Under these circumstances, regression on ranks becomes a useful alternative because it provides a

method for estimating a nonlinear relation without having to specify a particular nonlinear model. The procedure is based on the fact that when two variables have a monotonic relation, their ranks will have a linear relation (see, e.g., Conover 1980). The ranks serve as transformed variables, where the transformation converts the monotonic nonlinear relation into a linear equation. An additional advantage of regression on ranks is its relative insensitivity to non-normal distributions or outliers, which often exist in accounting data pooled over firms and time (see, e.g., Lee 1985).

The advantages of regression on ranks over the traditional ordinary least squares (OLS) regression in the context of the return/earnings relation were demonstrated by Cheng et al. (1992). They assess the effect of specification errors on accounting research that examines the return/earnings relation by first replicating the (traditional) analysis of Cornell and Landsman (1989, 592–5) and then comparing it to regression on ranks. The results show that the rank transformation was successful in substantially increasing the explanatory power of the model, as well as in alleviating specification errors of the traditional analysis (e.g., Table 2 demonstrates that the ranked regressions yielded stable and relatively large t-values for the parameter estimates, whereas the traditional regressions yielded erratic and generally smaller t-values).

This discussion clearly suggests the use of regression on ranks, rather than on the actual values themselves, for the current study. Replacing the explanatory variables by their ranks, however, results in parameter estimates whose values are (partially) dependent on the number of observations in the sample.[19] To address this undesirable consequence, the ranks, which are determined by year, are scaled by the annual number of observations so that the value of each of the ranked variables in each year ranges from $1/N_t$ to 1, where N_t is the number of observations in year t.[20]

The Sample
The sample covers the fifteen-year period from 1976 to 1990. This period is divided into two subperiods: an *SFAS* No. 8 period, 1976 through 1981, and an *SFAS* No. 52 period, 1984 through 1990. In the spirit of the extant literature in the area (e.g., Collins and Salatka 1993), data for the two-year period 1982–83 are omitted because (1) this was the transition period during which some companies adopted *SFAS* No. 52 early and others adopted it later (see, e.g., Ayers 1986), and (2) there is evidence in prior research that investors require time to understand the implications of a change in accounting standards for the relation between the resultant accounting numbers and firm value (e.g., Griffin and Castanias 1987).[21]

The data were retrieved from two sources. Abnormal returns were taken from the CRSP NYSE/AMEX Excess Return series, which contains daily returns for each stock in the database in excess of the daily returns on a portfolio of similar risk (i.e., same beta decile) stocks. Risk is determined by CRSP using beta values, which are estimated using the method developed by Scholes

Foreign Currency Exposure of Multinational Firms: Accounting Measures . . .   635

and Williams (1977). Accounting data were retrieved from the COMPUSTAT Expanded Annual Industrial and Full Coverage File.

Table 1 summarizes the sample selection procedure. First, COMPUSTAT was searched for firms with reported currency translation adjustments on their income statements, balance sheets, or both.[22] This search yielded 12,734 firm-year observations. Next, 1,693 firm years were dropped because they lacked the required accounting data on COMPUSTAT, which reduced the sample size to 11,041.[23] Missing return data in the CRSP NYSE/AMEX Excess Return series further reduced the sample size to 6,724 observations. Finally, the exclusion of the two-year transition period, 1982–83, decreased the sample size to 5,724 firm-year observations. The sample size for the *SFAS* No. 52 period (580 observations per year on average, 4,059 total observations) is more than double the sample size for the *SFAS* No. 8 period (277 observations per year on average, 1,665 total observations). This difference represents the increasing internationalization of US companies during the last decade.

TABLE 1
Sample selection

	SFAS No. 8	*SFAS* No. 52	Total
Firm years for the period 1976–90 with reported currency translation adjustments on their annual financial statements	2,845	9,889	12,734
Required COMPUSTAT data not available	341	1,352	1,693
Required CRSP data not available	580	3,737	4,317
Exclusion of transition period (1982–83)	259	741	1,000
Final sample size	1,665	4,059	5,724

Table 2 reports the distribution of sample firms by accounting rules for foreign currency translation and major standard industrial classification (SIC) groupings.

Two phenomena are evident. First, the industry distribution is roughly similar for both *SFAS* No. 8 and *SFAS* No. 52 as well as across different choices of functional currency under *SFAS* No. 52. Second, a broad cross-section of industries is represented in all subsamples.

TABLE 2

Industry distribution of sample firm-years by accounting rules for foreign currency translation and major standard industrial classification (SIC) groupings

Group	SIC Codes	SFAS # 8	%	SFAS # 52 by functional currency						
				Foreign currency	%	Dollar	%	Foreign currency and dollar	%
Agriculture	100–999	4	0.24	0	0	0	0	7	0.43
Mining	1000–1499	60	3.60	117	5.65	31	8.20	72	4.47
Construction	1500–1999	32	1.92	33	1.60	10	2.64	23	1.43
Food	2000–2199	89	5.34	98	4.74	20	5.29	74	4.60
Textile	2200–2399	12	0.72	52	2.52	1	0.26	10	0.62
Wood	2400–2599	10	0.60	18	0.87	0	0	7	0.44
Paper and printing	2600–2799	66	3.96	134	6.47	21	5.55	55	3.42
Chemicals	2800–2999	334	20.0	185	8.94	48	12.6	337	20.93
Plastic, glass, cement	3000–3299	51	3.06	86	4.15	4	1.05	57	3.54
Steel and machinery	3300–3999	722	43.3	845	40.80	142	37.5	785	48.76
Transportation and utilities	4000–4999	57	3.42	54	2.60	59	15.6	45	2.80
Wholesale	5000–5199	39	2.34	99	4.78	0	0	27	1.67
Retail	5200–5999	47	2.82	82	3.95	5	1.32	14	0.87
Financial services	6000–6999	60	3.60	63	3.04	22	5.82	30	1.86
Other services	7000–8999	82	4.92	205	9.89	15	3.96	62	3.85
Missing		0	0	0	0	0	0	5	0.31
Totals		1665	100	2071	100	378	100	1610	100

Table 3 displays a comparison between firms under *SFAS* No. 8 and firms under *SFAS* No. 52 with respect to four descriptive statistics: annual foreign currency translation adjustments, foreign currency exposure, market value of common equity, and leverage. Consistent with conventional wisdom that most US multinational firms have negative foreign currency exposure (see, e.g., Sease 1991), the mean and median reported currency translation adjustment are negative (positive) for the *SFAS* No. 8 (*SFAS* No. 52) period, corresponding to the positive (negative) change in the value of the dollar during the period. The (accounting) foreign currency exposure is economically significant for both subsamples; it is, however, larger for the *SFAS* No. 8 period. This result may

TABLE 3

Descriptive statistics for sample firm years by accounting standard for foreign currency translation

	SFAS No. 8 (1976–81)			SFAS No.52 (1984–90)			Two-sample z-statistic
	Mean	Median	Std	Mean	Median	Std	probability*
Percentage annual foreign currency translation adjustments†							
As reported	0.45	−0.13	3.41	0.20	0.08	7.19	0.00
In absolute values	1.10	0.39	3.26	1.48	0.55	7.04	0.00
Foreign currency exposure‡	0.55	0.11	1.52	0.39	0.08	2.52	0.00
Market value of common equity ($million)	1,345.92	318.69	3,352.44	2,057.27	488.13	5,209.47	0.00
Leverage¤	0.17	0.17	0.12	0.19	0.17	0.16	0.32
Percentage annual change in the US$#							
Actual	0.48	1.18	7.32	−4.91	−7.51	10.61	0.00
In absolute values	5.38	4.81	4.38	9.72	11.59	5.54	0.00

Notes:
* The z-statistic tests for equality of medians across the two accounting standards, using a two-sample median test.
† The annual foreign currency translation adjustment is per share and is scaled by the stock price at the beginning of the fiscal year.
‡ Foreign currency exposure is the foreign currency translation adjustment reported in the annual financial statement divided by the change in the value of the US dollar relative to the trade-weighted exchange rate index (see note (#) below). The foreign currency exposure is scaled by the market value of common equity at the beginning of the year.
¤ Leverage is the ratio of the book value of long-term debt to total assets.
The change in the value of the dollar is relative to a trade-weighted exchange rate index (among the G-7 countries) used by the International Monetary fund (IMF) in calculating its Multilateral Exchange Rate Model (MERM) exchange rate index.

reflect either more aggressive risk-management behavior by firms in the later subperiod or merely differences in accounting rules for calculating accounting exposure between the two standards.[24] Table 3 also shows that firm value is higher for the *SFAS* No. 52 period, in line with the general increase in firm value of COMPUSTAT firms between the late 1970s and the late 1980s, and that, as expected, US multinational firms are relatively large and have low leverage.

Finally, Table 4 reports the correlation coefficients for every pair of independent variables used in the analysis. The results clearly indicate that some of the explanatory variables are correlated. However, these correlation coefficients are rather small; the highest is −0.07, when the Pearson coefficient is

TABLE 4

Pairwise correlation among explanatory variables

Panel A: Pairwise correlation coefficients among the explanatory variables in
Table 5 ($n = 1665$)

	$R\Delta EPS$	$RCURADJ1$
$R\Delta EPS$	1.00	-0.07^*
$RCURADJ1$	-0.05^*	1.00

Panel B: Pairwise correlation coefficients among the explanatory variables in
Table 6 ($n = 4059$)

	$R\Delta EPS$	$RCURADJ1$	$RCURADJ2$
$R\Delta EPS$	1.00	$-0.02\dagger$	-0.06^*
$RCURADJ1$	$-0.01\dagger$	1.00	$0.02\dagger$
$RCURADJ2$	-0.04^*	$0.01\dagger$	1.00

Notes:

Spearman (Kendall) coefficients are reported above (below) the diagonal. $R\Delta EPS_i$ is the change in primary earnings per share before extraordinary items and discontinued operations, exclusive of foreign currency adjustment, for firm year i, scaled by beginning-of-the-year stock price. $RCURADJ1_i$ is the foreign currency translation adjustment reported in the annual income statement of firm year i, and $RCURADJ2_i$ is the change from year $t-1$ to year t in the cumulative translation adjustment entry reported on the balance sheet of firm year i; both variables are deflated by the market value of common equity at the beginning of the year. All variables are replaced by their ranks, which are calculated by year and then scaled by the number of yearly observations.

* Significant at the one-percent level for two-tailed tests.

† Insignificant at the five-percent level for two-tailed tests.

estimated for the correlation between $R\Delta EPS$ and $RCURADJ1$ (reported in panel A). This indicates that multicollinearity probably does not represent a serious problem for my sample.

Empirical results

Did SFAS No. 8 produce valuation relevant information?

Parameter estimates for equation (1) and their p-values based on the twelve-month return interval for firms using *SFAS* No. 8 appear at the top of Table 5.[25] The estimate of the coefficient on the annual earnings change is, as expected, positive and significant at conventional levels. In contrast, the estimate of the coefficient on the foreign currency adjustment is statistically insignificant at conventional levels. This finding is consistent with the claim that *SFAS* No. 8 produced numbers of low quality.

Foreign Currency Exposure of Multinational Firms: Accounting Measures . . .   639

TABLE 5

SFAS No. 8: Rank regression tests for the association between foreign currency translation adjustments and stock returns ($n = 1665$)

Model: $CAR_i = a_0 + a_1 R\Delta EPS_i + a_2 RCURADJ1_i + \varepsilon_i.$*

Expected sign:	?	+	+		
Estimation period	a_0	a_1	a_2	Model p-value†	Adjusted R^2
Second quarter of	−0.315	0.409	0.032	0.000	16.27%
year *t* through first	(0.00)	(0.00)	(0.11)		
quarter of year *t* + 1	[0.03]	[0.02]	[0.28]	[0.031]	[16.31]
Sixty trading days	−0.031	0.013	−0.016	0.136	0.12
from the beginning	(0.00)	(0.12)	(0.93)		
of the second quarter of year *t* + 1	[0.03]	[0.42]	[0.84]	[0.093]	[0.71]

Notes:
Observed significance levels (p-values) for one-tailed tests for a_1 and a_2 and two-tailed tests for
the intercept are in parentheses (standard errors are based on White's 1980 correction).
Alternative p-values and adjusted R^2, given in brackets, are calculated by estimating regressions
for each year in 1976–81 (using only firms with a December fiscal year end) and applying a
Wilcoxon signed rank test on each estimate's time series. Under the alternative hypothesis of
positive association between currency translation adjustments and stock returns, $a_2 > 0$.
* CAR_i is the sum of CRSP NYSE/AMEX's daily beta excess returns over the indicated
     estimation periods for firm year *i*. $REPS_i$ is the change in primary earnings per share before
     extraordinary items and discontinued operations, exclusive of foreign currency adjustment,
     for firm year *i*, scaled by the beginning-of-the-year stock price. $RCURADJ1_i$ is the foreign
     currency adjustment reported in the income statement of firm year *i*, scaled by the beginning-
     of-the-year stock price.
†   Tests the hypothesis that all model parameters (excluding the intercept) are zero.

     Table 5 also displays parameter estimates based on the sixty-trading-day
return interval. A positive estimate of the coefficient on the foreign currency
adjustment for this return interval would suggest that the failure to document a
positive association between foreign currency adjustments and changes in
stock prices using a twelve-month return interval represents a delayed disclosure of, or a delayed market reaction to, foreign currency adjustments, rather
than poor information. This estimate, however, is negative. This finding cor-
roborates the interpretation of the previous result and perhaps even suggests
that SFAS No. 8 produced accounting numbers at odds with economic reality.

Does SFAS No. 52 improve the reporting of foreign currency translation?
Preliminary evidence: the full sample
Parameter estimates for equation (1) and their p-values based on the twelve-
month return interval and the sixty-trading-day return interval for firms using
SFAS No. 52 appear in Table 6. The estimate of the coefficient on the foreign

currency translation adjustment reported when the dollar is the functional currency, a_2, is insignificant for the twelve-month interval and negative for the sixty-trading-day return interval. These results suggest that the temporal method under *SFAS* No. 52 fails to capture the effects of exchange rate changes, and thus they are consistent with the findings reported in the previous table, which indicated that the temporal method under *SFAS* No. 8 produced numbers of low quality. Still, these new results are somewhat surprising because they indicate that the temporal method provides a poor accounting measure even for the subset of firms that selected this method presumably on the basis of the guideline introduced by *SFAS* No. 52.[26]

Conversely, the estimate of the coefficient on the foreign currency translation adjustment reported when a foreign currency is the functional currency, a_3, is positive and significant at conventional levels for the sixty-day interval. Furthermore, an F-test indicates that a_3 is significantly larger than a_2 for that interval. These results clearly suggest that the option for managers to use the current rate method, introduced by *SFAS* No. 52, did indeed improve on the temporal method underlying *SFAS* No. 8. For the twelve-month return interval, however, the results in Table 6 show that the alternative t-test fails to reject $a_3 = 0$, and an F-test for the hypothesis $a_3 > a_2$ also fails.[27] One way to interpret this difference in the findings for a_3 between the two intervals is that there is a delay between the time in which financial statements are first released — sometime within the twelve-month interval — and the time (i.e., the ensuing sixty-day period) in which the effects of exchange rate changes captured by the reported translation gain or loss are incorporated into stock prices. This interpretation is consistent with findings in Bartov and Bodnar (1994), which indicated that investors experience difficulties in interpreting reported foreign currency adjustments. An alternative explanation for these findings is that the sample firms issue their annual report late. Finally, it is important to note that: (1) because the difference between a_2 and a_3 is observed in a cross-section, the alternative explanation — that the strengthening of the coefficients represents some temporal trend unrelated to the introduction of *SFAS* No. 52 — is unlikely,[28] and (2) the finding that a_1 and a_3 are significant as hypothesized, increases confidence that our regressions are able to detect correlations if they exist.

To study further the effects of *SFAS* No. 8 and *SFAS* No. 52 on the informativeness of financial statements, the ERCs reported in Table 5 are compared with those in Table 6. This comparison is along the lines of Holthausen and Verrecchia's (1988) model, which implies that the magnitudes of ERCs are positively related to the quality of earnings releases.[29] It is evident that the ERCs for the *SFAS* No. 8 period (Table 5) are quite similar to those for the *SFAS* No. 52 period (Table 6). This result means that, excluding the impact of foreign currency adjustments, there is no difference in the price response to a given amount of unexpected earnings between firms reporting under *SFAS* No. 8 and firms reporting under *SFAS* No. 52. In contrast to this result, Collins and Salatka (1993, Table 6) find that ERCs under *SFAS* No. 52 are higher than

TABLE 6
SFAS No. 52: Rank regression tests for the association between foreign currency translation adjustments and stock returns ($n = 4059$).

Model: $CAR_i = a_0 + a_1 R\Delta EPS_i + a_2 RCURADJ1_i + a_3 RCURADJ2_i + \varepsilon_i.$ *

Expected sign: ?   +   +   +

Estimation Period	a_0	a_1	a_2	a_3	Model p-value[†]	Adjusted R^2
Second quarter of	−0.244	0.384	0.012	0.030	0.000	12.32%
year t through first	(0.00)	(0.00)	(0.24)	(0.03)		
quarter of year $t + 1$	[0.01]	[0.01]	[0.97]	[0.41]	[0.015]	[15.00]

Test of alternative hypothesis: $a_2 < a_3$, $F(1,4055) = 0.53$, p-value $= 0.53$.

	a_0	a_1	a_2	a_3		
Sixty trading days	−0.031	0.031	−0.015	0.029	0.000	0.67
from the beginning	(0.00)	(0.00)	(0.95)	(0.00)		
of the second quarter of year $t + 1$	[0.10]	[0.07]	[0.98]	[0.01]	[0.031]	[0.64]

Test of alternative hypothesis: $a_2 < a_3$, $F(1,4055) = 13.04$, p-value $= 0.00$.

Notes:
Observed significance levels (p-values) for one-tailed tests for a_1, a_2, and a_3 and two-tailed tests for the intercept are in parentheses (standard errors are based on White's 1980 correction). Alternative p-values and adjusted R^2, given in brackets, are calculated by estimating regressions for each year in 1984–90 (using only firms with a December fiscal year end) and applying a Wilcoxon signed rank test on each estimate's time series. Under the alternative hypothesis of positive association between currency translation adjustments and stock returns, $a_2 > 0$, $a_3 > 0$; under the alternative hypothesis that a foreign currency as the functional currency produced more relevant and reliable currency translation adjustment numbers than the dollar ás the functional currency, $a_2 < a_3$.
* CAR_i is the sum over the indicated estimation periods of CRSP NYSE/AMEX's daily beta excess returns. $R\ EPS_i$ is the change in primary earnings per share before extraordinary items and discontinued operations, exclusive of foreign currency adjustment, for firm year i, scaled by the beginning-of-the-year stock price. $RCURADJ1_i$ is the foreign currency translation adjustment reported in the annual income statement of firm-year i, and $RCURADJ2_i$ is the change from year $t − 1$ to year t in the cumulative translation adjustment entry reported on the balance sheet of firm-year i; both variables are deflated by the market value of common equity at the beginning of the year. All regressors are replaced by their ranks, which are calculated by year and then scaled by the number of yearly observations.
†   Tests the hypothesis that all model parameters (excluding the intercept) are zero.

ERCs under *SFAS* No. 8. This difference probably results from the difference in research designs between the two studies — unlike Collins and Salatka, the unexpected earnings variable in this study excludes currency translation adjustments. These findings thus suggest that the differences with respect to measuring and reporting the currency translation adjustment, which captures a firm's exposed net asset position, fully account for the difference in the ERCs across the two accounting standards documented by Collins and Salatka. Other differences that might have led to distorted operating margins under *SFAS* No. 8 (e.g., sales revenues and cost of goods sold were translated into dollars at the same exchange rate under *SFAS* No. 52 but at different rates under *SFAS* No. 8) do not appear to have a significant impact on the relation between stock prices and income numbers.[30]

A closer look: Partitioning the sample by functional currency

The analysis so far has assumed that the switch to *SFAS* No. 52 had a uniform impact on all multinational firms. This assumption, however, may be invalid because different companies made different choices under *SFAS* No. 52. In particular, US multinational companies designated a foreign currency, the dollar, or a combination of the two as their functional currency. To determine whether the valuation relevance of the foreign currency adjustments varies across these three sets of firms, equation (1) is estimated by the choice of the functional currency under *SFAS* No. 52.

Table 7 reports the regression results for equation (1) by functional currency. Similar to the results reported in Table 6, panels A and C of Table 7 show that, when firms select either the foreign currency or a combination of the dollar and a foreign currency as their functional currency, the estimates of a_3 (the coefficient on the translation adjustment reported when the foreign currency is the functional currency) for the sixty-day return interval are positive and significant. Furthermore, the F-statistic reported in panel C demonstrates that a_3 exceeds a_2 (the coefficient on the translation adjustment reported when the dollar is the functional currency) for the subsample of firms selecting a combination of the dollar and a foreign currency as the functional currency. The tests reported in panels A and C for a_3 for the twelve-month return interval, however, appear inconclusive.

The results in panels B and C of Table 7 also demonstrate that, when firms select either the dollar or a combination of the dollar and a foreign currency as their functional currency, estimates of a_2 are insignificant at conventional levels for all intervals and appear similar to the estimates of a_2 given in both Table 6 and Table 5.[31] Overall, the findings in Table 7 reinforce the results in Table 5 and Table 6. Collectively, they suggest that *SFAS* No. 52 has improved on the method underlying *SFAS* No. 8. However, this improvement occurs only for firms selecting a foreign currency as the functional currency (i.e., switching to the current rate method); no improvement is observed for firms designating the dollar as the functional currency (i.e., as if they still reported under *SFAS* No. 8).

Foreign Currency Exposure of Multinational Firms: Accounting Measures . . .   643

TABLE 7
SFAS No. 52: Rank regression tests by functional currency for the association between foreign currency translation adjustments and stock returns

Model: $CAR_i = a_0 + a_1 R\Delta EPS_i + a_2 RCURADJ1_i + a_3 RCURADJ2_i + \varepsilon_i.$ [*]

Panel A: The functional currency is a foreign currency:

Expected sign:		?	+	NA	+		
Estimation						Model	Adjusted
period	n	a_0	a_1	a_2	a_3	p-value[†]	R^2
Second quarter of	2071	−0.273	0.423	NA	0.052	0.000	14.76%
year t through first		(0.00)	(0.00)	NA	(0.01)		
quarter of year $t + 1$		[0.02]	[0.01]	NA	[0.23]	[0.015]	[16.45]
Sixty trading days	2071	−0.047	0.042	NA	0.039	0.000	1.01
from the beginning		(0.00)	(0.00)	NA	(0.00)		
of the second quarter		[0.01]	[0.05]	NA	[0.04]	[0.218]	[1.08]
of year $t + 1$							

Panel B: The functional currency is the dollar:

Expected sign:		?	+	+	NA		
Estimation						Model	Adjusted
period	n	a_0	a_1	a_2	a_3	p-value[†]	R^2
Second quarter of	378	−0.233	0.446	−0.077	NA	0.000	13.47%
year t through first		(0.00)	(0.00)	(0.91)	NA		
quarter of year $t+1$		[0.04]	[0.01]	[0.85]	NA	[0.015]	[14.46]
Sixty trading days	378	−0.076	0.070	0.035	NA	0.046	1.09%
from the beginning		(0.00)	(0.02)	(0.13)	NA		
of the second quarter		[0.57]	[0.23]	[0.47]	NA	[0.046]	[4.86]
of year $t+ 1$							

Panel C: The functional currency is a combination of a foreign currency and the dollar:

Expected sign:		?	+	+	+		
Estimation						Model	Adjusted
period	n	a_0	a_1	a_2	a_3	p-value[†]	R^2
Second quarter of	1610	−0.192	0.311	0.017	0.012	0.000	8.69%
year t through first		(0.00)	(0.00)	(0.24)	(0.31)		
quarter of year $t + 1$		[0.03]	[0.01]	[0.66]	[0.04]	[0.015]	[12.77]

Test of alternative hypothesis: $a_2 < a_3$, $F(1,1606) = 0.02$, p-value $= 0.88$.

Sixty trading days	1610	−0.007	0.004	−0.029	0.026	0.011	0.50
from the beginning		(0.52)	(0.36)	(0.99)	(0.02)		
of the second quarter		[0.37]	[0.08]	[0.98]	[0.04]	[0.687]	[−0.27]
of year $t + 1$							

Test of alternative hypothesis: $a_2 < a_3$, $F(1,1606) = 10.68$, p-value $= 0.00$.

Notes:
Observed significance levels (*p*-values) for one-tailed tests for a_1, a_2, and a_3 and two-tailed tests for the intercept are in parentheses (standard errors are based on White's 1980 correction). Alternative *p*-values and adjusted R^2, given in brackets, are calculated by estimating regressions for each year in 1984–90 (using only firms with a December fiscal year-end) and applying a Wilcoxon signed rank test on each estimate's time series. Under the alternative hypothesis of positive association between currency translation adjustments and stock returns, $a_2 > 0$, $a_3 > 0$; under the alternative hypothesis that a foreign currency as the functional currency produced more relevant and reliable currency translation adjustment numbers than the dollar as the functional currency, $a_2 < a_3$.

* CAR_i is the sum over the indicated estimation periods of CRSP NYSE/AMEX's daily beta excess returns. $R\ EPS_i$ is the change in primary earnings per share before extraordinary items and discontinued operations, exclusive of foreign currency adjustment, for firm year *i*, scaled by the beginning-of-the-year stock price. $RCURADJ1_i$ is the foreign currency translation adjustment reported in the annual income statement of firm year *i*, and $RCURADJ2_i$ is the change from year $t - 1$ to year t in the cumulative translation adjustment entry reported on the balance sheet of firm year *i*; both variables are deflated by the market value of common equity at the beginning of the year. All regressors are replaced by their ranks, which are calculated by year and then scaled by the number of yearly observations.

† Tests the hypothesis that all model parameters (excluding the intercept) are zero.

Related research on foreign currency translation reporting: Soo and Soo (1994)
The sections that developed the research questions and described the previous findings already contrasted the methodologies and results of prior studies with those of the current study, highlighting its contribution. As might be expected, the results of the current study generally extend rather than contradict the results of previous research, and there is no reason to repeat the comparison here. As mentioned earlier, however, one exception is Soo and Soo (1994). Their results appear largely inconsistent with the results of this study. This section thus compares and attempts to reconcile the two sets of results.

Soo and Soo (1994, 630) claim that their results "are generally consistent with the market using the foreign currency gain and loss information reported in income, as well as the foreign translation gain and loss included in stockholders' equity." Conversely, for the full sample, I find no evidence that the market uses foreign currency translation information reported in income, nor did I expect to find such evidence. Can this difference be reconciled?

In an effort to provide such a reconciliation, I closely examine first the validity of the inference and then the validity of the findings of Soo and Soo(1994). Reading across their Table 4, I note that the estimate on their FORIS variable (foreign currency gain or loss reported in income statement) is statistically significant for the period 1976–82, but markedly smaller (it falls from 0.3610 to 0.0657) and statistically insignificant for the period 1981–87. So it seems that Soo and Soo document conflicting and puzzling findings that do not allow for the type of conclusion they reached.[32]

Of course, an interesting question concerns the inconsistency in findings between their two periods. It seems that one potential explanation lies in their research design, which uses a "one size fits all" type of rule for dealing with outlying observations. That is, they "exclude all firm years with scaled absolute explanatory variables in excess of 0.10" (p. 623). No explanation is provided as to why or how this arbitrary number was picked, nor do they explain why the same truncation rule was applied uniformly for all variables. Applying the same rule uniformly seems problematic, because the explanatory variables come from markedly different distributions (see their Table 2). Thus, for certain variables the truncation might be effective, for others it may not. Evidence in their Table 2 provides some idea of the effectiveness of this rule. For example, whereas the mean foreign currency in income for losses is –0.099, the minimum value is –7.21095, which lies 554 standard errors from the mean.[33] Thus, the instability in the estimates on FORIS between the two subsamples observed in their tables 4 and 5 may be caused by a few outlying observations. An additional clue that points in this direction is found in their footnote 12, which acknowledges that the parameter estimate on FORIS was insignificant for their full sample period (1976–87) when the untruncated data were used.

To evaluate further the validity of Soo and Soo's (1994) findings, I reestimate equation (1) of my study by using *CAR* accumulated over a three-day window around earnings announcements as the dependent variable and by handling outliers three different ways: ignoring the problem (using the original untruncated data), truncating the data using Soo and Soo's rule, and replacing the values of the explanatory variables by their ranks.[34] Table 8 reports the results, which clearly support the conjecture that Soo and Soo's findings for the early sample period are most likely driven by a few outliers. Although for all three regressions the parameter estimates on the unexpected earnings variable are highly significant, they are statistically insignificant on the foreign currency translation variable for the truncated and ranked data and statistically significant with the wrong sign for the original (untruncated) data.

TABLE 8
SFAS No. 8: Tests for the association between foreign currency translation adjustments and stock returns around earnings announcements

Model: $CAR_i = a_0 + a_1R \ EPS_i + a_2RCURADJ1_i + \varepsilon_i.^*$

Expected sign: ?   +   +

Method of dealing with outliers	n	a_0	a_1	a_2	Model p-value[†]	Adjusted R^2
Original sample (no truncation)	1626	–0.000 (0.44)	0.037 (0.00)	–0.086 (0.05)	0.000	2.46%
Outliers truncated by the Soo and Soo's rule	1373	–0.001 (0.29)	0.112 (0.00)	0.034 (0.43)	0.000	0.98
Original data replaced by ranks	1626	–0.123 (0.00)	0.023 (0.00)	0.000 (0.95)	0.000	2.43

Notes:
Observed significance levels (*p*-values) for two-tailed tests are in parentheses. The sample period is 1976–82. Under the alternative hypothesis of positive association between currency translation adjustments and stock returns, $a_2 > 0$.

646   Contemporary Accounting Research

* CAR_i is the sum of daily abnormal returns in the three days –2 to 0 relative to the earnings announcement date (day 0) of firm year i. Daily abnormal returns are the differences between daily returns of firm i and the returns for NYSE-AMEX firms of the same size decile, based on January 1 market values of equity. $R\Delta EPS_i$ is the change in primary earnings per share before extraordinary items and discontinued operations, exclusive of foreign currency adjustment, for firm year i, scaled by the beginning-of- the-year stock price. $RCURADJ1_i$ is the foreign currency adjustment reported in the income statement of firm year i, scaled by the beginning-of-the-year stock price. Soo and Soo's truncation rule excludes all firm years with explanatory variables in excess of 0.10 in absolute values. When using ranks, all regressors are replaced by their ranks, which are calculated by year and then scaled by the number of yearly observations.

† Tests the hypothesis that all model parameters (excluding the intercept) are zero.

Summary and interpretations

This article presents empirical tests of the association between foreign currency translation adjustments related to alternative translation methods employed by US multinational firms and changes in stock prices. A reported foreign currency translation adjustment measures the sensitivity of a firm's book value to changes in foreign exchange rates. If currency translation adjustments are relevant for valuing US multinational firms, they should be positively associated with changes in stock prices.

From the mid-1970s to the early 1980s under GAAP, foreign financial statements were translated into dollars using the temporal method (*SFAS* No. 8); since 1983, management has had a choice between the temporal method and the current rate method (*SFAS* No. 52). *SFAS* No. 8 had been widely perceived as producing inadequate accounting measures of the foreign currency economic exposure of US multinational firms. *SFAS* No. 52 sought to cure these inadequacies. However, extant evidence to support the inadequacy of *SFAS* No. 8 or an improvement in the quality of the reporting associated with *SFAS* No. 52 consists only of anecdotal and mixed indirect empirical findings. The two research questions addressed in this study are as follows: did *SFAS* No. 8 produce relevant information for valuing US multinational firms, and are the results reported under *SFAS* No. 52 more value relevant than those reported under *SFAS* No. 8?

The results show that for *SFAS* No. 8 there is no observed relation between currency translation adjustments and changes in stock prices. Thus, *SFAS* No. 8's foreign currency translation rules did produce a poor measure for valuing US multinational firms. For *SFAS* No. 52, however, there is a significant positive association between currency translation adjustments and changes in stock prices for firms designating the foreign currency as the functional currency, but no relation for firms choosing the dollar their functional currency (as if they still reported under *SFAS* No. 8).

These results suggest that the introduction of *SFAS* No. 52 resulted in a significant improvement in the quality of foreign currency translation reporting for those US multinational firms that designate a foreign currency as the functional currency. And, although a management choice of the dollar as the functional currency is warranted theoretically under certain circumstances, the val-

Foreign Currency Exposure of Multinational Firms: Accounting Measures . . .   647

uation relevance of the accounting numbers based on this choice cannot be supported empirically.

Endnotes

1   There are two differences between the two reporting methods for foreign currency translation: (1) measurement — the temporal exchange rate vs. the current rate (discussed later in detail) and (2) placement — reporting the translation gain or loss (i.e., the currency translation adjustment) in the income statement vs. directly on the balance sheet. Because the FASB has bundled the two issues together so that the translation adjustment associated with the temporal (current rate) method is reported in the income statement (balance sheet), I will identify each reporting method by its translation measurement method only.

2   According to the temporal method, monetary items (e.g., cash, receivables, and payables) are translated at the current rate, whereas nonmonetary items are translated at rates that preserve their original measurement bases: assets carried in the balance sheet of the foreign operation at historical cost (current values) are translated at the historical (current) rate. Conversely, the procedures of the current rate method involve translating all assets and liabilities at the current rate and capital accounts at the historical rate. For more details see Choi and Mueller (1992), for example.

3   A translation gain or loss (i.e., a foreign currency translation adjustment) arises from the restatement of a foreign operation's financial statements denominated in a foreign currency into the parent's (domestic) currency equivalents, such as when financial statements of a Japanese subsidiary, expressed in Japanese Yen, are restated into dollar-based statements for inclusion, by either consolidation or the equity method, in the parent company's financial statements.

4   See FASB *Statement of Financial Accounting Concepts* No. 2, 1980. Relevant accounting information helps users update expectations about the future prospects of a firm.

5   See FASB *Statement of Financial Accounting Concepts* No. 2, 1980.

6   For a detailed analysis of many potential drawbacks of *SFAS* No. 8. See, for example, Aggarwal (1978).

7   Findings of one study (Soo and Soo 1994) seem inconsistent with this conclusion. However, it appears that this study is plagued with serious flaws that make its findings unreliable. This study is discussed in detail later.

8   Beaver and Wolfson (1982) and Goldberg and Godwin (1994) analyze theoretically alternative combinations of accounting models and translation methods from two perspectives: economic interpretability and symmetry (for the definitions of these two notions see Beaver and Wolfson, 529). Although their analysis implies that in perfect and complete markets neither *SFAS* No. 8 nor *SFAS* No. 52 possesses the property of economic interpretability, it is silent as to which method is preferable from this perspective.

9   ERC is the slope coefficient from a return/earnings regression.

10 The paper's two research questions are positive (descriptive), not normative (prescriptive). In general, it is well known that normative statements about accounting policies are difficult to make outside a restrictive certainty framework (see, e.g., Beaver and Demski 1979).

11 Earnings surprises are included as explanatory variables because prior research (see, e.g., Ball and Brown 1968, and Beaver 1968) has demonstrated that they have significant explanatory power for changes in stock prices. Using earnings changes ($R\Delta EPS_i$) as a proxy for earnings surprises has been advocated by several studies (see, e.g., Ball and Watts 1972) and has widespread acceptance in

market-based accounting research. Few studies, however, have suggested the use of earnings levels, rather than or in addition to, earnings changes. Although this may be advantageous under some circumstances, I opted to use the more traditional and widely used procedure of regressing abnormal returns on earnings changes to allow comparison between my results and those of Collins and Salatka (1993). Still, I replicated the analysis using earnings levels, rather than earnings changes, and obtained similar results.

12　Two points: (1) all explanatory variables in this study are scaled by the market value of common equity at the beginning of the year to alleviate problems that might arise because of cross-sectional differences in firm size and to make them dimensionally consistent with returns (see, e.g., Christie 1987); (2) for some firms, $RCURADJ1_i$ represents gains or losses from foreign currency transactions as well as from foreign currency translation, whereas $RCURADJ2_i$ represents only gains or losses from foreign currency translation. This fact works against finding differences between the dollar and a foreign currency as functional currencies in the direction hypothesized, because foreign currency transaction gains or losses are easily measured and have a direct impact on cash flow. (Foreign currency transaction gains or losses result from a change in exchange rates between the reporting currency of the parent company and the currency in which a foreign currency transaction — for example, sales or purchases of goods or services — is denominated.)

13　These choices might not have been appropriate for Collins and Salatka (1993,121), because their purpose was to provide ("...evidence about the factors that contribute to differences in the return/earnings relation across firms and over time. Unlike the previous work in this area, however, the present analysis focuses on how differences in the perceived quality of earnings signals manifest themselves in different ERCs," which is different from the purpose of my study.

14　In an event study, returns are measured over a short interval (i.e., a few days) around the announcement date, whereas in an association study longer windows are used (e.g., fiscal quarters or even years). The choice of the length of the event window involves a tradeoff. Whereas windows that are too wide increase the noise-to-signal ratio and thereby decrease the power of the experiment, windows that are too narrow might exclude the event of interest and thereby bias the parameter estimate on the accounting variable that captures that event toward zero.

15　Firms are required to file their annual reports (10-K) with the Security and Exchange Commission (SEC) within 90 days of the end of their fiscal year.

16　Alford, Jones, and Zmijewski (1994) find that 19.8 per cent of companies file their 10-K Form with the SEC late. In addition, more than 40 per cent of the firms with a December fiscal year end that do comply with the 90-day rule file on March 31 (the very last day), and their reports become available publicly only in April.

17　This evaluation is absent from Collins and Salatka (1993), because their objective was to evaluate the effect of the choice of foreign currency translation method on earnings quality, not to evaluate the quality of the numbers produced under each method.

18　There are other, less important, differences between the research design of this study and that of Collins and Salatka (1993). Whereas I use a sample of over a thousand distinct firms, annual data, a statistical method that is robust to nonlinearity and outliers, standard as well as alternative p-values, and a sample period ending in 1990, they use 27 distinct firms, quarterly data, standard OLS analysis, standard p-values, and a sample period ending in 1987.

19   Along the lines of prior accounting research (e.g., Cheng,Hopwood, and McKeown 1992), the dependent variable was not transformed because unlike the independent (accounting) variables, returns (the dependent variable) are well-behaved, especially for long windows.

20   Two types of sensitivity tests were performed by replicating all regression tests (1) using the actual data (excluding outliers) for all variables, and (2) replacing the dependent as well as the independent variables by their ranks. These supplementary tests yielded qualitatively similar results. For parsimony, these results are not reported.

21   *SFAS* No. 52 was issued in December 1981 and became effective for fiscal years beginning on or after December 15, 1982, with early adoption encouraged. Unlike Collins and Salatka (1993), I did not eliminate 1981 because *SFAS* No. 52 was issued at the end of 1981 and became effective in 1983, and because I also report alternative *p*-values using yearly regressions. The elimination of 1981 had little effect on the results.

22   The first difference in the Retained Earnings,Cumulative Translation Adjustment was taken to identify the foreign currency translation adjustment reported directly on the balance sheet.

23   The accounting data include Retained Earnings-Cumulative Translation Adjustment (item 230), Foreign Currency Adjustment-Income Account (item 150), Price-Close- Fiscal-Year-End (item 199), Common Shares Used to Calculate Earnings per Share-Primary (item 54), Earnings per Share-Primary (item 58), Common Shares Outstanding (item 25), and Adjustment Factor-Cumulative (item 27).

24   The latter explanation is less plausible as in most cases *SFAS* No. 8 will produce smaller, not larger, accounting exposure than *SFAS* No. 52.

25   Due to concerns about cross-sectional dependence in stock returns that results in overstated standard *p*-values, the tables that follow display alternative *p*-values in addition to the standard *p*-values for the pooled data. These alternative *p*-values are calculated by first estimating yearly regressions (using only firms with a December fiscal year end) and then testing the regression estimates' time series.

26   A potential flaw underlying this test is that zero values are assigned to the variable *RCURADJ*1 for firms using only a foreign currency as the functional currency, which may reduce the power of the test. The analysis in panel B and panel C of Table 7, however, shows that this is not a severe problem, as a_2 remains insignificant in tests constructed in a manner that *RCURADJ*1 is assigned only its actual (nonzero) values.

27   The standard *t*-test for the pooled regression does reject $a_3 = 0$; however, this statistic seems unreliable because it is likely to be overstated due to cross-sectional dependence in stock returns.

28   In addition, this alternative explanation is inconsistent with the fact that there is no significant difference between the ERCs reported in Table 5 and Table 6.

29   This implication is conditional, however, on the (perhaps strong) assumption that a number of unobservable factors (e.g., the quality of predisclosure information and the variance of the underlying cash flows) are controlled. Also, their model specifically shows that the quality of earnings releases is positively associated with the variance of price changes, but the result can be extended to the relation between the quality of earnings and ERCs.

30   For a discussion of potential distortions in operating income caused by *SFAS* No. 8, see, for example, White, Sondhi, and Fried (1994, 958–60).

31   The estimate for a_2 in panel C, sixty-day interval, would have been significantly negative had two-tailed tests been used. This result is consistent with the claim,

discussed previously, that the numbers produced by the method associated with *SFAS* No. 8 and *SFAS* No. 52 with the dollar as the functional currency are at odds with economic reality.

32   The redundant results reported in their Table 5 do not clarify the issue. The results in panel A, for example, involve testing the stability of the parameter estimate on FORIS between the two sample subperiods. Although the results show that the dummy interaction variable for FORIS is significant (t-statistic of 1.63, which is significant at 5.15 per cent for one-tailed tests), they claim it is not. If one accepts their interpretation that the dummy is insignificant and that there is no change in the estimate on FORIS between the two periods, the inference that the FORIS variable is informative depends on the way the test is set up. If instead the dummy is set to one for the period 1976–81 and zero otherwise, the conclusion will be that FORIS is not informative.

33   Although in the their regressions Soo and Soo (1994) scaled all their explanatory variables by stock price at the beginning of the year, their Table 2 provides descriptive statistics scaled by absolute net income. This difference explains why the minimum value here is less then their cutoff point of 0.1. However, it is unlikely to resolve the problem of outliers in the regressions because a firm's net income and stock price are highly correlated.

34   Although for this analysis, the sample period (1976–82) and the return window (three days around earnings announcements) I use are identical to those of Soo and Soo (1994), there are some differences between my analysis and that of Soo and Soo. Specifically, I use earnings changes rather than errors in analyst forecasts of earnings as a proxy for earnings surprises. Also, I obtained earnings announcement dates and values for the *CAR* variable from a file that was created eight years ago for another project. Therefore, *CAR* is size adjusted, not risk adjusted. For three-day windows, this should not have an effect on the results.

References

Aggarwal, R. 1978. *FASB* no. 8 and reported results of multinational operations: Hazard for managers and investors. *Journal of Accounting, Auditing, and Finance* 3 (Spring): 197–216.

Alford, A., J. J. Jones, and M. E. Zmijewski. 1994. Extensions and violations of the statutory SEC form 10-k filing requirements. *Journal of Accounting and Economics* 17 (1/2): 229–54.

Ayers, F. L. 1986. Characteristics of firms electing early adoption of *SFAS* no. 52. *Journal of Accounting and Economics* 8 143–58.

Ball, R., and P. Brown. 1968. An empirical evaluation of accounting income numbers. *Journal of Accounting Research* 6 (2): 159–78.

Ball R., and R. L. Watts. 1972. Some time series properties of accounting income. *Journal of Finance* 27 (3): 663–81.

Bartov, E., and G. M. Bodnar. 1994. Firm valuation, earnings expectations and the exchange-rate exposure effect. *Journal of Finance* 49 (5): 1755–85.

Basu, S. 1983. The relationship between earnings yields, market value, and return for NYSE common stocks: Further evidence. *Journal of Financial Economics* 12 (1): 129–56.

Beaver, W. H. 1968. The Information Content of Annual Earnings Announcements. *Journal of Accounting Research* 6 (Supp.): 67–92.

———, and J. S. Demski. 1979. The nature of income measurement. *Accounting Review* 54 (1): 38–46.

———, and M. Wolfson. 1982. Foreign currency translation and changing prices in perfect and complete markets. *Journal of Accounting Research* 20 (2): 528–50.

Cheng, C. S. A., W. S. Hopwood, and J. C. McKeown. 1992. Non-linearity and
    specification problems in unexpected earnings response regression model.
    Accounting Review 67 (3): 579–98.
Choi, F. D. S., and G. G. Mueller. 1992. *International accounting.* 2nd ed. Englewood
    Cliffs, N.J.: Prentice-Hall.
Christie, A. A. 1987. On cross-sectional analysis in accounting research. *Journal of
    Accounting and Economics* 9 231–58.
Collins, D. W., and W. K. Salatka. 1993. Noisy accounting earnings signals and
    earnings response coefficients: The case of foreign currency accounting.
    Contemporary Accounting Research 10 (1): 119–60.
Conover, W. J. 1980. *Practical nonparametric statistics.* 2nd ed. New York: John
    Wiley & Sons.
Cornell, B., and W. A. Landsman. 1989. Security price response to quarterly earnings
    announcements and analysts' forecast revisions. *Accounting Review* 64 (4):
    680–92.
Financial Accounting Standards Board (FASB). *Statement of Financial Accounting
    Concepts* 1980. No. 2: Qualitative characteristics of accounting information.
    Norwalk, CT: FASB .
————.*Statement of Financial Accounting Standards* 1975. No. 8: Accounting for
    translation of foreign currency transactions and foreign currency financial
    statements. Norwalk, CT: FASB.
————. 1981. No. 52: Foreign currency translation. Norwalk, CT: FASB.
Freeman, R. N., and S. Y. Tse. 1992. A nonlinear model of security price responses to
    unexpected earnings. *Journal of Accounting Research* 30 (2): 185–209.
Frenkel, J. 1981. Flexible exchange rates, prices, and the role of news: Lessons from
    the 1970s. *Journal of Political Economy* 89 (4): 665–705.
Gilbert, L. R. 1989. The effect of *SFAS* 52 on earnings expectations. Ph.D. dissertation
    Boston University, Boston, Mass.
Goldberg, R. S., and J. H. Godwin. 1994. Foreign currency translation under two cases
    integrated and isolated economies. *Journal of International Financial
    Management and Accounting* 5 (2): 97–119.
Griffin, P. A., and R. P. Castanias. 1987. *Accounting for translation of foreign
    currencies: The effect of statement 52 on equity analysts.* Norwalk, CT: FASB.
Helns, John. 1986. Plenty of opportunity to fool around. *Forbes* (June 2): 139– 40.
Holthausen, R. W., and R. E. Verrecchia. 1988. The effect of sequential information
    releases on the variance of price changes in an intertemporal multi-asset market.
    Journal of Accounting Research 26 (1): 82–106.
Jorion, P. 1990. The exchange rate exposures of U.S. multinationals. *Journal of
    Business* 63 (3): 331–45.
Lee, C. J. 1985. Stochastic properties of cross-sectional financial data. *Journal of
    Accounting Research* 23 (1): 213–27.
Massaro, V. G. 1978. Corporate experience with FASB statement no. 8. *Conference
    Board Information Bulletin* No. 4 New York: Conference Board.
Ohlson, J. A., and S. H. Penman. 1992. Disaggregated accounting data as explanatory
    variables for returns. *Journal of Accounting, Auditing and Finance* 7 (4): 553–73.
Ou, J. A., and S. H. Penman. 1989. Financial statement analysis and the prediction of
    stock returns. *Journal of Accounting and Economics* 11 (4): 295–329.
Scholes, M., and J. Williams. 1977. Estimating betas from nonsychronous data.
    Journal of Financial Economics 5 (3): 309–27.
Sease, Douglas R. 1991. The dollar rally: Hit on profits may drag down stock market
    ... . *Wall Street Journal* (July 8): C1.

652   Contemporary Accounting Research

Selling, T. I., and G. H. Sorter. 1983. FASB statement no. 52 and its implications for financial statement analysis. *Financial Analysts Journal* 39 (3): 64–9.

Soo, B. S., and L. G. Soo. 1994. Accounting for the multinational firm: is the translation process valued by the stock market? *Accounting Review* 69 (4): 617–38.

White, G. I., A. C. Sondhi, and D. Fried. 1994. The analysis and use of financial statements. New York: Wiley & Sons, Inc.

White, H. 1980. A heteroskedasticity-consistent covariance matrix estimator and a direct test for heteroskedasticity. *Econometrica* 48: 817–38.

Wojciechowski, S. R. 1982. Du Pont evaluates *SFAS* 52. *Management Accounting* 64 (1): 31–5.

Ziebart, D. A., and D. H. Kim. 1987. An examination of the market reactions associated with *SFAS* no. 8 and *SFAS* no. 52. *Accounting Review* 62 (2): 343–57.

[8]

ELSEVIER Journal of Accounting and Economics 24 (1997) 69–97

JOURNAL OF
Accounting
& Economics

The valuation of the foreign income of US multinational firms: a growth opportunities perspective

Gordon M. Bodnar[a,*], Joseph Weintrop[b]

[a] *Department of Finance, Wharton School, University of Pennsylvania, Philadelphia, PA 19104-6367, USA*
[b] *Department of Accounting, School of Business Administration, Baruch College, New York, New York 10010, USA*

Received 1 January 1995; received in revised form 1 April 1997

Abstract

We demonstrate the value-relevance of foreign earnings for US multinational firms by examining the associations between annual abnormal stock performance and changes in firms' domestic and foreign incomes. For 2570 firm-year observations between 1985 and 1993, both foreign and domestic earnings changes have significant positive associations with annual excess return measures; however, the association coefficient on foreign income is significantly larger than the association coefficient on domestic income. We demonstrate this larger association coefficient for foreign income is consistent with differences in growth opportunities between domestic and foreign operations. © 1997 Elsevier Science B.V. All rights reserved.

JEL classification: F23; M41

Keywords: Association coefficients; Growth opportunities; Foreign income

1. Introduction

During the last 25 years, US firms have substantially expanded their operations outside of the United States. Accounting regulators such as the Securities and Exchange Commission (SEC) and the Financial Accounting Standards

*Corresponding author. Tel.: (215) 898 4260; fax: (215) 898 6200; e-mail: bodnarg@wharton.upenn.edu.

0165-4101/97/$17.00 © 1997 Elsevier Science B.V. All rights reserved.
PII S0165-4101(97)00016-5

70   *G.M. Bodnar, J. Weintrop / Journal of Accounting and Economics 24 (1997) 69–97*

Board (FASB) have mandated that firms provide data on foreign operations. The maintained belief is that more data about these expanding foreign operations will contribute to better informed investors and more precise valuation of firms. This paper provides direct evidence on the association between foreign earnings and firm value based upon the firm's disclosure of its domestic and foreign earnings components as required by SEC Regulation §210.4-08(h), General Notes to Financial Statements – Income Tax Expense.

Utilizing this data on the breakdown of earnings into domestic and foreign components, we consider two questions: (1) are changes in the domestic and foreign components of earnings significantly associated with changes in the market value of the firm? and (2) are the domestic and foreign components of earnings capitalized by the market at a similar rate? For a sample of 2570 firm-year observations over fiscal years 1985–1993, we find that changes in both the domestic and foreign earnings components of US multinational firms are significantly associated with annual abnormal returns. However, foreign earnings changes are capitalized into stock price at a significantly higher rate than domestic earnings changes. This suggests that the market views foreign and domestic income changes differently for purposes of firm valuation.

We consider several possible economic explanations for this latter finding. We first consider whether the properties of exchange rate changes embedded in foreign earnings changes make foreign income changes more permanent than domestic earnings changes, resulting in the larger foreign association coefficient. After adjusting foreign earnings changes for the change in an average annual exchange rate, we find the association coefficient on the adjusted foreign earnings change remains significantly larger than the domestic association coefficient. We also consider the possibility that this finding is due to economic differences in the earnings streams. As previous research has demonstrated that association coefficients are increasing with the growth opportunities of a firm's operations (see, e.g., Collins and Kothari, 1989), we conjecture that this difference between foreign and domestic association coefficients is the result of greater opportunities for growth in foreign operations. Using foreign and domestic sales growth as proxies for the foreign and domestic growth opportunities of the firm, we find that there is a significant positive relation between the incremental foreign association coefficient and relative foreign and domestic growth opportunities. This suggests that firms with greater foreign growth opportunities than domestic growth opportunities have significantly larger foreign association coefficients.

To demonstrate that the findings are due to economic factors and not problems with our empirical framework, we consider several specification tests to check the robustness of our basic finding. Specifically, we consider several issues that could lead to observed differences in the foreign and domestic association coefficients when one does not exist economically. These issues are the timing/length of the return interval and problems with the simple specification of

G.M. Bodnar, J. Weintrop / Journal of Accounting and Economics 24 (1997) 69–97   71

the earnings expectations process. Although we demonstrate that these issues do affect the estimation of the segmental association coefficients, the basic finding of a significantly larger foreign association coefficient remains robust to these issues.

There is limited prior research on the value-relevance of the disclosure of foreign financial data on a firm's foreign operations. Kinney (1972) examines the association between market risk and the number of foreign segments. He finds a positive relation between risk and the number of reported geographic segments. More recently, Balakrishnan et al. (1990) study 89 firms from 1979 to 1983 that complied with the *Statement of Financial Accounting Standards FASB No. 14: Financial Reporting for Segments of a Business Enterprise* (Financial Accounting Standards Board (1978)) (henceforth SFAS No.14) mandated disclosure requirements and find weak evidence that geographic segment data provide enhanced predictive ability of annual income and sales data. Most recently, and more closely related to this paper, Boatsman et al. (1993) address the issue of the value-relevance of selected geographic segments of income for a sample of 970 firm-year observations using data from SFAS No.14. They find no evidence of a difference among the changes in the estimates of the coefficients of segmental earnings and excess returns for a 15 month window extending from the beginning of the fiscal year to the time of the filing of the Form 10-K (see Table 4, p. 62).[1] Below we discuss possible explanations for the difference between their results and our own and suggest that our findings are likely due to the use of SEC Regulation §210.4-08(h) data which provide a larger sample and a more powerful test.

The rest of this paper is as follows. Section 2 discusses our methodology and develops the our two hypotheses. Section 3 describes the mandated disclosure requirements and our sample selection. Section 4 contains the basic empirical tests on the association coefficients while Section 5 considers economic explanations for the differences in size. Section 6 considers the specification issues related to our tests and Section 7 concludes.

2. Methodology and hypothesis development

The methodology for the analysis builds on the relation between earnings and returns documented by Ball and Brown (1968) and the subsequent literature that identifies a positive relation between the unexpected change in total annual

---

[1] Boatsman et al. (1993) examine the value relevance of geographic income disclosures from SFAS No. 14 looking at both price reactions around the time of the release of the 10-K as well as long window associations of changes in geographic earnings with stock returns. While they find a few cases suggesting some value relevance for geographic disclosures, they conclude that "... there is little evidence that these disclosures affect equity values." (p. 46.)

72   *G.M. Bodnar, J. Weintrop / Journal of Accounting and Economics 24 (1997) 69–97*

earnings, $\Delta TERN_{i,t}$, and some measure of the change in the value of the firm, $\Delta V_{i,t}$.

$$\Delta V_{i,t} = \alpha_0 + \alpha_1 \Delta TERN_{i,t} + \varepsilon_{i,t}. \tag{1}$$

Unlike event studies that examine short windows around earnings announcements (or other events), we are interested in the relation between earnings changes and price changes over the reporting periods. This approach is commonly referred to as an association study.[2]

Common extensions of the association literature have been to decompose the annual earnings change into its longitudinal components (e.g., revenues, expenses, gross profits, and taxes) and to examine the associations between each component and returns (see, e.g., Lipe, 1986; Rayburn, 1986; Wilson, 1986). In contrast, we are interested in examining the association of the cross-sectional components of earnings based upon the location where the income is earned: at home or abroad. This breakdown of earnings is of interest from an economic perspective as it is likely that investors do not see these income streams as perfectly similar. Foreign operations offer both additional risks (exchange rate, political, different business cycles) as well as opportunities (new markets for growth). In addition, foreign operations face the problems of conducting operations at a distance, making it more difficult for domestic investors to obtain information about a firm's economic situation. These unique features of foreign income can cause investors to incorporate foreign income into firm value differently than they do domestic income.

The decomposition of total income into domestic and foreign components based upon US GAAP leads to the following respecification of Eq. (1):

$$\Delta V_{i,t} = \gamma_0 + \gamma_1 \Delta DERN_{i,t} + \gamma_2 \Delta FERN_{i,t} + \varepsilon_{i,t}, \tag{2}$$

where $\Delta DERN_{i,t}$ is the change in the domestic component of total annual earnings and $\Delta FERN_{i,t}$ is the change in the foreign component of total annual earnings. This decomposition allows us to examine several questions about the market's valuation of multinational firms' activities. First, are changes in the domestic and foreign components of earnings associated with changes in the market value of the firm? This question considers whether the market incorporates each income stream individually when valuing the firm and involves testing $\gamma_1 = 0$ and $\gamma_2 = 0$. Second, are the association coefficients on domestic and foreign earnings changes equal? As mentioned above, because foreign operations have exposures to risks and rewards that differ significantly from those faced domestically, it is possible that the market capitalizes foreign income streams into price differently than domestic income streams. This involves testing the null hypothesis that $\gamma_1 = \gamma_2$.

---

[2] Association studies have a long history in accounting for measuring value-relevance (see, e.g., Beaver and Dukes. 1972; Gonedes. 1973). Collins and Kothari (1989) provide a summary of studies and implied assumptions in the association literature.

G.M. Bodnar, J. Weintrop / Journal of Accounting and Economics 24 (1997) 69–97   73

One interesting aspect of this second question is that there are several economic arguments as to the relative size of the foreign and domestic association coefficient. On one hand, foreign earnings could be valued less highly than domestic earnings by the market because they are perceived to be less reliable and/or more uncertain. Foreign earnings numbers may be less reliable than domestic earnings because US GAAP practices for foreign currency accounting combine non-cash flow adjustments with actual cash flow numbers making it difficult to determine the implications of reported foreign earnings for future cash flows.[3] In addition, foreign earnings streams can be more uncertain in economic value as they can face restrictions and uncertainties from foreign governments such that their availability to shareholders is less certain than domestic earnings.[4] Moreover, if investors perceive foreign operations as riskier, in terms of greater non-diversifiable risk, then they will require a higher rate of return on foreign operations. This higher required rate of return implies a higher discount rate for foreign earnings than domestic earnings.[5] All of these influences suggest the foreign association coefficients should be lower than domestic association coefficients as the market would value an additional dollar of foreign earnings less highly than an additional dollar of domestic earnings.

Alternatively, there are influences suggesting that foreign association coefficients should be larger than domestic association coefficients. An extant literature in international finance (Frankel and Rose, 1995) suggests that exchange rate changes are virtually unforecastable and have a significant permanent component. This implies that changes in the dollar value of foreign earnings resulting purely from exchange rate changes are both unforecastable and permanent. Thus, when an increase in the dollar value of foreign earnings results from a depreciation of the dollar (a pure price effect), this increase is both unanticipated and expected to be permanent, resulting in an unexpected increase in the dollar value of foreign earnings into perpetuity. If exchange rate changes are more unexpected and permanent than underlying earnings changes, the influence of exchange rates on foreign earnings will lead to a higher association between foreign earnings changes and stock returns than domestic earnings changes and stock returns.[6]

---

[3] This is true of the temporal method of foreign currency consolidation used by foreign operations that have designated the US dollar as functional currency. For more on this problem, see Bartov and Bodnar (1996).

[4] See Saudagaran (1993).

[5] In a simple model, where earnings streams are assumed to evolve randomly and the value of the firm is equal to the present discounted value of the earnings stream, it is possible to show that the association coefficient between an earnings change and the market value of the firm will be equal to one over the market discount rate for that stream of earnings (see, e.g., Collins and Kothari, 1989).

[6] Permanent changes in earnings by definition should lead to a larger impact on price today as the present value of the impact on cash flows is larger than for a similar-sized temporary change in

An additional reason for larger foreign association coefficients relates to differential growth opportunities perceived by the market in foreign versus domestic operations. Previous research (see, e.g., Collins and Kothari, 1989) demonstrates that association coefficients are an increasing function of the growth opportunities in the total firm's activities. The split between domestic and foreign income allows us to independently look at these two segments. In the evolution of the firm, foreign operations typically follow the development of successful domestic operations. Foreign operations represent expansions into new, less exploited markets (see, e.g., Kogut, 1983; Stopford and Wells, 1972). Since foreign operations generally represent a minority of most US firms' total operations, given the size of the potential foreign market, the foreign markets offer greater potential for growth than the already more exploited domestic market. Because the opportunities for growth are greater abroad, successful foreign operations can be interpreted by the market as indicating the expectation of higher future foreign earnings. If foreign operations hold the possibility of greater growth than domestic operations, and earnings changes 'are an indication of the realizations of such growth opportunities, then one should expect a larger association between changes in firm value and foreign earnings changes than domestic earnings changes.

3. Mandated accounting disclosure requirements and sample selection

3.1. Mandated accounting disclosure requirements

The source of segment data to determine the annual domestic and foreign income come from a firm's compliance with the disclosure requirements of SEC Regulation §210.4-08(h), General Notes to Financial Statements-Income Tax Expense (henceforth Rule 4-08(h)).[7] This regulation requires that "... disclosure shall be made in the income statement or a note thereto, of (i) the components of income (loss) before income tax expense (benefit) as either

---

earnings. An earnings change that is perfectly unanticipated and permanent, by definition, should result in an association coefficient of approximately $1/r$, where r is the firm's discount rate. Of course this will only result in larger foreign association coefficients to the extent that changes in domestic earnings are more predictable or perceived to be less permanent. Easton and Harris (1991) argue that under the specification of earnings as a random walk, changes in earnings represent permanent components and levels of earnings represent temporary components. They include both earnings levels and changes in a single regression with returns and find the earnings response coefficient for changes to be higher than it is for levels.

[7] This regulation can be traced back to the General Revision of Regulation SX (Securities and Exchange Commission (1980)) and was first included in Compustat in 1984.

G.M. Bodnar, J. Weintrop / Journal of Accounting and Economics 24 (1997) 69–97   75

domestic or foreign;[8] (ii) the components of income tax expense, including (A) taxes currently payable, and (B) the net tax effects, as applicable, of timing differences" (17 CFR §210.4-08(h)(1)). Timing differences arise from foreign income because the US tax liability on most income of foreign subsidiaries of U.S. corporations is payable only when the income is repatriated;[9] if income is not currently repatriated, a deferred tax timing difference is created. To provide information on the nature of a firm's tax status, Rule 4-08(h) requires disclosure of data on the domestic and foreign components of pre-tax income and the related tax calculations.[10] The disclosure of these data is subject to a 5% materiality requirement.

These data allow the calculation of domestic and foreign after-tax earnings which (in most cases) reconciles directly with net earnings reported in the income statement. Any differences arise from untaxed income recognitions (primarily equity in net income of affiliated companies) that some firms report as part of total income but not part of taxable income and/or the allocation of minority interests in subsidiaries. Since there is no indication of the allocation of these items between foreign and domestic income, when they are present they drive a wedge between the firm's actual after-tax income and the sum of our domestic and foreign after-tax income.[11]

The use of Rule 4-08(h) disclosure data differentiates this paper from previous research on geographic segment information (e.g., Balakrishnan et al., 1990; Boatsman et al., 1993). They use data from SFAS No. 14 which mandates the disclosure of a firm's geographic segments whenever a segment constitutes more than 10% of total assets, revenues or a broad-based definition of income.[12] For our study, we believe there are several reasons why Rule 4-08(h) data is superior to the SFAS No. 14. First, unlike SFAS No. 14 data on foreign income, Rule 4-08(h) domestic and foreign pre-tax income and the related taxes are applied on

---

[8] For the purposes of the regulation, foreign operations are defined as operations that are located outside of the registrant's home country. Export income of the domestic parent is defined to be part of the domestic income segment.

[9] One exception to this is income that falls under the definition of subpart F income. Such income, typically passive income or income from specific activities that may be associated with tax avoidance, does not receive US tax deferral and is taxable by the US in the year that it is earned.

[10] These data are calculated using US GAAP and is based on financial income from foreign sources and needs to be distinguished from the tax notion of foreign source income. Foreign source income denotes income from foreign sources that constitutes currently taxable income by the IRS.

[11] Below we discuss the frequency of this problem in our data and how we deal with this issue in our empirical framework.

[12] SFAS No. 14 supersedes the earlier disclosure requirements initiated by the SEC. In 1969, under SEC Release No. 33-4949, 33-4988, and 34-9000 (see, Swaminathan, 1991), the SEC required disclosure for firms that had revenues and/or earnings of greater than 10% outside of the United States. This supplemental disclosure data are prepared using US GAAP, and is found in the form 10-K and is used by Kinney (1972) among others.

a consistent basis through the time period of our study and allow us to calculate foreign and domestic after tax income. Whereas SFAS No. 14 income data may be " ... operating income, net income or some measure in between ... " (SFAS No. 14), our income measures are comparable across firms. Second, since the materiality criterion for this disclosure is lower than SFAS No. 14 (5% versus 10%), we have a larger sample than studies that use SFAS No. 14 data.

One drawback to the use of Rule 4-08(h) data is we are only able to obtain the total amount of income from foreign operations and thus are unable to study any associations between specific foreign segments (e.g., Europe, Asia, etc.) as in Boatsman et al. (1993). While it is plausible that there are differences across foreign activities, we believe these differences are economically less significant than the differences between domestic and foreign operations. Given the limited number of usable observations on distinct separate foreign segments, focusing on the broad categories should improve the power of tests on the value-relevance of foreign data.

3.2. Sample selection

To construct our sample, we first search the Compustat Expanded Annual Industrial File for firms with both current and one-year lagged observations for the SEC mandated disclosures of domestic and foreign pre-tax annual income (Compustat annual data items 272 and 273). Although multinational firms have made these disclosures in their annual reports in accordance with Rule 4-08(h) since the integration of disclosures in 1980, the data are not included on the Compustat database until 1984. We also require current and lagged data for total and foreign income taxes (Compustat annual data items 16, 64 and 270, respectively). These variables are used to calculate domestic and foreign after-tax income for current and prior years. These measures are converted into domestic earnings per share, $DEPS_{i,t}$, and foreign earnings per share, $FEPS_{i,t}$, upon dividing by shares outstanding at the end of the respective fiscal year.[13] From these variables we create the change in domestic earnings per share, $\Delta DEPS_{i,t}$, and the change in foreign earnings per share, $\Delta FEPS_{i,t}$, by differencing with the previous year. For our tests we also extract current and lagged annual earnings per share, $TEPS_{i,t}$ (Annual Compustat item number 58), and create the change in total earnings per share, $\Delta TEPS_{i,t}$.[14]

---

[13] The appropriate adjustment is made when definitional changes in shares outstanding occur.

[14] In order to avoid confusion about the definition of foreign operations, especially when we consider the impact of exchange rate changes, only firms incorporated in the United States were included. Foreign firms listed on US exchanges include US operations in their definition of foreign income. The foreign incorporation code in Compustat (FINC) is checked to insure only US firms are included in the sample.

G.M. Bodnar, J. Weintrop / Journal of Accounting and Economics 24 (1997) 69–97   77

We also require that firms have 60 months of stock price return available preceding the current fiscal year on the Center for Research in Security Prices (CRSP) database for calculating changes in firm value.[15] Cumulative abnormal returns for firm i are calculated over a 12-month period as

$$CAR_{i,t} = \prod_{k=t_1}^{t_2} (1 + (R_{i,k} - a_i - b_i R_{m,k})) - 1, \tag{3}$$

$CAR_{i,t}$	is the annual cumulative abnormal return to firm i over the 12 month period beginning with the fourth month of fiscal year t and ending with the third month of the fiscal year $t + 1$
$R_{i,k}$	is the monthly stock return for firm i in month k
$R_{m,k}$	is the monthly return to the value-weighted CRSP market index in month k
a_i, b_i	are the parameters from the estimation of a market model on firm i over the 60 months prior to the beginning of the fiscal year t
t_1, t_2	are the fourth month of fiscal year t and the third month of fiscal year $t + 1$

Finally, we require firms to have valid stock price data for the end of the first quarter of fiscal year t to normalize all the per share data.[16]

Later tests require data on the distribution of a firm's sales between domestic and foreign operations. We obtain foreign sales data from the 1994 Disclosure WorldScope database. This database contains information for the percentage of foreign (non-US) assets and sales. These data are provided under the disclosure requirements of SFAS No. 14. Due to the higher materiality requirement in SFAS No. 14 (10%) than Rule 4-08(h) (5%), these data are available only for a subset of our sample firms.

3.3. Descriptive statistics

The initial sample consists of 2671 firm-year observations for 471 distinct firms. Due to the sensitivity of previous results in this area to outlying observations (see Boatsman et al., 1993), we conduct a three step approach to ensure that our results are not driven by outliers. First we examine the data for

---

[15] All of the tests in Section 4 (below) are replicated on raw returns with similar statistical results, though lower overall explanatory power.

[16] See Christie (1987) and Collins and Kothari (1989) for a discussion of the benefits of deflating per share data by price. We also ran all of our tests deflating by price at the beginning of the first quarter and the results are fundamentally unchanged.

extreme observations. Three observations are eliminated based upon this criteria.[17] Second, we delete observations for which any regression variable is more than four standard deviations from its sample mean. This reduces the sample size by 93 to 2575 observations.[18] Finally, we carry out a Cook's Distance screen on Eq. (5) (below) to remove any remaining observations that have excessive influence on the reported results. This removes five additional observations.[19] Thus our final sample consists of 2570 firm-year observations for 459 distinct firms. Panel A of Table 1 contains descriptive statistics for this sample. Being multinational firms, the firm size of our sample is in all respects significantly greater than the Compustat universe. The medians of both total assets and market value are larger than the medians of the complete Compustat sample at the 1% level (tests not reported).

Our sample reveals substantial foreign activity. The foreign economic activity is measured in four different ways. For the full sample of 2570 observations we report foreign earnings (Rule 4-08(h)) as a percentage of total earnings. Since segment data are available only through SFAS No. 14, we report the percentage of foreign revenues, operating income, and assets for the subset of firms that make SFAS No. 14 disclosures reported on the Disclosure WorldScope database.

As displayed in Panel A of Table 1, the median proportion of foreign to total earnings for the full sample is 21.4%. The median percentage of foreign revenues, operating income, and assets for the subset of firms making SFAS No. 14 disclosures is higher at 26.7%, 26.5% and 24.9% respectively. Thus for the median firm, foreign activity accounts for approximately 20–25% of total activity, across measures. Panel B of Table 1 provides medians of these measures of foreign activity by fiscal year to indicate the changes in foreign activities over time. The values generally tend upwards over the first half of the sample, then flatten out and fall off slightly as the sample size increases (entry of smaller, less international firms) in the later years.

Table 2 contains summary statistics and correlations for the variables used in the regressions. It is interesting to note that the correlation between the change in domestic earnings variable (DEPS/P) and foreign earnings variable

---

[17] These observations report measures for DTEPS/P of 167.5 and − 17.8, and CAR of 8123%. Each of these observations is more than twice as large as the next closest observation.

[18] This 4 standard deviation criteria results in screens on DTEPS/P of approximately ± 1.30, DDEPS P of roughly ± 1.25, DFEPS P of approximately ± 0.40, and CAR of approximately − 75% and + 300%. Many of these data-determined cutoff points are consistent with cutoff criteria used in other association studies (see Collins and Kothari, 1989).

[19] Cook's distance tests identifies individual observations that have an excessive impact on the regression results. For more on this test, see, e.g., Belsley et al., 1980). The removal of these five observations results in an increase in R^2 of 0.002 and an increase in the foreign association coefficient of approximately 0.1. However, this screen does not affect the statistical significance of any of the tests.

Table 1
Sample characteristics

Panel A: Quartiles of pooled sample

Variable	Q1	Median	Q3	N
Assets ($MM)	308.6	1191.2	4013.2	2570
Market value ($MM)	205.3	976.6	3288.9	2570
Foreign earnings (% of total)	3.6	21.4	50.0	2570
Foreign revenues (% of total)	16.2	26.7	39.9	1970
Foreign operating inc. (% of total)	11.0	26.5	52.4	1979
Foreign assets (% of total)	14.9	24.9	36.7	1979

Panel B: Foreign economic activity over time

	Fiscal year								
Medians	1985	1986	1987	1988	1989	1990	1991	1992	1993
Foreign earnings (%)	23.3	17.6	22.1	22.5	25.9	24.6	20.9	19.7	15.9
N	125	245	262	284	305	318	329	347	354
Foreign revenues (%)	22.0	23.8	24.8	25.2	26.3	27.7	28.1	29.3	28.8
N	92	181	203	218	235	248	258	265	270
Foreign operating inc. (%)	23.8	22.6	25.1	26.0	26.6	28.9	28.4	26.7	26.3
N	93	182	204	219	236	249	259	266	271
Foreign assets (%)	22.8	21.5	23.6	22.8	24.0	27.3	26.5	26.2	26.3
N	93	182	204	219	236	249	259	266	271

Notes: Descriptive statistics for the sample are drawn from Compustat, CRSP, and Disclosure. Assets, market value, and foreign earnings are from the Compustat database. Foreign earnings are the percentage of earnings reported from foreign sources based upon SEC Regulation §210.4-08(h). Foreign revenues, operating income and assets are from SFAS No. 14 disclosures contained in the Disclosure WorldScope database. Panel A: Q1 is the 25th percentile, Median is the 50th percentile, and Q3 is the 75th percentile. N is the number of firm-year observations. Panel B: Reported numbers are medians for fiscal years. N is the number of observations for each year.

(FEPS/P), although statistically significant, is economically small, 0.094. This suggests that foreign operations provide a substantial degree of diversification to the firm's domestic income stream.

4. Empirical tests and results

4.1. The association of total earnings with abnormal return

We begin our empirical tests with an estimation of the association coefficient between cumulative abnormal stock returns and total earnings changes to verify whether our sample selection procedures produce results which are similar in nature

Table 2
Summary statistics for empirical variablesPanel A: Distributional Characteristics

Variable	Mean	Median	Min	Max	Q3–Q1	N
ΔTEPS/P	− 0.0017	0.0055	− 1.153	1.056	0.0395	2570
ΔDEPS/P	− 0.0011	0.0034	− 1.153	0.939	0.0392	2570
ΔFEPS/P	− 0.0006	0.0006	− 0.352	0.359	0.0137	2570
ΔFEPSVOL/P	− 0.0013	0.0003	− 0.355	0.353	0.0135	2570
CAR (%)	1.14	− 3.19	− 62.71	167.89	35.71	2570

Panel B: Correlations among regression variables

	ΔDEPS P	ΔFEPS/P	ΔFEPSVOL/P	CAR (%)
ΔTEPS/P	0.950	0.395	0.394	0.249
	[0.0001]	[0.0001]	[0.0001]	[0.0001]
ΔDEPS/P	—	0.094	0.095	0.209
		[0.0050]	[0.0040]	[0.0001]
ΔFEPS/P	—	—	0.996	0.177
			[0.0001]	[0.0001]
ΔFEPSVOL/P	—	—	—	0.176
				[0.0001]

Notes: Panel A: Distributional statistics for the variables used in the regression analysis. CAR is the cumulative abnormal return over the 12 month period running from the second quarter of the current fiscal year through the end of the first quarter of the subsequent fiscal year. ΔTEPS is the change in total earnings per share from fiscal year $t − 1$ to fiscal year t; ΔDEPS is the change in the domestic component of earnings per share from fiscal year $t − 1$ to fiscal year t; ΔFEPS is the change in the foreign component of earnings per share from fiscal year $t − 1$ to fiscal year t; ΔFEPSVOL is the change in the exchange rate adjusted foreign earnings per share. This represents the change in the volume of foreign currency earnings converted into dollars at a constant exchange rate (i.e., an exchange rate price-free volume change) from fiscal year $t − 1$ to fiscal year t; P is the price of the firm's share at the beginning of the second quarter of the fiscal year t. This price is used to normalize all the variables defined above. Q3–Q1 is the inter-quartile range and N is the number of firm-year observations. Panel B reports Pearson correlations among these variables. Spearman correlations. not reported, are similar. Significance (p-value) of the correlation coefficients is reported within brackets below each correlation.

to other association studies.[20] The standard association regression is given by

$$CAR_{i,t} = \alpha_0 + \alpha_1 \frac{\Delta TEPS_{i,t}}{P_{i,t}} + \varepsilon_{i,t}, \qquad (4)$$

---

[20] Kothari and Zimmerman (1994) argue that in situations where prices lead earnings, price-level regressions are better specified than return changes regressions for estimating the price earnings relation. Tests (not reported) of our hypotheses using price/level regressions lead to similar qualitative results for all regressions reported in Table 3. The relation between foreign earnings and price is significantly large than the relation between domestic earnings and price. Given the similarity of the basic results, we report results for return/change regressions only as these are more commonly used in the literature.

where the change in earnings, ΔTEPS, is normalized by the firm's share price at the end of the first quarter of the current fiscal year and ε is the error term.[21] Panel A of Table 3 contains the results of the estimation of Eq. (4). The association coefficient for the total earnings change, α_1, is 0.611 and is significant at the 1% level.[22] The adjusted R^2 of the regression is 6.1%. Both of these results are consistent with the results of previous studies that examine association coefficients for large samples of firms (e.g., Easton and Harris, 1991; Collins and Kothari, 1989).

4.2. The association of foreign and domestic earnings with abnormal returns

We next consider the value-relevance of foreign and domestic earnings changes using cumulative abnormal annual returns. To do this we substitute domestic and foreign earnings changes for total earnings changes in Eq. (4). This replacement results in Eq. (5):

$$\text{CAR}_{i,t} = \gamma_0 + \gamma_1 \frac{\Delta \text{DEPS}_{i,t}}{P_{i,t}} + \gamma_2 \frac{\Delta \text{FEPS}_{i,t}}{P_{i,t}} + \varepsilon_{i,t} \qquad (5)$$

where ΔDEPS and ΔFEPS are the changes in domestic and foreign earnings per share, respectively. As mentioned above, there are some cases in which the sum of domestic and foreign pre-tax income does not equal total pre-tax income on the income statement. There are 435 observations for which this difference is more than $100 000, of which 398 are due to the failure to allocate equity in net earnings of affiliates, minority interest in subsidiaries, and/or common expenses in pre-tax earnings.[23] As a result, the results of Eq. (5) are not directly comparable with the results of Eq. (4).

---

[21] The use of a naive prediction for the domestic and foreign components of earnings per share is consistent with Boatsman et al. (1993), Harris (1993) and Klassen et al. (1993). In order to maintain consistency with these measures, we continued to use the naive model for the total earnings per share estimate even though there are models that have higher predictive powers. Potential problems with this specification for our tests are considered below in Section 6.

[22] All t-statistics are based upon White (1980) heteroskedasticity consistent estimates of the standard errors and all significance levels are for one-tailed tests.

[23] These mis-matches are identified by a JJ footnote code in Compustat, data item 42. A total of 457 observations with the JJ footnote were found; however, 22 of these were differences of less than $100,000. Of the remaining 435,280 were due to a failure to allocate minority interest amongst foreign and domestic pre-tax income, 111 were due to a similar failure to allocate earnings in the net equity of affiliated companies, and 29 cases were due to failure to allocate common expenses when the geographic segment income disclosure was pre-tax income. The remaining 15 cases were found to be errors in Compustat's recording of the equity in earnings numbers. Dropping these 435 observations from the tests did not significantly alter the results from those reported.

82   *G.M. Bodnar, J. Weintrop / Journal of Accounting and Economics 24 (1997) 69–97*

Table 3
Results of pooled time-series cross-sectional association regressions of annual excess returns and changes in earnings

Panel A: Total earnings

$$\mathrm{CAR}_{i,t} = \alpha_0 + \alpha_1 \frac{\Delta \mathrm{TEPS}_{i,t}}{P_{i,t}} + \varepsilon_{i,t}^1$$

α_0	α_1	Adj R^2	N
0.012	0.611	0.061	2570
$(2.051)^a$	$(10.63)^b$		

Panel B: Domestic and foreign earnings

$$1_{i,t} = \gamma_0 + \gamma_1 \frac{\Delta \mathrm{DEPS}_{i,t}}{P_{i,t}} + \gamma_2 \frac{\Delta \mathrm{FEPS}_{i,t}}{P_{i,t}} + \varepsilon_{i,t}^2$$

γ_0	γ_1	γ_2	Adj R^2	N
0.013	0.517	1.235	0.068	2570
$(2.097)^a$	$(8.376)^b$	$(6.698)^b$		

Panel C: Total and foreign earnings

$$1_{i,t} = \delta_0 + \delta_1 \frac{\Delta \mathrm{TEPS}_{i,t}}{P_{i,t}} + \delta_2 \frac{\Delta \mathrm{FEPS}_{i,t}}{P_{i,t}} + \varepsilon_{i,t}^3$$

δ_0	δ_1	δ_2	Adj R^2	N
0.013	0.521	0.727	0.069	2570
$(2.104)^a$	$(8.408)^b$	$(3.626)^b$		

Notes: Panel A: $\mathrm{CAR}_{i,t}$ is the cumulative abnormal return for firm i over the 12-month period running from the beginning of the second quarter of the current fiscal year through the end of the first quarter of the subsequent fiscal year. Firm specific estimates of the market model were obtained from a 60 month period prior to the current fiscal year; $\Delta \mathrm{TEPS}_{i,t}$ is the change in total earnings for firm i from fiscal year $t-1$ to fiscal year t; $P_{i,t}$ is the price of firm i's equity at the end of the first quarter of the current fiscal year. In Panel B. $\Delta \mathrm{DEPS}_{i,t}$ is the change in the domestic earnings of firm i from fiscal year $t-1$ to fiscal year t; $\Delta \mathrm{FEPS}_{i,t}$ is the change in foreign earnings of firm i from fiscal year $t-1$ to fiscal year t. Panel C contains a re-specification of the equation in Panel B, restated to demonstrate the incremental association of $\Delta \mathrm{FEPS}$ over $\Delta \mathrm{DEPS}$. All regression are OLS. t-statistics are shown in parentheses based upon the White (1980) corrected standard errors. Superscripts a and b represent statistical significance at the 5% and 1% levels, respectively, for one-tailed tests.

G.M. Bodnar, J. Weintrop / Journal of Accounting and Economics 24 (1997) 69–97   83

Panel B of Table 3 displays the results of the estimation of Eq. (5). Focusing on our first research question, we examine whether domestic and foreign earnings are each significantly related to cumulative abnormal returns ($H_0:\gamma_1 = 0$, $\gamma_2 = 0$). Both the change in domestic earnings and the change in foreign earnings are positively associated with cumulative abnormal returns. The association coefficient for domestic earnings, γ_1, is 0.517, and the association coefficient for foreign earnings, γ_2, is 1.235. Both coefficients are significant at the 1% level. This indicates that US multinational firms' returns are significantly related to changes in both domestic and foreign income.

A striking feature about the results in Panel B is the relative size of the association coefficients. The larger foreign association coefficient suggests that foreign earnings are capitalized into price at a higher rate than domestic earnings. To directly test the significance of the difference in association coefficients, we modify Eq. (4) by adding the foreign earnings change to the total earnings change to obtain Eq. (6):

$$\text{CAR}_{i.t} = \delta_0 + \delta_1 \frac{\Delta \text{TEPS}_{i.t}}{P_{i.t}} + \delta_2 \frac{\Delta \text{FEPS}_{i.t}}{P_{i.t}} + \varepsilon_{i.t}. \tag{6}$$

In this specification, δ_1 captures the level of the association coefficient common to both domestic and foreign earnings (henceforth referred to as the domestic association coefficient). The coefficient on ΔFEPS, δ_2, is now the *difference* between the foreign and domestic association coefficients, and the significance of the difference between the foreign and domestic association coefficients can be gauged directly by the significance of δ_2. There are two important benefits of this specification. First, this specification is robust to those cases where the sum of domestic and foreign earnings do not equal total earnings. Second, this specification also allows us to test the difference between the domestic and foreign association coefficients controlling directly for possible heteroskedasticity through the use of White (1980) corrected standard errors.

Panel C of Table 3 displays the results of the estimation of Eq. (6). The foreign association coefficient, δ_2, is significantly larger than the domestic association coefficient. The difference between the association coefficients is 0.727, with a t-statistic of 3.626 which is significant at the 1% level. The other regression outputs are nearly identical to the regression outputs of Eq. (5) reported in Panel B, suggesting that any error in the decomposition of total income has little impact on the results. This result indicates that the market recognizes different implications of changes in foreign earnings versus domestic earnings for the value of the firm. More specifically, the value of the firm is more sensitive to changes in the foreign income than it is to changes in domestic income.

Table 4
Cross sectional regressions of excess annual returns on domestic and foreign earnings changes by fiscal year7

Panel A: Year-by-year regressions

$$CAR_{i,t} = \delta_0 + \delta_1 \frac{\Delta TEPS_{i,t}}{P_{i,t}} + \delta_2 \frac{\Delta FEPS_{i,t}}{P_{i,t}} + \varepsilon_{i,t}$$

Fiscal year	δ_0	δ_1	δ_2	Adj R^2	N
1985	0.027	0.754	1.047	0.103	126
	(1.150)	(3.119)[a]	(1.466)[c]		
1986	− 0.023	− 0.063	0.547	− 0.003	246
	(− 1.421)	(− 0.391)	(0.935)		
1987	0.049	0.431	0.259	0.037	261
	(2.600)[a]	(2.663)[a]	(0.312)		
1988	− 0.032	0.394	0.655	0.038	285
	(− 2.053)[b]	(2.082)[b]	(1.318)[c]		
1989	− 0.060	0.742	1.169	0.140	304
	(− 3.719)[a]	(4.072)[a]	(1.387)[c]		
1990	− 0.029	0.535	1.434	0.116	318
	(− 1.814)[b]	(2.727)[a]	(2.636)[a]		
1991	0.064	0.340	1.221	0.057	329
	(3.120)[a]	(1.763)[b]	(2.671)[a]		
1992	0.013	0.758	0.947	0.128	347
	(0.768)	(4.605)[a]	(2.062)[b]		
1993	0.103	0.659	− 0.124	0.062	354
	(5.370)[a]	(4.393)[a]	(− 0.248)		

Notes: The variables are as defined in Table 3. The estimates are from individual cross sectional OLS regressions by fiscal years. t-statistics are shown in parentheses based upon the White (1980) corrected standard errors. Superscripts a, b and c represent statistical significance at the 1%, 5% and 10% levels, respectively, for one-tailed tests.

4.3. Cross-sectional regressions

To demonstrate that the finding of a significantly larger foreign association coefficient is not driven by either positive cross-sectional correlation among the residuals (resulting in overstated t-statistics for the parameter estimates) or remaining outlying observations, we report cross-sectional regression results in Table 4. The table displays the results for nine year-by-year regressions of total and foreign earnings changes on abnormal returns. The estimate of the difference between the foreign and domestic association coefficient, δ_2, is positive in eight of the nine cross-sectional regressions. This difference is statistically significant for six years: two years at the 1% level; one year at the 5% level; and

G.M. Bodnar, J. Weintrop / Journal of Accounting and Economics 24 (1997) 69–97   85

three years at the 10% level (for one-tailed tests).[24] Thus our finding of a larger association coefficient on foreign earnings in the pooled regression does not appear to be driven by observations in a particular year or by the presence of positive cross-sectional correlation in the residuals.

5. Economic explanations for the results

The results from the previous section indicate that changes in the earnings from foreign operations are more highly associated with changes in firm value than changes in domestic earnings. This suggests that something about the foreign operations themselves may be responsible for this observed phenomena. In Section 2, we offered two possible economic explanations for larger foreign association coefficients: exchange rate impacts and growth opportunities. In this section we test these two possibilities.

5.1. Exchange rate effects

The first economic explanation for the larger foreign association coefficient we examine relates to the one important difference between foreign income and domestic income changes: that foreign income changes incorporate within them an exchange rate change. The change in foreign income measured in US dollars is a combination of the change in the amount of foreign currency income earned by the firm and the change in the appropriate dollar-foreign currency exchange rate over the year. As mentioned in Section 2, exchange rate changes are, to a first approximation, unexpected and permanent. As a result, the changes in dollar-measured foreign income resulting purely from exchange rate changes will be unexpected and permanent. The more unexpected and permanent an earnings change, the higher will be its association with returns. Theoretically, earnings changes that are completely unexpected and totally permanent should result in association coefficients of one over the firm's cost of equity capital (see, e.g., Collins and Kothari, 1989). If the other components of earnings changes (both foreign and domestic) are more predictable and/or less permanent than the exchange rate change component of foreign earnings changes, the association coefficient on foreign earnings change may be larger than the domestic association coefficient.

To consider whether the larger foreign association coefficient is due to the valuation impact of exchange rate changes on foreign income, we can adjust the

---

[24] The mean of the nine cross-sectional estimates of the domestic association coefficients, d_1 is positive, 0.505, with a t-statistic of 5.660. The mean of the cross sectional estimates of the incremental foreign association coefficient, d_2, is also positive, 0.794, with a t-statistic of 4.736.

change in foreign earnings for the change in exchange rate over the year. To do this correctly, we would need to know the proportion of income in different foreign currencies, the timing of the earnings flows, the extent to which the firms have hedged these foreign earnings, and the method used to consolidate foreign financial statements. Given that we only have information on unified foreign activities, we use an exchange rate index that measures the trade-weighted value of the US dollar relative to the currencies of the six other members of the G-7 countries (Canada, France, Germany, Italy, Japan, and the United Kingdom, (\$/FC)) for all firms and assume that foreign income is unhedged and earned smoothly over the fiscal year.[25]

For each fiscal year we calculate the difference in the average of this index over that fiscal year, ΔAVGXR. The reason for the difference across annual averages is because income flows are usually converted into dollars under US GAAP using period average exchange rates. The current foreign earnings change is then adjusted for the exchange rate change by subtracting the exchange rate-induced adjustment to the basis (the product of the dollar value of foreign earnings for fiscal year t-1 multiplied by change in the average exchange rate index over fiscal year t):

$$\Delta FEPSVOL_{i,t} = \Delta FEPS_{i,t} - (FEPS_{i,t-1} \cdot \Delta AVGXR_t).$$

The resulting value, ΔFEPSVOL, is a proxy for the change in the quantity of foreign currency earnings generated by the firm and represents the change in the dollar value of foreign earnings measured at a constant exchange rate. This variable measures only the change in the *volume* of the foreign currency earnings, which is a proxy for changes in fundamental foreign currency profitability analogous to the way domestic income measures the change in domestic profitability. Summary statistics for the adjusted foreign earnings and its correlation with the other regression variables are reported in Table 2. This adjustment results in a small downward shift in the distribution due to the fact that the dollar appreciated slightly against these currencies. Because the variation in ΔAVGXR is small compared to the variation in individual firm's foreign earnings, the correlation between ΔFEPS/P and ΔFEPSVOL/P is high.

To test whether the larger foreign association coefficient is the result of an exchange rate change component in the foreign earnings change, we substitute the adjusted foreign earnings change, ΔFEPSVOL, for the foreign earnings change variable, ΔFEPS, in Eq. (6). If the exchange rate change is causing the larger foreign association coefficient, then we should see no difference between

---

[25] The data on month-end exchange rates come from the International Financial Statistics database of the International Monetary Fund. Weights for the exchange rate index come from the weights used in the Multilateral Exchange Rate Model of the International Monetary Fund (see *International Financial Statistics*, 1985).

G.M. Bodnar, J. Weintrop / Journal of Accounting and Economics 24 (1997) 69–97   87

Table 5
Examination of the impact of exchange rate changes

$$CAR_{i,t} = \theta_0 + \theta_1 \frac{\Delta TEPS_{i,t}}{P_{i,t}} + \theta_2 \frac{\Delta FEPSVOL_{i,t}}{P_{i,t}} + \varepsilon_{i,t}$$

θ_0	θ_1	θ_2	Adj R^2	N
0.013	0.523	0.708	0.068	2570
(2.177)[a]	(8.451)[b]	(3.581)[b]		

Notes: The variables are as defined in Table 3. $\Delta FEPSVOL$ is the change in the exchange rate adjusted foreign earnings per share. This represents the change in the volume of foreign currency earnings converted into dollars at a constant exchange rate (i.e., a exchange rate-price free volume change), from fiscal year $t - 1$ to fiscal year t. Regressions are OLS. t statistics based upon the White (1980) corrected standard errors in are given parentheses. Superscripts a, and b represent statistical significance at the 1%, 5% and 10% levels, respectively, for one-tailed tests.

the domestic association coefficient and the association coefficient on the exchange rate adjusted foreign earnings change. This specification provides us with Eq. (7):

$$CAR_{i,t} = \theta_0 + \theta_1 \frac{\Delta TEPS_{i,t}}{P_{i,t}} + \theta_2 \frac{\Delta FEPSVOL_{i,t}}{P_{i,t}} + \varepsilon_{i,t}. \tag{7}$$

Table 5 contains the results of the estimation of Eq. (7). As expected, the domestic association coefficient changes little from the previous estimates; θ_1 is 0.523 with a t-statistic of 8.451 which is significant at the 1% level. Moreover, the same is true for the incremental foreign association coefficient on the adjusted measure of foreign earnings change. The estimate of θ_2 is 0.708, with t-statistic of 3.581 which is significant at the 1% level. Thus, given that our trade-weighted exchange rate change is a reasonable proxy for the exchange rate change for each firm, these results suggest the change in foreign earnings due to changes in the exchange rate is not responsible for the significantly larger foreign association coefficient of US multinational firms. The association of the change in the foreign currency volume component of foreign earnings is significantly larger than the association of domestic earnings changes.

5.2. Growth opportunities

As discussed in Section 2, growth opportunities have been demonstrated to be positively related to the size of association coefficients. Thus, a perception by the market of greater growth opportunities in foreign operations, compared to domestic operations, is a plausible explanation for our finding. If this economic

88   *G.M. Bodnar, J. Weintrop / Journal of Accounting and Economics 24 (1997) 69–97*

difference in the interpretation of earnings changes is driving our results, then we would expect that the difference between association coefficients should be systematically related to differences in the relative amount of growth opportunities between domestic and foreign operations.

It is common in the literature to use the market-to-book ratio as a surrogate for a firm's future growth opportunities (Collins and Kothari, 1989; Smith and Watts, 1992). Unfortunately market-to-book is not observable for foreign and domestic segments. Two alternative measures of growth opportunities available on a segmental basis are return-on-assets and sales growth (percentage change in sales). Both of these measures are significantly correlated on a firm-level basis with market-to-book and are reasonable indicators for higher future net cash flows. However, tests of the link between association coefficients and growth opportunities using return-on-assets pose several problems. First, return on assets is an income-based measure and may confound the interpretation of the tests since the changes in earnings are also in the independent variables.[26] In addition, segment return-on-assets can be distorted by the subjective allocation of assets across segments making it difficult to identify the appropriate base for the ratio.[27] Since segment sales are fully allocated across segments, we use segmental sales growth as our measure of growth opportunities.[28]

The changes in domestic and foreign sales growth (DSG and FSG) for firm i are defined as the percentage change in domestic and foreign sales between periods $t-1$ and t. The segment with the larger percentage change in sales is assumed to have relatively more growth opportunities. To test for a link between the relative growth opportunities of foreign and domestic operations and the size of the foreign and domestic association coefficients, we first divide our sample with available data into groups based upon the relative size of the changes in segmental sales. We expect a difference in the significance of the incremental foreign association coefficient between these groups. Firms with

---

[26] This issue is also a problem with any other income based proxy for growth opportunities such as income to sales ratios.

[27] For example, firms are not required to allocate corporate assets across segments nor do all firms provide data on the elimination of intercompany accounts. Given our data source, unallocated assets are defined as domestic assets. This has the effect of depressing the domestic ROA measure. For our sample, the mean foreign ROA is 0.068, which is nearly twice as high as the domestic ROA of 0.036. This may be an economic result of greater required rates of return on foreign operations due to greater risks; however, such an explanation would suggest a lower association coefficient for foreign income than the less risky domestic income. Instead, we find that much of this difference in measured ROA appears to be due to freedom in the allocation of common assets under SFAS No. 14. This issue is also a problem for any segment asset based ratio, such as sales-on-assets.

[28] Segmental sales data are taken from Disclosure's WorldScope database. Similar results to those displayed in Table 6 are found when we use changes in segment ROA (where the changes difference out any measurement allocation problems) as proxies for relative growth opportunities.

larger foreign sales growth are assumed to have greater opportunities for growth abroad than at home and are predicted to have a larger incremental foreign association coefficient than other firms.[29]

Panel A of Table 6 displays the results of the estimation of Eq. (6) on firms divided by relative sales growth for the foreign and domestic segments. For the 597 firm-years with the domestic sales growth (DSG) greater than the foreign sales growth (FSG), the estimate of the incremental foreign association coefficient, δ_2, is not significantly different from zero indicating that the domestic and foreign association coefficients are statistically similar. In contrast, for the 1066 firm-years when the FSG greater than or equal to DSG, we find that δ_2 is positive, 1.478, and significant at the 1 percent level. Thus, the finding of a significantly larger foreign association coefficient is conditional on whether foreign operations are indicating more growth than domestic operations (as measured by sales growth).

To further examine the relation between changes segmental sales growth and the incremental foreign association coefficient, we consider Eq. (8) where the incremental foreign association coefficient from Eq. (6), δ_2, is modeled as an intercept, π_0, and a linear relation, π_1, of the difference between FSG and DSG.

$$
CAR_{i,t} = \delta_0 + \delta_1 \frac{\Delta TEPS_{i,t}}{P_{i,t}} + \pi_0 \frac{\Delta FEPS_{i,t}}{P_{i,t}}
$$

$$
+ \pi_1 \frac{\Delta FEPS_{i,t}}{P_{i,t}} (FSG - DSG)_{i,t} + \varepsilon_{i,t}. \tag{8}
$$

The results of the estimation of Eq. (8) are displayed in Panel B of Table 6. The focus of attention is the parameter π_1 which is the slope coefficient on the relative foreign sales growth. If, as we hypothesize, the size of the incremental size of the foreign association coefficient is positively related to greater foreign than domestic growth opportunities, we expect this coefficient to be significantly positive. As seen from the table, the estimate of this coefficient is 0.430 and significant at the 5% level. This relation is significant despite our restriction that it be linear. The estimate of the coefficient π_0 is also positive, 0.952, and significant at the 1% level, suggesting either that our proxies for growth opportunities are not capturing all of the growth difference or that are other factors lead to larger foreign association coefficients.

Overall, these results agree with our predictions and support our claim that differential growth opportunities are part of the economic difference between domestic and foreign earning streams. We interpret these results as consistent with the general view that foreign association coefficients are larger because successful foreign operations offer firms greater opportunities for future growth.

---

[29] Firms for which sales growth for both domestic and foreign segments is negative are excluded from the analysis as these cases do not provide a clear indication of relative growth opportunities.

Table 6
Relation between annual excess return and total and foreign earnings based upon changes in relative growth opportunities

Panel A: Segmental Sales Growth – Split Sample

$$\text{CAR}_{i,t} = \delta_0 + \delta_1 \frac{\Delta \text{TEPS}_{i,t}}{P_{i,t}} + \delta_2 \frac{\Delta \text{FEPS}_{i,t}}{P_{i,t}} + \varepsilon_{i,t}$$

δ_0	δ_1	δ_2	Adj R^2	N
Domestic sales growth > foreign sales growth				
0.011	0.959	0.443	0.111	597
(0.907)	(6.152)[a]	(1.243)		
Foreign sales growth ≥ domestic sales growth				
− 0.004	0.503	1.478	0.067	1066
(− 0.521)	(3.904)[a]	(3.617)[a]		

Panel B: Difference in segmental sales growth – continuous specification

$$\text{CAR}_{i,t} = \delta_0 + \delta_1 \frac{\Delta \text{TEPS}_{i,t}}{P_{i,t}} + \pi_0 \frac{\Delta \text{FEPS}_{i,t}}{P_{i,t}} + \pi_1 \frac{\Delta \text{FEPS}_{i,t}}{P_{i,t}} (\text{FSG–DSG})_{i,t} + \varepsilon_{i,t}$$

δ_0	δ_1	π_0	π_1	Adj R^2	N
0.003	0.704	0.952	0.430	0.0822	1663
(0.479)	(7.047)[a]	(3.325)[a]	(1.830)[b]		

Notes: Variable definitions are as in Table 3. The firms in Panel A must report a breakdown of sales between foreign and domestic for the current and prior year to be included in the analysis. The firms are divided into two groups based upon relative domestic sales growth (DSG) and foreign sales growth (FSG) (defined as percentage change in segmental sales from year $t − 1$ to t). In Panel B the incremental component of the foreign association coefficient, δ_2, is modeled as a linear function of the difference between foreign sales growth (FSG) and domestic sales growth (DSG). t-statistics based upon White (1980) corrected standard error are reported in parentheses. Superscripts a, and b represent statistical significance at the 1% and 5% levels, respectively, for one-tailed tests. The number of observations is reduced relative to the previous tables due to a smaller number of firms disclosing information about the geographic breakdown of sales under SFAS No. 14 and the fact that firm-years where both FSG and DSG are negative are excluded.

6. Alternative explanations for differences in association coefficients

The evidence above supports the claim that the differences in association coefficients are due to economic differences between domestic and foreign earnings streams. However, there are several specification issues related to our tests that could be affecting our results. In this section we examine three possible specification errors in our framework that have the potential to generate larger foreign than domestic association coefficients.

6.1. Timing issues

One alternative reason for a difference between foreign and domestic association coefficients is the structure of the mapping between annual returns and earnings changes. Foreign operations are physically removed from the domestic market, and it is possible that information about their economic performance is not available to investors on as timely a basis. Ostensibly, the SEC and FASB mandates for expanded disclosure of foreign operations were made with the underlying belief that data about a firm's foreign operations are not publicly available as readily as information about a firm's domestic operations. If prices adjust currently in response to information about future earnings and information about the future performance of domestic operations is available to investors further in advance than information about foreign operations, then the temporal positioning and length of the return window can affect the estimate of the association coefficients.[30] In particular, if information about domestic earnings for period t is mostly known one year in advance, but information about foreign earnings in period t are learned about only during the fiscal year, the use of a fiscal year abnormal return would lead to a higher correlation between returns and foreign earnings changes than domestic earnings changes. This would not be because of a fundamental difference in the value-relevance of the earnings streams but rather a function of the timing of the information arrival. Thus tests examining the difference between domestic and foreign association coefficients need to be concerned about the placement and length of the window used to measure the change in firm value.

To address this possible explanation, we extend the excess return window backwards an additional 12 months in time (24 month window) to minimize any possible timing difference between domestic and foreign information revelation on the estimation of the association coefficients. This longer window increases the likelihood that we capture the complete relation between domestic earnings changes and firm value, relative to foreign earnings, if a greater proportion of information in the current year's domestic earnings is incorporated into price prior to the beginning of the year. If differences in the nature of the information environment are responsible for our results, we would expect to see the

---

[30] Prior studies, such as Collins and Kothari (1989) and Kothari and Sloan (1992), provide evidence on the relation between information environments and the earnings response coefficient.

difference between the foreign and domestic association coefficients disappear as we extend the window backwards in time.

6.2. Misspecification of earnings

Another possible explanation for our findings is that there are measurement errors in our earnings expectations. If these expectation errors are systematically different across domestic and foreign earnings, then our association coefficients can be differentially affected leading to an observed difference in association coefficients. We consider two basic specification problems for our naïve expectation assumption that last period's earnings realization is the expectation of next period's earnings: (i) negative earnings realizations and (ii) special charges to earnings.[31]

Hayn (1995) points out that the use of a naïve model of earnings expectations leads to a potential bias in the interpretation of the findings when negative earnings values are used as the expectation of next period's earnings. She demonstrates that the inclusion of negative realized earnings results in downward biased association coefficients. As losses were more prevalent in domestic earnings than foreign earnings in our sample (31%–18%), this problem could be responsible for the larger foreign association coefficients in our sample.[32]

In addition, the time period under investigation featured a significant amount of corporate downsizing and reorganization. These activities resulted in large special charges to pre-tax income. If most of this activity focused on domestic operations, with the related charges taken only against the domestic segment income, this would reduce the association between domestic earnings and stock returns as the reported domestic earnings would not be a good predictor of the expected domestic earnings next period. Again, such a problem would result in the finding of a larger foreign than domestic association coefficient.

To control for these earnings specification problems we make two adjustments to our tests. First, to control for negative earnings, we create dummy variables to partition out the earnings changes when either the current or lagged realization of earnings is negative. This allows us to determine an association coefficient for earnings changes involving only positive earnings realizations.

---

[31] Note that is not possible for us to use market forecasts of earnings as these are not commonly made on a segmental basis.

[32] A similar bias would be present if a manager adopted a more conservative accounting policy towards the treatment of domestic earnings (see Basu, 1997). In order to mitigate this problem, we conduct tests on changes in domestic and foreign income.

G.M. Bodnar, J. Weintrop / Journal of Accounting and Economics 24 (1997) 69–97   93

Second, to control for special charges, we include the change in special charges (per share) as an additional variable in our specification. This variable is intended to control for cases when a special charge influences earnings, making them a poor expectation for future earnings.

6.3. Re-testing

The result of incorporating these specification issues discussed above into our analytic framework is reflected Eq. (9):

$$CAR24_{i,t} = \lambda_0 + \lambda_1 \frac{\Delta TEPS_{i,t}}{P_{i,t-12}} + \lambda_2 TNEG_{i,t} \frac{\Delta TEPS_{i,t}}{P_{i,t-12}} + \lambda_3 \frac{\Delta FEPS_{i,t,j}}{P_{i,t-12}}$$

$$+ \lambda_4 FNEG_{i,t} \frac{\Delta FEPS_{i,t,j}}{P_{i,t-12}} + \lambda_5 \frac{\Delta SPEC_{i,t}}{P_{i,t-12}} + \varepsilon_{i,t}. \tag{9}$$

$CAR24_{i,t}$ is the cumulative abnormal return for firm i over a 24 month period ending with the first quarter of fiscal year $t + 1$.[33] $\Delta TEPS_{i,t}$ and $\Delta FEPS_{i,t}$ are, as before, the change in total and foreign earnings for firm i between over the fiscal year t and fiscal year $t - 1$. $TNEG_{i,t}$ ($FNEG_{i,t}$) are dummy variables for firm i set equal to one if the current total (foreign) earnings, for fiscal year t are negative and are zero otherwise. $\Delta SPEC_{i,t}$, is the change in the special charges for firm i in fiscal year t over that reported in fiscal year $t - 1$. All the variables are normalized by $P_{i,t-12}$, (the price of the firm at the end of the first quarter of the fiscal year $t - 1$), which is the beginning of the return cumulation period.

The estimation of Eq. (9) is displayed in Table 7. The first thing to note about the results is that the specification adjustments dramatically increase the "domestic" association coefficient, λ_1, compared to estimates from previous tables. The estimate of λ_1, which is the association for positive total earnings realizations, is 2.384 and significant at the 1% level. This compares to estimates for the association on total income of 0.521 in Panel C of Table 3 when we ignore the timing issues and the negative earning realizations and special charges problem. This suggests that these specification issues are important factor when comparing different earnings streams within a company. However, despite these adjustments to our empirical framework, Table 7 reveals that the incremental foreign association coefficient (for positive foreign income realizations), λ_3, is positive, 0.706, significant at the 10% level. This means that the foreign association coefficient remains larger than the domestic association coefficient after these adjustments, and thus our earlier finding is not

---

[33] To determine CAR24, we estimate the market model over a 48 month period ending three months before the return cumulation period.

Table 7
Joint specification tests of the relation between excess returns and changes in domestic and foreign income

$$CAR24_{i,t} = \lambda_0 + \lambda_1 \frac{\Delta TEPS_{i,t}}{P_{i,t-12}} + \lambda_2 TNEG_{i,t} \cdot \frac{\Delta TEPS_{i,t}}{P_{i,t-12}} + \lambda_3 \frac{\Delta FEPS_{i,t,}}{P_{i,t-12}}$$

$$+ \lambda_4 FNEG_{i,t} \cdot \frac{\Delta FEPS_{i,t}}{P_{i,t-12}} + \lambda_5 \frac{\Delta SPEC_{i,t}}{P_{i,t-12}} + \varepsilon_{i,t}$$

λ_0	λ_1	λ_2	λ_3	λ_4	λ_5	Adj R^2	N
− 0.0002	2.384	− 1.376	0.706	− 0.418	− 0.486	0.084	2409
(− 0.026)	(7.357)[a]	(− 4.066)[a]	(1.460)[b]	(− 0.685)	(− 2.752)[a]		

Notes: $CAR24_{i,t}$ is the cumulative abnormal return over the period beginning 24 months prior to the end of the first quarter of fiscal year $t + 1$. Parameters for the market model used to calculate abnormal returns for each firm are estimated with monthly data over a 48 month period beginning 60 months prior to the beginning of fiscal year t. $\Delta TEPS_{i,t}$ is the change in the total earnings of firm i from fiscal year $t - 1$ to fiscal year t; $\Delta FEPS_{i,t}$ is the change in foreign earnings of firm i from fiscal year $t - 1$ to fiscal year t. $TNEG_{i,t}$ ($FNEG_{i,t}$) is an indicator variable that is equal to one is the current or lagged total (foreign) income is less than zero and is equal to zero otherwise. $\Delta SPEC_{i,t}$ is the change in the reported special items (per share) in the firm'2s financial statement that flow through net income for the fiscal year t less the same item reported for fiscal year $t - 1$. All the variables are normalized by $P_{i,t-12}$, (the price of the firm at the end of the first quarter of the fiscal year $t - 1$. which is the beginning of the return cumulation period. t-statistics based upon the White (1980) corrected standard errors are in parentheses. Superscripts a, and b denote statistical significance at the 1% and 10% levels, respectively, for one-tailed tests. N is the number of firm-year observations; the number of observations differs from the previous tables because of progressively larger number of observations falling outside the outlier screening points.

driven purely by specification problems in our framework. As predicted by Hayn (1994). the coefficient estimates on the negative earnings dummy terms, λ_2 and λ_4. are both negative (though λ_4 is not significant). indicating that negative earning realizations bias the association coefficients downward. Lastly, the estimate on the special charge variable. λ_5. is also negative and statistically significant.[34]

Thus. our basic finding of a larger foreign association coefficient is robust to these three important specification issues. This points us back to the economic explanation offered above as an explanation for this finding. The results of these specification tests increase our confidence that this phenomenon

---

[34] Tests (not reported) with segmental sales growth similar to those displayed in Table 6 were carried out on a specification analogous to Eq. (9) with qualitatively similar results.

is not an outcome of the specific form of the testing framework, but has an explanation based in economic theory.[35]

7. Summary and conclusions

In this paper we investigate the association between domestic and foreign annual earnings changes and cumulative abnormal returns for a sample of US multinational firms over the period 1985–1993. We find that both domestic and foreign earnings are statistically significantly related to annual excess returns. Furthermore, the association coefficient for foreign earnings is significantly larger than it is for domestic earnings.

We present evidence consistent with a growth opportunity explanation for this result of a larger foreign association coefficient. We demonstrate that greater opportunities for growth in successful foreign operations are responsible for the larger foreign than domestic association coefficient. Using segment sales growth as a proxy for segment growth opportunities, we show that the difference in magnitudes of the association coefficients is related to differences in the relative growth opportunities in foreign and domestic operations over the period. We also carry out specification tests to demonstrate that our findings are not driven by other effects, such as differences in the timing of information dissemination, or problems with our naïve earnings expectation assumption.

Acknowledgements

The authors wish to acknowledge the helpful comments of Ray Ball, Jane Bozewicz, Alvin Carley, Paul Fisher, Ken Froot, Bernard Goodman, Gerry Lobo, Aditya Kaul, S.P. Kothari, Steve Lilien, Yaw Mensah, Dennis Patz, Eric Press, Victoria Shoaf, Adrian Tschoegl, Jerry Zimmerman (the editor), an anonymous referee, and participants at the Wharton finance lunch, and seminars at Frankfurt University (Germany), Rutgers University (New Brunswick), and Syracuse University. This paper has also been presented at the 1995

---

[35] A similar result on the differential nature of foreign income is documented in Hines (1996). He finds that dividend changes of US multinational firms are three times more sensitive to foreign income changes than to domestic income changes. His analysis suggests that this finding is not due to tax reasons and concludes by conjecturing that the effect may be related to the firm's desire to signal about future profitability of foreign operations. This signaling story is consistent with our evidence supporting a growth opportunities explanation for the greater association between foreign income and firm returns. Tests (not reported) verify that this increased dividend sensitivity to foreign income, while existent in our sample, is not the source of our differential association coefficients.

annual meeting of the American Accounting Association and the 7th Annual Conference on Financial Economics and Accounting. This research has been supported by a grant from the Center for International Business Education and Research (CIBER) at Columbia University and grants (Weintrop) from Stan Ross and PSC-CUNY. All errors are the responsibility of the authors.

References

17 CFR Regulation 210.4-08.paragraph (h) General Notes to Financial Statements – Income Tax Expense.

Balakrishnan, R., Harris, T., Sen, P.K., 1990. The predictive ability of geographic segment disclosures. Journal of Accounting Research 28, 305–325.

Ball, R., Brown, P., 1968. An empirical evaluation of accounting numbers. Journal of Accounting Research 6, 159–178.

Basu, S., 1997. The conservatism principle and the asymmetric timeliness of earnings. Baruch College Working Paper. Journal of Accounting and Economics 24, 3–37.

Bartov, E., Bodnar, G.M., 1996. Accounting methods, information asymmetry and liquidity: theory and evidence. Accounting Review 71, 397–418.

Beaver, W.H., Dukes, R.E., 1972. Interperiod tax allocation earning expectations, and the behavior of security prices. Accounting Review 47, 320–332.

Belsley, D.A., Kuh, E., Welsch, R.E., 1980. Regression Diagnostics. Wiley, New York.

Boatsman, J.R., Behn, B.K., Patz, D.H., 1993. A test of the use of geographical segment disclosures. Journal of Accounting Research 31 (Suppl.), 46–64.

Christie, A., 1987. On cross-sectional analysis in accounting research. Journal of Accounting and Economics 9, 231–258.

Collins, D.W., Kothari, S.P., 1989. An analysis of the inter-temporal and cross-sectional determinants of earnings response coefficients. Journal of Accounting and Economics 11, 143–181.

Easton, P., Harris, T., 1991. Earnings as an explanatory variable for returns. Journal of Accounting Research 29, 19–36.

Financial Accounting Standards Board, 1978. Statement of Financial Accounting Standards No. 14: Financial Reporting for Segments of a Business Enterprise. (FASB: Stamford, Conn).

Frankel, J., Rose, A., 1995. A survey of empirical research on nominal exchange rates. In: Grossman, G., Rogoff, K. (Eds.), Handbook of international economics. North-Holland, New York.

Gonedes, N.J., 1973. Properties of accounting numbers: models and tests. Journal of Accounting Research 11, 212–237.

Harris, D., 1993. Impact of tax law on capital location and income shifting. Journal of Accounting Research 31 (Suppl.), 111–140.

Hayn, C., 1995. The information content of losses. Journal of Accounting and Economics 20, 125–154.

Hines, J., 1996. Dividends and profits: some unsubtle foreign influences. Journal of Finance 51, 661–689.

International Financial Statistics, 1985. Supplement on exchange rates. International Monetary Fund: Washington DC.

Kinney, W., 1972. Covariability of segment earnings and multisegment company returns. Accounting Review 47, 339–345.

Klassen, K., Lang, M., Wolfson, M., 1993. Income shifting in response to tax rate changes. Journal of Accounting Research 31 (Suppl.), 141–173.

Kogut, B., 1983. Foreign direct investment as a sequential process. In: Kindleberger, C., Audretsch, A. (Eds.), The multinational corporation in the 1980s. MIT Press, Cambridge, MA.

Kothari. S.P., Sloan. R., 1992. Information in prices about future earnings: implications for earnings response coefficients. Journal of Accounting and Economics 15, 143–173.

Kothari. S.P., Zimmerman, J., 1994. Price and return models. Journal of Accounting and Economics 20, 1–34.

Lipe, R., 1986. The information contained in the components of earnings. Journal of Accounting Research 24, 37–64.

Rayburn. J., 1986. The association of operating cash flow and accruals with security returns. Journal of Accounting Research 24, 112–154.

Saudagaran, S.M., 1993. Discussion of a test of the use of geographical segment disclosures. Journal of Accounting Research 31 (Suppl.), 65–74.

Securities and Exchange Commission, 1980. General Revision of Regulation SX. In: Federal Register vol. 48 (188).

Smith, C.W., Watts, R., 1992. The investment opportunity set and corporate financing, dividend, and compensation policies. Journal of Financial Economics 32, 263–292.

Stopford. J.M., Wells, L.T., 1972. Managing the multinational enterprise: Organization of the firm and ownership of the subsidiaries. Basic Books, New York.

Swaminathan, S., 1991. The impact of SEC mandated segment data on price variability and divergence of beliefs. Accounting Review 66, 23–41.

White, H., 1980. A heteroskedasticity-consistent covariance matrix estimator and a direct test for heteroskedasticity. Econometrica 48, 817–838.

Wilson, G.P., 1986. The relative information content of accruals and cash flows: combined evidence at the earnings announcement and the annual report date. Journal of Accounting Research 24 (Suppl.), 165–200.

[9]

ELSEVIER   Journal of Accounting and Economics 28 (2000) 243–267

JOURNAL OF
Accounting
& Economics

www.elsevier.com/locate/econbase

A test of the market's mispricing of domestic and foreign earnings☆

Wayne B. Thomas*

School of Accounting, University of Utah, Salt Lake City, UT 84112, USA

Received 13 May 1999; received in revised form 17 March 2000

Abstract

This study investigates whether abnormal returns can be earned using public information about firms' domestic and foreign earnings. The results indicate that the market understates foreign earnings' persistence. As a result, it is possible to construct a zero-investment hedge portfolio that consistently earns positive returns across years. A disproportionate fraction of the positive abnormal returns to the long position is concentrated in the few days surrounding the subsequent year's quarterly earnings announcement dates. Furthermore, the abnormal returns do not appear to persist beyond the subsequent year. The results are consistent with market mispricing, and not mis-estimated risk. © 2000 Elsevier Science B.V. All rights reserved.

JEL classification: F23; G14; M41

Keywords: Capital markets; Market efficiency; Valuation; Multinational firms; Foreign earnings

☆I wish to thank Neil Bhattacharya, Dan Collins, Peter Easton, Don Herrmann, Marlene Plumlee, J Riley Shaw, James Wahlen and seminar participants at Arizona State University, Oklahoma State University, and the University of Utah for helpful comments relating to the paper. I am especially thankful for the comments provided by S.P. Kothari (the editor) and Art Kraft (the referee) that greatly improved this research. Eugene Fama and Mark Carhart generously provided factor model data.

* Corresponding author. Tel.: + 1-801-581-8790; fax: + 1-801-581-7214.

E-mail address: actwbt@business.utah.edu (W.B. Thomas).

244   *W.B. Thomas / Journal of Accounting and Economics 28 (2000) 243–267*

1. Introduction

This study investigates whether abnormal returns can be earned using public information about firms' domestic and foreign earnings. Specifically, I test whether the market accurately incorporates the pricing effects of the persistence of the domestic and foreign earnings components of total earnings reported by a firm. The tests in this study add to the existing literature on post-earnings-announcement drift, the pricing of accruals, and the pricing of domestic and foreign earnings components. The results indicate that the market understates foreign earnings' persistence and that positive abnormal returns can be earned using a trading strategy based on changes in foreign earnings. Further analysis indicates that the abnormal returns do not appear to be the result of risk mis-estimation.

SEC Regulation §210.4-08(h), General Notes to Financial Statements – Income Tax Expense, requires firms to disclose components of income (loss) before income tax expense (benefit) as either domestic or foreign. While domestic income refers to a single country (i.e., the United States), foreign income encompasses countries from around the world differing drastically in terms of economic conditions, political stability, competitive forces, growth opportunities, governmental regulations, etc. Therefore, Rule 4-08(h) may provide only limited information regarding the risks and opportunities of the firm's foreign operations.

Guidelines set forth in Statement of Financial Accounting Standards No. 14, *Financial Reporting for Segments of a Business Enterprise* (FASB, 1978) (SFAS 14) require firms to go beyond a simple breakdown of earnings into foreign operations domestic categories. SFAS 14 requires that firms disclose earnings by geographic area (e.g., Canada, Europe, Asia/Pacific), potentially providing information beyond that required by Rule 4-08(h). Many complain, however, that geographic segment earnings disclosures are not useful because of (1) the lack of comparability and consistency in segment definition both across firms and over time for the same firm, (2) insufficient disaggregation, (3) failure to group foreign operations according to similar risk and return characteristics, and (4) management manipulation through transfer pricing policies and common cost allocations. These criticisms come from both the financial community (e.g., Association for Investment Management Research, 1992 and American Institute of Certified Public Accountants, 1994) and the academic community (Bavishi and Wyman, 1980; Arnold et al., 1980; Roberts, 1989; Balakrishnan et al., 1990; Boatsman et al., 1993; Herrmann, 1996).[1,2] If the market fails to understand the

---

[1] See Pacter (1993) for a thorough discussion of the alleged shortcomings of segment reporting practices.

[2] The FASB recently issued SFAS 131, *Disclosures about Segments of an Enterprise and Related Information*, which supersedes SFAS 14. However, the new statement appears to have *reduced* the quantity and quality of disclosure of foreign operations compared to that provided under SFAS 14 (Herrmann and Thomas, 2000).

W.B. Thomas / Journal of Accounting and Economics 28 (2000) 243–267   245

time-series properties of domestic or foreign earnings, then stock prices will systematically understate/overstate the value of the firm in a predictable manner. That is, if the market perceives the persistence of domestic or foreign earnings to be different than their historical time-series patterns, then stock prices will move in a predictable manner in the subsequent year.

A growing body of literature questions the market's efficiency with respect to earnings and other accounting information (for reviews see Ball, 1992; Bernard et al., 1993; Bernard et al., 1997). Most of this research centers on the premise that the market does not fully understand the time-series behavior of earnings or its components. For example, Bernard and Thomas (1989, 1990) show that the well-documented post-earnings-announcement drift is characteristic of a market that expects (naively) seasonal changes in quarterly earnings to follow a random walk process, even though the time-series pattern over the past several decades shows that this is not the case. When subsequent earnings are released, the market acts 'surprised' and stock prices move in a predictable direction and magnitude.

In related work, Sloan (1996) investigates the accrual and cash flow components of earnings. Sloan (1996) finds that even though the cash flow component of earnings persists into future earnings more heavily than the accrual component, stock prices act as if the opposite were true. In the subsequent period, the market appears to revise its prior (incorrect) belief in a predictable manner. Furthermore, these adjustments are concentrated around future earnings announcements.

Abarbanell and Bushee (1997, 1998) examine nine of the fundamentals signals identified in Lev and Thiagarajan (1993). Abarbanell and Bushee (1997) find that (some of) these fundamentals are significantly associated with future earnings but analysts tend to underreact to the fundamental signals (i.e., analysts do not fully understand the impact that these fundamental signals have on future earnings). Abarbanell and Bushee (1998) devise an investment strategy based on these fundamental signals that earns significant abnormal returns in the following period. The market tends to underreact to fundamental signals about future earnings and in the subsequent period when earnings are different than expectations, the market corrects its apparent mispricing in a predictable manner.

This study adds to the existing literature by testing whether the market correctly incorporates the pricing effects of the persistence of domestic and foreign earnings components of total earnings reported by a firm. The results indicate the market understates foreign earnings' persistence, causing a positive relation between current changes in foreign earnings and future abnormal stock returns. As with any study in this area, conclusions should be made with the caveat that the apparent abnormal returns could be the result of the researcher's inability to adequately measure and control for underlying risk factors. The change in foreign earnings may be a proxy for (or source of) risk, and the positive

246 *W.B. Thomas / Journal of Accounting and Economics 28 (2000) 243–267*

relation with abnormal returns is the result of unidentified risk premia and not market mispricing.

To help disentangle these two competing hypotheses, I employ three additional tests. First, Bernard et al. (1997) suggest that any *risky* hedge portfolio that requires zero-investment should produce positive returns in some years and negative returns in other years. A zero-investment hedge portfolio that consistently produces positive returns is more likely to be the result of market mispricing and not unidentified risk. Using the relation between changes in total earnings and foreign earnings, a zero-investment hedge portfolio consisting of firms expecting to do well (poorly) is constructed. This hedge portfolio produces positive abnormal returns in nine out of ten years, which supports the conclusion of market mispricing and not omitted risk factors.

The second test suggested by Bernard et al. (1997) involves observing market reactions to future earnings announcements. If abnormal returns are the result of a market that does not fully understand the persistence of current earnings (or its components), then market corrections are most likely to occur when future earnings are announced. As such, abnormal returns should be concentrated in the few days surrounding subsequent earnings announcements. I do find that the abnormal returns to the long position of the hedge portfolio are concentrated in the few days surrounding the subsequent year's earnings announcements. For firms that experience a large, positive increase in foreign earnings in year t (holding the change in total earnings constant), a disproportionately large, positive reaction occurs in the few days surrounding the quarterly earnings announcements in year $t + 1$. This is characteristic of a market that underestimates the persistence of foreign earnings and corrects for this mispricing in the subsequent year when earnings are announced higher than expected.

The final test involves estimating the relation between long-term stock returns and current changes in foreign earnings. Long-term stock returns are defined as stock returns two or three years in the future. If the change in foreign earnings is a proxy for (or source of) risk, then one might expect abnormal returns to persist beyond the subsequent year. A permanent shift in the firm's systematic risk will be related to higher returns in subsequent years. If, however, the market does not fully understand the persistence of foreign earnings, then abnormal returns should exist in the immediate subsequent year only and should not continue. It is not likely that mispricing could occur for several subsequent years. The market will correct for its (incorrect) prior belief when earnings are realized above or below expectations in the subsequent year. The results in this study show no relation between long-term stock returns and current changes in foreign earnings. The market appears to correct fully for its mispricing in the subsequent year so that abnormal returns do not persist for more than one year. All three tests support the notion that the abnormal returns are the result of market pricing, and not mis-estimated risk.

The paper proceeds as follows. The research design is outlined in Section 2. The sample selection is discussed in Section 3. The results of the primary and supplemental tests are reported in Section 4 and the paper concludes in Section 5.

2. Research design

The primary focus of this paper is to test whether the market correctly prices multinational firms' securities relative to the persistence of the domestic and foreign earnings components. To test this, I use the Mishkin (1983) framework. Mishkin (1983) devises a test to determine whether the market rationally prices information. In the context of this study, the test for market rationality would involve simultaneously estimating the following equations.[3]

$$\Delta TOTX_{t+1} = \alpha_0 + \alpha_D \Delta DOMX_t + \alpha_F \Delta FORX_t + v_{t+1}, \tag{1}$$

$$ARET_{t+1} = \beta_0 + \beta_1(\Delta TOTX_{t+1} - \alpha_0 - \alpha_D^* \Delta DOMX_t$$
$$- \alpha_F^* \Delta FORX_t) + \varepsilon_{t+1}, \tag{2}$$

where $\Delta TOTX_{t+1}$ = the change in total earnings in year $t+1$, $\Delta DOMX_t$ = the change in domestic earnings in year t, $\Delta FORX_t$ = the change in foreign earnings in year t, and $ARET_{t+1}$ = the abnormal return in year $t+1$.

Eq. (1) represents the *actual* time-series relation of changes in domestic and foreign earnings to future changes in total earnings (i.e., the extent to which changes in domestic and foreign earnings persist into changes in total earnings in the subsequent year). α_D represents a measure of the persistence of changes in domestic earnings and α_F represents a measure of the persistence of changes in foreign earnings, controlling for one another. A slope coefficient equal to -1 would suggest that earnings are purely transitory whereas a slope coefficient equal to 0 would suggest that earnings follow a random walk. A slope coefficient greater than 0 would indicate growth in earnings. If α_F is greater than α_D, then foreign earnings are considered to be more persistent than domestic earnings.

Eq. (2) estimates the relation between unexpected movements in stock prices and the unexpected portion of the change in total earnings. The expected change in total earnings is based on last year's change in domestic and foreign earnings. Mishkin (1983) suggests that the second equation provides an estimate of the market's *perceived* time-series behavior of domestic and foreign earnings. The notion is that unexpected movements in stock prices in the current period are related only to unexpected information received that same period. Therefore, the second equation can be used to estimate the market's perception of the

---

[3] For a more extensive, generalized discussion of this test, see Mishkin (1983) or Sloan (1996).

248   *W.B. Thomas / Journal of Accounting and Economics 28 (2000) 243–267*

unexpected change in total earnings based on the change in domestic and foreign earnings in the previous year. α_D^* is an estimate of the extent to which the market perceives changes in domestic earnings to persist into future years. Likewise, α_F^* is an estimate of the extent to which the market perceives changes in foreign earnings to persist into future years. Since domestic and foreign earnings are public information, market efficiency requires that $\alpha_D = \alpha_D^*$ and $\alpha_F = \alpha_F^*$. If either equality does not hold, then the market's perception of earnings persistence differs from the historical time-series pattern.

The two equations are estimated simultaneously using non-linear least squares. Non-linear least squares is required because of Eq. (2). The equality of the coefficients across equations is tested using the likelihood ratio statistic suggested by Mishkin (1983).

$$2n \log(SSR^C/SSR^U) \sim \chi^2(q) \tag{3}$$

where n is the number of observations, SSR^C is the sum of squared residuals from the constrained weighted system, SSR^U is the sum of squared residuals from the unconstrained weighted system, and q is the number of constraints imposed by market efficiency. A significant χ^2 statistic would suggest that the coefficients are not equal across equations and market efficiency would be rejected.

3. Sample selection, variable measurement, and descriptive statistics

The sample consists of all firms that have the necessary data available in the intersection of the 1998 versions of the Compustat annual industrial and research files and the CRSP monthly stock returns file. Compustat contains data on firms' foreign and domestic earnings back to 1984. Since the tests require the change in foreign earnings, 1985 is the first year of usable observations. The sample is restricted to U.S. multinational firms so that domestic and foreign earnings are reported for each firm and have the same meaning across sample firms. To control for influential observations, any observation that has a change in total earnings, change in domestic earnings, or change in foreign earnings (scaled by average total assets) in year t greater than 0.25 is deleted. This criterion resulted in approximately 4% of the observations being deleted. The final sample consists of 8051 firm-year observations over the 1985–1995 period. No control for extreme observations of returns or earnings in $t + 1$ is made since this would introduce hindsight bias in the results.

Compustat reports both domestic and foreign earnings on a pretax basis (Compustat data item #272 and data item #273, respectively). To be consistent, total earnings is defined as pretax income (data item #122). To control for differences in size across firms and over time, all earnings variables are scaled by

W.B. Thomas / Journal of Accounting and Economics 28 (2000) 243–267 249

average total assets (data item #7). Average total assets are defined as total assets in year t plus total assets in year $t - 1$, divided by 2.[4]

The Mishkin (1983) test requires the use of abnormal returns. As in Daniel et al. (1997), I calculate abnormal returns using a comparison portfolio approach. This approach entails matching a firm's security return with the value-weighted return of a portfolio consisting of firms that are similar in size, book-to-market-ratio, and prior year return. The comparison portfolios are created by first selecting all stocks that have year end capitalization values available on CRSP and book value data available on COMPUSTAT. Only firms with positive book values are included. These stocks are then sorted into quintiles based on their capitalization values at the beginning of the year of portfolio formation. NYSE breakpoints are used so that there are an equal number of NYSE stocks in each quintile. Next, within each of the size quintiles, stocks are sorted into quintiles based on their industry-adjusted book-to-market ratios. The book-to-market ratio is defined as the book value at the end of the fiscal year prior to the year of portfolio formation divided by capitalization value at the beginning of the calendar year of portfolio formation. The book-to-market ratio is industry-adjusted by subtracting the mean industry book-to-market ratio over the sample period from the individual stock's book-to-market ratio, where industries are defined along two-digit SIC codes. Finally, within the 25 size/book-to-market portfolios, stocks are sorted based on their prior 12-month return ending one month prior to portfolio formation. Excluding the month just prior to the portfolio formation date avoids problems associated with the bid–ask spread bounce and monthly return reversals (Jegadeesh, 1990). Thus, there are 125 size/book-to-market/prior year return portfolios for each fiscal year.

Abnormal returns are calculated as the stock's 12-month buy-and-hold return beginning three months after the fiscal year-end minus the buy-and-hold value-weighted return of the comparable size/book-to-market/prior year return portfolio over the same 12-month period. Extending the return interval three months beyond the fiscal year end helps to ensure that information related to domestic versus foreign earnings is publicly available by the beginning of the return interval.

Table 1 reports descriptive statistics for the variables in this study. The average annual abnormal return for the firms in the sample is 0.92%. The

---

[4] For some firms, domestic earnings plus foreign earnings does not equal total earnings. To test the sensitivity of the results to this inequality, observations were eliminated if domestic earnings and foreign earnings did not sum to within 1% of total earnings (scaled by average total assets). This resulted in approximately 2.2% of the sample observations being eliminated. The results for this reduced sample are similar to those reported. The effect of this inequality was also tested by including the difference between total earnings and domestic plus foreign earnings (i.e., 'nonallocated' earnings) as an additional explanatory variable. Inclusion of this additional explanatory variable has no qualitative effect on the reported results.

250 *W.B. Thomas / Journal of Accounting and Economics 28 (2000) 243–267*

Table 1
Descriptive statistics during the period 1985–1995 ($n = 8051$)[a]

Variables	Mean (%)	Standard deviation	Min (%)	Q1 (%)	Median (%)	Q3 (%)	Max (%)
$ARET_{t+1}$	0.92	47.03	− 159.56	− 23.31	− 3.51	17.13	980.32
$\Delta TOTX_{t+1}$	0.43	9.99	− 187.74	− 2.52	1.13	4.06	123.69
$\Delta TOTX_t$	0.77	7.16	− 24.95	− 2.29	1.12	4.09	24.99
$\Delta DOMX_t$	0.46	6.31	− 24.97	− 2.11	0.69	3.26	24.91
$\Delta FORX_t$	0.31	2.75	− 24.97	− 0.53	0.17	1.05	24.76

[a] $ARET$ is the 12-month buy-and-hold security return beginning three months after the fiscal year end minus the value-weighted return of the comparable size/book-to-market/prior year return portfolio over the same 12-month period. The comparison portfolios are created by first sorting stocks into quintiles based on their capitalization values at the beginning of the year of portfolio formation. NYSE breakpoints are used so that there are an equal number of NYSE stocks in each quintile. Next, within each of the size quintiles, stocks are sorted into quintiles based on their industry-adjusted book-to-market ratios. The book-to-market ratio is defined as the book value at the end of the fiscal year prior to the year of portfolio formation divided by capitalization value at the beginning of the calendar year of portfolio formation. The book-to-market ratio is industry-adjusted by subtracting the mean industry book-to-market ratio over the sample period from the individual stock's book-to-market ratio, where industries are defined along two-digit SIC codes. Finally, within the 25 size/book-to-market portfolios, stocks are sorted based on their prior 12-month return ending one month prior to portfolio formation.
$\Delta TOTX$ is the change in total earnings scaled by average total assets.
$\Delta DOMX$ is the change in domestic earnings scaled by average total assets.
$\Delta FORX$ is the change in foreign earnings scaled by average total assets.

average change in domestic earnings is 0.46% while the average change in total foreign earnings is 0.31% (both scaled by average total assets). Total earnings has an average change of 0.77%.[5] The rank correlation between the change in domestic earnings and the change in foreign earnings is 0.15.

4. Empirical analysis

4.1. Primary results

Table 2 reports the results of the Mishkin (1983) test for total earnings alone (Panel A) and for domestic and foreign earnings (Panel B). Results are reported

---

[5] Average domestic earnings is 5.13% and average foreign earnings 2.36%.

W.B. Thomas / Journal of Accounting and Economics 28 (2000) 243–267   251

using (1) a pooled model and (2) estimated coefficients from the Fama–MacBeth (1973) procedure where the coefficient represents the mean of the annual regression coefficients and the standard error is based on the time-series variation of the annual coefficients. Assuming independence through time, the Fama–MacBeth procedure has the advantage of controlling for cross-sectional correlation in the residuals. In the presence of positive cross-correlation in the residuals, the standard errors can be biased downward and the t-statistics biased upward in the pooled regression. For this study, the results of these two procedures are similar.

In Panel A, the estimate of *actual* total earnings persistence (α_T) is -0.209 for the pooled model. The magnitude of the total earnings coefficient suggests that total earnings contain both transitory and permanent components. Positive (negative) changes in earnings tend to be followed by negative (positive) changes in earnings, but the subsequent reversal is less than the current change. The estimate of the market's *perceived* total earnings persistence (α_T^*) is -0.194. The difference in actual total earnings persistence and the market's perception of total earnings persistence is not significant $(\chi^2(1) = 0.162$ with p-value $= 0.687)$. The difference in the cross-sectional means is also not significant $(t = 0.073$ with

Table 2
Nonlinear least squares regression of the relation between future abnormal stock returns and information in current changes in total earnings (or domestic and foreign earnings) about future total earnings changes $(n = 8051)$.[a]

Panel A: Total earnings

$$\Delta TOTX_{t+1} = \alpha_0 + \alpha_T \Delta TOTX_t + v_{t+1}$$

$$ARET_{t+1} = \beta_0 + \beta_1(\Delta TOTX_{t+1} - \alpha_0 - \alpha_T^* \Delta TOTX_t) + \varepsilon_{t+1}$$

	Pooled[b]	Cross-sectional[c]
α_0	0.006	0.005
	(0.001)	(0.220)
α_T	-0.209	-0.230
	(0.001)	(0.001)
α_T^*	-0.194	-0.226
	(0.001)	(0.001)
β_0	0.009	0.008
	(0.077)	(0.380)
β_1	1.48	1.46
	(0.001)	(0.001)
Test of market efficiency:[d]		
$H_0: \alpha_T = \alpha_T^*$	0.162	0.073
	(0.687)	(0.943)

Table 2 (continued)

Panel B: Domestic and foreign earnings

$$\Delta TOTX_{t+1} = \alpha_0 + \alpha_D \Delta DOMX_t + \alpha_F \Delta FORX_t) + v_{t+1}$$

$$ARET_{t+1} = \beta_0 + \beta_1(\Delta TOTX_{t+1} - \alpha_0 - \alpha_D^* \Delta DOMX_t - \alpha_F^* \Delta FORX_t) + \varepsilon_{t+1}$$

	Pooled[b]	Cross-sectional[c]
α_0	0.006	0.005
	(0.001)	(0.223)
α_D	− 0.233	− 0.254
	(0.001)	(0.001)
α_D^*	− 0.168	− 0.199
	(0.002)	(0.002)
α_F	− 0.096	− 0.111
	(0.017)	(0.153)
α_F^*	− 0.338	− 0.367
	(0.006)	(0.004)
β_0	0.009	0.008
	(0.109)	(0.388)
β_1	1.47	1.45
	(0.001)	(0.001)
Test of market efficiency: [d]		
$H_0: \alpha_D = \alpha_D^*$	1.71	0.859
	(0.191)	(0.401)
$H_0: \alpha_F = \alpha_F^*$	5.62	2.09
	(0.018)	(0.049)

---

[a] *ARET* is the 12-month buy-and-hold security return beginning three months after the fiscal year end minus the value-weighted return of the comparable size/book-to-market/prior year return portfolio over the same 12-month period (see Table 1 for a description of the comparable portfolio construction).

$\Delta TOTX$ is the change in total earnings scaled by average total assets.

$\Delta DOMX$ is the change in domestic earnings scaled by average total assets.

$\Delta FORX$ is the change in foreign earnings scaled by average total assets.

[b] Amounts reported are coefficients from the pooled regression with the *p*-value of the Chi-square likelihood ratio statistic that the coefficient equals zero in parentheses.

[c] Amounts reported are mean coefficients from annual cross-sectional regressions with the *p*-value of the two-tailed *t*-test that the mean coefficient equals zero in parentheses.

[d] Amounts reported for the pooled model are the Chi-square likelihood ratio statistic that the coefficients are equal across equations and the corresponding *p*-value in parentheses. Amounts reported for the cross-sectional model are the *t*-statistic for the two-tailed difference of means test that the mean coefficients are equal and the corresponding *p*-value in parentheses.

W.B. Thomas / Journal of Accounting and Economics 28 (2000) 243–267 253

p-value $= 0.943$). The market appears to understand the time-series behavior of total earnings and incorporates this information into security prices appropriately.

In Panel B of Table 2, the total change in earnings in year $t + 1$ is regressed on changes in both domestic and foreign earnings in year t. The coefficient on the change in domestic earnings (α_D) is -0.233 for the pooled model, similar to the findings in Panel A for total earnings. The coefficient on the change in foreign earnings (α_F) is -0.096 for the pooled model. Foreign earnings show less reversal (i.e., are more persistent) than domestic earnings. α_D and α_F are statistically different ($\chi^2(1) = 9.17$ with p-value $= 0.003$).[6] The estimates of the market's perception of the persistence of domestic earnings (α_D^*) and foreign earnings (α_F^*) changes in the pooled model are -0.168 and -0.338, respectively. The difference in the domestic earnings coefficients ($\alpha_D - \alpha_D^* = -0.065$) is not significant for the pooled model ($\chi^2(1) = 1.71$ with p-value $= 0.191$) or for the means of the cross-sectional models ($t = 0.859$ with p-value $= 0.401$).

The difference in the foreign earnings coefficients ($\alpha_F - \alpha_F^* = 0.243$) is significant for the pooled model (($\chi^2(1) = 5.622$ with p-value $= 0.018$) and for the means of the cross-sectional models ($t = 2.09$ with p-value $= 0.049$). These results suggest that stock prices do not reflect accurately the time-series properties of foreign earnings. Specifically, stock prices underestimate the extent to which changes in foreign earnings persist. A market that fixates on changes in total earnings without considering whether the changes are attributable to domestic versus foreign earnings causes stock prices to lag earnings.

Finding that the market correctly prices the domestic component of earnings may seem inconsistent with the findings of extant research that the market fails to understand and price correctly the time-series trend of total earnings [e.g., Bernard and Thomas (1989, 1990) for the post-earnings-announcement drift]. The tests in this study are conducted based on annual earnings data. The post-earnings-announcement drift is more pronounced for quarterly earnings data (Ball et al., 1993). Furthermore, the firms in this study are larger than average and the post-earnings-announcement drift is less pronounced for larger firms (Bernard and Thomas, 1989). These two factors contribute to the insignificant relation between domestic earnings and future abnormal returns documented in this study.

4.2. Distinguishing between market mispricing and failure to control for risk

Given the results of the previous section, a positive relation should exist between the change in foreign earnings in the current year and stock returns in

---

[6] This result is consistent with that found by Bodnar and Weintrop (1997) who show that foreign operations provide greater growth opportunities than domestic operations. Greater growth opportunities should lead to more persistent earnings.

254   *W.B. Thomas / Journal of Accounting and Economics 28 (2000) 243–267*

the subsequent year (controlling for changes in total earnings).[7] This would be consistent with the evidence that the market does not fully understand (i.e., impound into security prices) the implications of foreign earnings on the value of the firm.

However, such a result is also consistent with the change in foreign earnings being a proxy for (or source of) risk. In rational markets, investors require higher returns on assets with greater risks. Since foreign operations likely have greater risk than domestic operations, the higher future returns may simply be compensation for risk. Even though commonly identified risk factors were controlled for in the measure of abnormal returns, there may be other unidentified risk factors. This is the classical problem for all studies in this area. Are abnormal returns the result of market mispricing or the researcher's inability to accurately specify and control for differences in risk?

Bernard et al. (1997) discuss how researchers may best disentangle the issues of market mispricing from premia for unidentified risks. They suggest two simultaneous tests. With respect to earnings information, they suggest that market mispricing is more likely when (1) abnormal returns on zero-investment hedge portfolios are consistently positive each period and (2) these abnormal returns are concentrated around subsequent earnings announcement dates.

The first test involves taking a long (short) position in stocks expecting to do well (poorly). If equal amounts are invested in each portfolio and the market prices securities correctly, then any nonzero average return must be attributable to differences in risk. However, a *risky* zero-investment portfolio should result in positive returns in some periods and negative returns in others, with the average return being perhaps positive. If the annual returns are consistently positive, it is difficult to attribute the results to unidentified risk.

The second test suggested by Bernard et al. (1997) determines whether the abnormal returns cluster around future earnings announcement dates. If abnormal returns are the result of the market failing to understand fully the time-series properties of earnings (or its components), then absent other information events, earnings announcements are the points at which the market realizes that earnings are different than expectations and the price corrects. Bernard et al. (1997) demonstrate that for the post-earnings-announcement drift anomaly about 25% of the abnormal returns occur around earnings announcements. They suggest that such a result is difficult to explain as risk-based. Instead, it is more reasonable to conclude that the market failed to understand the time-series properties of seasonal changes in quarterly earnings. When subsequent earnings are announced, the market revises its prior (incorrect) belief in a predictable manner. Bernard et al. (1997) show that risk-based anomalies (e.g., book-to-market, earnings-to-price) produce positive abnormal returns evenly

---

[7] Evidence for the positive relation between the change in foreign earnings in year t and abnormal returns in year $t + 1$ is shown in Table 4. These results will be discussed in more detail below.

W.B. Thomas / Journal of Accounting and Economics 28 (2000) 243–267 255

over the return interval with no disproportionate cluster of returns around earnings announcements.

In this section, the two tests suggested by Bernard et al. (1997) are conducted in the context of domestic and foreign earnings. A zero-investment hedge portfolio is created using firms' foreign earnings in year t. The abnormal returns to the long and short positions are then measured over the 12-month period beginning three months after year t. So that the variables used to create the hedge portfolios coincide chronologically and are publicly available at the time of portfolio creation, only firms with December year-ends are included in the test. The positions of the hedge portfolio are held for one year and then a new hedge portfolio is created. To insure that the length of the earnings announcement period relative to the nonannouncement period remains constant across firms, firms are required to have announcement dates for all four quarters in the subsequent year provided on the Compustat quarterly tapes and these dates must fall within the 12-month holding period. These criteria reduce the sample to 3614 firm/year observations.[8]

To create the long and short positions of the hedge portfolio, firms are first ranked on the magnitude of the change in total earnings and assigned in equal numbers to 20 portfolios each year. Next, within each of the 20 portfolios, firms are sorted evenly into quintiles based on the change in foreign earnings. Firms in the lowest quintile are firms that have experienced the most negative change in foreign earnings for a given change in total earnings. Firms in the highest quintile are firms that have experienced the most positive change in foreign earnings for that same change in total earnings. Creating the portfolios in this manner allows firms to be ranked on changes in foreign earnings while controlling for changes in total earnings. The long (short) position consists of all firms in the top (bottom) quintile of the change in foreign earnings and has an average of 67.5 (63.3) firms per year. The ranking procedure is performed each year and the number of observations in the long and short position in each year is approximately the same, except for sample size differences over time.[9]

If the market fixates on changes in total earnings, then those firms experiencing the largest increase in foreign earnings are more likely to have undervalued stocks. In the subsequent year when total earnings are higher than expected

---

[8] While requiring firms to have all four quarterly earnings announcement dates available within the one year return interval enhances interpretation of the results, it reduces the sample size. The requirement, however, has little affect on the results. The average abnormal return to the hedge portfolio after relaxing this requirement is similar to that reported. In addition, the average abnormal return of the firms deleted in this analysis is close to zero (0.3%).

[9] The hedge portfolio was also created by first sorting firms evenly into deciles based on the change in total earnings each year. Then, within each of the deciles, firms were sorted evenly into deciles based on their change in foreign earnings. The long (short) position consisted of all firms in the highest (lowest) change in foreign earnings decile. The results are similar to those reported.

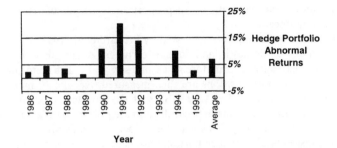

Fig. 1. Abnormal returns by calendar year to a hedge portfolio taking a long position in firms with large positive changes in foreign earnings and taking a short position in firms with a large negative changes in foreign earnings, controlling for changes in total earnings. The short and long positions have approximately an equal number of firms in each year. Abnormal returns are defined as the 12-month buy-and-hold security return beginning April 1 and ending March 31 minus the value-weighted return of a comparable size/book-to-market/prior year return portfolio over the same period (see Table 1 for a description of the comparable portfolio construction). The calendar year is the year in which the portfolio was formed (e.g., for 1986, changes in total and foreign earnings in 1986 are used to form the long and short position of the hedge portfolio and abnormal returns are then measured for the 12-month period beginning April 1, 1987 and ending March 31, 1988). (Firms are first ranked on the magnitude of the change in total earnings and assigned in equal numbers to 20 portfolios each year. Next, within each of the 20 portfolios, firms are sorted evenly into quintiles based on the change in foreign earnings. The long position consists of observations in the highest quintile of the change in foreign earnings and the short position consists of observations in the lowest quintile of the change in foreign earnings).

because of the higher persistence of foreign earnings, stock prices will correct upward. Likewise, firms that have experienced the largest decrease in foreign earnings are more likely to have overvalued stocks. These firms have experienced a shift in earnings from more persistent foreign sources to less persistent domestic sources. In the subsequent year when the market realizes that earnings expectations were too high, stock prices will correct downward. If the market fails to understand the persistence of foreign earnings versus domestic earnings in this manner, then it should be possible to exploit this to earn positive abnormal returns in each year.

The annual abnormal returns to the hedge portfolio are shown in Fig. 1.[10] The hedge portfolio produces a positive abnormal return in every year of the test

---

[10] To control for observations that have an extreme influence on the average portfolio returns, any observation that has an abnormal return greater than 200% is omitted from this analysis. This results in seventeen observations or 0.5% of the sample being deleted. The average abnormal return of the hedge portfolio when these observations are not deleted is 7.1%, which is similar to the reported average abnormal return of 6.8% when these observations are deleted. Extreme abnormal returns in the short position approximately offset those in the long position. Also, deleting observations with abnormal returns greater than 200% had no qualitative effect on the regression results reported in Tables 2, 4 and 5.

period except one.[11] The hedge portfolio abnormal returns for the single negative year is close to zero at -0.36%. The average abnormal return over the 10-year period is 6.8%. If the results were due to omitted risk factors, the portfolio would return both negative and positive returns with perhaps the net return being positive over the entire period. A consistent pattern of positive abnormal returns is more characteristic of a market that fails to understand the implications of current changes in foreign earnings for future earnings. The market corrects for its mispricing in the next year when subsequent earnings are reported different than expected.[12]

The next test involves determining whether the market corrections to the hedge portfolio are centered on future earnings announcements. If the market fails to understand differences in the persistence of domestic and foreign earnings and corrects any mispricing when future quarterly earnings are announced, then the correcting returns should be centered on future earnings announcements. Without other information, future earnings announcements are the points at which the market realizes that it has under or overestimated the extent to which last year's earnings would persist into the future. To perform this analysis, abnormal returns are separately measured in the announcement and nonannouncement periods.

The announcement period is defined as the four three-day intervals around the quarterly earnings announcement dates in the subsequent year. Each three-day interval begins two days before and ends on the day of the earnings announcement. The announcement period abnormal return for a given year is then defined as the 12-day compounded return surrounding the four quarterly earnings announcements minus the compounded value-weighted return of the comparable size/book-to-market/prior year return portfolio over the same 12-day interval.

The nonannouncement period includes all trading days over the 12-month period, excluding the 12 announcement period days. The nonannouncement period abnormal returns are measured as the compounded daily return over the nonannouncement period minus the compounded value-weighted return of the

---

[11] The hedge portfolio total return (i.e., the return unadjusted for the comparable portfolio performance) is positive in all ten years.

[12] An additional test to determine whether the hedge portfolio's positive abnormal returns were the result of already commonly identified risk premia was conducted by regressing the hedge portfolio total returns (i.e., the raw return of the long positive minus the raw return of the short position) on the Fama–French (1993) three-factor model and the Fama–French–Carhart (1997) four-factor model. For both models, the book-to-market factor was related to the hedge portfolio total return at the 0.06 significance level and the other risk factors were never significantly related. The intercept for both models is positive and significant at the 0.01 level, indicating that positive abnormal returns remain after controlling for commonly identified risk factors. These results can be obtained from the author upon request.

258   *W.B. Thomas / Journal of Accounting and Economics 28 (2000) 243–267*

Table 3
Average abnormal returns during the announcement and nonannouncement periods for the long and short positions of the hedge portfolio[a]

Return interval	Average number of trading days		Average abnormal return[b]		Average hedge portfolio abnormal return
	Long position	Short position	Long position	Short position	
Announcement period[c]	12	12	1.21% (0.011)	0.71% (0.304)	0.50% (0.347)
Nonannouncement period[d]	240.7	240.7	2.19% (0.034)	− 4.44% (0.061)	6.63% (0.010)
Total period[e]	252.7	252.7	3.21% (0.006)	− 3.61% (0.071)	6.82% (0.010)

[a]Firms are first ranked on the magnitude of the change in total earnings and assigned in equal numbers to 20 portfolios each year. Next, within each of the 20 portfolios, firms are sorted evenly into quintiles based on the change in foreign earnings. The long position consists of observations in the highest quintile of the change in foreign earnings and the short position consists of observations in the lowest quintile of the change in foreign earnings.
[b]Abnormal returns are calculated as the compounded daily return over the given interval minus the value-weighted return of the comparable size/book-to-market/prior year return portfolio over the same interval (see Table 1 for a description of the comparable portfolio construction). Average abnormal returns are shown with the p-value of the corresponding two-tailed t-test that the mean abnormal return is zero in parentheses.
[c]The announcement period consists of the four three-day periods surrounding the subsequent years quarterly earnings announcements. Each quarterly announcement period begins two days before the earnings announcement date and ends on the day of announcement.
[d]The nonannouncement period begins on the first trading day in April in year $t + 1$ and ends on the last trading day in March in year $t + 2$. Announcement period days are excluded.
[e]The total return period is the announcement period plus the nonannouncement period.

comparable size/book-to-market/prior year return portfolio over the corresponding days. The average number of trading days in the nonannouncement period is 240.7.

Table 3 reports the average abnormal returns of the long and short positions for the announcement period, nonannouncement period, and the total period. For the long position of the hedge portfolio, the average abnormal return for the announcement period is 1.21%. The average abnormal return for the total period for the long position is 3.21%. Approximately, 38% of the abnormal returns to this portfolio are concentrated around subsequent quarterly earnings announcement dates. The 12-day announcement interval represents approximately 5% of the annual return interval. The average positive abnormal return

W.B. Thomas / Journal of Accounting and Economics 28 (2000) 243–267   259

combined with an unusually large proportion of the return being centered on future earnings announcements provides evidence consistent with market mispricing.

To provide a benchmark as to how unusual the pattern of abnormal returns exhibited by the long position of the hedge portfolio is, I use a random portfolio design. That is, portfolios are created using a random sample of firms with characteristics similar to those of the firms in the long position. All firms on CRSP that have the necessary data to calculate abnormal returns and on Compustat that have all four quarterly earnings announcements between April 1 of the current year and March 30 of the following year are included. The announcement period abnormal return is measured over the 12-day interval, consisting of the four three-day periods around quarterly earnings announcements. The annual abnormal return is measured from April 1 of the current year to March 31 of the following year. The average annual and announcement period abnormal returns for each random portfolio are then computed. Such an analysis provides an expectation of how often the pattern of abnormal returns exhibited by the long position randomly occurs.

There are 13,544 firm/year observations over the 10-year test period meeting the necessary data requirements, excluding firm/years in the long position. So that the average size of the firms used to construct the random portfolios approximately equals the average size of the firms in the long position, firms in the two smallest NYSE capitalization deciles are eliminated. The mean (median) capitalization decile of firms in the random portfolios is 6.6 (7), which approximately equals the mean (median) capitalization decile of 6.3 (7) for the firms in the long position. The final sample used to create random portfolios consists of 8824 firm/year observations. Thirteen random portfolios are created each year for the 10-year hedge portfolio period. This allows the average number of firms in each random portfolio (67.9) approximately to equal the average number of firms in the long position (67.5). Thus, the data requirements, average firm size, average number of firms, length of the annual and announcement period return intervals, and the test period of the random portfolios are similar to those of the long position. The randomization procedure is repeated until 1000 random portfolios are created.

The results reveal that the pattern of abnormal returns for the long position is indeed unusual. In only 79 of the 1000 random portfolios does the average 12-day announcement period abnormal return exceed the twelve-day announcement period abnormal return of the long position. Furthermore, in only three of the 1000 random portfolios does the average annual abnormal return exceed 3.21% (i.e., the annual abnormal return of the long position) with at least 38% of the return occurring on earnings announcement dates. Thus, the significant, positive abnormal return of the long position along with a disproportionately large fraction of this abnormal return occurring around subsequent earnings announcement dates appears to be unusual.

260   *W.B. Thomas / Journal of Accounting and Economics 28 (2000) 243–267*

The results for the short position of the hedge portfolio are not as clear. The average abnormal return for the announcement period is a *positive* 0.71% (but not significant).[13] Recall that the short position consists of firms that are expected to do poorly. The average abnormal return for the nonannouncement period is −4.44% and the average abnormal return for the total period is −3.61%. Unlike the long position, the negative abnormal returns to the short position do not center on subsequent quarterly earnings announcements. Sloan (1996) and Collins and Hribar (1999) also find no significant abnormal returns centered on the four subsequent quarterly earnings announcements for their 'bad news' portfolios. The asymmetric announcement period returns for the 'good news' and 'bad news' portfolios is consistent with evidence that firms tend to preempt bad news earnings announcements (Chambers and Penman, 1984; Skinner, 1994; Kasznik and Lev, 1995; Francis et al., 1995). Thus, it may be difficult to detect systematically the market reaction to 'bad' earnings news.[14]

One potential alternative hypothesis for these results is the firm size anomaly. Chari et al. (1988) report that small firms tend to exhibit positive returns at earnings announcements *unconditional* of the news released at those dates. A portfolio that consists of smaller firms will have biased upward returns during earnings announcement dates. This size effect could explain the previous abnormal returns if the firms in the long position of the hedge portfolio tend to be smaller than average or smaller than the firms in the short position. This is not likely the case for the sample of firms in this study. Multinational firms tend to be larger than average. For the firms in the hedge portfolio, the mean (median) decile rank based on NYSE capitalization breakpoints is 6.0 (7). The mean (median) capitalization rank for firms in the long position of the hedge portfolio is 6.3 (7) compared to the mean (median) of 5.7 (6) for firms in the short position. Thus, the firms used in this analysis are larger than average and are less likely to be subject to the small firm size effect. Also, the firms in the long position are *larger* than the firms in the short position. This actually works against finding a positive return to the hedge portfolio during the announcement period as reported in Table 3.

As a final test of market mispricing versus unidentified risk premia, the relation between current changes in foreign earnings and one, two, or three year-ahead stock returns is estimated. If the abnormal returns in year $t + 1$ are the result of the market failing to understand how foreign earnings in year t relates to total earnings in year $t + 1$, then we should expect the market to correct fully for this mispricing when earnings in year $t + 1$ are reported. In this

---

[13] The announcement period abnormal return of the short position is approximately equal to the average announcement period abnormal return of the 1000 random portfolios (0.66%).

[14] Bernard et al. (1997) report an asymmetric announcement period return for the post-earnings-announcement drift. The quarter $t + 1$ three-day earnings announcement market-adjusted return for the good (bad) news portfolio is 1.3% (−0.3%).

W.B. Thomas / Journal of Accounting and Economics 28 (2000) 243–267 261

case, abnormal returns would not persist beyond year $t + 1$. If the abnormal returns are due to the change in foreign earnings being a measure of risk, then abnormal returns are more likely to persist beyond year $t + 1$. Thus, these tests operate under the assumption that a relation between current accounting variables and long-term abnormal returns is more characteristic of accounting variables representing risk factors and that no relation beyond $t + 1$ is more characteristic of market mispricing. However, it could be that the change in foreign earnings represents a risk factor that exhibits short-term reversal so that there is no relation with abnormal returns in the long-term. Likewise, it may also be possible for the market to fail to understand the impact of foreign earnings on long-term earnings, causing a long-term relation between current changes in foreign earnings and stock returns. While it is not possible to observe directly whether market mispricing or unidentified risk premia causes a relation between accounting variables and future abnormal returns, I proceed under the assumption that mispricing is more likely to cause only a short-term relation with abnormal returns while unidentified risk is more likely to cause a short- and long-term relation with abnormal returns. As an example, Stober (1992) shows that the abnormal returns to Ou and Penman's (1989) *Pr* trading strategy continue for up to 72 months. It is not likely that any market mispricing could continue for up to six years. Instead, this result is more consistent with *Pr* proxying for the effects of unidentified risk premia.

Table 4 reports the results of mean coefficients of cross-sectional regressions of abnormal returns in year $t + 1$, $t + 2$, or $t + 3$ on the change in total earnings and the change in foreign earnings in year t. As shown for year $t + 1$, the relation between the change in total earnings in year t and abnormal returns in year $t + 1$ is not significant, while the relation between the change in foreign earnings in year t and abnormal returns in year $t + 1$ is significant (controlling for the change in total earnings in year t). These results are consistent with the results reported previously in Table 2. For years $t + 2$ and $t + 3$, there is no statistically significant relation between long-term stock returns and either the change in total earnings alone or the change in foreign earnings while controlling for the change in total earnings.[15] In addition, the hedge portfolio's average abnormal returns for years $t + 2$ and $t + 3$ are close to zero at -0.5% and -0.2%, respectively. The evidence is consistent with the notion that the market fails to understand the persistence of foreign earnings in year t for total earnings in year $t + 1$ and then corrects fully for this mispricing in year $t + 1$ as total earnings are reported. Abnormal returns are no longer available beyond year $t + 1$.

---

[15] It should be noted that an additional, competing reason for the insignificant results in $t + 2$ and $t + 3$ could be the lower power of the tests relative to $t + 1$, as the number of observations has declined due to data requirements.

Table 4
Mean coefficients (p-values) of cross-sectional regressions of abnormal returns in year $t + \tau$ on the change in total earnings and the change in foreign earnings in year t[a]

$$ARET_{t+\tau} = \beta_0 + \beta_1 \Delta TOTX_t + \beta_2 \Delta FORX_t + \varepsilon_{t+\tau}$$

	$\tau = 1$ (n = 8051)		$\tau = 2$ (n = 7137)		$\tau = 3$ (n = 6273)	
β_0	0.008	0.008	0.003	0.005	0.010	0.010
	(0.380)	(0.385)	(0.757)	(0.634)	(0.273)	(0.266)
β_1	− 0.44	− 0.140	0.083	0.134	− 0.219	0.128
	(0.600)	(0.185)	(0.447)	(0.284)	(0.170)	(0.443)
β_2		0.495		− 0.374		− 0.478
		(0.045)		(0.345)		(0.316)
R^2		0.01		0.00		0.00

[a] $ARET$ is the 12-month buy-and-hold security return beginning three months after the fiscal year end minus the value-weighted return of the comparable size/book-to-market/prior year return portfolio over the same 12-month period (see Table 1 for a description of the comparable portfolio construction).

$\Delta TOTX$ is the change in total earnings scaled by average total assets.

$\Delta FORX$ is the change in foreign earnings scaled by average total assets.

Amounts reported represent mean coefficients of cross-sectional regressions. Amounts in parentheses are p-values of two-tailed t-tests that the mean coefficient is equal to zero. t-statistics are calculated using the time-series standard errors of the cross-sectional coefficients.

4.3. Incremental explanatory power beyond the accrual anomaly

As a final test, the market anomaly documented in this study is tested in the presence of the accrual anomaly documented in Sloan (1996). Sloan (1996) finds that the market overvalues (undervalues) firms with large positive (negative) accruals. If the change in foreign earnings (holding the change in total earnings constant) is negatively correlated with accruals, then the anomaly documented in this study may simply be the accrual anomaly in disguise. Sloan (1996, 293) estimates accruals using the following equation:

$$Accruals = (\Delta CA - \Delta Cash) - (\Delta CL - \Delta STD - \Delta TP) - Dep, \qquad (4)$$

where CA is the current assets, CL the current liabilities, STD the short-term debt, TP the income taxes payable, Dep the depreciation and amortization expense, and Δ denotes a change (all scaled by average total assets). Collins and Hribar (1999) suggest that this estimation of accruals can lead to serious errors, especially when the firm has been involved in mergers, acquisitions, and divestitures. Instead, Collins and Hribar (1999) estimate accruals as the difference between earnings and operating cash flows as reported on the statement of cash flows. They find that the accrual anomaly is more robust when using reported accruals rather than estimated accruals as in Sloan (1996). Limiting the estimation of accruals in this manner, however, limits the test period to 1988 and beyond since most firms did not begin reporting operating cash flows until Statement of Financial Accounting Standards No. 95 (SFAS 95) became effective.

To test for the incremental explanatory power of the foreign earnings anomaly beyond the accrual anomaly, the following regression models are estimated. First, using data over the 1988–1995 period, the existence of the accrual anomaly is tested for the sample of US multinational firms in this study in a regression of abnormal returns in year $t + 1$ on accruals in year t. Consistent with previous research, the coefficient on accruals should be negative. Since the test period has changed to coincide with the SFAS 95 reporting period, the results reported in Table 4 are replicated for this slightly different time period. The coefficient on the change in foreign earnings is expected to remain positive and significant. Results consistent with expectations in the first two regressions would separately support both anomalies. To test whether the anomalies are incremental to one another, the final regression includes both accruals and the change in foreign earnings. This allows the testing of one anomaly while controlling for the other.

The results are reported in Table 5. As expected and consistent with prior research, the first regression shows a significant negative relation between accruals in year t and abnormal returns in year $t + 1$. This result essentially replicates the anomaly documented in Sloan (1996) and Collins and Hribar (1999) for this sample of multinational firms. The second regression documents the existence of the foreign earnings anomaly in the SFAS 95 reporting period. The results are similar to those reported in Table 4. Finally, the third regression reveals that the coefficients on both accruals and the change in foreign earnings remain significant and have the predicted sign, controlling for each other. This result demonstrates that these anomalies are incremental to one another and additional abnormal returns could be earned using a combined strategy. For example, creating a hedge portfolio that consists of a long position in firms with large negative accruals and (holding total earnings constant) large positive changes in foreign earnings and a short position in firms with large positive accruals and (holding total earnings constant) large negative changes in foreign earnings should provide greater abnormal returns than those documented in the previous section. In fact, it does. Intersecting the long (short) position of the hedge portfolio created in Table 3 and Fig. 1 with firms in the lowest (highest) accrual quintile results in an average annual abnormal return of 12.8%.[16] This

---

[16] The average abnormal return of the long position is 5.0% and the average abnormal return of the short position is −7.8%.

264   W.B. Thomas / Journal of Accounting and Economics 28 (2000) 243–267

Table 5
Mean coefficients (p-values) of cross-sectional regressions of abnormal returns in year $t + 1$ on the change in total earnings, change in foreign earnings, and accruals in year t over the 1988–1995 period $(n = 6111)$[a]

$ARET_{t+1} = \beta_0 + \beta_1 \Delta TOTX_t + \beta_2 \Delta FORX_t + \beta_3 ACCRUALS_t + \varepsilon_{t+1}$		
β_0	− 0.019	0.004	− 0.021
	(0.055)	(0.691)	(0.036)
β_1		− 0.204	− 0.038
		(0.156)	(0.781)
β_2		0.632	0.607
		(0.052)	(0.048)
β_3	− 0.540		− 0.544
	(0.003)		(0.004)
R^2	0.01	0.01	0.02

[a] *ARET* is the 12-month buy-and-hold security return beginning three months after the fiscal year end minus the value-weighted return of the comparable size/book-to-market/prior year return portfolio over the same 12-month period (see Table 1 for a description of the comparable portfolio construction).

$\Delta TOTX$ is the change in total earnings scaled by average total assets.

$\Delta FORX$ is the change in foreign earnings scaled by average total assets.

ACCRUALS is the earnings before extraordinary items minus reported operating cash flows, divided by average total assets.

Amounts reported represent mean coefficients of cross-sectional regressions. Amounts in parentheses are p-values of two-tailed t-tests that the mean coefficient is equal to zero. t-statistics are calculated using the time-series standard errors of the cross-sectional coefficients.

compares to the average annual abnormal return of 6.8% when using the foreign earnings strategy alone, as reported in Table 3.

5. Conclusion

Prior research has shown that in certain contexts the market does not fully understand the extent to which current earnings persist to future earnings [e.g., Bernard and Thomas (1989, 1990) for the quarterly earnings series, Sloan (1996) for the cash flow versus accrual component of earnings, and Abarbanell and Bushee (1998) for various fundamental signals]. As a result, stock prices predictably overstate/understate the value of the firm. This study builds on this line of research by investigating whether abnormal returns can be earned using public information about firms' domestic and foreign earnings.

The results suggest that foreign earnings tend to be more persistent than domestic earnings. The market, however, underestimates the persistence of

W.B. Thomas / Journal of Accounting and Economics 28 (2000) 243–267 265

foreign earnings. As a result, there is a positive relation between current changes in foreign earnings and future abnormal stock returns, controlling for current changes in total earnings. A zero-investment hedge portfolio is constructed using the relation between changes in total earnings and changes in foreign earnings. This portfolio earns positive abnormal returns in nine out of ten years and the positive abnormal returns to the long position are concentrated in the few days surrounding the subsequent year's earnings announcement dates. Furthermore, the abnormal returns do not persist beyond the subsequent year. While it is not possible to observe directly whether the positive abnormal returns are the results of market mispricing or compensation for risk, the results of this study support the notion that market mispricing is more likely. However, the risk-based explanation cannot be ruled out. It could be that the abnormal returns are a combination of market mispricing and compensation for risk. It is also possible that risk factors other than those controlled for are the reason for the results.

One potential explanation for the existence of market mispricing is that it is difficult for investors to understand fully the origin of firms' foreign earnings. As discussed in the introduction, the investment and academic communities have heavily criticized firms' disclosures of foreign earnings. As a result of the low-quality disclosures, investors may not fully understand the implications of foreign earnings on the value of the firm. When facing considerable uncertainty, investors may cautiously underestimate the persistence of foreign earnings. Noise in disclosures alone, however, should not explain why investors underestimate the persistence of foreign earnings. Noise (or uncertainty) does not suggest a bias in either direction in setting security prices (Holthausen and Verrecchia, 1988). Future research is needed to investigate further why the market appears to underestimate the persistence of foreign earnings as the results of this study suggest. Additional research could investigate the source of foreign earnings or the type of disclosure that is associated with the market apparently underestimating the persistence of foreign earnings. For example, are earnings from riskier geographic areas such as South America or Asia more closely related to the foreign earnings anomaly? Is the level of disaggregation of geographic segment disclosures related to the foreign earnings anomaly? Unfortunately, given the high level of aggregation of foreign operations by many firms and the wide range of reporting practices across firms, it may be difficult to make any generalizations about the relation between geographic segment disclosures and the foreign earnings anomaly documented in this paper.

References

Abarbanell, J., Bushee, B., 1997. Fundamental analysis, future earnings, and stock prices. Journal of Accounting Research 34, 1–24.

Abarbanell, J., Bushee, B., 1998. Abnormal returns to a fundamental analysis strategy. The Accounting Review 73, 19–45.

American Institute of Certified Public Accountants, 1994. The Information Needs of Investors and Creditors. AICPA, New York.

Association for Investment Management and Research, Financial Accounting Policy Committee, 1992. Financial Reporting in the 1990's and Beyond: A Position Paper of the Association for Investment Management and Research, prepared by Peter H. Knutson, Charlottesville, Va., October.

Arnold, J., Holder, W., Mann, M., 1980. International reporting aspects of segment disclosures. International Journal of Accounting 15, 125–135.

Ball, R., 1992. The earnings-price anomaly. Journal of Accounting and Economics 15, 319–346.

Ball, R., Kothari, S., Watts, R., 1993. Economic determinants of the relation between earnings changes and stock returns. The Accounting Review 68, 622–638.

Bavishi, V., Wyman, H., 1980. Foreign operations disclosures by US-based multinational corporations: are they adequate? International Journal of Accounting 15, 153–168.

Balakrishnan, R., Harris, T., Sen, P., 1990. The predictive ability of geographic segment disclosures. Journal of Accounting Research 28, 305–325.

Bernard, V., Thomas, J., 1989. Post-earnings-announcement drift: Delayed price response or risk premium? Journal of Accounting Research 27, 1–36.

Bernard, V., Thomas, J., 1990. Evidence that stock prices do not fully reflect the implications of current earnings for future earnings. Journal of Accounting and Economics 13, 387–404.

Bernard, V., Thomas, J., Abarbanell, J., 1993. How sophisticated is the market in interpreting earnings news? Journal of Applied Corporate Finance 6, 54–63.

Bernard, V., Thomas, J., Whalen, J., 1997. Accounting-based stock price anomalies: separating market inefficiencies from risk. Contemporary Accounting Research 14, 89–136.

Boatsman, J., Behn, B., Patz, D., 1993. A test of the use of geographical segment disclosures. Journal of Accounting Research 31, 46–64.

Bodnar, G., Weintrop, J., 1997. The valuation of the foreign income of US multinational firms: a growth opportunities perspective. Journal of Accounting and Economics 24, 69–97.

Carhart, M., 1997. On persistence in mutual fund performance. Journal of Finance 52, 57–82.

Chambers, A., Penman, S., 1984. Timeliness of reporting and the stock price reaction to earnings announcements. Journal of Accounting Research 22, 21–47.

Chari, V., Jagannathan, R., Ofer, A., 1988. Seasonalities in security returns: the case of earnings announcements. Journal of Financial Economics 21, 101–121.

Collins, D., and Hribar, P., 1999. Earnings-based and accrual-based market anomalies: One effect or two? Unpublished working paper. University of Iowa.

Daniel, K., Grinblatt, M., Titman, S., Wermers, R., 1997. Measuring mutual fund performance with characteristic-based benchmarks. Journal of Finance 52, 1035–1058.

Fama, E., French, K., 1993. Common risk factors in the returns on stocks and bonds. Journal of Financial Economics 33, 3–56.

Fama, E., MacBeth, J., 1973. Risk, return, and equilibrium: empirical tests. Journal of Political Economy 71, 607–636.

Financial Accounting Standards Board, 1978. Statement of Financial Accounting Standards No. 14: *Financial Reporting for Segments of a Business Enterprise*. FASB, Stamford.

Francis, J., Philbrick, D., Schipper, K., 1995. Shareholder litigation and corporate disclosures. Journal of Accounting Research 33, 137–164.

Herrmann, D., 1996. The predictive ability of geographic segment information at the country, continent and consolidated levels. Journal of International Financial Management and Accounting 7, 50–73.

Herrmann, D., Thomas, W., 2000. An analysis of segment disclosures under SFAS No. 131 and SFAS No. 14. Forthcoming in Accounting Horizons.

Holthausen, R., Verrecchia, R., 1988. The effect of sequential information releases on the variance of price changes in an intertemporal multi-asset market. Journal of Accounting Research 26, 82–106.

Jegadeesh, N., 1990. Evidence of predictable behavior in security prices. Journal of Finance 45, 881–898.

Kasznik, R., Lev, B., 1995. To warn or not to warn: management disclosures in the face of an earnings surprise. The Accounting Review 70, 113–134.

Lev, B., Thiagarajan, R., 1993. Fundamental information analysis. Journal of Accounting Research 31, 190–215.

Mishkin, F., 1983. A Rational Expectations Approach to Macroeconomics: Testing Policy Effectiveness and Efficient Markets Models. University of Chicago Press for the National Bureau of Economic Research, Chicago.

Ou, J., Penman, S., 1989. Financial statement analysis and the prediction of stock returns. Journal of Accounting and Economics 11, 295–329.

Pacter, P., 1993. Reporting Disaggregated Information. FASB, Norwalk.

Roberts, C., 1989. Forecasting earnings using geographical segment data: some U.K. evidence. Journal of International Financial Management and Accounting 1, 130–151.

Skinner, D., 1994. Why firms voluntarily disclose bad news. Journal of Accounting Research 32, 38–60.

Sloan, R., 1996. Do stock prices fully reflect information in accruals and cash flows about future earnings? The Accounting Review 71, 289–315.

Stober, T., 1992. Summary financial statement measures and analysts' forecasts of earnings. Journal of Accounting and Economics 15, 347–372.

[10]

The International
Journal of
Accounting

The Difficulty of Achieving Economic Reality Through Foreign Currency Translation

David A. Ziebart and Jong-Hag Choi
University of Illinois at Urbana-Champaign

Key Words: Foreign Currency Translation; Purchasing Power Parity

Abstract: The Financial Accounting Standards Board attempted to alleviate the problems with the reporting of foreign operations and foreign currency translation adjustments by issuing SFAS No. 52. This study examines the sign and magnitudes of the reporting errors that result under the best translation approach—current cost translated at the current exchange rate. Accordingly, a benchmark is established regarding the "best" we will be able to accomplish when certain foreign currency market conditions exist. Unfortunately, the results demonstrate that a foreign currency translation that is economically interpretable is not easily achieved. To achieve economic interpretability, we suggest that supplemental information regarding current values, the timing of asset acquisitions, historical exchange rates at the time of the acquisitions, and the current exchange rates should be provided in financial statements or the accompanying footnotes.

> "The values in the Ledger must be reckoned in one kind of money.....ducats, or lire, or Florence, or gold scudi....you should always use the same kind of money...."

> Frater Lucas de Burgo Sancti Sepulchri, (1494, p. 210):
> translation by Geijsbeek (1914).

Foreign currency translation has been an issue in accounting since the days of Paccioli. In the United States, the Financial Accounting Standards Board (FASB) has been involved in developing accounting methods for U.S. multinational corporations to translate the results of foreign operations and financial position for inclusion in their financial statements. As the globalization of corporate activities as well as the volatility of foreign currency exchange rates increase, the FASB continues to face difficulties in developing translation methods that provide financial reporting information which is interpretable. Given the continued pressure for financial statements to portray economic reality, the current approach to foreign currency translation will continue to be questioned.

Direct all correspondence to: David A. Ziebart, Department of Accountancy, University of Illinois at Urbana-Champaign 215 Commerce West, 1206 S. Sixth Street, Champaign, IL 61820; E-Mail:ziebart@uiuc.edu.

The International Journal of Accounting, Vol. 33, No. 4, pp. 403-414   **ISSN: 0020-7063.**

404   THE INTERNATIONAL JOURNAL OF ACCOUNTING   Vol. 33, No. 4, 1998

It is difficult to develop foreign currency translation (FCT) methods that achieve "economic interpretability" by employing a translation method of just converting the amounts of transactions and balances of accounts from one currency to another using an exchange rate. As explained later, employing such a simple approach does not result in economic interpretability.

Given the recent emphasis on valuation and economic interpretability of the statement of financial position, foreign currency translation continues to be a concern. This concern is exacerbated since the degree of internationalization of many firms continues to increase and now includes hedging activities as well as transactions in derivative securities. Internationalization and the need for sound FCT methods are expected to increase as additional foreign markets are opened to U.S. corporations as well as foreign corporations expanding their presence into new markets.

Of the alternative foreign currency translation methods, the method that theoretically *best* achieves economic interpretability is current cost valuation translated at the current exchange rate (CCCE, hereafter) (Beaver & Wolfson, 1982; Ijiri, 1983). Unfortunately, Glick (1986) points out that this method, while theoretically superior to the alternatives, is flawed when conditions of market neutrality are violated—and these violations occur almost continuously. This problem may assist in explaining why recent evidence on the valuation implications of FCT adjustments (Soo & Soo, 1994; Collins & Salatka, 1993; Bartov & Bodnar, 1994), although generally supporting the theoretically expected effects, is inconsistent.

Using actual foreign currency exchange rates, this study investigates the degree that reported values of foreign subsidiary assets, translated using CCCE (current costs and current exchange rates—the best method for achieving economic interpretability), are biased relative to the economic value of the assets. This bias is due to the failure of exchange rate neutrality or purchasing power parity, one of the conditions of market neutrality assumed by Beaver and Wolfson (1982), to hold. Most economists take it for granted that purchasing power parity does not hold for exchange rates in today's markets and its failure is widely documented.

HISTORICAL BACKGROUND

The FASB's first attempt to regulate foreign currency translation methods for U.S. GAAP, SFAS No. 8, was issued in 1975. SFAS No. 8 standardized the various translation practices being used by multinational corporations into one general approach. SFAS No. 8 was met with strong opposition by the financial community since it disparately treated long term assets and increased the volatility of reported income. The FASB attempted to alleviate these problems by issuing SFAS No. 52 in December 1981.

SFAS No. 52 provided two methods of foreign currency translation; the temporal method when the functional currency is the U.S. dollar and the current method when the functional currency is the local currency of the foreign subsidiary. The temporal method is, in essence, the same as SFAS No. 8; all translation gains and losses are reflected in current income and different exchange rates are used for different items. The current rate approach does not require gains and losses from foreign currency translation to be reported as income and all items are translated at the current exchange rate.

SFAS No. 70, issued in 1982, added to and clarified SFAS No. 52 by requiring supplemental disclosure of the current market values of fixed assets and certain other foreign operation items. In 1986, the FASB issued SFAS No. 89 to supersede SFAS No. 33 and the related statement No. 70. Supplemental disclosure of current market values is no longer required; it is only encouraged.

Although SFAS No. 52 may have alleviated the significant controversies of SFAS No. 8, it does not result in financial statements that are economically interpretable. Selling and Sorter (1983) describe the effect of SFAS No. 52 on financial statement analysis as follows:

> ...the translation at current exchange rates of local currency-denominated historical cost items may be considered to result in a figure that is neither a meaningful description of past cash flows nor a description of future flows. The Statement further confounds interpretation of the effects of translation by requiring that these meaningless balances be consolidated with the parent company's accounts.

Wojciechowski (1982) describes the position of Du Pont regarding SFAS No. 52 by stating that "the current rate method...gives off potential false and misleading signals."

IDENTIFICATION OF "BEST" REPORTING METHOD

To evaluate alternative translation methods, Beaver and Wolfson (1982) introduced the concepts of *economic interpretability* and *symmetry* as desirable attributes of the financial statements produced using alternative FCT methods. Given some fairly restrictive assumptions regarding the nature of financial markets, Beaver and Wolfson concluded that the current cost and current exchange rate (CCCE) method results in financial statements that possess the properties of economic interpretability and symmetry. They note that other methods, such as historical cost translated at the historical exchange rate and historical cost translated at the current exchange rate, are deficient in achieving these attributes. The stylized economy used by Beaver and Wolfson assumed a nearly perfect market situation and they implied that alternative FCT methods are even more deficient in less perfect market situations.

The Beaver and Wolfson (1982) results require four conditions of market neutrality to hold (Glick, 1986). First, exchange rate neutrality, commonly referred to as purchasing power parity, prevails when the change in price of goods in the parent country is equal to the dollar-equivalent change in price of goods in the host country. Second, inflation neutrality exists when the input and output prices change at the same rate. Third, international interest parity holds when the domestic interest rate is equivalent to the effective dollar cost of borrowing in the foreign market. Fourth, domestic interest neutrality exists when the market rate of interest is equal to the real interest rate plus the rate of inflation. When these conditions are met, the CCCE provides an accurate assessment regarding the value of the foreign operations (Glick, 1986, 247)). However, when the neutrality conditions are not met, CCCE does not produce financial information that is readily interpretable.

From a practical point-of-view, the "best" FCT approach (using the criteria identified by Beaver & Wolfson) combines SFAS No. 52 with supplemental information such as was required by SFAS No. 70. Unfortunately, translating historical cost information falls fall short of achieving economic interpretability because the assets are not reported at current costs and the conditions of neutrality are not met in the real world. When neutrality conditions are not met, even translating current values at current exchange rates may not achieve complete economic interpretability. With financial statement information prepared using a historical cost basis, the failure to disclose current values results in financial statements which are even less interpretable.

SCOPE OF ANALYSIS

This study determines the extent to which the failure of the exchange rate neutrality condition (purchasing power parity) biases reported assets even when the assets are measured using current cost translated at the current exchange rate (CCCE). Evidence on the extent to which the most theoretically correct method of FCT is biased due to the failure of purchasing power parity is provided. In addition, the results of this study provide a benchmark as to the "best" we can hope to achieve with FCT. Accordingly, the analysis is conducted such that the computed bias is due solely to the violation of the exchange rate neutrality condition.

For a sample of 59 countries, the long-run deviation of the actual exchange rate from the theoretical purchasing power parity derived exchange rate is computed and the degree of long term asset misstatement is assessed for hypothetical asset acquisitions made from 1960 through 1996 and reported at year-end 1996.

For actual multinational corporations, the degree of actual misstatement will be most severe when foreign operations have a high ratio of fixed assets. Therefore, the degree of misstatement in actual financial statements depends on (1) the extent to which the purchasing power parity condition is violated; (2) the degree of investment in fixed assets; (3) the years in which the assets were acquired; and (4) the rate of asset turnover.[1]

The results of this study demonstrate that the reporting of assets using CCCE does not achieve economic interpretability in most cases. Glick (1986) suggests that more meaningful financial statements can be produced by adjusting the reported current values for the deviations of the actual exchange rates from the purchasing power parity exchange rates. The adjustments needed to offset the exchange rate purchasing power parity deviations in the reporting of assets are provided in this study.

If corporations were to provide supplemental information regarding acquisition dates and current costs of assets and liabilities, and either parity deviations or the exchange rates at the time of the acquisitions, financial statement users could adjust the historical cost information to be economically interpretable. Alternatively, these adjustments could be computed by the reporting entity and provided directly to the financial statement users in the financial statements or the accompanying notes.

The next section illustrates the effects purchasing power parity deviations may have on the economic interpretability of asset values measured using CCCE. The computed percentage amounts of misstatement are then reported. The fourth section summarizes the results and the implications of the findings to the accounting for foreign operations.

EFFECTS OF PURCHASING POWER PARITY DEVIATIONS ON REPORTED ASSET VALUES

The purchasing power parity theory, an integral assumption of Beaver and Wolfson (1982, pg. 531), links the change in the foreign exchange rate between two countries to the changes in the price levels of the two countries. A change in the equilibrium exchange rate is assumed to be proportional to the change in the ratio of the foreign price level to the domestic price level. Given the evidence by Frenkel (1981) and Branson (1983) (as well as others) that the purchasing power parity theorem does not hold in either the short or the medium term, this analysis focuses on the extent to which asset values translated using the "best" method, CCCE, may be biased.

To illustrate the effect of purchasing power parity deviations on the economic interpretability of reported asset values, let us assume the following. *XYZ* Corporation, a multinational corporation based in the United States, purchases fixed assets (land) in three countries during year t. At the time of the purchase the U.S. dollar value for each of the investments is $100.00. The exchange rates for the three countries at the time of acquisition are: Country A: 3.5 local currency units to $1.00; Country B: 20 local currency units to $1.00; and Country C: 1 local currency unit to $1.00.

In local currency units, the cost of the asset purchases is 350.00 in Country A, 2000.00 in Country B, and 100.00 in Country C. For simplicity, assume that during period T the foreign inflation rate is 10% in each of the three countries and there is no inflation in the United States. For simplicity, let us further assume that the current value of the assets in each of the countries rises at the general rate of inflation in that country.

The current values of the assets at time t+T in the local currency units are: Country A: 385.00 (350.00 * (1.10)); Country B: 2200.00 (2000.00 * (1.10)); and Country C: 110.00 (100.00 * (1.10)).

Assume that at time t+T the current exchange rates, foreign currency units to U.S. dollars, are: Country A: 4.50 local currency units to $1.00; Country B: 21.00 local currency units to $1.00; and Country C: 1.10 local currency units to $1.00. The foreign currency translated current values reported in the corporation's financial statements will be: Country A: $85.56 (385.00 / 4.50); Country B: $104.76 (2200.00 / 21.00); and Country C: $100.00 (110.00 / 1.10). Note that by construction of the example, the economic value of the asset measured in U.S. dollars is $100.00!

The value reported in the financial statements of the asset in Country A using CCCE translation understates the economic value of the asset by $14.44 (a positive parity error of 14.44%; (4.50 - 3.85) / 4.50) while the reported value of the asset in Country B overstates the economic value by $4.76 (a parity deviation of - 4.76%).[2] Only for Country C is the reported value of the asset consistent with its economic value.

The failure of the reported asset values (using CCCE) to portray the economic value of the assets is due to the purchasing power parity deviations for Country A and Country B. The purchasing power parity exchange rates are 3.85 local currency units per $1.00 and 22.00 local currency units per $1.00 for Country A and Country B, respectively. The actual exchange rates are 4.50 local currency units per $1.00 for Country A and 21.00 local currency units per $1.00 for Country B.

The preceding simple example illustrates the difficulty of developing a foreign currency translation method that achieves economic interpretability when the exchange rate neutral-

THE INTERNATIONAL JOURNAL OF ACCOUNTING   Vol. 33, No. 4, 1998

Table 1.   Mean, Standard Deviation, and Range of Reported Bias by Country

Country	Mean	Standard Deviation	Minimum	Maximum
Australia	-.06	.13	-.36	+.15
Austria	-.50	.37	-1.13	+.04
Belgium	-.23	.26	-.71	+.22
Bolivia	-5.18	25.37	-151.87	+.27
Brazil	-7.08	10.71	-45.37	-.15
Canada	+.14	.07	+.01	+.24
Chile	-.11	.74	-2.49	+.65
Columbia	-.09	.33	-.84	+.30
Costa Rico	+.12	.38	-1.08	+.49
Cyprus	+.05	.17	-.36	+.30
Denmark	-.37	.35	-1.07	+.07
Ecuador	+.01	.43	-1.09	+.42
Egypt	-.01	.23	-.50	+.33
El Salvador	-.85	.32	-1.37	-.07
Finland	-.12	.19	-.40	+.23
France	-.20	.20	-.64	+.09
Germany	-.27	.27	-.69	+.15
Guatemala	+.08	.27	-.81	+.31
Haiti	-.25	.22	-.96	+.06
Honduras	+.34	.21	-.30	+.55
Iceland	-.19	.27	-1.19	+.16
India	+.39	.23	-.11	+.63
Iran	+.18	.42	-1.34	+.65
Ireland	-.23	.20	-.52	+.10
Israel	-.66	1.22	-5.52	+.18
Italy	-.18	.18	-.57	+.14
Jamaica	-.00	.39	-1.37	+.42
Japan	-.81	.80	-2.53	+.19
Kenya	+.03	.22	-.86	+.35
Luxembourg	-.18	.22	-.67	+.22
Malaysia	+.12	.14	-.17	+.31
Malta	+.17	.14	-.11	+.38
Mexico	-.11	.52	-1.87	+.37
Morocco	+.07	.20	-.44	+.39
Netherlands	-.29	.33	-.90	+.19
Netherlands Antilles	+.04	.05	-.07	+.12
New Zealand	-.31	.20	-.88	+.01
Nigeria	-1.16	1.22	-4.82	+.24
Norway	-.22	.28	-.76	+.11
Pakistan	+.36	.24	-.07	+.65
Panama	+.30	.14	+.02	+.46
Paraguay	-.01	.32	-.69	+.42
Peru	-7.81	19.74	-102.01	-.07
Philippines	-.22	.24	-.92	+.35
Portugal	-.57	.37	-1.32	+.01
Sierra Leone	-.02	.34	-1.69	+.30
Singapore	-.18	.12	-.43	+.08
South Africa	+.02	.18	-.70	+.22
Sri Lanka	+.26	.41	-.25	+.87
Sweden	-.12	.20	-.53	+.17

(continued)

Table 1.   (Continued)

Country	Mean	Standard Deviation	Minimum	Maximum
Switzerland	-.59	.53	-1.47	+.09
Syria	-1.18	.55	-2.47	-.02
Thailand	.00	.09	-.17	+.14
Trinidad	+.04	.11	-.13	+.34
Turkey	-.13	.50	-1.41	+.42
United Kingdom	-.14	.16	-.38	+.17
Uruguay	-1.26	1.07	-4.37	+.75
Venezuela	+.17	.46	-1.04	+.62
Zambia	-.35	.79	-2.61	+.31

ity condition, assumed by Beaver and Wolfson (1982), is violated. Accordingly, this example portrays the practical significance of the problem pointed out analytically by Glick (1986).

One might presume from the example that the ideal is to maintain the dollar value of the asset over time. This would imply that the use of historical costs translated at the historical exchange rate would be appropriate. Unfortunately, this results in well known problems regarding the economic interpretability of historical cost data.

EMPIRICAL ANALYSIS

To determine the extent to which reported asset values may be misstated due to purchasing power parity deviations when CCCE is employed, the percentage deviation from parity is computed for a sample of 59 countries. This computation is based on a year-end 1996 reporting date and computes the percentage error that results if assets were acquired during each of the years from 1961 to 1996 and reported in 1996 using CCCE. The translation error and, accordingly the correction needed to reflect economic interpretability, is determined for each of the 36 years. Table 1 reports the average translation error, the standard deviation of the error across time, as well as the minimum and maximum errors for the 59 countries in this analysis.

Note that a positive parity error results in an understatement of asset values since more local currency units are required to purchase a U.S. dollar. Alternatively, when less (than parity) local currency units are required to purchase a U.S. dollar, a negative parity error occurs and the economic values of the assets are overstated in U.S. dollars.[3]

For example, the percentage parity deviation for an asset acquired in 1961 and reported using CCCE is −.17 for Australia. The reported asset value is overstated by about 17 percent, an amount that is probably material and certainly inconsistent with the accounting notion of conservatism. However, the reported value in 1996 for an asset purchased in 1973 is understated by about 11 percent. For the 36 years of potential asset acquisition, the reported asset value is overstated 23 times and understated 12 times.

In addition to the sign of the average parity errors across countries, the magnitude of the parity errors varies both across time and across countries. For instance, Australia has thirteen periods out of thirty-six in which the magnitude of the error is less than 10 percent.

410   THE INTERNATIONAL JOURNAL OF ACCOUNTING   Vol. 33, No. 4, 1998

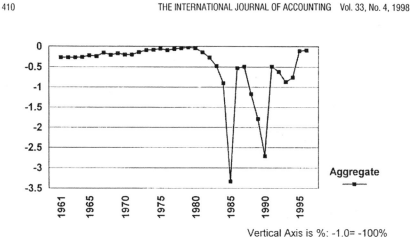

Vertical Axis is %: -1.0= -100%

Figure 1. Average Aggregate Parity Error

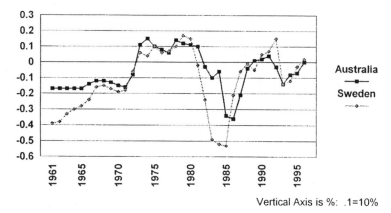

Vertical Axis is %: .1=10%

Figure 2. Parity Errors for Australia and Sweden

However, Brazil has twenty-six periods in which the magnitude of the error is greater than 100 percent.

The magnitude of the error is rather small for many countries. In instances in which the error is small, the current values of assets translated at current rates may be reasonably interpretable. Examples of countries with minor, on average, deviations from the parity exchange rate are Ecuador, Egypt, Jamaica, Kenya, Netherlands Antilles, Paraguay, Sierra Leon, South Africa, Thailand, and Trinidad. On the other hand, a number of countries have numerous years in which the magnitude of the error exceeds 100%—Bolivia, Nigeria, Peru, Syria, and Uruguay.

The patterns of the computed parity deviations indicate that the magnitudes of the errors as well as the signs of the errors are not consistent over time. If the errors are not system-

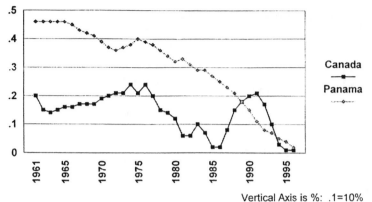

Vertical Axis is %: .1=10%

Figure 3. Parity Errors for Canada and Panama

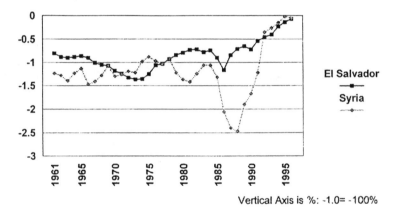

Vertical Axis is %: -1.0= -100%

Figure 4. Parity Errors for El Salvador and Syria

atic, one cannot easily adjust for the parity deviation without knowing the composition of the assets and the periods of acquisition.

Figure 1 portrays the mean percentage errors for each of the 36 years in this analysis. Generally speaking, these results suggest an overall negative error, which implies an over-statement of the reported values. However, these overall mean negative errors are driven by a few extreme negative outliers.

To illustrate the longitudinal patterns, the percentage parity errors are graphed for a few example countries. Figure 2 shows the patterns of two countries, Sweden and Australia, in which the pattern is mixed in sign over time. This indicates that one cannot readily know whether the reported assets are overstated or understated without knowing the years in which the particular assets were acquired. In essence, information regarding acquisition dates is needed in order to make the information economically interpretable. The information user cannot know the direction or the magnitude of the bias unless the acquisition date is known.

Figure 3 illustrates two countries, Panama and Canada, in which the parity deviation is positive over all the years analyzed. In this case, the current values of assets translated at current exchange rates are systematically understated. A financial statement user knows the general direction of the error and only needs the specific acquisition information to determine the magnitude.

Figure 4 depicts the patterns for El Salvador and Syria, two countries in which the deviations are negative over all of the years in the analysis. For these two countries, the economic values of the assets are overstated when the current values are translated at the current rate of exchange. Again, the sign of the error is known but acquisition information is required to determine the magnitude.

Table 2 classifies the 59 countries into the three types of patterns, positive deviations, mixed sign deviations, and negative deviations. For countries with a systematic pattern, the sign of the misstatement is known but the magnitude of misstatement is not known without detailed analysis. For the 59 countries studied, only two countries display a systematic positive parity deviation (understatement of economic values) while another four countries possess a systematic negative parity deviation (overstatement of economic values) when CCCE is applied. Fifty-three of the countries have a mixed pattern with both positive and negative parity errors. The financial statement user does not know either the sign of the misstatement or the magnitude unless more detailed information is provided.

One might expect the greatest deviations from purchasing power parity occurred when the Bretton Woods agreement was still intact; exchange rates were not allowed to float until the Smithsonian Agreement of 1971. This would result in greater parity deviations for the 1960's with smaller deviations from the early 1970's onward. However, many countries continued to lock their currency onto the dollar and maintained a relatively fixed exchange rate policy after the Smithsonian Agreement. The results in Figure 1 suggest that the deviations immediately following the Smithsonian Agreement, 1972 through 1980, were relatively small with larger deviations both in the earlier (pre-1972) and later (post-1980) periods.

Table 2. Countries Classified by Systematic Deviations (Errors)

Systematic Positive	Systematic Negative	Mixed
Canada	Brazil	Australia Austria Belgium Bolivia Chile
Panama	El Salvador	Colombia Cyprus Denmark Ecuador Egypt
	Peru	Finland France Germany Guatemala Honduras
	Syria	Iceland India Iran Ireland Israel Italy Jamaica
		Japan Kenya Luxembourg Malaysia Malta
		Mexico Morocco Netherlands Netherland
		Antilles New Zealand Nigeria Pakistan
		Paraguay Philippines Portugal Sierra Leone
		Singapore Sri Lanka Sweden Switzerland
		Thailand Trinidad & Tobago Turkey
		United Kingdom Uruguay Venezuela Zambia

SUMMARY AND CONCLUSIONS

This study demonstrates that the notion of economic interpretability is not achieved when foreign subsidiary financial statements are translated using the current cost and current exchange rate method advocated by Beaver and Wolfson (1982). As pointed out analytically by Glick (1986), when there are significant deviations from the conditions of exchange rate neutrality, the value of the foreign operations is misstated.

In addition, the results of this study indicate that the degree of misstatement is unique both across time and across countries. For many countries (53 out of 59) the sign of the misstatement varies across years and a financial statement user needs to know the date the asset was acquired in order to correctly understand its value when it is translated from the foreign currency to U.S. dollars.

From a policy point of view, these results imply that the Financial Accounting Standards Board may not be able to achieve economic interpretability in foreign currency translation when the conditions of market neutrality fail to exist. Purchasing power parity has not existed in foreign exchange rates in the past and it will probably not exist in the future. In fact, the magnitudes of the deviations have gotten even larger during the later 1980's and early 1990's.

The most promising foreign currency exchange rate method, CCCE (Beaver & Wolfson, 1982), fails when the exchange rates are not consistent with the underlying price level changes. For the current cost data translated at the current exchange rate to be made more meaningful, additional disclosures need to be provided regarding the historical exchange rates in effect when assets were acquired and the current exchange rate at the date of the financial statement. In addition, a schedule of when the assets of the entity were acquired is necessary. This information, in combination with the current costs of the assets, may allow the user to more accurately assess the results of operations and the financial position regarding foreign operations.

Given the complexity and volume of information that would need to be provided, we suggest two alternatives. One approach would be to provide the additional information only when the magnitude of the misstatement is greater than some threshold amount or percentage. A second approach would be to only provide the supplemental information only for periods in which a significant amount of assets was acquired.

NOTES

1. It is assumed that general price level changes and specific price level changes are the same This simplifying assumption is necessary in order to focus on the general effects that are introduced when purchasing power parity fails to hold and allows this analysis to focus on the assumptions made by Beaver and Wolfson (1982) and questioned by Glick (1986). Failure of this assumption to hold indicates that the reported asset values may be even less economically interpretable.
2. Percentage Parity Error = [(Actual Current Exchange Rate) - (Parity Current Exchange Rate)] / (Actual Current Exchange Rate). Parity Current Exchange Rate = Original Exchange Rate at Time of Acquisition * [(1 + Foreign Inflation Rate) / (1 + Domestic Inflation Rate)].
3. Percentage Parity Error = [(Actual 1996 Exchange Rate) - (Parity 1996 Exchange Rate)] / (Actual 1996 Exchange Rate) where Parity 1996 Exchange Rate = Original Exchange Rate * [(1 + Foreign Inflation Rate) / (1 + Domestic Inflation Rate)]

414   THE INTERNATIONAL JOURNAL OF ACCOUNTING   Vol. 33, No. 4, 1998

REFERENCES

Bartov, E. and G. Bodnar. 1994. "Firm Valuation, Earnings Expectations, and the Exchange-Rate Exposure Effect," *Journal of Finance, 49*(5): 1755–185.

Beaver, W. and M. Wolfson. 1982. "Foreign Currency Translation and Changing Prices in Perfect and Complete Markets," *Journal of Accounting Research*, (Autumn): 528–550.

Branson, W. 1983. "Macroeconomic Determinants of Real Exchange Risk," in *Managing Foreign Exchange Risk*, (edited by R. Herring). Cambridge: Cambridge University Press, pp. 33–74.

Collins D. and W. Salatka. 1993. "Noisy Accounting Earnings Signals and Earnings Response Coefficients: The Case of Foreign Currency Accounting," *Contemporary Accounting Research, 10*(1): 119–159.

Frenkel, J. 1981. "The Collapse of Purchasing Power Parities During the 1970's," *European Economic Review*, (May): 145–165.

Geijsbeek, J. 1914. *Ancient Double-Entry Bookkeeping*, Denver Colorado: 57.

Glick, R. 1986. "Market Neutrality Conditions and Valuation of a Foreign Affiliate," *Journal of Business, Finance, and Accounting*, (Summer): 239–249.

Ijiri, Y. 1983. "Foreign Currency Accounting and Its Transition," in *Managing Foreign Exchange Risk*, (edited by R. Herring). Cambridge: Cambridge University Press), pp. 181–212.

Selling, T. and G. Sorter. 1983. "FASB Statement No. 52 and Its Implications for Financial Statement Analysis," *Financial Analysts Journal*, (May–June): 64–69.

Soo B. and L. Soo. 1994. "Accounting for the Multinational Firm: Is the Translation Process Valued by the Stock Market?" *The Accounting Review*, (October): 617–637.

Wojciechowski, S. 1982. "Du Pont Evaluates FAS 52," *Management Accounting*, (July): 31–35.

Ziebart, D. 1985. "Exchange Rates and Purchasing Power Parity: Evidence Regarding the Failure of SFAS No. 52 to Consider Exchange Risk in Hyper-Inflationary Countries," *The International Journal of Accounting, 21*(1), (Fall): 39–51.

[11]

ACCOUNTING FOR BUSINESS COMBINATIONS AND FOREIGN CURRENCY TRANSLATION:
AN EMPIRICAL COMPARISON OF LISTED COMPANIES FROM DEVELOPED ECONOMIES

Ajay Adhikari and Emmanuel N. Emenyonu

ABSTRACT

This paper presents the results of a cross-national study to assess the degree of harmony in selected accounting measurement practices of large companies from France, Germany, Japan, the United Kingdom, and the United States. The accounting measurement practices examined in this study relate to accounting for business combinations, consolidations, and foreign currency transactions and translations. The results of the study suggest that there are substantial differences in the level of harmony achieved on the different measurement issues examined.

Advances in International Accounting, Volume 10, pages 45-62.
Copyright © 1997 by JAI Press Inc.
All rights of reproduction in any form reserved.
ISBN: 0-7623-0165-1

46 AJAY ADHIKARI and EMMANUEL N. EMENYONU

INTRODUCTION AND MOTIVATION

In the last decade we have witnessed the globalization of the capital markets. Deregulation and advances in technology and communication have effectively linked different parts of the world. Accounting practices, however, continue to be nationalistic, reflecting the different environmental conditions that exist in each country. This accounting diversity adds another layer of complexity in analyzing foreign financial statements and may impede the free flow of capital (Choi and Levich 1990).

Responding to this concern a number of organizations both regional (e.g., European Union [EU]) and international (e.g., International Accounting Standards Committee [IASC]) have launched international accounting harmonization initiatives. Although much has been written on the subject of international harmonization of accounting standards (Nobes 1980; Rivera 1989; Goeltz 1991; Chandler 1992), empirical research in this area has been less forthcoming. Prior to 1988 a few studies (Nair and Frank 1981; Evans and Taylor 1982; McKinnon and Janell 1984; Doupnik and Taylor 1985) used an empirical design to examine harmonization issues. These studies, however, have been criticized by Tay and Parker (1990) for lack of conceptual clarity and shortcomings in the data used.

More recently another strand of research pioneered by Van der Tas (1988) has emerged. It uses measurement approaches (C-index and I-index) derived and adapted from the Herfindahl concentration index (H-index) to assess the degree of harmony in accounting practices among countries.[1] A number of studies (Van der Tas 1988, 1992; Emenyonu and Gray 1992; Archer, Delvaille, and McLeay 1995; Herrmann and Thomas 1995) have used this methodology to examine accounting practices across countries but much work still needs to be done. This is because all the studies relate to a certain time frame and examine selected accounting practices in selected countries. Consequently, given the dynamic nature of accounting, there is a continuing need to fill the gaps of what we know about the state of accounting practices in the different countries of the world.

In this paper we use the I-index of international harmonization measurement complemented by the chi-square tests to assess the degree of harmony in selected accounting measurement practices of large companies from France, Germany, Japan, the United Kingdom, and the United

States. These countries were selected because France, Germany, and the United Kingdom are the leading economic powers in the EU and Japan and the United States are non-EU countries that have the strongest economies in the world. The five countries are founding members of the IASC and are current members of the IASC board. The sample of this study, therefore, is more international in nature than earlier studies that have been confined to European countries. Wallace and Gernon (1990) also suggest, to investigate similiarity (or indeed harmony), the sample under study must manifest significant differences (or heterogenity). All five countries boast strong, albeit, disparate accounting traditions making them interesting subjects for a study of harmony.

The accounting measurement practices examined in this study relate to accounting for business combinations, consolidations, and foreign currency transactions and translations. These three areas of accounting measurement were selected because there has traditionally been a great deal of diversity in national accounting rules governing these topics. Moreover, the globalization of business and the increase in international merger and acquisition activity has led to a heightened interest in the financial statement effects of accounting measurement choices related to these three areas. Accounting diversity related to business combinations, consolidation practices, and foreign currency transactions and translations can seriously impair international comparability of financial statements and potentially lead to capital market effects. Choi and Lee (1991), for example, found that U.K. acquirors of U.S. target firms were willing to pay a higher premium than U.S. acquirors of U.S. target firms. The higher premium appeared to be associated with the U.K. firms not having to amortize goodwill to earnings as is required in the United States.

The remainder of the paper is structured as follows: the second section is concerned with methodological aspects; in the third section the study findings are presented and discussed; this is followed by brief concluding remarks.

RESEARCH METHODOLOGY

This study embraced a total of 413 companies randomly selected. The national composition of the companies is as follows: France 70, Germany 73, Japan 90, U.K. 90, and United States 90.[2] Selected companies were required to have achieved a minimum turnover figure of at least

US\$250 million for the 1990/1991 financial year. In stipulating the minimum turnover threshold, care was taken to ensure that in each of the five countries only significantly large companies were selected for the study. Furthermore, the companies were selected from all industrial sectors except financial institutions. It is not expected that industrial factors should introduce any distortions since the sample is representative of a number of different industrial segments. The main source of data for this study was the annual reports of the companies in the sample for the 1990/1991 financial year.

Two major statistical tools of analysis were employed in analyzing the data. The chi-square test was used to ascertain whether significant differences can be said to exist in the pattern of using various profit measurement methods by large firms originating from each of these countries. On the other hand, the I-index, a variant of the Herfindahl concentration measure, was used to compute the degree of harmony that exists in the financial reporting practices among the countries included in the study.

It is important to point out that the results derived from the chi-square tests should not always be expected to accord with the rankings given by the I-index computations. For instance, it is quite possible that on a particular item the chi-square test might indicate that there are no significant differences between the practices of the companies, whereas the I-index calculation might lead to a relatively low score. The reason for this is that the tools measure different concepts of harmonization.

The chi-square test measures the extent to which the policy choices of companies from the five countries studied are matched. On the other hand, the I-index measures the extent to which the accounting practices of the companies are concentrated around one or more alternatives.

In order to illustrate the above point, assume that on a given accounting topic there are three alternative methods. If an equal proportion of companies from the different countries used the alternative methods equally, then the chi-square test will indicate that there are no significant differences in the accounting practices of the five countries. On the other hand, the I-index will result in a score of 33.3 percent, which might be lower (less harmonized) than the score on another topic whose chi-square test result might have indicated that there are significant differences between the different countries. Both concepts of harmonization are important. Therefore, we employ both techniques in this study.[3]

PRESENTATION AND DISCUSSION OF FINDINGS

In this section the status of the relevant accounting regulations in the five countries is first reviewed.[4] This is followed by the study results and a discussion of comparative practices. To facilitate discussion, the measurement issues examined in the study are categorized in three subsections: accounting for business combinations; accounting for consolidation practices; and accounting for foreign currency transactions and translations.

Accounting for Business Combinations

Table 1 reports the results for the measurement issues related to accounting for business combinations. Three measurement issues related to business combinations (purchase versus pooling, goodwill, and amortization of goodwill) were examined and are discussed below.

Table 1.   Accounting for Business Combinations

Panel A	Purchase vs. Pooling Accounting					
	France (%)	Germany (%)	Japan (%)	UK (%)	USA (%)	Total (%)
Purchase	65 (100.0)	50 (71.4)	73 (97.3)	86 (96.6)	82 (100.0)	356 (93.4)
Pooling	0 (0.0)	20 (28.6)	2 (2.7)	3 (3.4)	0 (0.0)	25 (6.6)
Total	65 (17.1)	70 (18.4)	75 (19.7)	89 (23.4)	82 (21.5)	381 (100.0)

Chi - Square - 68.96489;   D.F. = 4;   Sig. = .0000;   I-index = 0.9052

Panel B	Method of Accounting for Goodwill					
	France (%)	Germany (%)	Japan (%)	UK (%)	USA (%)	Total (%)
Capitalized	61 (100.0)	29 (52.7)	45 (83.3)	2 (2.4)	49 (100.0)	186 (61.4)
Written off	0 (0.0)	26 (47.3)	9 (16.7)	82 (97.6)	0 (0.0)	117 (38.6)
Total	61 (20.1)	55 (18.2)	54 (17.8)	84 (27.7)	49 (16.2)	303 (100.0)

Chi - Square - 205.28695;   D.F. = 4;   Sig. = .0000;   I-index = 0.5441

Panel C	Amortization Period for Goodwill					
	France (%)	Germany (%)	Japan (%)	UK (%)	USA (%)	Total (%)
1-5 years	1 (1.9)	9 (47.4)	24 (55.8)	0 (0.0)	0 (0.0)	34 (20.5)
6-10 years	6 (11.1)	2 (10.5)	5 (11.6)	0 (0.0)	0 (0.0)	13 (7.8)
11-15 years	5 (9.3)	6 (31.6)	0 (0.0)	0 (0.0)	2 (4.1)	13 (7.8)
16-20 years	13 (24.1)	1 (5.3)	8 (18.6)	1 (100.0)	3 (6.1)	26 (15.7)
21-40 years	29 (53.7)	1 (5.3)	6 (14.0)	0 (0.0)	44 (89.8)	80 (48.2)
Total	54 (32.5)	19 (11.4)	43 (25.9)	1 (0.6)	49 (29.5)	166 (100.0)

Chi - Square - 123.60272;   D.F. = 16;   Sig. = .0000;   I-index = 0.1097

50   AJAY ADHIKARI and EMMANUEL N. EMENYONU

Purchase versus Pooling Accounting

The regulatory requirements in all the countries, except France, allow for the use of both the purchase and the pooling of interests methods of accounting for business combinations. The IASC (IAS 22) requires that the purchase method be used except in the rare circumstances when a business combination is deemed as a "uniting of interests." In France only the purchase method is permitted. In Germany, Japan, the U.K., and the United States the pooling of interests method is also allowed if the combination meets certain restrictive criteria. The combination can be accounted as a pooling of interests in the four countries only when at least 90 percent of the outstanding voting common shares of one company is exchanged for voting common shares of the other company in a single transaction. In Japan and the United States there is the additional requirement that the two companies must have been autonomous for at least two years prior to the combination. There are also restrictions on the amount of cash consideration that can be paid. All forms of business combinations that do not meet these criteria must be accounted for by the purchase method.

The chi-square results reported in Table 1 (Panel A) suggest that there are significant differences in the accounting practices of companies from the five countries with respect to accounting for business combinations. The I-index value of 0.9052 for this measurement practice is, however, above most of the measurement issues examined and, thus, suggests the attainment of a relatively high level of harmonization on the topic of accounting for business combination. Furthermore, the results are also reflective of the regulatory stipulations. An overwhelming 93.4 percent of the companies adopted the purchase method for accounting for acquired businesses—a method strongly favored by the regulatory requirements of all the countries and also of the IASC.

Accounting for Goodwill

The regulatory provisions dealing with goodwill vary across the five countries. In the U.K. the immediate write-off of goodwill to stockholders' equity is preferred (though SSAP 22 allows companies the option of amortization over a period not exceeding the useful life of goodwill). In the United States goodwill must be capitalized and then written off to expense over a period not exceeding 40 years. In France goodwill is generally amortized over a period reflecting the assumptions and objectives prevailing at time of acquisition. No maximum period of amortization is stipulated. Internally generated goodwill (fonds de commerce) is generally accounted for separately.[5] It is not mandatory to amortize internally generated goodwill, but any decline in value should be reflected. In Germany goodwill may be capitalized as an intangible fixed asset and amortized either over four years or systematically over the period the company is likely to derive benefits from it. However, for tax purposes the amortization period is fixed at 15 years. Goodwill may also be written off against reserves in the consolidated balance sheet. In Japan goodwill should either be amortized on a straight-line basis over a reasonable period (usually five years) or charged immediately to income if it is not significant.

In its comparability project the IASC has recommended that goodwill be recognized as an asset and amortized on a systematic basis over five years and in exceptional circumstances up to 20 years maximum. The writing off of goodwill against reserves or shareholders' interest is specifically prohibited as an allowable alternative.

The chi-square test result (Table 1, Panel B) indicates that there are significant differences in the manner of treating goodwill across the five countries. The I-index value of 0.5441 is also low relative to the other measurement practices examined in the study, suggesting a low degree of harmony in the measurement practice related to goodwill among the five countries. The significant chi-square test result and the relatively low I-index value are being driven largely by the use of the immediate write-off method for goodwill used by European, especially German and U.K. companies. Emenyonu and Gray (1992) and Herrmann and Thomas (1995), using a sample comprised only of European companies, reported an even lower degree of harmony for goodwill measurement practices. In their study, Emenyonu and Gray obtained an I-index of 0.2636 and Herrmann and Thomas obtained an I-index of 0.2457 for goodwill accounting. This reinforces the assertion that the low degree of harmony in goodwill accounting is largely driven by the European countries.[6]

Amortization Period for Goodwill

Next in importance to the decision to capitalize and amortize goodwill is the question of the period over which goodwill should be amortized.

The link between the period of goodwill amortization and profit deter-mination is direct. A longer amortization period will, all things being constant, lead to a higher or more optimistic profit figure and vice versa. From Table 1 (Panel C), it can be seen that U.S. companies adopt the longest period of amortization with 89.8 percent of the U.S. companies that disclosed this item electing to amortize goodwill over a period of between 21-40 years. This is followed by France where 53.7 percent of the companies chose to amortize goodwill over the same time span. In contrast, a significant proportion of German companies (47.4%) and Japanese companies (55.8%) amortized goodwill over a time span of one to five years. This is reflective of the influence of taxation laws over financial reporting in the two countries. Interestingly, only one U.K. company disclosed the amortization period for goodwill. This reflects the prevalent practice in the U.K. of writing off goodwill to stockhold-ers' equity rather than capitalizing and amortizing it.

The chi-square test indicates that there are significant differences on the issue of the amortization period for goodwill in the financial state-ments of the companies from the five countries. The I-index of 0.1097 is the lowest of all measurement issues examined in the study. The low score on the I-index for amortization period can be partly attributed to the arbitrary time-period categorization used by the researchers to study this issue, but the results also mirror the wide scope for discretion allowed companies on this issue in the various national regulatory requirements.

Table 2.   Accounting for Consolidations

Panel A	Consolidated Financial Statements					
	France (%)	Germany (%)	Japan (%)	UK (%)	USA (%)	Total (%)
Non-consolidated	3 (4.3)	4 (5.5)	14 (15.6)	0 (0.0)	3 (3.3)	24 (5.8)
Consolidated	67 (95.7)	69 (94.5)	76 (84.4)	90 (100.0)	87 (96.7)	389 (94.2)
Column Total	70 (16.9)	73 (17.7)	90 (21.8)	90 (21.8)	90 (21.8)	413 (100.0)

Chi - Square - 22.48774;   D.F. = 4;   Sig. = .0002;   I-index = 0.9269

Panel B	Accounting for Investments in Associates					
	France (%)	Germany (%)	Japan (%)	UK (%)	USA (%)	Total (%)
Equity method	65 (100.0)	60 (95.2)	67 (87.0)	80 (95.2)	49 (98.0)	321 (94.7)
Cost method	0 (0.0)	3 (4.8)	10 (13.0)	4 (4.8)	1 (2.0)	18 (5.3)
Total	65 (19.2)	63 (18.6)	77 (22.7)	84 (24.8)	50 (14.7)	339 (100.0)

Chi - Square - 13.84864;   D.F. = 4;   Sig. = .0078;   I-index = 0.9376

Accounting for Consolidations

The two measurement practices examined that relate to accounting for consolidation practices are presentation of consolidated financial statements and accounting for investments in associates. The results for this section are presented in Table 2.

Consolidated Financial Statements

In all the five countries the preparation of consolidated financial statements for companies with subsidiaries is, generally speaking, mandatory. Control in most cases is determined by the ownership of more than half of the ordinary shares of a company. Control can also be said to exist if a company has the power to dominate the constitution of another company's board of directors or supervisory board, or if a company has the authority to exercise dominant influence over another via a control contract. In Japan and the United States, however, the existence of management control is not a sufficient basis for establishing control as the emphasis is more on ownership interest in a subsidiary. This contrasts with the practice in the U.K. where control, rather than legal ownership, receives more weighting in the determination of parent/subsidiary relationships. In all material particulars, the position of the International Accounting Standards Committee (IASC) is similar to that adopted by all the countries on the topic of consolidations. Control, under IAS 22 and IAS 27, can be established either through legal ownership or the existence of management control (IASC 1994).

Also, in all the countries there are provisions for the exclusion of some subsidiaries from consolidation under certain restrictive conditions. The most common reasons for excluding some subsidiaries from consolidation include the following:

1. the subsidiary is not material,
2. control is intended to be temporary,
3. unreasonable expense is likely to be incurred in order to consolidate a subsidiary,
4. substantial dissimilarity in the activities of a particular subsidiary such that consolidation would yield misleading information,
5. long-term restrictions hinder the parent company's ability to exercise control over a subsidiary, and

54   AJAY ADHIKARI and EMMANUEL N. EMENYONU

6. a subsidiary is not considered a going concern due to bankruptcy or liquidation.

The chi-square results reported in Table 2 (Panel A) indicate that there are significant differences between the countries on the issue of consolidated financial statements. Furthermore, from Panel A it can be seen that the country with the lowest proportion of companies practicing full consolidation is Japan with 84.4 percent, while the U.K. attained a 100 percent compliance with the requirement to prepare consolidated financial statements. The high compliance rates observed for France (95.7%) and Germany (94.5%) can partly be attributed to the implementation of the EU Seventh Directive that mandates consolidated financial statements in member countries.

The I-index value of 0.9269 is, relatively speaking, very high and signifies the achievement of an above normal level of de facto harmonization on this topic. The chi-square and I-index results seem to be in conflict because, as discussed earlier, the chi-square and I-index measure different concepts of harmonization. The significant chi-square is attributable to the lower percentage of Japanese companies which provide consolidated financial statements. If Japan is dropped from the sample, the chi-square becomes 7.597 (Sig. = .0782), which is no longer significant at the .05 level.

Accounting for Investments in Associates

In all the five countries both accounting regulations (as is the case with France, Germany, the U.K., the United States, and the IASC), and accounting conventions (as is the case with Japan), ordinarily encourage the use of the equity method of accounting for investments in associated companies. Associated companies are unanimously defined as companies over which another company exercises significant influence but not control. Significant influence is usually denoted by the holding of between 20 to 50 percent of the voting shares of a company.

Findings based on the chi-square tests (Table 2, Panel B), suggest that there are significant differences in the patterns of usage of methods between the five countries on the issue of accounting for investments in associates. On the other hand, the I-index score yields a value of 0.9376, which is the highest score obtained for any measurement issue examined in the study. As with consolidated financial statements, the lower

Business Combinations and Foreign Currency Translation   55

Table 3.   Accounting for Foreign Currency Transactions and Operations

Panel A   *Accounting for Foreign Currency Transactions*

	France (%)	Germany (%)	Japan (%)	UK (%)	USA (%)	Total (%)
Actual rates	14 (48.3)	22 (50.0)	22 (33.3)	7 (14.0)	2 (28.6)	67 (34.2)
Average rates	1 (3.4)	1 (2.3)	8 (12.1)	3 (6.0)	4 (57.1)	17 (8.7)
Closing rates	14 (48.3)	1 (2.3)	15 (22.7)	32 (64.0)	1 (14.3)	63 (32.1)
Other	0 (0.0)	20 (45.5)	21 (31.8)	8 (16.0)	0 (0.0)	49 (25.0)
Total	29 (14.8)	44 (22.4)	66 (33.7)	50 (25.5)	7 (3.6)	196 (100.0)

Chi - Square - 86.28420;   D.F. = 12;   Sig. = .0000;   I-index = 0.4039

Panel B   *Treatment of Foreign Exchange Differences for Foreign Currency Transactions*

	France (%)	Germany (%)	Japan (%)	UK (%)	USA (%)	Total (%)
In current income	25 (78.1)	39 (95.1)	52 (86.7)	48 (77.4)	19 (63.3)	183 (81.3)
Current & future income	6 (18.8)	1 (2.4)	1 (1.7)	1 (1.6)	6 (20.0)	15 (6.7)
Others	1 (3.1)	1 (2.4)	7 (11.7)	13 (21.0)	5 (16.7)	27 (12.0)
Total	32 (14.2)	41 (18.2)	60 (26.7)	62 (27.6)	30 (13.3)	225 (100.0)

Chi - Square - 33.18213;   D.F. = 8;   Sig. = .0001;   I-index = 0.8136

Panel C   *Foreign Currency Translation of Income Statement of Foreign Subsidiaries*

	France (%)	Germany (%)	Japan (%)	UK (%)	USA (%)	Total (%)
Average rates	50 (87.7)	33 (61.1)	33 (67.3)	73 (83.9)	17 (81.0)	206 (76.9)
Closing rates	7 (12.3)	21 (38.9)	16 (32.7)	14 (16.1)	4 (19.0)	62 (23.1)
Total	57 (21.3)	54 (20.1)	49 (18.3)	87 (32.5)	21 (7.8)	268 (100.0)

Chi - Square - 16.43371;   D.F. = 4;   Sig. = .0025;   I-index = 0.7039

Panel D   *Treatment of Translation Differences*

	France (%)	Germany (%)	Japan (%)	UK (%)	USA (%)	Total (%)
Taken to reserves	46 (88.5)	12 (24.0)	28 (52.8)	75 (88.2)	22 (64.7)	183 (66.8)
Taken to income	6 (11.5)	38 (76.0)	25 (47.2)	10 (11.8)	12 (35.3)	91 (33.2)
Total	52 (19.0)	50 (18.2)	53 (19.3)	85 (31.0)	34 (12.4)	274(100.0)

Chi - Square - 74.62922;   D.F. = 4;   Sig. = .0000;   I-index = 0.5063

percentage of Japanese companies using the equity method drives the chi-square results.

Accounting for Foreign Currency Transactions and Translations

The discussion in this section is broadly divided into two parts. The first part examines measurement issues pertaining to foreign currency transactions, while the second part deals with issues pertaining to the

56   AJAY ADHIKARI and EMMANUEL N. EMENYONU

translation of financial statements of foreign subsidiaries. Results for this section are presented in Table 3.

Accounting for Foreign Currency Transactions

In all five countries foreign currency transactions are recorded initially at the exchange rate in effect at the transaction date. However, there is a difference in the treatment of foreign currency transactions subsequent to initial recording. In Japan, on the balance sheet date, short-term foreign currency denominated receivables and payables arising from prior foreign currency transactions are revalued at the closing exchange rate, while long-term foreign denominated receivables and payables continue to be reported at historical (transaction date) exchange rates. France and Germany, in keeping with the conservative accounting traditions in those countries, require that foreign currency denominated receivables and payables be revalued at the closing exchange rate if unrealized losses accrue. However, if unrealized gains would accrue because of revaluation, the receivables and payables continue to be held at historical (transaction date) exchange rates. The policy in the U.K. and the United States is that, with few exceptions (e.g., hedge accounting), foreign currency denominated receivables and payables are revalued at closing rates on the balance sheet date. The position of the IASC is similar to that found in the U.K. and the United States.

Tests based on the data in Table 3 (Panel A) suggest that there are significant differences in the practices of companies from the five countries in relation to the issue of the rate for translating foreign currency transactions at the balance sheet date. Furthermore, the I-index of 0.4039 is the second lowest of all the topics covered in this study. This low index value is a reflection of the flexibility in regulations pertaining to this topic.

Treatment of Foreign Exchange Differences for Foreign Currency Transactions

In Japan, the U.K., and the United States companies are required to reflect gains or losses on foreign currency transactions in income in the period when the gains or losses arise. However, in France and Germany companies have a choice of either reflecting gains or losses on their foreign currency transactions in income or taking them to reserves. In all the countries there are also provisions for deferring the gains or losses on certain types of foreign currency transactions (e.g., certain hedging transactions).

Although, the chi-square tests (Table 3, Panel B) suggest that there are significant differences in the practices of the five countries in the treatment of exchange differences, the I-index value of 0.8136 is the highest for all of the measurement issues examined in this section, implying that a relatively high level of de facto harmonization has been attained on this item.

Translation of Foreign Currency Financial Statements

In France the issue of the most appropriate rate to be used in translating the financial statements of foreign subsidiaries is dependent to a large extent on whether the operations of the foreign subsidiaries are integral to those of the parent or not. For foreign operations that are not integral to those of the parent company, assets and liabilities are translated at the year-end exchange rate. Income and expense items are translated at either the year-end or the average rate for the year, according to the discretion of the responsible accounting officers of the company. If a foreign operation forms an integral part of the reporting company, the monetary items in its balance sheet are translated at the year-end exchange rate and nonmonetary items are translated at historical rates. Income and expense items are translated at the average exchange rate for the year. As for Germany, there is no particular requirement in German law or accounting principles covering this issue except the requirement that companies adhere to the principle of consistency in the usage of whichever method they prefer.

Japanese companies are required to translate income and expense items of foreign subsidiaries at either the effective rate when the transactions were entered into or at the average rate for the period. U.K. companies have the option of either using the average rate or the closing rate for the income and expense items of foreign subsidiaries that are not integral to the parent's operations, while balance sheet items are to be translated using the closing rate.

The U.S. requirement is that the financial statements of foreign affiliates whose functional currency is their reporting foreign currency be restated to dollar equivalents using the closing rate for balance sheet and

58   AJAY ADHIKARI and EMMANUEL N. EMENYONU

the average exchange rate for the income statements. For foreign affiliates whose functional currency is determined to be the dollar, the underlying measurement attribute of each account determines the exchange
rate at which it is restated. Monetary assets and liabilities are translated
at the closing rate while nonmonetary assets and liabilities are translated
at historical rates.[7] Average and historical exchange rates are used to
translate income statement items.

The International Accounting Standards Committee initially endorsed
the use of either the historical, average, or closing exchange rate for the
translation of the income statements of foreign subsidiaries. However,
the use of the closing rate was eliminated as part of the IASC's comparability project.

In this study we examine only the rates used for translating the income
statement of foreign subsidiaries. The reason for only examining
exchange rates for translating the income statement was largely due to
data limitations. Very few companies disclosed the exchange rates they
used for translating balance sheet items. By far the most common rate
for translating the income and expense items of foreign subsidiaries is
the average rate which was used by 76.9 percent of all the companies
tested, while 23.1 percent adopted the closing rate (Table 3, Panel C).
The chi-square test indicates that there are significant differences in the
rates employed by companies from the five countries in translating
income and expense items in the financial statements of foreign subsidiaries. The I-index value of 0.7039 is approximately in the middle for all
the topics covered in this study. The results are also generally consistent
with those obtained by Herrmann and Thomas (1995), albeit for a European sample. They reported an I-index of 0.6433 for this measurement
issue.

Treatment of Translation Differences

The two main choices confronting companies is whether to reflect
translation differences in the income of the period when they arise, or to
take them to stockholders' equity. In Germany companies have the
option to choose whichever method they deem fit. In France, for foreign
operations that are not an integral part of the parent, the translation differences should be taken to a separate component of shareholders'
equity. For those that are integral to the parent, the translation differences should be taken to income. The requirement under Japanese

financial reporting rules is that differences in translation should be taken to a translation adjustment account in the balance sheet as either an asset or a liability. The translation adjustment account can also be shown on the face of the income statement and statement of retained earnings.

For U.K. companies the translation differences from translating the financial statements of foreign subsidiaries that are not an extension of the parent company should be taken to movement in reserves. For foreign subsidiaries that are considered dependent on the parent company translation differences emanating from the foreign currency translation process are taken to the income statement. In the United States, gains or losses on the translation of the financial statements of foreign subsidiaries whose functional currency is the dollar should be taken to the income statement. For those subsidiaries whose functional currency is their local currency, translation gains or losses should be accumulated in a separate component of equity. The IASC requirement with regard to translation differences is similiar to those in France, the U.K., and the United States.

Of all the responding companies, 66.8 percent (see Table 3, Panel D) took translation differences to reserves while 33.2 percent reflected them in current income. The two countries with the greatest extremes of practice are France where 88.5 percent of the companies took the translation differences to reserves, and Germany where 76 percent of the companies credited or debited translation differences to the profit and loss account. The chi-square test suggests the existence of significant differences between the five countries on the treatment of translation gains and losses. The I-index of 0.5063 is relatively low compared to the other measurement issues examined in the study. This suggests that the level of harmony among the five countries is relatively low on this measurement issue.

CONCLUSIONS

All the chi-square results derived from the measurement issues covered in this study indicate that there still exist significant differences in the accounting practices of the five countries studied (see Table 4). This is surprising to some extent in view of the major international efforts that have been made by the IASC and other organizations to enhance the comparability of financial reporting practices worldwide.

With regard to the overall extent of international harmony, the I-index values ranged from 0.1097 for goodwill amortization period to 0.9376

60   AJAY ADHIKARI and EMMANUEL N. EMENYONU

Table 4. Summary Table of Chi-Square and I-index Values

Topics	Chi-Square Values	Significance	I-index Scores
Accounting for Business Combinations			
A. Purchase vs. Pooling Accounting	68.96489	0.0000	0.9052
B. Method of Accounting for Goodwill	205.28695	0.0000	0.5441
C. Amortization Period for goodwill	123.60272	0.0000	0.1097
Accounting for Consolidations			
A. Consolidated Financial Statements	22.48774	0.0002	0.9269
B. Accounting for Investments in Associates	13.84864	0.0078	0.9376
Accounting for Foreign Currency Transactions and Operations			
A. Accounting for Foreign Currency Transactions	86.28420	0.0000	0.4039
B. Treatment of Foreign Exchange Differences From Foreign Currency Transactions	33.18213	0.0001	0.8136
C. Foreign Currency Translation of Income Statement of Foreign Subsidiaries	16.43371	0.0025	0.7039
D. Treatment of Translation Differences	74.62922	0.0000	0.5063

for accounting for investments in associates. This suggests that there are substantial differences in the level of harmony achieved on the different measurement issues.

Of the main topical areas examined in this study, relatively lower levels of harmony were observed for accounting for business combinations and foreign currency transactions and translations. With the continuing trend toward globalization of business and international mergers and acquisitions, these two areas of accounting will become even more important. Accounting for business combinations, goodwill accounting in particular, has already become the focus of a spirited public policy debate in the United States. U.S. companies contend that because of national differences in the accounting treatment of goodwill, foreign companies enjoy a competitive advantage vis à vis U.S. companies when bidding for the same target company (Davis 1992).

In view of this controversy, the findings from this study can help regulatory bodies such as the IASC to further isolate those topics with relatively low levels of harmony such as "goodwill accounting" and "accounting for foreign currency transactions and translations." Such topics are potential targets for future harmonization initiatives.

The findings of this study should, however, be tempered by acknowledged limitations. This study was cross-sectional in nature and, therefore, measured the degree of harmony in the selected measurement practices at one particular point in time. The numerical (dollar or percentage) impact resulting from the measurement differences in each country is also not addressed in this paper. Additionally, due to data and resource constraints, the study only examined selected measurement issues for selected countries for a specified time frame. Nevertheless, the findings of the study do suggest that there are substantial differences in the extent of harmonization on the different accounting measurement issues examined. Consequently, there is a continuing need for research examining additional accounting measurement issues, different countries, and different time frames to fill the gaps in what we know about the state of accounting practice in the world.

NOTES

1.   Van der Tas (1988 and 1992) and Tay and Parker (1990) provide a detailed discussion of these indexes and how they could be applied to measure the degree of harmony and harmonization in accounting practices.

2.   A list of the companies included in the sample is available from the second author.

3.   Due to nondisclosure of accounting policy on certain topics by companies, the number of companies whose accounting measurement practices were tested using the two techniques was not always equal to the total sample of 413. Since nondisclosure of a particular accounting policy can either imply that the particular item is not applicable to the company or the company simply chose not to disclose, to avoid introducing bias, cases of nondisclosure were omitted from the sample for the particular item.

4.   The national accounting requirements for the five countries discussed in the paper reflect existing requirements as of 1991, the time period of the study.

5.   France is the only country among the five countries studied where the recognition of internally generated goodwill is permitted.

6.   Caution needs to be exercised in comparing I-indexes reported in different studies due to differences in the countries included in the sample, sample size, and time period evaluated.

7.   Inventories and marketable securities are translated at either historical or closing rates depending on whether they are carrried at cost or market.

REFERENCES

Archer, S., P. Delvaille, and S. McLeay. 1995. The measurement of harmonisation and the comparability of financial statement items: Within-country and between-country effects. *Accounting and Business Research* 25 (98): 67-80.

Chandler, R.A. 1992. The international harmonization of accounting: In search of influence. *International Journal of Accounting* 27: 222-233.

Choi, F. D.S., and R.M. Levich. 1990. *The Capital Market Effects of International Accounting Diversity.* Homewood, IL: Dow Jones-Irwin.

Choi, F. D.S., and C. Lee. 1991. Merger premia and national differences in accounting for goodwill. *Journal of International Financial Management and Accounting* (Autumn): 219-240.

Davis, M. 1992. Goodwill accounting: Time for an overhaul. *Journal of Accountancy* (June): 75-83.

Doupnik, S., and M.E. Taylor. 1985. An empirical investigation of the observance of IASC standards in Western Europe. *Management International Review* (Spring): 27-33.

Emenyonu, E.N., and, S.J. Gray. 1992. EC accounting harmonisation: An empirical study of measurement practices in France, Germany, and the UK. *Accounting and Business Research* 23 (89): 49-58.

Evans, T.G., and M.E. Taylor. 1982. Bottom-Line Compliance with the IASC: A Comparative Analysis. *International Journal of Accounting* (Fall): 115-128.

Goeltz, R.K. 1991. Commentary: International accounting harmonization: The impossible (and unnecessary?) dream. *Accounting Horizons* (March): 85-88.

Herrmann, D., and W. Thomas. 1995. Harmonisation of accounting measurement practices in the European community. *Accounting and Business Research* 25 (100): 253-265.

International Accounting Standards Committee. 1994. Accounting for business combinations (IAS 22) and consolidated financial statements and accounting for investments in subsidiaries (IAS 27). In *International Accounting Standards.* London: IASC.

McKinnon, S.M., and P. Janell. 1984. The international accounting standards committee: A performance evaluation. *International Journal of Accounting* (Spring): 19-34.

Nair, R.D., and W.C. Frank. 1981. The harmonization of international accounting standards, 1973-1979. *International Journal of Accounting* (Fall): 61-77.

Nobes, C.W. 1980. Harmonization of accounting within the European communities: The fourth directive on company law. *International Journal of Accounting* (Spring): 1-16.

Rivera, J.M. 1989. The internationalization of accounting standards: Past problems and current prospects. *International Journal of Accounting* 24: 320-341.

Tay, J.S.W., and R.H. Parker. 1990. Measuring international harmonization and standardization. *Abacus* 26 (1): 71-87.

Van der Tas, L.G. 1988. Measuring harmonisation of financial reporting practice. *Accounting and Business Research* 18 (70): 157-169.

_____. 1992. Evidence of European community financial reporting practice harmonization: The case of deferred taxation. *The European Accounting Review* 1 (1): 59-104.

Wallace, R.S.O., and H. Gernon. 1990. Frameworks for international comparative financial accounting. *Journal of Accounting Literature* 19: 209-264.

[12]

© 1995 American Accounting Association
Accounting Horizons
Vol. 9 No. 2
June 1995
pp. 1–16

Financial Reporting for Foreign Exchange Derivatives

Stephen R. Goldberg, Charles A. Tritschler, and Joseph H. Godwin

Stephen R. Goldberg is an Assistant Professor and Charles A. Tritschler is an Associate Professor both at Purdue University, and Joseph H. Godwin is an Assistant Professor at the University of Georgia.

SYNOPSIS: A major objective of the FASB's financial instruments project, inclusive of SFAS 105, SFAS 107 and SFAS 119, is to provide information useful to investors in assessing the credit and market risk associated with the use of off-balance-sheet financial instruments. We survey 1992 SFAS 105 and SFAS 107 disclosures on Foreign Exchange Derivatives (FXD) to: (1) benchmark current practice by summarizing quantitative and qualitative disclosures of FXD, and (2) examine the usefulness of current disclosures in assessing market and credit risk related to FXD. In achieving these objectives, we provide insight into how leading U.S. multinationals operationalize accounting standards related to off-balance-sheet financial instruments and identify disclosure attributes of footnotes unarticulated to the financial statements.

We conclude from our survey that (1) some firms make extensive use of FXD, (2) there is substantial compliance with SFAS 105 and SFAS 107 requirements, (3) large dealers comply with the FASB's credit risk disclosure requirements, (4) book and fair values of FXD are small relative to contract and notional amounts and (5) most importantly, disclosures providing information on market risk are deficient due to lack of both specificity and quantification. Additional disclosures required by SFAS 119 do not substantially address deficiencies related to disclosure of latent market risk.

Data Availability: Data used for this study are publicly available.

INTRODUCTION

The growth of off-balance-sheet financial instruments (i.e., derivatives), the dynamic state of financial markets, the complexity of financial engineering and the potential impact of derivatives on profitability and risk led the Financial Accounting Standards Board (FASB) to establish a financial instruments project in 1986. As a first step, the FASB issued an exposure draft (ED) *Disclosures about Financial Instruments* (1987) and then two statements requiring less disclosure than the ED. SFAS 105, *Disclosure of Information about Financial Instruments with Off-Balance-Sheet Risk and Financial Instruments*

with Concentrations of Credit Risk (FASB 1990a), requires disclosure of the contract amount of financial instruments with off-balance sheet (OBS) risk of loss. SFAS 107, *Disclosures about Fair Value of Financial Instruments* (FASB 1991b), requires disclosure of the fair value of all financial instruments. More

The authors gratefully acknowledge the support of Joe Kolman and *Derivatives Strategy* and the Center for International Business Education and Research at Purdue University. We also appreciate suggestions from workshop participants at the University of Wisconsin, DePaul University, the Ohio State University, Purdue University and the American Accounting Association's 1994 Annual Meeting and anonymous referees.

Submitted July 1994
Accepted January 1995

recently, SFAS 119, *Disclosure about Derivative Financial Instruments and Fair Value of Financial Instruments* (FASB 1994b) requires disclosure of average fair value of and net trading gains and losses for derivatives held for trading purposes. For derivatives held for purposes other than trading, it requires disclosure about purposes, how the instruments are reported in the financial statements and additional information for hedges of anticipated transactions.

SFAS 105 and SFAS 107 disclosures provided the first mandated source of public information about off-balance-sheet financial instruments. SFAS 119 disclosures were not yet available for this survey. Footnotes appearing in 1992 annual reports reveal how firms deal with both the expanded content and the unstructured format of the new disclosures which extend the scope of financial reporting to unarticulated positions rather than just providing details of existing account balances.

The disclosures provide some details of these previously unreported instruments used extensively by financial companies to service customers and generate income and by both financial and nonfinancial companies to manage foreign currency exposure. The six banks which dominate U.S. markets held contract values of foreign exchange derivatives (FXD) totaling $3.2 ($4.2) trillion dollars. This is 4.2 (4.7) times total assets, at December 31, 1992 (1993). In contrast, multinational manufacturers in our sample held foreign exchange derivatives with contract value equal to 10.3% of their total assets at December 31, 1992.

We cite two FASB distinctions to clarify discussion. First, foreign exchange (FX) risk can be viewed from the perspective of either the individual transaction as in SFAS 52 micro linked hedges or the portfolio (i.e., firm) consisting of all assets and liabilities whether on or off balance sheet as in SFAS 80 enterprise level hedges. As discussed later, some firms manage FX exposure at the level of the transaction. However, investors are concerned with exposure of their investment. Therefore, the appropriate view for public disclosure purposes is the effect of foreign exchange derivatives on portfolio or firm level risk.

Second, risk can be viewed as the likelihood of loss from either an historical cost or replacement cost (i.e., economic) perspective. From an historical cost perspective the exposure to risk of loss related to purchased call or put options is limited to their initial cost. Economically, purchased options (as well as other derivatives) are at risk of loss of market value due to price changes reversing previous gains.

Derivatives, if naked at the enterprise level, increase the leverage and risk of the firm. The same level of derivatives, if covered, reduces the risk of the firm. Under present reporting, neither quantification of exposure nor consistent disclosure of firms' approach to risk management is provided. In some cases, interrelated transactions (the hedged transaction, such as an FX payable, and the hedging instrument, an FX forward) appear separately in financial statements. In other cases, interrelated transactions appear as one (e.g., a foreign currency borrowing and a currency swap). In still other cases, only one side of the interrelated transaction is disclosed (e.g., an FX forward disclosed in the footnotes that hedges an unbooked and undisclosed FX purchase commitment). Lack of quantification and failure to clearly link the hedge instrument with the hedged item make it difficult for anyone to measure the firm's exposure to exchange rate changes and determine to what extent FXD increase or decrease exposure.

The next section discusses the general nature of disclosures. The third section reviews extant and developing GAAP related to foreign exchange derivatives. The fourth section provides analysis of existing disclosures by firms in our sample. The final section presents our conclusions.

THE NATURE OF DISCLOSURES

GAAP-required footnote disclosures differ in the degree to which they are quantifiable and testable. A disclosure asserting a firm "never speculates" is different from one that asserts "the foreign currency position value at risk has not exceeded $xxx at a 99 percent confidence level in 1993." The latter statement, in turn, is less quantified than one providing maximum, minimum, and average foreign currency values at risk at some confidence level for a specific period.

GAAP-required footnote disclosures also differ in that they may or may not provide the constituents of a control account articulated into the income statement and balance sheet. An articulating footnote "deepens" an existing line item disclosure. By contrast, a footnote may "broaden" disclosure by introducing data points not constituents of an account articulated into the general ledger. Requiring a footnote that extends the architecture of financial reporting "off-balance sheet" (OBS), as the slang goes, means the standard cannot presume that firms already have the model and the experience for reporting such data. To the extent a firm is given *carte blanche* to respond, open-ended responses may not be commensurable or even yield summary statistics. Footnote disclosures of derivative fair values have the undifferentiated alternatives of duplicating, adjusting or augmenting booked accruals of gains or losses. The disclosures are not uniform and frequently not explicit as to which of these functions are performed.

A broadening type footnote containing information unarticulated to the financial statements cannot merely be a fishing expedition whose net benefit is a matter of chance, any more than scientific research can test without a model. A "disclosure" type SFAS differs methodologically from a Discussion Memorandum (DM) surveying the same issues. If a disclosure standard is to generate an inductive inference, then the design calls for respondents to answer the same questions and interpret them equivalently. The OBS disclosure of operating leases presents a successful analogy. The FASB hypothesis is that footnote disclosure of prospective uncapitalized, noncancellable commitments inhibits evasion of capitalization requirements and expands the empirical data for estimating leveraging risk. One purpose of our study is to determine what inferences can be drawn from the 1992 data on FXD. Our survey leads us to conclude that the lack of clearly specified quantification of market risk has led to disclosures of limited benefit to investors.

FXD THEORY AND PRACTICE

Off-balance-sheet risk exists when a possible loss is not reflected on the balance sheet because a derivative contract is not reported as an asset or liability. Since open derivative contracts are executory in nature, they are not booked (i.e., no asset or liability is recorded) and the notional or contract amount is not articulated on the balance sheet. Exposed derivatives may increase OBS risk whereas enterprise level hedging derivatives decrease risk. Therefore, deciding whether FXD expose or cover risk is of substantial concern to investors and regulators. Accelerating use of FXD by financial institutions particularly, and by nonfinancial entities also, is a major motivation for the FASB undertaking their financial instruments projects.

SFAS 105 (FASB 1990a) was the initial response to calls for expanded disclosure under the FASB's financial instruments project. It "applies to all financial instruments with off-balance-sheet risk of accounting loss and all financial instruments with concentrations of credit risk except those specifically excluded ...." Disclosures required by SFAS 105 consists of the following information about financial instruments with risk of accounting loss: (a) the face or contract amount (or notional principal amount), and (b) the nature and terms, including a discussion of (1) the credit and market risk of those instruments, (2) the cash requirements of those instruments, and (3) the related accounting policy. If the financial instrument has off-balance-sheet credit risk, two additional disclosures are required, (1) the potential loss due to nonperformance by the counterparty, and (2) information about collateral. SFAS 105 was issued in March 1990 and is effective for fiscal years ending after June 15, 1990.

This study surveys only foreign currency contracts with OBS risk (FXD) and not other financial instruments addressed by SFAS 105. Foreign exchange exposures for nonfinancial firms are generally managed at the transaction or account level. Therefore, corporate hedging objectives are more narrowly defined and it is more feasible for firms to monitor usage of foreign exchange contracts as compared to interest rate contracts. FXD are usually "plain vanilla" forwards, options, or currency swaps in comparison to complex interest rate contracts. Risk and return management with interest rate contracts is analogous to capital structure decisions and is therefore more difficult to define and to monitor than FX risk exposure reduction.

SFAS 107 (FASB 1991b) "requires disclosures about fair value for all financial instruments, whether recognized or not recognized in the statement of financial position, except for those specifically listed ...." Similar to SFAS 105, items covered by other SFAS such as pensions, insurance contracts, warranty obligations, lease contracts and investments accounted for under the equity method are excluded from the disclosure requirements.

Fair value is quoted market value where available. Otherwise, it is management's best estimate using the quoted market price of similar financial instruments, present value of estimated cash flows, option pricing models, or other valuation models. The FASB chose the term *fair value* as opposed to *market value* to avoid any misunderstanding that the statement applies both to actively traded financial instruments where a clear market price does exist and to those where no active market exists. Where it is not possible or practical (e.g., too costly) to determine market value, available information to proxy for market value should be disclosed (carrying amount, interest rate, and maturity). The FASB valuation definition is flexible in that neither spot nor forward rates are specified. SFAS 107 is effective for fiscal years ending after December 15, 1992. For entities with total assets less than $150 million, the standard is effective for fiscal years ending after December 15, 1995.

In October 1994, the FASB issued SFAS 119, *Disclosure about Derivative Financial Instruments and Fair Value of Financial Instruments*, as a response to criticism of derivatives disclosure. It requires a distinction be made between derivatives held for trading purposes and those held for purposes "other than trading." The FASB explains that this distinction is not one between speculation and

hedging, which is what everyone recommends in theory but no one has operationalized in practice. Segregating trading and nontrading instruments (risk management or asset-liability management (ALM)) is what banks already do as a matter of business practice and nonbanks may choose to ignore.

Additional disclosures required for derivatives held for trading purposes are average and end-of-period fair values, and gains and losses on trading activities disaggregated into categories consistent with how the business is managed. The FASB dropped a requirement from the related disclosure draft to disclose minimum and maximum fair values, and gains and losses from derivatives shown separately from other financial instruments. Additional disclosures required for derivative financial instruments held for purposes other than trading consist of (a) a description of the objectives for holding the derivatives, (b) a description of how each class of derivatives is reported in the financial statements, and (c) for derivatives held and accounted for as hedges of anticipated transactions "(1) a description of the anticipated transactions whose risks are hedged, including the period of time until the anticipated transactions are expected to occur, (2) a description of the classes of derivatives used to hedge the anticipated transactions, (3) the amount of hedging gains and losses explicitly deferred, and (4) a description of the transactions or other events that result in the recognition in earnings of gains or losses deferred by hedge accounting." The disclosures required under (c) are an attempt to clarify the gray area between derivatives used to hedge anticipated transactions and to speculate.

Additional encouraged but not required disclosures include average fair values of other financial instruments or nonfinancial assets held for trading purposes, and quantitative information about market risks of derivatives "that is consistent with the way in which the entity manages or adjusts those risks." Although this is the first time the FASB encouraged market risk disclosures, SFAS 119 requires neither quantification of exposure to market risk nor a discussion of management's controls on currency risk management. Dealer banks use value at risk for internal control, but typically have not reported it publicly. SFAS 119 is effective for fiscal years ending after December 15, 1994 (December 15, 1995 for entities with less than $150 million in total assets).

Derivatives are subject to the same types of liquidity, market, credit, and operational risks as other financial instruments (CITICORP 1994, 26). Market risk is the risk of loss due to unexpected changes in interest and exchange rates. Credit risk is the potential loss from counterparty nonperformance. Liquidity risk is related to market liquidity of instruments held and therefore, closely related to market risk. Operating risk is linked to inadequate controls that ensure following a properly defined corporate policy.

Whether companies are dealers or end-users, FXD manage and adjust market and credit risks. Market risk on an exposed position can be eliminated (hedged) by FXD with the opposite exposure. In a pure sense, hedging is risk reduction without intent to profit. A speculative FXD, however, is one that does not hedge an identified exposure or perversely unhedges natural offsetting positions. A company's risk management policy determines the portfolio of exposures which they identify. For example, is *every* foreign-currency denominated receivable, payable, contractually committed future sale or purchase, and anticipated revenue or expenditure (for the next three months, one year, five years, etc.) identified as exposed to exchange rate changes? Or, is only some decentralized entity's net amount identifiable as exposed? Definition, measurement of market risk, and determination of an acceptable level of exposure are complex issues about which treatment may differ by industry, geography, technical feasibility, and management policy.

FASB disclosure requirements address credit and market risks. Recent disclosures in the financial press (e.g., Procter & Gamble, Gibson Greetings) suggest market risk is less understood and less controlled than credit risk but not necessarily less important. Long before 1994 revelations of derivative losses, the

FASB issued the exposure draft *Disclosures about Financial Instruments* (1987). This proposal omitted notional and market values of derivative contracts and relied instead on quantification of cash flows and tableaux of position profiles over time. These numerical specifications at the enterprise level have been dropped from subsequent standards and proposals in favor of verbalized descriptions and nonstandardized views of historical data resulting in inconsistent content and formats.

Credit risk, which relates to the possibility of nonperformance by a counterparty, applies to FXD entered into by both dealers and end-users, and to those entered both for hedging exposures and for speculating. The maximum potential accounting loss at a balance sheet date, SFAS 105's (FASB 1990a) measure of credit risk, is the gross amount of contracts in a *gain* position (modified by losses that can be offset under a binding agreement). Credit risk, measured by observed gains on derivatives, is not a proxy measure of market risk, which is measured by potential, unobservable derivative *losses*. The FASB, regulators, and rating agencies set thresholds of credit risk because business practice deems it measurable and avoidable, whereas market risk is viewed as neither. Thus, outside regulators neither monitor nor restrict market risk-taking directly yet.

The four cells of table 1 relate to disclosure as follows. For credit risk (two bottom cells), SFAS 105 requires disclosure of the maximum potential accounting loss due to counterparty nonperformance and a discussion of the firm's credit controls. By contrast, FXD reduce net enterprise market risk exposure when other exposures are hedged (upper left cell). The major uncertainty, and therefore need for disclosure, is exposure to market risk of FXD held for speculation (upper right cell), whether intentional or not. The disclosure challenge is to distinguish between enterprise level exposures and hedges and then to measure the speculative value at risk. The FASB requires disclosure of FXD contractual amounts and fair values and a "discussion" of their market risk. The remainder of the paper shows that while the required dis-

---

TABLE 1
Summary of Exposure to Risks
from Foreign Exchange Derivatives (FXD)

Type of Risk	Hedge	Speculate
Market Risk+	No*	Yes***
Credit Risk++	Yes**	Yes**

+ Market risk is the risk of loss due to unexpected changes in the foreign exchange rate.
++ Credit risk is the potential loss resulting from counter-party non-performance.
* Net effect of hedge instrument and exposed position that is being hedged.
** From an historical cost perspective, there is credit risk exposure only for OTC unrealized gains on FXD. If there is an unrealized loss, the firm's counter-party is exposed to credit loss. Gains and losses on futures contracts traded on exchanges are settled in cash daily. Therefore, credit risk is minimal. The counterparty to a written option has no performance obligations under the option.
*** From an historical cost perspective, the maximum possible loss on purchased options are the premiums paid for the options.

---

closures are a step in the right direction, quantifying the exposure of unhedged derivatives to market risk is a necessary but missing component of FXD disclosure.

FXD DISCLOSURES

This study includes a descriptive analysis of the SFAS 105 and SFAS 107 disclosures of six large banks that dominate U.S. derivative markets and 98 large U.S. multinational manufacturing companies for fiscal years ending December 1992 through March 1993. To obtain a purposive sample of major FXD users, we selected (1) the 100 firms on Forbes' list of the largest U.S. multinationals, (2) the firms on Fortune's list of the 50 largest U.S. exporters not included in Forbes' list, and (3) U.S. companies not yet included that are in the Standard & Poor 500 and classified as banks, chemicals, computers, electronic components, pharmaceuticals, and oils. To focus the survey on large U.S. manufacturing mul-

tinationals, we excluded firms with ratios of foreign assets to total assets or foreign sales to total sales less than ten percent (22 firms) and retailers (eight firms).

SFAS 105 and SFAS 107 disclosures by firms in our survey vary greatly in format and content. One area where companies showed inconsistency is in use of terminology. The primary example is the distinction between contract and fair value. Several companies used terminology treating contract values and fair values as equivalent (e.g., Intergraph, Cray). Contract (notional) value is the amount of currency to exchange at a defined time in the future. Fair value of a contract is determined by changes in exchange rates (and possibly by interest rates and other factors) applied to the notional base. Changes in a contract's fair value impacts income, if the contract is not construed as hedged. If there is no change in exchange rates since the inception of the contract, its fair value is within transactions costs of zero. Fair value disclosures are also frequently unclear about whether the amount is an asset or liability, a deficiency addressed in SFAS 119 (FASB 1994b).

Dealer Bank FXD Disclosures

The total notional value of foreign exchange contracts of the six dominant U.S. banks is $3.2 ($4.2) trillion or 4.2 (4.7) times total assets at December 31, 1992 (1993). Foreign exchange trading income totaled $2.7 ($2.3) billion, which was 30.3% (17.4%) of pretax income in 1992 (1993). Table 2 summarizes reported FXD for 1992 and 1993 for comparison.

Banks foreign exchange dealings are exposed to market (or price), liquidity, operational, and credit risks. Banks apply similar credit procedures to customers with whom they enter into forward contracts as with loan agreements. In terms of amount at risk in case of default, it is approximately equal to the unexpected change in the exchange rate since the contract was signed times the notional amount for all contracts in a gain position. The maximum exposure to credit loss reported by the six banks is $80.4 ($54.0) billion in 1992

TABLE 2
Summary of Foreign Exchange (FX) Derivative Disclosures: Six Major Dealer Banks

	1993		1992		Percent Change 1993/1992
	$ million	% total assets	$ million	% total assets	
Notional principal amount					
FX forwards, spots, futures	$3,277,512	371.8%	$2,639,892	344.9%	+24.2%
FX swaps	$233,712	26.5%	$244,553	31.9%	–4.4%
FX options	$672,716	76.3%	$345,748	45.2%	+94.6%
Total FXD	$4,183,940	474.7%	$3,230,193	422.1%	+29.5%
Total assets on balance sheet	$881,468	100.0%	$765,313	100.0%	+15.2%
Maximum Exposure to Credit loss for FXD (Unrealized exchange gains)	$53,998	6.1%	$80,357	10.5%	–32.8%
% of Stockholders' equity	85.6%		149.1%		
% of notional principal	1.3%		2.5%		
FX Trading Income	$2,330	0.3%	$2,701	0.4%	–13.7%
% of Income before taxes	17.4%		30.3%		

Includes Citicorp, J.P.Morgan, Chemical Bank, Bankers Trust, Chase Manhattan, and BankAmerica.

(1993) or 2.5% (1.3%) of notional value and 10.5% (6.1%) of total assets. Nonfinancial companies entering into FXD generally do so with financial institutions, so that their credit risk is the risk of insolvency of the financial institution. The "too big to fail" rule may protect banks' customers, but not U.S. taxpayers.

Dealer banks, as well as end-users, failed in their 1993 disclosures to address vital issues surfacing in 1994 related to market risk and liquidity risk. Disclosures do not provide (a) amounts exposed to market risk, (b) the effect of FXD on exposure to market risk, and (c) any information, qualitative or quantitative, on liquidity risk.

CITICORP (10-Q for quarter ended June 30, 1994) provides the first reported quantification of market risk.

Earnings at risk measures the potential impact on the nontrading portfolios of a specified movement in interest rates for a given period. The earnings at risk for each currency is calculated by multiplying the gap between interest sensitive items by the specified rate movement, and then taking into account the impact of options, both explicit and embedded. The specific rate movements are statistically derived from a two standard deviation rate movement ...

... The price risk of the trading portfolios is measured using the potential loss amount

method, which estimates the sensitivity of the value of the trading positions to changes in the various market factors, such as interest and foreign exchange rates, over the period necessary to close the position (generally one day). The method considers the probability of movements of these market factors (as derived from a two standard deviation movement), adjusted for correlation among them. (CITICORP 1994, 24)

Reported amounts calculated for market risk at CITICORP are small relative to credit risk. Disclosed earnings at risk from changes in market rates for the *nontrading* portfolio ranges from a high of $90 million to a low of $10 million dollars in the first half of 1994. This market risk range is from 4.24% to .47% of the first six months pretax income and .58% to .06% of stockholders' equity. The potential loss to the *trading* portfolio ranges from $90 million to $50 million (4.24% to 2.36% and .58% to .32%). CITICORP's maximum exposure to credit loss (i.e., gross unrealized gains net of netting agreement offsets) on FXD only was $32.0 billion or 205% of stockholders' equity at June 30, 1994 (1509% of six months pretax income).

Industry practice is for banks to accrue unrealized gains and losses on foreign exchange contracts, interest rate swaps, and interest rate protection contracts, offset on a net basis through 1993. Beginning in 1994, FASB Interpretation 39, *Offsetting of Amounts Related to Certain Contracts* (FASB 1992), requires banks to report separately their unrealized gains as assets and unrealized losses as liabilities. Unrealized gains and losses on multiple contracts may continue to be shown on a net basis only when the contracts are executed with the same counterparty and a legally enforceable master netting agreement is in place and where the intent to settle net exists. Federal Reserve and Group of Thirty (1993) surveys document banks are planning to substantially increase the use of master netting agreements. While application of FASB Interpretation 39 does not affect net income or net assets, it does increase total assets and liabilities. This disaggregation enables analysts to better discern the scale of hedging and speculation.

CITICORP's (1994) second quarter, 1994 10-Q provides insight into the effect of Interpretation 39 on the balance sheet. At June 30, 1994 Trading Account Assets ($52 billion) and Total Assets ($254 billion) are $30 billion higher than previously reported because gross unrealized gains of $32 billion (asset) and gross unrealized losses of $30 billion (liability) were separately reported. The result is to reduce the ratio of Stockholders Equity to Total Assets from 6.9% under previous GAAP to 6.1% under current GAAP. Similarly, the ratio of Net Income to Total Assets falls from .64% to .56%.

Since banks mark-to-market their *trading* portfolios of foreign exchange contracts, there are no reported differences between book value and fair value, except for their Asset Liability Management (ALM) *end-user* positions. The SFAS 105 disclosures provide new information on the open interest of OBS instruments. By the nature of their usage, bank foreign exchange contracts substantially offset, reduce the bank's exposure or "gap," and thus reduce the risk premium to recover from customers. Where end-user companies use foreign exchange contracts to hedge operating exposure however, SFAS 105 tabulations do not display their offset against foreign currency assets and liabilities on the balance

sheet. The result is either of limited value or misleading.

End-User Manufacturing Companies FXD Disclosures

End-user firms in the manufacturing sector provide a rigorous test of FASB derivative disclosure standards in that these firms have limited experience with disclosures or footnotes related to foreign exchange risk. To develop a more relevant survey, we restrict the sample to companies which are multinational and therefore more likely to use FXD to manage risk. Identical to the SFAS 14 requirement for providing geographic disclosures, we define companies as multinational if foreign revenue is ten percent or more of consolidated revenue or identifiable foreign assets are ten percent or more of consolidated total assets. The sample analyzed in this section consists of 98 U.S. multinational manufacturing firms.

FXD disclosures are located in a variety of footnotes including one or more covering accounting policies, foreign exchange, debt, financial instruments, commitments, contingencies, and geographic disclosures. Footnotes are frequently not cross-referenced making it difficult to know if all FXD disclosures have been identified.

We tabulated currency swap agreements when they were identifiable separately from interest rate swaps. Johnson & Johnson's annual report, for example, did not include currency swaps with OBS activity. Instead, ECU and Swiss Franc notes payable were listed under *borrowings* with a note indicating "These debt issues were converted to fixed or floating rate U.S. dollar liabilities via interest rate and currency swaps." This contract interdependence highlights the need to link disaggregated disclosure of OBS instruments in order to understand exposures. (SFAS 119 addresses this concern.) Some companies describe separately the type of foreign exchange contract and others combine amounts for different types of contracts.

Table 3 shows the incidence of revelation (panel A) and descriptive statistics for Notional (panel B), Book (panel C), and Fair (panel D) values for FXD user firms in the

TABLE 3

Summary of 1992 Foreign Exchange Derivatives Disclosures

Panel A: Number of U.S. Manufacturing Firms in Sample Reporting Notional Values (NV), Book Values (BV), and Fair Values (FV)

Number of Companies in Sample	Number of Companies Reporting Amounts							
	NV, BV, FV	NV, FV, Only	NV, BV Only	FV, BV Only	NV Only	FV Only	BV Only	No Disclosure
98	29	11	0	2	42	1	0	13
100%	30%	11%	0%	2%	43%	1%	0%	13%

Panel B: Notional Amount of Disclosed FXD

Category of FXD—% of Total Sample of 98	No. of Companies Reporting $ Amounts	Notional Amount ($000,000)		Ratio of Notional Value to Total Assets			
		Mean	Median	Mean	Median	Min	Max
Forwards—65%	64	$1261	$340	.077	.048	0.000	.636
Swaps—26%	26	351	161	.035	.011	.004	.120
Options—12%	12	508	234	.038	.022	0.000	.137
Not disclosed separately—21%	21	1497	701	.104	.072	.011	.443
Total Users—84%	82	$1554	$569	.103	.068	0.000	.636

Out of the total sample of 98 U.S. companies 82 reported using FXD. FXD are foreign currency financial instruments with off-balance-sheet risk of accounting loss. NV, BV, and FV are notional, book and fair values, respectively.

(Continued on next page)

TABLE 3 (Continued)

Panel C: Book Value of Disclosed FXD

Category	Book Values of Reported FXD ($000,000)			Ratio of Book to Notional Values		
	No. Reporting	Mean Amount	Median	No. Reporting	Mean Amount	Median
Forwards	16	$37	$4	12	.062	.008
Swaps	3	64	11	0	—	—
Options	4	30	38	0	—	—
Not Separated	8	32	6	6	.025	.009
Total	31	$38	$4	27	.029	.006

Panel D: Fair Value of Disclosed FXD

Category	Fair Values of Reported FXD ($000,000)			Ratio of Fair to Notional Values		
	No. Reporting	Mean Amount	Median	No. Reporting	Mean Amount	Median
Forwards	25	$32	$6	21	.108	.009
Swaps	6	35	6	0	—	—
Options	5	22	23	0	—	—
Not Separated	11	66	21	9	.043	.027
Total Reporting	43	$43	$8	38	.041	.018

Panels C and D present summary statistics on companies that disclosed both notional and book (C) or fair (D) values for the indicated category. Some companies reported different levels of detail of notional and fair values or amounts in non-matching categories. Therefore, Total Reporting the Ratio of Book (Fair) to Notional Values, 27 (38) companies exceeds the sum of the number of companies reporting individual ratio categories, 12+6 or 18 (21+9 or 30). Two companies reported $0 for notional, book, and fair values. These two companies are considered as reporting amounts but are not included in the ratio statistics.

sample. Since SFAS 107 requires fair value disclosures, we assume that no disclosure of book and fair values implies book approximates fair value for firms disclosing notional amounts of FXD.

Panel A of table 3 shows that 82 of the 98 U.S. companies disclosed only the notional value of FXD. Only 29 companies disclosed notional, book and fair values separately. Forty-two companies disclosed only notional value. Frequently book and fair values were not disclosed. In summary, notional values were generally reported, but the reporting of book and fair values was inconsistent. However, three companies reported no notional value but did report fair and/or book values. Since SFAS 105 requires disclosure of notional amounts of FXD, these three companies did not appear to be in compliance with GAAP.

The mean (median) notional amount of FXD for users in our sample was $1.54 ($.57) billion dollars (table 3, panel B). The mean (median) ratio of notional value of FXD to total assets is .103 (.068) for the 82 manufacturing firms that report usage of FXD. Of those firms reporting type of FXD, about two-thirds use OTC forward contracts and one-fourth use swaps. Since some companies did not identify currency and interest rate swap amounts separately, the incidence of FX swaps and total FXD is understated. This survey confirms that although FXD usage is frequently substantial, it is not systematically material across manufacturers.

Panels C and D of table 3 show approximately only three percent of the notional or contract amounts of FXD are reported on the balance sheet and replacement cost or fair value of FXD is four percent of the contract amount. Because of inconsistencies in reporting, only approximately one-third of sample firms report enough information to calculate these ratios. Whether these amounts are debits (receivables subject to credit risk), credits, both, or net is rarely clear. Manufacturing firms generally do not report separate credit risk amounts as banks do. Some manufacturing firms do, however, indicate risk of credit loss is remote since counterparties are large credit-worthy financial institutions.

The FASB's hypothesis that FXD credit risk is a major concern for users and therefore should be a major disclosure component is perhaps misguided because amounts at risk are small (for the manufacturing firms) and the counterparties are credit-worthy. If compliance costs are constrained, why should the FASB waste resources by requiring extensive disclosures of credit risk, when market risk and liquidity risk are the perils to end-user firms? Our conclusion is that dealer banks complied fully with SFAS 105 and SFAS 107 and could have provided a model for manufacturing firms whose compliance was spotty.

Appendix B of SFAS 105 provides an example of inconsistent financial reporting treatment by presenting a concept of credit risk contrary to bank practice, regulations, and the predecessor FASB ED. Setting aside any questions as to how "credit risk" is actually measured, the table on pages 22–23 of SFAS 105 shows no OBS credit risk for swaps and forwards, yet shows market risk for all derivatives. By contrast, banks report credit risk for all over-the-counter derivatives, except options. Recall that Interpretation 39 generally requires gross, not net, unrealized gains and losses be reported on the balance sheet and thus unrealized gains (FASB's measure of maximum credit loss) are now on the balance sheet. Thus, it is not until Interpretation 39 that financial reporting is consistent with the appendix to SFAS 105, whereby only market risk is OBS.

Liquidity risk, in the sense of market failure, is perhaps the greatest problem of all in reporting the fair value of derivative positions. While the ED preceding SFAS 105 identifies liquidity risk using a cashflow definition, SFAS 105 drops it from the appendix entirely. The market in 1994 however, has demonstrated that only plain vanilla derivatives can be resold without significant cost when the market begins to inflict losses. In summary, it appears the FASB hypothesizes that a measure of usage (i.e., notional amount) serves as a metric for market risk.

Appendix A to the ED preceding SFAS 107 enumerates prior FASB, AICPA and SEC precedents requiring disclosure of "fair value."

Such an appendix of precedents is essential to any research process and reveals a persistent characteristic of FASB standard setting, although that entire reference appendix is ultimately omitted in SFAS 107. Bank regulation and international precedents are persistently omitted from accounting standard background citations. For example, neither the 1994 ED nor SFAS 119 revising SFAS 105 and SFAS 107 refer to bank regulatory precedent (e.g. the Federal Deposit Insurance Corporation (FDIC) Call Report, Schedule RC-L, Off Balance Sheet Items, FFIEC 031, 032, 033, and 034, and Item no. 12, which defines determination of notional amounts of forward contracts for reporting purposes). This level of guidance is also omitted from FASB or EITF publications. Because of omitted relevant regulatory accounting principles (RAP), the FASB gives less guidance to itself and to "nonbanks," who need help the most, if only by analogy.

DISCLOSURE OF HEDGING POLICIES

Belk and Glaum (1990) provide evidence that balance sheet exposure is managed primarily by adjusting the currencies of lending and borrowing (i.e., hedging with "primitives"). By contrast, exposure on future purchases and sales transactions is primarily managed by hedging with derivatives (FXD). The implication for the present study is to remind us that FXD are likely to be a significant, but not necessarily the primary FX hedging and positioning strategy. To determine if positions are exposed or not, a firm would have to summarize balance sheet positions, off-balance-sheet positions (i.e., firm commitments), and anticipated transactions (i.e., operating transactions or exposure) before reporting complementary derivative positions.

SFAS 105 requires a discussion of the market risk of financial instruments with OBS risk of accounting loss. In response to this requirement, most firms briefly summarize how FXD are used only to hedge foreign exchange risk. Table 4 summarizes these disclosures. There are 59 references to hedges of balance sheet exposures (45 balance sheet items plus

14 net investments in international operations). There are 19 indications of hedging commitments and 28 indications of hedging anticipated transactions, i.e., operating exposure. Our results are consistent with Rodriguez (1981) who finds that companies do not appear to be speculating, because of asymmetric rewards associated with negative derivatives performance. We classified a policy as one of hedging whenever a company used any wording implying such. Three companies clearly indicate that they do not speculate as a matter of policy.

It is likely that companies take an active currency position in anticipation of rate changes and view this as hedging anticipated transactions. For example, Coca Cola "engages in hedging to enhance income and cash flows denominated in foreign currencies" and Halliburton enters into FXD "in its selective hedging of its exposure." This suggests that differences between selectively hedging future transactions and speculation, or "taking a view," may be in the eye of the beholder. The FASB, in SFAS 119, gives up on robust criteria for hedging and settles for euphemisms like "end-user risk management" or "nontrading activities."

Some companies disclose the maturity and currency profile of derivatives. Thirty-eight companies disclosed maximum maturities of open forwards. Seventeen reported maturities of less than one year. Twelve reported forwards maturing in one year. Nine reported maturities of greater than one year, with the maximum maturity being 13 years. Multiple long-term forwards which hedge debt are equivalent to swaps designed for the same purpose.

Seven companies disclosed the maturities of currency options. Five matured within one year, the other two reported maximum maturities of 15 and 36 months. SFAS 119 encourages, but does not require, "gap" analysis for interest rate positions by duration and illustrates a format for a financial entity to report exposure by repricing intervals.

Information was provided on the currency of FXD by 19 companies. However, the level of detail varies from a description that FXD

TABLE 4
Summary of Manufacturing Companies' Policy Statements on
Hedging of Foreign Exchange Exposures—1992

Reported Description of What is Hedged (Alternative wording in annual reports interpreted as equivalent)	No. of References
Balance Sheet Exposure	
Assets- Receivables	3
Inventories	2
Assets	1
Foreign currency investments (Foreign currency denominated securities)	3
Liabilities- Payables	1
Short term borrowings	1
Long term debt (Foreign currency bonds and warrants)	1
Liabilities (Debts)	9
To provide local currency debt to subs	1
Balance Sheet- Net monetary assets (Receivables and payables, Receivables, payables and other commitments, Monetary assets and liabilities)	11
Balance Sheet (Assets and liabilities)	8
Net investments in international operations	14
Interco transactions (Interco payables and receivables)	2
Interco dividends and royalties (Dividends from sub)	2
Total policy references to hedged balance sheet items	**59**
Firm Commitments	
Firm commitments (Commitments)	15
Sales commitments	1
Inventory purchase commitments with specific supplier	1
Commitments for Property, Plant and Equipment	1
Sale of German sub	1
Total policy references to hedged commitments	**19**
"Does not hedge non-transaction exposure"	1
Total Balance Sheet (from above)	59
Total Policy References to Accounting Exposures	**79**
Anticipated transactions (i.e., Operating exposure):	
Revenues (Anticipated sales commitments, probable anticipated sales, anticipated interco sales, future export commitments, future exports)	5
Expected inventory purchases	1

Income and cash flows (Anticipated transactions, cash flow transactions,
  operating activities, economic exposure, operational exposure, currency
  fluctuations on operations, operating income, sales and purchases)
	22

Total policy references to anticipated transactions	**28**
General comments to reduce exposure with no specifics	17
Specific statement indicating no speculation	3
Total Policy References to All Hedged Exposures	**127**
No statement on hedging policy	17
Reported statement indicating speculation	1
Total Policy References plus No References	**145**

are "primarily European" to specification of amounts of currencies purchased or sold forward and amounts of currency for buy or sell options. Except for debt instruments, in no cases were the amounts of foreign currency exposed assets or liabilities identified. SFAS 119 illustrates an "encouraged" format that provides limited information on currency-specific exposures.

The Group of Thirty (1993) estimates that from 1985 to 1989, the volume of international new issues that were swap-driven increased steadily, reaching 70 percent of international U.S. dollar new issue volume and 53 percent of total international new issue volume. Major borrowers monitor funding opportunities regularly by evaluating the relative pricing for new issues and swaps across markets worldwide. Commonly, currency swap agreements effectively establish U.S. dollar-denominated principal and interest obligations over the terms of foreign currency denominated debt. Swaps are entered simultaneously with debt transactions and are integral to the debt transaction. Reporting debt and swaps separately, as is done by many companies, confuses the investor as to the substance of debt transactions. One example of showing the economic substance of transactions, and not just legal form, is Procter & Gamble's long-term-debt summary table that describes each major issuance of debt with a description of the related swap in parentheses and the effective borrowing amount, currency, and interest rate. However, Procter & Gamble did not reveal the *market risk* of their derivative activities in 1992 or 1993 only to have that risk emerge in 1994 as a significant loss and negative publicity.

One argument against requiring quantitative market-risk disclosures such as are now reported by CITICORP (1994), is that some companies do not have the capacity to produce such information (SFAS 119, ¶72). Conventional business wisdom however, is not to sign contracts when management does not understand the risks involved. "Plain vanilla" derivatives, simple forwards, swaps, and options are relatively easy to value. If management chooses to enter complex derivative transactions, then it is incumbent upon them to ac-

quire the expertise and technology to undertake a sensitvity analysis of changes in value in response to changes in interest and exchange rates. The complaint filed in Gibson Greetings (GG) Vs. Bankers Trust (BT) and BT Securities Incorporated (1994) presents a clear admission of a company entering into transactions without adequately understanding the attendant risks. Allegedly, BT, as adviser and banker, sold GG complex derivatives and GG had "no capacity independently to evaluate the benefits or risks involved in derivative transactions or to value the transactions themselves." In short, at the time the complaint was filed GG had lost $23 million and GG's liability was "potentially without limit, a situation which threatened the survival of the Company" (¶ 27).

CITICORP provides a quantification of market risk previously only described verbally and abstractly. The dollar numbers are remarkable because market risk is reported by the industry leader to be of low magnitude, especially compared to the credit risk numbers. However, there is a counterparty to each of CITICORP's positions, who may not be so consistently hedged or diversified. Interest rate and FX databases and software are available to facilitate quantification of exposure to market risk. (For example, see Guldimann 1994.) Since the need for quantification of market risk exposure has been identified and the technology exists for calculation, perhaps the time has come for the FASB or the SEC to require its disclosure.

CONCLUSIONS

Three factors likely reduce the willingness of management to support requirements for disclosure of enterprise exposure to currency risks and the effect of FXD on this exposure. First, is concern that disclosures may convey strategic information to competitors. Second, and perhaps more specious, specific information on the use of derivatives increases management exposure to shareholder lawsuits alleging misuse of corporate resources. For example, shareholders sued Procter & Gamble following their disclosure of $102 million losses on interest rate swaps in the first quarter of 1994. Third, disclosures impose a level of costs which are not always commensurate with their materiality to nonfinancial entities.

Even after SFAS No. 119, quantitative disclosures consist primarily of notional principal amounts of FXD outstanding at year-end. The Group of Thirty (1993) concludes that notional principal amounts of FXD measure activity level but do not measure risk exposure (either credit or market risk) for three main reasons. First, notional principal outstanding fails to account for offsetting exposures. Second, transactions of various maturities are simply added without accounting for the differing sensitivities of the values of the contracts to changes in the value of the underlying (e.g., the exchange rate risk of a one year option is not equal to that of a ten-year swap despite SFAS 105 treating the notional principal amounts the same). Finally, different types of derivatives (e.g., options versus swaps) have substantially different risk profiles.

Derivatives disclosures are relatively new and are evolving with the encouragement and guidance of the FASB (e.g., SFAS 119) and the SEC. SFAS 119 (FASB 1994) provides clarification and expansion of qualitative disclosures on derivatives and new quantitative information on average fair values of derivatives held for trading purposes. Other quantitative disclosures are either optional or have been withdrawn. Average fair values of derivatives used for trading purposes are additional information about level of usage of derivatives, not about market risk. Also, a large majority of non-financial companies do not use derivatives for trading purposes and are thus unaffected by the additional fair value disclosures. A major concern to investors is quantifying market risk which has yet to be directly addressed. The result is that empirical research potential is limited and aggregation of derivative disclosures to test cross-sectional and time series variation for policy inferences is delayed.

Large corporate losses reported in 1994 (e.g., Procter & Gamble and Gibson Greetings, reported in Kolman 1994) resulted from rapid market movements (market risk) and from management not properly controlling exposure to market risk (operating risk) of complex derivative contracts into which they had entered. The analysis of our survey, leads to several conclusions. First, all major dealers and some users report the quantified credit risk information required by the FASB. Considering the lack of reported problems to date and the magnitudes disclosed by manufacturers, credit risk does not appear to be a primary disclosure issue. Second, market risk disclosure is deficient because of inadequate quantification of some measure of value-at-risk in view of the reporting of large derivatives losses. Third, revelations by some managements that they were unaware of and were not controlling risks involved in derivative contracts undertaken (see the press release of Procter & Gamble and the 1994 law suit of Gibson Greetings against Bankers Trust) suggest internal control and operating risk is an area of concern. Arguably, operating risk relates to corporate controls and therefore is not directly within the FASB 's jurisdiction. However, requiring quantification of market risk (as well as credit risk) would educate users in decision making, thus reducing operating risk and providing useful information to investors and management.

REFERENCES

Belk, P. A., and M. Glaum. 1990. The management of foreign-exchange risk in UK multinationals: An empirical investigation. *Accounting and Business Research* (Winter): 3–13.

CITICORP. 1994. *FORM 10-Q, Quarterly Report Under Section 13 or 15(d) of the Securities Exchange Act of 1934, For the Quarterly Period Ended June 30, 1994.* Securities Exchange Commission file number 1-5738.

Federal Deposit Insurance Corporation. 1993. Reporting of Condition, Schedule RC-L. Washington: FDIC.

Financial Accounting Standards Board. 1981. *Foreign Currency Translation.* Statement of Financial Accounting Standards No. 52. Stamford: FASB.

———. 1984. *Accounting for Futures Contracts.* Statement of Financial Accounting Standards No. 80. Stamford: FASB.

———. 1987. *Proposed Statement of Financial Accounting Standards, Disclosures about Financial Instruments.* Stamford: FASB.

———. 1989. *Proposed Statement of Financial Accounting Standards, Disclosure of Information about Financial Instruments with Off-Balance-Sheet Risk and Financial Instruments with Concentrations of Credit Risk.* Stamford: FASB.

———. 1990a. *Disclosure of Information about Financial Instruments with Off-Balance-Sheet Risk and Financial Instruments with Concentrations of Credit Risk.* Statement of Financial Accounting Standards No. 105. Norwalk: FASB.

———. 1990b. *Proposed Statement of Financial Accounting Standards, Disclosures about Market Value of Financial Instruments.* Norwalk: FASB.

———. 1991a. *EITF Abstracts Issue No. 90-17, Hedging Foreign Currency Risks with Purchased Options.* Norwalk: FASB.

———. 1991b. *Disclosures about Fair Value of Financial Instruments.* Statement of Financial Accounting Standards No. 107. Norwalk: FASB.

———. 1992. *Offsetting of Amounts Related to Certain Contracts.* Interpretation No. 39. Norwalk: FASB.

———. 1994a. *Proposed Statement of Financial Accounting Standards, Disclosure about Derivative Financial Instruments and Fair Value of Financial Instruments.* Norwalk: FASB.

———. 1994b. *Disclosure about Derivative Financial Instruments and Fair Value of Financial Instruments.* Statement of Financial Accounting Standards No. 119. Norwalk: FASB.

Gibson Greetings Inc. vs. Bankers Trust Co and BT Securities Incorporated. 1994. Case No. 0-1-94-620, U.S. District Court, Southern District of Ohio, Western Division, Sept 12.

Group of Thirty. 1993. *Derivatives: Practices and Principles.* Washington, D.C.: Group of Thirty.

Guldimann, T. M. 1994. *RiskMetrics—Technical Document.* New York: J.P. Morgan.

Kolman, J., ed. 1994. Gibson Greetings, thank you. *Derivatives Strategy* (September 19).

Rodriguez, R. M. 1981. Corporate exchange risk management: Theme and aberrations. *The Journal of Finance* (May): 427–439.

Part III
Financial Reporting and Stock Markets

[13]

Journal of Accounting Research
Vol. 34 No. 1 Spring 1996
Printed in U.S.A.

Disclosure Choices of Foreign Registrants in the United States

CAROL A. FROST* AND WILLIAM R. KINNEY, JR.†

1. Introduction

This study provides descriptive evidence on the nature and timing of disclosures of foreign registrants (hereafter "issuers") in filings with the U.S. Securities and Exchange Commission (*SEC*). The *SEC* has exempted foreign issuers from some disclosure requirements applicable to U.S.-based registrants in order to encourage foreign firms to enter U.S. capital markets (Silkenat [1994]).[1] For example, under current *SEC* annual reporting rules, a foreign issuer that does not wish to make a public offering of securities in the United States may omit disclosures about income taxes, leases, pensions, nonconsolidated affiliates, related parties, and complete industry and geographic segment information. While these exemptions may stimulate listing in the U.S., they may also impair investors' ability to evaluate the financial performance of the affected firms. In particular, the *SEC* has relaxed disclosure requirements in areas cited by the *AICPA* Special Committee on Financial Reporting as the most useful to financial

*Washington University, St. Louis; †University of Texas at Austin. We are grateful for financial support from the Price Waterhouse Foundation, the Olin School of Business at Washington University (St. Louis), and the KPMG Peat Marwick Research Fellowship Program. We also thank Eli Amir, Andrew Alford, Bruce Behn, Christine Botosan, Curt Coffer, Nick Dopuch, Ed Etter, Trevor Harris, Eric Hirst, Norm Walker, and workshop participants at Southern Methodist University, the universities of Colorado, Michigan, Missouri at Columbia, North Carolina at Chapel Hill, and Notre Dame for helpful comments, and Roger Martin and Lorani Orobitg for their research assistance.

[1] In 1992, 94 nondomestic companies entered the U.S. market for the first time, offering $32 billion (U.S.) in new securities (Breeden [1994]).

68   JOURNAL OF ACCOUNTING RESEARCH, SPRING 1996

statement users (*AICPA* [1993]).[2] For example, the Special Committee concluded that financial statement users place a high value on segment reporting and that they want more information about risks associated with financial instruments, off-balance-sheet financing arrangements, and other items disclosed in footnotes required by U.S. *GAAP*.[3] The Special Committee also concluded that users prefer that one set of accounting standards be applied by all foreign registrants wishing to raise capital in the United States (*AICPA* [1993]).

To compare disclosures of U.S. and foreign-based private (nongovernment) issuers, we examine annual reports filed with the *SEC* by 126 (of a total of 128) *SEC*-registered non-Canadian foreign issuers with securities traded on major U.S. stock exchanges during all of 1990, and a random sample of 30 of the 171 Canadian issuers who also met this trading requirement. We also examine dates of annual report filings and media announcements of annual earnings, and the frequency and filing dates of sample firms' interim reports. A size-matched sample of U.S. firms in the same industries is used as a benchmark. The evidence is relevant for assessing the extent to which *SEC* accommodations result in fewer and/or less timely accounting disclosures made by foreign issuers, as compared to disclosures made by domestic firms.

This study differs in several respects from recent studies of the value relevance of foreign issuers' reconciliation disclosures (e.g., Amir, Harris, and Venuti [1993], Bandyopadhyay, Hanna, and Richardson [1994], Barth and Clinch [1994], and McQueen [1993]). First, it focuses on firms' disclosure practices generally, rather than the value relevance of one type of disclosure (reconciliations to U.S. *GAAP* accounting numbers). As a result, the foreign firm sample is not limited to firms that provide reconciliation disclosures or firms from domiciles with selected accounting principle characteristics. Second, we provide a comparative disclosure analysis of foreign and U.S. firms while the other studies focus exclusively on foreign firms. Third, we present evidence on disclosure differences both among and within filing status partitions (Form 20-F, Item 17; Form 20-F, Item 18; and Form 10-K). Related 20-F studies do not distinguish among filing status groups, since *SEC* reconciliation rules do not vary among those groups.

There are four main findings. First, for fiscal years 1989 and 1990, the foreign firms file fewer interim reports, their reports are filed later, they announce earnings later, and more than 80% of them use non-U.S. *GAAP*. Second, the differences in disclosure are related to their filing status. The

---

[2] The *SEC* recently issued rule changes and proposals for rule changes to further reduce the reporting burden for foreign issuers (SEC [1994*a*; 1994*c*; 1994*d*; 1994*e*] and Kosnik [1994]) and has requested views and empirical data about the costs and benefits associated with the proposals (SEC [1993*a*; 1994*b*], and Harlan [1993]).

[3] Also, the Association for Investment Management and Research (*AIMR*) has emphasized the importance of segment reporting, has expressed concern over the possible lowering of accounting standards to promote the internationalization of capital markets and has stressed the importance of frequent and timely financial reporting (*AIMR* [1993]).

least stringent filing status (Form 20-F, Item 17) filers file annual reports significantly later than do foreign firms filing under Form 20-F, Item 18 or Form 10-K. Third, within each Form 20-F filing status category, a substantial number of firms do not comply with disclosure requirements of their category. Finally, there is significant variation in the earnings/ stock returns and earnings change/stock return correlations among domicile, filing status, and disclosure groups. However, when compared to the earnings and earnings change/stock return correlations for an industry-matched U.S. sample, the correlations are similar.

Section 2 presents relevant background on *SEC* disclosure requirements. Section 3 discusses sample selection and description. We present results in section 4 and conclusions in section 5.

2. SEC Disclosure Requirements

During the period studied (fiscal years 1989 and 1990), most Canadian issuers were required to file annual reports on Form 10-K and quarterly reports on Form 10-Q. Non-Canadian foreign issuers could file annual reports on Form 20-F, which allow two levels of financial statement disclosure referred to as Item 17 and Item 18. Item 18 of Form 20-F generally requires disclosure of all information required by U.S. *GAAP* and Regulation S-X. In contrast, Item 17 is less burdensome with regard to conformance with U.S. *GAAP* and Regulation S-X (Warren, Gorham & Lamont [1994]).[4]

A foreign registrant's disclosure choices are dictated by the firm's method of entering the U.S. capital market. A company seeking to issue new shares through a public offering in the United States must prepare and file Item 18 financial statements in the registration statement. A foreign company can avoid U.S. *GAAP* disclosures required under Item 18 by filing Item 17 statements and choosing "public listing" of its existing shares on a U.S. exchange, but it cannot make a public offering of securities. Murray, Decker, and Dittmar [1993] state that non-U.S. issuers rarely use the Form 20-F, Item 17 option except when a U.S. *GAAP* disclosure (e.g., segment profits) is sensitive or when certain information is unavailable or costly to obtain (also see *SEC* [1987, chap. 4] and Bloomenthal [1989, sec. 5.07(1)]). Decker [1994] finds that sensitivity is the

---

[4] For example, Item 17 does not require an issuer to furnish the geographic market and industry segment information required by Regulation S-X. However, Item 1 of Form 20-F requires limited segment information about sales revenue. Also, the *SEC* permits a registrant to omit information about subsidiaries outside the registrant's home country if the disclosure would be harmful to the registrant (Form 20-F, General Instructions, Part E in Warren, Gorham & Lamont [1994]). Finally, Item 17 filers whose annual financial statements otherwise follow U.S. *GAAP* are not required to make *SFAS No. 14* segment profit disclosures but are allowed to state that their financial statements conform to U.S. *GAAP* (Form 20-F, Item 17 in Warren, Gorham & Lamont [1994]). This special accommodation reflects the *SEC*'s response to numerous comment letters from foriegn issuers, particulary Japanese issuers, requesting that Form 20-F segment disclosure rules be relaxed (see *SEC* [1987, chap. 4] and McKinnon [1984]).

70   CAROL A. FROST AND WILLIAM R. KINNEY

greater issue in practice. For example, foreign issuers may be reluctant to provide disclosures that might reveal an aggressive revenue recognition approach, "hidden reserves," or a substantially underfunded pension plan (see "Bridging the GAAP to Germany" [1994]).

Disclosure levels may also vary considerably among firms nominally facing the same financial statement requirements (either Form 10-K; Form 20-F, Item 18; or Form 20-F, Item 17 requirements). First, the *SEC* occasionally grants disclosure relief to a foreign issuer in areas that are especially burdensome and sometimes makes accommodations to foreign issuers in interpreting what is "equivalent to" U.S. *GAAP* in Item 18 footnote disclosures (see Cochrane [1994], *SEC* [1993a], and Bergman [1993]). Second, foreign issuers may simply not comply with the disclosure requirements. Thus, Item 18 filers may fail to provide the required segment profit disclosures, or an issuer in any one of the three filing status categories may fail to provide the full five years of summary reconciliation disclosures.[5]

3. Sample Selection and Description

The initial sample consisted of the 369 foreign companies traded on the *NYSE, ASE,* or *NASDAQ* during all of calendar year 1990, based on lists of non-U.S. listed firms supplied by the two exchanges and *NASDAQ.* This 1990 census was reduced by excluding: (*a*) 51 "grandfathered" companies exempted by the *SEC* from filing Forms 20-F,[6] (*b*) 19 non-Canadian Form 10-K filers probably considered domestic issuers according to the *SEC*'s definition,[7] (*c*) two U.K. holding companies (to avoid duplication with closely related Netherlands holding companies), and (*d*) 141 Canadian firms remaining after 10 firms were randomly selected from Canadian firms listed on each of the two exchanges and *NASDAQ.* A size- and industry-matched comparison sample of U.S. firms was obtained by selecting from *Compustat,* for each of the 156 foreign firms, the

---

[5] The legal and regulatory consequences of noncompliance with *SEC* disclosure requirements are potentially significant. The federal securities acts contain provisions that create potential liability for non-U.S. issuers and directors and officers of non-U.S. issuers. The securities acts also give the *SEC* considerable enforcement powers, and criminal sanctions may apply in some cases (Brown & Wood [1994]). Although several *SEC* lawsuits, *SEC* enforcement cases, and class action lawsuits related to financial reporting have been brought against foreign issuers or their directors or officers in recent years, foreign issuers probably face lower expected costs of noncompliance than do U.S. issuers, ceteris paribus, due to difficulties and added costs that the *SEC* often faces in seeking information, gathering evidence, and enforcing judgments against foreign parties (see *SEC* [1993b; 1994f; 1995], Mann and Mari [1990], and the American Law Institute [1991]).

[6] Non-Canadian issuers traded on *NASDAQ* as of October 6, 1983 are eligible to use an exemption from *SEC* registration (*SEC* [1984]).

[7] Foreign companies meeting two conditions are considered to be essentially U.S. issuers and are subject to the same requirements as U.S. companies. The first condition is that 50% of the issuer's shares are held by U.S. persons; the second is that either the issuer's business is headquartered in the U.S., or most of the senior executives or directors are U.S. citizens, or 50% of the assets are located in the U.S. (*SEC* [1984]).

U.S. firm in the same *SIC* code that was closest in revenues.[8] Thus, this matched sample should reflect variation in disclosure due to industry and size factors. It does not, of course, reflect other factors such as customs, laws, regulations, or any other differences due to being domiciled outside the United States.

Panel A of table 1 shows that the final sample of 156 foreign firms consists of the random sample of 30 firms from Canada, 21 firms from Israel, 16 from Japan, 34 from the United Kingdom, 35 from all other European countries, and 20 firms from all other non-European countries. Mean revenues for fiscal 1990 (from Forms 20-F and 10-K) vary among domicile groups, ranging from $135.4 million (U.S. dollars throughout) for Israeli firms to $26,134.7 million for Japanese firms. As to geographic concentration, Form 20-F and 10-K disclosures made by 117 of the 156 foreign firms indicate that about 28% of these firms' revenues and 21% of their total profits were attributed to U.S. operations. In contrast, only 53 of the matched U.S. comparison firms reported foreign segment results, and these indicated that U.S. revenues and profits were 59% and 60% of the respective totals. Thus, almost half of the U.S. firms appear not to have had substantial foreign operations, and those that did had most of their activities within the United States.

Table 1 panel A also indicates the numbers of U.S. and non-U.S. analysts following the foreign issuers vary among domicile groups (U.S. [non-U.S.] analysts are those whose business addresses are within [outside of] the U.S.). For example, the mean number of U.S. analysts ranges from 1.2 for Israeli firms to 7.4 for U.K. firms. In contrast, U.S. analyst following for the U.S. comparison firms averages 17.7, similar to a mean analyst following of 17.6 for 751 firms studied in Lang and Lundholm [1993*b*]. Several studies document positive associations between firms' disclosure policies and both their size and analyst following (e.g., Botosan [1995], Lang and Lundholm [1993*a*; 1993*b*], and Kasznik and Lev [1995]). Therefore, the evidence in table 1, panel A suggests that foreign firms' disclosure practices may vary among the domicile groups represented in the sample, and between foreign firms and the U.S. comparison firms.[9]

---

[8] The comparison sample consists of 136 different firms. Due to the limited range of industries for the foreign issuers, 10 firms are used twice in this comparison sample, and 5 firms are used three times, with the result that these comparison firms are double- or triple-counted, respectively. Double- and triple-counting some of the match firms violates the assumption of independent observations and raises the probability that peculiar characteristics of one or more match firms are overweighted in the analyses. In the analyses to follow, results are presented with and without the double- and triple-counted U.S. firms.

[9] In table 1, panel A, mean and median revenues, but not analyst following, are substantially affected by the inclusion of 20 double- and triple-counted U.S. firm observations. The 20 U.S. double- and triple-counted firm-observations had mean (median) revenues (in millions) of $13,108.9 ($924.9), compared to $5,859.9 ($573.8) for the 136 single-counted firm-observations. The 20 had mean (median) U.S. analyst followings of 16.8 (11) versus 17.8 (11.5) for the 136 firms and 0.95 (0) versus 1.0 (0) non-U.S. analysts, respectively.

TABLE 1

Descriptive Statistics for Overall Sample of Foreign Firms Trading on the NYSE, ASE, or NASDAQ during Calendar Year 1990 and Size and Industry-Matched U.S. Firms

Panel A: Revenues and Analyst Following by Domicile

Domicile	Number of Firms	Revenues[1] ($ U.S. millions) Mean	Median	U.S.[2] Analysts Mean	Median	Non-U.S.[2] Analysts Mean	Median
Canada	30	1,520.4	245.1	4.3	0.5	6.4	0.5
Israel	21	135.4	74.5	1.2	0	0	0
Japan	16	26,134.7	13,241.0	2.4	2	11.2	12.5
United Kingdom	34	6,783.5	2,622.2	7.4	5	22.3	27.5
Other (European)[3]	35	9,830.8	3,896.2	4.5	2	16.8	20
Other (Non-European)[4]	20	2,278.7	254.6	3.8	1.5	3.9	0
All Foreign Firms	**156**	**6,967.32**	**1,287.4**	**4.2**	**2**	**11.5**	**7.5**
U.S. Comparison Firms Matched on Revenues and Industry	156	6,789.15	573.8	17.7	11	1.0	0

Panel B: Accounting Principles Used in Primary Financial Statements, Auditor, and Filing Status by Domicile

Domicile	No. of Firms	GAAP Home	U.S.	Home and U.S.[5]	Other[6]	Auditor Big Six	Other	Filing Status 10-K	20-F	20-F
Canada	30	28	—	2	—	24	6	23	3	4
Israel	21	10	1	10	—	—	21	—	9	12
Japan	16	—	16	—	1	16	4	—	11	5
United Kingdom	34	32	—	1	1	30	4	—	4	30
Other (European)	35	28	—	2	—	33	2	—	13	22
Other (Non-European)	20	12	7	—	1	16	4	—	5	15
All Foreign Firms	**156**	**110**	**29**	**15**	**2**	**119**	**37**	**23**	**45**	**88**

[1]Revenues and other data for all panels are from fiscal 1990 Forms 20-F and 10-K (fiscal year-ends July 1, 1990 through June 30, 1991). Translation to U.S. dollars is based on exchange rates in effect at the fiscal year-end date.

[2]U.S. (non-U.S.) analysts are those whose business addresses are within (outside of) the United States. Data on analyst following are from Nelson Publications [1992].

[3]Includes Denmark, Finland, France, Ireland, Italy, Luxembourg, the Netherlands, Norway, Spain, and Sweden.

[4]Includes Australia, the Bahamas, the British Virgin Islands, the British West Indies, the Cayman Islands, Hong Kong, Liberia, Mexico, the Netherlands Antilles, and the Philippines.

[5]Firm states that financial statements conform with both home and U.S. accounting principles or that differences are not material. Israeli firms that state differences are not material, but whose primary financial statements are price-level adjusted, are classified in the Home GAAP category.

[6]One U.K. firm based its financial statements on Canadian GAAP, and one firm domiciled in the Cayman Islands (a British Crown colony) reported using U.K. GAAP.

Panel B of table 1 presents the type of *GAAP* used in annual reports, auditor (Big Six vs. non-Big Six), and filing status (Form 10-K; Form 20-F, Item 18; Form 20-F, Item 17) by domicile. The type of *GAAP* used was disclosed in notes to the financial statements, the Management's Discussion and Analysis, selected financial data (Item 8 of Form 20-F), and audit reports. Most firms' annual reports (110 out of 156, or 70.5%) disclosed that the primary financial statements were based on home domicile accounting principles. Forty-four registrants used U.S. *GAAP* or both U.S. and home country *GAAP.* The two remaining firms used accounting principles different from home *GAAP* and U.S. *GAAP.*

Panel B of table 1 also shows that 119 (76.3%) of the 156 sample firms used Big Six audit firms, and that use of Big Six audit firms varies by domicile, ranging from 0% for Israeli firms to 100% for Japanese firms. Twenty-three of the 30 Canadian firms file Forms 10-K. A mix of Form 20-F, Item 18 and Item 17 filers comprise firms in the other domicile groups. Analysis of the association between filing status and auditor (not shown in table 1) indicates that 21 of the 23 (91.3%) Form 10-K filers (all Canadian) use Big Six auditors. The lowest frequency of Big Six auditors is observed for Form 20-F, Item 17 filers (30 out of 45, or 66.7%). Thus, companies electing to file "low disclosure" Form 20-F, Item 17 annual reports are less likely to choose the expertise associated with large international audit firms.[10] Smaller firms do not appear to be more likely to choose the Item 17 filing status, however. Mean (median) revenues are larger for Item 17 filers than for Item 18 filers ($8,697.5 [$1,395.4] and $7,385.6 [$1,557.7], respectively, all in millions).

4. *Empirical Results*

4.1 FREQUENCY AND TIMING OF ACCOUNTING DISCLOSURES

SEC filing dates for fiscal year 1990 filings for foreign issuers and U.S. comparison firms were obtained as follows. Dates for foreign issuers' and U.S. comparison firms' annual Forms 20-F, 10-K, and interim Forms 10-Q for fiscal 1990 (fiscal year-ends July 1, 1990–June 30, 1991) were determined from the *SEC* date stamps and from Disclosure Inc.'s *SEC* filing histories. Interim report filing dates of the Form 20-F filers were tabulated using Form 6-K data from Disclosure Inc. Media disclosures of fiscal year 1990 annual earnings for 141 (90%) of the 156 foreign issuers and for 147 (94%) of the 156 U.S. comparison firms were obtained from the *Wall Street Journal* and/or the *Dow Jones News Retrieval Service.*

---

[10] An alternative view is that a firm raising new capital in the United States is encouraged by its investment banker to use a Big Six auditor. If a firm not raising new capital has a non-Big Six auditor, it may not want to change auditors. Hence, auditor choice by foreign firms entering U.S. capital markets may be related to reputation effects as well as auditor expertise.

74   CAROL A. FROST AND WILLIAM R. KINNEY

TABLE 2

Frequency and Timing of Financial Reports and Media Disclosures of
Annual Earnings for Fiscal Years Ending July 1, 1990 through June 30, 1991

	Foreign Firms Trading on NYSE, ASE, or NASDAQ				U.S. Comparison Firms
	Form 20-F Filers				
	Form 10-K Filers	Item 18	Item 17	All Foreign Firms	Form 10-K Filers
Annual Reports on Forms 10-K and 20-F[1]					
No. of Firms Analyzed	23	88	45	156	156
Mean Lag[2]	85.1	160.6	173.5	153.2	86.0
Median Lag[2]	87	178	180	176	88
Range (min., max. lag)[2]	(46, 106)	(60, 334)	(89, 249)	(46, 334)	(51, 137)
Interim Reports[3]					
No. of Firms Analyzed	23	88	45	156	156
No. of Interim Reports per Firm					
Mean	3.0	1.2	1.4	1.9	3.0
Median	3	1	1	2	3
Range (min., max.)	(2, 3)	(0, 3)	(0, 3)	(0, 3)	(2, 3)
Mean Lag[2]	44.9	58.2	81.4	54.6	43.1
Median Lag[2]	44	55	72	45	44
Range (min., max. lag)[2]	(12, 164)	(4, 127)	(44, 167)	(4, 167)	(15, 137)
Media Disclosures of Annual Earnings					
No. of Firms with Disclosures	22	82	37	141	147
Mean Lag[4]	47.5	72.3	78.5	70.1	43.4
Median Lag[4]	47.5	66	75	64	38
Range (min., max. lag)[4]	(21, 87)	(23, 144)	(17, 199)	(17, 199)	(15, 138)

[1]The Forms 10-K were filed by 23 Canadian firms.
[2]Calendar days between filing date and fiscal period end.
[3]Includes Forms 10-Q filed by Canadian registrants, and half-yearly and quarterly reports filed by Form 20-F filers.
[4]Calendar days between disclosure issuance date and fiscal period end.

Table 2 presents evidence on the frequency and timing of annual and interim reports, and annual earnings announcements of the foreign and U.S. comparison firms. Forms 10-K, 10-Q, and 20-F were filed on average within the 90-day, 45-day, and 180-day allowable periods, respectively, and all filing dates cluster at their respective filing deadlines.[11] Table 2 indicates that foreign issuers file annual and interim reports and announce annual earnings with longer lags, and file interim reports less frequently than do U.S. firms. Mean (median) annual report filing lags for foreign and U.S. firms are 153.2 (176) days and 86.0 (88) days, respectively.[12] Mean and median differences in filing lag are significant at $p = .000$ (all tests are two-sided). Interim reports of foreign registrants are significantly less frequent and also less timely than Forms 10-Q filed

---

[11] For further evidence on reporting lags, see Easton and Zmijewski [1993], Alford, Jones, and Zmijewski [1994], Amir, Harris, and Venuti [1993], and Frost and Pownall [1994].

[12] Amir, Harris, and Venuti [1993] report a mean reporting lag of 154.4 days for 467 Forms 20-F filed during 1981–91.

by the U.S. firms ($p = .000$). Mean (median) interim report frequencies are 1.9 (2) and 3.0 (3) for foreign and U.S. firms, respectively, and mean (median) filing lags are 54.6 (45) days and 43.1 (44) days, respectively.[13] Table 2 also shows that media disclosures of earnings were made by foreign firms, on average, 70.1 days after the fiscal year-end, in contrast to a mean lag of 43.4 days for the U.S. firms. Both mean and median disclosure lags are significantly greater for the foreign firms than for the U.S. firms at $p = .000$.[14]

Analysis of differences in filing lags of Item 17 and Item 18 Form 20-F filers reveals that Item 17 (low disclosure) filers release financial information on a less timely basis than do Item 18 filers. Mean (median) Form 20-F filing lags for Item 17 and Item 18 filers are 173.5 (180) days and 160.6 (178) days, respectively, and the mean and median differences in reporting lag are significant at the 0.05 level or better. Mean and median interim reporting lags are also significantly longer for the Item 17 filers than for the Item 18 filers at the 0.01 level; the mean (median) lags are 81.4 (72) days and 58.2 (55) days, respectively. Although Item 17 filers announce annual earnings to the media about a week later than do Item 18 filers, the mean and median lag differences are not statistically significant at conventional levels. The longer annual and interim reporting lags observed for Item 17 filers relative to Item 18 filers may be due to deliberate delays in releasing the reports for competitive reasons or difficulty in obtaining the required financial information, consistent with Decker's [1994] assertion that foreign issuers self-select into the "low disclosure" Item 17 filing status when financial information is sensitive or costly to obtain.

4.2 DISCLOSURES WITHIN FILING CATEGORIES

Disclosure levels within filing categories were assessed by comparing foreign issuers' disclosures to benchmarks based on Form 20-F and 10-K instructions and on Regulation S-X. In this analysis, substance was emphasized over form. For example, Items 17 and 18 specify a tabular format for reconciliation to U.S. *GAAP,* but a firm was considered to have met the reconciliation requirement if it provided the proper information, even

---

[13] Most non-U.S. countries either do not require interim reports or require only one semiannual report. Nine of the Form 20-F filers did not file any interim reports with the *SEC* during fiscal year 1990. Israeli companies listed on the Tel-Aviv Stock Exchange are required to submit quarterly financial statements to the Securities Authority (Coopers & Lybrand [1993]), but only 6 of our 21 Israeli firms are listed in Israel. Five of these companies filed three quarterly reports each with the *SEC,* and one firm filed two quarterly reports. The Ontario Securities Act of 1980, which applies to most of the publicly traded equity in Canada, requires the filing of three interim reports per year (Orsini, McAllister, and Parikh [1994]). The 23 Canadian 10-K filers filed three quarterly reports each. Six of our seven Canadian sample firms filing Forms 20-F are publicly traded in Canada, but only one of the companies filed three quarterly reports with the *SEC.*

[14] Results in table 2, which are based on 156 U.S. firm-observations, are almost identical to results obtained using a sample of 136 firm-observations, after deleting the 20 double- and triple-counted observations.

76   CAROL A. FROST AND WILLIAM R. KINNEY

TABLE 3

Segment and Reconciliation Disclosures for Fiscal Years Ending July 1, 1990 through
June 30, 1991 by Foreign Issuers Trading on the NYSE, ASE, or NASDAQ during Calendar Year 1990

Domicile	No. of Firms	Segment Disclosures[1]		Reconciliation Disclosures[2]	
		Comply	Do Not Comply	Comply	Do Not Comply
Canada	30	28	2	22	8
Israel	21	15	6	15	6
Japan	16	16	0	16	0
United Kingdom	34	28	6	33	1
Other (European)	35	32	3	34	1
Other (Non-European)	20	18	2	15	5
All Foreign Firms	**156**	**137**	**19**	**135**	**21**
(*p*-value)[3]			(.105)		(.001)

[1]The 137 compliers include 57 firms that did not disclose either or both industry or geographic segment information about revenues, operating profits, or identifiable assets. Eighteen segment disclosure noncompliers were Form 20-F, Item 18 filers that disclosed some information about industry or geographic segments (e.g., revenues) but failed to disclose operating profits (four firms), identifiable assets (five firms), or both profits and assets (nine firms) for industry and/or geographic segments. The nineteenth segment noncomplier was a Form 20-F, Item 17 filer that disclosed identifiable assets and operating profits, but not revenues, for industry segments.

[2]The 135 compliers include 29 firms using U.S. *GAAP*, 15 firms that stated that financial statements conform with both home and U.S. accounting principles (or that differences are not material), and 91 firms that presented reconciliation disclosures in conformance with *SEC* requirements. The 21 noncompliers presented incomplete reconciliation information. Seventeen firms presented some reconciliation information, but either did not present the required earnings or earnings per share (*EPS*) reconciliation, did not disclose five years of reconciled results, or did not discuss material variations from U.S. *GAAP*. Three firms stated that reconciliation to U.S. *GAAP* amounts was impossible, and one firm did not disclose the type of *GAAP* used.

[3]Probability of the observed association given independence using Fisher's Exact Test (Mehta and Patell [1983]).

though not in a tabular format. Noncompliance was coded only for those cases that we believed would lead to a comment letter or further inquiry if noted by *SEC* staff during a filings review (for example, disclosure of segment revenues but not profits by a Form 10-K or Form 20-F, Item 18 filer should lead to some action by the *SEC* staff).[15]

Table 3 presents segment and reconciliation disclosure results. The table shows that 137 firms complied with the segment disclosure requirements, including 57 firms that did not make either or both geographic or industry segment disclosures, presumably because the characteristics of their products and/or markets were not appropriately described by segment breakdowns. Nineteen of the 156 foreign firms did not meet the *SEC*'s segment disclosure requirements for their filing status. Eighteen segment noncompliers were Item 18 filers that disclosed *some* information about industry or geographic segments (indicating that segment breakdowns were meaningful) but failed to disclose segment operating profit

---

[15] Foreign issuers' disclosures that fall short of *SEC* written benchmarks do not necessarily indicate noncompliance. As noted earlier, the *SEC* occasionally grants accommodations to individual registrants, and a low disclosure level that might appear to be noncompliance could be the result of an *SEC* exemption granted in the past. The *SEC* does not release information about the accommodations.

(four firms), identifiable assets (five firms), or both profit and assets (nine firms). The nineteenth segment noncomplier was an Item 17 filer that disclosed identifiable assets and operating profits, but not revenues, for industry segments.

Table 3 also shows that 135 of the 156 non-U.S. firms complied with the reconciliation disclosure requirements, including 29 firms using U.S. *GAAP*, 15 firms that stated that financial statements conform with both home and U.S. accounting principles (or that differences were not material), and 91 firms that presented reconciliation disclosures in conformance with *SEC* written requirements. Twenty-one firms did not meet the *SEC*'s written reconciliation rules. Seventeen firms presented some reconciliation information but either did not present the required earnings or earnings per share (*EPS*) reconciliation, presented reconciliation disclosures for three or fewer years (rather than the required five years), or did not discuss material variations from U.S. *GAAP* or the type of *GAAP* used. Three firms stated that reconciliation to U.S. *GAAP* amounts was impossible, and one firm did not disclose the type of *GAAP* used. Finally, the cross-classifications of accounting disclosure compliance levels with domicile shows that firms' disclosure choices appear to be positively correlated with their size. The Japanese domicile group, which consists of relatively large firms, exhibits full compliance, and low compliance is concentrated in the Israeli and Canadian groups, which have the smallest firms.

Not reported in table 3 are the associations between disclosure compliance level, filing status, and auditor. There were highly significant associations between filing status and disclosure level measures. Eighteen of the 19 firms that did not meet their chosen filing forms' written segment rules filed using Form 20-F, Item 18, which requires segment disclosures in full conformance with Regulation S-X. Ten of 21 firms that did not comply with the reconciliation rules were Item 17 filers, consistent with possible self-selection into the lower disclosure requirements for Item 17. A final result is that for both segment and reconciliation disclosures, non-Big Six auditors are associated with a significantly greater relative frequency of noncompliance than would be expected by chance (at $p = .002$ and $.000$ for segment and reconciliation noncompliance, respectively). This evidence is consistent with the view that disclosure and accounting practices, auditor size choice, and filing status (Item 17 vs. Item 18 financial statements) are jointly determined elements of a foreign issuer's financial reporting strategy.

4.3 DISCLOSURE LEVEL AND EARNINGS/RETURN ASSOCIATION

As a final set of descriptive analyses, Spearman rank correlations were calculated for 15-month stock returns with both earnings and earnings changes for the foreign firms and their U.S. counterparts overall, and for various domicile- and disclosure-based partitions. Due to the small sample size and the short time period, the results are only suggestive of the possible relations between disclosure and the earnings/return correlations (e.g., see King, Pownall, and Waymire [1990] and Lang and Lundholm [1993a]). However, if the *SEC*'s objective of "full and fair disclosure" is being met for every group and subgroup, then the associations of earnings and stock returns for foreign issuers should be similar to those of U.S. firms, ceteris paribus. Rank correlations for the size- and industry-matched U.S. firms serve as the "other things equal" condition.[16]

The association analyses are based on annual U.S. *GAAP*-based *EPS* and change in *EPS* from the prior year, deflated by stock price on the first day of the year (all figures translated to U.S. $ at year-end rates).[17] Stock returns were computed for each foreign and matched U.S. firm using daily returns and a buy-and-hold strategy with data from the *CRSP* daily returns file. *CRSP* returns were not available for 43 of the foreign registrants on *NASDAQ*, since *CRSP* does not supply returns data for foreign common share issues on *NASDAQ*. For these 43 firms, returns were computed using price, dividend, and split data from the Standard and Poor's *Daily Stock Price Record and Dividend Record* (Standard and Poor's [1990; 1991; 1992]). The returns cumulation period for all foreign and U.S. comparison firms began 90 days after the start of the fiscal year and ended 15 months later. For example, returns for a December 31, 1990 fiscal year-end firm were accumulated from April 1, 1990 to June 30, 1991.[18] Fourteen foreign firms (and their U.S. matches) which had stock prices of $2.00 or less at the start of the cumulation period were excluded due to the expected error in measuring these firms' returns caused by large bid–ask spreads relative to their stock prices. In addition, 20 firms were deleted for 1989 due to lack of earnings or stock price data. Thus, the analyses are based on 264 firm-year observations for each group.

Table 4 presents the earnings/returns correlations. Panel A presents correlations between returns and earnings, and returns and earnings changes for all foreign firm-observations and all U.S. firm-observations. The correlations for both groups are about .40 for earnings and about .30 for earnings changes. All four correlations are highly significant ($p = .000$,

---

[16] As noted above, the matched sample does not control for different customs, laws, regulations, and other factors related to being domiciled outside the U.S., nor does it control for the percentage of U.S. revenues and profits.

[17] U.S. *GAAP*-based earnings are used for the 108 firms that reconcile to U.S. *GAAP*. For the 48 foreign firms which either use U.S. *GAAP*, state that differences between home and U.S. *GAAP* are not material, or do not disclose U.S. *GAAP*-based earnings, net income is from the primary financial statements. The term "U.S. *GAAP*" is used for convenience and should be interpreted with caution. As one example, several Israeli firms state that their earnings are the same as U.S. *GAAP* earnings, even though their financial results are price-level adjusted (also see n. 4).

[18] We also used 12-month cumulation periods beginning either 3 months after the fiscal year-end for all firms, or 6 months after year-end for foreign firms and 3 months after year-end for U.S. firms. In these diagnostic analyses, most of the estimation results were similar to those in the primary analysis.

TABLE 4

Spearman Correlations between 15-Month U.S. Stock Returns and Deflated Earnings and Earnings Change for Foreign Firms Trading on the NYSE, ASE, or NASDAQ during Calendar Year 1990 and U.S. Comparison Firms (two-sided p-values shown in parentheses)

	n^1	Foreign Firms Deflated Earnings[2]	Foreign Firms Deflated Earnings Change	U.S. Comparison Firms Deflated Earnings	U.S. Comparison Firms Deflated Earnings Change	Difference[3] (Foreign–U.S. Comparison) Deflated Earnings	Difference[3] (Foreign–U.S. Comparison) Deflated Earnings Change
Panel A: All Firms							
	264	.399	.320	.393	.294	.006	.026
		(.000)	(.000)	(.000)	(.000)	(.935)	(.743)
Panel B: By Domicile							
Canada	45	.702	.216	.640	.337	.062	−.121
		(.000)	(.154)	(.000)	(.024)	(.605)	(.548)
Israel	33	.230	.222	.316	.344	−.086	−.122
		(.199)	(.215)	(.073)	(.050)	(.719)	(.607)
Japan	31	.417	.276	.432	.291	−.015	−.015
		(.020)	(.133)	(.015)	(.112)	(.946)	(.951)
United Kingdom	57	.397	.306	.311	.345	.086	−.039
		(.002)	(.020)	(.018)	(.008)	(.609)	(.820)
Other	64	.077	.252	.387	.276	−.310	−.024
(European)		(.543)	(.044)	(.002)	(.027)	(.067)	(.887)
Other	34	.270	.444	.181	.353	.089	.091
(Non-European)		(.122)	(.008)	(.305)	(.040)	(.712)	(.669)
Panel C: By Filing Status							
Form 10-K	42	.662	.277	.620	.322	.042	−.045
		(.000)	(.076)	(.000)	(.037)	(.753)	(.827)
Form 20-F,	75	.189	.268	.422	.428	−.230	−.160
Item 17		(.103)	(.020)	(.000)	(.000)	(.120)	(.273)
Form 20-F,	147	.432	.348	.305	.213	.127	.135
Item 18		(.000)	(.000)	(.000)	(.000)	(.211)	(.213)
Panel D: By Compliance[4]							
Segment Rules							
Compliers	234	.402	.319	.415	.286	−.013	.033
		(.000)	(.000)	(.000)	(.000)	(.867)	(.697)
Noncompliers	30	.041	.304	.130	.352	−.089	−.048
		(.829)	(.103)	(.494)	(.056)	(.742)	(.843)
Reconciliation Rules							
Compliers	238	.396	.283	.406	.300	−.010	−.017
		(.000)	(.000)	(.000)	(.000)	(.897)	(.841)
Noncompliers	26	.378	.539	.342	.414	.036	.125
		(.062)	(.004)	(.088)	(.036)	(.889)	(.582)

[1]The overall sample of 264 firm-year observations from 142 foreign firms and 142 U.S. comparison firms matched on *SIC* code and size (1990 revenues in U.S. dollars) for 1989 and 1990 fiscal years. For all firms, the stock returns are based on a buy-and-hold trading strategy with a cumulation period that begins 3 months after the beginning of the fiscal year and ends 15 months later. *EPS* and change in *EPS* are deflated by beginning-of-year price, where all amounts are in U.S. dollars, based on translation at the fiscal year-end exchange rates.

[2]U.S. *GAAP*-based earnings are used for the 108 firms that reconcile to U.S. *GAAP*. For the 48 foreign firms that either use U.S. *GAAP*, state that differences between home and U.S. *GAAP* are not material, or do not disclose U.S. *GAAP*-based earnings, net income is from the primary financial statements.

[3]Difference is the Spearman correlation for foreign firms minus the Spearman correlation for the U.S. comparison firms. The p-values in parentheses assume that the samples are drawn from populations with equal correlations and are calculated following Morrison [1976, pp. 104–5].

[4]Compliance was assessed by comparing foreign issuers' disclosures to benchmarks based on Form 20-F and 10-K instructions, and on Regulation S-X. In this analysis, substance was emphasized over form. For example, Items 17 and 18 of Form 20-F specify a tabular format for reconciliation to U.S. *GAAP*, but a firm was considered to have met the reconciliation requirement if it provided the proper information even though not in a tabular format (also see the notes to table 3).

two-sided), and they are statistically indistinguishable between foreign and U.S. groups (Morrison [1976, pp. 104–5]). Panels B, C, and D of table 4 present correlations for the six domicile partitions, three foreign firm filing status groups, and the segment and reconciliation disclosure partitions, respectively.

Table 4, panel B shows significant variation in earnings/return correlations among domicile groups. For example, earnings and earnings change correlations are both less than .25 and not significant at conventional levels for Israeli firms, but are greater than .30 and significant at conventional levels for U.K. firms. For the other domiciles, correlations for foreign firms tend to be lower and less significant than their U.S. counterparts. However, the within-match results are generally consistent, with two-sided p-values on the difference in correlations greater than .5 for all except deflated earnings for the other European group. The latter was statistically indistinguishable from zero and significantly less than that of its U.S. comparison group at $p = .067$ (two-sided). The 12 correlations for the foreign firms vary from .077 to .702, while their U.S. counterparts are within .10 of the foreign firms for 9 of the 12 correlations, and within .13 for 11 of the 12. Thus, the industry and size matching appear to control for differences that might be obscured if foreign firms' disclosures are analyzed without considering firms' economic characteristics (see Alford et al. [1993] for related evidence).

Panel C of table 4 shows that correlations for Form 20-F, Item 17 filers are lower than for Form 20-F, Item 18 filers and Form 10-K filers, consistent with the lower disclosure levels of Item 17 financial statements. Within Form 20-F filing status groups, the differences in correlation approach significance at conventional levels but are in the opposite directions for Items 17 and 18. Panel D of table 4 shows highly significant positive correlations for both segment and reconciliation rules compliers and varied results for noncompliers. In particular, the correlations for segment rules noncomplier earnings are near zero and insignificant for these foreign firms, but correlations of their U.S. counterparts are also near zero, and all p-values for differences in correlation exceed .5. Thus, as with the other analyses, industry and size factors may be more important than the disclosure compliance differences.[19] For example, the segment disclosure noncompliers are substantially smaller than the complying firms. The mean (median) revenues (all in millions) are $4,318.4 ($362.7) and $8,414.7 ($1,946.9) for noncompliers and compliers, respectively, and 14 (74%) of the 19 noncompliers are traded on *NASDAQ*, in contrast to only 53 (39%) of the 137 foreign firms.

---

[19] Correlations for the 156 U.S. comparison firm-observations in table 4 are the same as, or qualitatively similar to, results using 136 firm-observations (after deleting the 20 double- and triple-counted observations), with the exception of the Japan domicile comparison firm correlations, which are approximately twice as large in table 4 as those computed using only single-counted firm-observations.

5. *Summary and Conclusions*

This study documents differences in disclosure practices between foreign and U.S. issuers whose securities are registered with the *SEC* and trade in U.S. markets, and among foreign issuers in different filing status categories. The main results are as follows. First, on average, foreign issuers file fewer interim reports and file interim and annual reports and announce annual earnings on a less timely basis than do U.S. comparison firms. One hundred and twenty-seven (81%) of the 156 foreign firms studied filed financial statements based on non-U.S. accounting principles. In addition, U.S. and non-U.S. analyst followings differ substantially among the foreign domicile groups. For the foreign issuers as a whole, U.S. analyst following is smaller, and non-U.S. following is larger, than for the U.S. comparison firms. To the extent that analyst following is associated with the demand for public disclosure, the relatively low U.S. analyst following observed for foreign issuers is consistent with the relatively low disclosure levels observed for these firms.

Second, there are differences in disclosure among foreign firms in different filing status groups. Firms that file Form 20-F, Item 17 financial statements face the least onerous disclosure rules, since they are exempt from making U.S. *GAAP* footnote disclosures. Also, these firms file annual and interim financial statements significantly later than do Form 20-F, Item 18 and Form 10-K foreign issuers. This evidence is consistent with the view that some foreign issuers "self-select" into the Form 20-F, Item 17 filing status because they do not have information available to meet the Item 18 disclosure requirements, because they prefer not to disclose certain types of sensitive information (such as segment profits), or both.

Third, foreign firms *within* filing status categories made different disclosure choices. For example, 18 of the 88 Form 20-F, Item 18 filers did not meet their chosen filing forms' written segment disclosure rules, and 10 of the 45 Form 20-F, Item 17 filers did not comply with the written U.S. *GAAP* reconciliation rules. This evidence suggests that some foreign issuers view the costs of meeting written disclosure requirements as exceeding the expected costs of noncompliance. However, the descriptive evidence on earnings/return associations for foreign issuers and the U.S. comparison firms suggests that foreign issuers' lower disclosure levels may not, on average, impair the usefulness of earnings for valuing these firms.

Finally, we observe substantial variation in earnings/stock returns and earnings change/stock returns correlations among different domicile and disclosure groups. Relatively low rank correlations are observed for firms in the Israel and Other European domicile groups; Form 20-F, Item 17 filers; and firms that do not comply with the segment disclosure rules. However, there are few substantial earnings/returns correlation differences between foreign firms and their U.S. comparison firms. The foreign firm and U.S. firm correlations are similar and have similar significance levels for almost all domicile and disclosure partitions.

REFERENCES

ALFORD, A.; J. JONES; AND M. ZMIJEWSKI. "Extensions and Violations of the Statutory SEC Form 10-K Filings Requirements." *Journal of Accounting and Economics* (January 1994): 229–54.

ALFORD, A.; J. JONES; R. LEFTWICH; AND M. ZMIJEWSKI. "The Relative Informativeness of Accounting Disclosures in Different Countries." *Journal of Accounting Research* (Supplement 1993): 183–223.

AMERICAN INSTITUTE OF CERTIFIED PUBLIC ACCOUNTANTS. *The Information Needs of Investors and Creditors: A Report on the AICPA Special Committee's Study of the Information Needs of Today's Users of Financial Reporting, November, 1993.* New York: AICPA, 1993.

AMERICAN LAW INSTITUTE. *Internationalization of the Securities Market: Business Experience and Regulatory Policy. ALI-ABA* Course of Study Materials, September 23, 1991. Washington, D.C.: American Law Institute, 1991.

AMIR, E.; T. S. HARRIS; AND E. K. VENUTI. "A Comparison of the Value Relevance of U.S. versus Non-U.S. *GAAP* Accounting Measures Using Form 20-F Reconciliations." *Journal of Accounting Research* (Supplement 1993): 230–64.

ASSOCIATION FOR INVESTMENT MANAGEMENT AND RESEARCH, FINANCIAL ACCOUNTING POLICY COMMITTEE. *Financial Reporting in the 1990s and Beyond.* Charlottesville, Va.: AIMR, 1993.

BANDYOPADHYAY, S. P.; J. D. HANNA; AND G. RICHARDSON. "Capital Market Effects of U.S.–Canada *GAAP* Differences." *Journal of Accounting Research* (Autumn 1994): 262–77.

BARTH, M. E., AND G. CLINCH. "International Accounting Differences and Their Relation to Share Prices: Evidence from U.K. and Australian Firms." Working paper, Harvard Business School, February, 1994.

BERGMAN, M. "SEC Announces New Initiatives for Foreign Issuers." *Euromoney* (December 1993): 20.

BLOOMENTHAL, H., ed. *International Capital Markets and Securities Regulation.* 1st ed., Release no. 7, rev. 10/89, vol. 10A. New York: Clark Boardman, 1989.

BOTOSAN, C. A. "The Impact of Disclosure Level on the Cost of Equity Capital and Stock Market Liquidity." Ph.D. dissertation proposal, University of Michigan, March 1995.

BREEDEN, R. C. "Foreign Companies and U.S. Securities Markets in a Time of Economic Transformation." *Fordham International Law Journal* (Symposium 1994): S77–S96.

"Bridging the GAAP to Germany." *The Economist* (September 17, 1994): 89.

BROWN & WOOD. *Accessing the U.S. Capital Markets: An Introduction to United States Securities Laws for Non-U.S. Issuers of Securities.* New York: Brown & Wood, 1994.

COCHRANE, J. L. "Are U.S. Regulatory Requirements for Foreign Firms Appropriate?" *Fordham International Law Journal* (Symposium 1994): S58–S67.

COOPERS & LYBRAND. *International Accounting Summaries: A Guide for Interpretation and Comparison.* 2d ed. New York: Wiley, 1993.

DECKER, W. E. "The Attractions of the U.S. Securities Markets to Foreign Issuers and the Alternative Methods of Accessing the U.S. Markets: from the Issuer's Perspective." *Fordham International Law Journal* (Symposium 1994): S10–S24.

EASTON, P. D., AND M. E. ZMIJEWSKI. "SEC Form 10K/10Q Reports and Annual Reports to Shareholders: Reporting Lags and Squared Market Model Prediction Errors." *Journal of Accounting Research* (Spring 1993): 113–29.

FROST, C. A., AND G. POWNALL. "Accounting Disclosure Practices in the United States and the United Kingdom." *Journal of Accounting Research* (Spring 1994): 75–102.

HARLAN, C. "SEC Tries to Ease Disclosure Rules for Foreign Firms." *Wall Street Journal* (November 4, 1993): A12.

DISCLOSURE CHOICES OF FORIEGN REGISTRANTS 83

KASZNIK, R., AND B. LEV. "To Warn or Not to Warn: Management Disclosures in the Face of an Earnings Surprise." *The Accounting Review* (January 1995): 113–34.

KING, R.; G. POWNALL, AND G. WAYMIRE. "Expectations Adjustment via Timely Management Forecasts: Review, Synthesis, and Suggestions for Future Research." *Journal of Accounting Literature* (1990): 113–44.

KOSNIK, R. "The Role of the SEC in Evaluating Foreign Issuers Coming to U.S. Markets." *Fordham International Law Journal* (Symposium 1994): S97–S111.

LANG, M., AND R. LUNDHOLM. "Cross-Sectional Determinants of Analyst Ratings of Corporate Disclosures." *Journal of Accounting Research* (Autumn 1993a): 246–71.

———. "The Effect of Corporate Disclosure Policy on Analysts." Working paper, Stanford University, 1993b.

MANN, M. D., AND J. G. MARI. "Developments in International Securities Law Enforcement and Regulation." Prepared for the Securities Regulation Seminar of October 24, 1990, Los Angeles, California, 1990.

MCKINNON, J. L. "Application of Anglo-American Principles of Consolidation to Corporate Financial Disclosure in Japan." *Abacus* 20 (1984): 16–33.

MCQUEEN, P. D. "The Information Content of Foreign and U.S. GAAP Earnings in SEC Form 20-F." Working paper, AIMR, January 1993.

MEHTA, C. R., AND N. R. PATELL. "A Network Algorithm for Performing Fisher's Exact Test in $r \times c$ Contingency Tables." *Journal of the American Statistical Association* (1983): 427–34.

MORRISON, D. F. *Multivariate Statistical Methods.* 2d ed. New York: McGraw-Hill, 1976.

MURRAY, R. J.; W. E. DECKER, JR.; AND N. W. DITTMAR, JR. *The Coopers & Lybrand SEC Manual.* 6th ed. Englewood Cliffs, N.J.: Prentice-Hall, 1993.

NELSON PUBLICATIONS. *Nelson's Directory of Investment Research 1992.* Chester, N.Y.: Nelson, 1992.

ORSINI, L. L.; J. P. MCALLISTER; AND R. N. PARIKH. *World Accounting.* New York: Matthew Bender, 1994.

SILKENAT, J. R. "Overview of U.S. Securities Markets and Foreign Issuers." *Fordham International Law Journal* (Symposium 1994): 54–59.

STANDARD & POOR'S CORPORATION. *Daily Stock Price Record–New York Stock Exchange, American Stock Exchange,* and *Over-the-Counter.* New York: Standard & Poor's, 1990; 1991; 1992.

———. *Dividend Record.* New York: Standard & Poor's, 1990; 1991; 1992.

SECURITIES AND EXCHANGE COMMISSION. *Memorandum of the Office of International Corporate Finance, Division of Finance, Securities and Exchange Commission on the Application of the Securities and Exchange Act of 1934 to Foreign Private Issuers.* Washington, D.C.: SEC, January 1984.

———. *Internationalization of the Securities Markets: Report of the Staff of the U.S. Securities and Exchange Commission to the Senate Committee on Banking, Housing and Urban Affairs and the House Committee on Energy and Commerce.* Washington, D.C.: SEC, July 17, 1987.

———. *Simplification of Registration and Reporting Requirements for Foreign Companies; Safe Harbors for Public Announcements of Unregistered Offerings and Broker-Dealer Research Reports.* Securities Act Release no. 7029 (November 3, 1993), Securities Exchange Act Release no. 33139; 58 Fed. Reg. 60, 307–01, November 5, 1993a.

———. *1992 Annual Report.* Washington, D.C.: SEC, 1993b.

———. *Simplification of Registration and Reporting Requirements for Foreign Companies; Safe Harbors for Public Announcements of Unregistered Offerings and Broker-Dealer Research Reports.* Securities Act Release no. 7053, Securities Exchange Act Release no. 33918; 59 Fed. Reg. 21,644, April 26, 1994a.

———. *Selection of Reporting Currency for Financial Statements of Foreign Private Issuers and Reconciliation to U.S. GAAP for Foreign Private Issuers with Operations in a Hyperinflationary Economy.* Securities Act Release no. 7054, Securities Exchange Act Release no. 33919; 59 Fed. Reg. 21,810, April 26, 1994b.

———. *Selection of Reporting Currency for Financial Statements of Foreign Private Issuers and Reconciliation to U.S. GAAP for Foreign Private Issuers with Operations in a Hyperinflationary Economy.* Securities Act Release nos. 33-7117 and 34-35093; Fed. Reg. 43, December 13, 1994c.

84   CAROL A. FROST AND WILLIAM R. KINNEY

_____. *Financial Statements of Significant Foreign Equity Investees and Acquired Foreign Businesses of Domestic Issuers and Financial Schedules.* Securities Act Release nos. 33-7118, 34-35094, and IC-20766; Fed. Reg. 44, December 13, 1994*d.*

_____. *Reconciliation of the Accounting by Foreign Private Issuers for Business Combinations.* Release nos. 33-7119 and 34-35095; Fed. Reg. 45, December 13, 1994*e.*

_____. *1993 Annual Report.* Washington, D.C.: SEC, 1994*f.*

_____. *1994 Annual Report.* Washington, D.C.: SEC, 1995.

WARREN, GORHAM & LAMONT. *SEC Guidelines: Rules and Regulations.* Boston: Warren, Gorham & Lamont, 1994.

[14]

N·H

ELSEVIER   Journal of Accounting and Public Policy 20 (2001) 129–153

Journal of
Accounting
and
Public Policy

www.elsevier.com/locate/jaccpubpol

Non-US Firms' Accounting Standard Choices

Hollis Ashbaugh *

*School of Business, Grainger Hall, University of Wisconsin at Madison, 975 University Avenue,
Madison, WI 53706-1323, USA*

Abstract

My study investigates the factors associated with non-US firms voluntarily reporting
financial information prepared in accordance with International Accounting Standards
(IAS) or United States (US) Generally Accepted Accounting Principles (US-GAAP).
Documenting the factors associated with non-US firms' disclosures of IAS or US-
GAAP financial information is important in that many equity market regulators are
now allowing, or considering allowing, registrants to report under alternative sets of
accounting standards. The annual reports of 211 non-US firms listed with the London
Exchange are examined to determine firms' disclosure of IAS or US-GAAP financial
information. Using multivariate logit regression, I found systematic differences in firm
characteristics associated with non-US firms disclosing IAS or US-GAAP financial
information rather than or in addition to financial information prepared in accordance
with their domestic generally accepted accounting principles (domestic-GAAP). The
results are consistent with the hypotheses that non-US firms are more likely to disclose
IAS or US-GAAP financial information as their shares trade in more equity markets. In
addition, I found that firms are more likely to disclose IAS or US-GAAP financial
information when by doing so they can provide more standardized financial information relative to the information generated via their domestic-GAAP. I also found that
firms are more likely to report IAS financial information when they participate in
seasoned equity offerings and when US-GAAP requires more accounting policy changes
relative to what is required under firms' domestic-GAAPs. These results suggest that
non-US firms report IAS financial information to receive some benefits of providing
more standardized financial information at costs less than what are incurred to implement US-GAAP. © 2001 Elsevier Science Ltd. All rights reserved.

---

* Tel.: +1-608-263-7979; fax: +1-608-265-9412.
  E-mail address: hashbaugh@bus.wisc.edu (H. Ashbaugh).

0278-4254/01/$ - see front matter © 2001 Elsevier Science Ltd. All rights reserved.
PII: S0278-4254(01)00025-4

130	*H. Ashbaugh / Journal of Accounting and Public Policy 20 (2001) 129–153*

1. Introduction

This study investigates the factors associated with non-United States firms reporting financial information prepared in accordance with International Accounting Standards (IAS) or United States (US) Generally Accepted Accounting Principles (US-GAAP). IAS promulgated by the International Accounting Standards Committee (IASC) are a set of accounting standards intended to be used as a basis for cross-border capital raising and listing purposes in global markets (e.g., International Accounting Standards Committee, 1995). A competing international accounting regime, US-GAAP is derived from a hierarchy of US standard setting organizations, including the Financial Accounting Standards Board (FASB). The objective of an international set of accounting standards is to standardize firms' financial disclosures and accounting method choices among different nations (Ashbaugh and Pincus, 2001; Financial Accounting Standards Board, 1996, pp. 16–19). Proponents of international standards claim that if all firms follow the same set of accounting standards, firms' external financial reports would provide more uniform disclosures and accounting variables would be more useful to investors (Purvis et al., 1991, p. 43). It is also claimed that firms, in addition to investors, would benefit from disclosing financial information prepared in accordance with an internationally acceptable set of accounting standards (see e.g., Financial Accounting Standards Board, 1996, p. 3), i.e., IAS or US-GAAP. However, the majority of non-US firms do not disclose IAS or US-GAAP financial information (Speidell and Bavishi, 1992, pp. 58–66). This suggests that for the majority of non-US firms the costs associated with reporting IAS or US-GAAP financial information outweigh the benefits.

The scope of my study is to document factors associated with non-US firms voluntarily reporting IAS or US-GAAP financial information in their annual financial reports. Identifying the firm-specific characteristics associated with firms' disclosure of IAS or US-GAAP financial information is important in that many equity market regulators are now allowing, or considering allowing, registrants to report under alternative sets of accounting standards. For example, German laws were changed in 1998 to allow listed firms to prepare their consolidated financial reports in accordance with IAS or US-GAAP (Eggert, 1998, pp. 61–62) and the US Securities and Exchange Commission (SEC) is currently reviewing IAS as an alternative reporting regime for foreign registrants (Securities and Exchange Commision, 2000). Documenting the factors associated with non-US firms voluntarily reporting IAS or US-GAAP financial information contributes to our understanding of firms' financial reporting strategies in the global market.

Non-US firms listed with the London Exchange and quoted on the Stock Exchange Automated Quotation System (SEAQ) International Equity Market of London in 1993 are used to investigate the factors associated with non-US

H. Ashbaugh / Journal of Accounting and Public Policy 20 (2001) 129–153   131

firms' IAS or US-GAAP reporting. I use this setting for several reasons. First, the London Exchange (1994a, pp. 35–40) allows foreign registrants to prepare financial reports in accordance with IAS, US-GAAP, UK-GAAP, or firms' domestic generally accepted accounting principles, i.e., domestic-GAAP. Second, as the largest international equity market (Zeff, 1998, p. 74), SEAQ International provides a more generalized setting to examine firms' accounting standard choices than a national equity market. Third, the London Exchange was the first to specifically identify IAS as an internationally acceptable set of accounting standards (International Accounting Standards Committee, 1992, p. 4). Since 1993 many domestic standard setters have incorporated IAS, or a subset of IAS, into their set of generally accepted accounting principles (International Accounting Standards Committee, 1995, pp. 8–10) suggesting that in periods after 1993, firms' choices may be influenced by their domestic standards alignment with IAS.

I examined the annual reports of 211 non-US firms to determine firms' accounting standard choices. Less than half of my sample firms (43.6%) disclose IAS or US-GAAP financial information in their annual reports. [1] After controlling for relative firm size and US-listings, the results of the multivariate logit regression indicate that the probability of disclosing IAS or US-GAAP financial information is positively associated with the number of foreign equity markets in which a firm's shares trade. The results also indicate that IAS or US-GAAP reporting is positively associated with the number of accounting measurement methods and disclosure changes imposed by the international accounting regimes relative to firms' domestic-GAAP. These results suggest that non-US firms use IAS or US-GAAP to disseminate standardized financial information to diverse financial information users.

To better understand why non-US firms disclose IAS financial information, I repeated the logit analysis excluding firms that report US-GAAP financial information. I found a positive association between firms' disclosures of IAS financial information and the number of foreign equity markets in which their shares trade. In addition, firms are more likely to disclose IAS financial information when IAS requires more financial disclosures and restricts their accounting method choices relative to their domestic-GAAPs. I also found that non-US firms are more likely to disclose IAS financial information when they are raising additional capital via the issuance of equity shares, i.e., participating

---

[1] The firms identified as disclosing IAS (US-GAAP) financial information state that the financial information that they are presenting complies with IAS (US-GAAP). Street et al. (1999) suggest that non-US firms do not implement IAS on a consistent basis. Ashbaugh and Olsson (2001, pp. 10–15) indicate that their sample of non-US firms reporting under IAS have done so for more than five years and, in addition, contract with the large international auditing firms, suggesting that non-US firms do apply IAS on a consistent basis. It is beyond the scope of this study to attest to my sample firms' compliance with IAS or US-GAAP.

132 *H. Ashbaugh / Journal of Accounting and Public Policy 20 (2001) 129–153*

in seasoned equity offerings. These findings are consistent with the suggestion that non-US firms voluntarily disclose IAS financial information in an attempt to lower the information asymmetry component of their costs of capital (Leuz and Verrecchia, 2001).

My study's final analysis investigates the firm-specific characteristics associated with non-US firms voluntarily reporting IAS or US-GAAP financial information in their annual reports. The majority of my sample firms reporting US-GAAP financial information in their annual reports are required to file such information with the SEC because their shares trade in the New York, American, or NASDAQ market. However, 33.3% of my sample firms reporting US-GAAP financial information have no SEC filing requirements. While the results of the logit analysis indicate that non-US firms are more likely to disclose IAS financial information when they do not have to file US-GAAP financial information with the SEC, the results also indicate that non-US firms are more likely to disclose IAS financial information when they trade in fewer equity markets relative to US-GAAP firms. Furthermore, I found that non-US firms are more likely to disclose IAS financial information when the disclosure requirements and accounting method constraints of US-GAAP increase relative to IAS and their domestic-GAAP. Collectively, these findings suggest that non-US firms not required to adhere to the stringent reporting standards of US-GAAP prefer IAS as the means to provide standardized financial information because IAS allows greater flexibility in firms' accounting measurement choices and requires fewer disclosures relative to US-GAAP.

My study provides evidence on the factors associated with non-US firms deviating from their traditional reporting practices, i.e., domestic-GAAP, and reporting financial information prepared in accordance with IAS or US-GAAP. These factors proxy for some of the benefits associated with non-US firms reporting financial information prepared in accordance with IAS or US-GAAP. The fact that not all non-US firms voluntarily report IAS or US-GAAP financial information implies that firms incur non-trivial costs to report financial information prepared in accordance with an internationally acceptable set of accounting standards. The remainder of the paper is organized as follows. Section 2 develops the hypotheses and Section 3 sets forth the research design. The results are presented in Section 4. Section 5 concludes the study.

2. Factors influencing firms to disclose IAS or US-GAAP financial information

Welker (1995) suggests that firms engage in differential disclosure practices, and that firms' disclosure strategies and changes thereof can impact capital market participants. Firms have discretion over the financial disclosures they provide to capital markets (Lang and Lundholm, 1996). The annual report is one mechanism firms use to disseminate discretionary financial information

H. Ashbaugh / Journal of Accounting and Public Policy 20 (2001) 129–153   133

(Botosan, 1997, p. 326). My general hypothesis is that non-US firms will disclose financial information prepared in accordance with IAS or US-GAAP when the benefits related to such disclosures outweigh their costs. More specifically, I posit three factors that proxy for the benefits associated with non-US firms voluntarily disclosing IAS or US-GAAP financial information in their annual reports.

2.1. To communicate with foreign financial information users

With the globalization of capital markets and the increase in world trade, firms are more likely to communicate with foreign as well as domestic financial information users. Firms acknowledge the importance of providing useful financial information to foreign as well as domestic investors (see e.g., Bayer, 1997, p. 60). Firms conducting business outside their native country are also concerned with communicating with diverse suppliers and customers. Such firms have used foreign listings as a mechanism to gain public recognition in a foreign market (Saudagaran, 1988, p. 106). Managers have identified the increase in company visibility as a benefit of foreign listings (Mittoo, 1994, pp. 33–35). Furthermore, as a firm's securities trade in more foreign equity markets, there is a wider distribution of equity shares and a greater demand for financial information (Biddle and Saudagaran, 1991, p. 71). [2] Therefore, I hypothesize that the greater the number of foreign equity markets in which a firm's shares trade, the more likely it is that the firm discloses IAS or US-GAAP financial information. [3] Formally, the first hypothesis is (in alternative form):

H1: The probability of disclosing IAS or US-GAAP financial information is positively related to the number of foreign equity markets in which a firm's shares trade.

---

[2] The proportion of equity shares held by foreign investors may be an alternative measure of foreign financial information users. However, this measure does not address the diversity of foreign shareholders or capture the other potential users of firms' financial reports. For example, suppose two French firms each have 20% of their stock held by foreign investors. Assume the first firm's foreign investors reside in Germany because this firm is listed on the Frankfurt exchange. Assume the other firm has a uniform distribution of foreign investors residing in Sweden, Switzerland, the UK, Norway, Finland, and Germany because this firm is listed on six foreign exchanges. It is assumed the latter firm is more likely to present internationalized financial information in its annual report.

[3] Recall that the London Exchange was the only exchange to specifically accept IAS as a basis for financial reporting in 1993. Since then, more exchanges are accepting IAS as a basis for financial reporting (Choi et al., 1999, 255–266). Thus, a tangential benefit firms may currently receive by reporting IAS or US-GAAP financial information is the minimization of financial reporting costs across equity markets.

134   *H. Ashbaugh / Journal of Accounting and Public Policy 20 (2001) 129–153*

2.2. To facilitate raising equity capital

Prior research suggests that firms benefit from providing voluntary disclosures (Welker, 1995; Botosan, 1997). Moreover, prior research suggests that firms time their voluntary disclosures to preempt investors' private information search activities (Choi, 1973). For example, Cooper and Grinder (1996, pp. 470–472) report US firms have significantly higher information flows in the month prior to announcing new equity offerings. I hypothesize that non-US firms incorporate the reporting of IAS or US-GAAP financial information into their disclosure strategies to facilitate raising equity capital. That is:

H2: The probability of disclosing IAS or US-GAAP financial information is positively related to the occurrence of firms' stock issuances.

2.3. To provide more standardized financial information in the annual financial report

Fishman and Hagerty (1989, pp. 635–642) demonstrate that firms expend more resources on disclosure than is socially optimal because firms must compete for the attention of traders since it is too costly for a trader to study the disclosures of every firm. In the context of this study, firms may choose to provide standardized financial disclosures and measures of accounting variables (e.g., net income, stockholders' equity) to reduce traders' information processing costs related to understanding alternative domestic-GAAP. If so, firms preparing financial information in accordance with IAS or US-GAAP may be better able to attract the attention of traders and increase the efficiency of the market prices of their securities.

2.3.1. Disclosure requirements

In some countries, domestic-GAAP varies from IAS and US-GAAP because there are fewer disclosure requirements and/or firms have more discretion in the informativeness of the disclosures provided in their annual reports (Coopers and Lybrand, 1993, pp. 1–37). Table 1 reports the comparisons between eight IAS (11 US-GAAP) disclosures in force in 1993 to the 1993 disclosure requirements of domestic-GAAP of countries in which the firms used in the empirical analysis are domiciled. The disclosure items, while not all-inclusive, represent the more significant variation in financial disclosure requirements across national boundaries (International Accounting Standards Committee, 1993, pp. 6–7). A domestic-GAAP is considered less stringent than IAS or US-GAAP in its disclosure requirements if (1) it has no re-

Table 1
Matrix of required disclosures: IAS and US-GAAP compared to domestic accounting standards[a]

Country[c]	Addition disclosures required under IAS[b]									Additional disclosures required under US-GAAP			
	1	2	3	4	5	6	7	8	IASDIS[d]	9	10	11	USDIS[d]
Australia	X				X[c]				1				1
Belgium		X				X		X	3		X		4
Bermuda									0			X	1
Denmark					X	X			2		X	X	3
Finland	X		X	X	X	X	X		6	X		X	8
France	X			X	X	X			4			X	5
Germany	X				X	X			3		X	X	5
Hong Kong	X				X		X		3			X	4
Japan				X	X				2	X			3
Luxembourg	X			X	X		X		4		X	X	6
Netherlands	X			X	X				2		X	X	4
New Zealand				X	X				2			X	3
Norway	X	X		X	X	X	X	X	7		X	X	9
Singapore	X	X		X					2				2
Spain				X	X	X	X		3	X	X		5
Sweden	X			X	X	X		X	5	X	X	X	7
Switzerland	X			X	X			X	4		X	X	6

[a] *Sources*: Coopers and Lybrand (1993) and Price Waterhouse (1996).
[b] Disclosure items: 1 = required statement of funds/cash flows; 2 = required disclosure of accounting policies; 3 = required disclosure of effect of change in accounting policy; 4 = required disclosure of effect of change in accounting estimate; 5 = required disclosure of prior period adjustment; 6 = required disclosure of post balance sheet events; 7 = required disclosure of related party transactions; 8 = required disclosure of segmental information; 9 = required disclosure of discontinued operations; 10 = required disclosure of earnings per share; 11 = required disclosure of allowance of doubtful accounts.
[c] The countries examined are based on where the firms used in the empirical analysis are domiciled.
[d] IASDIS and USDIS are the sum of the additional disclosures required under IAS and US-GAAP, respectively, relative to a country's GAAP disclosure requirements.
[e] X = when (1) domestic-GAAP has no disclosure requirement or (2) the domestic-GAAP requirement is less stringent than IAS or US-GAAP.

136   *H. Ashbaugh / Journal of Accounting and Public Policy 20 (2001) 129–153*

quirement or (2) the requirement is less restrictive than the IAS or US-GAAP requirement. [4]

The IASDIS (USDIS) value in Table 1 is the sum of differences in the disclosure requirements of a domestic-GAAP relative to IAS (US-GAAP). IASDIS (USDIS) represents the increasing standardization of firms' required financial disclosures by choosing to comply with IAS (US-GAAP) rather than their domestic-GAAP. In general, firms domiciled in Finland, France, Luxembourg, Norway, Sweden, and Switzerland provide more standardized financial disclosures by complying with IAS than by complying with their domestic-GAAP. [5] Because US-GAAP has more stringent disclosure requirements than IAS, i.e., USDIS, firms domiciled in these countries would also provide more standardized financial disclosures by complying with US-GAAP.

2.3.2. Accounting method restrictions

Choi and Levich (1992) suggest that the differences in the number of accounting measurement methods within and across domestic-GAAP result in disparities in information across markets. Ashbaugh and Pincus (2001) document that the differences in domestic-GAAP relative to IAS are positively associated with analysts' forecast errors. The differences in accounting measurement methods across domestic-GAAP potentially impacts other users of firms' financial reports as they may find it too costly to become (and remain) informed about alternative domestic-GAAP accounting measurement methods. Hence, firms have incentives to provide more standardized measures of net income and stockholders' equity.

Table 2 compares four IAS (seven US-GAAP) accounting measurement rules in force in 1993 to the 1993 domestic-GAAP measurement rules for countries where my sample firms are domiciled. IAS (US-GAAP) is considered to be more restrictive than domestic-GAAP when IAS (US-GAAP) has fewer acceptable methods of accounting for an economic event relative to the

---

[4] For example, IAS requires post-balance sheet events having evidence of existence at the balance sheet date to be disclosed in the footnotes to the financial statements (Coopers and Lybrand, 1993, pp. IAS-8–IAS-9). French-GAAP only requires disclosure if the going-concern assumption might be affected by the post-balance sheet event (Coopers and Lybrand, 1993, pp. F-39–F-40). Thus French-GAAP is considered to be less stringent than IAS.

[5] Since the public accounting profession in Bermuda was governed by the Institute of Chartered Accountants of Bermuda, which was formally affiliated with the Canadian Institute of Chartered Accountants, firms domiciled in Bermuda in 1993 generally followed Canadian-GAAP (Price Waterhouse, 1996, p. 2). As such, the Bermuda indices reported in Tables 1 and 2 are based on comparisons between Canadian-GAAP and IAS (US-GAAP).

Table 2
Restriction of accounting measurement choices: IAS and US-GAAP compared to domestic accounting standards[a]

Country[c]	Accounting measurement restrictions under IAS[b]					Accounting measurement restrictions under US-GAAP			
	1	2	3	4	IASCON[d]	5	6	7	USCON[d]
Australia	X		X[e]	X	2	X		X	4
Belgium	X		X	X	3	X			4
Bermuda					0			X	1
Denmark		X	X	X	2		X		3
Finland	X	X	X	X	4	X	X		6
France	X	X	X		3	X	X	X	6
Germany	X				1				1
Hong Kong				X	1	X	X	X	4
Japan		X	X		2				2
Luxembourg			X	X	2		X		3
Netherlands			X		1	X	X	X	4
New Zealand				X	1	X	X	X	4
Norway			X		1	X	X	X	4
Singapore					0	X	X	X	3
Spain			X		1		X		3
Sweden		X	X		2	X	X	X	4
Switzerland	X	X	X	X	4		X	X	6

[a] *Sources*: Coopers and Lybrand (1993) and Price Waterhouse (1996).

[b] Accounting measurement restrictions; 1 = domestic-GAAP allows firms to report additional depreciation that has been recorded to reduce firms' tax liability or to setup replacement reserves; 2 = accounting for leases; 3 = accounting for pensions; 4 = accounting for research and development costs; 5 = required use of historical cost accounting for property, plant, and equipment; 6 = accounting for intangible assets other than research and development; 7 = accounting for investments.

[c] The countries examined are based on where the firms used in the empirical analysis are domiciled.

[d] IASCON and USCON are the sum of the accounting measurement constraints under IAS and US-GAAP, respectively, relative to a country's GAAP measurement methods.

[e] X = when adopting IAS restricts the accounting measurement choices relative to the accounting measurement choices available under domestic-GAAP.

138   *H. Ashbaugh / Journal of Accounting and Public Policy 20 (2001) 129–153*

methods acceptable under domestic-GAAP. [6] IASCON (USCON) represents the increasing restrictions on a firm's accounting measurement choices by complying with IAS (US-GAAP) rather than the domestic-GAAP of its country of domicile. IAS compliance results in greater restrictions on accounting measurement choices for firms domiciled in Belgium, Finland, France, and Switzerland. Firms from these countries will report more standardize measures of net income and stockholders' equity by complying with US-GAAP.

It is reasonable to conjecture that firms incur differential costs to disclose IAS or US-GAAP financial information since not all firms report such information in their annual reports. The more restrictive IAS or US-GAAP is in its accounting measurement methods relative to domestic-GAAP, the more costly it is to report standardized measures of net income and stockholders' equity. Explicit costs are due, in part, to the information collection and processing costs associated with the number of changes needed to convert a domestic-GAAP accounting system into a system that produces earnings and stockholders' equity in accordance with IAS or US-GAAP (see e.g., Biddle and Saudagaran, 1991, p. 71). The increase in required standardized disclosures can also impose costs on firms. Firms incur out-of-pocket costs to produce the additional disclosures if the data are not already produced for internal reporting purposes. The additional disclosures may also impose implicit costs on a firm if such disclosures place a firm at a competitive disadvantage when competitors do not publish similar information. Hence, for some firms the costs will dominate the perceived benefits associated with reporting IAS or US-GAAP financial information. Since the costs and benefits of reporting IAS or US-GAAP financial information is unclear due to the variation in domestic-GAAP, the following hypothesis is tested:

H3: The probability of disclosing IAS or US-GAAP financial information is associated with the financial reporting requirements of a firm's domestic-GAAP.

3. Research design

The sample selection is as follows. The London Exchange provided me the names of all 484 non-US/non-UK firms admitted to listing as of March 31, 1994. Of these, 184 firms were eliminated because they were not in the *Global Vantage*

---

[6] For example, a French firm may elect to capitalize leases in its consolidated financial statements (Coopers and Lybrand, 1993, pp. F-43–F-44). IAS requires leases to be capitalized when substantially all the risks and rewards incident to ownership are transferred to the lessee (Coopers and Lybrand, 1993, pp. IAS-11–IAS-12). Thus, lease accounting under IAS is judged to be more constrained than under French-GAAP.

database, the source of financial and market data, and 15 firms were eliminated because they were approved for listing but did not trade on SEAQ International in 1993. [7] I deleted eight Italian firms and 26 South African firms because IAS was the basis for those countries' domestic-GAAP in 1993 (International Accounting Standards Committee, 1995, p. 9). Letters were sent to the remaining 251 SEAQ International firms requesting a copy of their 1993 and 1994 annual reports. Annual reports of 211 firms were received (an 84.1% response rate). [8]

Based on my examination of their annual reports, firms were classified as IAS firms, US-GAAP firms, or domestic-GAAP firms. [9] Non-US firms are classified as IAS (US-GAAP) firms if it was stated in their summary of accounting policies or audit reports that the financial statements were prepared in accordance with IAS (US-GAAP). [10] Firms providing IAS (US-GAAP) footnote reconciliations are also classified as IAS (US-GAAP) firms. [11] The domestic-GAAP firms use the accounting standards of their country of domicile. Table 3 presents the distribution of the three categories of sample firms by country. The majority of IAS firms are domiciled in France (11 firms), Finland (8), Switzerland (8), and Sweden (7). [12] The US-GAAP firms are domiciled primarily in Japan (16 firms), France (6), and Sweden (4). [13]

---

[7] The London Exchange did not identify any Canadian firms as being listed with the Exchange and quoted on SEAQ International in 1993.

[8] The London Exchange's listing requirements require non-UK firms listed with the Exchange to prepare their annual report in English (London Exchange, 1994a, p. 34).

[9] None of the firms used UK-GAAP.

[10] Details on how firms implement IAS are provided in the Appendix.

[11] To gain some insight into the impact of adopting IAS or US-GAAP, I calculate the changes in net income and stockholders' equity for the few firms that provide footnote reconciliations from domestic-GAAP to either IAS ($n = 9$) or US-GAAP ($n = 17$). The median change from domestic-GAAP net income to IAS (US-GAAP) net income is 0% (−12%), although the changes range from −367% to 372% (−79 to 185%). The median change from domestic-GAAP stockholders' equity to IAS (US-GAAP) stockholders' equity is 22% (6%). Overall, the variation in earnings and stockholders' equity measured in accordance with an internationally acceptable set of standards suggests the implementation of IAS or US-GAAP may differentially impact firms' financial statements.

[12] There are five firms that are domiciled in Bermuda where firms generally follow Canadian accounting standards (Price Waterhouse, 1996, p. 12.1). I performed two sensitivity tests related to these firms. First, I set SET (USSET) equal to 12 (18) under the assumption that Bermuda firms would have to make all the changes to adhere to the disclosure requirements and accounting standards choices under IAS (US-GAAP). Second, I deleted Bermuda firms from the statistical analyses. The results reported in Tables 5, 6, and 8 are robust to these two sensitivity tests.

[13] To provide some evidence about business operations, I examined firms' SIC codes (not tabled). The distribution of SIC codes appears similar across the three types of firms. Regardless of accounting standard choice, the majority of firms are engaged in manufacturing operations. Descriptive statistics of other firm-specific characteristics (e.g., sales, total assets) are dependent on firms' accounting standard choices and as such are not prepared.

140   *H. Ashbaugh / Journal of Accounting and Public Policy 20 (2001) 129–153*

Table 3
Distribution of firms by country of domicile

Country	IAS		US-GAAP		Domestic-GAAP		Total	
	n	%	n	%	n	%	n	%
Australia	5	9	1	3	13	11	19	9
Belgium	1	2	1	3	3	3	5	2
Bermuda	5	9	0	0	0	0	5	2
Denmark	1	2	1	3	0	0	2	1
Finland	8	14	0	0	1	1	9	4
France	11	20	6	16	11	9	28	14
Germany	0	0	0	0	22	18	22	11
Hong Kong	1	2	1	3	8	7	10	5
Japan	5	9	16	43	34	28	55	26
Luxembourg	0	0	1	3	0	0	1	0
Netherlands	0	0	2	6	14	12	16	8
New Zealand	0	0	1	3	1	1	2	1
Norway	3	5	1	3	5	4	9	4
Singapore	1	2	0	0	0	0	1	0
Spain	0	0	1	3	1	1	2	1
Sweden	7	12	4	11	5	4	16	8
Switzerland	8	14	0	0	1	1	9	4
Total	56	100	36	100	119	100	211	100

Accounting Standard Choice classifications are based on the examination firms' 1993 annual report prepared in English in accordance with the London Exchange's listing requirements (London Exchange, 1994b, pp. 8–9).

Firms were classified as IAS firms if (1) they prepared financial reports in accordance with IAS as described in the summary of significant accounting policies or the audit report or (2) they prepared financial reports in accordance with their domestic-GAAP and provided IAS footnote reconciliations; Firms were classified as US-GAAP firms if (1) they prepared financial reports in accordance with US-GAAP as described in the summary of significant accounting policies or the audit report or (2) they prepared financial reports in accordance with their domestic-GAAP and provided US-GAAP footnote reconciliations; Firms were classified as Domestic-GAAP firms if their financial reports were prepared in accordance with the generally accepted accounting principles of their country of domicile and they did not provide any IAS or US-GAAP financial data in their financial reports.

The factors hypothesized as being associated with firms' decisions to disclose IAS or US-GAAP financial information are tested using the following logit regression:

$$P(\text{CHOICE}) = \beta_0 + \beta_1 \text{NMARKETS} + \beta_2 \text{ISSUE} + \beta_3 \text{SET}$$
$$+ \beta_4 \text{RELSIZE} + \beta_5 \text{USXCH} + \varepsilon, \tag{1}$$

where Choice equals one if a firm reports IAS or US-GAAP financial information in its 1993 annual financial report ($n = 92$) and zero if a firm reports

H. Ashbaugh / Journal of Accounting and Public Policy 20 (2001) 129–153 141

only domestic-GAAP financial information ($n = 119$), NMARKETS is the number of foreign equity markets in which a firm's shares are traded, ISSUE equals one if a firm issues stock in 1993 or 1994, and zero otherwise, SET is the sum of IASDIS and IASCON from Tables 1 and 2, respectively, REL-SIZE is the market value of a firm's shares listed on its domestic exchange divided by the total capitalization of its domestic equity market at December 31, 1993, USXCH equals one if a firm is required to file Form 20-F and zero otherwise.

The number of foreign equity markets in which a firm's shares are traded, NMARKETS, is identified through the *Bloomberg Financial Services* database. [14] Firms raising capital through equity offerings, i.e., ISSUE = 1, are identified by reading the firms' 1993 and 1994 financial reports. Equity offerings in 1993 and 1994 are considered because my sample firms adopted IAS prior to 1993. Specifically, 5.4%, 19.6%, and 75.0% of the IAS sample firms adopted IAS in 1990, 1991, and 1992 respectively. The value assigned to SET represents the potential number of accounting policy changes firms made by providing IAS financial information. SET reflects the fact that each set of domestic-GAAP is a unique combination of disclosure and accounting measurement policies (Ashbaugh and Pincus, 2001). [15] The same classifications are assumed for firms using US-GAAP in this phase of the analysis.

---

[14] It could be that firms decide jointly to change their financial reporting strategies and list on foreign exchanges. If so, the number of foreign exchanges may not be exogenous to the model of accounting standard choice. To test for exogeneity, I applied the Hausman test (Hausman, 1978) as follows. First, I used absolute firm size as the instrumental variable in the first stage regressions where the dependent variable is NMARKETS. Absolute firm size is defined as the firm's market value of equity. The market value of equity is statistically significant (at the 0.01 level, two-tailed test) in each model and the R^2s range from 0.10 to 0.22. Second, the predicted values from the first stage regressions are added as instrumental variables (call the variable NMARKET-HAT) to the original logit equations. The results of the second stage regressions fail to reject the hypothesis that the coefficients on NMARKET-HAT are zero. Thus, the number of exchanges can be considered an exogenous variable.

[15] Doupnik and Salter (1993) argue that countries' legal classifications are aligned with countries' accounting objectives, suggesting that common law countries' domestic-GAAP objectives are to produce transparent financial information. In this sense, domestic-GAAP from common law countries would be similar to IAS since IAS are intended to produce information that allows users to properly value firms (International Accounting Standards Committee, 1999, pp. 38–46). Using the common versus code law country classifications reported in Haskins et al. (1996, p. 19), I found the SET variable to be highly positively correlated with a categorical variable, coded 1 for firms domiciled in countries classified as having a code law legal system and one for firms domiciled in countries classified as having a common law legal system. As a sensitivity test, I substituted the legal classification categorical variable for SET in my regression analyses and obtained quantitatively similar results.

142   *H. Ashbaugh / Journal of Accounting and Public Policy 20 (2001) 129–153*

Two control variables are included in the regression equation. RELSIZE is a relative size measure where the numerator is equal to a firm's price per share multiplied by the number of shares outstanding as of December 31, 1993. The denominator of RELSIZE is the total equity market capitalization of the firm's country of domicile as reported in the *London Exchange 1994 Fact Book* (1994b, p. 36). Wyatt (1992, p. 13.9) suggests that non-US firms will use IAS to facilitate the cross-border flow of capital when they exhaust their ability to raise capital in their home markets. I use RELSIZE to proxy for a firm's demand for foreign capital (Saudagaran, 1988, p. 108). USXCH controls for firms' required filing of US-GAAP financial data with the SEC when they trade on a major US exchange.

4. Results

Table 4 presents summary statistics. Likelihood ratio χ^2 tests indicate that IAS/US-GAAP firms (1) trade in more foreign equity markets than domestic-GAAP firms, (2) issue more equity in 1993 or 1994 than domestic-GAAP firms, (3) provide more standardized information by complying with IAS or US-GAAP relative to their domestic-GAAP, and (4) more often file Form 20-F than domestic-GAAP firms. The mean value of RELSIZE for IAS/US-GAAP firms is significantly larger (at the 0.01 level in a one-tailed test) than the mean value of RELSIZE for domestic-GAAP firms. [16]

The results of logit regression (1) are reported in Table 5. Overall, the model is highly significant ($\chi^2 = 62.93$; significance level <0.001) and has a Pseudo R^2 of 0.22. [17] The positive and significant coefficient on NMARKETS (at the 0.02 level, one-tailed test) indicates that firms are more likely to disclose IAS or US-GAAP financial information when their shares trade in more foreign equity markets. The positive and significant coefficient on SET (at the <0.01 level, two-tailed test) indicates that firms from countries with less stringent reporting requirements are more likely to report financial information prepared in accordance with an internationally acceptable set of accounting standards. The positive and significant coefficient on ISSUE (at the 0.08 level, one-tailed test) indicates that firms seeking additional equity capital are more likely to disclose IAS or US-GAAP financial information. The coefficients on the control variables RELSIZE and USXCH are also

---

[16] Spearman correlations (not tabled) for the explanatory variables range from −0.258 to 0.392. In general, the pattern of significant correlations is similar across the three firm classifications.

[17] The Pseudo R^2 is calculated as $1 - (\log L_{UR} / \log L_R)$ (Maddala, 1988, pp. 277–279).

H. Ashbaugh / Journal of Accounting and Public Policy 20 (2001) 129–153 143

Table 4
Summary statistics

Variable	IAS/US-GAAP firms ($n = 92$)				Domestic-GAAP firms ($n = 119$)			
	Mean	Median	S.D.	Min./Max.	Mean	Median	S.D.	Min./Max.
NMARKETS++	3.64	3.00	1.99	1/9	2.77	2.00	1.68	1/8
ISSUE++	0.35	0.00	0.48	0/1	0.21	0.00	0.41	0/1
SET+++	5.93	5.00	2.38	0/10	4.76	5.00	1.55	3/10
USXCH+++	0.35	0.00	0.47	0/1	0.07	0.00	0.25	0/1
RELSIZE	0.03***	0.01###	0.04	0.00/0.24	0.01	0.00	0.01	0.00/0.05

Variable descriptions: NMARKETS is the number of foreign markets in which a firm's shares are traded in 1993. ISSUE equals 1 if a firm issues stock in 1993 or 1994 and 0 otherwise. SET is the sum of IASDIS and IASCON from Tables 1 and 2, respectively. USXCH equals 1 if a firm is required to file Form 20-F and 0 otherwise. RELSIZE is the market value of a firm's shares listed on its domestic exchange divided by the total capitalization of its domestic equity market at December 31, 1993.
++ Likelihood ratio χ^2 tests reject the hypotheses of no difference in the values of the discrete and binary variables across IAS/US-GAAP and domestic-GAAP firms (significant at the 0.05 level).
+++ Likelihood ratio χ^2 tests reject the hypotheses of no difference in the values of the discrete and binary variables across IAS/US-GAAP and domestic-GAAP firms (significant at the 0.01 level).
*** A *t*-test rejects the hypothesis of no difference in the means of RELSIZE for IAS/US-GAAP and domestic-GAAP firms (significant at the 0.01 level, one-tailed test.)
A Wilcoxon rank sum test rejects the hypothesis of no difference in the distributions of RELSIZE (significant at the 0.01 level, one-tailed test).

positive and significant (at the 0.09 and <0.01 levels, respectively, one-tailed tests). These results suggest, in general, that non-US firms with culturally diverse shareholders, less demanding domestic reporting practices, and relatively large domestic market capitalization perceive benefits associated with reporting financial information prepared in accordance with an internationally acceptable set of accounting standards.

To investigate the characteristics that are associated with firms disclosing IAS financial information, I re-estimate Eq. (1) excluding US-GAAP firms from the analysis. Specifically, I code the dependent variable in Eq. (1) as 1 if the firm discloses IAS financial information in its annual report ($n = 56$) and 0 if a firm reports only domestic-GAAP financial information ($n = 119$). The results are reported in Table 6. The model is significant ($\chi^2 = 38.41$; significance level < 0.001; Pseudo $R^2 = 0.18$).

The positive and significant coefficient on SET (at the 0.01 level, two-tailed test) indicates that firms from countries with less stringent reporting requirements are more likely to use IAS, suggesting IAS is viewed as a mechanism to disseminate more standardized financial information than what is provided under the firms' domestic-GAAP. The significant coefficient on ISSUE (at the

144   *H. Ashbaugh / Journal of Accounting and Public Policy 20 (2001) 129–153*

Table 5
Probability of disclosing IAS or US-GAAP financial information

	Explanatory variable	Predicted sign	Parameter estimate	Standard error
	Intercept	Unsigned	$-3.676^{\#\#\#}$	0.691
H1	NMARKETS	+	0.227^{**}	0.104
H2	ISSUE	+	0.510^{*}	0.365
H3	SET	±	$0.375^{\#\#\#}$	0.094
	RELSIZE	+	15.782^{**}	9.441
	USXCH	+	1.706^{***}	0.468
Maximum likelihood estimates			Goodness-of-fit measures	
χ^2	62.93		Pseudo R^2	0.22
Significant level	0.00		Concordant	80%

Dependent variable: Probability of IAS or US-GAAP, coded 1 for firms that disclose IAS or US-GAAP financial information in their annual reports ($n = 92$) and 0 otherwise ($n = 119$). NMARKETS is the number of foreign markets in which a firm's shares are traded in 1993. ISSUE equals 1 if a firm issues stock in 1993 or 1994 and 0 otherwise. SET is the sum of IASDIS and IASCON from Tables 1 and 2, respectively. RELSIZE is the market value of a firm's shares listed on its domestic exchange divided by the total capitalization of its domestic equity market at December 31, 1993. USXCH equals 1 if a firm is required to file Form 20-F and 0 otherwise.
$^{\#\#\#}$ Significant at the 0.01 level (two-tailed test).
* Significant at the 0.10 level (one-tailed test).
** Significant at the 0.05 level (one-tailed test).
*** Significant at the 0.01 level (one-tailed test).

0.01 level, one-tailed test) indicates a positive relation between IAS reporting and seasoned equity offerings. Recall that my sample of IAS firms adopted IAS in 1990, 1991, or 1992, i.e., the years immediately preceding the analysis period. This result suggests firms incorporate IAS into their disclosure strategies in order to increase their externally reported information flows prior to issuing additional shares. [18] The positive and significant coefficient on NMARKETS (at the 0.08 level, one-tailed test) indicates that non-US firms more likely to adopt IAS as their shares trade in more foreign equity markets, suggesting that firms view IAS financial information as being useful to foreign financial

---

[18] Due to data limitations, I was not able to discern from the financial reports if firms were issuing stock in their domestic or in foreign equity markets. However, anecdotal evidence suggests firms have incentives to standardize and/or increase their disclosures to meet the information needs of both domestic and foreign shareholders. For example, prior to 1991, domestic institutional investors in Switzerland were not as active in their domestic equity market as their US counterparts. Evidence suggests, however, that after 1992, domestic institutional investment has increased in Switzerland due, in part, to the improvements in corporate disclosures by Swiss companies (Euromoney, 1994, pp. 29–30).

Table 6
Probability of disclosing IAS financial information

	Explanatory variable	Predicted sign	Parameter estimate	Standard error
	Intercept	Unsigned	−3.690###	0.747
H1	NMARKETS	+	0.163*	0.118
H2	ISSUE	+	0.943***	0.388
H3	SET	±	0.321###	0.099
	RELSIZE	+	22.777**	11.351
	USXCH	unsigned	0.480	0.610

Maximum likelihood estimates		Goodness-of-fit measures	
χ^2	38.41	Pseudo R^2	0.18
Significant level	0.00	Concordant	76%

Dependent variable: Probability of IAS, coded 1 for firms that disclose IAS financial information in their annual report ($n = 56$) and 0 for firms that disclose only domestic-GAAP financial information ($n = 119$). NMARKETS is the number of foreign markets in which a firm's shares are traded in 1993. ISSUE equals 1 if a firm issues stock in 1993 or 1994 and 0 otherwise. SET is the sum of IASDIS and IASCON from Tables 1 and 2, respectively. RELSIZE is the market value of a firm's shares listed on its domestic exchange divided by the total capitalization of its domestic equity market at December 31, 1993. USXCH equals 1 if a firm is required to file Form 20-F and 0 otherwise.
Significant at the 0.01 level (two-tailed test).
* Significant at the 0.10 level (one-tailed test).
** Significant at the 0.05 level (one-tailed test).
*** Significant at the 0.01 level (one-tailed test).

statement users. Turning to the two controls variables, the coefficient on RELSIZE is positive and significant (at the 0.04 level, one-tailed test) whereas the coefficient on USXCH is now insignificant.

Recently, the debate over the acceptability of IAS has centered on the US capital markets (Pownall and Schipper, 1999). The SEC requires foreign registrants to prepare US-GAAP financial information if their equity shares trade in the New York, American, or NASDAQ markets. Instead of preparing their annual report in accordance with US-GAAP, firms can elect to provide a reconciliation of domestic-GAAP earnings and stockholders' equity to US-GAAP earnings and stockholders' equity as a supplement to their domestic-GAAP annual report. The SEC is considering allowing registrants' financial information to be prepared in accordance with IAS without reconciliation to US-GAAP (Securities and Exchange Commision, 2000, p. 1). Non-US firms trading or wanting to trade their equity shares in the US capital markets may prefer IAS to US-GAAP because they perceive US-GAAP to be too restrictive in its accounting method choices and/or too demanding in its disclosure requirements. Non-US firms may use IAS as the mechanism to report more standardized financial information until they have

146   *H. Ashbaugh / Journal of Accounting and Public Policy 20 (2001) 129–153*

to bear the additional costs of preparing US-GAAP financial information for the SEC. [19]

Table 7 reports the sample distribution of IAS and US-GAAP firms across US equity markets (domestic-GAAP firms are included for completeness). Of the 88 firms using IAS or US-GAAP, 23 (26.2%) did not trade equity shares in the US. A larger proportion of IAS firms (29.6%) than US-GAAP firms (9.1%) traded American Depository Receipts (ADRs) in the Over-the-Counter Bulletin Board market. [20] Of the 39 sample firms required to file US-GAAP financial information with the SEC, because they traded their ADRs in the New York, American, or Nasdaq markets, 24 elected to report US-GAAP information in their annual report while seven firms elected to report IAS financial information. A likelihood ratio χ^2 test rejects the null hypothesis of no difference in the frequencies of US equity market listings across IAS and US-GAAP firms. The distribution suggests that the required filing of Form 20-F influences a firm's choice between reporting IAS or US-GAAP information, but does not dictate the choice.

Recall that Tables 1 and 2 summarize the additional disclosures and accounting measurement restrictions of US-GAAP relative to IAS when a firm deviates from its domestic-GAAP. For the majority of firms, preparing US-GAAP financial reports results in two additional required disclosures beyond IAS requirements. In addition, US-GAAP materially restricts most firms' accounting measurement choices relative to the choices available under IAS (Financial Accounting Standards Board, 1996, pp. 25–37). The additional reporting requirements of US-GAAP suggest that US-GAAP reporting may be a more costly disclosure strategy for non-US firms than the strategy of disseminating IAS financial information.

To investigate the firm-specific characteristics of IAS versus US-GAAP firms, the following logit regression is estimated:

---

[19] Anecdotal evidence consistent with this conjecture can be found. For example, Saga Petroleum (1993, p. 45) applied IAS in its 1993 financial report by providing a footnote reconciling Norwegian GAAP net income and shareholders' equity to IAS net income and stockholders' equity. However, in 1994, Saga presents a footnote reconciling its domestic-GAAP to US-GAAP because of the company's interest in obtaining a New York Stock Exchange listing during the next year (Saga Petroleum, 1994, p. 49). Prior to having to file US-GAAP financial information with the SEC, Saga arguably believed financial information prepared in compliance with IAS to be beneficial to the readers of its 1993 financial report. Because Saga incurred costs to generate US-GAAP financial information for 1994, it may not have been worth the additional cost to prepare its annual financial reports using IAS.

[20] The Over-the-Counter Bullettin Board market is an electronic quotation system sponsored by Nasdaq. Non-US firms trading ADRs on the Bulletin Board in 1993 were not required to file financial information with the SEC (Frost and Lang, 1996, pp. 98–99).

H. Ashbaugh / Journal of Accounting and Public Policy 20 (2001) 129–153   147

Table 7
Distribution of firms across US equity markets

	Not traded in the US	US Bulletin Board market[a]	US Form 20-F market[b]	Total
IAS firms				
Frequency	19	26	7	52[c]
Percent of total	21.6	29.6	7.9	
Row percent	36.5	50.0	13.5	
US-GAAP firms				
Frequency	4	8	24	36
Percent of total	4.6	9.1	27.3	
Row percent	11.1	22.2	66.7	
Domestic-GAAP firms				
Frequency	53	58	8	119
Percent of total	25.6	28.0	3.9	
Row percent	44.6	48.7	6.7	
Total	76	92	39	207

A likelihood ratio χ^2 test rejects the hypothesis of no difference in the frequencies of equity market listings across IAS and US-GAAP firms (significant at the 0.01 level).
Accounting Standard Choice classifications are defined in Table 3.
[a] Non-US firms that trade American Depository Receipts in the Nasdaq's Over-the-Counter (OTC) Bulletin Board market did not have to file US-GAAP financial information with the SEC in 1993 (Frost and Lang, 1996, pp. 98–99).
[b] Non-US firms trading in the New York, American, or NASDAQ markets must file Form 20-F with the SEC.
[c] Four IAS firms were deleted from the analysis because they also reported US-GAAP reconciliations in their annual reports.

$$P(IAS^*) = \beta_0 + \beta_1 NMARKETS + \beta_2 ISSUE + \beta_3 USSET$$
$$+ \beta_4 RELSIZE + \beta_5 USXCH + \varepsilon, \qquad (2)$$

where IAS* equals 1 if a firm discloses IAS financial information in its annual financial report ($n = 52$) and zero if the firm chooses US-GAAP ($n = 36$), USSET is the sum of USDIS and USCON from Tables 1 and 2, respectively.

Table 8 presents the results of estimating multivariate logit regression (2). The model is significant ($\chi^2 = 58.86$; significance level < 0.001; Pseudo $R^2 = 0.49$). As expected, the negative and significant coefficient on USXCH (at the 0.01 level, one-tailed test) is consistent with the notion that firms are more likely to disclose IAS financial information when they are not required to file US-GAAP financial information with the SEC. The negative and significant coefficient on NMARKETS (at the 0.02 level, two-tailed test) indicates that IAS firms' shares trade in fewer equity markets relative to firms that disclose US-GAAP financial information in their annual reports. The negative and

Developments in Financial Reporting by Multinationals

148   *H. Ashbaugh / Journal of Accounting and Public Policy 20 (2001) 129–153*

Table 8
Probability of disclosing IAS versus US-GAAP financial information

Explanatory variable	Predicted sign	Parameter estimate	Standard error
Intercept	Unsigned	6.310###	1.666
NMARKETS	Unsigned	−0.493##	0.220
ISSUE	Unsigned	2.571###	0.834
USSET	±	−0.602###	0.180
RELSIZE	Unsigned	20.633##	9.302
USXCH	−	−3.142***	0.808
Maximum likelihood estimates		Goodness-of-fit measures	
χ^2	58.86	Pseudo R^2	0.49
Significance level	0.00	Concordant	92%

Dependent variable: Probability of IAS, coded 1 for firms that disclose IAS financial information in their annual reports ($n = 52$) and 0 for firms that disclose US-GAAP, ($n = 36$). Four IAS firms were eliminated from the analysis because they also reported US-GAAP reconciliations in their annual reports. NMARKETS is the number of foreign markets in which a firm's shares are traded in 1993. ISSUE equals 1 if a firm issues stock in 1993 or 1994 and 0 otherwise. USSET is the sum of USDIS and USCON reported in Tables 1 and 2, respectively. RELSIZE is the market value of a firm's shares listed on its domestic exchange divided by the total capitalization of its domestic equity market at December 31, 1993. USXCH equals 1 if a firm is required to file Form 20-F and 0 otherwise.
Significant at the 0.05 level (two-tailed test).
Significant at the 0.01 level (two-tailed test).
*** Significant at the 0.01 level (one-tailed test).

significant coefficient on USSET (at the 0.01 level, two-tailed test) documents that firms are more likely to disclose IAS financial information when US-GAAP requires more disclosures and restricts accounting measurement methods relative to the policies of their domestic-GAAP. [21] The positive and significant coefficient on ISSUE (at the 0.01 level, two-tailed test) indicates that firms are more likely to disclose IAS financial information when they are issuing seasoned equity.

The positive and significant coefficient on RELSIZE (at the 0.02 level, two-tailed test) indicates that relatively larger firms, in terms of domestic market capitalization, are more likely to disclose IAS financial information than US-GAAP financial information. Recall that RELSIZE is a size measure that proxies for a firm's demand for foreign capital (Saudagaran, 1988, p. 108). It could be that such relatively large firms demand more foreign capital because their domestic markets are smaller or less sophisticated than other countries' capital

---

[21] One of the criticisms of IAS is that the IAS accounting measurement choice set is too large (Financial Accounting Standards Board, 1996, pp. 34–37). The IASC has had two major overhauls of the set of standards comprising IAS. The first was the Comparability Project implemented in January 1, 1995 (International Accounting Standards Committee, 1993, pp. 8–9). The second was the Core Project completed in 1998 (Zeff, 1998, pp. 67–70).

H. Ashbaugh / Journal of Accounting and Public Policy 20 (2001) 129–153 149

markets and reporting IAS financial information is the first step in providing more standardized financial information to capital market participants. [22] To investigate this conjecture, I partitioned my sample firms into quartiles based on RELSIZE. Examining the upper quartile (where the expectation is that 25% of the sample firms from each country would appear), I found that 60.0%, 50.0%, 66.7%, 70.0%, 55.6%, 100%, 50.0%, 31.3%, and 33.3% of the sample firms from Belgium, Denmark, Finland, Hong Kong, Norway, New Zealand, Spain, Sweden, and Switzerland, respectively, have RELSIZE upper quartile values. In general, the number of listings and trading volume in these countries' equity markets are less relative to other countries represented in my sample, e.g., France, Germany, Japan (Euromoney, 1994, pp. 9–10, 11–13, 55–57, respectively). [23]

Alternatively, large firms, in absolute terms, may have incentives to disclose IAS or US-GAAP financial information because there is a greater demand for information about large firms (Lang and Lundholm, 1993, pp. 250–251). I explored the incentives large firms have to disclose IAS or US-GAAP financial information by re-estimating the regression equations using an absolute size measure; the market value of a firm's shares listed on its domestic exchange at December 31, 1993, measured in millions of US dollars. The estimated coefficients on the absolute size variable (not reported) were insignificant in each analysis. This suggests that absolute firm size does not influence a firm's decision to disclose IAS or US-GAAP financial information.

5. Conclusions

My study develops and tests hypotheses explaining why non-US firms voluntarily report financial information prepared in accordance with IAS or US-GAAP. The evidence presented in this paper indicates that non-US firms are more likely to disclose IAS or US-GAAP financial information when their equity shares trade in more foreign equity markets and when IAS or US-GAAP results in more standardized financial information relative to their domestic-GAAP reports. The results also document that firms are more likely to disclose IAS financial information when they are participating in seasoned equity offerings. I also found that firms are more likely to disclose IAS financial information when US-GAAP requires more disclosures and restricts accounting measure methods relative to the policies of their domestic-GAAP. Overall, the factors documented as being associated with non-US firms' ac-

---

[22] I thank a reviewer for positing this explanation of the positive association between non-US firms' disclosure of IAS financial information and their relative size.

[23] The remaining countries (Australia, Bermuda, France, Germany, Luxemburg, Japan, Netherlands, and Singapore) had relatively equal distribution of sample firms across the RELSIZE quartiles.

150   *H. Ashbaugh / Journal of Accounting and Public Policy 20 (2001) 129–153*

counting standard choices suggest that non-US firms select increasingly stringent sets of accounting standards when the expected benefits exceed the expected costs.

Documenting the factors associated with non-US firms' accounting standard choices is important because market regulators, accounting standard setters, accounting researchers, and capital market participants are interested in the quality of accounting standards. One characteristic of high quality accounting standards is that the standards result in transparent and comparable financial information (Securities and Exchange Commision, 2000, pp. 3–4). However, firms' implementation of accounting standards can influence the transparency and comparability of the resulting financial statements. Without knowing what motivates non-US firms to report IAS or US-GAAP financial information, it is difficult to assess the comparability of the alternative sets of standards because firms' incentives may influence the implementation of the standards. To this end, the results of my study provide insights into what motivates non-US firms' to deviate from their domestic-GAAP and implement an internationally acceptable set of accounting standards. Further research can assess whether the factors documented in my study as being associated with non-US firms' reporting of IAS or US-GAAP financial information result in differential implementation of the sets of standards and, ultimately, differential transparency and comparability of firms' financial information.

Acknowledgements

This paper is based on my dissertation titled Non-US Firms' Accounting Standard Choices in Accessing Foreign Capital Markets. I thank my chair, Morton Pincus and other members of my dissertation committee, Tom Carroll, Dan Collins, Amy Dunbar, George Neumann, and Grace Pownall, for their comments. In addition, I appreciate the comments of Robert Dosch, W. Bruce Johnson, Tom Linsmeier, Per Olsson, Mohan Venkatachalam, R.S. Olusegun Wallace, Terry Warfield, and workshop participants at the American Accounting Association/KPMG 1997 International Accounting Research Conference, Purdue University, Ohio State University, Oklahoma State University, and the University of Wisconsin–Madison. I also thank the Ernst & Young Foundation for their funding of this project.

Appendix A. IAS implementation

Firms implement IAS differently and, in general, the cost of IAS implementation is dependent on a firm's domestic-GAAP. Firms from developing countries where IAS have become the national standards do not incur any

H. Ashbaugh / Journal of Accounting and Public Policy 20 (2001) 129–153 151

incremental costs to report IAS financial information because they can prepare financial reports that conform with national and international requirements (International Accounting Standards Committee, 1995, pp. 8–9). In some developed countries, IAS is the basis for domestic-GAAP (Cairns, 1995, pp. 53–56), suggesting that firms incur minimal incremental costs in preparing IAS financial information. In countries with sets of financial reporting standards that are independent of IAS, firms can incur substantial incremental costs to report IAS financial information (Leuz and Verrecchia, 2001). These firms can provide footnote reconciliations of domestic-GAAP net income and shareholders' equity to IAS-based net income and shareholders' equity (see e.g., Bergesen, 1997, p. 25) or they can provide two sets of financial statements within the annual report; one prepared in accordance with domestic-GAAP and the other prepared in accordance with IAS (see e.g., Huhtamaki, 1997, pp. 24–26). Alternatively, a firm can apply IAS to the financial statements taken as a whole and disseminate only IAS financial statements to capital market participants (see e.g., Bayer, 1997). The incremental costs of reporting IAS financial information are assumed to be minimized when firms choose the subset of measurement and disclosure practices that meet their domestic requirements and that also comply with IAS. [24]

References

Ashbaugh, H., Olsson, P., 2001. An exploratory study of the valuation properties of cross-listed firms' IAS and US-GAAP earnings and book values. The Accounting Review (forthcoming).

Ashbaugh, H., Pincus, M., 2001. Domestic accounting standards, International Accounting Standards, and the predictability of earnings. Journal of Accounting Research (forthcoming).

Bayer, 1997. Annual Report. Bayer AG, Germany.

Bergesen, 1997. Annual Report. Bergesen ASA, Norway.

Biddle, G., Saudagaran, S., 1991. Foreign stock listings: Benefits, costs, and the accounting policy dilemma. Accounting Horizons 5 (3), 69–80.

Botosan, C., 1997. Disclosure level and the cost of equity capital. The Accounting Review 72 (3), 323–349.

Cairns, D., 1995. A Guide to Applying International Accounting Standards. Accountancy Books, London.

Choi, F., 1973. Financial disclosure and entry to the European capital market. Journal of Accounting Research 11 (2), 159–175.

Choi, F., Levich, R., 1992. International accounting diversity and capital market decisions. In: Frederick, C. (Ed.), Handbook of International Accounting. Wiley, New York, pp. 7.1–7.29.

---

[24] For example, 1993 IAS require firms to expense all research costs but allow firms to capitalize some development costs (International Accounting Standards Committee, 1994, pp. 140–146). Norwegian-GAAP permitted firms to capitalize research and development costs (Coopers and Lybrand, 1993, pp. N-91–N-92). By capitalizing only its development costs, a Norwegian firm can comply with its domestic-GAAP and IAS.

Choi, F., Frost, C., Meek, G., 1999. International Accounting, third ed. Prentice-Hall, Englewood Cliffs, NJ.

Cooper, D., Grinder, B., 1996. Voluntary information disclosure during periods of stock price vulnerability. Journal of Business Finance and Accounting 23 (3), 461–472.

Coopers & Lybrand, 1993. International Accounting Summaries, second ed. Wiley, New York.

Doupnik, T., Salter, S., 1993. An empirical test of a judgmental international classification of financial reporting practices. Journal of International Business Studies 28 (1), 41–60.

Eggert, R., 1998. German corporate law and accounting legislation. International Tax Review 9 (7), 61–62.

Euromoney, 1994. World Equity Markets, Euromoney, London.

Financial Accounting Standards Board, 1996. The IASC-U.S. Comparison Project: A Report on the Similarities and Differences between IASC Standards and U.S. GAAP, Financial Accounting Standards Board, Norwalk, CT.

Fishman, M., Hagerty, K., 1989. Disclosure decisions by firms and the competition for price efficiency. The Journal of Finance 44 (3), 633–646.

Frost, C., Lang, M., 1996. Foreign companies and US securities markets: Financial reporting policy issues and suggestions for research. Accounting Horizons 10 (1), 95–109.

Haskins, M., Ferris, K., Selling, T., 1996. International Financial Reporting and Analysis. Irwin, Chicago.

Hausman, J., 1978. Specification tests in econometrics. Econometrica 46, 1251–1271.

Huhtamaki, 1997. Annual Report 1997. Huhtamaki Oy, Finland.

International Accounting Standards Committee, 1992. IASC Annual Review 1991/1992, International Accounting Standards Committee, London.

International Accounting Standards Committee, 1993. IASC Insight: December, International Accounting Standards Committee, London.

International Accounting Standards Committee, 1994. International Accounting Standards 1994, International Accounting Standards Committee, London.

International Accounting Standards Committee, 1995. IASC Annual Review 1994, International Accounting Standards Committee, London.

International Accounting Standards Committee, 1999. International Accounting Standards 1999, International Accounting Standards Committee, London.

Lang, M., Lundholm, R., 1993. Cross-sectional determinants of analyst ratings of corporate disclosures. Journal of Accounting Research 31 (2), 246–271.

Lang, M., Lundholm, R., 1996. Corporate disclosure policy and analyst behaviour. The Accounting Review 71 (4), 467–492.

Leuz, C., Verrecchia, R., 2001. The economic consequences of increased disclosure. Journal of Accounting Research (forthcoming).

London Stock Exchange, 1994a. A listing in London, second ed. The International Stock Exchange of the United Kingdom and the Republic of Ireland, London.

London Stock Exchange, 1994b. Fact Book 1994. The International Stock Exchange of the United Kingdom and the Republic of Ireland, London.

Maddala, G., 1988. Introduction to Econometrics. Macmillan, New York.

Mittoo, U., 1994. Evaluating the foreign listing decision in a capital budgeting framework. Managerial Finance 20 (8), 22–35.

Pownall, G., Schipper, K., 1999. Implications of accounting research for the SEC's consideration of international accounting standards for U.S. securities offerings. Accounting Horizons 13 (3), 259–280.

Price Waterhouse, 1996. Doing Business in Bermuda, Price Waterhouse, NJ.

Purvis, S., Gernon, H., Diamond, M., 1991. The IASC and its comparability project: Prerequisites for success. Accounting Horizons 5 (2), 25–44.

Saga Petroleum, 1993. Annual Report. Saga Petroleum, Norway.

H. Ashbaugh / Journal of Accounting and Public Policy 20 (2001) 129–153   153

Saga Petroleum, 1994. Annual Report. Saga Petroleum, Norway.

Saudagaran, S., 1988. An empirical study of selected factors influencing the decision to list on foreign stock exchanges. Journal of International Business Studies 19 (1), 101–127.

Speidell, L., Bavishi, V., 1992. GAAP arbitrage: Valuation opportunities in international accounting standards. Financial Analysts Journal 48 (6), 58–66.

Street, D., Gray, S., Bryant, S., 1999. Acceptance and observance of International Accounting Standards: An empirical study of companies claiming to comply with IASs. The International Journal of Accounting 34 (1), 11–48.

United States Securities and Exchange Commission (SEC), 2000. SEC Concept Release No. 1215: International Accounting Standards, Securities and Exchange Commission, Washington, DC.

Welker, M., 1995. Disclosure policy, information asymmetry, and liquidity in equity markets. Contemporary Accounting Research 11 (2), 801–827.

Wyatt, A., 1992. International Accounting Standards and organizations: Quo Vadis? In: Frederick, C. (Ed.), Handbook of International Accounting. Wiley, New York, pp. 13.1–13.20.

Zeff, S., 1998. The IASC's core standards: What will the SEC do? Journal of Financial Statement Analysis 4 (1), 67–78.

[15]

The International
Journal of
Accounting

Disclosure Level and Compliance with IASs: A Comparison of Companies With and Without U.S. Listings and Filings

Donna L. Street and Stephanie M. Bryant
James Madison University, Harrisonburg, VA, USA

Key Words: International accounting standards; Compliance with IASs; IASC; Voluntary disclosure

Abstract: This research investigates the extent to which the disclosure requirements of the IASC are complied with or exceeded for companies claiming to use International Accounting Standards (IASs). Additionally, the research seeks to identify significant differences between those companies with U.S. listings, U.S. filings, and those with no U.S. listings or filings with regard to (1) compliance with IASC-required disclosures, and (2) level of disclosure (including both mandatory and voluntary items). The findings reveal the overall level of disclosure is greater for companies with U.S. listings. Additionally, greater disclosure is associated with an accounting policies footnote that specifically states that the financial statements are prepared in accordance with IASs and an audit opinion that states that International Standards of Auditing (ISAs) were followed when conducting the audit. Further, the findings indicate the extent of compliance with IASs is greater for companies with U.S. listings or filings. A higher level of compliance is associated with an audit opinion that states the financial statements are in accordance with IASs and that ISAs were followed when conducting the audit.

The research highlights the significance of the enforcement issue for the International Accounting Standard Committee (IASC) as it seeks an International Organization of Securities Commissions (IOSCO) endorsement. The findings indicate enforcement of IASs may be less of an issue for companies with listings and filings in the U.S. However, for companies without U.S. listings and filings, compliance is indeed of great concern.

Currently, the International Organization of Securities Commissions (IOSCO) and its member bodies are reviewing the International Accounting Standard Committee's (IASC) application for endorsement of International Accounting Standards (IASs). This critical decision will determine whether IASs may be used for cross-border offerings of securities

---

Direct all correspondence to: Donna L. Street, School of Accounting, James Madison University, Mail Stop Code 0203, Harrisonburg, VA 22807, USA; E-mail: streetdl@jmu.edu

The International Journal of Accounting, Vol. 35, No. 3, pp. 305–329

in all the world's major capital markets, including the U.S. To this end, the SEC Chief Accountant has encouraged research to assist the Commission in its assessment of the IASC's Core Standards and related topics. This research addresses a key question posed by Chief Accountant Turner (SEC, 1999):

> What are typical footnote disclosures by companies currently using IASC filings (a) in non-U.S. countries, (b) in U.S. filings using reconciliation, and (c) similar U.S. GAAP filings?

For a sample of companies claiming to use IASs, the current research investigates the extent to which the disclosure requirements of the IASC are complied with or exceeded. Additionally, the research seeks to identify any significant differences between those companies with U.S. listing, U.S. filings, and those with no U.S. listings or filings with regard to (1) compliance with IASC-required disclosures, and (2) level of disclosure (including both mandatory and voluntary items). To the extent that such differences are not significant, particularly with regard to compliance with IASs, the argument for accepting IASs for cross-border listings will be supported. On the other hand, evidence to the contrary is likely to strengthen the argument against an IOSCO endorsement of IASs for cross-border listings.

IOSCO'S Review of IASs

As part of IOSCO's commitment to facilitate cross-border offerings and listings by multinationals, the Commission's Technical Committee actively participated in the IASC Core Standards Project (IASC, 1999). Following the 1999 publication of the interim standard on financial instruments, which resulted in the IASC substantially completing all key parts of the core standards, the IOSCO Technical Committee began an assessment of the core standards, focusing on whether the core standards are of sufficiently high quality to warrant permitting foreign issuers to utilize IASs to access a country's capital markets as an alternative to domestic standards. Upon completion of its analysis, the IOSCO Working Group will make a recommendation to the IOSCO Technical Committee. The Technical Committee will then decide whether to recommend that members of IOSCO permit foreign issuers to use IASs in lieu of national standards for cross-border offering and listing purposes.

With regard to IOSCO's evaluation of IASs, the SEC (1996) has indicated that there are three primary elements to acceptance of IASs. The standards must:

(a) Include a core set of standards that constitute a comprehensive, generally accepted basis of accounting
(b) Be of high quality and result in comparability, transparency, and full disclosure; and
(c) Be rigorously interpreted and applied.

This research addresses the issues of full disclosure (item b) and rigorous application of IASs (item c).

LITERATURE REVIEW AND RESEARCH ISSUES

Several studies have addressed the impact of various corporate characteristics on annual report disclosures. These characteristics include size, listing status, leverage, profitability, industry, type of auditor, size of the equity market, degree of economic development, type of economy, activity on the equity market, dispersion of stock ownership, and culture.

Studies based on capital markets in developed countries include Singhvi and Desai (1971), Buzby (1975), Belkaoui and Kahl (1978), Firth (1979), McNally et al. (1982), Cooke (1989a,b, 1991, 1992, 1993), Wallace and Naser (1995), Wallace et al. (1994), Inchausti (1997), and Dumontier and Raffournier (1998). Overall, these studies indicate that size and listing status are significantly associated with the level of disclosure.[1] Cooke (1989b) concluded that while size, as measured by total assets, sales, and number of shareholders, is an important variable, it does not matter which of the three measures of size is selected. Additionally, prior research consistently suggests that leverage (gearing) is not significantly associated with level of disclosure.

Findings regarding the relationship between level of disclosure and other corporate variables have been mixed. Singhvi and Desai (1971), Belkaoui and Kahl (1978), Wallace and Naser (1995), and Wallace et al. (1994) provide evidence of an association between profitability (rate of return) and level of disclosure. However, their findings are not supported by the work of Cerf (1961), McNally et al. (1982), Inchausti (1997), and Dumontier and Raffournier (1998). While Cooke (1991, 1992) reports that manufacturing companies report more information than other types of corporations, Inchausti's (1997) findings do not support an association between industry and level of disclosure. Research by Singhvi and Desai (1971), Inchausti (1997), and Dumontier and Raffournier (1998) suggest an association between audit firm and level of disclosure; alternatively, Firth (1979) and McNally et al. (1982) provide no evidence of this association.

Adhikari and Tondkar (1992) report significant variations in the overall quality and level of detail disclosure that are required as part of the listing and filing requirements of stock exchanges around the world. Among a total of 35 stock exchanges, the NYSE was clearly the leader in terms of disclosure requirements, with London not far behind. The findings revealed a significant association between size of the equity market and disclosure requirements. However, no significant associations were identified for the degree of economic development, type of economy, activity on the equity market, and dispersion of stock ownership.

Accounting standards, such as IASs, set forth the minimum disclosure guidelines, which companies are obligated to follow. However, the IASC and International Federation of Accountants (IFAC) are concerned that some companies claiming to comply with IASs may not in fact be complying with all of the requirements of IASs. In this regard, the President of the IFAC has criticized auditors for asserting that financial statements comply with IASs when the accounting policies and other notes show otherwise (Cairns, 1997). Research by Cairns (1999) and Street et al. (1999) supports the assertions of the IASC and IFAC by providing evidence that the degree of compliance by companies claiming to comply with IASs is very mixed and somewhat selective. The findings of these studies reinforce the significance of the acceptance and observance issue for the IASC. The current research extends these previous studies by examining the factors that may be associated with noncompliance.

In addition to the information companies are obligated to disclose (although as previously noted some may not fully comply), in many instances, companies voluntarily disclose information *beyond* that required by accounting standards and listing authorities. Hence, this research also addresses the extent of voluntary disclosure provided by companies claiming to follow IASs and seeks to identify the factors associated with voluntary disclosures.

Based on this discussion and prior literature, four primary research questions are considered in this article:

> *Research Question #1*: For companies that claim to comply with IASs, does the overall level of disclosure differ significantly for companies with (1) U.S. listings, (2) U.S. filings, and (3) without U.S. listings or filings?

> *Research Question #2*: For companies that claim to comply with IASs, does the degree of compliance with IASC-required disclosures differ significantly for companies with (1) U.S. listings, (2) U.S. filings, and (3) without U.S. listings or filings?

> *Research Question #3*: What are the factors associated with the overall level of disclosure provided by companies that claim to comply with IASs?

> *Research Question #4*: What are the factors associated with the degree of compliance with IASC-required disclosures for companies that claim to comply with IASs?

HYPOTHESES AND INDEPENDENT VARIABLES

The following hypotheses, stated in alternative form, were developed to test the four research questions.

Hypotheses Associated with Research Questions 1 and 2

As noted previously, the SEC has requested research to determine whether disclosure levels vary for those companies utilizing IAS filings (a) in non-U.S. countries, (b) in U.S. filings using reconciliation, and (c) similar U.S. GAAP filings. In line with this inquiry, prior research suggests that disclosure levels are significantly different for companies listed on major exchanges than for other companies.

H_a1: The level of disclosure is significantly different for (1) companies with U.S. listings, (2) U.S. filings, and (3) without U.S. listings or filings.

H_a2: Compliance with mandatory IASC disclosures differs significantly for (1) companies with U.S. listings, (2) U.S. filings, and (3) without U.S. listings or filings.

Hypotheses Associated with Research Questions 3 and 4

Prior research addressing the association between disclosure levels and corporate characteristics has focussed primarily on companies domiciled in one country that use domestic GAAP. For example, Cooke (1989b), Cooke (1991, 1992), and Buzby (1975) examined Swedish, Japanese, or U.S. companies, respectively. The current research examines a sample of companies representing many countries that claim to use IASC GAAP. Additionally, the current research extends studies by Cairns (1999) and Street et al. (1999) relating to noncompliance with IASs by examining factors that may be associated with the degree of compliance with IASs.

Prior research has consistently identified company size and listing status as positively significantly associated with level of disclosure. Cooke (1989b) concluded that while size, as measured by total assets, sales, and number of shareholders, is an important variable, it does not matter which of the three measures of size is selected. In this study, the variable ASSETS is chosen to measure size, and is defined as total assets in U.S. dollars.

To explore the questions posed by the SEC Chief Accountant, the variable listing status (LISTING) is defined, as follows:[2]

- U.S. listings: NYSE or NASDAQ listings (file form 20-F)
- Companies with U.S. filings: 12g3-2(b) exempt, 144A, and OTC filings
- Companies without U.S. listings or filings

The following hypotheses test the associations described above utilizing a sample of global companies that claim to use IASs.

H$_a$3a: Company size is significantly positively related to the overall level of disclosure (including both voluntary and mandatory disclosure).

H$_a$4a: Company size is significantly positively related to the degree of compliance with IASC-required disclosures.

H$_a$3b: Listing status is significantly positively related to the overall level of disclosure (including both voluntary and mandatory disclosure).

H$_a$4b: Listing status is significantly positively related to the extent of compliance with IASC-required disclosures.

Prior research regarding the association between profitability and level of disclosure is mixed. For example, research by Singhvi and Desai (1971), Belkaoui and Kahl (1978), Wallace and Naser (1995), and Wallace et al. (1994) indicates a significant association. Alternatively, Cerf (1961), McNally et al. (1982), Inchausti (1997), and Dumontier and Raffournier (1998) provide no evidence of an association. Due to the mixed findings from prior research, no prediction of direction of association is made in the current study. Hence, a two-tailed test is conducted. In this research, the variable profitability (PROFIT) is measured as the ratio of net income before tax to total shareholder's equity.

H_a3c: Profitability is significantly associated with level of disclosure.

H_a4c: Profitability is significantly associated with the extent of compliance with IASC-required disclosures.

Prior research yields mixed results regarding the association between industry and level of disclosure. The current research further explores the relationship between industry and level of disclosure. The variable INDUSTRY is coded as manufacturing or non-manufacturing.

H_a3d: Type of industry is significantly associated with level of disclosure.

H_a4d: Type of industry is significantly associated with the extent of compliance with IASC-required disclosures.

The current research explores the association between compliance and/or disclosure level and the manner in which companies refer to IASs in their accounting policies footnote. In line with Cairns' (1999) discussion of approaches to the use of IASs and domestic GAAP, the variable POLICY categorizes companies as follows:

- Uses IASs as the primary reporting standards (i.e., makes no reference to compliance with domestic GAAP and no exceptions are noted),
- Makes reference to IAS, but not as the primary reporting standards and/or exceptions to IAS are noted (i.e., claims financial statements prepared in accordance with national GAAP and IAS; claims financial statements in accordance with IAS with exceptions as noted; claims financial statements prepared according to national GAAP and that they also comply with IAS in all material aspects or are consistent with IAS).

H_a3e: The manner in which companies refer to the use of IAS in the accounting policies footnote is significantly associated with level of disclosure.

H_a4e: The manner in which companies refer to the use of IAS in the accounting policies footnote is significantly associated with the extent of compliance with IASC-required disclosures.

Prior research provides some evidence that the level of disclosure may be associated with the type of auditor. However, this variable is not considered in the current study because, with the exception of six companies, the sample companies are audited by one of the Big 5+2. However, the current research does explore the association between compliance and/or disclosure level, and the manner in which the audit opinion addresses (1) the type of accounting standards used by the companies and (2) the auditing standards adhered to. The variable OPACCT categorizes companies as follows:

- Audit report states financial statements in compliance with IASs.
- Audit report makes reference to IASs with noted exceptions or the audit report makes no reference to IASs.

H_a3f: The type of accounting standards used by the company, as stated in the audit report, is significantly associated with level of disclosure.

H_a4f: The type of accounting standards used by the company, as stated in the audit report, is significantly associated with the extent of compliance with IASC-required disclosures.

The variable OPAUDIT categorizes companies as follows:

- Audit report states International Standards of Auditing (ISAs) were followed
- Audit report makes no reference to ISAs.

H_a3g: The audit standards adhered to, as stated in the audit report, is significantly associated with the level of disclosure.

H_a4g: The audit standards adhered to, as stated in the audit report, is significantly associated with the extent of compliance with IASC-required disclosures.

METHODOLOGY

Sample Selection

Companies claiming to comply with IASs that have U.S. listings or filings were identified by comparing *The ADR Investor* (issued by the Bank of New York, 2000) list of companies selling U.S. ADRs to the IASC's (2000) *Companies Referring To Their Use of IAS. The ADR Investor* specifies listings as NYSE or NASDAQ and filings as 144A or OTC. Additionally, 12g3-2(b) companies were identified by comparing the SEC's (2000) list of 12g3-2b companies with the IASC's *Companies Referring To Their Use of IAS*. For all IAS companies identified with U.S. listings or filings, 1998 annual reports were obtained. Inclusion in the sample was contingent on the accounting policies note indicating that the financial statements were in accordance with IASs or consistent with IASs and/or the audit opinion indicating the financial statements were prepared in accordance with IASs. Companies were excluded from the sample if they operated in the finance industry, the natural resource industry, or a regulated industry.

A group of IAS companies that does not have listings or filings in the U.S. was selected from the remaining companies on the IASC's *Companies Referring To Their Use of IAS*. Selection was based on matching to the companies with U.S. listings or filings based on country and to the extent possible industry.[3] For all companies included in the group without U.S. listings or filings, the accounting policies note and/or audit opinion referred to the use of IAS as described above. A list of sample companies is provided in Table 1.

Table 1. Sample Companies

Company	Country
Panel A: U.S. listed companies (20-F) that claim to comply with IASs, $n = 11$	
Aramax	Jordan
Bejing Yanhua Petrochemical	China
Gucci Group NV	Netherlands
Hoechst	Germany
Jilin Chemical	China
New Holland	Netherlands
Nokia	Finland
Scania	Sweden
Shanghai Petrochemical	China
Sulzer Medica	Switzerland
Usinor Sacilor-18	France
Panel B: U.S. filing (12g3-2(b) exempt) companies that claim to comply with IASs ($n = 12$)	
ABB AG	Switzerland
Boehler–Uddeholm	Austria
Dairy Farm Int'l	Hong Kong
Holderbank Financiere Glarus AG	Switzerland
Jardine Matheson Holdings	Hong Kong
Lafarge SA	France
Mandarin Oriental	Hong Kong
Nestle	Switzerland
Novartis	Switzerland
Puma	Germany
Technip	France
Vtech Holdings 16	Hong Kong
Panel C: U.S. filing (OTC/144A) companies that claim to comply with IASs, $n = 18$	
Adidas–Salomon	Germany
AECI Ltd.	South Africa
Bayer AG	Germany
Borsod	Hungary
Canal +	France
Esselte AB	Sweden
Fotex	Hungary
Henkel	Germany
Kemira	Finland
Lagardere SCA	France
Merck KGAA	Germany
C.P. Pokphand Co.	Hong Kong
Renault SA	France
Richemont	Switzerland
Roche Holding AG	Switzerland
Toray Industries	Japan
Torkett Summer	Germany
Yizheng Chemical	China

(continued on next page)

Table 1. *(Continued)*

Company	Country
Panel D: Non-U.S. listing or filing companies that claim to comply with IASs, $n = 41$	
Algroup	Switzerland
Anhui Conch Cement	China
Ares Serono Group	Switzerland
Articon	Germany
BB Med Tech	Switzerland
Beijing Orient Electronics	China
Bongrain	France
Calida	Switzerland
Cementia Holding	Switzerland
China Motor Telecom	China
Christian Dalloz	France
Danisco	Denmark
Danubius	Hungary
Dyckerhoff	Germany
Essilor	France
Gintian	China
Heidelberger Druckmaschinen	Germany
Heidelberger Zement	Germany
Jardine International Motor Holding	Hong Kong
Lectra	France
MB Software	Germany
Metra	Finland
Moevenpick Holding	Switzerland
Moulinex SA	France
Oriflame	Belgium
Perstorp AB	Sweden
Phoenix Mecano	Switzerland
Pliva	Croatia
Saint Gobain	France
Schering AG	Germany
Shanghai Dajiang	China
Sherzhen Textile	China
Shijiazhuang Baoshi	China
Sihl	Switzerland
Technotrans	Germany
Tiszai Vegyi Kombinat	Hungary
Trelleborg	Sweden
Voest-Alpine Stahl	Austria
Weiju Fuel Injection	China
Zimbabwe Sun Limited	Africa
Zwach Unicum	Hungary

In order to test H_a1 and H_a2, analysis of variance (ANOVA) was used. This procedure tests overall group differences between U.S. listed companies, companies with U.S. filings, and companies with no U.S. listings or filings with respect to (1) overall level of disclosure and (2) compliance with IASs. The results of each ANOVA were then used to determine model specifications for testing of the remaining hypotheses related to company characteristics. Stepwise regression was first used to determine which factors are associated with the overall level of disclosure, with follow-up ordinary least squares (OLS) regression based on the results of the stepwise regression. The regression equation for the overall level of disclosure is specified as:

$$INDEX_j = \beta_0 + \beta_1 ASSETS + \beta_2 PROFIT + D_1 OPAUDIT + D_2 OPACCT + D_3 POLICY + D_4 INDUSTRY + D_5 LISTING + e_j$$

Where: INDEX=jth observation of disclosure index by company;
β_0=constant;
β_1=size as measured by total assets in U.S. dollars;
β_2=profit, as measured by rate of return (Net income before tax/total stockholders' equity);
D_1=dummy variable
1 if audit opinion indicates company follows international standards of audit,
0 if otherwise;
D_2=dummy variable
1 if audit opinion indicates company's financial statements are prepared in accordance with international accounting standards (IASs),
0 if otherwise;
D_3=dummy variable
1 if accounting policy footnote indicates IASs are the basis for the financial statements,
0 if otherwise;
D_4=dummy variable
1 if company is a manufacturing company,
0 otherwise;
D_5=dummy variable[4]
1 if company is a 20-F company,
0 if otherwise;
e_j=stochastic error term;
β=parameter.

For the compliance tests, the same regression equation was estimated, with the following change for LISTING:[4]

D_5=dummy variable (1 if company is a U.S.-listed or U.S. filing company, 0 if otherwise).

Dependent Variable

A checklist for IASC-required disclosures was developed for IASs 1 through 38.[5] For IASs that have been revised, but were not yet mandatory for fiscal year 1998, the disclosure list included the original disclosures and the additional disclosures included in the recent revision of the IAS. To tap voluntary disclosures, items were added to capture disclosures as follows:

- Required by U.S. GAAP but not by IASC GAAP,
- Cited in previous literature as items frequently provided by companies seeking the benefits associated with full disclosure.

The disclosure checklist focused on items disclosed in the financial statements and footnotes. Items disclosed elsewhere in the annual report were not considered. The only exception was the items referred to in IAS 1 that may be disclosed in the financial statements, footnotes, or elsewhere (i.e., dividend per share and number of employees).

Based on a review of the company's complete annual report, each disclosure item was coded as disclosed, not disclosed, or not applicable, following Cooke (1989b):

$$\text{Disclosed (TD)} = \sum_{i=1}^{m} d_i$$

Where $d = 1$ if the item d_i is disclosed;
0 if the item d_i is not disclosed, and
$m \leq n$ (see below).

A review of the complete annual report minimized the possibility that companies would be penalized for disclosures that were not applicable or immaterial. Failure to adopt such an approach would have resulted in larger, more diversified companies being more likely to disclose more information (See Buzby, 1975; Cooke, 1989b, 1991, 1992). The overall disclosure index (INDEX) for each company was calculated by dividing the total number of mandatory and voluntary disclosures provided by the number of applicable disclosures. Adjustments were made to the data set so that disclosures noted in more than one IAS were not double-counted (i.e., research and development charged to expense is required by both IAS 9 and IAS 38).

$$\text{Total Applicable } (M) = \sum_{i=1}^{n} d_i$$

Where d = expected item of disclosure;
n = the number of items which the company is expected to disclose.

The disclosure index for compliance (INDEX) for each company was measured by the number of mandatory disclosures provided divided by the number of applicable mandatory disclosures.

$$\text{INDEX} = \frac{TD}{M}$$

Table 2. Analysis of Variance on Overall Level of Disclosure and Compliance

Source	df	SS	MS	F	Prob>F
Panel A: Overall level of disclosure, test of H_a1					
Group	2	1.08033403	0.54016702	5.60	0.0038
Error	2,037	196.61548414	0.09652208		
Total	2,039	197.69581817			
Panel B: Compliance, test of H_a2					
Group	2	2.30275136	1.15137568	12.97	0.0001
Error	1,792	159.03610736	0.08874783		
Total	1,794	161.33885871			

With respect to mandatory disclosures, for those IASs that had been revised but were not yet effective for fiscal year 1998, the number of applicable mandatory disclosures was based on the original version of the IAS unless the company specifically indicated early adoption of the standard. For early adoptors of recently revised or new IASs, the expanded disclosure requirements were treated as mandatory.[6,7]

RESULTS

Level of Disclosure—H_a1

ANOVA allows for an examination of differences between (1) the U.S. listings group (20-F), (2) the U.S. filings group, and (3) the group with no U.S. listings or filings.[8] The null of no significant difference in group means is rejected ($F = 5.60$, $p<0.004$, See Panel A, Table 2).

Follow-up multiple comparisons using Duncan's Multiple Range Test of differences in cell means indicates that the overall level of disclosure is not significantly different for companies with U.S. filings and those companies without U.S. listings or filings. However, at $\alpha=0.05$, the overall level of disclosure for the U.S. filings group and the group without U.S. listings or filings combined (74.9%) is less than the level of overall disclosure for the U.S. listing (20-F) group (81.3%) (See Table 3).

The results of the ANOVA indicate how to best group the data in the stepwise regression. Hence, in the stepwise regression examining factors associated with overall level of disclosure, listing status is coded as U.S. listed (20-F) versus not U.S. listed (U.S. filings and no U.S. listings or filings).

Compliance—H_a2

ANOVA was used to examine any differences in compliance between (1) the U.S. listings group (20-F), (2) the U.S. filings group, and (3) the group without U.S. listings or filings.[8] The null of no significant difference is rejected at $p<0.0001$ ($F = 12.97$) (See Panel B, Table 2). Follow-up multiple comparisons using Duncan's Multiple Range Test of differences in cell means indicates compliance with IASC mandatory disclosures is not

Table 3.   Mean Disclosure Index by Group

Group	Mean disclosure index
Panel A: Overall level of disclosure	
U.S. listings	0.813
No U.S. listings (includes U.S. filings and No U.S. listings of filings)	0.749
Panel B: Compliance	
U.S. listings and U.S. filings	0.843
No U.S. listings or filings	0.774

significantly different for 20-F companies and companies with U.S. filings. However, at $\alpha =$ 0.05, compliance for the U.S. listings and filings groups combined (84.3%) is significantly greater than compliance for the group with no U.S. listings or filings (77.4%) (See Table 3). Thus, in the stepwise regression that examines factors associated with the degree of compliance with IASs, listing status is coded as U.S. listings or filings versus no U.S. listings or filings.

Level of Disclosure—H_a3

Stepwise regression (See Table 4) was utilized to determine the factors associated with overall level of disclosure. Examination of Pearson correlation coefficients suggests no problems associated with multicollinearity.[9] Additionally, variance inflation factors (VIFs) were run to measure "how much the variances of the estimated regression coefficients are inflated as compared to when the independent variables are not linearly related" (Neter et al., 1989). The larger the VIF, the greater the difference between the coefficient estimated in the regression equation and the true coefficient. A VIF greater than 10 indicates a serious multicollinearity problem (Neter et al., 1989). The largest VIF noted was for OPAUDIT at 1.516. Thus, there appears to be no serious problems with multicollinearity in the data. Based on a significance level of 0.15, stepwise regression selected the variables POLICY, LISTING, and OPAUDIT (See Panel A, Table 4). These three variables were then input into an OLS regression model. The OLS regression confirms that the best model includes the variables LISTING (H_a3b), POLICY (H_a3e), and OPAUDIT (H_a3g) ($F = 14.492$, $p < 0.0001$, See Panel B, Table 4). The model explains approximately 34 percent of the variance attributable to the independent variables. Panel C of Table 4 shows the parameter estimates and t-statistics for the OLS model. Thus, the null hypothesis for H_a3b, H_a3e, and H_a3g is rejected.

The results of the regression do not support a size (H_a3a), profitability (H_a3c), industry (H_a3d), or audit opinion stating that IASs were followed (H_a3f) effect. Thus, the null hypotheses for H_a3a, H_a3c, H_a3d, and H_a3f cannot be rejected.

Compliance—H_a4

Stepwise regression (see Table 5) was utilized to determine the factors associated with compliance. Pearson correlation coefficients suggest no problems associated with multi-

Table 4. Regression Models Estimated Factors Associated with Overall Level of Disclosure (Tests of H_a3)

Panel A: Stepwise regression on level of disclosure

Step	Variable entered	Removed	Model R^2	F	Prob>F
1	POLICY		0.2682	28.5873	0.0001
2	OPACCT		0.3149	5.2505	0.0247
3	LISTING		0.3358	2.3875	0.1265
4	OPAUDIT		0.3768	4.9359	0.0293
5		OPACCT	0.3639	1.5538	0.2165

Panel B: Analysis of variance on stepwise model

Source	df	SS	MS	F	Prob>F
Model	3	0.31197	0.10399	14.492	0.0001
Error	76	0.54536	0.00718		
Total	79	0.85733			
Adjusted $R^2 = 0.3388$					

Panel C: OLS regression model

Variable	df	Parameter estimate	Standard error	T for HO: Parameter = 0	Prob>T
INTERCEPT	1	0.657838	0.01777449	37.010	0.0001
LISTING	1	0.075764	0.02957955	2.561	0.0124
OPAUDIT	1	0.070530	0.02380615	2.963	0.0041
POLICY	1	0.072056	0.02350550	3.066	0.0030

Model: $INDEX_j = \beta_0 + \beta_1 ASSETS + \beta_2 PROFIT + D_1 OPAUDIT + D_2 OPACCT + D_3 POLICY + D_4 INDUSTRY + D_5 LISTING + e_j$.

collinearity.[10] VIFs were examined as a formal test of multicollinearity. The highest VIF was noted to be OPACCT, with a VIF of 2.27. Again, since the VIFs are not 10 or above, we conclude that there is no significant problem with multicollinearity.

Based on a significance level of 0.15, stepwise regression selected the variables OPACCT, LISTING, OPAUDIT, and POLICY (See Panel A, Table 5).

A second OLS regression model was run with the variables OPACCT, LISTING, and OPAUDIT. POLICY was excluded in the reduced model as it was only marginally significant in the stepwise regression model ($p<0.0704$). Based on the OLS regressions, the best model includes the variables OPACCT (H_a4f), LISTING (H_a4b), and OPAUDIT (H_a4g) ($F = 19.461$, $p<0.0001$, See Panel B, Table 5). This model explains approximately 41 percent of the variance attributable to the independent variables. Panel C of Table 5 shows the parameter estimates and t-statistics for the OLS model. Thus, the null hypothesis of no effect for H_a4f, H_a4b, and H_a4g is rejected. No evidence is provided for a size (H_a4a), profitability (H_a4c), industry (H_a4d), or policy (H_a4e) effect. Thus, the null hypothesis for H_a4a, H_a4c, H_a4d, and H_a4e cannot be rejected. A summary of the findings for H_a3a–H_a3g and H_a4a–H_a4g is reported in Table 6.

Table 5. Regression Models Estimated Factors Associated with Compliance with IASs (Tests of $H_a 4$)

Panel A: Stepwise regression on compliance

Step	Variable entered	Removed	Model R^2	F	Prob>F
1	OPACCT		0.2955	32.7193	0.0001
2	LISTING		0.3783	10.2462	0.0020
3	OPAUDIT		0.4345	7.5533	0.0075
4	POLICY		0.4588	3.3702	0.0704

Panel B: Analysis of variance on stepwise reduced model (excludes POLICY variable)

Source	df	SS	MS	F	Prob>F
Model	3	0.51833	0.17278	19.461	0.0001
Error	76	0.67472	0.00888		
Total	79	1.19304			
Adjusted $R^2 = 0.4121$					

Panel C: OLS regression model on reduced model

Variable	df	Parameter estimate	Standard error	T for HO: Parameter = 0	Prob>T
INTERCEPT	1	0.663141	0.02223488	29.824	0.0001
LISTING	1	0.078411	0.02128964	3.683	0.0004
OPAUDIT	1	0.073110	0.02660163	2.748	0.0075
OPACCT	1	0.098599	0.02709670	3.639	0.0005

Model: $INDEX_j = \beta_0 + \beta_1 ASSETS + \beta_2 PROFIT + D_1 OPAUDIT + D_2 OPACCT + D_3 POLICY + D_4 INDUSTRY + D_5 LISTING + e_j$.

DISCUSSION OF FINDINGS

For a sample of companies referring to the use of IASs, this research addresses four primary research questions. In response to an inquiry by the SEC Chief Accountant, research questions #1 and #2 explore the extent to which U.S. listing or filing status is associated with the overall level of disclosure provided and the extent of compliance with IASC-required disclosures. Research questions #3 and #4 address the factors associated with the overall level of disclosure provided by companies and the extent of compliance with IASC-required disclosures.

An analysis of research questions #1 and #2 provides a response to an inquiry by the SEC Chief Accountant. The findings reveal that the overall level of disclosure provided by companies that file Form 20-F (81%), in association with a listing on the NYSE or NASDAQ, significantly exceeds the disclosures provided by companies with U.S. filings or with no U.S. listings or filings (75%). This finding is in line with previous research that consistently suggests an association between listing status and the overall level of disclosure.

A series of protected *t*-tests identifies any significant differences in the overall levels of disclosure for each IAS.[11] These indicate that 20-F companies provide significantly more disclosure (See Panel A, Table 7) with respect to IAS 9 (Research and Development Cost),

Table 6. Summary of Findings for Factors Related to Overall Level of Disclosure and Compliance

Variable name	Definition	Hypothesis	Finding
Panel A: Level of disclosure			
ASSETS	Total assets in U.S. dollars	H_a3a	Not supported
LISTING	1 if U.S. filing 0 otherwise	H_a3b	Supported
PROFIT	*NI before tax/Total SE*	H_a3c	Not supported
INDUSTRY	1 if manufacturing 0 otherwise	H_a3d	Not supported
POLICY	1 if accounting policy footnote indicates IASs are the basis for the financials 0 otherwise	H_a3e	Supported
OPACCT	1 if audit opinion indicates company's financials are prepared in accordance with IASs 0 otherwise	H_a3f	Not supported
OPAUDIT	1 if audit opinion indicates company follows international standards of audit 0 otherwise	H_a3g	Supported
Panel B: Compliance			
ASSETS	Total assets in U.S. dollars	H_a4a	Not supported
LISTING	1 if U.S. listing or U.S. filing 0 otherwise	H_a4b	Supported
PROFIT	*NI before tax/Total SE*	H_a4c	Not supported
INDUSTRY	1 if Manufacturing 0 otherwise	H_a4d	Not supported
POLICY	1 if accounting policy footnote indicates IASs are the basis for the financials 0 otherwise	H_a4e	Not supported
OPACCT	1 if audit opinion indicates company's financials are prepared in accordance with IASs 0 otherwise	H_a4f	Supported
OPAUDIT	1 if audit opinion indicates company follows international standards of audit 0 otherwise	H_a4g	Supported

IAS 12 (Income Taxes), IAS 19 (Employee Benefits), IAS 33 (Earnings Per Share), and IAS 37 (Provisions, Contingent Liabilities, and Contingent Assets).

For IAS 19, the disclosure checklist includes items required by the version effective for 1998 financial statements, items where disclosure is encouraged but not required, and the additional disclosures required by the 1998 revision of the IAS. 20-F companies supplied 80 percent of the employee benefit disclosures while the other companies provided only 54 percent. This difference is linked to 20-F companies exhibiting higher levels of compliance with IAS 19 (discussed in more detail under research question #2), and voluntarily supplying some of the additional disclosures that will be required by the 1998 revision (effective for periods beginning on or after January 1, 1999). For example, USINOR early-adopted IAS 19, thereby considerably increasing the company's overall level of disclosure in association with IAS 19.

Table 7. Mean Disclosure Index by Standard

IAS number	Subject of Standard	F	Pr>F
Panel A: Overall level of disclosure			
1	Accounting policies	0.22	0.6402
2	Inventories	0.29	0.5931
7	Cash flow statement	0.19	0.6620
8	Net profit/loss, errors, and changes in policy	1.61	0.2044
9	Research and development	4.44	0.0353*
10	Subsequent events	2.33	0.1275
12	Income taxes	6.69	0.0098**
13	Presentation of current assets and current liab	0.52	0.4697
14(a)	Segment reporting (geographic)	0.23	0.6343
14(b)	Segment reporting (line of business)	0.05	0.8152
16	Property, plant, and equipment	2.09	0.1489
17	Leases	0.27	0.6010
18	Revenue	1.15	0.2828
19	Employee benefits	9.21	0.0024**
20	Government grants and government assistance	1.41	0.2351
21	Foreign exchange rates	0.64	0.4235
22	Business combinations	0.16	0.6916
23	Borrowing costs	0.52	0.4704
24	Related party disclosures	0.01	0.9047
25	Accounting for investments	1.26	0.2611
27	Consolidated financial and inv. in subsidiaries	2.38	0.1234
28	Investments in associates	0.35	0.5514
29	Hyperinflationary economies	4.79	0.0287*
31	Interests in joint ventures	2.65	0.1038
32	Financial instruments: Disclosure and presentation	0.55	0.4572
33	Earnings per share	8.37	0.0038**
34	Interim financial reporting	0.53	0.4678
35	Discontinuing operations	0.01	0.9301
36	Impairment of assets	0.69	0.4065
37	Provisions, contingent liabilities and assets	7.67	0.0056**
38	Intangible assets	0.14	0.7103
Panel B: Compliance			
1	Accounting policies	0.6825	0.4089
2	Inventories	0.8758	0.3495
7	Cash flow statement	0.7528	0.3857
8	Net profit/loss, errors, and changes in policy	5.5966	0.0181*
9	Research and development	0.5669	0.4516
10	Subsequent events	1.1897	0.2755
12	Income taxes	11.3374	0.0008***
13	Presentation of current assets and current liab	2.2738	0.1318
14(a)	Segment reporting (geographic)	1.0641	0.3024
14(b)	Segment reporting (line of business)	1.8921	0.1691
16	Property, plant, and equipment	2.2685	0.1322
17	Leases	12.2944	0.0005***
18	Revenue	0.8792	0.3486
19	Emloyee benefits	7.2755	0.0071**
20	Government grants and government assistance	0.0855	0.7700
21	Foreign exchange rates	0.1116	0.7384

(continued on next page)

Table 7. (*Continued*)

IAS number	Subject of Standard	F	Pr>F
Panel B: Compliance			
22	Business combinations	0.0001	0.9940
23	Borrowing costs	4.0513	0.0443*
24	Related party disclosures	0.0000	1.0000
25	Accounting for investments	2.2136	0.1370
27	Consolidated financials and Inv. in subsidiaries	0.8494	0.3569
28	Investments in associates	0.3590	0.5491
29	Hyperinflationary economies	0.0000	1.0000
31	Interests in joint ventures	1.0928	0.2960
32	Financial instruments: Disclosure and presentation	3.1332	0.0769
33	Earnings per share	5.1078	0.0239*
35	Discontinuing operations	3.1583	0.0757
36	Impairment of assets	0.9870	0.3206
37	Provisions, contingent liabilities and assets	0.7167	0.3973
38	Intangible assets	0.4797	0.4887

* $p < 0.05$.
** $p < 0.01$.
*** $p < 0.001$.

Some of the significant differences in the overall level of disclosure are solely associated with higher levels of noncompliance for companies without U.S. listings. The disclosure checklist included only IASC-required disclosures for IASs 12 and 33. While 20-F companies exhibit relatively high levels of compliance with IAS 12 (96%), the level of compliance is only 74 percent for the other companies. IAS 12 Revised became mandatory for 1998 financial statements and was not well-received by several sample companies, particularly those without U.S. listings. For example, in the accounting policies notes, Bongrain (French), China Motion Telecom (Chinese), Lafarge (French), and Lectra (French), acknowledged noncompliance with IAS 12. None of these companies have NYSE or NASDAQ listings. Additionally, for companies utilizing the liability method required by IAS 12 Revised, several companies with U.S. filings or without U.S. listings or filings omitted disclosures, such as:

- The expiration date of deductible temporary differences,
- The amount of deferred tax income/expense in respect of each type of temporary difference.

Our analysis reveals that 20-F companies provided 89 percent of the disclosures required by IAS 9, but other companies provided only 70 percent of the IASC-required disclosures. For IAS 33, 20-F companies provided 94 percent of the disclosures while other companies provided only 70 percent. Examples of disclosures omitted more frequently by companies that do not file Form 20-F include:

- IAS 9: amount of R&D charged as expense; for those capitalizing some development cost, the useful lives of assets used in R&D activities or the amortization rates used;

- IAS 33: amounts used in the numerators and denominators for basic and diluted EPS; a few did not disclose EPS.

IAS 37 becomes effective for periods beginning on or after July 1, 1999. Therefore, the companies were not required to provide these disclosures in their 1998 financial statements, but the 20-F companies voluntarily provided 82 percent of the disclosures. For example, USINOR early-adopted the standard and provided all the required disclosures. The other companies without a U.S. listing voluntarily provided only 59 percent of the disclosures. IAS 37 will require disclosures such as a reconciliation of the beginning and ending balance for each class of provision and an indication of the uncertainties about the amount and timing of cash flow associated with provisions.

The findings associated with research question #2 address noncompliance with IASs, which is an area of great concern to the IASC, IFAC, and securities market regulators such as the SEC. In line with Cairns (1999) and Street et al. (1999), the findings indicate that compliance with IASs is very mixed and somewhat selective.

The findings reveal that compliance with IASC-required disclosures for companies with U.S. listings or filings (84%) significantly exceeds the extent of compliance exhibited by companies without U.S. listings or filings (76%). A series of protected t-tests identifies significant differences in the compliance measures for each IAS.[11] The t-tests indicate significant differences associated with (See Panel B, Table 7):

- IAS 8 (net profit or loss for the period; 84% vs. 65%),
- IAS 12 (income taxes; 87% vs. 66%),
- IAS 17 (leases; 82% vs. 59%),
- IAS 19 (employee benefits; 77% vs. 60%),
- IAS 23 (borrowing costs; 60% vs. 46%), and
- IAS 33 (earnings per share; 80% vs. 66%).

While the extent of noncompliance with IASs 8, 17, 19, and 23 is more pronounced for companies without U.S. listings or filings, it is problematic for the entire sample and is accordingly discussed below.

As noted in the discussion of research question #1, some companies acknowledged noncompliance with IAS 12 Revised. Three of the four (Bongrain, Lectra, and China Motion Telecom) have no U.S. listings or filings. Additionally, for companies utilizing the liability method required by IAS 12 Revised, companies without U.S. listings or filings more frequently omitted disclosures such as those noted above.

As noted in the discussion of research question #1, some companies without U.S. listings or filings did not disclose the amount used in the numerator to calculate basic and diluted EPS or the weighted average number of shares used as the denominator in calculating basic and diluted EPS. Additionally, some companies without U.S. listings or filings simply did not disclose EPS.

A review of the average level of compliance with IASs for the entire sample indicates several standards where compliance is less than 75 percent. These include:

IAS 8 (net profit or loss for the period; 75%),
IAS 14 in regard to geographic disclosures (segment reporting; 60%),

IAS 17 (leases; 71%),
IAS 19 (employee benefits; 69%),
IAS 23 (borrowing costs; 53%),
IAS 29 (financial reporting in hyperinflationary economies; 56%),
IAS 31 (joint ventures; 57%).

While the degree of compliance with IAS 29 gives reason for concern, it is important to note that the standard was not applicable for the majority of sample companies. Of the nine companies for which IAS 29 is applicable, only one (a 20-F company) provided all the required IAS disclosures.

With respect to IAS 8, several companies, particularly those without U.S. listings or filings, failed to provide the disclosures required for a change in accounting policy that should have been provided in association with the adoption of IAS 12 Revised. For example, several did not provide the amount of the adjustment related to each period presented.

With respect to IAS 14, noncompliance was particularly evident with regard to geographic disclosures. For example, several companies provided only sales data by geographic region as required by the European Union Directives although information contained elsewhere in the annual report strongly suggested additional disclosures such as operating profit and assets by geographic region were warranted.

Among the companies that disclosed material amounts of assets subject to finance leases, several failed to provide other IAS 17-required disclosures such as commitments for minimum leases payments. In association with operating leases, some companies reported rental expense for the period and indicated continuing commitments for several years; however, several of these companies did not disclose the amounts of these future commitments as required by IAS 17. Further, several companies claimed to early-adopt the standard, but failed to provide relevant new disclosures.

A troubling number of companies with defined benefit pension plans failed to provide all the disclosures required by IAS 19. Compliance was particularly low in regard to disclosure of the fair value of the plan assets, the actuarial present value of the promised benefits, and a description of the principle actuarial assumptions used in determining the cost of retirement benefits.

With the exception of some Chinese companies, most companies utilizing the IAS 23 allowed alternative did not disclose the capitalization rate used to determine the amount of borrowing costs eligible for capitalization. Some utilizing the allowed alternative also failed to disclose the amount of borrowing costs capitalized for the period. A few companies with significant amounts reported under construction in progress failed to even disclose the accounting policy for borrowing costs.

For several companies with material interests in joint ventures, compliance with IAS 31-required disclosures is limited or nonexistent. Most, but not all, provided a list of the significant joint ventures. However, many of the companies failed to disclose the aggregate amounts of current assets, current liabilities, long-term assets, income, and expenses related to these joint ventures.

The findings associated with research question #3 indicate the overall level of disclosure is significantly associated with:

- Listing status,

- The type of auditing standards adhered to as stated in the audit opinion, and
- The manner in which the accounting policies footnote makes reference to the use of IASs.

Specifically, the overall level of disclosure provided by companies with U.S. listings (20-F companies) exceeds the overall level of disclosure provided by companies with U.S. filings and companies with no U.S. listings or filings. Additionally, more disclosure is associated with an accounting policies footnote stating that IASs are the primary reporting standards used by the company and where no exceptions to the use of IASs are noted. Alternatively, lower disclosure is associated with an accounting policies footnote that refers to IASs in another manner. For example, the company may note compliance with domestic GAAP and IAS, note exceptions to compliance with IASs, or claim the financial statements are based on domestic GAAP but that they also comply with IAS in all material aspects or are consistent with IAS. More disclosure is also associated with an audit opinion that makes a specific reference to the utilization of ISAs issued by IFAC. Alternatively, lower disclosure is associated with an audit opinion that makes reference to the use of domestic auditing standards, professional standards, generally accepted auditing standards, or principles of proper annual account audit.

These findings are consistent with prior research that indicates a significant association between listing status and overall level of disclosure. While prior studies also indicate that variables including size and profitability may be associated with overall level of disclosure, our results suggest a different scenario for companies that refer to the use of IASs. In addition to listing status, our findings indicate that the accounting policies footnote and the audit opinion provide a better indication of the overall level of disclosure.

Extending prior research by Cairns (1999) and Street et al. (1999), the findings associated with research question #4 indicate the degree of compliance with IASs is significantly associated with:

- Listing status,
- The manner in which the audit opinion addresses the type of accounting standards used by the company, and
- The manner in which the audit opinion addresses the auditing standards adhered to.

Specifically, compliance with IASs for companies that file Form 20-F to achieve a NYSE or NASDAQ listing or with U.S. filings exceeds compliance for those companies with no U.S. listings or filings. Greater compliance is also associated with an audit opinion that specifically states that the financials are prepared in accordance with IAS. Alternatively, lower compliance is associated with an audit opinion that either makes reference to IASs with noted exceptions or makes no reference to IASs. Greater compliance is also associated with an audit opinion that makes a specific reference to the utilization of ISAs as issued by IFAC. Alternatively, lower compliance is associated with an audit opinion that makes reference to the use of domestic auditing standards, professional standards, generally accepted auditing standards, or principles of proper annual account audit.

CONCLUSION

For companies that make reference to the use of IASs, this research reveals that the overall level of disclosure is greater for companies with U.S. listings. Additionally, greater disclosure is associated with an accounting policies footnote that specifically states the financial statements are prepared in accordance with IASs and an audit opinion that states that ISAs were followed when conducting the audit.

The findings also indicate that the extent of compliance with IASs is greater for companies with U.S. listings or filings. Additionally, a higher level of compliance is associated with an audit opinion, which states that the financial statements are in accordance with IASs and that ISAs were followed when conducting the audit. These findings highlight the significance of the enforcement issue for the IASC as it seeks an IOSCO endorsement. Our findings indicate enforcement of IASs may be less of an issue for companies with listings and filings in the U.S. However, for companies without U.S. listings and filings, compliance is indeed of great concern. In light of this problem, the IFAC has criticized auditors for asserting that financial statements comply with IASs when the accounting policies and other notes show otherwise.

For companies making reference to IASs, the findings suggest that auditors have not addressed this issue directly. Instead of insisting that companies remove any reference to IASs unless the statements are indeed in full compliance with IASs, auditors indirectly signal the extent of compliance via wording in the audit opinion. The findings suggest that the financial statement user should question compliance with IASs unless the audit opinion specifically says the statements are prepared in accordance with IASs and the audit was conducted in accordance with ISAs. However, this situation needs to change.

Recently, the Big 5+2 international accounting firms joined forces to address accounting and auditing issues associated with globalization of business and capital markets, chaos in financial reporting, and the Asian Financial Crisis (Blanchet, 2000). A report by the United Nations Conference on Trade and Development noted that an analysis of the causes of the financial crisis that affected East Asia raises serious questions about transparency, *disclosure*, and the role of accounting and reporting in producing reliable and relevant information. The UN report clearly stated that *inadequate disclosure* was a contributing factor to the depth and breadth of the crisis. Additionally, the UN report stated that the local member firms of the Big 5 were involved in auditing most of the large corporations and banks in the East Asian countries. Many of the East Asian companies that received a clean bill of health from their auditors proved to be "not a going concern" within a few months from the completion of the audit.

According to Muis (Vice President and Controller of the World Bank), the World Bank has asked the Big 5 to make sure they do not confuse the world by associating their international good name with financial statements prepared and/or audited far below international standards. The World Bank argues it is in the long-term interest of the Big 5 in terms of quality brand naming, and at the same time, useful for the clarity of the less initiated financial statement users that these problems be addressed.

In response to concerns expressed by not only the UN and World Bank, but also the SEC, the Big 5+2 have agreed to address the issues of noncompliance and limited disclosure of accounting information. Indeed, the findings of this research reveal that the problem is widespread and not limited to Asia. The Big 5+2 plan is revolutionary as it encompasses all countries, all companies, and all auditors (Blanchet, 2000). The plan focuses on strengthening the accounting profession's international organizations and further developing international accounting standards and international standards of auditing. The goal is to prepare all financial information following a single worldwide framework, with common measurement and fair and *comprehensive disclosure*, which provides a transparent representation of the economics of transactions, and is consistently applied. To achieve this goal, the Big 5+2 will continue to work towards the development of high quality IASs, promote the IASC as the international accounting standards setter, and work to raise auditing standards and practices in all countries to common high standards with ISA as the benchmark.

If successfully implemented, the Big 5+2 plan should greatly assist in addressing several of the problems highlighted by the current research. Our findings suggest that raising the quality of auditing standards internationally is of the utmost importance. As all the sample companies made reference to IASs, and most were audited by Big 5+2 firms, it is reasonable for users to assume that at a minimum, the financial statements provide all IASC-required disclosures. However, the findings reveal numerous troubling instances of noncompliance particularly for companies with no U.S. listings or filings. The findings also indicate that voluntary disclosures tend to be limited unless the company has a U.S. listing.

With the issuance of 1999 financial statements, companies should no longer refer to the use of IAS unless they comply with each and every IAS (via a recent revision of IAS 1). The Big 5 + 2 must insist on compliance with IAS 1 Revised and refuse to sign clean audit opinions unless the financials statements are indeed in total compliance with all IASs and provide all IASC-required disclosures. The Big 5+2 have suggested this can be achieved by having companies that utilize standards that are "similar" to IASs provide legends in the accounting footnotes. A legend verbally describes significant differences with IAS. A legend would replace companies stating in the accounting policies footnote that the financial statements are "in compliance with IAS with noted exceptions" or "are consistent with IASs in all material aspects."

Given the rapid growth in cross-border listings and U.S. holdings of foreign securities, it is crucial that the Big 5+2 raise audit quality to a commonly high standard throughout the world and promote the enforcement of IASs. An IOSCO endorsement of IASs could further stimulate cross-border listings in the world's major capital markets. Additionally, acceptance of one set of high quality global accounting standards would greatly enhance the understandability of financial statements for analysts and other users. However, an IOSCO endorsement of IASs is unlikely to occur in the foreseeable future if the limited disclosure and noncompliance with IASC-required disclosures revealed by this research continue to be the norm. Enforcement and acceptance of IASs on a global basis is likely contingent on the successful and timely implementation of the Big 5+2 vision.

Acknowledgment: The authors wish to thank Barry Moser for his guidance regarding the use of HOLM's step-down analysis.

Editors Note: The editor invited this paper for publication in The International Journal of Accounting.

NOTES

1. In line with Cerf (1961), Buzby (1975) reported that the extent of disclosure was not significantly associated with listing status. Buzby defined listed companies as those with common stock traded on the NYSE or AMEX. Unlisted companies included those with stock traded in the U.S. OTC market.

2. While the findings of Adhikari and Tondkar (1992) suggest that a London listing may be associated with greater levels of disclosure, our analysis indicates that the levels of disclosure and compliance with IASs for London-listed companies are not in line with those provided by companies with U.S. listings or filings. Thus, companies with London listings (that do not also have a U.S. listing or filing) are included in the group with no U.S. listings or filings, but no further analysis is reported for these companies.

3. For four companies it was not possible to match on country. In these instances, the match was selected from a country with a similar culture.

4. It was not known until the ANOVA results were obtained from testing H_a1 and H_a2 how to identify the grouping for the LISTING variable for the regression equation.

5. IAS 11 (Construction Contracts), IAS 15 (Information Reflecting Effects of Changing Prices), IAS 26 (Accounting and Reporting by Retirement Benefit Plans), and IAS 30 (Disclosures in the Financial Statements of Banks and Similar Financial Institutions) were excluded as these standards are not applicable for the sample companies. IAS 3 (Superseded by IAS 27 and 28), IAS 5 (Superseded by IAS 1), and IAS 6 were excluded in that they have been superseded by newer IASs.

6. These included IAS 1 (Presentation of Financial Statements), IAS 14 (Segment Reporting), IAS 17 (Leases), IAS 19 (Retirement Benefits), and IAS 22 (Business Combinations).

7. These included IAS 35 (Discontinued Operations), IAS 36 (Impairment of Long-Lived Assets), IAS 37 (Provisions, Contingent Liabilities, and Contingent Assets), IAS 38 (Intangible Assets).

8. SAS's PROC GLM procedure was used due to the unbalanced design.

9. A major (in excess of 0.90) correlation coefficient is generally indicative of a multicollinearity problem. The highest correlation coefficient was 0.70, between POLICY and OPACCT.

10. The highest correlation coefficient was again 0.70 between POLICY and OPACCT.

11. SAS's PROC MULTTEST using HOLM's step-down method was used to adjust for multiplicity in testing.

REFERENCES

Adhikari, Ajax and Ross H. Tondkar. 1992. "Environmental Factors Influencing Accounting Disclosure Requirements of Global Stock Exchanges." *Journal of International Financial Management and Accounting, 3*(2) (Summer).

Bank of New York 2000. *ADR Investor.* (http://site-by-site.com/adr/).

Belkaoui, Ahmed and A. Kahl, 1978. *Corporate Financial Disclosure in Canada*, Research Monograph of the Canadian Certified General Accountants Association, Vancouver.

Blanchet, Jeannot. 2000. "Globalization and the Future of Accounting and Auditing." In Presented at AAA International Accounting Section Mid-Year Meeting, January 9–10, Tampa, FL.

Buzby, Stephen L. 1975. "Company Size, Listed Versus Unlisted Stocks, and the Extent of Financial Disclosure." *Journal of Accounting Research,* (Spring) *13*(1): 16–37.

Cairns, David. 1997. "IFAC—20 Years On." *World Accounting Report,* (October): 2.

Cairns, David. 1999. *The FT International Accounting Standards Survey 1999.* London: Financial Times.

Cerf, R. A. 1961. *Corporate Reporting and Investment Decisions*. Berkley, CA: University of California Press.

Cooke, T. 1989. *An Empirical Study of Financial Disclosure by Swedish Companies*. New York: Garland Publishing.

Cooke, T. 1989. "Disclosure in the Corporate Annual Reports of Swedish Companies." *Accounting and Business Research, 19*(74): 113–124.

Cooke, T. 1991. "An Assessment of Voluntary Disclosure in Annual Reports of Japanese Corporation." *International Journal of Accounting, 26*(3): 174–189.

Cooke, T. 1992. "The Impact of Size, Stock Market Listing and Industry Type on Disclosure in the Annual Reports of Japanese Listed Corporations." *Accounting and Business Research, 22*(87): 229–237.

Cooke, T. 1993. "Disclosure in Japanese Corporate Reports." *Journal of Business Finance and Accounting*, June *20*(4): 521–535.

Dumontier, Pascal and Bernard Raffournier. 1998. "Why Firms Comply Voluntarily with IAS: An Empirical Analysis with Swiss Data." *Journal of International Financial Management and Accounting, 9*(3): 216–245.

Firth, Michael. 1979. "Impact of Size, Stock Market Listing and Auditors on Voluntary Disclosure in Corporate Annual Reports." *Accounting and Business Research, 9*(36): 273–280.

IASC 1999. "IOSCO Aims for a Timely Review of Core Standards." *IASC Insight*, June: 1–2.

IASC 2000. *Companies Referring To their Use of IAS*. http://www.iasc.org.uk./frame/cen1_7.htm.

Inchausti, B. 1997. "The Influence of Company Characteristics and Accounting Regulation on Information Disclosed by Spanish Firms." *European Accounting Review, 6*(1): 45–68.

McNally, Graeme, Lee Hock Eng, and C. Roy Hasseldine. 1982. "Corporate Financial Reporting in New Zealand: An Analysis of Users Preferences, Corporate Characteristics and Disclosure Practices for Discretionary Information." *Accounting and Business Research*, (Winter): 11–20.

Neter, John, William Wasserman, and Michael Kutner. 1989. *Applied Linear Regression Models*, 2nd edn. Boston, MA: Irwin.

SEC. 1996. Press Release 11, April.

SEC. 1999. "A Message from the Chief Accountant of the U.S. Securities Exchange Commission." *COSMOS Accountancy Chronicle, 11*(1), January: 5.

SEC. 2000. *List of Foreign Issuers which have Submitted Information Under the Exemption Relating to Certain Foreign Securities*. http://www.sec.gov/rules/othern/34-39681.htm.

Singhvi, Surendra and Harsha Desai. 1971. "An Empirical Analysis of the Quality of Corporate Financial Disclosure." *Accounting Review*, January *46*(1): 129–138.

Street, Donna L., Sid J. Gray, and Stephanie M. Bryant. 1999. "Acceptance and Observance of International Accounting Standards: An Empirical Study of Companies Claiming to Comply with IASs." *The International Journal of Accounting, 34*(1): 11–48.

Wallace, R. S. Olusegan and Kamal Naser. 1995. "Firm-Specific Determinants of the Comprehensiveness of Mandatory Disclosure in the Corporate Annual Reports of Firms Listed on the Stock Exchange of Hong Kong." *Journal of Accounting and Public Policy, 14*(4): 311–368.

Wallace, R. S. Olusegan, Kamal Naser, and Araceli Mora. 1994. "The Relationship Between the Comprehensiveness of Corporate Annual Reports and Firm Characteristics in Spain." *Accounting and Business Research, 25*(97): 41–53.

[16]

The International
Journal of
Accounting

Acceptance and Observance of International Accounting Standards: An Empirical Study of Companies Claiming to Comply with IASs

Donna L. Street,* Sidney J. Gray,† and Stephanie M. Bryant*
James Madison University and University of New South Wales†

Key Words: International Accounting Standards; IASC: Comparability Project; Compliance with IASs

Abstract: *This article reports on an empirical study of the accounting policies and disclosures of a sample of major companies from around the world claiming to comply with IASs in 1996. Specifically, the research addresses the extent of compliance with the IASs revised during the Comparability Project. The findings reveal significant noncompliance with IASs including: use of LCM for inventories; violation of the all-inclusive requirement for reporting profit/loss and of the strict definition of extraordinary items; failure to capitalize certain development costs; failure to provide all required disclosures for property, plant, and equipment, particularly those associated with revaluations; failure to comply with pension disclosure requirements; for companies operating in hyperinflationary economies, failure to restate foreign entities in accordance with IAS 29; and charging goodwill to reserves or amortizing goodwill over a period in excess of the 20 year limit. Noncompliance, as evidenced by the current research, is very problematic for the IASC as it strives to achieve an IOSCO endorsement and as IAS 1 Revised becomes effective for 1999 financial statements.*

Currently, the International Accounting Standards Committee (IASC) is completing an intensive work program to develop a core set of accounting standards for the purpose of cross-border securities market listings and capital raisings. The IASC and several of its major constituents hope these standards will be endorsed by the International Organization of Securities Commissions (IOSCO) and thus provide significant support for the acceptance and observance of International Accounting Standards (IASs). During the Comparability Project, the IASC revised ten IASs, effective 1995, to incorporate a more uniform approach. Additional standards have been and are currently being developed and introduced in accordance with the agreement with IOSCO to complete a core set of IASs by 1999.

Direct all correspondence to: Donna L. Street, School of Accounting MSC 0203, James Madison University. Harrisonburg, VA 22807. U.S.A.; E-mail: streetdl@jmu.edu.

The International Journal of Accounting, Vol. 34, No. 1, pp. 11-48   ISSN: 0020-7063.

It would seem opportune at this critical point in the 25-year history of the IASC to assess the extent to which IASs are currently being accepted and observed by companies in practice. While compliance is an issue of substantial importance, the IASC is also concerned that companies claiming compliance may not in fact be complying with all of the requirements of IASs. In this regard, the President of the International Federation of Accountants (IFAC) has also criticized auditors for asserting that financial statements comply with IASs when the accounting policies and other notes show otherwise (Cairns, 1997). The recent revision of IAS 1 to require companies stating that they are in compliance with IASs to comply with all IASs without exception reflects these concerns.

The purpose of this research is to report on an empirical study of the accounting policies and disclosures of a sample of major companies from around the world claiming to comply with IASs in 1996. Companies that have voluntarily adopted IASs and claim to comply with them should provide a good test of IAS's relevance and feasibility in practice. The key research questions addressed are as follows:

- To what extent are companies claiming to comply with IASs doing so in practice?
- What are the most important areas of measurement and disclosure noncompliance?
- What are the implications of noncompliance for the acceptance and observance of IASs in the future?

INTERNATIONAL HARMONIZATION PRESSURES

Pressures for the international harmonization of accounting have grown rapidly since the early 1970s when the IASC was established, along with the development of stock markets internationally and the growth of international investment. The benefits of international accounting standards include the reduction of investment risks and cost of capital worldwide, the lowering of costs arising from multiple reporting, the elimination of confusion arising from different measures of financial position and performance across countries, the encouragement of international investment, and the more efficient allocation of savings worldwide (Sharpe, 1998). However, while IASs issued during the 1970s and 1980s were recognized to have made some progress towards international harmonization, by the late 1980s the performance of the IASC was increasingly criticized because of the flexibility of IASs and a continuing lack of comparability across country borders.

An important development at this time was the agreement of the IASC and IOSCO in 1988 to work together to find a way to allow a company to list its securities in any foreign stock market on the basis of one set of financial statements conforming to IASs (Cairns, 1995). The IASC responded with its 1989 Comparability Project defined in Exposure Draft (E) 32, *Comparability of Financial Statements* (IASC, 1989). The aim of the proposals in E 32 was to eliminate most of the choices of accounting methods then permitted so as to enhance the credibility and acceptability of IASs by the international investment community.

The outcome of the Comparability Project was the revision of ten IASs, effective 1995, including the elimination of twenty hitherto permitted accounting methods (IASC, 1993). However, subsequent to completion of the Comparability Project,

Table 1.   Sample Selection

Companies	Number
Number of companies in initial sample provided by the IASC	221
Companies that do not claim to comply with international accounting standards in the annual report or are in noncompliance on more than two relevant standards	(32)
Companies that were acquired or otherwise merged with other companies that do not claim to comply with international accounting standards	(5)
Companies for which Worldscope Disclosure or Financial Times is not available	(82)
Companies in a regulated industry, banks, and nonprofit companies	(16)
Companies with sales less than 1 billion annually for 1995	(33)
Duplicate companies	(3)
Companies for which an English annual report is not readily available	(1)
Final sample	**49**

IOSCO indicated that further work would be required and provided a list of core standards that it might be willing to accept subject to the full program being completed by the end of 1999. This deadline was subsequently brought forward by the IASC to March 1998 and now late 1998 with the completion of the core standard on financial instruments.

While the endorsement of IOSCO's technical committee is yet to be received, the prospect of such an endorsement has led to growing support for the IASC by national standard-setters. IASs have been adopted by law in some countries (e.g., Malta) and by accountancy bodies (e.g., Malaysia and Singapore). In a recent noteworthy move, Belgium, France, Germany, and Italy have agreed to permit certain companies to use IASs in their consolidated financial statements instead of existing national requirements (IASC, 1998a). Perhaps most importantly, a growing number of companies are voluntarily adopting IASs, including multinationals such as Bayer, Fiat, Lafarge, Nestle, and Nokia. The nature and extent of compliance with IASs by these companies is the focus of this research.

METHODOLOGY

Sample Selection

A list of 221 companies claiming to comply with IASs in one or more years was obtained from the IASC in late 1996. The IASC has publicized the fact that these companies have stated their voluntary commitment to comply with IASs. A search was conducted in *WorldScope* and the *Financial Times* databases for information on each of these companies. Companies not represented in at least one of these databases were excluded on significance grounds. Annual reports for 1996 were requested for companies that met the following additional significance criteria:

- 1995 sales of at least $1 billion
- Nonregulated, nonfinancial industry, by reference to SIC code

14   THE INTERNATIONAL JOURNAL OF ACCOUNTING   Vol. 34, No. 1, 1999

Table 2. Companies in Final Sample (by Country), $n = 49$

Company	Country	1995 Sales (in U.S. dollars)
Alcan Aluminum	Canada	9,287,000,000
Dominion Textile	Canada	1,041,193,000
Huhtamaki	Finland	1,788,162,000
Metra	Finland	2,422,906,000
Nokia	Finland	8,400,410,000
Aerospatiale	France	10,035,705,000
Bongrain	France	2,022,888,000
Eridania Beghin-Say	France	10,357,819,000
Essilor	France	1,332,902,000
Lafarge	France	6,772,154,000
Moulinex	France	1,599,017,000
Renault	France	37,525,332,000
Saint-Gobain	France	14,334,100,000
Usinor	France	15,988,097,000
Valeo	France	5,143,640,000
Bayer	Germany	31,022,776,000
Heidelberger Zement	Germany	4,202,161,000
Schering	Germany	3,234,122,000
Jardine Matheson	Hong Kong	10,636,000,000
Fiat	Italy	47,101,950,000
Olivetti	Italy	6,160,292,000
Pirelli	Italy	6,862,794,000
Fujitsu	Japan	37,626,504,000
Kirin Brewery	Japan	15,794,011,000
Toray	Japan	10,400,798,000
Multi-Purpose Holdings	Malaysia	1,131,061,000
Kvaerner	Norway	4,682,922,000
AECI	South Africa	1,838,980,000
South African Breweries	South Africa	7,189,845,000
AGA	Sweden	1,984,015,000
Astra	Sweden	5,352,100,000
Atlas	Sweden	3,655,873,000
Autoliv	Sweden	1,525,050,000
Esselte	Sweden	1,687,020,000
Perstorp	Sweden	1,918,347,000
Stora	Sweden	8,537,347,000
Trelleborg	Sweden	3,184,948,000
Alusuisse-Lonza	Switzerland	6,490,460,000
Electrowatt	Switzerland	2,501,036,000
Forbo	Switzerland	1,548,005,000
Georg Fischer	Switzerland	1,958,403,000
Holderbank	Switzerland	7,166,369,000
Jelmoli	Switzerland	1,623,741,000
Nestle	Switzerland	48,946,210,000
Oerlikon-Buhrle	Switzerland	3,129,112,000
Saurer	Switzerland	1,127,091,000
Sika	Switzerland	1,166,264,000
Sulzer	Switzerland	4,973,997,000
Von Roll	Switzerland	1,530,327,000

TABLE 3. Statements Regarding Compliance with IASs

Company	Footnote on Accounting Principles	Audit Opinion
PANEL A: COMPANIES THAT NOTE FULL COMPLIANCE WITH IASs		
AGA	Recommendations of Swedish Financial Accounting Standards Board (in all essential aspects in accordance with IASC rules; differences do not concern AGA)	Swedish Companies Act
Alcan Aluminum	• Canada GAAP • In all material respects with principles established by IASC (Responsibility for annual report)	Canadian GAAP
Alusuisse-Lonza	Current IAS, published by IASC	• IASs of the IASC • 4th and 7th EU Directives • Swiss Law • Listing Rules of Swiss Exchange
Bayer	• German law • Rules issued by IASC (current version)	• Fully complied with IASs • German law
Bongrain	• Internationally accepted principles set forth by IASC • Provisions of the Law	True and fair view
Dominion Textile	• Canadian GAAP • In all material respects with standards of IASC	Generally accepted accounting principles
Essilor	Accounting principles recommended by the IASC	Present fairly…
Forbo	• IASs as issued by IASC • Swiss Code of Obligations	The law and articles of incorporation
Heidelberger Zement	• German Commercial Code • Standards of IASC (Significant items requiring different treatment under IAS and HGB not present)	Standards of IASC
Holderbank	• IASs as published by IASC (since 1991) • Swiss Accounting and Reporting Recommendations	The law and articles of incorporation.
Jardine Matheson	IASs	• IASs • Bermuda Companies Act
Jelmoli	IASs issued by IASC	The law and articles of incorporation
Moulinex	• French GAAP • Principles formulated by IASC	True and fair view
Multi-Purpose Holdings	• Companies Act 1965 • IASs adopted by Malaysian Institute of Accountants	Companies Act 1965
Nestle	IASs issued by IASC	• IAS • The law
Pirelli	• Legislative Decree No. 127 • Standards issued by the IASC…	True and fair view
Saurer	• IASs • Swiss Accounting and Reporting Recommendations	The law and articles of incorporation.

(continued)

THE INTERNATIONAL JOURNAL OF ACCOUNTING   Vol. 34, No. 1, 1999

16

TABLE 3.   (Continued)

Company	Footnote on Accounting Principles	Audit Opinion
PANEL A: COMPANIES THAT NOTE FULL COMPLIANCE WITH IASs		
Sika	Regulations of IASC	IASs The law
Sulzer	Standards formulated by IASC	Full compliance with IASs (for first time)
Trelleborg	Swedish Financial Accounting Council's recommendations (in substance correspond with IASC's regulations)	Swedish Companies Act
PANEL B: COMPANIES THAT NOTE FULL COMPLIANCE WITH IASs WITH LIMITED EXCEPTIONS		
Aerospatiale	Internationally accepted accounting principles as recommended by IASC (except IAS 8, profit and loss, and IAS 32, financial instruments)	Present fairly…
AECI	• GAAP in South Africa • In most respects conform to IASs	• GAAP • Companies Act
Astra	• Swedish Financial Accounting Standards Council • In most respects IASs (exception, IAS 19 pensions)	Swedish Companies Act
Atlas	With few exceptions, IAS (Exceptions, translation of foreign subsidiaries and amortization of goodwill)	Swedish Companies Act
Autoliv	In all material respects, IASs (Exception, for reasons of competition, sales and income are not by country)	Swedish Companies Act
Eridania Beghin-Say	• French legislation • Standards formulated by IASC (exception, IAS 22 concerning amortization periods for goodwill)	True and fair view
Electrowatt	• EU's 4th and 7th Directives • Guidelines of IASC (exception, goodwill)	• 4th and 7th Directives of EU • IAS of IASC
Esselte	• Recommendations of Financial Accounting Standards Council • Guidelines formulated by IASC (exception pensions reported per accounting practices in countries where Esselte has operations)	Swedish Companies Act

(continued)

TABLE 3. (Continued)

Company	Footnote on Accounting Principles	Audit Opinion
PANEL B: COMPANIES THAT NOTE FULL COMPLIANCE WITH IASs WITH LIMITED EXCEPTIONS		
Fiat	Italian legislation (consistent with IASs, except IAS 9 requirement that development costs be capitalized)	True and fair view
Fujitsu	IASs (exceptions, translation of foreign currency accounts -and IAS 2 LCNRV—both not significant	Accounting principles generally accepted in Japan
Georg Fischer	• IASs (since 1993) (exception, for structural reasons information per segment on operating income and total assets) • 4th and 7th directives of the EU • Swiss shareholding law • Swiss Accounting and Reporting Recommendations	• IASs of IASC • 4th and 7th Directives of the EU • Swiss law • Accounting principles for Listing Rules of the Swiss Exchange
Huhtamaki	• Accounting standards issued by IASC • Finnish Accounting Standards (differences between FAS and IAS have largely disappeared except for depreciation on revalued tangible assets, untaxed reserves and taxation, and associated companies	Finnish accounting act
Kirin	Japanese Accounting Principles (differs from IASs for Consolidation and equity method of accounting, Tax effect accounting, Leases, and Marketable and investment securities)	IAS in all material respects, expect as described in Note 2
Kvaerner	• Norwegian GAAP • Broadly in compliance with IASs thus a note for reconciliation has not been made	Kjoint Stock Companies Act
Lafarge	• IAS (exception maximum amortization period for goodwill) • Provisions of French accounting legislation	• Accounting principles generally accepted in France • IASs, except for amortization of goodwill
Metra	Finnish accounting legislation and regulations (which in all essential respects correspond with IASs)	Accounting Act governing preparation of financial statements in Finland
Nokia	IASs and Finnish Accounting Standards (two sets of accounts of separate pages) Reconciliation between the financial statements under FAS and IAS presented	• IAS • Regulations governing preparation of financial statements in Finland • (Provides Finnish and IAS accounts)

(continued)

18   THE INTERNATIONAL JOURNAL OF ACCOUNTING   Vol. 34, No. 1, 1999

TABLE 3.   (Continued)

Company	Footnote on Accounting Principles	Audit Opinion
PANEL B: COMPANIES THAT NOTE FULL COMPLIANCE WITH IASs WITH LIMITED EXCEPTIONS		
Oerlikon-Buhrle	IAS (exceptions, segment information includes results by product groups, but not the results by geographic region and development costs at Group risk are not capitalized)	IAS with exceptions described in financial statements
Olivetti	Legislation by Italian accounting profession and, in absence thereof, by IASC	True and fair view
Perstorp	• Swedish Financial Accounting Standards Council's recommendations • In all important respects, IASC's recommendations, which fulfill requirements imposed on foreign companies listed on London Stock Exchange (exception, for practical reasons, does not fully adhere to IAS 7 regarding statements of changes in financial position)	Swedish Companies Act
Renault	• French regulations • IASs (exception, IAS 9 which requires capitalization of development costs, like other worldwide automobile manufacturers expenses such costs)	True and fair view
Saint- Gobain	• French law • IASs (exception, IAS 22 on goodwill amortisation period)	Accounting principles described in the notes
Schering	• German Commerical Code • Standards of IASC observed where they do not conflict with German Code (Differences due to principles of recognition and prudence —not material)	Standards of IASC
South African Breweries	• GAAP in South Africa • Standards of IASC (Exception goodwill)	Generally accepted accounting practice Companies Act
Stora	• Recommedations of Swedish Financial Accounting Standards Council • Recommendations issued by IASC (exceptions, reporting of hydropower assets sold on a sale and leaseback basis, capitalization of interest expense in connection with major investments, revaluations of fixed assets, reporting of proposed dividend as a liability, statement of changes in financial position)	Swedish Companies Act

(continued)

TABLE 3. (Continued)

Company	Footnote on Accounting Principles	Audit Opinion
PANEL B: COMPANIES THAT NOTE FULL COMPLIANCE WITH IASs WITH LIMITED EXCEPTIONS		
Toray	• Accounting principles generally accepted in Japan. • Overseas subsidiaries accounting practices prevailing in their respective domicile countries, but any significant departures from IASs which affect net income and net assets, are adjusted to comply with IAS and such adjusted financial statements are used for the purpose of consolidation	• Generally accepted accounting principles in Japan
Unisor	• French generally accepted accounting principles • IASs as prescribed by the IASC (exception, a non-recurring adjustment) • Summarizes differences with US GAAP	Conform with GAAP in France
Valeo	• French GAAP • IASs, (exception, IAS 9, like other international groups in automotive sector continues to expense these costs as incurred)	In accordance with French and international GAAP
Vonroll	• IASs as published by IASC • Recommended Swiss accounting principles.	• IASs (exception, value adjustment for steel activities recorded to equity without affecting the 1996 income statement, not in accordance with IAS 8 • Accounting Reporting Recommendations • The law

Data Collection

Each annual report was reviewed to confirm that the company claimed to comply with IASs in 1996. This information was located in the note on accounting principles and/or in the audit opinion. Companies were included in the sample if the annual report stated that IASs were followed, that IASs were followed with limited exceptions, or that exceptions to IASs were immaterial in nature. Companies noting noncompliance with more than two relevant IASs (i.e., one of the ten revised IASs resulting from the Comparability Project) were excluded.[1] Table 1 summarizes the sample selection procedure. The final sample consists of the 49 companies listed in Table 2. The companies are geographically dispersed, with

20   THE INTERNATIONAL JOURNAL OF ACCOUNTING   Vol. 34, No. 1, 1999

Table 4. Compliance with IASs Revised During the Comparability Project

	Number in Compliance	Number in Noncompliance	Comments
PANEL A: IAS 2, INVENTORIES			
Method			
Cost Formula	• 18 FIFO • 12 Weighted Average • 12 combination of IASC benchmark methods	• 1 industry practice (market price) • 1 Simplified procedures and market value where permissible	5 ND
Impairment	• 34 LCNRV • 1 Both LCNRV and LCM (immaterial)	• 13 LCM • 1 Both LCNRV and LCM	
Disclosures			
Any reversal of write-down recognized as expense reduction in period reversal occurs	2	0	47 Likely NA
Amount of any reversals of write-downs recognized in period	1	0	48 Likely NA
Circumstances leading to any reversals of write-downs	1	0	48 Likely NA
Carrying amount of inventories carried at NRV	14	1	34 Likely NA
Carrying amount of inventories pledged as collateral	11	0	38 Likely NA
Either cost of inventories recognized as expense during the period, or operating costs, applicable to revenues, recognized as an expense during the period, classified by their nature	• 44 • 1 operating profit before interest (interest charges, which were significant, classified in a footnote)	4 disclosed sales less operating costs applicable with no breakdown of operating expenses	
Total carrying amount of inventory	49	0	
Accounting policies, including cost formula	44	5	
Carrying amount of inventories in classifications appropriate to enterprise	45	2	2 Likely NA
PANEL B: IAS 8, NET PROFIT/LOSS			
Method			
All items of income/ expense included in net profit/loss for period	36	13	
Profit/loss from ordinary activities disclosed on income statement	49	0	

(continued)

Table 4. (Continued)

PANEL B: IAS 8, NET PROFIT/LOSS			
Extraordinary items disclosed on income statement		10 in noncompliance with the IASC's strict definition. See Table 5.	39 NA
Disclosure			
Both amount and nature of each extraordinary item	10	0	39 NA
PANEL C: IAS 9, RESEARCH AND DEVELOPMENT			
Method			
Research	40 expenses all	3 ND despite significant R&D activity (1 acknowledges non-compliance)	6 NA
Development	• 1 expenses all development costs • 8 capitalize development costs	• 3 ND despite significant R&D activity (1 acknowledged noncompliance) • 4 acknowledge noncompliance and expense all development costs	• 27 expense all development cost (cannot ascertain compliance or noncompliance) • 6 NA
Any capitalized development costs amortized on a systematic basis over 5 years or less	4 (of 8)		• 2 ND • 2 NA
Any capitalized development costs tested for impairment in subsequent periods and discussion of write-back of previously written-down capitalized development costs	2 (of 8)		• 6 ND
Disclosure			
Accounting policy	33 (of 43)	10	
Amount of R&D charged to expense during the period	33 (of 43)	10	
Amortization methods used	4 (of 8)	2	2 NA
Useful lives of assets used in R&D activities or amortization rates used	4 (of 8)	2	2 NA
Reconciliation of the balance of unamortized development costs at the beginning and end of the period	1 (of 8)	5	2 NA
PANEL D: IAS 16, PROPERTY, PLANT, AND EQUIPMENT			
Method			
Measurement after initial recognition	• 25 historical cost, benchmark • 11 revaluations for specific groups of PPE, alternative	1 revaluing fixed assets acknowledges noncompliance	12 revaluations per company law or tax regulations

(continued)

Table 4. (Continued)

PANEL D: IAS 16, PROPERTY, PLANT, AND EQUIPMENT			
Revaluations made with sufficient regularity	6 (of 12 electing to revalue fixed assets)	6	Likely not possible for revaluations per company law or tax regulations
Revaluations applied to the entire class of PPE	11 (of 12 electing to revalue fixed assets)		• Likely not possible for revaluations per company law or tax regulations • 1 ND
Depreciation allocated on systematic basis over useful life	49	0	
Disclosure			
Measurement base	49	0	
When more than one measurement base used, carrying amount for that basis in each category	15 (of 24)	9 (8 per company law or tax regulations)	
Depreciation Methods	• 37 straight-line • 9 straight-line plus an accelerated method • 2 declining balance • 1 rates for asset groups	0	
Depreciation Disclosure			
Useful lives or depreciation rates	43	6	
Gross carrying amount and accumulated depreciation at beginning and end of each period	47	2	
Reconciliation of carrying amount at beginning and end of each period	34	15	
General Disclosures			
Whether in determining recoverable amount of items of PPE, expected future cash flows discounted	0	6	43 Likely NA
Existence and amounts of title restrictions and PPE pledged as collateral	26	0	23 Likely NA
Accounting policy for restoration costs related to PPE	2	0	47 Likely NA
Amount of expenditures on account of PPE in course of construction	41	0	8 Likely NA
Amount of commitments for the acquisition of PPE	28	0	21 Likely NA
Revaluation Disclosures			
Basis used to revalue assets	• 8 (of 12 electing to revalue) • 12 (of 12 revaluing due to company law or tax regulations)	4 (of 12 electing to revalue)	

(continued)

Table 4. (Continued)

PANEL D: IAS 16, PROPERTY, PLANT, AND EQUIPMENT			
Effective date of revaluation	• 6 (of 12 electing to revalue) • 5 (of 12 revaluing due to company law or tax regulations)	6 (of 12 electing to revalue) 7 (of 12 revaluing due to company law or tax regulations)	
Whether an independent valuer was involved	• 4 (of 12 electing to revalue) • 12 (of 12 revaluing due to company law or tax regulations)	8 (of 12 electing to revalue)	
Nature of indices used to determine replacement costs	• 4 (of 12 electing to revalue) • 1 (of 12 revaluing due to company law or tax regulations)	8 (of 12 electing to revalue)	May be viewed as NA for most (11) of the 12 revaluing due to company law or tax regulations
Carrying amount of each class of PPE if the assets had been carried at cost less depreciation	• 11 (of 12 electing to revalue) • 4 (of 12 revaluing due to company law or tax regulations)	• 1 (of 12 electing to revalue) • 8 (of 12 revaluing due to company law and tax regulations)	
Revaluation surplus, indicating movement for the period and any restrictions on the distribution of the balance to shareholders	• 10 (of 12 electing to revalue) • 2 (of 12 revaluing due to company law or tax regulations)	2 (of 12 electing to revalue)	May be viewed as NA for most (10) of the 12 revaluing due to company law or tax regulations
PANEL E: IAS 18, REVENUE			
Disclosure			
Accounting policy	22	27	
PANEL F: IAS 19, RETIREMENT BENEFITS			
Defined Contribution Plans			
General Description of Plan	5 (of 10)	5	
Amount recognized as expense	7 (of 10)	3	
Any significant matters that affect comparability			Likely NA
Defined Benefit Plans			
Method			
Amortization period for past service cost and plan amendments	11 (of 23)		Cannot ascertain if remaining 12 NA or noncompliance
Actuarial valuation period	• 12 (of 23) accrued benefit (benchmark) • 2 projected benefit (alternative)		9 ND
Actuarial assumptions, incorporate projected salary levels	21 (of 23)		2 ND
Actuarial assumptions, all to be based on long-term considerations	16 (of 23)		7 ND

(continued)

Table 4. (Continued)

PANEL F: IAS 19, RETIREMENT BENEFITS			
Defined Benefit Plans Disclosures			
General description of plan	9 (of 23)	14	
Accounting policies	17 (of 23)	6	
Whether or not plan is funded	22 (of 23)	1	
Amount recognized as expense	15 (of 23)	8	
Actuarial present value of promised retirement benefits	18 (of 23)	5	
Fair value of plan assets	21 (of 23)	2	
If amounts funded since inception of plan differ from amounts recognized as expense/income over the same period, amount of liability/assets and funding approach adopted. When more than one plan exists and this results in both a liability and an asset, both are presented (no netting)			Likely NA for all sample companies
The principal actuarial assumptions used in determining cost of retirement benefits and any significant changes in assumptions	19 (of 23)	4	
Date of the most recent actuarial valuation and the frequency with which valuations are made	16 (of 23)	7	
Any other significant matters, including effects of a plan termination, curtailment, or settlement, that affect comparability			Likely NA for all sample companies
PANEL G: IAS 21, FOREIGN CURRENCY			
Method			
Foreign Currency Transactions	35	2 method eliminated by Comparability Project	• 10 hedge to minimize impact • 2 NA
Foreign Enterprises	3 temporal method	None	46 NA
Foreign Entities	45 current rate method	3 (one immaterial)	1 NA
Hyperinflationary economies	7 (of 20)	• 5 temporal • 5 current rate • 3 monetary/nonmonetary	29 do not mention operations in hyperinflationary economies
Disclosure			
Amount of exchange differences included in the net profit/loss	33	15	1 NA

(continued)

Table 4.   (Continued)

PANEL G: IAS 21, FOREIGN CURRENCY			
Net exchange differences classified as equity as a separate component of equity and reconciliation of amount of such exchange differences at beginning and end of period	44 (1 omits reconciliation)	3	2 NA
Amount of exchange differences arising during period which is included in carrying amount of an asset			49 Likely NA
When reporting currency is different from currency of country in which enterprise is domiciled, reason for using a different currency and reason for any change in reporting currency	1 (of 2)	1	47 Report in local currency, thus NA
PANEL H: IAS 22, BUSINESS COMBINATIONS			
Method			
Accounting for business combinations	31 report combinations accounted for as purchases		• 0 report combinations accounted for as poolings • 18 provide no footnote information on business combinations
Goodwill recognized as asset and amortized on systematic basis	42	4 charge to reserves	3 NA (no goodwill on books)
Goodwill amortization method	42 (of 42), benchmark straight line		
Goodwill amortization period	• 4 (of 42), benchmark 5 years • 33, alternative 20 years or less	5, 40 years	
Disclosures for all business combinations			
Names and descriptions of combining enterprises	30 (of 31 disclosing that a business combination was accounted for as a purchase)	1	
Method of accounting	25 (of 31)	6	
Effective date for accounting purposes	26 (of 31)	5	
Any operations resulting from combination the enterprise has decided to dispose of	13 (of 31)	0	18 likely NA

(continued)

Table 4. (Continued)

PANEL H: IAS 22, BUSINESS COMBINATIONS			
Disclosures for acquisitions			
Percentage voting shares acquired	30 (of 31)	1	
Cost of acquisition	20 (of 31)	11	
Nature and amount of provisions for restructuring and other plant closure expenses arising as a result of the acquisition and recognized at date of acquisition	5 (of 31)		26 likely NA
Disclosures goodwill			
Accounting treatment	42 (of 42)		
Period of amortization	42 (of 42)		
When useful life or amortization period exceeds 5 years, justification for period adopted	24 (of 38—only 9 provide a specific justification thereby adhering to the spirit of the IASC disclosure requirement)	14	
When not amortized on straight line basis, basis used and why			Likely NA for all sample companies
Reconciliation at beginning and end of period	29 (of 42)	13	
PANEL I: IAS 23, BORROWING COSTS			
Accounting Method	• 6 benchmark, expense • 14 alternative, capitalize		29 NA
Disclosure			
Accounting method	20 (of 20)	0	
For alternative, amount capitalized	6 (of 14)	8	
For alternative, capitalization rate	0 (of 14)	14	

Notes: ND: not disclosed;
         NA: not applicable.

the most companies coming from Switzerland (12), France (10), and Sweden (8). Nine additional countries are represented in the sample (i.e. Canada, Finland, Germany, Hong-Kong, Italy, Japan, Malaysia, Norway and South Africa).

The 1996 annual reports for the 49 companies meeting our selection criteria were comprehensively examined to determine the extent of compliance with IASs. Our tests for compliance focused on both measurement and disclosure issues for the IASs revised during the Comparability Project. IAS 11, *Construction Contracts,* was not applicable for most companies in our sample, and was excluded from the anlaysis.

One researcher carefully examined each annual report using a survey instrument and noted the measurement practice utilized and the disclosures provided. The survey instrument was based on a review of the text of the revised IASs and summaries prepared by the IASC regarding key modifications resulting from the Comparability Project (IASC March 1995a and December 1995b). To increase reliability, another researcher compared the data to that provided by *WorldScope.*[2] In instances where inconsistencies were identified, the annual report was examined by the second researcher. Discrepancies between the original data set and *WorldScope* were identified and resolved by the second researcher revisiting the annual report. The second review confirmed the original data and very few modifications to the data set were required. The second researcher also carefully examined the data set to confirm the consistency and logic of the entries.[3]

While summarizing the findings, a researcher other than the one who initially collected the data revisited several annual reports to provide illustrations. This exercise provided an additional check on the accuracy of the data. When the data set indicated widespread noncompliance, detailed lists of disclosures provided by the companies were compiled and carefully reviewed by the researchers to further ensure data accuracy. Such lists were compiled for the all-inclusive income requirement of IAS 8; extraordinary items; translation of foreign entities operating in hyperinflationary economies; pensions; capitalization of development costs; and revaluations of property, plant, and equipment.

FINDINGS

The note disclosing the company's accounting policies and/or the audit opinion were the sources of information about compliance with IASs. From this it was evident that only 20 companies noted full compliance with IASs (see Table 3, Panel A) while 29 companies noted compliance with some limited exceptions (see Table 3, Panel B).

The results of the analysis of the extent of compliance with IASs in respect of both measurement issues and disclosure requirements are summarized in Table 4. Each of the relevant IASs will now be discussed in the context of the survey results.

IAS 2 Inventories

Measurement

As issued in 1975, IAS 2 allowed use of the FIFO, weighted average, LIFO, and base stock costing methods (Epstein and Mirza, 1997). During the Comparability Project, it was determined that LIFO and base stock should be eliminated. However, the IASC found it

28   THE INTERNATIONAL JOURNAL OF ACCOUNTING   Vol. 34, No. 1, 1999

necessary to accept the continued existence of LIFO due to its popularity in certain countries. As revised, IAS 2 endorses FIFO and weighted average as the benchmark methods; LIFO is now the allowed alternative.

Most sample companies use an IASC benchmark method or some combination of benchmark methods (see Table 4, Panel A). None use the IASC allowed alternative for financial statement preparation. However, one company indicates that adjustments are made for inventories valued on a LIFO basis (to arrive at weighted average). Other methods utilized by two companies included:

- Industry practice whereby the cost of dairy products is valued according to dairy-market price
- Simplified valuation procedures, where permissible, and current market value

These two companies are not in compliance in that IAS 2 Revised specifically eliminated current cost as an acceptable inventory costing method. Five companies do not disclose their inventory costing method.

Impairment: Lower of cost or net realizable value (LCNRV)

Most comply with the IAS 2 requirement that inventories be carried at LCNRV. Alternatively, 13 carry inventories at lower of cost or market (LCM). Two carry some inventories at LCNRV and others at LCM. One company, which acknowledges noncompliance in its accounting policy footnote, states: "IAS 2 requires that inventories be valued at lower of historical cost or NRV. Had IAS 2 been applied, the difference...would not have been significant."

Disclosures

There are very few examples of noncompliance with IAS 2 disclosures (Table 4, Panel A). Of the 14 that disclose the carrying amount of inventories carried at LCNRV (or LCM), three provide a footnote listing inventories by classification (raw materials, work-in-process, finished products, etc.) and for each classification disclose the gross value. write-downs (allowance), and net inventory. Ten disclose a provision for obsolescence for total inventories, and one notes the amount of stocks carried at lower market prices as compared to purchase or production costs. The disclosure is likely not applicable for most of the remaining companies.

Only two companies disclose that the reversal of a write-down is recognized in income in the period the reversal occurs. One of the two companies discloses the amount of such reversals recognized during the period. In a footnote on supplemental income, this company includes a section on inventories that discloses "new provisions" and "writebacks" for 1995 and 1996. The circumstances leading to the reversals can be inferred from the company's inventory valuation method whereby dairy products are valued according to the year's dairy market price. The other company recognizes no reversals during 1996; thus, the additional disclosures are not applicable. For the 47 remaining companies, in that economic events that justify reversals of write-downs are rare and the IASC allows but does not require reversals when such events occur, disclosures regarding reversal of inventory write-downs are likely not applicable.

In summary, notable examples of noncompliance include:

- Two use inventory valuations not endorsed by IAS 2;
- Thirteen use LCM as opposed to LCNRV;
- Some disclosures are not provided. For example, five fail to disclose their valuation method.

IAS 8 Net Profit/Loss for the Period

As a new requirement under IAS 8 Revised, all items of income/expense must be included in net profit/loss unless prohibited by an IAS. Exceptions to the all-inclusive requirement are: revaluation surplus, gain/loss on translation of foreign currency statements, correction of fundamental errors, and effects of changes in accounting policy. Thirteen companies (Table 4, Panel B) violate the all-inclusive requirement by allowing at least one of the following non-owner changes in equity to bypass income:

- Captive insurance contingency reserve
- Legal and statutory reserves
- Consolidated goodwill charged to reserves
- Operating subsidies
- Bonuses to directors and statutory auditors
- Untaxed reserves
- Reserves provided by Company's By-Laws
- Ordinary reserves and sundry reserves
- Capital redemption reserve fund
- Income reserves
- Restricted reserves

In its accounting policy footnote, one of these companies acknowledges violating the all-inclusive requirement and states that it complies with IASs with the exception of a value adjustment for steel activities recorded to equity without affecting the 1996 income statement, which is not in accordance with IAS 8.

Profit/loss from Ordinary Activities and Extraordinary Items

IAS 8 requires that profit/loss from ordinary activities and extraordinary items each be separately reported on the face of the income statement and that the amount and nature of each extraordinary item be disclosed either on the face of the income statement or in the notes. All 49 companies disclose profit/loss from ordinary activities on the face of the income statement.

While extraordinary items should be rare under the IASC's revised definition, ten companies report extraordinary items in 1996. Indicative of noncompliance with the

30   THE INTERNATIONAL JOURNAL OF ACCOUNTING   Vol. 34, No. 1, 1999

TABLE 5.   Extraordinary Items And Special Items Reported By Sample Companies

PANEL A: EXTRAORDINARY ITEMS
French Income on **sale or scrapping of fixed assets** (96/95/94) Differences between **restructuring costs** and provisions set aside previously (96 and 95) Provisions for **restructuring** at subsidiaries (96/95) Provisions for litigation (96 and 95) Other extraordinary items/expenses (96, 95, and 94)
French Subsidies and other (96 and 95) • capital **gains and losses on the disposal of fixed assets**
French **Gains on disposals of investments** (96/95)and fixed assets (96/95) Other income including out of period income (96/95) **Losses on disposals of investments** (96/95) **and fixed assets** (96/95) Taxes related to prior years (96/95) Other expenses including extraordinary accrual (96/95) Out of period expenses (96/95)
French **Restructuring** costs and provisions (94/95/96) **Disposals of businesses** (94/95/96) Write off of capitalized research and development costs (94/95/96) Miscellaneous charges and provisions (94/95/96)
Swiss Gains on sales of real estate (96/95) **Gains on sales of investments** (96/95) Other extraordinary income (96/95) Loss on sales of real estate (96/95) **Loss on sales of investments** (96) Amortization of goodwill (96/95) Other extraordinary expenses (96/95). • Complete closing expenses for a joint venture and extraordinary expenses in excess of provisions previously made for capacity adjustments in a US operation whose operations are substantially independent of the other activities of the Group.
Swiss Extraordinary income (96, 95) • Liquidation of no longer necessary provisions for contingent risks and pending legal disputes Extraordinary expense (96, 95) • Reorganization expenses for a division as well as losses from divestitures of participations Extraordinary depreciation (96, 95) **Liquidations of unnecessary plant and equipment**
Italian **Gains on disposals** (96/95) Other income (96/95) Losses on disposals (96/95) Other expense (96/95) **(losses arising from the sale of assets)** Financial review: for an improved understanding of performance, a reclassified consolidated statement of income prepared after re-elaboration by reclassification and regrouping of the statement of income as required by the provisions of Italian Legislative Decree no 127/1991. The new format does not provide for separation of operations from financial and extraordinary components (in the past, the latter were identified by excluding from operations all events not directly relatable to turnover), assuming instead the ordinary nature of almost all the company's operational activities (as indicated by IAS no. 8). A distinction is however made between recurring and non-recurring economic items to facilitate interpretations of the result for the year.

(continued)

TABLE 5. (Continued)

PANEL A: EXTRAORDINARY ITEMS
Italian **Gains on disposals** (96/95) Miscellaneous (96/95) • (exchange gains on reimbursement to X of a part of the share capital of Y) **Losses on disposals** (96/95) Miscellaneous (96/95) • reorganization and **restructuring costs**, amounts accrued by US companies to comply with FAS 106   and connected to land reclamation of abandoned areas and other expenses
Finnish Discontinued operations (96) **Gain on sale of fixed assets** (95) Write off of shares (95) Other expenses (95/96)
Malaysian **Profit on sale of land and buildings** (95/96) and minority interests (96/95) **Profit/loss on the sale** of quoted subsidiary, other **investments**, and **land and buildings** (96) Surplus on compulsory acquisition of freehold land (96) Provision for diminution in value of plant and machinery (96) Retrenchment benefits (96) Other (96)
PANEL B: SPECIAL ITEMS LISTED ON INCOME STATEMENT FOLLOWING OPERATING INCOME
Abnormal items: • long term provisions (explosive closures, environmental remediation, post-employment medical and ben-   efits, net costs of business closures and disposals and other costs) • liquidation dividend
Non-recurring expense, net
Exceptional income (restructuring costs, provisions for group risks, prior year adjustment, disposals of assets, other income-net)

Exceptional income:
• gains on sold businesses less realized divestment expenses and potential future expenses, expenses
   arising from changes in corporate structure and the effect of change in accounting policy relating to
   those divestments are also deducted
Exceptional expense:
• changes related to current and forthcoming restructurings
• loss on exiting the collectible cards business
Effect of change in accounting policy

Special credits or charges • loss on disposal of property, plant, and equipment • loss/gain on sale or write down of investment securities • special severance payments and other restructuring costs Special contributions for retirement pension plans

Note: Bold print designates items that other sample companies argue no longer may be considered as extraordinary items.

revised guidelines, each of these ten report several extraordinary items and/or report items as extraordinary that fail to meet the IASC's strict definition. A list of extraordinary items reported by the ten companies is provided in Table 5 (Panel A). All ten provide the required IASC disclosures for extraordinary items. One of the ten states in its accounting policy footnotes that the company complies with IASs with two exceptions, one being IAS 8.[4]

Some companies specifically acknowledge the IASC's revised rules regarding extraordinary items. For one such company, a footnote states that extraordinary items are clearly distinct from the ordinary activities of the Group and are not expected to recur frequently or regularly. In its Five-Year Review, the company reports gains/losses on disposal of investments and restructuring costs for financial year 1994 and before as extraordinary income/expense. The company explains that the change in policy, whereby these items are no longer considered extraordinary, is due to the requirements of the revised IAS 8, effective January 1, 1995. In contrast, six of the ten companies listed in Table 5 report either gains/losses on the sale of investments or restructuring costs as extraordinary.

Another company states that it applies a strict interpretation of the concept of extraordinary income/expense. Gains/losses in the sale of businesses and fixed assets, as well as costs relating to restructuring, are considered to be a natural element of the Group's business and are therefore included as a part of the operating result, with a note of disclosure as to nature and amount. Again referring to Table 5, all ten companies report either gains/losses in the sale of businesses, gains/losses on the sale of fixed assets, or restructuring costs as extraordinary.

With the revision of IAS 8, IASC guidelines on extraordinary items are in some instances stricter than national requirements. Illustrative of this scenario, in its 1996 and 1995 financial statements prepared according to Finnish GAAP, one company reports discontinued operations as extraordinary items on the 1996 and 1995 profit/loss statements. In its 1995 profit/loss statement, the company also reports the cumulative effect of a change in accounting principle as an extraordinary item. However, the profit/loss account prepared according to IASs includes no extraordinary items. Such deviations between national guidelines and IASs can be confusing for users of financial statements and illustrate the need for harmonization of standards.

Several companies, while technically complying with the IASC's strict guidelines on extraordinary items, use other ways to distinguish "unusual" items and as such may not be complying with the "spirit" of IAS 8. For example, while one company does not report any extraordinary items in the income statement, in "Overview of Activities in 1996" (prior to the financial statements), it lists extraordinary items for 1996, 1995, and 1994. The "extraordinary items" include net gains on disposals and other non-recurrent income. Other companies list several types of "unusual" items in a separate category following profit from ordinary activities; a summary appears in Table 5 (Panel B).

In summary, our analysis reveals the following examples of noncompliance:

- Thirteen violate the all-inclusive requirement of IAS 8;
- Ten violate the IASC's strict guidelines on extraordinary items. The noncompliers included four of ten French, two of twelve Swiss, two of three Italian, the only Malaysian, and one of three Finnish companies.[5]

IAS 9 Research and Development Costs (R&D)

Measurement

Originally, IAS 9 required the expensing of research costs but allowed either the capitalization or expensing of defined development cost. Following the Comparability Project,

IAS 9 continues to require that research costs be expensed but now sets standards for cap-italization of certain development costs. If the capitalization criteria are met, the costs must be capitalized and amortized. Otherwise, the costs must be expensed immediately.

R&D disclosures are likely not applicable for six companies (Table 4, Panel C) because the annual report includes no significant discussion of R&D activity. While R&D disclo-sures appear applicable for three other companies, none of the IASC required disclosures are provided. One of the three states that the application of IAS 9, which requires the cap-italization of development costs meeting certain criteria, has been "postponed pursuant to authorization given by the French Stock Exchange Authorities in a letter dated May 19, 1995." Another includes an entire page in the annual report devoted to a discussion of R&D and states that 300 employees work in R&D. The final company provides a page of R&D discussion in the annual report with no financial statement disclosures. Thus, these three companies are not in compliance.

All 40 companies providing R&D disclosures expense research costs as required by the IASC. While eight companies capitalize at least some development costs, 32 expense all development costs. Some of the 32 are not in full compliance with IAS 8 which requires that (as opposed to allows) development costs be capitalized when incurred if certain con-ditions are met.

Four companies acknowledge that they do not comply with IAS 9 in regard to capitali-zation of certain development costs. Three companies state in their accounting policy foot-note that they expense all development costs like other companies in the worldwide automotive industry. The audit report of the final company, which received a qualified opinion for 1996 and 1995, notes that the financial statements give a true and fair view in accordance with IASs with the exceptions described in the financial statements. The accounting policies footnote states that development costs at Group risk are not capitalized.

Most companies expensing all development costs provide vague R&D policy descrip-tions making it impossible to ascertain compliance or noncompliance. For example, one states that "R&D is not capitalized but is charged continuously to income" and another notes that "R&D are charged as an expense in the income statement in the period in which they are incurred without exception."

Companies whose development costs do not meet the capitalization criteria set forth in IAS 9 should consider disclosures similar to that provided by Bayer. In its footnote on R&D, Bayer states:

> According to IAS 9,...Research costs cannot be capitalized but must always be expensed in the periods in which they are incurred. Development costs, too, normally have to be recognized as expenses, but they have to be capitalized if it is sufficiently certain that the future economic benefits to the company will cover not only the usual production, selling and administrative costs but also the development costs themselves. There are also several other criteria relating to the development project and the product being developed, all of which have to be met according to IAS 9 if the development costs are to be recognized as an asset.

> The conditions for asset recognition are not satisfied in the Bayer Group, because the very nature and scale of the economic risk attaching to chemical and pharmaceutical products under development means it cannot be assessed reliably until:

34   THE INTERNATIONAL JOURNAL OF ACCOUNTING   Vol. 34, No. 1, 1999

- Development of a product or process has been completed
- In the case of chemical products, subsequent premarketing as a trial product has demonstrated that the product meets the technological and economic requirements of the market.

An additional factor in the health care and agriculture areas, for example, is that marketing is impossible without regulatory approval, even if the product's efficacy is proven.

The above disclosure clearly informs the financial statement reader of the requirements of IAS 9 and provides assurance that Bayer is in compliance.

Disclosures provided by the eight companies capitalizing some development costs suggest compliance with IAS 9. For example, one states: "R&D costs are charged to the income statement insofar as the conditions for capitalization in accordance with IAS 9 are not fulfilled. In this connection, only the costs for the development of new products and the further development of existing products are included." Another states, "Research costs are charged to income when incurred. Development costs are expensed if they do not meet the capitalization criteria set out in international accounting principles."

In an interesting twist, one company's R&D disclosure indicates compliance with IAS 9; however, further investigation suggests noncompliance with IAS 8. The company's R&D footnote states, "in accordance with the provision of IAS 9, capitalized R&D are reviewed each year-end and any costs that no longer meet the criteria for capitalization are written off to the profit and loss account. Costs that continue to meet the criteria for capitalization are amortized over a period not exceeding five years, as from the dates on which the related products are marketed." An examination of the income statement reveals that this company wrote off capitalized R&D as an extraordinary item in 1994, 1995, and 1996. Thus, the company is not complying with the IASC's strict definition of an extraordinary item.

Disclosure

Regarding disclosures, ten companies do not disclose their accounting policy for R&D and the amount of R&D charged to expense (See Table 4, Panel C). For the eight that capitalize some development costs, only two note that a test for impairment is conducted and discuss the write-back of previously written-off development costs. However, the latter is likely not applicable for most companies. Four of the eight disclose their amortization policy, and the disclosure is not applicable for two companies (i.e. there is no capitalized development costs on the books). Four disclose the useful life of capitalized development costs, and again, the disclosure is not applicable for two companies. Only one company provides the new IASC disclosure requiring a reconciliation of the balance of unamortized development costs at the beginning and end of the period. Again, the disclosure is not applicable for two companies.

While *WorldScope's* three-year comparative data suggest that three companies changed from expensing all R&D to a mix of expensing and capitalizing between 1994 and 1996, our analysis indicates two of these companies charged all R&D to expense in 1996. For the third, the annual report states that the 1996 accounts have been stated for the first time in full compliance with IASs, and R&D are normally charged directly to income as incurred. Development costs for major projects are only capitalized and amortized over the period of use (maximum five years) to the extent that the antici-pated yield will exceed the development costs with reasonable certainty. At the end of 1996, there are no capitalized development costs.

In summary, the analysis reveals some noncompliance:

- Three companies with significant R&D activity provide no R&D disclosures;
- Four acknowledge noncompliance in regard to capitalization of certain development costs;
- Several examples of noncompliance with disclosure requirements are revealed.

IAS 16 Property, Plant, and Equipment (PPE)

Measurement After Initial Recognition

Initially, IAS 16, as issued in 1982, permitted either historical cost or revalued amounts as the basis for reporting plant assets. As revised via the Comparability Project, the IAS 16 benchmark suggests that PPE be carried at cost less accumulated depreciation. The allowed alternative states that PPE may be carried after initial recognition at its revalued amount. As modified, IAS 16 requires that any revaluations be to fair value and that these be updated regularly (at least every three years).

Twenty-five companies (Table 4, Panel D) utilize historical cost exclusively. Of these, while stating in a footnote that PPE is stated at historical cost, one company, in another footnote providing a schedule of depreciation and amortization, discloses depre-ciation per IAS and then adjusts for depreciation on revalued assets to arrive at total depreciation per Finnish GAAP. Thus, per Finnish standards some items of PPE are revalued, but the company's IAS statements utilize historical cost only. Again, such dif-ferences between national GAAP and IASs may be confusing to financial statement users.

Another company states that PPE is carried at purchase or production costs. A schedule for PPE indicates that at the end of 1995 there was a balance for revaluations; however, the balance was zero at the end of 1996. Thus, it appears that the company switched to the IASC benchmark during 1996.

In addition to measuring some items of PPE using historical cost, 12 companies revalue certain items in association with company law or tax regulations. For example, one com-pany states that PPE are "recorded at acquisition cost, except those within the scope of a legal revaluation." Another company states that PPE are carried, "at cost, except those items acquired by French companies which are stated at revalued cost, in accordance with the provisions of the laws of Dec. 29, 1976 and Dec. 30, 1977."

Twelve other companies utilize revalued amounts for specific groups of PPE and histor-ical costs for all other items. For example, one company states "investment properties are valued from time to time by sworn appraisers. The basis of valuation is their open market value and any surplus arising on valuation is transferred to a non-distributable reserve." Another company states:

36   THE INTERNATIONAL JOURNAL OF ACCOUNTING   Vol. 34, No. 1, 1999

...land and buildings are stated at valuation. Independent valuations are performed every three years on an open market for existing use basis. In the intervening years, the Directors review the carrying value of land and buildings and adjustment is made where there has been a material change. Revaluation surpluses and deficits are dealt with in capital reserves except for movements on individual properties below depreciated cost which are dealt with in the profit and loss account. Other tangible fixed assets are stated at cost less amount provided for depreciation.

Of the companies revaluing certain assets, one acknowledges in a section on deviations from IASC Recommendations that it has made a revaluation to fixed assets in a manner not in accordance with IASs.

The IASC requires that revaluations be made with sufficient regularity and that revaluations are applied to the entire class of PPE. Revaluations associated with company law and tax regulations may make it difficult, if not impossible, to comply with these IASC requirements. For example, several French companies, or those with significant French subsidiaries, revalued assets only as required by law in the 1970s. A similar situation holds for certain Italian companies (i.e., the Italian monetary revaluation laws of 1991 in relation to property). For the 12 companies electing to revalue certain items of PPE, six indicate that valuations are made with sufficient regularity, and 11 indicate the specific classes of PPE revalued. It is impossible to determine if the remaining companies are complying with the IASC guidelines.

WorldScope's three-year comparative disclosures reveal that one company switched from historical cost with revaluations to historical cost in 1996. The annual report states that the change moved the company in compliance with IASs. *WorldScope's* comparative data also indicate that one company moved from historical cost to historical cost with revaluations in 1996, and another made a similar switch in 1995. Thus, following completion of the IASC Comparability Project, these two companies moved from the IASC preferred benchmark to the IASC allowed alternative.

Disclosures for Revalued PPE

Of the 24 companies using the IASC allowed alternative, 15 companies disclose the carrying amount for each measurement basis. Of the nine companies not providing this disclosure, eight revalued assets only in association with company law or tax regulations. For the 12 companies utilizing the IASC allowed alternative (other than for revaluations associated with company law or tax regulations), Table 4 (Panel D) presents numerous examples of noncompliance with IASC required disclosures.

For companies following the allowed alternative only in association with company law or tax regulations, all 12 companies provide information regarding the basis used to revalue the assets (government indices) and whether an independent valuer was used. For five of the six French companies in this group the effective date is provided or can be inferred, given that the 1978 required government revaluation is general knowledge. The sixth French company reported revaluations based only on its Mexican subsidiaries. All the other French companies state that their financial statements are based exclusively on the historical cost principle. For example, one company specifically states that French and foreign legal revaluations are not reflected in the consolidated financial statements.

Overall, the disclosures provided by companies revaluing due to company law and tax regulations may be viewed as problematic. Lack of compliance for this group may be tied to conflicts between IASs and national requirements, and in some instances compliance may indeed not be possible. This issue requires further consideration by the appropriate parties.

Depreciation

As required by IAS 16, all the companies charged depreciation expense on fixed assets on a systematic basis over the assets' useful lives. Table 4 (Panel D) lists the depreciation methods utilized by the 49 companies.

Disclosures

As a result of the Comparability Project, IASC disclosure requirements for PPE were expanded considerably. Table 4 illustrates the degree of compliance and reveals few examples of noncompliance for disclosures other than those associated with revaluations (discussed separately). Noncompliance is noted primarily in three areas. Fifteen fail to provide a complete reconciliation of the carrying amount at the beginning and end of each period, and six do not disclose the useful lives or depreciation rates utilized.

While it appears that six should disclose information regarding the impairment test (i.e. whether in determining the recoverable amount of items of PPE expected future cash flows have been discounted to present value), none provide such disclosures. In 1996, one of these six includes amounts written off in its tangible asset reconciliation (for land and buildings and plant and machinery) and states that deficits on individual properties below depreciated cost had been charged to the consolidated profit/loss account. The other five also include a line for write-offs in their PPE reconciliation.

In summary, for PPE, noncompliance includes:

- One company made a revaluation to fixed assets in a manner not in accordance with IASs;
- Several examples of noncompliance with disclosures are noted.

Noncompliance with disclosures is particularly problematic for the 12 electing to revalue certain classes of assets.

IAS 18 Revenue

IAS 18 Revised requires that companies disclose the accounting policy adopted for revenue recognition and if applicable the methods used to determine the stage of completion for services rendered.[6] Twenty-seven companies (Table 4, Panel E), representing the majority, are not in compliance with the IASC disclosure requirement regarding accounting policy used for revenue recognition.

38   THE INTERNATIONAL JOURNAL OF ACCOUNTING   Vol. 34, No. 1, 1999

IAS 19 Retirement Benefit Costs

In the 1983 version of IAS 19, the guidance for defined benefit plans was very general and essentially only required that costs be rationally allocated to the periods benefited. The standard indicated either an accrued or a projected benefit valuation method should be used consistently for defined benefit plans. Following the Comparability Project, IAS 19 contained much more detail. However, the standard continued to permit flexibility by presenting the accrued benefit valuation method as the benchmark but also set forth a projected benefit valuation method as an allowed alternative.

Analysis suggests that many companies view IAS 19 as not applicable for their retirement plans or alternatively chose not to comply with the requirements. Thus, compliance is discussed separately for companies providing 1) limited disclosures (26 companies), and 2) a significant portion of the IASC required disclosures (23 companies).

Limited Pension Disclosures Group

The companies providing limited disclosures include four of ten French, seven of eight Swedish, the only Malaysian, two of three Japanese, all three Finnish, all three Italian, both South African, and four of 12 Swiss companies. Of the 26, only two acknowledge that they do not comply with IAS 19. For example, one states that the company complies with the guidelines of the IASC with the exception of pensions which are reported per accounting practices in countries where the company has operations.

Disclosures for the limited disclosure group range from none to a few short statements or paragraphs including vague descriptions of the plans. For example, while one company's balance sheet includes a liability for pensions, no disclosures are provided. All three Finnish, three of the Swedish, and one Swiss company state that the pensions plans are contracted with insurance companies and provide very limited additional disclosure. Five Swedish companies and one Swiss company with significant plans based in Sweden, provide very limited disclosures for PRI (Pension Registration Institute) plans. For example, one simply discloses liabilities to the PRI and the calculated rate of interest for the PRI liability. Another only discloses the amount of PRI pensions and other commitments.

Although IAS 19 appears applicable for most, if not all, of the 26 companies, none disclose the actuarial present value of promised retirement benefits, the fair value of the plan assets, or the principal actuarial assumptions used in determining the cost of retirement benefits. Few disclose the actuarial valuation method used or discuss the actuarial assumptions used.

Although, some companies in our sample imply that IAS 19 is not applicable for their pension plans, a recent statement by the IASC indicates that several such companies are not complying with IAS 19. In announcing the recent revision of IAS 19, the IASC (1998b) states that some argued that the old IAS 19 (as revised during the Comparability Project) did not work well for plans in countries such as Germany, Japan, and the Netherlands. However, the IASC now holds that as these countries were represented on the Retirement Benefits Steering Committee, such arguments will have little force in the future. The significance of this statement is magnified by the revision of IAS 1. Paragraph 1 of IAS 1 now states that "financial statements should not be described as complying with IAS unless they comply with each applicable Standard and each applicable Interpretation issued by the Standing Interpretations Committee."

Significant Pension Disclosures Group

The 23 other companies provide a significant portion of the IASC required disclosures for pensions. Table 4 (Panel F) provides a summary of compliance. For the ten companies with defined contribution plans, the table provides several examples of noncompliance.

Of the 23 with defined benefit plans, 11 amortize past service cost over the expected remaining working life of employees unless a shorter time period is more appropriate. Amortization of past service costs is either not disclosed or not applicable for the remaining companies. The IASC benchmark, accrued benefit, is the actuarial valuation method used by 12 of the companies. Two use the IASC allowed alternative, projected benefit method (which has since been eliminated with the 1998 revision of IAS 19). Twenty-one companies state that actuarial assumptions incorporate projected salary levels. Sixteen state that all assumptions (such as interest rates) are based on long term assumptions. For the above items, the remaining companies do not disclose their policies; thus it is not possible to determine whether or not they are complying with IAS 19.

Disclosures

For the IASC required disclosures associated with defined contribution plans, Table 4 indicates that compliance is problematic. For example, only nine (of 23) provide a general description of the plan and only 15 disclose the amount recognized as an expense during the period. While none of the companies provide information regarding terminations, curtailments, or settlements, this is likely because they are not applicable.

Noncompliance may be summarized as follows:

- Twenty six provide very limited disclosures
- For the 23 providing the majority of the IAS 19 information, compliance with disclosures is problematic

IAS 21 The Effects of Changes in Foreign Exchange Rates

As issued in 1983, the initial version of IAS 21 allowed several choices. Only modest changes were made during the Comparability Project. For example, certain choices such as those relative to the deferral and amortization of exchange differences on long-term monetary items, on translation of income statements of foreign entities at the closing rate, and on translation of financial statements of foreign entities that report in the currency of a hyperinflationary economy without prior restatement were narrowed (Epstein and Mirza 1997). IAS 21 prescribes that the statements of self-sustaining operations be translated using the current rate method and statements of integrated operations be translated using the temporal method. The revision yielded additional disclosure requirements.

Foreign Currency Transactions

The Comparability Project eliminated the option of deferring recognition of foreign exchange gains/losses on long-term monetary items. The IAS 21 benchmark now requires that on settlement of monetary items, or on reporting monetary items at rates different from those at which they were initially recorded, the entity recognize any income/expense during the period in which they arise.

Ten companies (Table 4, Panel G) utilize hedging to minimize exchange gains/loss arising from foreign currency transactions. Three of these note that those gains/losses not hedged are recognized per the IAS 21 benchmark.

Thirty-five companies use only the IASC benchmark. Alternatively, two Canadian companies note that unrealized exchange gains/losses on translation of long-term monetary items are deferred and amortized over the life of those items; thus, these companies are using a method eliminated by the Comparability Project. Section 1501 of the Canadian Handbook notes that this is an inconsistency with IAS GAAP. For two other sample companies gains/losses arising from foreign currency transactions are not applicable.

Foreign Enterprises

For 46 companies, there is no indication that the company has subsidiaries operating as foreign enterprises (i.e. functional currency is reporting currency). The other three, as required by the IASC, use the temporal method to account for the translation of subsidiaries operating as foreign enterprises.

Foreign Entities

Forty-five companies utilize the IASC benchmark, the current rate method, to account for the translation of foreign entities (i.e. functional currency is foreign currency). One company indicates that all its subsidiaries depend on the Parent for their product and supply and operate as integrated parts of the Parent; thus the company has no foreign entity subsidiaries.

Three are not in noncompliance with IAS 21. One, which acknowledges that it does not comply with IAS 21 in its accounting policy note, states that current receivables/payables denominated in foreign currencies are translated into the Parent currency at the exchange rates in effect at the respective balance sheet dates. Noncurrent monetary items denominated in foreign currencies are translated at historical exchange rates. Had noncurrent receivables/payables been translated at the exchange rates in effect at the balance sheet dates pursuant to IAS 21, the differences would not be significant. Another of the noncompliers uses the current-noncurrent method. The other translates balance sheet items at year end rates except for shareholders' equity items, which are translated at historical rates. Income/expense items are converted at average exchange rates for the year. Any resulting translation differences are posted to shareholder's equity.

Foreign Entities Operating in Hyperinflationary Economies

For subsidiaries operating in a hyperinflationary economy, the original version of IAS 21 required that the financial statements be translated without prior restatement. Following the Comparability Project, the IASC now requires that the financial statements be restated via IAS 29, *Financial Reporting in Hyperinflationary Economies*, before translation.

Twenty companies discuss their policy for translating subsidiaries operating in highly inflationary countries. Five companies utilize the temporal method; five others use the current rate method or a modified version of this method. Three companies use the monetary/nonmonetary method or a modified version of this method. Only one company acknowledges noncompliance in its annual report. This company states in a section on exceptions to IAS:

> In a couple of instances, the monetary/non-monetary method has been applied in the translation of foreign subsidiaries in countries with high inflation. According to IAS recommendations, such translations are based on the application of an inflation index. In terms of the effect on earnings, the difference is considered marginal.

Only seven companies are in compliance with IAS 21. Of the seven, only two make specific reference to IAS 29. One company states, "those subsidiaries operating in high-inflation countries (cumulative inflation in excess of 100% in three years) are translated at year-end exchange rates in accordance with IAS No. 29. The effects of inflation on monetary assets are allocated among various income statement captions." The second company notes that Turkish undertakings followed IAS 29.

Disclosures

Table 4 indicates few examples of noncompliance with IAS 21 disclosure requirements with one exception. Fifteen companies fail to disclose the amount of exchange differences included in net profit/loss for the period.

While most companies disclose the net exchange differences classified as equity as a separate component of equity, some of these may not be complying with the spirit of IAS 21. In several instances, the information is not supplied in a true reconciliation form and the balance sheet and footnotes must both be viewed to reconstruct the activity. The disclosure is not applicable for two companies. One of these uses only the temporal method. The other hedges shareholder's equity in non-domestic countries; thus, the Group's shareholders' equity is not impacted by the translation effect.

The IASC requires that when the reporting currency is different from the currency of the country of domicile the reason for using a different currency and the reason for any change in the reporting currency must be disclosed. All but two companies report in the local currency. A Canadian company discloses that the consolidated statements are expressed in US dollars, the principal currency of the company's business, thereby, satisfying the IASC disclosure requirement. However, a holding company based in Hong Kong, with its primary listing in London, reports in US dollars but does not provide a rationale for stating its financial statements in a currency different from the currency of the country of domicile.

42   THE INTERNATIONAL JOURNAL OF ACCOUNTING   Vol. 34, No. 1, 1999

Noncompliance with IAS 21 may be summarized as follows:

- Two Canadian companies defer and amortize unrealized exchange gains/losses on translation of long-term monetary items over the life of those items, thereby using a method eliminated by the Comparability Project;
- Two do not follow IASC guidelines for translating foreign entities;
- Thirteen of 20 with operations in hyperinflationary economies, do not restate these foreign entities in accordance with IAS 29;
- Several fail to provide all required disclosures.

IAS 22 Business Combinations

The original version of IAS 22 was issued in 1983. As revised following the Comparability Project, IAS 22 now more clearly defines which combinations are accounted for using the purchase method and which must be accounted for as a pooling (Epstein and Mirza 1997). Purchase accounting must be used for acquisitions, and pooling may only be used for a uniting of interest. As expected given the IASC's strict position on pooling, none of the sample companies accounted for a business combination using the pooling method during 1996.[7]

As revised, IAS 22 prohibits the immediate write-off of goodwill against equity, which was previously allowed (Epstein and Mirza 1997). Goodwill must be recognized as an asset and amortized to income on a systematic basis over its useful life. IAS 22 requires the amortization period not to exceed five years, unless a longer period (not to exceed 20 years) can be justified. Recently, goodwill was revisited as part of the IASC's intangible assets project.

Purchase Method

Thirty-one companies (Table 4, Panel H) report business combinations accounted for as purchases during 1996. For an additional company, the annual report states that the company had newly consolidated three companies. Disclosures for one of these subsidiaries indicate that ownership went from zero percent in 1995 to over 84 percent in 1996. Yet, the financial statements are silent regarding several IASC disclosures. Based on the schedule reconciling goodwill on acquisition, it is possible that the combinations are immaterial.

A few companies do not strictly adhere to the IASC's distinction of the terms acquisition/purchase and merger/pooling, thereby creating confusion. For example, one company discusses its treatment of goodwill (charged to reserves) arising from a 1996 business combination. However, "merger" is utilized elsewhere in the annual report to describe this same business combination.

Disclosures

Overall, disclosures for business combinations reveal few examples of noncompliance (see Table 4). A notable exception is that 11 of 31 companies fail to clearly disclose the cost of the acquisition. The cost cannot be determined by examining the footnotes or by consulting the cash flow statement.

Goodwill

Forty-two companies state that goodwill is recognized as an asset and amortized over a straight-line basis. For those following the capitalize and amortize approach, four utilize an amortization period of five years or less. Thirty-three use an amortization period of more than five but equal to or less than 20 years. Of these 33, 22 provide some explanation of why the amortization period exceeds five years. However, 15 of the 22 simply state that goodwill is amortized based on the estimated useful life or that circumstances justify amortization over a period exceeding 20 years. Only seven comply with the "spirit" of the IASC disclosure requirement and provide a specific rationale for utilizing an amortization period in excess of five years. For example, one states that goodwill related to gas operations will be amortized over 20 years since it pertains to gas companies in stable markets and that other goodwill will be written off over five to ten years.

Five amortize goodwill over periods of up to 40 years. Four of the five acknowledge that they are in violation of IAS 22 in their accounting policy footnotes. Two of the four state that while awaiting clarification of the new IASC standard covering the amortization of intangible assets, they have postponed application of IAS 22. The two (French) companies further state that amortization of goodwill over a 40-year period is allowed by the Commission des Operations de Bourse. The audit opinion of one of the two also acknowledges this exception to compliance with IASs.

Only two of the five provide a justification for using an amortization period in excess of five years. One indicates that a 40-year amortization period provides the most accurate picture of the acquisition's impact on earnings and financial position and also notes that applying a longer amortization period may be attributed to competitive factors. The second argues that the 40-year amortization period reflects the subsidiary's future prospects at the time of acquisition.

Seven companies have no goodwill on the books. This omission may be due to non-compliance (i.e. goodwill is charged to reserves) or because it is not applicable. For two of these companies, there is no evidence to indicate noncompliance. For one company, this omission may be viewed as a violation of IASs in that business combinations accounted for as purchases occurred during the year.

Four of the seven companies with no goodwill on the books write off goodwill to reserves. One states in a footnote on subsidiary companies that goodwill is dealt with in capital reserves. Another states in the goodwill footnote that goodwill acquired was offset against consolidated reserves without any impact on the income statement in accordance with prevailing European practice. The company further notes that this treatment is in compliance with the directives of the European Union, but in contrast, IAS 22 requires acquired goodwill to be capitalized and written off via the income statement over a period of five to 20 years. The company's audit opinion states that the financial statements comply with the "IAS of the IASC" while the accounting policy note indicates that it complies with IASs with the exception of goodwill. Two companies state that goodwill is eliminated against retained surplus at the date of acquisition. In the note on accounting policies, one of these companies states that it complies with the standards of the IASC with the exception of goodwill.

44   THE INTERNATIONAL JOURNAL OF ACCOUNTING   Vol. 34, No. 1, 1999

The analysis provides evidence that seven companies changed their method of accounting for goodwill to come in line with the revised IAS. These companies changed from charging goodwill to reserves to the capitalize and amortize approach. One states:

> Goodwill on acquisitions occurring on or after 1st January 1995 is reported in the balance sheet as an intangible asset or included within associates or non-current liabilities, as appropriate....Goodwill on acquisitions which occurred prior to 1st January 1995 was taken directly to reserves.

Another company states that goodwill was charged against shareholder's equity in the years through 1993. Starting from 1994, as a consequence of Italian Decree no. 127/1991, positive differences arising on purchase are capitalized and amortized during the period that such goodwill is expected to benefit. *WorldScope's* three-year comparative data indicate that two additional companies changed to the capitalize and amortize approach between 1994 and 1996. These changes may be viewed as a response to the Comparability Project whereby the method of charging goodwill to reserves was eliminated.

One company notes a change in accounting method that involves amortizing goodwill over a maximum of 20 years, versus 40 years previously, effective from January 1, 1995. The company states that this method was adopted in compliance with the provisions of IAS 22 Revised. Another states that goodwill is capitalized in accordance with IAS 22 and is being written off over twenty years beginning in 1994, thereby suggesting the new policy is a response to the Revision of IAS 22.

Goodwill Disclosures

Compliance with the IASC required disclosures for goodwill is mixed (see Table 4). On one extreme, a company includes no footnote on goodwill, and amortization is revealed only via a schedule reconciling the beginning and ending balance of goodwill. No other goodwill disclosures are provided by the company.

As noted previously, a key area of noncompliance is that 14 companies that amortize goodwill over a period exceeding five years fail to provide a justification for using a longer period. And, several others do not comply with the "spirit" of the IASC disclosure requirement. Also notable is that 13 companies fail to provide a reconciliation for goodwill at the beginning and end of the period.

In summary, areas of noncompliance with IAS 22 include:

- Four companies charge goodwill to reserves;
- Five amortize goodwill over a period in excess of the IASC 20 year limit;
- Some companies fail to provide all the IASC required disclosures for business combinations and goodwill.

IAS 23 Borrowing Costs

The 1984 version of IAS 23 provided a flexible approach with capitalization or expensing of borrowing costs permitted. The Comparability Project proposed flexibility be reduced. E 39 favored capitalization of borrowing costs which met certain criteria; however, a last minute change resulted in 1993's IAS 23 incorporating capitalization as an allowed alternative for borrowing costs that are directly attributable to the acquisition, construction, or production of a qualifying asset. Under the IAS 23 benchmark treatment, borrowing costs related to expenditures on assets that take a substantial period to get ready for their intended use are expensed. All other borrowing costs must be expensed.

In the sample, six companies follow the benchmark (Table 4, Panel I). All six specifically disclose their policy for borrowing costs thereby satisfying the only IASC required disclosure. One notes:

> French accounting principles exclude financial interest from capitalizable costs of constructing fixed assets. Under US GAAP, an appropriate portion of financial interest would be included in the capitalizable costs. The reconciling adjustment includes the amortization of previously capitalized interest.

This company also provides a reconciliation of shareholder's equity and the statement of income under French GAAP and US GAAP. This scenario illustrates the consequences associated with differences between IASs, other "internationally recognized standards," and/or national GAAP, particularly the confusion users may face when presented with two versions of GAAP for one company.

In an interesting twist, a company expensing borrowing costs states in "Important Deviations From IASC Recommendations:"

> The acquisition value of machinery and buildings does not include interest expense paid during construction and assembly time. According to the IASC, such interest expense should be included in acquisition value.

Thus, this company is confessing to a deviation from IASs, when it appears to be following the IASC benchmark.

Fourteen companies follow the IASC allowed alternative. As required, all 14 disclose their accounting policy for borrowing costs. However, only six disclose the amount of borrowing costs capitalized. None disclose the capitalization rate used to determine the amount of borrowing costs eligible for capitalization.

In that 29 companies made no mention of borrowing costs, the issue is likely not applicable for most of these. However, some may not be complying with the IASC required disclosures in that a few of these mention significant construction projects in their annual reports.

In summary, given the flexibility permitted by IAS 23 most companies appear to be complying with the recognition guidelines. The preference for the allowed alternative treatment may be linked to its consistency with US GAAP. Indeed one company using the benchmark is doing so only because of French national requirements and indicates a preference for the allowed alternative in order to be in line with US GAAP. With regard to disclosures, there are several examples of noncompliance among those using the allowed alternative method.

SUMMARY

The research questions addressed in this article concern the extent to which companies claiming to comply with IASs are doing so in practice and the nature and significance of

46 THE INTERNATIONAL JOURNAL OF ACCOUNTING Vol. 34, No. 1, 1999

measurement and disclosure noncompliance. Our study of the reporting practices of 49 major companies from 12 countries in 1996 reveals that there is significant noncompliance with IASs. Only 20 (41%) of the 49 companies surveyed note compliance with all IASs. More importantly, even where compliance with all or most IASs is indicated in the accounting policy footnote and/or audit opinion, there are notable examples of noncompliance with the measurement and disclosure requirements of individual IASs in practice.

The main areas of noncompliance in respect of IAS 2, *Inventory*, are the use by some companies (4%) of inventory valuations not endorsed by the standard, the use of LCM (29%) rather than LCNRV and a lack of disclosure of the methods used. For IAS 8, *Net Profit or Loss for the Period*, many companies (27%) violate the all inclusive requirement and the IASC's strict guidelines on extraordinary items (20%). In the case of IAS 9, *Research and Development Costs*, some companies with significant R&D activity do not make any disclosures. In addition, several companies (8%) acknowledge their noncompliance in regard to capitalization of development costs. Noncompliance in respect of disclosures is also notable for IAS 16, *Property, Plant and Equipment*, and especially problematic for those companies (24%) making revaluations. The majority of companies (55%) are not in compliance with the disclosure requirements of IAS 18, *Revenue*. In respect of IAS 19, *Retirement Benefit Costs*, disclosure by the majority of companies (53%) is very limited. For IAS 21, *The Effects of Changes in Foreign Exchange Rates*, some companies use methods eliminated by the standard while a significant number of companies (65%) with operations in hyperinflationary economies do not restate these foreign entities in accordance with IAS 29. Failure to provide the required disclosures is also evident for IAS 22, *Business Combinations*. In addition, some companies (9%) still charge goodwill to reserves despite the elimination of this practice by IAS 22. Further, a number of companies (11%) amortize goodwill over a period in excess of the IASC 20 year limit, though this is no longer an issue following the 1998 revision of IAS 22. Disclosure is again an issue for some companies in the case of IAS 23, *Borrowing Costs*.

CONCLUSIONS

Overall, the degree of compliance by companies claiming to comply with IASs is very mixed and somewhat selective. Important areas of noncompliance with the measurement and disclosure requirements of IASs have been highlighted. The extent of noncompliance discovered by our research supports IFAC's view that auditors are asserting that financial statements comply with IASs when the accounting policies footnotes and other notes show otherwise. The research reinforces the significance of the acceptance and observance issue for the IASC. It also suggests that while many companies may appear anxious to seek the international investment status that comes with the adoption of IASs they are not always willing to fulfil all of the requirements and obligations involved.

Our research suggests that national standard-setters and regulators need to work more closely with the IASC to eliminate significant differences between national accounting guidelines and IASs. For example, one sample company includes both Finnish and IASC statements in its annual report. A comparison of the two sets of statements reveals several significant differences including the disclosure of profit/loss and the revaluation of fixed assets.

A similar situation arises when companies, including several in our sample, provide reconciliations to US GAAP. Reporting two (or more) sets of numbers for net income, stockholder's equity, and so on, may be confusing to financial statement users. Attainment of an IOSCO endorsement of IASs would eliminate the need for reconcilations to US GAAP.

Our research suggests that, in addition to working with IOSCO, the IASC needs to encourage national regulators to support IASs without exception, particularly as more and more countries allow for the use of IASs. For example, a French company in our sample states that the application of IAS 9 (R&D) has been postponed pursuant to authorization given by the French Stock Exchange Authorities. Differences between IASC requirements and national guidelines will be even more troublesome under IAS 1 Revised (effective for periods beginning on or after July 1, 1998). In 1999 financial statements, legislated conflicts with IASC GAAP will prohibit companies from noting compliance with IASs.

Additional research is needed to explore the impact of IAS 1 on the "selective compliance" identified by our research. When combined with the revision of (i.e. pensions revised 1998 and segment reporting revised 1997) and addition of (i.e. provisions and contingencies 1998 and recognition of financial instruments forthcoming) several IASs, IAS 1 Revised may force some, if not many, companies to reconsider adoption of IASs.

NOTES

1. Several companies followed IASs except for goodwill or research and development. These companies were retained in the final sample.
2. Only 32 of the sample companies were included in the Lexis-Nexus version of *WorldScope* database.
3. This involved addressing a series of questions such as:

    - If the company reported a business combination as a purchase during 1996 are the disclosure requirements for purchases marked as either "yes" or "no;" alternatively, if there were no purchases during 1996, are the disclosures required marked "not applicable"?
    - Are the IASC disclosure requirements for revalued property, plant, and equipment marked as "yes" or "no" when the company revalues certain assets, and alternatively marked as "not applicable" if the company uses only historical cost to value property, plant, and equipment?

4. The company appears to be in compliance with IAS 8's all inclusive requirement. Thus, the violation referred to in the accounting policy footnote is likely associated with the reporting of extraordinary items.
5. In that only six companies appropriately reported changes in accounting principle and given the diverse nature of the items reported, few, if any, meaningful generalizations can be made. Thus, no discussion is included.
6. Measurement issues are not discussed given the diversity of revenue sources for the sample. The major change associated with the Comparability Project in relation to revenue recognition is that while the original version of IAS 18 permitted either percentage-of-completion or completed contract accounting for the recognition of revenue related to rendering of services, as revised, IAS 9 now endorses only the percentage-of-completion method.
7. A few companies indicate, outside the financial statements, that members of the group merged or that subsidiaries merged with other entities. There is no discussion of the pooling method in the financial statements.

48   THE INTERNATIONAL JOURNAL OF ACCOUNTING   Vol. 34, No. 1, 1999

REFERENCES

Cairns, David. 1995. *"A Guide to Applying International Accounting Standards."* London: Accountancy Books, 1995.

Cairns, David. 1997. "IFAC – 20 Years On." *World Accounting Report* (October): 2.

Epstein, B.J. and A. A. Mirza, 1997. *IAS 97: Interpretation and Application of International Accounting Standards.* New York: John Wiley & Sons.

IASC. 1989. *Exposure Draft E32. Comparability of Financial Statements: Proposed Amendments to International Accounting Standards 2, 5, 8, 9, 11, 16, 17, 18, 19, 21, 22, 23 and 25.*

IASC. 1993. *Statement of Intent: Comparability of Financial Statements.*

IASC. 1995a. "Revised Standards Now Effective." *IASC Insight* (March): 15–16.

IASC. 1995b. "Revised Standards - The Main Changes." *IASC Insight* (December): 14–15.

IASC. 1998a. "Europe Opens to IAS" IASC Insight (March): 1.

IASC. 1998b. "IASC Board Approves Revised IAS 19." *IASC Insight*, (March): 4–5.

Sharpe, Michael. 1998. "Looking for Harmony: Building a Global Framework." *Australian Accountant* (March).

[17]

Journal of Accounting Research
Vol. 39 No. 3 December 2001
Printed in U.S.A.

Domestic Accounting Standards, International Accounting Standards, and the Predictability of Earnings

HOLLIS ASHBAUGH* AND MORTON PINCUS†

Received 2 March 1998; accepted 19 April 2000

We investigate (1) whether the variation in accounting standards across national boundaries relative to International Accounting Standards (IAS) has an impact on the ability of financial analysts to forecast non-U.S. firms' earnings accurately, and (2) whether analyst forecast accuracy changes after firms adopt IAS. IAS are a set of financial reporting policies that typically require increased disclosure and restrict management's choices of measurement methods relative to the accounting standards of our sample firms' countries of domicile. We develop indexes of differences in countries' accounting disclosure and measurement policies relative to IAS, and document that greater differences in accounting standards relative to IAS are significantly and positively associated with the absolute value of analyst earnings forecast errors. Further, we show that analyst forecast accuracy improves after firms adopt IAS. More specifically, after controlling for changes in the market value of equity, changes in analyst following, and changes in the number of news reports, we find that the convergence in firms' accounting policies brought about by adopting IAS is positively associated with the reduction in analyst forecast errors.

* The University of Wisconsin-Madison; †The University of Iowa. We wish to thank Donal Byard, Ole-Kristian Hope, Per Olsson, the anonymous referee, and workshop participants at the University of Northern Iowa, the University of Wisconsin, and the 1998 American Accounting Association annual meeting for their helpful comments.

417

Copyright ©, University of Chicago on behalf of the Institute of Professional Accounting, 2001

1. Overview

We investigate the impact of differences in countries' accounting standards relative to International Accounting Standards (IAS) on the accuracy of financial analyst earnings forecasts for a sample of non-U.S. firms before and after they adopt IAS. IAS are a set of accounting standards promulgated by the International Accounting Standards Committee (IASC). The IASC's goal is to develop an internationally acceptable set of reporting standards that will generate more comparable financial information across national boundaries by minimizing, if not eliminating, differences in countries' domestic generally accepted accounting principles (domestic-GAAP) (FASB [1996]). For most of the firms included in our sample, IAS adoption leads to increased disclosure and/or a restricted set of measurement methods. To the extent this causes an IAS adopter's financial information to become more predictable, we expect improved accuracy of analysts' earnings forecasts. However, there is some controversy regarding the degree of stringency of IAS (Davis-Friday and Rueschhoff [1998]) and firms' compliance with IAS (Street, Gray, and Bryant [1999]). Moreover, it is unclear how changing accounting polices, as implied by IAS adoption, impacts the ability of analysts to accurately forecast earnings (e.g., Brown [1983]; Elliott and Philbrick [1990]). For example, if managers were trying to smooth earnings, adoption of IAS might reduce their ability to do so, in turn leading to more volatile earnings and analyst forecast errors.

We develop indexes that reflect differences in countries' measurement and disclosure policies relative to IAS. We then test whether (1) differences in countries' accounting policies relative to IAS and (2) the subsequent accounting standard convergence brought about by firms' IAS adoptions affect analyst earnings forecast accuracy. We use a sample of non-U.S. firms that adopted IAS during the 1990–93 period. We focus on these firms and this period for several reasons. First, a surge of voluntary IAS adoptions occurred during this period. While Ashbaugh [2001] finds that firms are more likely to use IAS when their securities are traded on more foreign exchanges and when they engage in seasoned equity offerings, the specific costs and benefits associated with firms' voluntary adoptions of IAS remain unclear. Finding a statistically reliable association between changes in accounting policies due to IAS adoption and improvements in analysts forecast accuracy provides some evidence of the benefits firms receive from adopting IAS. Specifically, after firms adopt IAS, financial analysts are better able to predict a variable highly relevant to firm valuation. Second, studying firms that have voluntarily adopted IAS is particularly interesting since many countries and securities exchanges recently have given firms the option of preparing IAS financial reports; e.g., Germany (Eggert [1998]). Third, the set of policies comprising IAS was relatively static during the 1990–93 period. Since then, however, the IASC has completed two major overhauls of IAS,[1] and many countries now base their reporting standards on IAS (IASC [1998]).

Our indexes of differences in countries' measurement and disclosure standards relative to IAS are positively associated with analyst earnings forecast errors. This evidence is consistent with the claim that the variation in accounting standards across national borders impacts the predictions of financial analysts. We also document that, on average, the absolute value of analyst forecast errors decreases following firms' adoptions of IAS.

Ashbaugh [2001] provides evidence that large firms are more likely to use IAS, and that firms typically issue additional shares of stock within a year or two of adopting IAS. We posit that IAS adoption is part of a concerted effort by managers to satisfy the increased demand for information that typically occurs as firms issue additional equity. In support of this claim, we find that our sample firms issue additional stock in the year of or the year following IAS adoption. We also detect a significant increase in the number of news reports about our sample firms in the year following IAS adoption. Thus, several endogenous events that likely affect a firm's information environment, such as the issuance of equity shares and an increase in news reports, often occur when a firm adopts IAS. We posit that the adoption of IAS is a response to an anticipated or realized shift in the firm's environment.

Accordingly, we control for changes in (1) market capitalization, (2) analyst following, and (3) news reports in our empirical analyses. We find that the improved forecast accuracy following IAS adoptions is significantly associated with changes in firms' accounting policies. Specifically, the more changes in measurement and disclosure reporting standards implied by moving from firms' domestic-GAAPs to IAS, the larger the reduction in analyst earnings forecast errors. This enhanced forecast accuracy associated with IAS adoptions suggests that analysts can more accurately predict a key variable, i.e., earnings, which is relevant to firm valuation.

2. Hypotheses

Prior research suggests that the differences in countries' accounting standards affect the informativeness of reported financial information (Alford et al. [1993]). However, the empirical evidence is mixed with regard to whether the convergence of countries' accounting standards increases the informativeness of firms' financial reports (Joos and Lang [1994]; Auer [1996]).

Our first hypothesis relates the differences in countries' accounting standards relative to IAS to the accuracy of analysts' earnings forecasts. We focus on the period prior to IAS adoption since firms, in this time period, are reporting in accordance with their domestic-GAAP, which reflect a variety of disclosure requirements and measurement methods. To the extent greater

---

[1] Specifically, the IASC's 1995 Comparability Project and 1998 Core Project.

differences in domestic-GAAPs relative to IAS result in more variation in the information reflected in firms' financial reports, we expect such reporting differences to impair the ability of analysts to forecast earnings. Our first hypothesis is:

> H1: The absolute values of analyst earnings forecast errors are positively associated with greater differences in countries' accounting measurement and disclosure standards relative to IAS.

Our second hypothesis examines the impact of IAS adoptions. Switching to IAS typically increases the type and quantity of financial information a firm discloses. Lang and Lundholm [1996] document that analysts' forecast accuracy improves as firms' disclosure levels increase. Adopting IAS generally also restricts a firm's choices of accounting measurement methods. With fewer measurement rules to deal with, analysts should be better able to master the existing set. Hence, restrictions on measurement methods as well as expanded disclosures that result from adopting IAS should enable analysts to more accurately predict firms' earnings.

However, while firms' choices of measurement methods under IAS generally are restricted as compared to their domestic-GAAP, some degree of flexibility may remain. This suggests that some firms can adopt IAS without changing many (or any) accounting measurement methods.[2] Alternatively, if adopting IAS requires a firm to change its measurement methods, analysts' abilities to accurately forecast earnings might be impaired. Brown [1983] and Elliott and Philbrick [1990] report evidence consistent with this possibility for U.S. firms. One plausible explanation for reduced forecast accuracy concerns earnings volatility. The restricted set of measurement method choices under IAS might require firms to report more volatile earnings series as compared to the earnings series generated when using the accounting methods that are acceptable under their domestic-GAAP. If the manager's choice is constrained under IAS, there are fewer ways for managers to disguise volatility.

Yet another factor that may hamper forecast accuracy is the extent to which analysts rely more on public rather than private information. Barron et al. [1998] model how analyst earnings forecasts are related to analysts' public and private information, and how these two types of information map differently into forecast errors. The common component of forecast error

---

[2] Firms comply with IAS measurement standards in various ways, depending upon their domestic-GAAPs (Ashbaugh [2001]). Firms domiciled in countries where in 1993 there were relatively few accounting measurement choice restrictions (e.g., Switzerland) are able to implement IAS without violating their domestic-GAAPs. Alternatively, some domestic-GAAPs are quite similar to IAS. Thus, Canadian firms are able to meet the requirements of their domestic-GAAP and IAS by choosing measurement methods that satisfy both sets of standards. Some countries (e.g., France) permit a firm to use domestic-GAAP in the parent company's financial statements and IAS in its consolidated statements. Finally, in other countries, accounting standards and tax laws are highly aligned (e.g., Finland, Sweden), and firms typically use footnote reconciliations to meet IAS measurement requirements.

arises from errors in public information while the idiosyncratic component of forecast error is due to errors in the private information analysts hold. Relevant to our study is the result that the mean forecast error primarily reflects common error since idiosyncratic error can be diversified away as more forecasts are made. Thus, if under IAS errors in public information increase, we expect analyst forecast accuracy to decrease following IAS adoptions.

Because *a priori* arguments can be made for either enhanced or impaired forecast accuracy following the adoption of IAS, our second hypothesis is non-directional. It is:

> H2: The accuracy of analyst earnings forecasts changes after firms adopt IAS.

A firm may adopt IAS in anticipation of or concurrent with an increase in the demand for more information about the firm. For example, in addition to adopting IAS, a firm might provide additional voluntary disclosures as part of the process of raising capital in the equity markets. Firms might also change their operating activities at the same time they are adopting IAS, and such operating changes might impact the ability of analysts to forecast earnings. Consequently, several endogenous factors, in addition to the adoption of IAS, may impact the ability of analysts to predict a firm's earnings. We consider such factors in our empirical analyses.

3. Sample and Data

We identify non-U.S. firms using IAS and their year of adoption based on a list provided by the IASC.[3] The IASC list identified 163 firms that adopted IAS by 1993.[4] We eliminated seven firms from Italy and 22 firms from South Africa since firms from these countries could use IAS selectively rather than fully adopt IAS when their domestic-GAAP was silent on an accounting measurement or disclosure issue. In addition, we deleted one firm from Bermuda because Bermuda did not have a set of domestic-GAAP to benchmark to IAS. We deleted 53 of the remaining 133 firms voluntarily using IAS in 1993 because they were missing data (specifically analyst earnings forecasts) in the Historical I/B/E/S International database.[5] The final sample consists of 80 firms, 64% of which are engaged in manufacturing. Two percent of the sample adopted IAS in 1990, 50 percent in 1991, 33 percent in 1992, and 15 percent in 1993. Table 1 reports the distribution of sample firms across countries. The countries most highly represented in the sample are Switzerland (28.75%), France (21.25%), and Canada (15.00%).

---

[3] A similar list is on the IASC's Web site (IASC [1999]). On a random basis, we examined more than half of our sample firms' 1990–1994 annual reports to verify their year of adoption.

[4] Since 1994, many countries have adopted IAS as their national financial accounting standards or as the basis for their reporting standards (IASC [1998]). Prior to that, Italy and South Africa were among the few countries that used IAS as a basis for their national GAAP (Coopers and Lybrand [1993]).

[5] We gratefully thank I/B/E/S International, Inc., for providing us with earnings forecast data.

422   H. ASHBAUGH AND M. PINCUS

TABLE 1

*Distribution Across Countries of the Sample of 80 Non-U.S. Firms
That Adopted International Accounting Standards Between 1990
and 1993. We Identify Non-U.S. Firms Using IAS and Their Year of
Adoption Based on a List Provided by the IASC of 163 Firms That
Adopted IAS by 1993. We Eliminated Seven Firms from Italy and 22
Firms from South Africa Since Firms from These Countries Could
Adopt IAS Selectively Rather Than Fully Adopt IAS When Their
Domestic-GAAP Was Silent on an Accounting Measurement or
Disclosure Issue, One Firm from Bermuda Because Bermuda Did Not
Have a Set of Domestic-GAAP to Benchmark to IAS, and 53 Firms
with Missing Data (Analyst Earnings Forecasts as Well as Actual
Earnings, Share Prices, Shares Outstanding, and Analyst Following)
in the Historical I/B/E/S International Database*

Country	Number	Percent
Australia	5	6.25
Canada	12	15.00
Denmark	2	2.50
Finland	6	7.50
France	17	21.25
Hong Kong	2	2.50
Japan	3	3.75
Malaysia	4	5.00
Norway	1	1.25
Singapore	1	1.25
Spain	2	2.50
Sweden	2	2.50
Switzerland	23	28.75
Total	80	100.00

We use three indexes to capture differences in countries' accounting standards relative to IAS. Table 2 summarizes the differences in disclosure requirements (DISCLOSE) and measurement methods (METHODS) of IAS versus sample firms' domestic-GAAPs (see appendix A for details). Table 2 also presents IASSET, which is the summary measure of potential disclosure and measurement policy changes a firm in a given country commits to by adopting IAS. The larger an index value, the greater the potential difference between a firm's domestic-GAAP and the reporting requirements of IAS. We use DISCLOSE, METHODS, and IASSET to test whether reporting differences relative to IAS impair analyst forecast accuracy prior to IAS adoption. After adopting IAS, however, the differences in accounting regimes should be substantially reduced. Hence, we use the change in disclosure policies (CHDISCLOSE), the change in measurement methods (CHMETHODS), and the change in reporting policies taken as a whole (CHIASSET) to investigate the impact of IAS adoption on analyst forecast errors. The change in each index equals the negative of the pre-change index value (e.g., CHIASSET = 0 − IASSET).

We define forecast error (FERROR) as the absolute value of the difference between a firm's reported earnings per share in year t and the median analyst forecast of earnings per share for year t, deflated by the firm's stock price

TABLE 2

Variation in Accounting Standards: IAS versus Domestic-GAAPs.
DISCLOSE and METHODS Are the Sum of the Additional IAS Disclosure
Requirements and Measurement Method Restrictions, Respectively,
Relative to the Accounting Policies of Firms' Domestic-GAAPs (see
Appendix A). IASSET is the Sum of DISCLOSE and METHODS.
Comparisons Are Based on Standards in Effect as of January 1, 1993.

Country	DISCLOSE	METHODS	IASSET
Australia	1	2	3
Canada	0	0	0
Denmark	2	2	4
Finland	6	4	10
France	4	3	7
Hong Kong	3	1	4
Japan	2	2	4
Malaysia	2	0	2
Norway	7	1	8
Singapore	2	0	2
Spain	3	1	4
Sweden	5	2	7
Switzerland	4	4	8

at the beginning of year t (Lang and Lundholm [1996]).[6] We obtain actual and forecasted earnings, as well as share prices, shares outstanding, and analyst following from the I/B/E/S database.

Table 3 presents descriptive statistics of firm characteristics for the 80 sample firms. Compared to our sample firms' domestic-GAAPs, IAS requires additional disclosures in approximately three reporting areas (i.e., mean DISCLOSE = 3.12 and median = 2) and restricts management's choices of measurement standards in an average of two areas (i.e., mean METHODS = 2.45 and median = 2). There is a correlation of 0.78 between DISCLOSE and METHODS (not reported), suggesting that countries' disclosure and measurement standards tend to be similar in rigor relative to IAS. Overall, as reflected in IASSET, sample firms make approximately six (median = 7.00) disclosure and/or measurement method changes (out of the 12 financial reporting areas we consider) when adopting IAS.

In the year preceding IAS adoption, the average number of analysts following a firm (NUM) is approximately 14. In the year after IAS adoption, the mean (median) number of analysts following a firm rises to approximately

---

[6] The time between non-U.S. firms' fiscal year-ends and the public reporting of annual earnings varies due to differences in reporting or filing requirements across national boundaries and equity markets (e.g., Alford et al. [1993]; Frost and Kinney [1996]). As a consequence, the forecast horizon and thus the number of forecasts of annual earnings can vary by firm. To standardize, we calculate the median analyst forecast of earnings per share for year t using consensus forecasts in the six-month period prior to firms' fiscal year-ends. As a sensitivity check, we repeat the analysis using analyst forecasts starting in the first month they become available on I/B/E/S in the year for which the forecasts are being made; i.e., we allow forecast horizons to vary by firm. The results are similar.

424		H. ASHBAUGH AND M. PINCUS

TABLE 3

Descriptive Statistics of Firm Characteristics. A Sample Firm Appears Once in the Pre-IAS Adoption Period and Once in the Post-IAS Adoption Period. In the Pre-IAS Adoption Period, DISCLOSE and METHODS Are Indexes Reflecting the Differences in Disclosure Requirements and Measurement Choices of Firms' Domestic-GAAPs, Respectively, Relative to IAS (see Appendix A). IASSET is the Overall Index of Accounting Standard Differences and Equals the Sum of DISCLOSE and METHODS. In the Post-IAS Adoption Period, the Accounting Difference Indexes Equal Zero. NUM is the Number of Analysts Providing an Annual Earnings Forecast for the Month of the Firm's Fiscal Year-End, Obtained from I/B/E/S. MVE is the Log of the Firm's Market Value of Equity Measured in Millions of U.S. Dollars at Calendar Year-End in the Pre- and Post-IAS Adoption Years. We Calculate This Variable by Using Share Price and Shares Outstanding from I/B/E/S and Exchange Rates from Worldscope. Foreign Listings Are the Number of Foreign Exchanges on Which a Firm's Shares Trade as Reported in the Bloomberg Database at the End of a Firm's Fiscal Years in the Pre- and Post-Adoption Years. Foreign Sales as well as the Number of Business Segments and Geographic Segments are Collected from the Worldscope Database for the Pre- and Post-IAS Adoption Years. The % Foreign Sales Calculated by Dividing a Firm's Foreign Sales by Its Total Sales. The Sample Is 80 Firms Adopting IAS in 1990, 1991, 1992, or 1993.

		Pre-IAS Adoption			Post-IAS Adoption		
Variable	N	Mean	Standard deviation	Median	Mean	Standard deviation	Median
DISCLOSE	80	3.12	1.79	2.00	0	0	0
METHODS	80	2.45	1.55	2.00	0	0	0
IASSET	80	5.56	3.16	7.00	0	0	0
NUM	80	13.79	7.83	13.50	17.11***	8.80	15.00###
MVE	80	13.24	1.37	13.14	13.67**	1.24	13.66##
Foreign listings	80	2.16	1.66	2.00	2.20*	1.68	2.00
Business segments	64	3.74	2.62	3.00	3.91	2.26	3.00
Geographic segments	64	3.20	2.52	3.00	3.56	2.47	3.00
% Foreign sales	54	59	29	64	56	30	59

*, **, *** A t-test of paired differences rejects the hypothesis of no difference from zero (two-tail p-*value* < .10, < .05, and < .01, respectively).
##, ### A Wilcoxon rank sum test rejects the hypothesis of no difference in the distributions (two-tail p-*value* < .05 and < .01, respectively).

17 (15). The increases in NUM are significant at conventional levels. We define firm size as the log of market value of equity (MVE) measured in millions of U.S. dollars at calendar year-end. We calculate this variable by using share price and shares outstanding from I/B/E/S and exchange rates from *Worldscope*. We find that firm size increases significantly from the pre-IAS period to the post-IAS adoption period. Expressed in millions of U.S. dollars (not reported), mean (median) market value of equity increases from $2,069 ($530) million in the year prior to IAS adoption to $2,925 ($886) million in the year after adoption.[7] Ashbaugh [2001] documents that firms

---

[7] Changes in exchange rates between firms' domestic currencies and the U.S. dollar may influence the measurement of non-U.S. firms' market values at two points in time. To investigate whether such changes might confound the measurement of changes in market values, we calculate a firm's market value of equity using a constant exchange rate; specifically, the exchange rate in effect at the end of the year prior to the firm's IAS adoption. We find this measure of change in market value is highly correlated (0.98) with our original measure, and there is a significant increase in average market value even when controlling for exchange rate changes. Similarly, the results of our regression analyses based on our original MVE measures

adopt IAS in anticipation of engaging in seasoned equity offerings, and we find that firms in our sample have significantly more shares outstanding after adopting IAS (not reported). In particular, our sample firms have, on average, 1.2 million additional shares outstanding one year after IAS adoption compared to the year preceding adoption (with 78% of sample firms having more shares outstanding). Table 3 also indicates that the average number of foreign listings increases slightly from the year prior to IAS adoption to the year following adoption, although the median sample firm's equity shares are traded in two foreign equity markets during both the pre- and post-IAS adoption periods.

To investigate whether sample firms' operating environments change in the years surrounding IAS adoption, we calculate the number of business and geographic segments in which they operate. Of the 80 sample firms, 64 firms have segment data in the *Worldscope* database. For this sub-sample of firms, we find no significant difference in the number of business segments or geographic segments in the year following IAS adoption relative to the year preceding adoption (see table 3). Furthermore, the percentage of foreign sales, defined as a firm's foreign sales divided by its total sales, also does not change over the analysis period. To the extent that changes in business and geographic segments and foreign sales reflect changes in sample firms' overall operating activities, the lack of significant changes in these variables suggests an absence of operational changes that potentially impact analysts' abilities to forecast earnings.

4. Empirical Design and Results

4.1 THE IMPACT OF DOMESTIC-GAAP DIFFERENCES FROM INTERNATIONAL ACCOUNTING STANDARDS ON ANALYST FORECAST ERRORS

To test H1, i.e., whether differences in domestic accounting standards relative to IAS adversely affect analyst earnings forecast accuracy, we estimate the following regression model:

$$\text{FERROR}_{it-1} = \alpha + \beta_1 \text{NUM}_{it-1} + \beta_2 \text{MVE}_{it-1} + \beta_3 X_i + \varepsilon_{it-1} \qquad (1)$$

where

$t-1$	= the year prior to IAS adoption;
FERROR_{it-1}	= $|\text{EPS}_{it-1} - \text{Median Analyst Forecast}_{it-1}|/\text{Price}_{it-1}$;
NUM_{it-1}	= the number of analysts providing earnings forecasts of firm i for year $t-1$;
MVE_{it-1}	= the natural log of firm i's market value of equity at December 31 of year $t-1$, measured in millions of U.S. dollars;
X_i	= the index of differences in firm i's disclosure polices (DISCLOSE), measurement methods (METHODS), or overall reporting standards (IASSET) relative to IAS.

(reported below) are qualitatively unchanged when substituting the change in MVE variable that reflects a constant exchange rate.

426   H. ASHBAUGH AND M. PINCUS

Prior research examining analyst earnings forecast accuracy argues for controlling for differences in disclosure levels across firms. Following Lang and Lundholm [1996], we use the extent of analyst following (NUM) to control for differences in firms' disclosure practices that can impact analyst earnings forecasts. A negative coefficient on NUM suggests that analyst earnings forecast accuracy improves (i.e., forecast errors fall in absolute value) as more analysts follow a firm. We use MVE to control for differential information due to firm size (Lang and Lundholm [1993]). A negative coefficient on MVE suggests that analysts can predict the earnings of larger firms more accurately.

Our test of H1 focuses on the coefficient of X in equation (1), which represents the coefficient on DISCLOSE, METHODS, and IASSET. If accounting standard differences hamper the ability of analysts to accurately predict firms' earnings, the coefficient (β_3) should be reliably positive; i.e., larger earnings forecast errors (in absolute value) should be associated with greater differences between IAS and domestic-GAAPs.[8]

Table 4 reports the results of the estimations of equation (1).[9] The models have adjusted R^2s of 19.40%, 16.32%, and 18.87% for the disclosure, measurement, and overall accounting policy differences, respectively.[10] The coefficients on NUM are not significantly different from zero in any of the regressions, while the coefficients on MVE are negative, as expected, and significant. The coefficient on DISCLOSE is reliably positive (t = 2.909, one-tail p-*value* <.01). This result suggests that analysts earnings forecast accuracy declines as firms provide fewer disclosures in accordance with their domestic-GAAPs relative to those required under IAS. Likewise, the positive and significant coefficient (t = 2.313, one-tail p-*value* < .05) on METHODS indicates that the absolute value of analyst forecast errors increases as the flexibility in the choices of measurement methods under firms' domestic-GAAPs increases. Finally, considering the set of disclosure and measurement policies as a whole, the positive coefficient on IASSET (t = 2.811, one-tail p-*value* < .01) documents that analyst earnings forecast errors are higher the more firms' domestic-GAAPs depart from IAS. When we use mean analysts forecasts in place of median forecasts to compute FERROR, the results (not reported) are similar.[11] Thus, the results support the hypothesis that analyst earnings forecast accuracy is impaired by cross-country differences in accounting standards relative to IAS.

---

[8] Pearson (Spearman) correlations between FERROR and, respectively, DISCLOSE, METHODS, and IASSET are 0.37 (0.48), 0.32 (0.38), and 0.37 (0.44).

[9] The extremely high correlation (0.78) between DISCLOSE and METHODS (and CHDISCLOSE and CHMETHODS) means that if both variables were included in the same regression, inferences about their marginal effects would be suspect.

[10] We winzorize all variables in the regression analyses to their 1st and 99th percentile values. The results are virtually identical if variables are not winsorized.

[11] We also perform standard collinearity diagnostics (Belsey, Kuh, and Welsch [1980]) and find no evidence that multicollinearity is a serious problem in our regression analyses.

TABLE 4

Results of Testing H1: The Impact of Differences in Domestic-GAAPs Relative to IAS on Analyst Earnings Forecast Accuracy. FERROR Is the Absolute Value of the Difference Between Actual Earnings Per Share and the Median Analyst Forecast of Earnings Per Share for the Year, Deflated by Stock Price (all Data Obtained from I/B/E/S). NUM is the Number of Analysts Providing an Annual Earnings Forecast for the Month of the Firm's Fiscal Year End (Obtained from I/B/E/S). MVE Is the Log of the Firm's Market Value of Equity Measured in Millions of U.S. Dollars at Calendar Year-End. We Calculate This Variable by Using Share Price and Shares Outstanding from I/B/E/S and Exchange Rates from Worldscope. DISCLOSE and METHODS Are the Sum of the Additional IAS Disclosure Requirements and Measurement Method Restrictions, Respectively, Relative to the Accounting Policies of Firms' Domestic-GAAPs (see Appendix A). IASSET Is the Overall Occounting Standard Index for the Firm's Country of Domicile (Reported in Table 2). All Regression Variables Are Winzorized to the 1st and 99th Percentile Values. The Sample is 80 Firms Adopting IAS in 1990, 1991, 1992, or 1993 and t − 1 is the Year Prior to IAS Adoption

(a) Disclosure model: $FERROR_{it-1} = \alpha + \beta_1 NUM_{it-1} + \beta_2 MVE_{it-1} + \beta_3 DISCLOSE_i + \varepsilon_{it-1}$

(b) Methods model: $FERROR_{it-1} = \alpha + \beta_1 NUM_{it-1} + \beta_2 MVE_{it-1} + \beta_3 METHODS_i + \varepsilon_{it-1}$

(c) Set model: $FERROR_{it-1} = \alpha + \beta_1 NUM_{it-1} + \beta_2 MVE_{it-1} + \beta_3 IASSET_i + \varepsilon_{it-1}$

Predicted		Model		
	Sign	(a)	(b)	(c)
α	?	0.1192	0.1356	0.1187
		(2.088)**	(2.349)**	(2.055)**
NUM_{it-1}	−	−0.0008	−0.0008	−0.0008
		[−0.876]	[−0.821]	[−0.883]
MVE_{it-1}	−	−0.0077	−0.0083	−0.0076
		[−1.725]*	[−1.842]*	[−1.694]*
$DISCLOSE_i$	+	0.0094		
		[2.909]***		
$METHODS_i$	+		0.0088	
			[2.313]**	
$IASSET_i$	+			0.0052
				[2.811]***
N		80	80	80
Adj. R^2		19.40	16.32	18.87

t-statistics are in brackets for one-tail tests; *, **, *** one-tail p-*value* < .10, < .05 and < .01, respectively.
t-statistics are in parentheses for two-tail tests; ** two-tail p-*value* < .05.

4.2 THE IMPACT OF IAS ADOPTIONS ON ANALYST FORECAST ACCURACY

For descriptive purposes, we calculate the unconditional change in analyst forecast accuracy after firms adopt IAS. Panel A of table 5 indicates that the absolute value of forecast errors falls significantly, from a mean of 3.58% (median = 1.28%) in the year prior to IAS adoption to a mean of 1.73% (median = 0.76%) in the year following adoption. We also separate the sample into two groups: the 68 firms whose accounting policies should be affected most by the adoption of IAS (i.e., firms for which CHIASSET < 0); and the 12 Canadian firms whose CHIASSET = 0. For the former group of firms, forecast errors are reliably smaller after IAS adoption. Specifically, panel B of table 5 shows that the mean FERROR is 1.82% in year t + 1 as opposed to 3.97% in year t − 1, and the median is 0.72% in year t + 1 versus 1.60% in year t − 1. For the Canadian firms, mean and median FERROR remain essentially unchanged over the adoption period

428   H. ASHBAUGH AND M. PINCUS

TABLE 5

Univariate Tests of Change in Analysts' Forecast Errors. FERROR Is the Absolute Value of the Difference Between Actual Earnings Per Share and the Median Analyst Forecast of Earnings Per Share for the Year, Deflated by Stock Price. Year t − 1 (t + 1) Is the Year Prior to (Post) IAS Adoption. CHIASSET = 0 − IASSET; i.e., the Change in Differences in Domestic-GAAP Vis-à-Vis IAS Where IASSET Is the Accounting Standard Index for the Firm's Country of Domicile (Reported in Table 2)

Year	N	Mean	Median	Std. Dev.	Minimum	Maximum
Panel A: All Firms (Variable = FERROR)						
t − 1	80	0.0358	0.0128	0.0566	0.0000	0.2870
t + 1	80	0.0173	0.0076	0.0281	0.0000	0.1567
t-statistic		−3.135***				
z-statistic			−2.592###			
Panel B: Firms for which CHIASSET < 0 (Variable = FERROR)						
t − 1	68	0.0397	0.0160	0.0601	0.0001	0.2870
t + 1	68	0.0182	0.0072	0.0302	0.0001	0.1567
t-statistic		−3.154***				
z-statistic			−2.944 ###			
Panel C: Canadian Firms (CHIASSET = 0) (Variable = FERROR)						
t − 1	12	0.0141	0.0087	0.0196	0.0000	0.0673
t + 1	12	0.0123	0.0123	0.0098	0.0000	0.0307
t-statistic		−0.270				
z-statistic			0.375			

*** A t-test of paired differences rejects the hypothesis of no difference from zero (two-tail *p-value* < .01).
A Wilcoxon rank sum test rejects the hypothesis of no difference in the distributions (two-tail *p-value* < .01).

(see panel C of table 5). In addition, we note that the standard deviation of analyst forecast errors for both the Canadian firms and for the CHIASSET < 0 group is approximately cut in half in the year following IAS adoption relative to the pre-IAS period. Hence, both subsamples reflect reductions in the standard deviation of FERROR, while only the CHIASSET < 0 group exhibits a significant reduction in the average absolute value of forecast errors.

To formally test H2, and thus examine the relation between IAS adoptions and changes in analyst forecast errors, we use our sample of 80 firms and estimate the following regression:

$$CHFERROR_i = \alpha + \beta_1 CHNUM_i + \beta_2 CHMVE_i + \beta_3 CHX_i + \varepsilon_i \quad (2)$$

where
$CHFERROR_i$ = $FERROR_{it} - FERROR_{it-1}$;
$CHNUM_i$ = the change in the number of analysts providing earnings forecasts of firm i in year t + 1 relative to year t − 1 ;
$CHMVE_i$ = the change in the natural log of firm i's market value of equity at December 31 of year t + 1 versus December 31 of year t − 1, measured in millions of U.S. dollars;
CHX_i = the change in the index of differences in firm i's disclosure polices ($CHDISCLOSE_i$), measurement methods ($CHMETHODS_i$), or overall reporting standards ($CHIASSET_i$) relative to IAS (i.e., $CHX_i = 0 - X_i$).

DOMESTIC AND INTERNATIONAL ACCOUNTING STANDARDS   429

TABLE 6

Results of Testing H2: The Impact of IAS Adoptions on Analyst Earnings Forecast Accuracy. Changes Are Calculated from the Year Prior to IAS Adoption (t − 1) to the Year Post-IAS Adoption (t + 1). CHFERROR Is the Change in the Absolute Value of the Difference Between Actual Earnings Per Share and the Median Analyst Forecast of Earnings Per Share for the Year, Deflated by Stock Price. CHNUM Is the Change in the Number of Analysts Providing an Annual Earnings Forecast for the Month of the Firm's Fiscal Year End. CHMVE Is the Change in the Log of the Firm's Market Value of Equity Measured in Millions of U.S. Dollars at Calendar Year-End. CHDISCLOSE Is Zero Minus DISCLOSE, the Differences in Disclosures Required Under IAS Vis-à-Vis a Firm's Domestic-GAAP. CHMETHODS Is Zero Minus METHODS, the Difference in Measurement Method Restrictions Under IAS Vis-à-Vis a Firm's Domestic-GAAP. CHIASSET Is Zero Minus IASSET, the Overall Accounting Standard Index for the Firm's Country of Domicile in the Pre-IAS Adoption Period Reported in Table 2

(a) Change in disclosure: $CHFERROR_i = \alpha + \beta_1 CHNUM_i + \beta_2 CHMVE_i + \beta_3 CHDISCLOSE_i + \varepsilon_i$

(b) Change in methods: $CHFERROR_i = \alpha + \beta_1 CHNUM_i + \beta_2 CHMVE_i + \beta_3 CHMETHODS_i + \varepsilon_i$

(c) Change in policies: $CHFERROR_i = \alpha + \beta_1 CHNUM_i + \beta_2 CHMVE_i + \beta_3 CHIASSET_i + \varepsilon_i$

Predicted	Sign	Model (a)	(b)	(c)
α	?	0.0008	0.0007	0.0023
		(0.093)	(0.077)	(0.260)
$CHNUM_i$	−	0.0018	0.0013	0.0017
		[1.454]	[1.171]	[1.429]
$CHMVE_i$	−	−0.0180	−0.0189	−0.0184
		[−1.939]**	[−2.093]**	[−1.896]*
$CHDISCLOSE_i$	−/+	0.0055		
		(1.823)*		
$CHMETHODS_i$	−/+		0.0061	
			(1.952)*	
$CHIASSET_i$	−/+			0.0033
				(2.029)**
N		80	80	80
Adj. R^2		10.18	10.73	11.07

All regression variables are winzorized to the 1st and 99th percentile values.

t-statistics are in brackets for one-tail tests; *, ** one-tail p-*value* < .10 and .05, respectively.

t-statistics are in parentheses for two-tail tests; *, ** two-tail p-*value* < .10 and < .05, respectively.

The variables used to test H2 are CHDISCLOSE, CHMETHODS, and CHIASSET, which are represented by CHX in equation (2). Recall that H2 is a non-directional hypothesis, and thus predicts that $\beta_3 \neq 0$; i.e., that change in analyst forecast errors is related to changes in, respectively, disclosure policies, measurement methods, or accounting standards taken as a whole.[12] Changes in market value and analyst following are expected to be negatively related to CHFERROR.

Table 6 reports the results of estimating equation (2). Adjusted R^2s are approximately 10–11%. The coefficients on CHNUM are not significant, while the coefficients on CHMVE are negative and significant, indicating that as

---

[12] Pearson (Spearman) correlations between CHFERROR and, respectively, CHDISCLOSE, CHMETHODS, and CHIASSET are 0.25 (0.20), 0.28 (0.25), and 0.28 (0.23).

430   H. ASHBAUGH AND M. PINCUS

TABLE 7

Univariate Tests of Changes in News Reports. Changes Are Calculated from the Year Prior to IAS Adoption (t − 1) to the Year After IAS Adoption (t + 1). CHTOT Is the Change in the Total Number of News Reports About the Firm, and CHEA Is the Change in the Number of Earnings-Related News Reports About the Firm (Both Obtained from the Financial Times Index).

Variable	N[1]	Mean	Std. Dev.	Minimum	Maximum
Firms for which CHIASSET < 0:					
CHTOT	65	4.2461***	12.8938	−23.0000	42.0000
CHEA	65	1.8000***	4.7374	−5.0000	15.0000
Canadian Firms (CHIASSET = 0):					
CHTOT	12	2.5000	4.9810	−2.0000	15.0000
CHEA	12	2.3333*	3.7979	−1.0000	10.0000

[1] Three firms for which CHIASSET < 0 were not covered in the *Financial Times Index*.

*, *** A t-test rejects the hypothesis of no difference from zero (two-tail p-*value* < .10 and .01 respectively).

Changes are calculated from the year prior to IAS adoption (t − 1) to the year after IAS adoption (t + 1). CHTOT is the change in the total number of news reports about the firm, and CHEA is the change in the number of earnings-related news reports about the firm (both obtained from the *Financial Times Index*).

firms grow in market value, analysts forecast errors decrease. Turning to the variables of primary interest, we find that the coefficients on CHDISCLOSE and CHMETHODS are positive and significant (t = 1.823 and 1.952, respectively, two-tail p-*values* < .10), as is the coefficient on CHIASSET (t = 2.029, two-tail p-*value* < .05). These results indicate that analyst forecast errors decrease as the number of accounting policy differences from IAS decrease as a result of firms adopting IAS.[13] This suggests that firms domiciled in countries with accounting standards that require less disclosure and/or have more measurement method choices as compared to IAS benefit relatively more from adopting IAS because sophisticated users of their financial reports are now able to predict with greater accuracy a key valuation-relevant factor.[14]

4.3 THE IMPACT OF CHANGES IN NEWS REPORTS

We posit that IAS adoptions are part of a broader strategy by firms to expand their financial disclosures. For instance, at the same time they adopt IAS, firms may also increase press releases or more generally promote greater news coverage of their earnings-related activities. If so, an increase in news reports, rather than the adoption of IAS, might explain the improvement in analyst forecast accuracy.

We investigate this possibility by collecting news reports from the *Financial Times Index* for our sample firms in the years surrounding IAS adoption. We find news items for all but three sample firms in the *Index*. Table 7 reports

---

[13] We winsorize all variables in the regression analyses to their 1st and 99th percentile values. When we do not winsorize variables, two-tail p-*values* are .20, .16, and .15, respectively, for the t-statistics on the coefficients for CHDISCLOSE, CHMETHODS, and CHIASSET.

[14] Sixteen firms that adopted IAS were listed on a U.S. stock exchange that required the firms to file U.S.-GAAP data in supplemental filings with the Securities and Exchange Commission. These firms are from Australia (3), Canada (9), Finland (1), France (2), and Spain (1). We include them in our sample since analysts typically do not forecast alternative earnings measures included in supplemental reports. We conduct sensitivity tests excluding these 16 firms and find that the results are at least as significant as the results based on the full sample.

the change from year $t - 1$ to year $t + 1$ in the average number of earnings-related news reports (CHEA) and of all news reports (CHTOT) for the firms having CHIASSET < 0 and for the Canadian firms. Both subsamples reflect a reliable increase in news reports over the period surrounding IAS adoption, with firms having CHIASSET < 0 exhibiting a larger increase in overall news reports. To assess the impact of the increase in news items on the test of H2, we augment equation (2) with the change in news reports. The results (not reported) indicate that the coefficient on CHTOT is insignificant, while the coefficient on CHIASSET continues to be significant.

5. Conclusion

In this study we investigate whether differences in countries' accounting measurement and disclosure standards relative to IAS affect analyst forecast accuracy of non-U.S. firms' annual earnings. In addition, we examine whether adoption of IAS changes the absolute value of analyst forecast errors.

Using a sample of 80 non-U.S. firms, we find that, prior to adopting IAS, the extent of differences in countries disclosure and measurement policies relative to IAS is positively associated with analysts' earnings forecast errors. We also document a decrease in the absolute value of analyst forecast errors after firms adopt IAS. We find no evidence of significant changes in adopting firms' business and geographic segments and extent of foreign sales, but we observe increases in firms' market capitalizations and analyst following. After controlling for changes in market capitalization and analyst following, the results indicate that analyst earnings forecast errors decrease when the differences in accounting measurement and disclosure policies decline as a result of firms' adoptions of IAS. Furthermore, this result holds after controlling for the concurrent growth in news reports.

Choi and Levich [1992] argue that differences in domestic-GAAPs contribute to a continuum of information sets reported by firms. Our results indicate that those differences in reporting standards across countries relative to the benchmark of IAS affect the ability of financial analysts to accurately forecast non-U.S. firms' earnings. Prior studies report mixed results regarding whether the convergence of countries' accounting standards to a more uniform set of standards increases the informativeness of firms' financial reports (Joos and Lang [1994]; Auer [1996]). Our results are consistent with firms' financial information becoming more predictable following their adoptions of IAS and the consequent reduction in the variation in measurement and disclosure practices.

APPENDIX A

The tables included in this appendix provide additional details about the calculation of DISCLOSE, METHODS, and IASSET, which capture, respectively, the differences in financial reporting standards across countries relative to IAS due to the differences in disclosure requirements,

TABLE A1

DISCLOSE: Variation in Disclosure Standards of IAS versus Domestic-GAAPs. X = When a Domestic-GAAP Has No Disclosure Requirement or the Domestic-GAAP Requires Less Disclosure Than IAS. Comparisons Are Based on Standards in Effect as of January 1, 1993. Disclosure Items Are as Follows: (1) Providing a Statement of Cash Flows; (2) Disclosure of Accounting Policies; (3) Disclosure of the Effect of a Change in Accounting Policy; (4) Disclosure of the Effect of a Change in Accounting Estimate; (5) Disclosure of Prior Period Adjustments; (6) Disclosure of Post Balance Sheet Events; (7) Disclosure of Related Party Transactions; and (8) Disclosure of Segment Information. The Countries Examined Are Based on Where the Firms Used in the Empirical Analysis Are Domiciled.

Country	Disclosure Items								Total
	1	2	3	4	5	6	7	8	
Australia					X				1
Canada									0
Denmark					X	X			2
Finland	X		X	X	X	X	X		6
France	X			X	X	X			4
Hong Kong	X				X		X		3
Japan				X	X				2
Malaysia	X			X					2
Norway	X	X		X	X	X	X	X	7
Singapore	X			X					2
Spain				X	X		X		3
Sweden	X			X	X	X		X	5
Switzerland	X			X	X			X	4

TABLE A2

METHODS: Variation in Measurement Methods of IAS versus Domestic-GAAPs. X = When IAS Restricts the Accounting Measurement Methods Relative to the Measurement Methods Available Under Domestic-GAAP. Comparisons Are Based on Standards in Effect as of January 1, 1993. The Countries Examined Are Based on Where the Firms Used in the Empirical Analysis Are Domiciled.

Country	Measurement Method Restrictions				Total
	Additional Depreciation	Accounting for Leases	Accounting for Pensions	Research & Development	
Australia			X	X	2
Canada					0
Denmark		X		X	2
Finland	X	X	X	X	4
France	X	X	X		3
Hong Kong				X	1
Japan		X	X		2
Malaysia					0
Norway			X		1
Singapore					0
Spain			X		1
Sweden		X	X		2
Switzerland	X	X	X	X	4

measurement method restrictions, and reporting standards overall (see Ashbaugh [2001]). Table A1 compares eight IAS disclosure requirements in force in 1993 to the 1993 disclosure requirements of the domestic-GAAPs of the sample firms' countries of domicile. A domestic-GAAP's disclosure requirement is considered less demanding than IAS if (1) there is no domestic-GAAP requirement or (2) the requirement is for less disclosure than IAS.

Table A2 compares four IAS measurement rules in force in 1993 to the 1993 domestic-GAAP measurement rules for countries where firms in our sample are domiciled. IAS are considered to be more restrictive than domestic-GAAP when IAS has fewer acceptable accounting methods for an economic event relative to the methods acceptable under domestic-GAAP.

The IASSET index values presented in table 2 of the text equal the sum of the additional disclosure requirements (i.e., DISCLOSE) reported in table A1 and the measurement choice restrictions (i.e., METHODS) reported in table A2.

REFERENCES

ALFORD, A.; J. JONES; R. LEFTWICH; AND M. ZMIJEWSKI. "The Relative Informativeness of Accounting Disclosures in Different Countries." *Journal of Accounting Research* (Supplement 1993): 183–223.

ASHBAUGH, H. "Non-U.S. Firms' Accounting Standard Choices." *Journal of Accounting and Public Policy* (2000): 129–53.

AUER, K. "Capital Market Reactions to Earnings Announcements: Empirical Evidence on the Difference in the Information Content of IAS-Based Earnings and EC Directives-Based Earnings." *The European Accounting Review* (1996): 587–623.

BARRON, O.; O. KIM; S. LIM; AND D. STEVENS. "Using Analysts' Forecasts to Measure Properties of Analysts' Information Environment." *The Accounting Review* (October 1998): 421–33.

BELSEY, D. A.; E. KUH; AND R. E. WELSCH. *Regression Diagnostics*. New York: John Wiley & Sons, 1980.

BROWN, L. "Accounting Changes and the Accuracy of Analyst Earnings Forecasts." *Journal of Accounting Research* (Autumn 1983): 432–43.

CHOI, F., AND R. LEVICH. "International Accounting Diversity and Capital Market Decisions." In *Handbook of International Accounting*, edited by F. Choi, pp. 7.1–7.29. New York: John Wiley & Sons, 1992.

COOPERS LYBRAND. *International Accounting Summaries*, Second edition. New York: John Wiley & Sons, 1993.

DAVIS-FRIDAY, P., AND N. RUESCHHOFF. "International Accounting Standards versus U.S. GAAP: How Do They Compare?" Working paper, University of Notre Dame, 1998.

EGGERT, R. "German Corporate Law and Accounting Legislation." *International Tax Review* (July/August 1998): 61–2.

ELLIOTT, J., AND D. PHILBRICK. "Accounting Changes and Earnings Predictability." *The Accounting Review* (January 1990): 157–74.

FINANCIAL ACCOUNTING STANDARDS BOARD (FASB). *The IASC–U.S. Comparison Project: A Report on the Similarities and Differences Between IASC Standards and U.S. GAAP*, 1996.

FRANKEL, R., AND C. LEE. "Accounting Diversity and International Valuation." Working paper, University of Michigan, 1997.

FROST, C., AND W. KINNEY. "Disclosure Choices of Foreign Registrants in the United States." *Journal of Accounting Research* (Spring 1996): 67–84.

INTERNATIONAL ACCOUNTING STANDARDS COMMITTEE (IASC). *International Accounting Standards*, 1998.

434   H. ASHBAUGH AND M. PINCUS

INTERNATIONAL ACCOUNTING STANDARDS COMMITTEE (IASC). *http://www.iasc.org* (October 30, 1999).

JOOS, P., AND M. LANG. "The Effects of Accounting Diversity: Evidence from the European Community." *Journal of Accounting Research* (Supplement 1994): 141–68.

LANG, M., AND R. LUNDHOLM. "Cross-Sectional Determinants of Analyst Ratings of Corporate Disclosures." *Journal of Accounting Research* (Autumn 1993): 246–71.

LANG, M., AND R. LUNDHOLM. "Corporate Disclosure Policy and Analyst Behavior." *The Accounting Review* (October 1996): 467–92.

STREET, D.; S. GRAY; AND S. BRYANT. "Acceptance and Observance of International Accounting Standards: An Empirical Study of Companies Claiming to Comply with IASs." *The International Journal of Accounting* (1999): 11–48.

[18]

The European Accounting Review 1996, 5:4, 587–623

Capital market reactions to earnings announcements: empirical evidence on the difference in the information content of IAS-based earnings and EC-Directives-based earnings

Kurt V. Auer
University of Innsbruck, Austria

ABSTRACT

Listing on a foreign stock exchange and the aim to attract international investors usually forces European quoted companies to adapt information supplied in financial statements to different information needs of international investors. Because of the dominance of the American stock market, this adaptation raises especially the question whether Anglo-American-oriented accounting standards (for instance IAS – International Accounting Standards) convey a higher information content for investors than continental-Europe-oriented accounting standards (for instance EC-Directives). The study examines the information content of earnings announcements, i.e. abnormal returns resulting from un-expected earnings, for a sample of Swiss quoted companies which have changed the accounting standard used for presenting Swiss GAAP consolidated financial statements to either EC-Directives or IAS and can therefore contribute to this discussion. The results of the study suggest that IAS-based earnings announce-ments convey a statistically significant higher information content than earnings announcements based on the Swiss GAAP if a variance-approach is used. For investors in the Swiss capital market, the switch from Swiss GAAP to IAS has therefore increased the information content of financial statements. But comparing IAS-based and EC-Directives-based earnings announcements, the results suggest that for investors IAS-based earnings do not possess a statistically significant higher information content than EC-Directives-based earnings. This result has been achieved despite the fact that for Swiss financial analysts financial statements based on IAS convey a significant higher information content than financial statements based on EC-Directives. Avoiding problems in specifying a model for unexpected earnings by standardizing the mean of the abnormal returns of each event window to a positive value does not lead to a different conclusion if the variance approach is used.

Address for correspondence
Institut für Finanzwirtschaft und Controlling Universität Innsbruck, Bozner Platz 4, A-6020 Innsbruck, Austria

© 1996 European Accounting Association   0963-8180

INTRODUCTION

Companies raise capital and/or list their stocks outside their home country for a number of reasons: a) domestic capital markets are often too small to provide the capital required by internationally oriented companies, b) international capital markets are now more accessible, c) companies wish to match the currency of their operations and profits with the currency of their dividend flows by attracting foreign shareholders, d) international listings may provide increased liquidity of the securities and can therefore increase the attractiveness to investors and e) a listing on a foreign stock exchange can help to raise the profile of the company in the country of listing. But listing on a foreign stock exchange and/or the aim to attract international investors usually forces European quoted companies to adapt information supplied in financial statements to different information needs of international investors. Especially of great importance for investors are differences between local accounting traditions, which could have a negative impact on international portfolio decisions. For instance, Choi and Levich (1990) show that nearly one half of the institutions in their sample (representatives of 51 institutions with headquarters in Japan, Switzerland, the UK, the USA, and Germany) feel that their capital market decisions are affected by accounting diversity (see Table 1). The results of Choi and Levich also suggest that more than half of the investors examined are affected in their investment decisions by differences between their national and the internationally required accounting standard. They either try to adjust the national accounts to their home accounts as far as possible or to adapt an investment strategy that reduces the effect of such differences, for instance an underweighting in these markets (see Table 2).

In order to avoid negative impacts resulting from international accounting diversity on portfolio decisions of national investors, the SEC (Securities and Exchange Commission) in the USA forces foreign companies which seek listing on the NYSE to reconcile their financial statements from the home GAAP to US GAAP. For example, for the listing of ADRs on the NYSE the German company Daimler-Benz had to reconcile the net income and the

Table 1 Key question: Does accounting diversity affect your capital market decisions?

	Yes	No	Not available	Total
Investors	9	7	1	17
Issuers	6	9		15
Underwriters	7	1		8
Regulators	0	8		8
Raters and others	2	1		3
Total	24	26	1	51

Table 2 Capital Market Effects of Accounting Diversity: Investors (Choi and Levich, 1990, p. 129)

	From GAAP differences	From disclosure differences
Geographic spread of investments	3	3
Types of companies/securities selected	6	7
Information processing costs	5*	2[†]
Assessment of security return or valuation	8	8

* Two reported these costs were significant
[†] Both feel this cost is significant

stockholders' equity from the home GAAP (dHGB) to US GAAP. The listing of Daimler also gives a public transparency of possible differences in the impact of various accounting standards on earnings and owners' equity, i.e. for Daimler between US GAAP and German GAAP. In contrast to a published net income of DM 168 Mio under home GAAP for the first half of 1993, Daimler reported a net loss of DM 949 Mio based on US GAAP. Based on dHGB, the stockholders' equity amounted to DM 18.938 Mio, based on US GAAP to DM 26.231 Mio.

The disclosure of a reconciliation, for example the reconciliation of a continental-Europe-oriented accounting standard (e.g. EC-Directives), to an Anglo-American-oriented accounting standard (e.g. US GAAP or IAS), raises the question, whether such a reconciliation or whether the resulting differences provide information to investors not yet reflected in current stock prices or increases the explanatory power of accounting earnings for stock prices. Up to now, only few studies give some indication, whether different GAAPs possess different information content to investors. Despite the fact that final results cannot be achieved, empirical studies can be of interest in several aspects: a) it is possible to interpret the information content of accounting figures measured under different GAAP rules to investors, b) empirical studies can give an indication of the success of standard setters in different countries in meeting information needs of capital markets, c) they show from an economic point of view, whether it is necessary to require restatements for a listing on stock exchanges abroad (for instance in the USA) or not and finally d) empirical results are important for the harmonization discussion.

Empirical studies on the information content of earnings based on various local standards have shown only a weak correlation between stock prices and earnings. Lev (1989) has therefore proposed further research on the quality of earnings, which could increase this relationship. But the quality of earnings is a multi-dimensional concept and is also affected by international accounting diversity. Since a complete discussion of such a concept is beyond the scope of this paper, this research is limited to the question whether different GAAP regimes possess different information content to investors. As a proxy for the information content of financial statements, the information content of earnings announcements based on different accounting standards is used (see point a) above).

Because of the dominance of the US capital market and the listing requirements of the NYSE, the US GAAP are still the dominating 'benchmark' in capital market research. But previous studies have shown no clear indication of statistically significant differences in the information content of US GAAP and various accounting standards outside the USA. Therefore, these studies also give no clear indication of the usefulness of a reconciliation from various home GAAPs to US GAAP to the capital market (Meek, 1983; Meek, 1991; Pope and Rees (1993); Amir, Harris and Venuti (1993); Harris, Lang and Möller, 1994). However the SEC has recently accepted cash flow statements based on IAS 7 as fully equivalent to US GAAP. If SEC is going forward in easing the listing requirements on the NYSE and will accept also full financial statements based on IAS as fully equivalent to financial statements based on US GAAP in the future, this would rapidly increase the importance of IAS for listed companies in Europe. Examples for the increasing popularity of IAS can be found in Switzerland and in Germany.[1] For investors and for European companies the increasing importance of IAS also raises the question of differences in the information content of IAS-based accounting figures and accounting figures based on EC-Directives.

It has to be mentioned that a result which provides evidence that an accounting standard η_2 (e.g. IAS) conveys a higher information content to the needs of investors than an accounting standard η_1 (e.g. EC-Directives) cannot be interpreted in the way that accounting standard η_2 is in every respect superior to η_1. The development of national accounting standards is influenced by a number of factors. For instance, the information needs can differ between countries because of a higher portion of credit-financing in German-speaking countries in contrast to a higher portion of stock-market financing in the USA or differences between financial statements can result from a higher or lower influence of tax law on financial accounting. Therefore, differences between national accounting standards have also to be regarded as a result of differences in the socio-economic environment of these countries. If such differences are taken into consideration, local accounting standards can represent best solutions for a specific socio-economic environment of a country.

MOTIVATION FOR THE RESEARCH

Within the international accounting harmonization process, most effort has been done by the IASC (International Accounting Standards Committee) during the last years.[2] Up to now, the IASC has released 31 IAS (International Accounting Standards),[3] one proposed revised IAS (Income Taxes) and one proposed new IAS (Financial Instruments). In the past, IAS were mainly adapted by countries which did not have their own standard-setting bodies either as their national standards or as an acceptable basis for financial reporting. In addition, some stock exchanges have already recognized IAS as an acceptable basis for financial reporting. The London Stock Exchange, for example, encourages foreign companies to use IAS for presenting financial information. But as mentioned above, if the SEC is going forward in easing listing requirements on the NYSE and would also accept full financial statements based on IAS as fully equivalent to financial statements based on US GAAP, international adaptation of IAS would rapidly increase. A significant step forward in the world-wide acceptance of IAS has been issued recently:

> The IASC and IOSCO's technical committee, in a joint statement issued in Paris, said their goal was that international accounting standards 'can be used worldwide in cross border offerings and listings as an alternative to the use of national accounting standards.' The agreement, while stopping short of immediate recognition of a batch of 14 standards already acceptable in theory to IOSCO, marks a significant step forward in the long-term project to provide companies with an accounting framework for foreign markets.[4]

For investors and for European quoted companies this progress now raises the question of differences in the information content of accounting figures based on IAS and on EC-Directives. The study is the first empirical study on the information content of IAS-figures and gives therefore first results on differences in the information content of earnings based on IAS, EC-Directives and Swiss GAAP. The Swiss capital market has been chosen for research, as within a few years, companies – representing more than half of the capitalization of the Swiss stock market – have changed the accounting standard used for presenting consolidated statements from the local Swiss GAAP to either IAS or EC-Directives. Because of the low regulation of measurement and disclosure rules by Swiss GAAP, financial statements which are based on IAS or EC-Directives also fulfil the requirements of Swiss GAAP (Bertschinger, 1991; Thiel, 1991; Vischer, 1991). Neglecting the pressure from the capital market, the decision of Swiss companies to base their consolidated statements on IAS or EC-Directives is purely on a voluntarily basis.

> The willingness of continental companies to tap the international capital markets for new equity has greatly increased in recent years, a trend accelerated by Germany's shift from net exporter of capital to net importer. ... In order to tap those markets continental companies have had to offer international investors Anglo-Saxon standards of accounting disclosure. The rush towards frankness has been most noticeable in Switzerland.[5]

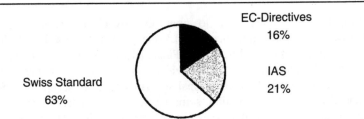

Figure 1 Swiss stock market: accounting standards used by companies (Fiscal year 1993): Based on the number of companies

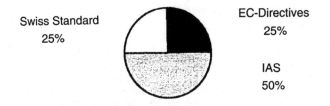

Figure 2 Swiss stock market: accounting standards used by companies (Fiscal year 1993): Based on the market capitalization

At the end of the fiscal year 1993, about 21% of the Swiss quoted companies have based their financial statements on IAS and about 16% on EC-Directives (see Figure 1).

But if the stock market capitalization is taken into consideration, the picture is clearly changing: companies, representing about 50% of the total market capitalization, base their financial statements on IAS and about 25% on EC-Directives (see Figure 2). This result can be explained by the fact that internationally oriented, higher capitalized Swiss companies usually prefer IAS in order to attract international investors. Neglecting high capitalized banks and insurance companies, which are not included in the sample examined, increases the share of IAS to 68%, and reduces the share of EC-Directives to 19%.

In contrast to the countries of the European Union, Switzerland has not transformed the EC-Directives into local law. Therefore, financial statements of Swiss companies only rely on the EC-Directives as a framework including all alternative measurement and disclosure treatments permitted to the member states of the European Union. Despite, measurement and disclosure practices of Swiss companies, which base their financial statements on EC-Directives, show, that they are more oriented on continental-Europe accounting traditions than on Anglo-American accounting traditions, which also form part of the 'culture' of the EC-Directives.[6] Neglecting the influence of Anglo-American traditions on the EC-Directives, major differences between IAS and EC-Directives result for Swiss companies from:

- A different definition of users of financial statements: In contrast to the EC-Directives, which try to serve different information needs of various users, the IAS only focus on the information needs of investors:

   > While all of the information needs of the users, i.e. investors, employees, lenders, suppliers and other trade creditors, customers, governments and their agencies as well as public,[7] cannot be met by financial statements, there are needs which are common to all users. As investors are providers of risk capital to the enterprise, the provision of financial statements that meet their needs will also meet most of the needs of other users that financial statements can satisfy.[8]

- Focusing on the information needs of investors results in an under-weighting of the prudence principle. For instance, the IAS use a more optimistic view in building contingencies, the EC-Directives a more pessimistic view.[9]
- In contrast to the EC-Directives, there is no significant impact of capital maintenance on the decision usefulness of financial statements based on IAS. Which means, that also the interpretation of the realization principle differs between EC-Directives and IAS. For instance, not yet 'realized' profits resulting from currency translation,[10] construction contracts,[11] deferred taxes[12] or investments[13] are shown in financial statements based on IAS but not or only in later periods in financial statements based on EC-Directives.
- Differences between IAS and EC-Directives also result from disclosure requirements: for instance, the EC-Directives only require the reporting of segment sales and employees, whereas IAS also require disclosure of segment results and segment assets employed.

A more detailed description of differences between IAS and EC-Directives can be seen from SVFV/Arthur Andersen (1991). As mentioned above, measurement and disclosure rules of Swiss GAAP are only low regulated. Because of the resulting heterogeneous measurement and disclosure practices in Swiss financial statements, it is not possible to specify precisely the average impact of the change in the accounting standard from Swiss GAAP to IAS or EC-Directives on the earnings. But generally speaking, in contrast to EC-Directives, the switch to IAS should result in an increase of the profit, mainly due to the differences between EC-Directives and IAS as mentioned above. For instance, the switch from Swiss GAAP to IAS resulted for Ciba-Geigy, a leading company in the pharmaceutical and chemical sector, in an increase of the profit from SFr 1.500 Mio to SFr 1.600 Mio. This change in the profit of Ciba-Geigy was mainly influenced by:[14]

- A change in the scope of consolidation (inclusion of companies outside the traditional scope of Ciba, i.e. reinsurance): SFr + 50 Mio.
- A switch to historical cost accounting: impact on depreciation: SFr + 350 Mio, impact on cost of goods sold (FIFO instead of current value): SFr + 100 Mio.
- A change in capitalization rules (more capitalized assets): SFr + 100 Mio.
- Exchange rate effects: SFr – 50 Mio.
- Impact of market valuation on marketable securities: SFr + 50 Mio.
- A change in the rules of building contingencies, primarily for retirement benefits, deferred taxes, inventory write-offs: SFr – 200 Mio.
- Inclusion of extraordinary items in the profit and loss account: SFr – 200 Mio.
- Other items: SFr – 200 Mio.

INFORMATION DIFFERENCES BETWEEN IAS, EC-DIRECTIVES AND SWISS GAAP FROM A FINANCIAL ANALYST PERSPECTIVE

One explanation for the popularity of the IAS in Switzerland seems to be a standard which is close to US GAAP but does not, at least at that time, impose the quantity and the strength of regulations of US GAAP. In addition, pressure results from Swiss financial analysts which declared IAS as the preferred benchmark: every year, the information content of financial statements (including the quality of consolidated statements, the number of detail information given and interim reporting) of a sample of Swiss quoted companies is evaluated by the analysts and the results officially released. As can be seen from Table 3, companies which base their financial statements (including interim reporting) on IAS are on average higher ranked than companies which base their financial statements on EC-Directives. Companies which base their financial statements on Swiss GAAP are ranked clearly below IAS-statements and EC-Directive-statements.

Swiss financial analyst define the objective of financial statements as to give a true and fair view or to present information fairly. The information given in the financial statements should correspond to reliability, materiality, relevance, neutrality, prudence and comparability (SVFV and Arthur Andersen, 1991, 89). Characteristics, which all are included in the framework of the IASC (IASC, 1995, framework). Even though the framework of the IASC, which is widely influenced by the framework of the American FASB (Baetge and Ross, 1995, 27), does not deal directly with the concept of true and fair view or the fair presentation, the application of the principle qualitative characteristics (i.e. understandability, relevance, reliability and comparability) and of appropriate accounting standards normally results, in

Table 3 Ranking of Swiss industrial and services companies by the Swiss Financial Analysts Association[23]

Company	Standard 1993	Results in % (maximum 100%)						
		86/87	87/88	88/89	89/90	91[24]	92	93
Adia	IAS	45	51	50	59	40.4	55.2	56.9
Alusuisse	ISA/EC-Dir	64	68	72	75	84.8	86.7	87.7
Ares Serono	IAS	–	69	68	75	–	64.1	59.5
Ascom	IAS	–	47	59	63	62.0	68.7	83.9
BBC	IAS	62	66	82	86	78.6	76.6	87.1
Bührle	IAS/EC-Dir	52	56	78	80	61.6	86.7	94.7
Ciba-Geigy	IAS	62	68	71	73	46.3	49.5	75.9
Elco Looser	EC-Dir	–	79	89	94	–	68.6	80.7
Elektrowatt	EC-Dir	–	–	–	–	50.4	66.4	77.2
Ems	IAS	55	70	77	85	–	60.4	71.9
Escor	Swiss GAAP	–	73	82	83	–	25.3	29.7
Fischer	EC-Dir	74	84	88	88	59.8	60.7	58.3
Forbo	IAS	71	70	83	85	–	68.8	73.2
Gavazzi	US GAAP	61	59	61	61	–	72.8	76.5
Globus	Swiss GAAP	70	75	77	78	–	56.9	69.0
Hero	EC-Dir	47	56	63	79	–	63.2	70.1
Holderbank	IAS/EC-Dir	68	85	86	81	56.3	79.5	83.0
Interdiscount	Swiss GAAP	95	98	98	98	–	21.9	30.4
Jelmoli	FER	75	77	78	88	–	23.7	56.5
Landis & Gyr	IAS	92	92	92	92	–	62.6	70.8
Lindt & Sprüngli	EC-Dir	42	49	53	55	–	47.4	53.9
Merck	EC-Dir	–	–	41	56	–	53.1	63.0
Merkur	Swiss GAAP	65	68	77	74	–	55.2	74.2
Mikron	IAS/EC-Dir	87	88	90	90	–	65.6	63.4
Nestlé	IAS	53	54	56	70	75.6	76.8	80.3
RIG-Rentsch	EC-Dir	57	56	56	56	–	39.2	–
Roche	IAS	64	72	73	77	56.3	63.2	63.3
Sandoz	IAS	57	58	64	64	23.9	67.4	73.4
Schindler	Swiss GAAP	41	42	42	50	25.0	23.6	23.2
Sika	IAS	70	79	89	93	–	52.4	67.1
Sulzer	IAS/EC-Dir	63	65	64	69	–	70.5	82.0
Surveillance	IAS	–	–	–	–	19.5	26.6	68.0
Swissair	EC-Dir	72	81	90	93	46.8	58.2	69.9
Von Roll	EC-Dir	68	69	86	87	–	57.1	61.3
Walter Meier	EC-Dir	91	94	71	84	–	70.5	69.8
Walter Rentsch	Swiss GAAP	91	94	71	84	–	40.7	47.4

the opinion of the IASC, in financial statements that convey what is generally understood as a true and fair view of, or as presenting fairly such information.[15] Deviations from this concept and deviations from the disclosure level defined as necessary for analysing financial statements result in a lower ranking by Swiss financial analysts. For instance, a more pessimistic view underlying the building of contingencies do not correspond to the objective of financial statements to give a true and fair view and results

596　The European Accounting Review

Table 4 Assessment approach of Swiss financial analysts: information content of financial statements including interim reporting (SVFV and Arthur Andersen, 1991, p. 116)

Part 1	Part 2	Part 3	Part 4	Total
Quality of consolidated statements 0–10	Number of detail information given in consolidated statements 0–500 Points	Other parts of financial statements	Interim Reporting	Total points are calculated as follows: (part 1 × part 2) + part 3 + part 4
Part 1 × Part 2 = Interim result of quality and information content of consolidated financial statements				
		0–2000 points	0–3000 points	0–10000 points
0–5000 points (maximum 10 × 500 points)				
50%		20%	30%	100%

therefore in a lower ranking (see for differences between IAS and EC-Directives the previous section.).

Differences in the information content between financial statements based on IAS, EC-Directives and Swiss GAAP, in the opinion of Swiss financial analysts, are also apparent from a breakdown of the results in Table 3. Table 4 shows the maximum points of the various parts of the assessment approach, Table 5 the average results for companies which base their financial statements on EC-Directives, IAS and Swiss GAAP.

For this study, the most interesting part of the assessment approach is the criterion 'quality of consolidated statements and detail information given', which, for instance, includes the true and fair view-concept, the consistency of measurement practices, the use of measurement practices which do not result in building up hidden reserves, the disclosure of related party transactions and the disclosure of segment reporting. Regarding only this part of the assessment approach, companies in the EC-Directives-sample show on average for the fiscal year 1993 a fulfilment of 64% of maximum points, companies in the IAS-sample on average 84%. Companies which base their financial statements on Swiss GAAP show on average a fulfilment of only 32%. Hence, the results suggest that financial analysts regard IAS-based financial statements to convey (at least in Switzerland) a higher information-content than EC-Directives-based financial statements. Only a low informa-tion content is supposed for companies which base their financial statements on Swiss GAAP.

Assuming that the assessment approach of Swiss financial analysts results in a true picture of the differences in the information content of financial statements based on various accounting standards it can be assumed:

Table 5 Assessment approach of Swiss financial analysts: information content of financial statements including interim reporting for fiscal year 1993 (SVFV, 1994)

	Total	Quality of consolidated statements	Detail information given	Other information	6-Months interim reporting	Other interim reporting
Maximum points	10 000	10	500	2000	2000	1000
EC-Directives		8.94	359.40	1081.60	310.50	722.00
IAS		9.52	439.75	1291.75	775.00	786.25
Others		4.87	276.44	927.67	365.56	552.22
EC-Directives	5327		3213	1082	311	722
IAS	7040		4187	1292	775	786
Others	3192		1347	928	366	552
Fulfilment in % of maximum						
EC-Directives	53		64	54	16	72
IAS	70		84	65	39	79
Others	32		27	46	18	55

- that earnings (earnings announcements) based on IAS convey a higher information content for financial analysts in the Swiss stock market than earnings (earnings announcements) based on the Swiss GAAP,
- that earnings (earnings announcements) based on EC-Directives convey a higher information content for financial analysts in the Swiss stock market than earnings (earnings announcements) based on the Swiss GAAP,
- that earnings (earnings announcements) based on IAS convey a higher information content for financial analysts in the Swiss stock market than earnings (earnings announcements) based on EC-Directives.

Table 5 also shows, that on average, information content of interim reporting is low for both the EC-Directives sample and the IAS-sample. This result is mainly due to the fact, that the majority of Swiss quoted companies did not release interim earnings in the fiscal years examined. For this reason, interim reporting should not have a significant impact on the information content of the fiscal-year (year-end) earnings announcements examined.

INFORMATION CONTENT DIFFERENCES BETWEEN IAS, EC-DIRECTIVES AND SWISS GAAP FROM A CAPITAL MARKET PERSPECTIVE

The differences in the information content of financial statements based on IAS, EC-Directives and Swiss GAAP for financial analysts as presented above raise the question, whether the switch from Swiss GAAP to IAS or

EC-Directives results not only in a higher ranking by Swiss financial analysts but also in a higher information content of earnings (as a proxy for the information content of financial statements) to investors.

The information content is usually defined as the potential for an event, such as the earnings announcements, to change extant market expectations. These underlying expectations are formed on the set of publicly available information in an informationally efficient market. Therefore, in a setting where market efficiency in a semi-strong form (Fama, 1970, 383F) holds, the unexpected element of an event (information not yet anticipated by the market) will have an impact on expectations and in consequence on capital market reactions as soon as it enters the public domain.

A comparison of the capital market reactions to unexpected earnings in the years preceding and subsequent to the change in the accounting standard gives an indication of differences in the information content of the new standard (IAS or EC-Directives) in contrast to the old standard (Swiss GAAP). In addition, a comparison of the information content of IAS-based earnings and EC-Directives-based earnings allows conclusions on differences in the information content of earnings based on Anglo-American accounting traditions versus the information content of earnings based on continental-Europe accounting traditions (see Motivation for the research).

Hypotheses tested

Empirical results have shown, that abnormal returns are higher for periods surrounding earnings announcements than for periods without new information announcements (Ball and Brown, 1968; Gonedes, 1974; Collins, 1975; Patell, 1976; Foster, 1977). For instance, Ball and Brown (1968) have tested the hypothesis that annual earnings announcements convey information to the market by using the abnormal returns (for a definition of abnormal returns see below) of a specific period surrounding the announcement. If earnings announcements convey information content for the capital market, the subsample of positive unexpected earnings (see below) should show positive abnormal returns in the period examined (event-window) and the negative subsample negative abnormal returns.

Based on this research methodology, also differences in the information content of various accounting standards can be tested by comparing the abnormal returns based on an accounting standard η_1 and the abnormal returns based on an accounting standard η_2 (see Figure 3).

A result which shows, that the mean abnormal return resulting from unexpected earnings $(\overline{AR})$ for the period examined (event-window) is higher for earnings based on accounting standard η_2 than for earnings based on accounting standard η_1, i.e.: $\overline{AR}_{\eta 1} < \overline{AR}_{\eta 2}$ could be interpreted as accounting standard η_2 conveying a higher information content to investors than accounting standard η_1 (see for Germany, Coenenberg and Möller, 1979).

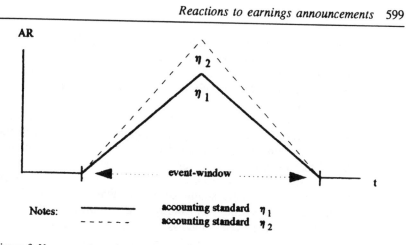

Figure 3 Unexpected earnings and abnormal returns

For Switzerland, if earnings based on the new accounting standard η_2 (in the study IAS or EC-Directives) convey a higher information content to investors than earnings based on the old accounting standard η_1 (Swiss GAAP), unexpected earnings based on the new accounting standard should lead to a higher mean of abnormal returns for the event-window than unexpected earnings based on the former standard. If IAS-based earnings convey more information to investors than EC-Directives-based earnings, unexpected earnings based on IAS should result in a higher mean of abnormal returns for the event-window than unexpected earnings based on EC-Directives.

Based on the results of Table 3 and Table 5, which suggest a higher information content of IAS-based/EC-Directives-based earnings than earnings based on the Swiss GAAP and a higher information content of IAS-based earnings than EC-Directives-based earnings, the following hypotheses are examined in the empirical tests. Formally the hypotheses tested, stated in the null form, are:

H_{01}: For investors, earnings announcements based on the new accounting standard η_2 (IAS or EC-Directives) convey a higher information content than earnings announcements based on the Swiss GAAP: i.e., the mean of the abnormal returns resulting from unexpected earnings of companies that have changed to IAS or EC-Directives for the event-window in the year y (the year of the change) is statistically significant higher than the corresponding mean of the abnormal returns resulting from unexpected earnings based on Swiss GAAP for the event-windows in the years y–5 to y–1:

$$H_{01}: \overline{AR}_{\eta 1} < \overline{AR}_{\eta 2}$$

where $\overline{AR}_{\eta 1}$ is the mean abnormal return resulting from unexpected earnings based on Swiss GAAP for the event windows in the years

y–5 to y–1, i.e. the years preceding the change, $\overline{AR}_{\eta 2}$ the mean abnormal return resulting from unexpected earnings based on the new accounting standard (IAS or EC-Directives) for the event window in the year y, i.e. the year in which the new accounting standard is used for the first time.

H_{02}: For investors, earnings announcements based on the new accounting standard (IAS or EC-Directives) convey a higher information content than earnings announcements based on the Swiss GAAP, i.e. the mean of the abnormal returns resulting from unexpected earnings based on IAS or EC-Directives for the event-windows in the years y+1 to y+5 is statistically significant higher than the mean of the abnormal returns resulting from unexpected earnings based on the Swiss GAAP for the event-windows in the years y–5 to y–1:

$$H_{02}: \overline{AR}_{\eta 1} < \overline{AR}_{\eta 3}$$

where $\overline{AR}_{\eta 1}$ is the mean abnormal return resulting from unexpected earnings based on the Swiss GAAP for the event windows in the years y–5 to y–1, i.e. the years preceding the change, $\overline{AR}_{\eta 3}$ the mean abnormal return resulting from unexpected earnings based on the new accounting standard (IAS or EC-Directives) for the event windows in the years y+1 to y+5, i.e. the years subsequent to the change.

H_{03}: For investors, earnings announcements based on IAS convey a higher information content than figures based on EC-Directives, i.e. the mean of the abnormal returns resulting from unexpected earnings for the event-windows in the years y+1 to y+5 (based on the new standard) is statistically significant higher for IAS-based earnings than for EC-Directives-based earnings:

$$H_{03}: \overline{AR}_{EC\text{-}Dir} < \overline{AR}_{IAS}$$

where $\overline{AR}_{EC\text{-}Dir}$ is the mean abnormal return resulting from unexpected earnings based on EC-Directives for the event-windows in the years y+1 to y+5, i.e. the years subsequent to the change, $\overline{AR}_{IAS}$ the mean abnormal return resulting from unexpected earnings based on IAS for the event–windows in the years y+1 to y+5, i.e. the years subsequent to the change.

To avoid measurement and disclosure problems which could arise for companies from the switch to IAS or EC-Directives during the change, the year of the change (y) is excluded in the hypotheses H_{02} and H_{03}.

Errors associated with specifying a model for expected earnings (see section below) could have a biasing effect on the results. To control for these effects, the study also uses the variance of the abnormal returns for the period surrounding the earnings-announcements (event-windows) as a proxy for the information content. Using the variance now allows to examine the information content of earnings releases independently on the distinction between positive and negative abnormal returns. Analogously to H_{01}, H_{02} and H_{03}, higher abnormal returns are expected for periods surrounding earnings announcements than for periods without any new information release. But whereas H_{01}, H_{02} and H_{03} use the mean of the abnormal returns as a proxy for the information content of earnings releases, the variance approach uses the squared deviation of these abnormal returns from their mean, i.e. the volatility of the abnormal returns. Now, a higher volatility (variance) suggests a higher information processing of the market within the event-window and therefore a higher information content of earnings releases (unexpected earnings). It is assumed, that if an accounting standard η_2 conveys a higher information content to investors than an accounting standard η_1, the variance of the abnormal returns resulting from unexpected earnings for the event-window is higher for earnings releases based on accounting standard η_2 than for earnings releases based on accounting standard η_1.

The following hypotheses are tested:

H_{04}: For investors, earnings announcements based on the new accounting standard η_2 (IAS or EC-Directives) convey a higher information content than earnings announcements based on the Swiss GAAP: i.e., the variance of the abnormal returns resulting from unexpected earnings based on IAS or EC-Directives for the event-window in year y (the year of the change) is statistically significant higher than the variance of the abnormal returns resulting from unexpected earnings based on Swiss GAAP for the event-windows in the years y–5 to y–1:

$$H_{04}: \text{Var}(AR_{\eta 1}) < \text{Var}(AR_{\eta 2})$$

where $\text{Var}(AR_{\eta 1})$ is the variance of abnormal returns resulting from unexpected earnings based on Swiss GAAP for the event windows in the years y–5 to y–1, i.e. the years preceding the change, $\text{Var}(AR_{\eta 2})$ the variance of abnormal returns resulting from unexpected earnings based on the new accounting standard (IAS or EC-Directives) for the event window in the year y, i.e. the year in which the new accounting standard is used for the first time.

H_{05}: For investors, earnings announcements based on the new accounting standard (IAS or EC-Directives) convey a higher information content than earnings announcements based on the Swiss GAAP, i.e. the variance of the abnormal returns resulting from unexpected earnings based on IAS or EC-Directives for the event-windows in the years y+1 to y+5 is statistically significant higher than the variance of the abnormal returns based on the Swiss GAAP for the event-windows in the years y–5 to y–1:

$$H_{05}: \text{Var}(AR_{\eta 1}) < \text{Var}(AR_{\eta 3})$$

where $Var(AR_{\eta 1})$ is the variance of abnormal returns resulting from unexpected earnings based on Swiss GAAP for the event windows in the years y–5 to y–1, i.e. the years preceding the change, $Var(AR_{\eta 3})$ the variance of abnormal returns resulting from unexpected earnings based on the new accounting standard (IAS or EC-Directives) for the event window in the years y+1 to y+5, i.e. the years subsequent to the change.

H_{06}: For investors, earnings announcements based on IAS convey a higher information content than earnings announcements based on EC-Directives, i.e. the variance of the abnormal returns resulting from unexpected earnings for the event-windows in the years y+1 to y+5 (based on the new standard) is statistically significant higher for IAS-based earnings than for EC-Directives-based earnings:

$$H_{06}: Var(AR_{EC\text{-}Dir.}) < Var(AR_{IAS})$$

where $Var(AR_{EC\text{-}Dir.})$ is variance of abnormal returns resulting from unexpected earnings based on EC-Directives for the event-windows in the years y+1 to y+5, i.e. the years subsequent to the change, $Var(AR_{IAS})$ the variance of abnormal returns resulting from unexpected earnings based on IAS for the event-windows in the years y+1 to y+5, i.e. the years subsequent to change.

Again, to avoid measurement and disclosure problems which could arise for companies from the switch to IAS or EC-Directives during the change, the year of the change (y) is excluded in the hypotheses H_{05} and H_{06}.

Data and research method

The sample consists of Swiss quoted non-financial companies which have changed their accounting standard used for presenting consolidated statements from the Swiss GAAP to either IAS (20 companies) or EC-Directives (15 companies) within the period 1985–1993.[16] In total, this corresponds to 247 earnings announcements.

The event study methodology is used for examining the information content of earnings announcements. The return data are the dividend-adjusted logarithmic daily stock returns, R_{it},[17] and the dividend-adjusted logarithmic daily market returns (R_{mt}). The information content of earnings announcements is measured by the standardized abnormal returns SAR_{it}, using Scholes-Williams-coefficients.

Definition of abnormal returns

The abnormal returns for a stock i in period t, AR_{it}, are defined as the difference between the actual return in period t, R_{it}, and the predicted return for stock i in period t, $E(R_{it})$:

$$AR_{it} = R_{it} - E(R_{it}) \tag{1}$$

where AR_{it} is the abnormal return for stock i in period t and $E(R_{it})$ is the expected return for stock i in period t

and

$$R_{it} = \ln(P_{it}) - \ln(P_{it-1}) \tag{2}$$

where R_{it} is the actual return for stock i in period t and P_{it}, P_{it-1} are the prices for stock i in period t and $t-1$.

The market model is used to determine the expected return for stock i in period t, $E(R_{it})$. The market model assumes the following statistical description of the relation between the return for stock i in period t (R_{it}) and the return for the market index in period t:

$$R_{it} = \alpha_i + (\beta_i * R_{mt}) + \varepsilon_{it} \tag{3}$$

where α_i is the normal unsystematic return for stock i, β_i the systematic risk of stock i, R_{mt} the return for the market index in period t and ε_{it} the prediction error for stock i in period t.

Whereas asset pricing theory suggests the use of a value-weighted index as a proxy for the market, the literature suggests for detecting abnormal returns the use of an equally-weighted index.[18] An equally-weighted index is especially used due to the fact, that the sample examined includes low capitalized companies. In this case, an equally-weighted index is more likely expected to detect abnormal returns for all companies examined than a value-weighted index, in which lower capitalized companies are represented only with a lower share.

Using Equations 1 and 3, the abnormal return AR_{it} can now be defined as:

$$AR_{it} = \varepsilon_{it} = R_{it} - \alpha_i - (\beta_i * R_{mt}) \tag{4}$$

An ordinary least squares (OLS) model is used to estimate the firm-specific parameters. For securities traded with trading delays different than those of the market, OLS β_i estimates are biased. Likewise, for securities with trading frequencies different than those of the market index, OLS β_i estimates are biased. In order to avoid distorting impacts of trading delays and trading frequencies different than those of the market index on the results, especially the impact from lower capitalized stocks, the adjustment technique proposed by Scholes/Williams is used.[19] This procedure involves for every company and for every year examined the estimate of three simple OLS regressions using the J daily security returns within the estimation period:

$$R_{ij} = \alpha_{i1} + \beta_{i1} R_{mj} + \varepsilon_{1j} \qquad \text{for } j = 1, 2, \ldots, J \tag{5}$$
$$R_{ij} = \alpha_{i2} + \beta_{i2} R_{mj+1} + \varepsilon_{2j} \qquad \text{for } j = 1, 2, \ldots, J-1 \tag{6}$$
$$R_{ij} = \alpha_{i3} + \beta_{i3} R_{mj+1} + \varepsilon_{3j} \qquad \text{for } j = 2, 3, \ldots, J \tag{7}$$

where R_{mj} is the return for the market index in period j, R_{mj+1} is the return for the market index in period $j+1$ and R_{mj-1} the return for the market index in period $j-1$.

The Scholes-Williams-beta (Scholes and Williams, 1977, 317) is formed as:

$$\hat{\beta}_{iSW} = \frac{(\beta_{i1} + \beta_{i2} + \beta_{i3})}{(1 + 2 \hat{\rho}_M)} \tag{8}$$

where $\hat{\beta}_{iSW}$ is the estimated Scholes-Williams beta, β_{i1}, β_{i2}, β_{i3} the estimated OLS coefficients for Equations 5, 6 and 7, and $\hat{\rho}_M$ the estimated serial correlation of R_{mj} from $j = 2$ to $j = J-1$.

The corresponding Scholes-Williams-alpha is defined as:

$$\hat{\alpha}_{iSW} = \frac{1}{J-2} \sum_{j=2}^{J-1} R_{ij} - \hat{\beta}_{iSW} \frac{1}{J-2} \sum_{j=2}^{J-1} R_{mj} \tag{9}$$

where $\hat{\alpha}_{iSW}$ is the estimated Scholes-Williams alpha.

Typical lengths of the estimation period for the parameters range from 100 to 300 days for daily studies. The benefit of a longer period is an improved prediction of model parameters, the cost of a longer period a possible instability of these parameters. This study uses an estimation period of 200 days. The estimation period falls on both sides of the event window, each 10 days beyond the event window. It is assumed, that there is not instability of the model parameters within this period.[20]

The dates of the events (earnings announcements) are based on firm announcements or – if not available – the dates of the earnings announcements in the NZZ (Neue Züricher Zeitung). In the maximum, the event-windows of five years preceding the change to the new accounting standard ($y-5$ to $y-1$), the event-window in the year of the change (y) and the event-windows of five years subsequent to the change to the new accounting standard ($y+1$ to $y+5$) are examined. Less than 11 event-windows for every company are included in the study for companies which changed the accounting standard towards the end of the period examined (1985–1993) or for companies, for which no precise announcement date is available for a specific year.

For the total sample examined, the abnormal return on a day t for the event-window, AR_{Nt}, is the mean of the AR_{it} for this day t:

$$AR_{Nt} = \frac{1}{N} \sum_{i=1}^{N} AR_{it} \tag{10}$$

where N is the number of events examined, e.g., if 30 companies are examined and five years preceding the change are available for each company, N amounts to 150 for a day t within the event-window.

Abnormal returns are expected to occur on the day of the event, i.e. the day of the earnings announcement, and due to the fact that information could have entered the market earlier than the official announcement date and due to a possible post-earnings-announcement drift, on a number of days preceding and subsequent to the event (event-window). Typical lengths of the event window range from 21 to 121 days for daily studies.[21] This study uses an event-window of 30 days on each side of the event-date. It is assumed that any capital market reactions due to the event occur within this period. The total capital market reactions due to the event (CAR_N) are measured by the cumulative abnormal returns for the event window:

$$CAR_N = \sum_{t=-30}^{t=+30} AR_{Nt} \tag{11}$$

where CAR_N is the total cumulative abnormal return for the event-window.

Definition of standardized abnormal returns

To reflect statistical error in the determination of expected returns and to control for the effect of beta reliability on abnormal returns (Ziebart, 1985), the abnormal returns are standardized by the standard deviation of the abnormal returns within the estimation period (Peterson, 1989, 43ff):

$$S_{ie} = \left[\sum_{j=1}^{J} (R_{ij} - E(R_{ij}))^2 / J - 2 \right]^{\frac{1}{2}} \tag{12}$$

where S_{ie} is the standard deviation of the abnormal returns for stock i over J periods within the estimation period and $E(R_{ij})$ is the predicted return for stock i in period j within the estimation period. Dividing the abnormal return for a day t within the event-window by the standard deviation of the abnormal returns for the estimation period yields a standardized abnormal return for a stock i on a day t within the event-window:[22]

$$SAR_{it} = \frac{AR_{it}}{S_{ie}} \tag{13}$$

where SAR_{it} is the standardized abnormal return for stock i for day t within the event-window. The standardized abnormal returns for a given day t within the event-window are summed up over the shares and divided by the square root of the number of events in the sample:

$$SAR_{Nt} = \frac{1}{\sqrt{N}} \sum_{i=1}^{N} SAR_{it} \tag{14}$$

where SAR_{Nt} is the total standardized abnormal return for day t within the event-window. Using Equation 11, we now get

$$CAR_{NS} = \sum_{t=-30}^{t=+30} SAR_{Nt} \qquad (15)$$

where CAR_{NS} is the total cumulative standardized abnormal return for the event-window.

As pointed out above it is assumed that unexpected increases in earnings result in positive standardized abnormal returns and unexpected decreases in negative standardized abnormal returns (Ball and Brown, 1968). Prior research has shown that when annual data are used to predict earnings, the random walk model performs as well as more complex time-series prediction models (Watts and Zimmerman, 1986, 43f). Hence, it is assumed that the best expectation of the earnings of company i in year y is the earnings in year $y-1$:

$$E(A_{iy}) = A_{iy-1} \qquad (16)$$

where $E(A_{iy})$ is the expected (accounting) earnings of company i in year y and A_{iy-1} is the (accounting) earnings of company i in year $y-1$. Using equation 16, the unexpected earnings of company i in year y (UA_{iy} can now be defined as the difference between the earnings in year y and the earnings in year $y-$1:

$$UA_{(iy)} = A_{iy} - A_{iy-1} \qquad (17)$$

where $UA_{(iy)}$ is the unexpected earnings of company i in year y.

A positive CAR-curve (using standardized abnormal returns) is expected for the event-window ($t-n$ to $t+n$) for positive unexpected earnings and a negative CAR-curve for negative unexpected earnings (see Figure 4).

In order to examine the total information content of earnings announcements, the differentiation between positive and negative abnormal returns is

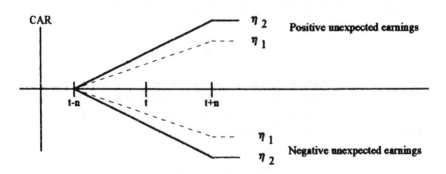

Figure 4 Unexpected earnings and *CAR* based on different accounting standards

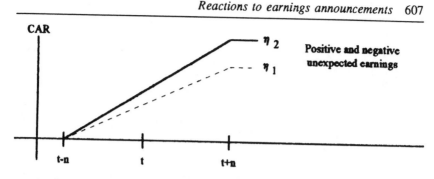

Figure 5 Unexpected earnings (positive and negative) and *CAR* based on different accounting standards

not followed further and it is assumed, that investors will buy stocks with positive unexpected earnings and will sell stocks with negative unexpected earnings. We now get the total, i.e. positive and negative *CAR*-curve illustrated in Figure 5.

If earnings announcements based on accounting standard η_2 convey more information to investors than earnings announcements based on accounting standard η_1, the *CAR*-curve for accounting standard η_2 is expected to lie above the CAR-curve for accounting standard η_1.

Results

The results of the regression analysis and hypotheses tests are shown in Tables 6–11. The results in Table 9 (using a *t*-test) and Table 10 (using an *f*-test) suggest, that there is no statistically significant difference in the mean of the abnormal returns comparing the event windows:

- in the years preceding the change to the new accounting standard (based on Swiss GAAP) and the year of the change to the new accounting standard (based on IAS or EC-Directives),
- in the years preceding the change to the new accounting standard (based on Swiss GAAP) and the years subsequent to the change to the new accounting standard (based on IAS or EC-Directives),
- based on EC-Directives and based on IAS.

The results also suggest that investors do not respond to earnings announcements (unexpected earnings) based on Swiss GAAP, IAS and EC-Directives in a statistically significant different way. Therefore, H_{01}, H_{02} and H_{03} have to be rejected at a $\alpha = 0.05$ confidence level.

These results are also apparent from Figures 6–8. The *CAR*-curves preceding and subsequent to the change in the accounting standard are very close, indicating no substantial differences in the information content of IAS/EC-Directives-based earnings and Swiss GAAP-based earnings. A higher

Table 6 Cumulative abnormal returns

t	Sample EC-Dir. preceding change	Sample EC-Dir. change	Sample EC-Dir. subsequent change	Sample IAS preceding change	Sample IAS change	Sample IAS subsequent change	Sample total preceding change	Sample total change	Sample total subsequent change
-30	0.0928	-0.0013	0.1614	-0.1665	0.2667	-0.0372	-0.0460	0.1411	0.0571
-29	0.1428	-0.3659	-0.0015	-0.3479	0.1952	0.0340	-0.1198	-0.0678	0.0172
-28	-0.1309	-0.2933	-0.0903	-0.4736	0.4924	0.1975	-0.3143	0.1241	0.0609
-27	-0.1102	-0.3960	-0.2071	-0.4250	0.4880	0.3465	-0.2787	0.0737	0.0838
-26	-0.1502	-0.1185	-0.2801	-0.4351	0.1229	0.3036	-0.3027	0.0097	0.0266
-25	-0.4495	-0.3866	-0.7815	-0.4298	0.4459	0.1017	-0.4389	0.0557	-0.3174
-24	-0.4922	-0.3515	-0.9174	-0.3845	0.4762	0.0548	-0.4345	0.0882	-0.4066
-23	-0.6244	-0.3412	-0.9702	-0.2120	0.5788	0.0001	-0.4037	0.1476	-0.4604
-22	-0.3267	-0.3651	-0.5852	-0.2697	0.7025	0.0199	-0.2962	0.2020	-0.2672
-21	-0.4389	-0.2261	-0.4715	-0.2912	1.6384	-0.1137	-0.3598	0.7644	-0.2835
-20	-0.5529	-0.3352	-0.2357	-0.2606	1.4233	0.1740	-0.3964	0.5990	-0.0205
-19	-0.6914	-0.3083	-0.3448	-0.3886	1.2099	-0.1732	-0.5293	0.4983	-0.2547
-18	-0.6323	-0.1818	-0.3083	-0.3717	1.0390	-0.2446	-0.4928	0.4668	-0.2748
-17	-0.5399	-0.2664	-0.4767	-0.3484	1.0671	-0.0884	-0.4374	0.4420	-0.2727
-16	-0.6585	-0.4584	-0.2922	-0.3190	0.9081	-0.2536	-0.4768	0.2676	-0.2719
-15	-0.7245	-0.2576	-0.3330	-0.3984	0.6621	-0.0160	-0.5499	0.2310	-0.1664
-14	-0.7524	-0.3078	-0.3651	-0.4638	0.4912	0.0137	-0.5979	0.1167	-0.1661
-13	-0.8750	-0.1736	-0.3125	-0.3701	0.5076	0.5830	-0.6048	0.1883	0.1580
-12	-0.6996	-0.3434	-0.5624	-0.2524	0.0093	0.7174	-0.4603	-0.1082	0.1100
-11	-0.6142	-0.6377	-0.5639	-0.2557	0.3006	0.5316	-0.4223	-0.1392	0.0117
-10	-0.5474	-0.9121	-0.4935	-0.2489	0.6194	0.8238	-0.3876	-0.0985	0.1986
-9	-0.4476	-0.6420	-0.6659	-0.2875	0.5913	0.9689	-0.3620	0.0132	0.1930
-8	-0.3201	-0.4726	-0.5892	-0.1482	0.8187	1.1148	-0.2281	0.2134	0.3062
-7	-0.2968	-0.2082	-0.6719	0.0056	0.9320	0.9933	-0.1350	0.3975	0.2030
-6	-0.1942	-0.0088	-1.1658	0.0939	1.2783	0.9298	-0.0400	0.6749	-0.0647
-5	-0.1655	0.0574	-0.9642	0.1086	1.3833	1.0405	-0.0188	0.7618	0.0891
-4	-0.2030	-0.2507	-0.7795	0.2617	1.6439	0.9519	0.0457	0.7558	0.1302
-3	-0.2183	-0.0100	-0.7285	0.5402	1.7372	1.0942	0.1876	0.9182	0.2292
-2	-0.0806	0.0315	-0.7263	0.6121	1.3598	1.3365	0.2901	0.7372	0.3576
-1	-0.0835	0.1134	-0.6710	0.7444	1.5349	1.2396	0.3596	0.8686	0.3346

0	0.1265	0.5663	-0.5058	1.1699	1.6294	1.0936	0.6849	1.1311	0.3346
1	0.2360	0.3726	-0.1508	1.3032	2.1471	1.4370	0.8072	1.3153	0.6835
2	0.1161	0.2643	-0.3082	1.3814	2.3612	1.5970	0.7933	1.3783	0.6928
3	0.0835	0.1651	-0.3514	1.3792	2.4297	1.7102	0.7770	1.3682	0.7318
4	0.2079	0.0438	-0.6242	1.2057	2.6448	1.7012	0.7419	1.4256	0.5976
5	0.3839	-0.0853	-0.7700	1.3509	2.5422	1.6866	0.9015	1.3106	0.5208
6	0.4758	0.1486	-0.8581	1.3398	2.9203	1.7246	0.9382	1.6211	0.4989
7	0.5624	-0.1634	-0.7217	1.3152	3.0762	1.4638	0.9653	1.5576	0.4266
8	0.5294	-0.4712	-0.6991	1.3910	2.9661	1.6627	0.9905	1.3549	0.5418
9	0.3312	-0.3847	-0.7309	1.3208	2.6245	1.8115	0.8609	1.2139	0.6049
10	0.2979	-0.4769	-0.7933	1.2425	2.5750	1.5552	0.8035	1.1445	0.4407
11	0.2545	-0.3841	-0.6164	1.2561	2.6407	1.7558	0.7906	1.2228	0.6300
12	0.2758	-0.4210	-0.7153	1.2164	2.6082	1.8434	0.7793	1.1883	0.6291
13	0.1432	-0.6091	-0.9805	1.1674	2.4994	1.8322	0.6914	1.0423	0.4973
14	0.1163	-0.3395	-1.0738	1.1684	2.0747	1.3305	0.6794	0.9430	0.1895
15	0.0973	-0.3657	-1.0656	1.0990	1.8272	1.2532	0.6334	0.7993	0.1528
16	0.2744	-0.4171	-1.0112	0.9182	1.7843	1.2282	0.6190	0.7524	0.1654
17	0.5149	-0.3463	-1.1022	0.7732	2.0241	1.2772	0.6532	0.9130	0.1480
18	0.3030	-0.1174	-0.9972	0.8881	1.7106	1.0696	0.6162	0.8537	0.0888
19	0.2440	-0.0304	-0.7055	0.9026	1.2095	1.4624	0.5965	0.6283	0.4336
20	0.0356	0.0250	-0.7713	0.9102	1.3844	1.4587	0.5037	0.7472	0.4004
21	0.1863	-0.0160	-0.6603	1.0463	1.4394	1.4291	0.6466	0.7572	0.4375
22	-0.0784	0.1779	-0.6105	0.9661	1.7366	1.1832	0.4806	1.0059	0.3320
23	0.1144	0.2124	-0.5558	0.8293	1.9395	1.2165	0.4970	1.1299	0.3755
24	0.2818	0.2150	-0.6385	0.8464	2.7127	0.9499	0.5840	1.5419	0.1961
25	0.1796	0.2457	-0.5455	0.9436	2.7443	1.1006	0.5885	1.5731	0.3194
26	0.2088	-0.1906	-0.3138	1.0668	2.9684	1.1702	0.6680	1.4876	0.4660
27	0.3844	-0.3924	-0.4853	1.0958	2.9739	1.5024	0.7651	1.3959	0.5591
28	0.5220	-0.2893	-0.4964	1.2211	3.0035	1.3357	0.8962	1.4600	0.4662
29	0.5269	-0.2365	-0.5402	1.0144	2.8371	1.3716	0.7879	1.3963	0.4643
30	0.2616	-0.0855	-0.6355	0.9366	2.8298	1.5274	0.6229	1.4633	0.5009

610 *The European Accounting Review*

Table 7 Kolmogorov-Smirnov goodness of fit test (abnormal returns)

Variable	Cases	K-S-Z	2-Tailed p	*Sign
Sample EC-Directives: preceding change	61	0.6420	0.8043	*
Sample EC-Directives: change	61	0.5373	0.9350	*
Sample EC-Directives: subsequent change	61	0.6956	0.7185	*
Sample IAS: preceding change	61	0.6820	0.7409	*
Sample IAS: change	61	0.5490	0.9238	*
Sample IAS: subsequent change	61	0.5687	0.9029	*
Sample total: preceding change	61	0.6928	0.7232	*
Sample total: change	61	0.6120	0.8480	*
Sample total: subsequent change	61	0.8198	0.5123	

Table 8 Descriptive statistics (abnormal returns)

Variable	N Cases	Mean	Std.dev.	Variance	Min	Max
Sample EC-Directives: preceding change	61	0.00	0.14	0.02	−0.2993	0.2977
Sample EC-Directives: change	61	0.00	0.19	0.03	−0.4363	0.4529
Sample EC-Directives: subsequent change	61	−0.01	0.17	0.03	−0.5014	0.3851
Sample IAS: preceding change	61	0.02	0.12	0.01	−0.2067	0.4255
Sample IAS: change	61	0.05	0.27	0.07	−0.5011	0.9359
Sample IAS: subsequent change	61	0.03	0.19	0.04	−0.5017	0.5693
Sample total: preceding change	61	0.01	0.09	0.01	−0.1945	0.3253
Sample total: change	61	0.02	0.16	0.03	−0.2965	0.5624
Sample total: subsequent change	61	0.01	0.14	0.02	−0.3440	0.3489

information content is shown for the IAS-sample only for the year of the change to IAS.

Using the variance-approach, the results in Table 11 suggest, that there is a statistically significant difference in the variance of abnormal returns comparing the event windows:

- in the years preceding the change to the new accounting standard (based on Swiss GAAP) and the year of the change to the new accounting standard (based on EC-Directives or IAS),

Table 9 t-Test (test of the mean of abnormal returns)

Variable	DF	t-value	2-tail sig	*Sign. at .05 level*
Sample EC-Directives: preceding change/ change	60	−0.19	0.853	
Sample EC-Directives: preceding change/ subsequent change	60	−0.56	0.579	
Sample IAS: preceding change/change	60	0.84	0.402	
Sample IAS: preceding change/subsequent change	60	0.34	0.732	
Sample total: preceding change/change	60	0.62	0.540	
Sample total: preceding change/subsequent change	60	−0.10	0.920	
Sample EC-Directives/sample IAS: preceding change	60	−0.50	0.615	
Sample EC-Directives/sample IAS: change	60	−1.09	0.279	
Sample EC-Directives/sample IAS: subsequent change	60	−1.18	0.242	

Table 10 Analysis of variance (abnormal returns)

Variable	DF	Sum of squares	f-ratio	f-prob	*Sign at .05 level*
Sample EC-Directives: preceding change/change	121	3.2213	0.0368	0.8482	
Sample EC-Directives: preceding change/subsequent change	121	2.8947	0.2741	0.6016	
Sample IAS: preceding change/ change	121	5.1985	0.6820	0.4105	
Sample IAS: preceding change/ subsequent change	121	3.0534	0.1125	0.7379	
Sample total: preceding change/ change	121	2.0813	0.3347	0.5640	
Sample total: preceding change/ subsequent change	121	1.7097	0.0086	0.9265	
Sample EC-Directives/sample IAS: preceding change	121	1.9598	0.2292	0.6330	
Sample EC-Directives/sample IAS: change	121	6.5030	1.2994	0.2566	
Sample EC-Directives/sample IAS: subsequent change	121	4.0209	1.1555	0.2846	

612   *The European Accounting Review*

Table 11 Levene test for homogeneity of variances (abnormal returns)

Variable	DF1	DF2	Statistic	2-tail sig	*Sign. at .05 level*
Sample EC-Directives: preceding change/change	1	120	4.5614	0.035	*
Sample EC-Directives: preceding change/subsequent change	1	120	1.0739	0.302	
Sample IAS: preceding change/ change	1	120	21.9958	0.000	*
Sample IAS: preceding change/ subsequent change	1	120	12.5003	0.001	*
Sample total: preceding change/ change	1	120	12.7182	0.001	*
Sample total: preceding change/ subsequent change	1	120	4.2652	0.041	*
Sample EC-Directives/sample IAS: preceding change	1	120	3.1194	0.080	
Sample EC-Directives/sample IAS: change	1	120	4.0378	0.047	*
Sample EC-Directives/sample IAS: subsequent change	1	120	1.0463	0.308	

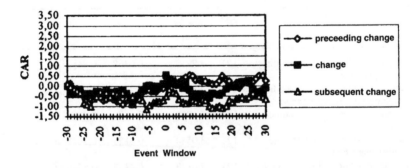

Figure 6 CAR – Sample EC-Directives

- in the years preceding the change to the new accounting standard (based on Swiss-GAAP) and the years subsequent to the change to the new accounting standard (based on IAS).

The results therefore also suggest a statistically significant higher information content of IAS-based earnings than earnings based on Swiss-GAAP. Hence, H_{04} and H_{05} (for the IAS sample) cannot be rejected at an $\alpha = 0.05$ confidence level. But the results also suggest, that there is no statistically significant difference in the variance of abnormal returns comparing EC-

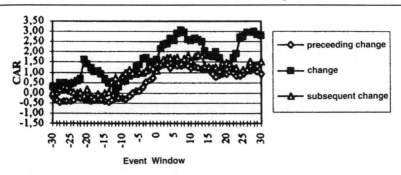

Figure 7 CAR – Sample IAS

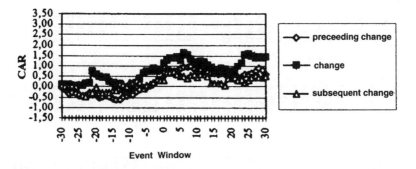

Figure 8 CAR – Total sample

Directives-based earnings and IAS-based earnings (except the year of the change). H_{06} has therefore to be rejected at an $\alpha = 0.05$ confidence level.

Alternatively to the variance approach, problems in specifying a model for expected earnings can be avoided by standardizing the mean of the abnormal returns of each event window to a positive value: i.e., if the mean of the abnormal returns of the event-window is negative, positive abnormal returns in the periods t–30 to t+30 are transformed in negative values and negative abnormal returns in positive values which results in a positive mean of the abnormal returns. This procedure assumes perfect information of an investor on the direction of unexpected earnings and enables that errors in specifying the direction of abnormal returns can be avoided. But also, the results of such a perfect model (see Tables 12–17) show no significant difference to the results presented in Tables 6–11. Based on the size of the mean of the abnormal returns, the results of the f-test (Table 15) show no statistically significant difference in the information content of earnings based on Swiss GAAP and EC-Directives or IAS. The results only suggest a statistically significant difference subsequent to the change in the accounting standard

Table 12 Cumulative abnormal returns (standardized to positive mean values)

t	Sample EC-Dir, preceding change	Sample EC-Dir, change	Sample EC-Dir, subsequent change	Sample IAS preceding change	Sample IAS change	Sample IAS subsequent change	Sample total preceding change	Sample total change	Sample total subsequent change
-30	0.0962	0.4504	0.1500	0.0976	0.1437	0.3437	0.0969	0.2875	0.2518
-29	0.1837	0.5526	0.0234	0.0548	0.0760	0.4076	0.1147	0.2994	0.2252
-28	0.3836	1.1310	0.0201	0.0013	0.3926	0.5560	0.1790	0.7387	0.3017
-27	0.5106	1.1433	-0.0480	0.0030	0.3024	0.7731	0.2389	0.6966	0.3834
-26	0.7300	0.9328	0.1747	0.1179	0.3989	0.6540	0.4024	0.6492	0.4266
-25	0.6860	1.0387	0.4601	0.1259	0.7202	0.5513	0.3862	0.8695	0.5080
-24	0.8365	1.0198	0.5236	0.2694	0.8924	0.7178	0.5330	0.9521	0.6256
-23	0.8635	1.1184	0.4189	0.4015	1.5102	0.8067	0.6162	1.3266	0.6227
-22	0.9072	1.5035	0.4846	0.3979	1.9001	0.8674	0.6346	1.7142	0.6857
-21	0.9399	2.0517	0.7092	0.5928	2.2808	0.8962	0.7542	2.1734	0.8074
-20	0.9625	2.2787	1.0481	0.6267	2.2787	0.9995	0.7828	2.2787	1.0226
-19	1.0240	2.6316	1.1227	0.6624	2.0187	0.9986	0.8304	2.3060	1.0575
-18	1.1839	2.3689	1.0985	0.7639	1.9545	1.0545	0.9591	2.1488	1.0754
-17	1.1828	2.4555	1.0743	0.8939	2.1442	1.2215	1.0282	2.2901	1.1516
-16	1.3472	2.2336	1.1354	1.0419	2.0755	1.2978	1.1838	2.1496	1.2207
-15	1.3902	2.3250	1.2929	1.0308	2.1605	1.6615	1.1978	2.2376	1.4866
-14	1.4328	2.4587	1.4616	1.0711	2.2127	1.6892	1.2392	2.3280	1.5812
-13	1.6137	2.4571	1.6628	1.1642	2.4179	1.9831	1.3732	2.4363	1.8311
-12	1.5562	2.4753	1.7831	1.2900	2.1550	2.0791	1.4137	2.3052	1.9386
-11	1.7346	2.5142	1.9127	1.4605	2.5436	1.9332	1.5879	2.5298	1.9235
-10	1.5261	2.3441	1.9871	1.6224	2.6865	2.3169	1.5776	2.5260	2.1604
-9	1.8251	2.3393	2.0460	1.7879	2.9481	2.6262	1.8052	2.6627	2.3508
-8	1.8242	2.6930	2.0768	1.9240	2.8418	2.5118	1.8776	2.7721	2.3054
-7	1.9570	2.8780	2.1234	2.0858	3.0849	2.7664	2.0259	2.9879	2.4612
-6	2.0513	2.9409	2.0861	2.1597	3.7104	3.0337	2.1093	3.3497	2.5840
-5	2.0559	2.7501	2.2383	2.1223	3.8026	3.3104	2.0915	3.3093	2.8016
-4	1.9658	3.0158	2.2754	2.1245	3.8386	3.4077	2.0508	3.4530	2.8703
-3	2.0303	3.0926	2.4338	2.2962	3.9420	3.5500	2.1726	3.5438	3.0203
-2	2.0727	3.2475	2.6251	2.4267	3.9058	3.7047	2.2622	3.5972	3.1923
-1	1.8850	3.1170	2.5618	2.5753	4.1753	3.6824	2.2545	3.6792	3.1506

0	2.1690	3.9191	2.7623	2.8365	3.9353	4.0142	2.5263	3.9277	3.4201
1	2.3866	4.5277	2.9536	3.1608	4.3545	4.3564	2.8010	4.4357	3.6906
2	2.3539	4.3137	2.8806	3.2456	4.6450	4.4642	2.8312	4.4897	3.7127
3	2.3646	4.5762	2.8982	3.5253	4.5167	4.9731	2.9858	4.5446	3.9884
4	2.5644	4.6410	3.2518	3.6761	4.5993	5.0293	3.1594	4.6188	4.1858
5	2.6836	4.6494	3.0949	3.6695	3.6531	5.3956	3.2113	4.6514	4.3038
6	2.7139	4.5373	2.9504	3.8236	5.1054	5.4330	3.3078	4.8391	4.2548
7	2.6665	4.6998	3.1488	3.8913	5.3635	5.3399	3.3220	5.0524	4.3001
8	2.8296	4.7640	3.1361	4.0219	5.2623	5.2177	3.4677	5.0287	4.2299
9	2.8416	4.9816	3.1782	4.0895	5.1378	5.2491	3.5095	5.0646	4.2663
10	2.8367	4.8867	3.2769	4.1788	5.1696	5.1630	3.5550	5.0370	4.2679
11	3.1424	4.7660	3.3425	4.3204	5.5674	5.3048	3.7729	5.1918	4.3735
12	3.1489	4.9221	3.4698	4.5013	5.3064	5.3535	3.8727	5.1263	4.4595
13	3.2123	5.2998	3.1798	4.5877	5.6594	5.2838	3.9484	5.4909	4.2853
14	3.4485	4.9384	3.1622	4.8176	5.5801	5.4562	4.1813	5.2793	4.3675
15	3.4876	5.2658	3.4078	4.9264	5.6702	5.5218	4.2577	4.8806	4.5185
16	3.6298	5.0050	3.6022	5.0355	5.5106	5.7443	4.3822	5.2736	4.7277
17	3.7074	4.7746	3.6718	5.1629	5.7503	5.8815	4.4864	5.2929	4.8328
18	3.7657	4.9061	3.6352	5.3674	5.4866	5.9609	4.6229	5.2145	4.8572
19	3.8319	5.0389	3.7709	5.4741	4.9173	5.9562	4.7108	4.9743	4.9248
20	3.8809	5.1529	3.9010	5.6455	5.0145	6.2180	4.8253	5.0794	5.1184
21	3.9878	5.5412	3.9532	5.9309	5.1372	6.2691	5.0277	5.3266	5.1700
22	3.9597	5.3581	4.2190	5.9771	5.6461	6.4491	5.0394	5.5111	5.3907
23	4.1664	5.5729	4.3851	5.9257	6.1499	6.4903	5.1080	5.8794	5.4912
24	4.2323	5.7896	4.2814	6.1921	6.6393	6.6616	5.2812	6.2410	5.5162
25	4.3735	5.8681	4.3792	6.3105	6.6583	7.2165	5.4102	6.2879	5.8700
26	4.7102	5.9701	4.4506	6.4931	6.5763	7.6872	5.6644	6.2921	6.1512
27	4.4873	5.5754	4.5725	6.7083	6.8679	7.8445	5.6760	6.2620	6.2917
28	4.5770	5.2427	4.5879	6.8403	7.1205	7.7624	5.7883	6.2403	6.2559
29	4.6544	5.8228	4.6756	6.9111	7.4756	7.9628	5.8622	6.7008	6.4028
30	4.6846	6.0681	5.0135	6.8640	7.7272	8.1860	5.8510	6.9495	6.6804

Table 13 Kolmogorov-Smirnov goodness of fit test (abnormal returns, standardized to positive mean values)

Variable	Cases	K-S-Z	2-Tailed p	*Sign
Sample EC-Directives: preceding change	61	0.7074	0.6989	*
Sample EC-Directives: change	61	0.5834	0.8854	*
Sample EC-Directives: subsequent change	61	0.5339	0.9380	*
Sample IAS: preceding change	61	0.5465	0.9263	*
Sample IAS: change	61	0.5537	0.9191	*
Sample IAS: subsequent change	61	0.6202	0.8365	*
Sample total: preceding change	61	0.4736	0.9784	*
Sample total: change	61	0.7849	0.5688	
Sample total: subsequent change	61	0.6776	0.7481	*

Table 14 Descriptive statistics (abnormal returns, standardized to positive mean values)

Variable	N Cases	Mean	Std.dev.	Variance	Min	Max
Sample EC-Directives: preceding change	61	0.08	0.11	0.01	-0.2229	0.3367
Sample EC-Directives: change	61	0.10	0.26	0.07	-0.3947	0.8021
Sample EC-Directives: subsequent change	61	0.05	0.14	0.02	-0.3300	0.3337
Sample IAS: preceding change	61	0.11	0.09	0.01	-0.0534	0.3243
Sample IAS: change	61	0.13	0.25	0.06	-0.5693	0.6254
Sample IAS: subsequent change	61	0.13	0.16	0.03	-0.1459	0.5850
Sample total: preceding change	61	0.10	0.08	0.01	-0.0407	0.2747
Sample total: change	61	0.11	0.18	0.03	-0.2402	0.5080
Sample total: subsequent change	61	0.09	0.11	0.01	-0.1821	0.3425

between earnings announcements based on EC-Directives and IAS. But using a variance-approach, no statistically significant difference in the information content between EC-Directives-based earnings and IAS-based earnings can be found (See Table 17). These results are also apparent from Figures 9–11. Again, the CAR-curves preceding and subsequent to the change in the accounting standard are very close, indicating no substantial differences in the information content of earnings based on Swiss GAAP and EC-Directives or IAS.

Interim earnings announcements could create some problems in interpreting the results. If interim earnings are announced, the market changes its expectations of annual earnings. Which means that the annual earnings

Table 15 *t*-Test (test of the mean of abnormal returns, standardized to positive means values)

Variable	DF	t-value	2-tail sig	*Sign. at .05 level
Sample EC-Directives: preceding change/ change	60	0.67	0.505	
Sample EC-Directives: preceding change/ subsequent change	60	−1.16	0.250	
Sample IAS: preceding change/change	60	0.42	0.679	
Sample IAS: preceding change/subsequent change	60	0.97	0.335	
Sample total: preceding change/change	60	0.74	0.464	
Sample total: preceding change/subsequent change	60	−0.08	0.937	
Sample EC-Directives/sample IAS: preceding change	60	−2.07	0.042	*
Sample EC-Directives/sample IAS: change	60	−0.60	0.550	
Sample EC-Directives/sample IAS: subsequent change	60	−3.08	0.003	*

Table 16 Analysis of variance (abnormal returns, standardized to positive mean values)

Variable	DF	Sum of squares	f-ratio	f-prob	*Sign at .05 level
Sample EC-Directives: preceding change/change	121	4.7170	0.4005	0.5281	
Sample EC-Directives: preceding change/subsequent change	121	1.9173	1.2891	0.2585	
Sample IAS: preceding change/ change	121	4.0793	0.1799	0.6722	
Sample IAS: preceding change/ subsequent change	121	2.0651	0.8382	0.3617	
Sample total: preceding change/ change	121	2.2375	0.5328	0.4669	
Sample total: preceding change/ subsequent change	121	1.0388	0.0053	0.9419	
Sample EC-Directives/sample IAS: preceding change	121	1.2899	3.7347	0.0556	
Sample EC-Directives/sample IAS: change	121	7.5461	0.3599	0.5497	
Sample EC-Directives/sample IAS: subsequent change	121	2.9081	9.4059	0.0027	*

Table 17 Levene test for homogeneity of variances (abnormal returns, standardized to positive mean values)

Variable	DF1	DF2	Statistic	2-tail sig	*Sign. at .05 level*
Sample EC-Directives: preceding change/change	1	120	21.2558	0.000	*
Sample EC-Directives: preceding change/subsequent change	1	120	1.6010	0.208	
Sample IAS: preceding change/change	1	120	45.0357	0.000	*
Sample IAS: preceding change/subsequent change	1	120	16.8502	0.000	*
Sample total: preceding change/change	1	120	29.5089	0.000	*
Sample total: preceding change/subsequent change	1	120	6.4777	0.012	*
Sample EC-Directives/sample IAS: preceding change	1	120	2.4672	0.119	
Sample EC-Directives/sample IAS: change	1	120	0.0351	0.852	
Sample EC-Directives/sample IAS: subsequent change	1	120	1.8451	0.177	

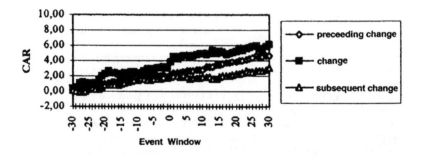

Figure 9 CAR – Sample EC-Directives (abnormal returns standardized to positive mean values)

expectation implicit in the stock price at the beginning of the announcement period is not the expectation implicit in the stock price at the beginning of the year. But Table 5 shows, that on average the information content of interim reporting in Switzerland is low for both the EC-Directives-sample and the IAS-sample. This is mainly due to the fact, that the majority of Swiss quoted companies did not release interim earnings within the period examined. For this reason, influences of interim reporting on the information content of annual earnings announcements should not have a significant impact on the

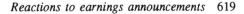

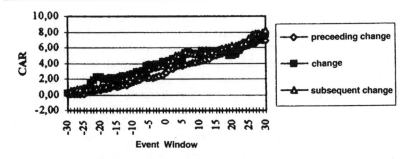

Figure 10 CAR – Sample IAS (abnormal returns standardized to positive mean values)

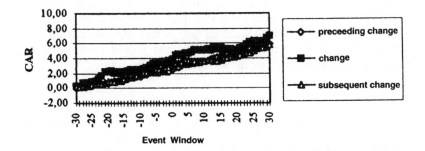

Figure 11 CAR – Total sample (abnormal returns standardized to positive mean values)

empirical results of the study and are therefore neglected in interpreting the results.

It also has to be pointed out that the earnings examined rely on the IAS before the harmonization and improvement project of the IASC (E32) has come into force. Since January 1995, the harmonization and improvement project of the IASC has reduced or eliminated a significant number of alternative accounting treatments in existing IASs and could therefore has an impact on the results of future research. In addition in the period examined financial statements of Swiss companies only relied on the EC-Directives as a framework including all alternative measurement and disclosure treatments permitted to the member states of the European Union. Transforming the EC-Directives into national law could therefore lead to different results.

CONCLUSION

To sum up, for investors in the Swiss stock market the switch from Swiss GAAP to IAS has increased the information content of earnings, if the information content is measured by a variance approach. This result cannot be achieved by comparing the differences in the mean of the abnormal returns resulting from unexpected earnings based on the former Swiss GAAP and the new GAAP (either EC-Directives or IAS). IAS are the preferred GAAP for Swiss quoted companies in the period examined. In addition, Swiss financial analysts suggest that for investors IAS-based financial statements possess a higher information content than EC-Directives-based financial statements. In contrast to these results, the empirical results of the study suggest, that there is no statistically significant difference in the information content between EC-Directives-based earnings and IAS-based earnings. Therefore, the results of the study also substantiate the hypothesis of no statistically significant difference in the information content of earnings based on Anglo-American accounting traditions (IAS) and earnings based on continental-Europe accounting traditions (EC-Directives) to investors. Despite these empirical results, for Swiss quoted companies especially the switch from Swiss GAAP to IAS should help to meet the information needs of international (Anglo-American) investors and should therefore reduce possible negative impacts in an international portfolio context.

NOTES

The author would like to thank Lombard Odier & Cie, Geneva, and Swiss Bank Corporation – Investment Consulting, Basel, for providing stock price data. I have benefited from comments of Hans Peter Möller, Alfred Wagenhofer and participants of the EIASM-Workshop on Corporate Financial Communication and the Stock Market in Brussels 1995.

1 See for instance Schering and Bayer
2 The objective of the IASC, formed in 1973, are a) to formulate and publish in the public interest accounting standards to be observed in the presentation of financial statements and to promote their world-wide acceptance and observance b) to work generally for the improvement and harmonization of regulations, accounting standards and procedures relating to the presentation of financial statements – IASC (1995), 7
3 See the full text of the International Accounting Standards in: IASC (1995)
4 Kelly/Lapper (1995)
5 Financial Times, 20.1.1994, 2
6 For instance, EC-Directives as a framework allow the inclusion of unrealized profits in financial statements
7 IASC Framework (1995), Par. 9
8 IASC Framework (1995), Par. 10
9 IAS 10, Par. 8 ff.
10 For the parent company, see IAS 21
11 See IAS 11
12 See IAS 12
13 See IAS 25
14 See Ciba-Geigy (1993), 2 ff
15 See IASC Framework (1995), Par. 46
16 Banks and insurance companies are excluded in the sample

17 I.e. continuously compounded rates of return; see for using logarithmic returns Dubacher/Zimmermann (1989, 67)
18 See Peterson (1989), 50 f., May (1991), 323; The only officially published equally-weighted index in Switzerland, the SKA-index, includes only 25 stocks. In order to reach a better proxy for the market, the SKA-index has been extended in this study to 60 stocks
19 Scholes/Williams (1977); Brown/Warner (1985) point out that neither the Dimson (1979) nor the Scholes/Williams procedures improve the power of tests for abnormal returns. In contrast, McInish/Wood (1986) show that the adjustment techniques proposed by Scholes/Williams, Dimson and others reduce a portion (29 per cent) of the bias in β_i arising from thin trading and delays in price adjustments.
20 Further research on the sample examined has shown that there is no statistically significant change in the beta of the stocks, comparing a period of 200 days preceding and 200 days subsequent to the event window in the year of the change to the new accounting standard – see Auer (1995)
21 Peterson (1989), 38; An example for the use of a –30/+30-day window-length in empirical research can be found in Conrad (1989)
22 Examples for using standardized abnormal returns can be found in Peterson (1989), 44
23 SVFV several years
24 This sample is not fully identical to the sample examined in this study. Due to a change in the ranking technique of the Swiss Financial Analyst Association ('Kommission Information der Aktionäre') the results of the years 1991, 1992 and 1993 are not comparable to those of preceding years

REFERENCES

Amir, E., Harris, T. S. and Venuti, E. K. (1993) 'A comparison of the value-relevance of U.S. versus non-U.S. GAAP Accounting Measures Using Form 20-F Reconciliations', *Journal of Accounting Research*, 31 Supplement, 230–64.
Auer, K. (1995) 'The Impact of a Change in the Accounting Standard on the Risk Parameters of a Company – Some Empirical Evidence for Changes to IAS and EC-Directives from Switzerland', Working Paper, Department of Finance, University of Innsbruck.
Baetge, J./Ross, H.-P. (1995) 'Was bedeutet "fair presentation"?', in W. Ballwieser (ed.) *US-Amerikanische Rechnungslegung*. Stuttgart: Schaeffer-Poeschel, 27–44.
Ball, R. and Brown, Ph. (1968) 'An empirical evaluation of accounting income numbers,' *Journal of Accounting Research*, 6 Autumn, 159–78.
Bertschinger, P. (1991) 'Konzernrechnung und konzernprüfung nach neuem Aktienrecht', *Der Schweizer Treuhänder*, 11: 564–72.
Brown, St. J. and Warner, J. B. (1985) 'Using daily stock returns: the case of event studies', *Journal of Financial Economics*, 14: March, 3–32.
Choi, F. D. S. and Levich, R. M. (1990) *The Capital Market Effects of International Accounting Diversity*, Homewood Ill: DowJones-Irwin.
Ciba-Geigy (1993) 'Restatement of the Group Financial Results 1992 according to International Accounting Standards (IAS)', Basel: Ciba-Geigy, 15 June.
Coenenberg, A. and Möller, P. (1979) 'Entscheidungswirkungen von Jahresabschlußinformationen vor und nach der Aktienrechtsreform von 1965,' *BFuP* 5: 438–54.
Collins, D. W. (1975) 'SEC product-line reporting and market efficiency', *Journal of Financial Economics*, 2: 125–64.

Conrad, J. (1989) 'The price effect of option introduction', *The Journal of Finance*, 44: June, 487–98.

Dimson, E. (1979) 'Risk measurement when shares are subject to infrequent trading', *Journal of Financial Economics*, 7, June, 197–226.

Dubacher, R. and Zimmermann, H. (1989) 'Risikoanalyse schweizerischer Aktien: Grundkonzepte und Berechnungen', in: *Finanzmarkt und Portfolio Management*, 3: 66–85.

Fama, E. F. (1970) Efficient capital markets: a review of theory and empirical work, *The Journal of Finance*, 25: March 383–417.

Foster, G. (1977) 'Quarterly accounting data: time series properties and predictive-ability results', *The Accounting Review*, 52: 1–21.

Harris, T. S., Lang M. and Möller, H. P. (1994) 'The value-relevance of German accounting measures: an empirical analysis', *Journal of Accounting Research*, 32, Autumn, 187–209.

Gonedes, N. J. (1974) 'Capital market equilibrium and annual accounting numbers: empirical evidence', *Journal of Accounting Research*, 12: 26–62.

IASC (1995) *International Accounting Standards 1995*, London IASC.

Kelly, J. and Lapper, R. (1995) 'Plan for global accounting standards', *Financial Times*, 12 July.

Knight R. F. (1991) 'The Information content of Swiss corporate earnings and dividend announcements', Working Paper, Studienzentrum Gerzensee.

Kommission Information der Aktionäre der SVFV: 'Tätigkeitsberichte', several years, Basel.

Lev, B. (1989) 'On the usefulness of earnings and earnings research: lessons and directions from two decades of empirical research', *Journal of Accounting Research*, 27 Supplement, 153–92.

May, A. (1991) 'Zum Stand der empiricshen Forschung über Informations-verarbeitung am Aktienmarkt – Ein Überblick', zfbf, 4, 313–35.

Meek, G. K. (1983) 'US securities market responses to alternate earnings disclosures of non-US multinational corporations', *The Accounting Review*, LVIII, 2, 349–402.

Meek, G. K. (1991) 'Capital market reactions to accounting earnings announcements in an international context', *Journal of Financial Management and Accounting*, 93–109.

McInish, Th. H. and Wood, R. A. (1986) 'Adjusting for beta bias: an assessment of alternative techniques: a note', *The Journal of Finance*, 41, March, 277–86.

Patell, J. M. (1976) 'Corporate forecasts of earnings per share and stock price behaviour: empirical tests', *Journal of Accounting Research*, 14, Autumn 246–76.

Peterson, P. P. (1989) 'Event studies: a review of issues and methodology', *Quarterly Journal of Business and Economics*, 28, Summer, 36–66.

Pope, P. F. and Rees, W. P. (1993) 'International differences in GAAP and the pricing of earnings', Working Paper, University of Strathclyde.

Scholes, M. and Williams, J. (1977) 'Estimating betas from nonsynchronous data', *Journal of Financial Economics*, 5, December, 309–28.

SVFV (Schweizerische Vereinigung für Finanzanalyse und Vermögensverwaltung) and Arthur Andersen (1991): *Information der Aktionäre – Rechnungslegung und Berichterstattung*, Zürich: SVFV.

SVFV (Schweizerische Vereinigung für Finanzanalyse und Vermögensverwaltung) (1994): *Informationspolitik börsenkotierter Unternehmen im Jahre 1993*, Basel: SVFV.

Thiel, H. (1991) 'Stille Reserven als ungelöstes Problem' *Der Schweizer Treuhänder*, 11: 556–59.

Vischer, F. (1991) 'Würdigung der Reform' *Der Schweizer Treuhänder*, 11: 525–29.

Watts, R. L. and Zimmerman, J. L. (1986) *Positive Accounting Theory*, Englewood Cliffs, N.J.

Ziebart, D. A. (1985) 'Control of beta reliability in studies of abnormal return magnitudes: a methodological note', *Journal of Accounting Research*, 2: 920–6.

[19]

The European Accounting Review 2000, **9:4**, 499–517

To whom are IAS earnings informative? Domestic versus foreign shareholders' perspectives

Juha Kinnunen
Helsinki School of Economics

Jyrki Niskanen
University of Tampere

Eero Kasanen
Helsinki School of Economics

ABSTRACT

Using a sample from the Helsinki Stock Exchange, this paper analyses the information content of dual disclosures of IAS (International Accounting Standards) and LAS (Local Accounting Standards) earnings. Their information content to foreign and domestic shareholders can be distinguished from each other as the unrestricted shares (available to foreign and domestic investors) and the restricted shares (available to domestic investors only) of the same set of companies were listed separately during 1984–92. The information content is tested with regressions using market-adjusted stock returns measured from the fifty-week period ending in the week of financial statements release. The overall findings suggest that restating local GAAP earnings according to the IAS helps to meet foreign investors' information needs, but is of limited use to domestic investors.

1. INTRODUCTION

In this paper we examine the information content of Local Accounting Standards (LAS) and International Accounting Standards (IAS) earnings to foreign and domestic investors separately. The empirical evidence is from Finland during 1984–92, when restricted and unrestricted shares were listed separately on the Helsinki Stock Exchange. The partially segmented stock market (that ceased to exist after 1992) makes it possible to distinguish between the information content of earnings to foreign and domestic investors.

Address for correspondence
Juha Kinnunen, Helsinki School of Economics, Runeberginkatu 22-24, 00100
Helsinki, Finland. E-mail: jkinnune@hkkk.fi; fax: +358-9-4313-8678.

Copyright © 2000 European Accounting Association
ISSN 0963-8180 print/1468-4497 online   DOI: 10.1080/09638180020025330
Published by Routledge Journals, Taylor & Francis Ltd on behalf of the EAA

Regulatory requirements of international financial markets have forced companies in different countries to publish financial statement information that differs from their usual reporting to domestic audiences. Virtually all European stock exchanges currently allow foreign listed companies to follow IAS. In contrast, the stock exchanges in the US and Canada have so far not accepted foreign listed companies to follow IAS without a reconciliation to local (US or Canadian) GAAP in the notes.[1]

There are several studies on the information content or value relevance of earnings numbers computed under two or more different GAAPs for the same set of firms (Pope and Rees, 1992; Amir *et al.*, 1993; Niskanen *et al.*, 1994; Auer, 1996; Barth and Clinch, 1996; Harris and Muller, 1999; Niskanen *et al.*, 2000). In addition, some studies have compared the information content of earnings reported by different firms in different countries (Alford *et al.*, 1993; Harris *et al.*, 1994).

Dual disclosure situations arise when domestic GAAP earnings are restated to reconcile to the GAAP of another country where the firm has a dual listing of its shares. In essence, prior studies have estimated the earnings response coefficients for the domestic GAAP earnings and for the restated (alternative GAAP) earnings, after controlling for the effect of each other. In such tests, the statistical significance of the coefficient estimated for the domestic GAAP earnings indicates incremental information content to the stock market beyond the target country earnings, and vice versa. Overall, the conclusions that can be drawn from these prior studies are mixed. For example, Pownall and Schipper (1999) note that when annual stock returns of non-US firms listed in US stock exchanges are regressed on their domestic GAAP earnings and their reconciliations to US GAAP, the results vary across empirical specifications, time periods and firm samples.

Recently, Niskanen *et al.* (2000) examined the value relevance of Finnish accounting standards earnings and their voluntarily disclosed IAS counterparts. In the study, annual stock returns from fiscal (reporting) years were regressed on the levels and changes of Finnish GAAP earnings and their reconciliations to the IAS. After controlling for Finnish GAAP earnings, the results showed that the aggregate reconciliations from Finnish GAAP to IAS did not provide significant value relevance to either domestic or foreign investors.

Instead of measuring stock returns from fiscal years, this paper analyses the information content of Local (Finnish) and International Accounting Standards earnings (LAS and IAS, respectively) using return windows defined individually for each firm on the basis of their financial statement release dates. Unlike in Niskanen *et al.* (2000), this approach allows for the possibility that investors may not anticipate the information content of IAS reconciliation until the financial statements are disclosed and, therefore, their information content is not fully reflected in share prices by the fiscal year end.

The hypotheses tested in this paper are divided into three groups. First, we hypothesize that both LAS and IAS earnings contain significant (incremental) information to both investor groups. Second, we hypothesize that the information content of the earnings measures differs *between* the investor groups. We expect that LAS (IAS) earnings are more informative to domestic (foreign) investors than to foreign (domestic) investors. Correspondingly, our third hypothesis is that the information content of the earnings measures differs *within* each investor group. Our expectation is that LAS (IAS) earnings are more informative than IAS (LAS) earnings to domestic (foreign) investors.

The Helsinki Stock Exchange (HeSE) was a partially segmented stock market during the period 1984–92, as unrestricted shares (available to both foreign and domestic investors) and restricted shares (available only to domestic investors) were listed separately. At the same time, a number of firms listed on the HeSE voluntarily disclosed both Local (Finnish) Accounting Standards earnings and International Accounting Standards earnings.

Our empirical results show that while domestic investors find information content only in LAS earnings (after controlling for IAS earnings), both IAS and LAS earnings are incrementally informative to foreign investors. Consistent with our hypothesis, we find that the response coefficient estimated for IAS earnings is significantly larger for foreign investors than for domestic investors. However, we cannot find any significant difference in the coefficients of LAS earnings between the investor groups. Moreover, the results are consistent with our hypothesis that, in the group of foreign investors, the response coefficient of IAS earnings is significantly larger than the coefficient of LAS earnings. In contrast, we find no significant difference between the response coefficients of LAS and IAS earnings estimated for domestic investors. Overall, the findings of this paper suggest that restating local GAAP earnings to conform to the IAS helps to meet foreign investors' information needs, but is of limited use to domestic investors. This general conclusion contrasts with Niskanen *et al.* (2000) and is presumably explained by the use of individually identified return windows that include the (dual) financial statement releases.

2. INSTITUTIONAL BACKGROUND AND HYPOTHESES

From the perspective of this study, the Finnish stock market was characterized by two important features during 1984–92. First, the ownership of foreign investors in Finnish firms was limited to a maximum of 20%. That is, at least 80% of a Finnish firm's shares had to be restricted, i.e. they were not allowed to be owned by foreigners. The purpose of this law was to prohibit foreign investors from achieving control in strategically important industries.[2]

Second, Finnish investors' possibilities to invest abroad were very limited until 1990. Before January 1986 they were not allowed to buy foreign securities without the permission of the Bank of Finland. From January 1986 onwards, the Bank of Finland allowed individual investors to invest 10,000 Finnish markkas (approximately 1,700 euros) in foreign securities. This limit was subsequently raised to 300,000 markkas (approximately 50,000 euros) until the limit was abolished in July 1990.

The investment restrictions implied that there were two investor groups with different opportunity sets. As a result, during 1984–92, restricted and unrestricted shares of the same set of companies were listed separately on the HeSE. The only difference between the two share classes was that restricted shares were available only to domestic investors, while both domestic and foreign investors could hold unrestricted shares. There were no differences in voting power or dividends between the share classes.

Hietala (1989) argues that foreign investors required a lower *risk premium* than Finnish investors, whose investment opportunities were limited to domestic stocks. Foreign investors' lower risk premium was due to a small correlation between the returns of Finnish shares and the world market portfolio (the world market portfolio was available to international but not to Finnish investors). A lower foreign investors' required return led to a situation where *price premiums* were paid for unrestricted shares. Hietala (1989) shows that unrestricted shares are traded at a premium *if and only if foreign investors determine their prices.* Therefore, since unrestricted shares in fact were traded at a premium, it is possible to measure foreign investors' use of earnings information with the price changes of unrestricted shares.

Simultaneously as the Helsinki Stock Exchange started to list separately restricted and unrestricted shares, many internationalized Finnish firms began to disclose dual financial statements following the Local Accounting Standards (LAS) and the International Accounting Standards (IAS). The voluntary disclosures of IAS-based financial statements were attributable to the growing importance of foreign ownership and the listings of Finnish firms in foreign stock exchanges. As foreign investors could not interpret Finnish earnings numbers without familiarity with the Finnish accounting and tax practices, they had informational disadvantage relative to domestic investors. In the following, we discuss the informational roles of LAS and IAS earnings during our research period, and conclude with our hypotheses.

The IASC survey (1988) of financial accounting practices in fifty-four countries worldwide indicates that Finnish accounting rules had the lowest conformity with the International Accounting Standards. Before the reform of Finnish accounting legislation in 1992, the main differences between the Finnish accounting rules and the IAS related to accounting for manufacturing overhead, depreciation of fixed assets, financial leases, 20–50%-owned affiliates, pension obligations, untaxed reserves and long-term construction projects. (For more detailed descriptions of the Finnish accounting rules and their differences from the IAS, see Näsi, 1992; Troberg, 1992; and Kasanen *et al.*, 1996.)

LAS earnings

During the research period, Finnish accounting rules have given firms ample opportunities for earnings management. At the same time, the corporate income tax system has been tied to corporate financial reporting. In principle, the taxable income of a firm has been approximately the same as the earnings before taxes reported to the shareholders. Especially, firms have not been allowed to deduct expenses in taxation beyond the expenses deducted in their books. Therefore, the tax laws have put certain practical limits on earnings management by defining maximum (but not minimum) depreciations and untaxed reserves. However, even after taking into account these tax-related constraints, firms typically have had a lot of 'reporting slack' left.

Kasanen *et al.* (1996) show that two major factors have influenced Finnish firms' propensity to manage LAS earnings. First, the nominal corporate tax rate has been high until quite recently, so firms have had a strong motive to minimize reported earnings. Second, to pay dividends, firms need to report positive (LAS) earnings and cannot therefore always take full cash-flow advantage of the linkage between financial accounting and tax rules. The importance of dividends accentuates, because in the thin Finnish market it has been difficult to sell or buy large blocks of shares without a share price effect.

The motivation of Finnish firms to pay dividends can be considered highly demand-driven because of the dominant role of institutional owners. The financial institutions such as banks, insurance companies, foundations and the government (through the Ministry of Trade and Industry) have been the largest owner groups of industrial and commercial firms. The first mutual funds in Finland were not launched until late 1987, and they played an insignificant role throughout our research period. In our sample, the average share of institutional ownership (defined as shares owned by others than individuals) is about 65%.

Manufacturing firms in Finland have traditionally been grouped around the financial institutions. In these groups, banks and other financial institutions have had a lot of influence upon the managers' decision-making in the member firms. Usually, the institutions have been also the main suppliers of long-term debt capital to the manufacturing firms in their groups. Until the most recent years, Finnish institutions have been unwilling to relinquish control in the firms of their financial block, and transfers of firms from one block to another have been rare. The ownership and control structures have been stable for a long time.

Because the capital market has been thin, the institutions have needed to collect a significant part of their revenue in the form of dividends. This situation has forced firms to follow stable dividend policies. Therefore, and because firms were able to manage their domestic earnings, reported LAS earnings have followed usually stable patterns over time. Consistent with Kasanen *et al.* (1996), we argue that investors consider unexpected LAS earnings a signal of a dividend change that has an effect on the market value of the firm's shares.

However, international investors may prefer dividends and capital gains differently from domestic investors. As an indication of this, the statistics of the Helsinki Stock Exchange show that unrestricted shares were more actively traded than restricted shares (the average turnover of unrestricted shares in 1987–92 was 38.5% of their year-end market value, whereas the corresponding ratio for restricted shares was only 18.4%). This suggests that, compared to domestic investors, international investors at the HeSE are short-term traders for which capital gains have played a more important role than cash dividends.

Moreover, domestic and international investors may be subjected to different tax rules, which provides one potential reason for differing preferences towards capital gains and dividends. Some evidence of such a difference is provided by Hietala and Keloharju (1995), who examine the ex-dividend ratios of Finnish firms during 1984–90. They find that the ex-dividend ratios of restricted shares have been statistically significantly larger than those of unrestricted shares. In conclusion, we hypothesize that while the LAS earnings are informative to both investor groups, they are a more important earnings measure for the domestic equity holders than for foreign investors.

In addition, we argue that domestic investors have been more familiar with LAS than with IAS earnings measures. As already noted, investments in foreign securities by Finnish investors were effectively restricted by the Bank of Finland until 1990. Because of this restriction, all individual and most institutional domestic investors operated mainly in the domestic capital market and thus were used to analysing LAS earnings information. Moreover, financial analysts and the financial press in Finland have rarely paid attention to the IAS-based financial statements.[3] Furthermore, while IAS earnings have been available only from major companies that attract foreign investors, domestic investors have also analysed other (non-listed) companies that disclose only LAS-based financial statements. Overall, it is reasonable to hypothesize that domestic investors are more accustomed to analysing and interpreting earnings information based on LAS than on IAS.

IAS earnings

IAS earnings aim to convey what is generally understood as a 'true and fair view' of the firms' performance (*IASC Framework*, para. no. 46). This earnings information is in contrast with the institution-dependent LAS earnings on which the dividends and taxable income are based.[4] Being a performance-related earnings measure, IAS earnings provide value-relevant information for both domestic and foreign investors. Thus we expect stock returns to be positively correlated with unexpected IAS earnings.

We hypothesize that IAS earnings are a more informative earnings concept to foreign investors than to domestic investors. In contrast with domestic investors, whose investment opportunities were restricted by the law, foreign investors needed to compare Finnish companies with other firms in their international portfolios. For this reason, IAS earnings are expected to be more useful for foreign than for domestic investors.

We hypothesize also that foreign investors prefer IAS earnings to LAS earnings information. Given the large differences between the LAS and IAS accounting rules and the small share of Finnish securities in their portfolios, foreign investors have had a limited motive to analyse the idiosyncrasies of LAS earnings information in detail. Therefore, we expect that, in our setting, IAS earnings information has easily found its way to the foreign audience. This argument is inconsistent with the 'single-domicile' notion, according to which financial statements restated in terms of different accounting standards lose the viewpoints of the original statements (Mueller, 1967: 162; Choi, 1980).

In conclusion, we test the following hypotheses.

- *Incremental information content of the earnings measures:* to both domestic and foreign investors, LAS and IAS earnings have incremental information content over each other.
- *Clientele effect between the investor groups:* the incremental information content of LAS earnings is larger to domestic investors than to foreign investors. Correspondingly, the incremental information content of IAS earnings is larger to foreign investors than to domestic investors.
- *Relevance effect within the investor groups:* to domestic investors, the incremental information content of LAS earnings is larger than the incremental information content of IAS earnings. Correspondingly to foreign investors, the incremental information content of IAS earnings is larger than the incremental information content of LAS earnings.

Our research design and hypotheses are summarized in Table 1.

Table 1 Summary of research design and hypotheses

	Earnings measure:	
Investor group:	Local Accounting Standards (LAS)	International Accounting Standards (IAS)
Domestic	$\beta_{D,L}$ = domestic investors' response to LAS earnings information	$\beta_{D,I}$ = domestic investors' response to IAS earnings information
Foreign	$\beta_{F,L}$ = foreign investors' response to LAS earnings information	$\beta_{F,I}$ = foreign investors' response to IAS earnings information

Hypotheses:

Incremental information content of the earnings measures:
$\beta_{D,L} > 0, \ \beta_{D,I} > 0, \ \beta_{F,L} > 0, \ \beta_{F,I} > 0$

Clientele effect between the investor groups:
$\beta_{D,L} > \beta_{F,L}, \ \beta_{F,I} > \beta_{D,I}$

Relevance effect within the investor groups:
$\beta_{D,L} > \beta_{D,I}, \ \beta_{F,I} > \beta_{F,L}$

3. METHODS AND DATA

To measure the information content of the Local and International Accounting Standards earnings, we estimate the earnings response coefficients separately for domestic and foreign investors. Initially, we have more observations available for tests with restricted stocks than for tests with unrestricted stocks. This is because all firms in the sample did not have a series of unrestricted shares (the company rules may prohibit foreign ownership), and because a few disclosures of LAS and IAS earnings are from years preceding the start of separate listing (1984) of restricted and unrestricted shares. However, to be able to compare the earnings response coefficients between the domestic and foreign investor groups, we must use price data that are available for both stock series. Thus, the sample of restricted shares gives up a little, but gains a perfectly matched set of sample pairs (restricted–unrestricted shares).

In the empirical tests, we use our matched-pairs sample pooled across firms and years. To control for the potential year effect, we add corresponding dummy variables in our regressions.[5]

We estimate the following two regressions for domestic and foreign investors, respectively.

$$AR^D_{i,t} = \beta_{0,D} + \beta_{D,L} ULAS_{i,t} + \beta_{D,I} UIAS_{i,t} + \sum_{t=85}^{91} \beta_{1,t} D_t + \varepsilon_{1,i,t} \qquad (1)$$

$$AR^F_{i,t} = \beta_{0,F} + \beta_{F,L} ULAS_{i,t} + \beta_{F,I} UIAS_{i,t} + \sum_{t=85}^{91} \beta_{2,t} D_t + \varepsilon_{2,i,t} \qquad (2)$$

where

$AR^D_{i,t}$ = the market-adjusted return (abnormal return) for the restricted shares available only to domestic investors of firm i in year t. The return is measured from the fifty-week period ending at the end of the week of the financial statement release.

$AR^F_{i,t}$: as $AR^D_{i,t}$ but for the unrestricted shares available to foreign investors.

$ULAS_{i,t}$ = the unexpected Local (Finnish) Accounting Standards earnings of firm i in year t, deflated by the market value of the firm's equity at the beginning of the year. Assuming a random walk-type process for earnings,[6] the unexpected earnings are measured with earnings changes between consecutive years.

$UIAS_{i,t}$: as $ULAS_{i,t}$ but for the International Accounting Standards (IAS) earnings.

D_t = a dummy variable indicating the observation year t in question.

$\varepsilon_{1,i,t}$ and $\varepsilon_{2,i,t}$ = regression residuals with usual assumptions.

$\beta_{D,L}$ and $\beta_{D,I}$ = the domestic investors' response coefficients for the unexpected Local and International Accounting Standards earnings, respectively.

$\beta_{F,L}$ and $\beta_{F,I}$ = the foreign investors' response coefficients for the unexpected Local and International Accounting Standards earnings, respectively.

Market-adjusted returns $AR_{i,t}^{D}$ and $AR_{i,t}^{F}$ are computed by deducting the market index return from the individual stock returns. Risk-adjusted returns are not used, because that would significantly reduce the sample size. The main reason for this is that there are no market data available for beta estimation for the unrestricted stock series before 1984. (See also Brown and Warner, 1980, who find that the method of market adjustment is not crucial for the results.)

Association studies typically use identical return periods for all sample stocks. Most commonly, reporting year return windows are used (for example, see Niskanen *et al.*, 2000, and Lev, 1989, for a review of market-based earnings research). These studies assume a lead association between prices and earnings Some studies (for example, Beaver and Dukes, 1972; Rayburn, 1986; and Bowen *et al.*, 1987) use fixed March–April windows, thereby attempting to match the return measurement period with the release of the financial statements in a simplified manner.

Moreover, some other studies use long-return windows identified individually for each sample firm on the basis of their actual financial statement release dates. Such studies include Board and Day (1989) and Kinnunen and Niskanen (1993), which are both studies on the information content of cash flows. These association studies resemble the present study in the sense that, unlike conventional earnings, cash flow (in our case IAS earnings) information is not available to the market before complete financial statements are disclosed. To make sure that IAS earnings information is available by the end of our return window, we measure stock returns from a fifty-week period ending in the week of the financial statement release.[7]

Our earnings data were obtained from the annual reports of those listed Finnish firms which have published dual financial statements prepared according to the Local (Finnish) Accounting Standards and the International Accounting Standards. Initially, all 137 dual disclosures by the firms listed on the Helsinki Stock Exchange in the 1980s and early 1990s were included. The earliest disclosure was from March 1981, but the major part of the disclosures was from later years, the last observation being from May 1992. The earnings announcement dates were obtained from the files of the HeSE.

The initial sample of the dual earnings disclosures was then screened to find those cases for which the firm had both restricted and unrestricted shares listed on the HeSE at the time of the earnings announcement. This resulted in 86 matched-pairs observations from 18 firms.[9] In 1987, for example, the sample firms represent 44% of all manufacturing firms listed on the HeSE, and their market capitalization is 41 milliard Finnish markkas (approximately 6.8 milliard euros) which is nearly 80% of the total market capitalization of all manufacturing companies on the HeSE in that year.

During the whole research period 1984–92, unrestricted shares sold at a premium compared to restricted shares. In 1984, i.e. the first year of separate listing of restricted and unrestricted shares on the HeSE, the median premium was 42.8%. Thereafter the median premium decreased, being only 1.4% in 1992, the last year of separate listing of restricted and unrestricted shares. In the period of separate listing of restricted and unrestricted shares, the lower quartile, the median and the upper quartile of the premium were 2.7%, 9.1% and 23.5%, respectively

4. EMPIRICAL RESULTS

The descriptive statistics for the market-adjusted returns of the restricted and unrestricted shares and for the Local and the International Accounting Standards earnings are given in Table 2. The upper panel of the table shows that the average market-adjusted returns for the domestic and foreign investors are −0.019 and −0.024, respectively. These average returns are not, however, significantly different from zero. In addition, the statistics indicate that the average change in LAS earnings −0.011 is somewhat higher than the average change in IAS earnings −0.037. These average earnings changes are neither significantly different from zero.

The lower panel of Table 2 shows a (very) significant positive correlation of 0.743 between the returns of the two share classes and a significant correlation of 0.300 between the two earnings variables. Moreover, the correlation of the LAS earnings change with the domestic investors' return is higher than with the foreign investors' return (0.239 versus 0.195). Correspondingly, the correlation of the IAS earnings change with the foreign investors' return is clearly higher than with the domestic investors' return (0.185 versus 0.096). In addition, the correlation of the domestic investors' return with the LAS earnings change is higher than with the IAS earnings change (0.239 versus 0.096).

The estimation results of regressions (1) and (2) are shown in Table 3. In panel A of Table 3 the results for *domestic investors* (Equation (1)) reveal incremental information content in LAS earnings after controlling for IAS earnings. The estimated earnings response coefficient is 0.329 and it is very significant. The response coefficient of 0.403 for IAS earnings is slightly larger but not yet significant at the conventional level of 5%. The adjusted R^2 for the model is 0.142 and the F-statistic for the model is significant at the 1.2% level. Overall, the findings are consistent with the hypothesis that, after controlling for IAS earnings, LAS earnings provide significant incremental information to domestic investors.

In panel B, the response coefficients estimated for *foreign investors* (Equation (2)) are 0.302 and 0.854 for the two earnings variables, respectively. The t-values and related marginal probabilities indicate that both earnings variables have significant incremental information content over each other. The adjusted R^2 is 0.314, and the F-statistic for the model is very significant. Overall, the findings

Table 2 Descriptive statistics on earnings and returns data

The table shows distributional statistics (panel **A**) and Pearson product–moment correlation matrix (panel **B**) for the share return and earnings variables. The share returns are market-adjusted returns of restricted shares (available to domestic investors only) and unrestricted shares (available also to foreign investors) measured from the fifty-week period ending at the end of the week of financial statement release. The earnings variables are unexpected LAS (Local Accounting Standards) and IAS (International Accounting Standards) earnings measured by earnings change divided by market value of equity at the beginning of the year.

A. Distributional statistics ($N = 86$)

	AR^D	AR^F	$ULAS$	$UIAS$
Average	−0.019	−0.024	−0.011	−0.037
Standard deviation	0.277	0.328	0.219	0.171
Lower quartile	−0.187	−0.249	−0.026	−0.090
Median	−0.023	−0.020	0.007	−0.014
Upper quartile	0.145	0.234	0.043	0.075

B. Correlation matrix ($N = 86$)

	AR^D	AR^F	$ULAS$	$UIAS$
AR^D	1.000	0.743 (0.000)	0.239 (0.027)	0.096 (0.379)
AR^F		1.000	0.195 (0.072)	0.185 (0.088)
$ULAS$			1.000	0.300 (0.005)
$UIAS$				1.000

Legend:
AR^D = market-adjusted return of restricted shares (domestic investors);
AR^F = market-adjusted return of unrestricted shares (foreign investors);
$ULAS$ = unexpected LAS earnings (earnings change divided by market value of equity);
$UIAS$ = unexpected IAS earnings (earnings change divided by market value of equity).
Parenthesized numbers in the correlation matrix (panel **B**) are two-tail significance levels.

are consistent with the hypothesis that both IAS and LAS earnings convey significant incremental information to the foreign investors.

Panel C shows the results from the tests comparing estimated earnings response coefficients *vis-à-vis* each other.[10] First, it turns out that although the coefficient of LAS earnings for domestic investors is larger than for foreign investors (0.329 versus 0.302), the difference remains statistically insignificant (*t*-value 0.409). Nevertheless, the corresponding difference between the earnings response coefficients of IAS earnings for foreign and domestic investors (0.854 versus 0.403) is significant at the 1% level (*t*-value 2.643). Thus, this finding is consistent with our hypothesis on the clientele effect in IAS earnings for the foreign investor audience.

When the response coefficients of the two earnings measures are compared in the group of domestic investors (Equation (1)), the difference in the estimated coefficients (0.329 versus 0.403) is insignificant (t-value -0.290). In contrast, the corresponding difference in the group of foreign investors (0.854 versus 0.302) is significant at the 3% level (t-value 2.206). The finding is consistent with our hypothesis on the relevance effect of IAS earnings for the foreign investor audience.

Finally, the importance of the earnings variables can be compared with the beta coefficients shown in panels A and B of Table 3. These betas are standardized regression coefficients measuring the relative magnitudes of the effects of the independent earnings variables on the dependent return variables (see, e.g., Snedecor and Cochran, 1980).

Overall, it can be seen that the standardized betas are consistent with our hypotheses on the clientele and relevance effects. Between the regressions, the

Table 3 Regression results

The table reports results from OLS regressions of returns of restricted shares available only to domestic investors (panel **A**) and unrestricted shares available also to foreign investors (panel **B**). The independent variables are unexpected LAS (Local Accounting Standards) and IAS (International Accounting Standards) earnings measured by earnings change divided by market value of equity at the beginning of the year. The share returns are market-adjusted returns measured from the fifty-week period ending at the end of the week of financial statement release.

A. Regression of restricted shares (domestic investors) ($N = 86$)

$$AR_{i,t}^{D} = \beta_{0,D} + \beta_{D,L}ULAS_{i,t} + \beta_{D,I}UIAS_{i,t} + \sum_{t=85}^{91}\beta_{1,t}D_{t} + \varepsilon_{1,i,t} \qquad (1)$$

	$\beta_{0,D}$	$\beta_{D,L}$	$\beta_{D,I}$	$\beta_{1,85}$	$\beta_{1,86}$	$\beta_{1,87}$	$\beta_{1,88}$	$\beta_{1,89}$	$\beta_{1,90}$	$\beta_{1,91}$
Estimate	-0.087	0.329	0.403	0.074	0.146	0.070	-0.074	0.243	-0.088	0.259
Std error	0.054	0.071	0.226	0.098	0.117	0.083	0.064	0.097	0.114	0.120
Beta	—	0.260	0.249	0.078	0.162	0.088	-0.099	0.326	-0.107	0.337
t-Value	-1.611	4.634	1.783	0.755	1.248	0.843	-1.156	2.505	-0.772	2.158
Prob(t)	0.111	0.000	0.079	0.453	0.216	0.402	0.251	0.014	0.443	0.034

Adj. $R^2 = 0.142$; Model $F = 2.57$; Prob(F) $= 0.012$.

B. Regression of unrestricted shares (foreign investors) ($N = 86$)

$$AR_{i,t}^{F} = \beta_{0,F} + \beta_{F,L}ULAS_{i,t} + \beta_{F,I}UIAS_{i,t} + \sum_{t=85}^{91}\beta_{2,t}D_{t} + \varepsilon_{2,i,t} \qquad (2)$$

	$\beta_{0,F}$	$\beta_{F,L}$	$\beta_{F,I}$	$\beta_{2,85}$	$\beta_{2,86}$	$\beta_{2,87}$	$\beta_{2,88}$	$\beta_{2,89}$	$\beta_{2,90}$	$\beta_{2,91}$
Estimate	-0.058	0.302	0.854	0.050	0.121	-0.174	-0.118	0.366	-0.138	0.351
Std error	0.182	0.063	0.221	0.234	0.218	0.195	0.184	0.194	0.199	0.204
Beta	—	0.202	0.446	0.045	0.114	-0.185	-0.134	0.414	-0.141	0.385
t-Value	-0.316	4.753	3.862	0.215	0.554	-0.894	-0.643	1.882	-0.692	1.718
Prob(t)	0.753	0.000	0.000	0.830	0.581	0.374	0.522	0.064	0.491	0.090

Adj. $R^2 = 0.314$; Model $F = 5.32$; Prob(F) $= 0.000$.

Table 3 Continued

C. Comparison between earnings response coefficients

Hypothesized relationship	t-Value	Prob(t) (two-tailed)
$\beta_{D,L} > \beta_{F,L}$	0.409	0.684
$\beta_{F,I} > \beta_{D,I}$	2.643	0.010
$\beta_{D,L} > \beta_{D,I}$	−0.290	0.772
$\beta_{F,I} > \beta_{F,L}$	2.206	0.030

Legend:
AR^D = market-adjusted return of restricted shares (domestic investors);
AR^F = market-adjusted return of unrestricted shares (foreign investors);
$ULAS$ = unexpected LAS earnings (earnings change divided by market value of equity);
$UIAS$ = unexpected IAS earnings (earnings change divided by market value of equity);
D = dummy variable indicating observation year.
$\beta_{D,L}$ and $\beta_{D,I}$ = the domestic investors' response coefficients for unexpected LAS and IAS earnings, respectively.
$\beta_{F,L}$ and $\beta_{F,I}$ = the foreign investors' response coefficients for unexpected LAS and IAS earnings, respectively.
Beta is the standardized regression coefficient comparing the strengths of the relations between different independent variables and the dependent variable. All t-values are based on heteroscedastic-consistent (White-adjusted) standard errors.

beta of LAS earnings for domestic investors is larger than for foreign investors (0.260 versus 0.202) and the beta of IAS earnings for foreign investors is larger than for domestic investors (0.446 versus 0.249). Within the regressions, the beta of LAS earnings is slightly larger than the beta of IAS earnings for domestic investors (0.260 versus 0.249). Respectively for foreign investors, the beta of IAS earnings is larger than the beta of LAS earnings (0.446 versus 0.202).

Additional tests

To examine how sensitive our general findings are to the selection of the return window, we re-estimated the regressions using market-adjusted stock returns from fiscal (reporting) years as dependent variables. In addition, we iterated the regressions with market-adjusted returns measured from periods [−50; −4], [−50; −3], [−50; −2], [−50; −1], [−50; +1] and [−50; +2] weeks relative to the week of financial statement release. The adjusted R^2's and related F-statistics are shown in Table 4.

The table indicates remarkable differences in the R^2's and significance levels of the estimated regressions conditional on the measurement of the dependent stock return variable. For both restricted and unrestricted shares, the results are clearly weakest for fiscal year returns (see the R^2 of 0.077 and 0.108 in panels A and B, respectively). When we use return windows ending closer to the week of financial

Table 4 The effect of return windows on adjusted *R*-squares of the regressions

The table reports adjusted *R*-squares from regressions where the dependent market-adjusted returns are measured from fiscal (reporting) years and from periods [−50; −4], ..., [−50; +2] weeks relative to financial statement release. The independent variables in each regression are unexpected LAS (Local Accounting Standards) and IAS (International Accounting Standards) earnings measured by earnings change divided by market value of equity at the beginning of the year (see Equations (1) and (2)).

A. Regressions of restricted shares (domestic investors) (*N* = 86)

	Fiscal year	Return window						
		[−50; −4]	[−50; −3]	[−50; −2]	[−50; −1]	[−50; 0]	[−50; +1]	[−50; +2]
Adj. R^2	0.077	0.102	0.126	0.186	0.183	0.142	0.138	0.139
Model *F*	1.79	2.07	2.37	3.16	3.12	2.57	2.52	2.53
Prob(*F*)	0.084	0.043	0.020	0.003	0.003	0.012	0.014	0.014

B. Regressions of unrestricted shares (foreign investors) (*N* = 86)

	Fiscal year	Return window						
		[−50; −4]	[−50; −3]	[−50; −2]	[−50; −1]	[−50; 0]	[−50; +1]	[−50; +2]
Adj. R^2	0.108	0.283	0.283	0.295	0.291	0.314	0.301	0.306
Model *F*	2.14	4.73	4.73	4.95	4.88	5.32	5.06	5.16
Prob(*F*)	0.036	0.000	0.000	0.000	0.000	0.000	0.000	0.000

statement release, the R^2's and significance levels improve substantially. For restricted shares, the R^2 peaks (0.186) when the return window $[-50; -2]$ ending two weeks before financial statement release is used. For unrestricted shares, the R^2 is largest (0.314) for the window $[-50; 0]$ ending in the week of financial statement release. These results are consistent with the notion that the information content of (dual) earnings disclosures is not properly measured through return windows limited to fiscal years. Thus, it seems plausible that the insignificant value relevance of the IAS earnings reconciliation reported by Niskanen *et al.* (2000) is driven by the earnings information not being fully reflected in share prices at the fiscal year end.

To control for the effect of potential outliers, we re-estimated Equations (1) and (2) using WLS (weighted least squares) instead of the OLS method. While the estimated regression coefficients were slightly different (the WLS-estimated coefficients were 0.314 and 0.400 for the *ULAS* and *UIAS* variables in Equation (1), and the corresponding coefficients in Equation (2) were 0.347 and 0.760), the broad tenor of the results were qualitatively the same as those reported in Table 3.

Furthermore, we re-estimated the regressions using raw returns instead of market-adjusted returns as dependent variables. In brief, the general findings proved to be insensitive with respect to the use of raw returns versus market-adjusted returns.

Finally, we estimated our regressions using both earnings changes and earnings levels as independent variables. These regressions were estimated for both raw returns and market adjusted returns. It appeared that IAS earnings change was the only statistically explanatory variable, and this was the case only in the model(s) estimated for foreign investors. However, these results were obviously affected by collinearity among the independent variables. The correlation between the changes and levels of LAS earnings was as high as 0.963, and the corresponding correlation for IAS earnings was 0.715. Because of severe collinearity problems, regressions including both earnings levels and changes as independent variables thus did not prove useful in our data.

5. SUMMARY AND CONCLUSIONS

This paper presents empirical findings on the information content of IAS (International Accounting Standards) versus LAS (Local Accounting Standards) earnings to foreign and domestic investors separately. Our data come from Finland, where a number of firms listed on the Helsinki Stock Exchange started the practice of disclosing dual financial statements in the mid-1980s.

Until 1992, Finnish law limited foreign investors' ownership of Finnish corporate shares to a maximum of 20%. Both domestic and foreign investors could invest in unrestricted shares, whereas restricted shares were held by domestic investors. Finnish investors' possibilities to invest abroad were negligible. Under such circumstances, the prices of unrestricted shares were determined by foreign investors and the prices of restricted shares were determined by domestic investors. Thus, because of dual earnings disclosures *and* a partially segmented stock market, we are able to measure the information content of the IAS- and LAS-based earnings information to foreign and domestic investors separately.

We argue that, in our institutional setting, the voluntarily reported IAS earnings provide independent information on the firms' performance, whereas earnings based on the Finnish LAS are related to firms' dividends. Our first research hypothesis is that, due to their different informational roles, both earnings variables are *incrementally informative* to both investor groups. In addition, we hypothesize that the two earnings measures have a *clientele effect* between the investor groups implying that the incremental information content of LAS (IAS) earnings is larger to domestic (foreign) investors than to foreign (domestic) investors. Finally, we hypothesize that there is also a *relevance effect* between the earnings concepts implying that, to domestic (foreign) investors, LAS (IAS) earnings have a larger incremental information content than IAS (LAS) earnings.

To test these hypotheses, we regressed stock returns on IAS and LAS earnings using a matched-pairs sample of unrestricted and restricted shares. The results from these regressions showed that, consistent with our hypothesis, both IAS and LAS earnings have significant incremental information content to foreign investors. To domestic investors, however, our findings indicated significant incremental information content only in LAS earnings.

The results also showed that IAS earnings did have a clientele effect, as indicated by the significant difference between the response coefficients of the investor groups for IAS earnings information. Consistent with our expectation, the information content of IAS earnings turned out to be greater to foreign investors than to domestic investors. However, we could not find a corresponding clientele effect in LAS earnings measure for the domestic audience.

In addition, the results indicated the existence of a significant relevance effect of IAS earnings for foreign investors. This finding is consistent with the view that foreign investors are more interested in the performance-related information based on the tax- and institutions-independent IAS earnings than in the idiosyncratic LAS earnings on which dividend distributions are based. Contrary to our expectation, however, we could not find a significant difference in domestic investors' responses to the two earnings measures. Thus, the results are not indicative of a relevance effect of LAS earnings measure for the domestic audience.

Overall, our findings are consistent with the view that foreign and domestic investors use earnings information based on the Local and International Accounting Standards differently in the valuation of shares. The results do *not* support the view that tax and dividend-driven earnings have no information content, nor do they fall in line with the 'single-domicile' notion of financial reporting, according to which the restatement lowers the information content of earnings. Rather, when the restatements are made towards internationally recognized accounting standards that provide performance-related earnings information they may increase the information content of earnings especially to foreign audiences.

ACKNOWLEDGEMENTS

The authors are grateful to an anonymous referee for helpful comments. Financial support for this project has been provided by the Foundation for Economic Education (Finland) and by Jenny and Antti Wihurin Rahasto, which is gratefully acknowledged.

NOTES

1 For the list of stock exchanges allowing foreign companies to follow IAS, see the IASC web page at http://www.iasc.org.uk/frame/cen1_10.htm

2 There are currently no restrictions on foreign ownership due to the legislative reform, which became effective in 1993. This reform was necessary because Finland applied for membership of the European Union.

3 For example, the full-text on-line database of a major Finnish business newspaper (*Kauppalehti*) covering the period 1988–92 includes only fifty references to IAS-based earnings, whereas the total number of references to LAS-based earnings amounts to 1,086.

4 It was not until the reform of the Accounting Act in 1992 that the concept of 'true and fair view' was included in the Finnish accounting legislation.

5 For discussions on pooling time-series and cross-sectional data using dummy variables, see Judge *et al.* (1987) and Greene (1993). In our data the null hypotheses that the effect of all dummies is zero can be rejected at the levels of 2.4% (restricted shares) and 0.0% (unrestricted shares).

6 For empirical evidence that the annual earnings of (listed) Finnish firms follow a random walk-type process, see Kinnunen (1991).

7 Like cash flows, IAS earnings are derivative numbers that firms compute by reconciling LAS earnings to the differences between LAS and IAS accounting rules. There are, for instance, no analyst forecasts for the voluntarily disclosed IAS earnings, and we cannot expect that the market can anticipate (e.g., at the end of the reporting year) the magnitude of the differences between LAS and IAS earnings before the dual financial statements are disclosed.

8 Because the exact announcement dates were not available from these files for twenty-two observations (16% of the initial sample), we use the deadlines of the calls for the shareholders' annual meetings in these cases. The actual announcements generally take place before these deadlines, and the deadline dates are therefore biased. To estimate the magnitude of this bias, a sample of exact announcement dates was analysed. The results indicated that the median time lag between the actual announcements and the deadlines for shareholder meetings is 6.5 days. To see whether this bias might affect our results, we re-estimated our regressions from alternative fifty-week periods ending from -4 to $+4$ weeks relative to the financial statement releases and the calls for shareholder meetings. The overall findings turned out to be insensitive to these return measurement periods.

9 The distribution of our 86 matched-pairs observations across the years is as follows: 5 (1984), 8 (1985), 9 (1986), 12 (1987), 14 (1988), 14 (1989), 11 (1990), 13 (1991). While the sample size is relatively small, it is qualitatively unique. This is because we have observations of dual (LAS and IAS) earnings disclosures by firms for which, at

the same time, we can separately observe domestic and foreign investors' market responses.

10 The differences between the coefficients *within* the regressions can be tested using the variance–covariance matrix of the parameter estimates in the computation of the standard errors for the differences (see, e.g., Gujarati, 1988; 227–8). The differences in the coefficients *between* the regressions, in turn, can be tested by estimating an equation obtained by subtracting Equation (1) from Equation (2). The resulting equation has a 'premium' return (return on unrestricted shares minus return on restricted shares) as the dependent variable. By definition, the coefficients of the independent earnings variables are equal to the differences of coefficients in the original equations (1) and (2). Thus, the differences in the original coefficients in (1) and (2) can be directly tested by estimating coefficients (and related *t*-values) of the new equation.

REFERENCES

Alford, A., Jones, J., Leftwich, R. and Zmijewski, M. (1993) 'The relative informativeness of accounting disclosures in different countries', *Journal of Accounting Research*, 31 (Supplement): 183–223.

Amir, E., Harris, T. S. and Venuti, E. K. (1993) 'A comparison of the value-relevance of US versus non-US GAAP accounting measures using Form 20-F reconciliations', *Journal of Accounting Research*, 31 (Supplement): 230–75.

Auer, K. (1996) 'Capital market reactions to accounting earnings announcements – empirical evidence on the difference in the information content of IAS-based earnings and EC-directives-based earnings', *European Accounting Review*, 5(4): 587–623.

Barth, M. E. and Clinch, G. (1996) 'International accounting differences and their relation to share prices: evidence from UK, Australian, and Canadian firms', *Contemporary Accounting Research*, 13(1) Spring: 135–70.

Beaver, W. H. and Dukes, R. E. (1972) 'Interperiod tax allocation, earnings expectations and the behavior of stock returns', *Accounting Review*, April: 320–32.

Board, J. L. G. and Day, J. F. S. (1989) 'The information content of cash flow figures', *Accounting and Business Research*, 19(77), 3–11.

Bowen, R. M., Burgstahler, D. and Daley, L. A. (1987) 'The incremental information content of accrual versus cash flow', *Accounting Review*, 62 (October): 723–47.

Brown, S. J. and Warner, J. B. (1980) 'Measuring security price performance', *Journal of Financial Economics*, 8 (September): 205–58.

Choi, D. S. (1980) 'Primary–secondary reporting: a cross-cultural analysis', *International Journal of Accounting*, 16 (Fall): 84–104.

Greene, W. H. (1993) *Econometric Analysis*. New York: Macmillan.

Gujarati, D. N. (1988) *Basic Econometrics*. Singapore: McGraw-Hill.

Harris, M. S. and Muller III, K. A. (1999) 'The market valuation of IAS versus US GAAP accounting measures using Form 20-F reconciliations', *Journal of Accounting and Economics*, 26(1–3): 285–312.

Harris, T. S., Lang, M. and Möller, H. P. (1994) 'The value relevance of German accounting measures: an empirical analysis', *Journal of Accounting Research*, 32 (Autumn): 187–209.

Hietala, P. (1989) 'Asset pricing in partially segmented markets: evidence from the Finnish market', *Journal of Finance*, 44 (July): 697–718.

Hietala, P. and Keloharju, M. (1995) 'The ex-dividend day behavior of Finnish restricted and unrestricted shares', *Applied Economics Letters*, 2: 467–8.

International Accounting Standards Committee (IASC) (1988) *Survey of the Use and Application of International Accounting Standards*. London: IASC.

International Accounting Standards Committee (IASC) (1991) *International Accounting Standards 1991/1992*. London: IASC.

Judge, G. G., Hill, R. C., Griffiths, W. E., Lutkepohl, H. and Lee, T.-C. (1987) *Introduction to the Theory and Practice of Econometrics*, 2nd edn. New York: John Wiley.

Kasanen, E., Kinnunen, J. and Niskanen, J. (1996) 'Dividend-based earnings management: empirical evidence from Finland', *Journal of Accounting and Economics*, 22(1–3): 283–312.

Kinnunen, J. (1991) 'The importance of accrual accounting as a determinant of submartingale behaviour in annual income numbers: empirical evidence from Finland', *Journal of Business Finance and Accounting*, 18 (November): 861–83.

Kinnunen, J. and Niskanen, J. (1993) 'The information content of cash flows and the random walk: evidence from the Helsinki Stock Exchange', *Accounting and Business Research*, 23: 263–72.

Lev, B. (1989) 'On the usefulness of earnings research: lessons and directions from two decades of empirical research', *Journal of Accounting Research*, 27 (Supplement): 153–92.

Mueller, G. G. (1967) *International Accounting*. New York: Macmillan.

Näsi, S. (1992) 'Finland', in *The European Accounting Guide*. London: Harcourt Brace Jovanovich, pp. 733–49.

Niskanen, J., Kinnunen, J. and Kasanen, E. (1994) 'The association of stock returns with International Accounting Standards earnings: evidence from the Finnish capital market', *International Journal of Accounting*, 29(4): 283–96.

Niskanen, J., Kinnunen, J. and Kasanen, E. (2000) 'The value relevance of IAS reconciliation components: empirical evidence from Finland', *Journal of Accounting and Public Policy*, 19(2): 119–37.

Pope, P. F. and Rees, W. P. (1992) 'International differences in GAAP and the pricing of earnings', *Journal of International Financial Management and Accounting*, 4(3): 190–219.

Pownall, G. and Schipper, K. (1999) 'Implications of accounting research for the SEC's consideration of International Accounting Standards for US securities offerings', *Accounting Horizons*, 13(3): 259–80.

Rayburn, J. (1986) 'The association of operating cash flow and accruals with security returns', *Journal of Accounting Research*, 24 (Supplement): 112–33.

Snedecor, G. W. and Cochran, W. G. (1980) *Statistical Methods*, 7th edn. Ames, IA: Iowa State University Press.

Troberg, P. (1992) 'Recent developments in financial reporting in Finland', *Advances in International Accounting*, 5: 25–45.

[20]

The Information Content of U.S. Versus Japanese GAAP Annual and Quarterly Earnings Announcements and their Relative Informativeness to Japanese Investors: A Small Sample Case Study

Edwin R. Etter

This study examines U.S. GAAP Japanese annual and quarterly earnings announcements to determine whether they convey information to Japanese investors. Also, a comparison is conducted to investigate the relative informativeness to Japanese investors of Japanese GAAP unconsolidated and U.S. GAAP consolidated earnings announcements, and U.S. GAAP consolidated annual and quarterly earnings announcements. Using an event methodology with unexpected returns, the results indicate that U.S. GAAP consolidated annual and quarterly earnings announcements have information content. Furthermore, Japanese GAAP unconsolidated earnings announcements are not more informative to Japanese investors than U.S. GAAP consolidated earnings announcements, nor are U.S. GAAP consolidated annual earnings announcements more informative to Japanese investors than U.S. GAAP consolidated quarterly earnings announcements.

Key Words: *Japan; earnings announcements; U.S. GAAP*

INTRODUCTION

Japanese companies, subject to the Japanese Securities and Exchange Law, are required to prepare unconsolidated (parent-only) semiannual, unconsolidated annual, and consolidated annual financial statements (Sakurai 1988; Tondkar,

Edwin R. Etter • University of South Florida, 5700 N. Tamiami Trail, PMC 101, Sarasota, FL 34243-2197.

Journal of International Accounting, Auditing & Taxation, 7(2):233-249   ISSN: 1061-9518

Adhikari and Coffman 1989). Typically, these financial statements are based on Japanese GAAP; however, most Japanese companies listed on a primary exchange in the U.S. also prepare their consolidated annual financial statements in accordance with U.S. GAAP to satisfy reporting requirements of the U.S. Securities and Exchange Commission (SEC). Prior to April 1, 1995, these U.S. GAAP consolidated annual financial statements were accepted by the Japanese Ministry of Finance as meeting Japanese consolidated reporting requirements (Cooke 1993). In addition, although not required by the U.S. SEC, many of these same Japanese companies announced U.S. GAAP consolidated quarterly earnings. Therefore, unlike other non-U.S. companies listed in the U.S., many Japanese companies have historically announced annual and semiannual unconsolidated earnings based on their domestic (Japanese) GAAP, and annual and quarterly consolidated earnings based on U.S. GAAP.

Recently, many studies have investigated the value-relevance of U.S. GAAP annual earnings information released by non-U.S. companies (Amir, Harris and Venuti 1993; Barth and Clinch 1996; Pope and Rees 1992). These studies have detected an association between the companies' U.S. GAAP earnings information and security returns, suggesting that U.S. GAAP earnings information is utilized by U.S. investors. However, although a non-U.S. company's U.S. GAAP earnings information is likely to be useful to U.S. investors, investors in the home market may have difficulties with income measures based on GAAP with which they are unfamiliar. Furthermore, most major foreign markets do not require quarterly reporting of earnings (Choi and Levich 1990, 112-113). Consequently, Choi, Harris, Leisenring and Wyatt (1992) question whether investors in the home market find non-U.S. companies' U.S. GAAP accounting information and reporting requirements useful. They call for research that examines issues regarding the cross-national transferability of U.S. accounting principles and reporting practices.

Based on the above discussion, and due to the unique manner in which U.S.-listed Japanese companies announce earnings based on U.S. GAAP, this study investigates whether Japanese investors find information content in U.S. GAAP Japanese consolidated annual and quarterly earnings announcements. Also, a comparison is conducted to determine the relative informativeness to Japanese investors of (1) Japanese GAAP unconsolidated and U.S. GAAP consolidated earnings announcements; and (2) U.S. GAAP consolidated annual and quarterly earnings announcements. Based on the nature and timing of these announcements, and since the announcement of quarterly earnings is not a common practice among Japanese companies, except for those listed in the U.S. (Choi and Hiramatsu 1987, 119), it is possible that there could be significant differences in the informativeness of these announcements to Japanese investors.[1]

The next section of this paper explores the motivation for the study and examines related research. The third section describes the research design. The fourth section discusses the sample selection criteria and data sources. Results are reported in the fifth section, and the last section provides the conclusion.

MOTIVATION FOR THE STUDY AND PRIOR RESEARCH

Consolidated Earnings

Sakurai (1988) examines the unexpected price reaction of Japanese investors to Japanese GAAP unconsolidated and consolidated, annual earnings announcements. The unconsolidated earnings in his study were, on average, announced one and one-half months prior to the consolidated earnings. Sakurai finds an increase in the unexpected price reaction of Japanese investors at the times of both the unconsolidated and consolidated, annual earnings announcements. He concludes that Japanese investors find information content in both types of announcements. Sakurai, however, does not test for any difference in the informativeness of the two types of earnings announcements.

Although Sakurai finds Japanese GAAP earnings announcements informative to Japanese investors, the same may not be true of U.S. GAAP consolidated earnings announcements. Significant differences between Japanese and U.S. consolidated GAAP exist, such as restatement of foreign subsidiaries' accounting information, valuation of marketable securities, accounting for reserves, and computation of earnings per share.[2] Cooke (1993), using published data and data secured from five Japanese corporations, compares each of the companies' consolidated earnings computed under Japanese and U.S. GAAP. Cooke finds that the consolidated earnings computed under Japanese GAAP were different (generally lower) than the consolidated earnings computed under U.S. GAAP. As a result of differences in GAAP, McKinnon (1984) argues that the information content in U.S. GAAP consolidated earnings to Japanese investors may be limited.

However, even if Japanese investors find the U.S. GAAP consolidated earnings of U.S.-listed companies informative, they may find the announcements significantly less informative than the companies' Japanese GAAP unconsolidated earnings announcements for the following reasons. First, a portion of the U.S. GAAP consolidated earnings may be anticipated or repetitious. Historically, unconsolidated earnings announcements have preceded consolidated earnings announcements in Japan. Sakurai (1988) notes that, in general, a Japanese company releases its unconsolidated annual earnings approximately 50 or more days after its fiscal year end, and its consolidated annual earnings 100 or more days after its fiscal year end. Furthermore, holding companies are banned in Japan, usually causing the parent company to dominate the reported financial information of the consolidated group.

Second, unconsolidated financial statements, with investments in affiliated companies carried at cost, have traditionally been considered the primary financial statements in Japan (Lowe 1990; McKinnon and Harrison 1985). This tradition is the result of Japanese businesses historically obtaining most of their financing in the form of debt as opposed to equity. Consequently, many Japanese perceive consolidated financial statements as secondary or supplemental statements, and consider them less relevant or reliable when compared to unconsolidated financial statements (Cooke and Kikuya 1992, 133; Lowe 1990). This perception is evidenced in practice by sending unconsolidated financial statements directly to shareholders, and by only making consolidated financial statements available to shareholders indirectly, through the Ministry of Finance and the stock exchanges (Cooke 1991; Hudack and Orsini 1992). Shigekazu Kurishima, general manager of Nikko International, suggests that because they deem them as less reliable, Japanese investors put less emphasis on consolidated results (Berton 1990).

Quarterly Earnings

The informativeness of quarterly earnings is often suspect due to the use of frequent estimates (e.g., inventory valuation, interim revenues and expenses, income tax allocation), seasonality of income, and the lack of external auditor verification of quarterly results (McEwen and Schwartz 1992).[3]

Specific Japanese environmental and institutional conditions may further minimize the informativeness of publicly reported quarterly earnings to Japanese investors. Japanese companies have long been characterized as being more interested in long-term market share and growth than in short-term profits (Choi and Hiramatsu 1987, 19; Hudack and Orsini 1992; Lowe 1990). Also, influential corporate insiders, such as employees, major shareholders, directors, unions, affiliated companies, creditors, institutional investors and Japanese brokers, have inside access to Japanese corporate accounting information (Choi and Hiramatsu 1987, 29; Cooke and Kikuya 1992, 40). Conversely, small investors are considered unimportant outsiders and have little influence with the company (Cooke and Kikuya 1992, 36; Jacobs 1991, 66). As a result, management does not feel obligated to provide essential financial information to small investors unless required to do so (Hudack and Orsini 1992). These practices could reduce the informativeness of quarterly earnings for two reasons. First, Hudack and Orsini (1992) suggest that management policies of long-term growth and selective sharing of financial information may not be compatible with short-term reporting of income. Second, management may not feel as obligated to present substantive consolidated quarterly accounting information to small outside investors since this information is not required of Japanese companies by either Japanese or U.S. authorities.[4]

Japanese investment strategy may also limit the informativeness of quarterly accounting information to Japanese investors. The view of the Japanese Business Accounting Deliberation Council, which sets accounting and reporting standards in Japan, is that the purpose of interim financial statements is to provide results for the period covered and information which will allow investors to predict the profitability of the company for the fiscal year (Choi and Hiramatsu 1987, 48). Thus, Japanese regulators do not perceive interim accounting information as an important source for long-run financial information for Japanese investors. In addition, Jacobs (1991, 37) argues that interim statements are relied upon primarily by short-term investors who spend little time understanding the long-term plans of corporations and who do not have inside access to corporate information. Most Japanese investors, however, are interested in long-term investments, and do not invest for short-term profits or dividends (Cooke and Kikuya 1992, 40). Therefore, due to their long-term investment strategy and inside access to corporate accounting information, many Japanese investors may have little to no reaction to quarterly earnings announcements.

Studies of U.S. quarterly earnings announcements by Ball and Kothari (1991), Morse (1981), Kiger (1972) and May (1971) have all found that U.S. investors are able to overcome the limitations inherent in quarterly earnings announcements and find information content in them. In addition, Kross and Schroeder (1990), Foster (1977), Brown and Kennelly (1972) and May (1971) did not detect any seasonality in return responses to earnings announcements for large U.S. companies. However, no study has yet determined if Japanese investors are able to find information content in quarterly earnings announcements or the relative informativeness of the announcements. Although the quarterly earnings of U.S.-listed Japanese companies are often based on U.S. GAAP, given the differences between U.S. and Japanese investment strategy, and environmental and institutional conditions, the findings of the U.S. studies are not automatically transferable to Japan.

Research Hypotheses

Consistent with the above arguments, the following three research hypotheses are tested: (1) there is no stock price response by Japanese investors to U.S. GAAP Japanese annual or quarterly earnings announcements; (2) there is a greater price response by Japanese investors to Japanese GAAP unconsolidated earnings announcements than to U.S. GAAP consolidated earnings announcements; and (3) there is a greater price response by Japanese investors to U.S. consolidated annual earnings announcements than to U.S. GAAP consolidated quarterly earnings announcements.

238   INTERNATIONAL ACCOUNTING, AUDITING & TAXATION, 7(2)   1998

RESEARCH DESIGN

An event study methodology, using test variables similar to that used by Beaver (1968), Patell (1976), and Frost and Pownall (1994a) was employed to determine whether there is information content in the respective Japanese earnings announcements. The unexpected price return in the announcement period is compared to those in the nonannouncement period to see if there has been a significant change.

The unexpected price return is calculated based on the following equation:

$$R_{it} = a_i + b_i R_{mt} + u_{it} \tag{1}$$

The variables in the above equation are defined as follows:

$$R_{it} = \ln\left(\frac{P_{it}}{P_{i,\,t-1}}\right) \tag{2}$$

$$R_{mt} = \ln\left(\frac{M_t}{M_{t-1}}\right) \tag{3}$$

where

R_{it} = the daily return of firm i on day t;
R_{mt} = the daily return of the market index on day t;
P_{it} = closing price per share of firm i on day t, adjusted for stock splits and stock dividends; and
M_t = closing value of the market index on day t.

R_{it} represents the natural log of the price relative, which can be thought of as a measure of the price change, or as a continuously compounded rate of return. The Durbin-Watson test is performed to test for first-order autocorrelation in the residuals. No first-order autocorrelation is detected in the residuals from Equation 1.

Equation 1 is used to estimate the coefficients for the nonannouncement period. The nonannouncement period consists of the 200 trading days prior to the announcement period. The estimated coefficients are then used to compute the unexpected price return ($\hat{u}_{i\tau}$) for the announcement period as follows:

$$\hat{u}_{i\tau} = R_{i\tau} - (\hat{a}_i + \hat{b}_i R_{m\tau}) \tag{4}$$

A three day announcement period is used, with $\tau = -1, 0, 1$, where $\tau = 0$ is the date when the earnings announcement was published.

Next the announcement period unexpected price returns are standardized, squared and averaged as follows:

$$[\bar{u}_i]^2 = \left(\frac{1}{3}\right) \sum_{\tau = -1}^{1} \left(\frac{\hat{u}_{i\tau}}{\hat{s}_i}\right)^2 \tag{5}$$

where $\hat{s}_i$ is the standard deviation of the residuals from Equation 1.

Two frequently used methods in analyzing earnings announcements are those employed by Beaver (1968) and May (1971). In his analysis of earnings announcements, Beaver (1968) uses the ratio of the squared announcement period residual over the average of the squared nonannouncement period residuals (Beaver's U) as his test statistic. While May (1971) uses the ratio of the absolute value of the announcement period residual over the average of the absolute values of the nonannouncement period residuals (May's U) as his test statistic. Rohrbach and Chandra (1989) provide evidence that cross-sectional correlation between the residuals could affect the reliability of the normal approximation to both Beaver's U and May's U. They also show that normal approximations using either Beaver's U or May's U are biased against the null for leptokurtic (heavy tailed) residuals. Rohrbach and Chandra's test corrects for cross-sectional correlation, and is unbiased against the null for leptokurtic residuals. Also, since daily residuals are being used in this study, there is little, if any, loss in power because Rohrbach and Chandra find that 99 observations from the nonannouncement period are adequate to provide power comparable to the theoretical distribution of Beaver's U and May's U.

The nonparametric test of Rohrbach and Chandra (1989) is employed to determine whether there is an increase in the residual, $[\bar{u}_i]^2$, at the time of the earnings announcements, and is implemented as follows. First, the standardized, squared, unexpected price residuals $([\hat{u}_{it}/\hat{s}_i]^2)$ from the nonannouncement period ($i = 1,...,N$ firm-years and $t = 1,...,T$, days, where $T = 200$) and the residuals $([\bar{u}_i]^2)$ from the announcement period are grouped together constructing a $(T + 1)$ X N matrix. Next, r_{it} is defined to be the within-firm rank of the current elements in each column (where $1 \leq r_{it} \leq T + 1$), and the current column elements are replaced with their within-firm rank. Since there are 200 nonannouncement period residuals and one announcement period residual in each column, the maximum within-firm rank is 201. Third, the ranks are summed across firm-years (i.e., summed across the rows) to obtain C_t. $C_{T + 1}$ is the test statistic, and $\{C_t | t = 1,...,T\}$ is the empirical null distribution. Finally, the empirical significance level of the test is determined. For a right-tailed test, this is k/T, where k is the number of observations in the empirical null distribution (number of C_ts) that exceed the test observation ($C_{T + 1}$). The null, $C_{T+1} \leq \{C_t | t = 1,...,T\}$, is rejected if $k/T \leq \alpha$ for a test with size α.

The second analysis investigates whether Japanese investors find Japanese GAAP unconsolidated earnings more informative than U.S. GAAP consolidated earnings, and whether they find U.S. GAAP consolidated annual earnings more informative than U.S. GAAP consolidated quarterly earnings. The methodology utilized is similar to that used by May (1971), in which he compares the relative informativeness of U.S. annual and quarterly earnings announcements to U.S. investors. The first step in this analysis is to group the announcement periods' residuals into pairs based on company, year, and type of earnings announcement (e.g., unconsolidated annual versus consolidated annual) or period being tested (e.g., consolidated annual versus consolidated first quarter). If either of the announcement period residuals is not available for a firm-year, that firm-year is not included in the analysis. Next the difference between the paired residuals is taken. For the analysis of the unconsolidated and consolidated residuals, each consolidated residual is subtracted from its corresponding unconsolidated residual. For the analysis of the annual and quarterly residuals, each quarterly residual is subtracted from its corresponding annual residual. Finally, the nonparametric Wilcoxon Signed Rank test is used to determine if the difference between the paired residuals is greater than zero (i.e., whether the unconsolidated residuals are greater then the consolidated residuals, and whether the annual residuals are greater than the quarterly residuals). The test statistic T^* is approximately standard normal, and equals the sum of the positively signed ranks less the expected value of this sum, all divided by the standard deviation of the sum.

SAMPLE AND DATA SOURCES

The sample in this study comprises the annual and quarterly, unconsolidated and consolidated earnings announcements of Japanese companies which met the four following conditions:

1. the Japanese companies are required to have been listed on one of the three primary U.S. exchanges (NYSE, ASE or NASDAQ) anytime during the period 1981–1990;
2. their consolidated earnings are based on U.S. GAAP;
3. the consolidated earnings announcements are released at least seven days subsequent to the release of the unconsolidated earnings announcements; and
4. earnings announcements are deleted if any other major announcement was made during the announcement period (e.g., an acquisition, change in corporate officer, sale of a segment, a lawsuit initiated against the company, etc.).

The first criterion is necessary for three reasons. First, Japanese companies listed in the U.S. are chosen since they typically announce consolidated earnings based on U.S. GAAP and release quarterly earnings announcements. Second, Japanese companies listed on a primary U.S. exchange, as opposed to a secondary U.S. exchange, are more likely to have their earnings announcements published. Therefore, any Japanese companies listed on the Over-the-Counter (OTC) market are not included. Finally, during the period chosen, unconsolidated earnings are typically announced prior to consolidated earnings. The timing of the announcements allows the study to consider the effect each type of earnings announcement had on Japanese investors. In the final sample, the Japanese GAAP unconsolidated annual earnings announcements preceded the U.S. GAAP consolidated annual earnings announcements by an average of 34 days. The Japanese GAAP unconsolidated semiannual earnings announcements preceded the U.S. GAAP consolidated semiannual earnings announcements by an average of 27 days.

The initial sample of companies was identified through the following sources: (1) the daily CRSP tapes; (2) Compustat; (3) reference to the annual editions of the NYSE Fact Book, AMEX Fact Book, and the NASDAQ Fact Book; and (4) correspondence with the individual exchanges. The daily price data for the Japanese shares was obtained from the Center for Japanese Economy and Business at Columbia University.[5] The Japanese market index used was the Nikkei Dow, and was secured from Reuters Information Services, Incorporated.

The earnings announcement dates were collected from the *Wall Street Journal Index*, Compustat, the *Financial Times Index (London)*, and the *Predicasts F&S Index, International Annual*. The *Predicasts F&S Index, International Annual* includes references for the *Financial Times (Frankfurt)* and the *Wall Street Journal Europe*. Frost and Pownall (1994b) note that U.S.-listed Japanese companies make frequent earnings disclosures in the U.S. In addition, they argue that non-U.S. companies take timely disclosure in the U.S. seriously due to pressure from U.S. investors and analysts. Given the high demand for public disclosure in the U.S. relative to that in Japan, it is unlikely that U.S.-listed Japanese companies would announce earnings in the U.S. in a less timely manner than they do in Japan. Also, Meek (1983) notes that frequently U.S. earnings announcements are published in the U.S. one day after they are announced to the public, since the announcements are typically made after the financial publications have been printed for the day. Given that there is a significant time difference between Tokyo and New York or Europe, any earnings announcement made in Tokyo is likely to be published in New York and Europe the same day the announcement was made. Therefore, although all of the earnings announcement dates were taken from non-Japanese sources, it is assumed that these dates are not significantly different from the dates the announcements were made in Japan. Earnings announcements that were published in more than one of the above sources were found to be

TABLE 1
Unexpected Price Reaction to U.S. GAAP Japanese
Earnings Announcements, Rohrbach and Chandra Test

	1st Quarter	Semiannual	3rd Quarter	Annual
Number of companies	7	15	7	17
Number of observations	56	114	52	135
Mean rank of announcement period squared residuals[a]	140.75[**]	134.46[**]	138.08[**]	126.54[**]
Standard deviation of rank of announcement period squared residuals	38.62	43.94	39.79	43.42
Mean of announcement period squared residuals	1.3346	1.3205	1.2489	1.0786
Standard deviation of announcement period squared residuals	0.4476	0.3925	0.5304	0.2895

Note: [a]Maximum possible value is 201
    [**]Significant at the $\alpha = 0.01$ level using a one-tailed test

consistent with regards to the announcement date. The above indexes were also examined for confounding events during the announcement period.

There are 18 Japanese companies included in the final sample (see appendix for companies included and excluded from final sample). The majority of Japanese companies listed in the U.S. during the sample period that also announced consolidated earnings based on U.S. GAAP are included in the sample. It is believed the sample is appropriate for examining the informativeness of U.S. GAAP consolidated earnings announcements. However, given the small number of companies in the sample the results should be interpreted carefully.

The sample is split between NYSE and NASDAQ companies, with two companies (Hitachi and TDK) switching from NASDAQ to the NYSE during 1982. The sample companies are all manufacturing companies except for CSK (service), Ito-Yokado (retail), Marubeni (trading) and Mitsui (trading). All sample companies are listed in the U.S. during the entire sample period (1981–1990), except for Marubeni which was listed in the U.S. from 1982–1984. Finally, the sample consists of relatively large companies with average net sales, average total assets and average market value during 1990 of $24.9 billion, $19.4 billion and $10.9 billion, respectively.[6]

EMPIRICAL RESULTS

Table 1 presents the results of the analysis of the unexpected price returns. The results of this analysis indicate that Japanese investors find information con-

TABLE 2
Comparison of the Announcement Period Squared Residuals Between
Types of Announcement or Periods, Wilcoxon Signed Rank Test

	Number of companies	Number of observations	Value of T*	p-value
Japanese GAAP annual residuals > U.S. GAAP annual residuals	12	68	0.0428	0.4801 $< \overline{\alpha} <$ 0.4840
Japanese GAAP semiannual residuals > U.S. GAAP semiannual residuals	9	54	0.6242	0.7324 $< \overline{\alpha} <$ 0.7357
U.S. GAAP annual residuals > U.S. GAAP 1st quarter residuals	7	50	0.7288	0.7642 $< \overline{\alpha} <$ 0.7673
U.S. GAAP annual residuals > U.S. GAAP semiannual residuals	14	89	1.0576	0.8531 $< \overline{\alpha} <$ 0.8554
U.S. GAAP annual residuals > U.S. GAAP 3rd quarter residuals	7	51	0.9373	0.8238 $< \overline{\alpha} <$ 0.8264

tent in both U.S. GAAP consolidated annual and quarterly earnings announcements. For all periods (i.e., 1st quarter, semiannual, 3rd quarter and annual) the sum of the ranks of the announcement period residuals is the greatest (i.e., $C_{T+1} > \{C_t | t = 1, \ldots, T\}$), resulting in the announcement period residuals for all periods being significant at the $\alpha = 0.01$ level.[7]

As noted previously, Sakurai (1988) finds information content in Japanese GAAP consolidated annual earnings announcements. The above results extend Sakurai's results by finding that Japanese investors find information content in U.S. GAAP consolidated annual earnings announcements, even though U.S. consolidation policies are significantly different, in many respects, from those of Japan. Furthermore, the results indicate that Japanese investors also find information content in U.S. GAAP consolidated quarterly earnings announcements. Therefore, it appears that Japanese investors are able to find information content in consolidated quarterly earnings announcements in spite of the intrinsic limitations associated with quarterly earnings, and the previously mentioned environmental and institutional conditions in Japan.[8]

Since all of the Japanese companies included in this study are listed in the U.S., another possible explanation for the above results is that Japanese investors are simply reacting to the response of investors in the U.S. market who find the U.S. GAAP consolidated earnings informative. However, Park (1990) using a Vector Autoregression (VAR) analysis, demonstrates that Japanese American Depository Receipts (ADRs) are more sensitive to a shock, such as an earnings announcement, in the underlying stocks on the Japanese market than to a shock in the U.S. market. Therefore, even if U.S. investors react to U.S. GAAP consolidated earnings announcements it is likely that the majority of the Japanese price reaction is a result of Japanese investors finding the announcements informative.

The results of the comparisons of the unexpected price reactions between announcement types (unconsolidated and consolidated) and between periods (annual and quarterly) are presented in Table 2. To judge the relative informativeness of the Japanese GAAP unconsolidated earnings announcements versus the U.S. GAAP consolidated earnings announcements, the unexpected price reactions to the Japanese GAAP unconsolidated annual and semiannual earnings announcements are compared to the unexpected price reactions to the U.S. GAAP consolidated annual and semiannual earnings announcements, respectively. In neither case are the unexpected price reactions to the Japanese GAAP unconsolidated earnings announcements statistically greater than the unexpected price reactions to the U.S. GAAP consolidated earnings announcements.

To assess the relative informativeness of the consolidated annual earnings announcements versus the consolidated quarterly earnings announcements, the unexpected price reactions to the U.S. GAAP consolidated annual earnings announcements are compared to the unexpected price reactions to the U.S. GAAP consolidated first quarter, semiannual and third quarter earnings announcements. The results indicate that the unexpected price reaction to the U.S. GAAP consolidated annual earnings announcements is not statistically greater than the unexpected price reaction to the U.S. GAAP consolidated semiannual or quarterly earnings announcements in any of the three comparisons.[9]

It can be inferred from the above analysis that Japanese investors find U.S. GAAP consolidated earnings at least as informative as Japanese GAAP unconsolidated earnings. Also, they find U.S. GAAP consolidated quarterly earnings at least as informative as U.S. GAAP consolidated annual earnings .

LIMITATIONS AND CONCLUSION

This study indicates that Japanese investors find information content in U.S. GAAP consolidated annual and quarterly earnings announcements. Also, Japanese investors do not find Japanese GAAP unconsolidated and U.S. GAAP consolidated annual earnings more informative than U.S. GAAP consolidated and quarterly earnings, respectively. However, the results of this study should be interpreted carefully due to the relatively small number of companies that were available to comprise the sample.

This study also does not address the issue of whether U.S. GAAP consolidated earnings, as calculated and reported by Japanese companies, are optimal for Japanese investors. Lowe (1990), McKinnon and Harrison (1985) and McKinnon (1984) argue that changes in Japanese environmental and institutional conditions, and consolidation policies would significantly increase the quality and level of information contained in both Japanese and U.S. GAAP consolidated earnings announcements. For example, many large Japanese companies are members of industrial groups called *keiretsu*. A characteristic of these industrial groups is mutual share ownership of greater than 50 percent of each company. Although through mutual ownership a *keiretsu* owns a majority of the outstanding stock of its member companies, many companies in the industrial group are not included in the consolidated group since no individual company owns a majority interest.

In addition, during the time period studied, the majority of Japanese companies listed in the U.S. only released consolidated earnings based on U.S. GAAP. Therefore, it was not possible to compare the relative informativeness to Japanese investors of Japanese and U.S. GAAP consolidated earnings. However, beginning April 1, 1995, most Japanese companies listed in the U.S. are now required to prepare two sets of consolidated annual statements. One set is based on U.S. GAAP to satisfy U.S. SEC reporting requirements. The other set is based on Japanese GAAP to meet the reporting requirements of the Japanese Ministry of Finance (Cooke 1993). Thus, an examination of the value-relevance to both Japanese and U.S. investors of Japanese GAAP and U.S. GAAP consolidated annual earnings appears to be a feasible and interesting avenue for future research.

It has been suggested that given the diversity of financial statement format and calculation of account balances using Japanese GAAP, Japanese corporations should prepare, for international investors, financial statements that adhere to the standards of the International Accounting Standards Committee (IASC) (Choi and Hiramatsu 1987, 128). These financial statements would also be available to Japanese investors who often face the same comparability problems with regard to Japanese GAAP financial statements. Choi, Harris, Leisenring and Wyatt (1992) note, however, that many critics of IASC standards believe the conceptual framework of the IASC is biased in favor of the Anglo-American approach of tailoring accounting information to the needs of shareholders and creditors, and is therefore ill-suited to countries whose accounting standards are strongly influenced by tax law and government regulations, such as Japan. Results of this study, however, provide evidence that not only is Anglo-American earnings information, namely U.S. GAAP consolidated annual and quarterly earnings announcements, informative to Japanese investors, but it is as informative to Japanese investors as the Japanese GAAP unconsolidated earnings information they receive. Mueller, Gernon and Meek (1997, 64) and Harris (1995) argue that there are few significant differences between U.S. GAAP and IASC standards. Therefore, it appears that some accounting standards and reporting practices with an Anglo-American bias promulgated by the IASC may be useful to investors in non-Anglo-American countries. However, further research is required to determine the characteristics of such standards and reporting practices, and which countries' investors would find them useful.

Acknowledgments: I wish to thank John Anderson of Syracuse University; Dan Jensen and Douglas Schroeder of The Ohio State University; Jean Bias; Molly Voorheis; and the participants of both the 1996 American Accounting Association Ohio Regional Conference and the Syracuse University Accounting Workshop for their helpful comments. Also, I would like to thank Joyce Zadzilka for her research assistance. This paper is based in part on my dissertation completed at The Ohio State University, which was financially supported by a dissertation grant from the American Institute of Certified Public Accountants.

NOTES

1.   Based on a discussion with Professor Masatoshi Gotoh of Kobe University, Japanese manage- ment are also required to issue forecasts for unconsolidated semiannual earnings, unconsoli- dated annual earnings and consolidated annual earnings, but not consolidated quarterly earnings. These forecasts are typically released at the same time as the corresponding earnings announcement. Thus, it is possible that any reaction by Japanese investors on the announce- ment date is a joint reaction to the earnings results from the previous period and the forecasted earnings for the current period. However, the significance of the "joint effect" problem in this study is uncertain. No attempt was made to exclude an earnings announcement if there was also a concurrent forecast announcement, since forecast announcements were not noted in any of the periodical indexes used to locate the earnings announcement dates. Also, the essence of the "announcement" remains unchanged with Japanese GAAP unconsolidated earnings (results and forecast) announced on one day, and U.S. GAAP consolidated earnings (results and forecast) announced on another day.

2.   See Choi and Hiramatsu (1987, 125-126) for a more detailed discussion of the differences between U.S. and Japanese consolidation policies.

3.   Unconsolidated semiannual financial statements of listed Japanese companies are required by the Tokyo Stock Exchange and the Japanese Ministry of Finance to be audited (Tondkar, Adhikari and Coffman 1989). Consequently, the problem of lack of external auditor verifica- tion does not apply to Japanese unconsolidated semiannual earnings announcements.

4.   However, U.S. GAAP consolidated quarterly earnings are voluntarily announced primarily for U.S. investors. Also, Japanese companies listed in the U.S. are competing for capital with U.S. companies that have historically provided substantive quarterly accounting information to U.S. investors. Therefore, it is possible that for the Japanese companies in this study the incli- nation of their management to withhold substantive consolidated quarterly earnings informa- tion from the public is mitigated.

5.   I would like to thank Professor Masako Darrough for her assistance in obtaining the data. A special thanks goes to Professor Won Choi for the actual task of data extraction. At the time, Professor Choi was a Ph.D. candidate at Columbia University.

6.   The range of values were: net sales, $677.1 million to $123.3 billion; total assets, $1.1 billion to $60.8 billion; and market value, $1.3 billion to $32.4 billion.

7.   Similar results (significant at the $\alpha = 0.01$ level) are found for the Japanese GAAP unconsoli- dated annual (consistent with the results of Sakurai 1988) and semiannual earnings annound- cements. These results were not included in Table 1 since this study was primarily concerned with the information content of U.S. GAAP consolidated earnings.

8.   For fiscal years ending on or after March 31, 1988, Japanese companies were required to file unconsolidated and consolidated statements with Japanese authorities on the same date.

Although based on the sample data, it appears that either the announcement of consolidated and unconsolidated earnings was not required to be made on the same date or even if they were, many Japanese companies listed in the U.S. did not follow the new regulation. The information content analysis was conducted again without consolidated annual and semiannual earnings announcements, from fiscal years ending on or after March 31, 1988, where a corresponding unconsolidated earnings announcement could not be located. The results of this examination were similar to those furnished in Table 1. The announcement residuals for both the consolidated annual and semiannual earnings announcements were significant at the $\alpha = 0.01$ level.

9. A similar result ($0.6700 < \overline{\alpha} < 0.6736$) was found when comparing the unexpected price reaction of Japanese GAAP unconsolidated annual and semiannual earnings announcements. Again, these results were not included in Table 2, since this study was primarily concerned with U.S. GAAP consolidated earnings.

APPENDIX

Japanese Firms in Sample (U.S. Exchange)

CSK Corp. (NASDAQ)
Canon Inc. (NASDAQ)
Fuji Photo Film Co., Ltd. (NASDAQ)
Hitachi Ltd. (NASDAQ/NYSE)
Honda Motor Ltd. (NYSE)
Ito-Yokado Co., Ltd. (NASDAQ)
Kubota Corp. (NYSE)
Kyocera Corp. (NYSE)
Makita Electric Works Ltd. (NASDAQ)
Marubeni Corp. (NASDAQ)
Matsushita Electric Industrial Co., Ltd. (NYSE)
Mitsui and Co., Ltd. (NASDAQ)
NEC Corp. (NASDAQ)
Pioneer Electronic Corp. (NYSE)
Sanyo Electric Co., Ltd. (NASDAQ)
Sony Corp. (NYSE)
TDK Corp. (NASDAQ/NYSE)
Wacoal Corp. (NASDAQ)

Japanese Companies Not in Sample

Do Not Announce Earnings Based on U.S. GAAP
Dai'ei Inc.
Japan Air Lines Co., Ltd.
Kirin Brewery Co., Ltd.
Nissan Motor Co., Ltd.
Shiseido Ltd.
Toyota Motor Corp.

Daily Price Data Unavailable
Mitsubishi Bank Ltd.
Tokio Marine and Fire Insurance Co., Ltd.
Trio Kenwood Corp.

248   INTERNATIONAL ACCOUNTING, AUDITING & TAXATION, 7(2)   1998

REFERENCES

Amir, E., T. Harris, and E. Venuti. 1993. A comparison of the value-relevance of U.S. versus non-U.S. GAAP accounting measures using Form 20-F reconciliations. *Supplement to Journal of Accounting Research* 31: 230-264.

Ball, R., and S.P. Kothari. 1991. Security returns around earnings announcements. *The Accounting Review* 66: 718-738.

Barth, M., and G. Clinch. 1996. International accounting differences and their relation to share prices: evidence from U.K., Australian, and Canadian firms. *Contemporary Accounting Research* 13: 35-170.

Beaver, W. 1968. The information content of annual earnings announcements. *Supplement to Journal of Accounting Research* 6: 67-92.

Berton, L. 1990, March 22. U.S. Investors devise strategies to value secretive Japan firms. *Wall Street Journal*: C1, C2.

Brown, P., and J. Kennelly. 1972. The information content of quarterly earnings: An extension and some further evidence. *Journal of Business* 45: 403-415.

Choi, F.D.S., T. Harris, J. Leisenring and A. Wyatt. 1992. *International financial reporting*. AAA/ FASB Annual Financial Reporting Research Conference.

Choi, F.D.S., and K. Hiramatsu (Eds). 1987. *Accounting and Financial Reporting in Japan*. Berkshire UK: Van Nostrand Reinhold Co., Ltd.

Choi, F.D.S., and R. Levich. 1990. *The Capital Market Effects of International Accounting Diversity*. Homewood, Illinois: Dow Jones-Irwin.

Cooke, T. 1991. An assessment of voluntary disclosure in the annual reports of Japanese corporations. *The International Journal of Accounting* 26: 174-189.

———. 1993. The impact of accounting principles on profits: the U.S. versus Japan. *Accounting and Business Research* 23: 460-476.

Cooke, T., and M. Kikuya. 1992. *Financial Reporting in Japan: Regulation, Practice and Environment*. Oxford, UK: Blackwell Publishers Ltd.

Foster, G. 1977. Quarterly accounting data: Time-series properties and predictive-ability results. *The Accounting Review* 52: 1-21.

Frost, C., and G. Pownall. 1994a. A comparison of the stock price response to earnings disclosures in the United States and the United Kingdom. *Contemporary Accounting Research* 11: 59-84.

———. 1994b. Accounting disclosure practices in the United States and the United Kingdom. *Journal of Accounting Research* 32: 75-102.

Harris, T. 1995. *International Accounting Standards Versus US-GAAP Reporting: Empirical Evidence Based on Case Studies*. Cincinnati: South-Western College Publishing.

Hudack, L., and L. Orsini. 1992. A note of caution to users of Japanese financial reports: A demonstration of an enlarged exogenist approach. *The International Journal of Accounting* 27: 15-26.

Jacobs, M. 1991. *Short-Term America: The Causes and Cures of Our Business Myopia*. Boston: Harvard Business School Press.

Kiger, J. 1972. An empirical investigation of NYSE volume and price reaction to the announcement of quarterly earnings. *Journal of Accounting Research* 10: 128-133.

Kross, W., and D. Schroeder. 1990. An investigation of seasonality in stock price responses to quarterly earnings announcements. *Journal of Business Finance & Accounting* 17: 649- 675.

Lowe, H. 1990. Shortcomings of Japanese consolidated financial statements. *Accounting Horizons* 4: 1-9.

May, R. 1971. The influence of quarterly earnings announcements on investor decisions as reflected in common stock price changes. *Supplement to Journal of Accounting Research* 9: 119-171.

McEwen, R., and B. Schwartz. 1992. Are firms complying with the minimum standards for interim financial reporting? *Accounting Horizons* 6: 75-87.

McKinnon, J. 1984. Application of Anglo-American principles of consolidation to corporate financial disclosure in Japan. *Abacus* 20: 16-33.

McKinnon, J., and G. Harrison. 1985. Cultural influence on corporate and governmental involvement in accounting policy determination in Japan. *Journal of Accounting & Public Policy* 4: 201-223.

Meek, G. 1983. U.S. securities market responses to alternate earnings disclosure of non-U.S. multinational corporations. *The Accounting Review* 58: 394-402.

Morse, D. 1981. Price and trading volume reaction surrounding earnings announcements: A closer examination. *Journal of Accounting Research* 19: 374-383.

Mueller, G., H. Gernon, and G. Meek. 1997. *Accounting: An International Perspective* (4th ed.). Chicago: Irwin.

Park, J. 1990. *The Impact of Information on ADR Returns and Variances: Some Implications*. Dissertation. University of Iowa.

Patell, J. 1976. Corporate forecasts of earnings per share and stock price behavior: Empirical tests. *Journal of Accounting Research* 14: 246-276.

Pope, P., and W. Rees. 1992. International differences in GAAP and the pricing of earnings. *Journal of International Financial Management & Accounting* 4: 190-219.

Rohrbach, K., and R. Chandra. 1989. The power of Beaver's U against a variance increase in market model residuals. *Journal of Accounting Research* 27: 145-55.

Sakurai, H. 1988. Market efficiency and the information content of annual accounting announcements. In S. Sakakibara, H. Yamaji, H. Sakurai, K. Shiroshita and S. Fukuda, (Eds.), *The Japanese Stock Market: Pricing Systems and Accounting Information*. New York: Praeger Publishers.

Tondkar, R., A. Adhikari, and E. Coffman. 1989. The internationalization of equity markets: motivations for foreign corporate listing and filing and listing requirements of five major stock exchanges. *The International Journal of Accounting* 24: 143-163.

Part IV
Case Studies of Financial Reporting Practices

The current issue and full text archive of this journal is available at
http://www.emerald-library.com

Corporate disclosure and the deregulation of international investment

Corporate
disclosure

David Bailey

Research Centre for Industrial Strategy, University of Birmingham and
Institute for Industrial Development Policy, Birmingham, UK

George Harte

Department of Accounting and Finance, University of Glasgow,
Glasgow, UK, and

Roger Sugden

Institute for Industrial Development Policy and University of
Birmingham, Birmingham, UK

197

Submitted June 1998
Revised March 1999
Accepted July 1999

Keywords Accountability, Deregulation, Disclosure, Foreign investment

Abstract Drawing on evidence of major Western governments' concerns with the wider
economic, social and environmental impact and performance of transnational firms, we argue
that recent emphasis on deregulating industrial development, such as in the proposed Multilateral
Agreement on Investment and ongoing discussions over a multilateral framework on investment,
necessitates a fuller and regulated, rather than voluntaristic, corporate accountability, covering
further details of the impact and performance of transnationals.

Introduction

This paper examines the accountability of transnational corporations in the
light of recent "deregulation" of international investment and trade flows.
Drawing on evidence of major Western governments' interest in
transnationals[1], which revealed a concern with the wider economic, social and
environmental impact and performance of such firms, we consider recent
proposals which threaten national and local government sovereignty in
industrial development. Ironically, the emphasis on markets, in contrast to the
regulation of industrial development, is argued to necessitate a fuller and
regulated corporate accountability, with further details of the impact and
performance of transnationals. The preference for market based solutions to
the problems of industrial development is seen to necessitate the regulation of
corporate reporting so as to facilitate the monitoring of transnational
corporations. In the following section we consider the nature of transnational
corporations, before outlining proposals for the monitoring of such firms.

We would like to acknowledge the helpful comments of a number of colleagues, including
participants at seminars at the University of Birmingham and Glasgow Caledonian University,
Carol Adams, David Cooper, Andrew Hawker, Ken McPhail, Martin O'Donnell, the late Tony
Puxty, Colin Rickwood, Fenton Robb and, in particular, the two anonymous referees. We would
also like to thank Kirsty MacCallum, Wards Librarian, for her research assistance.

Accounting, Auditing &
Accountability Journal,
Vol. 13 No. 2, 2000, pp. 197-218.
© MCB University Press, 0951-3574

AAAJ
13,2

Transnational corporations

The key characteristic of transnational corporations (transnationals) is their international production. Such firms are involved in capital accumulation on a global scale, operating global strategies to produce continued growth (Sklair, 1991). Various theories of the transnational have been put forward, including the monopolistic advantage approach of Hymer (1960) and Kindleberger (1969), and the eclectic analysis of Dunning (1977, 1979, 1980, 1981) (see the surveys by Cantwell (1991), Dunning (1993) and Dicken (1998)). Particularly influential has been transaction cost analysis (see, for instance, Buckley and Casson (1976) and Hennart (1991)), with its roots in Coasian theory of the firm (Coase, 1937). The basic premiss of this analysis is that a transnational firm involves co-ordination of production across national boundaries, in order to save transaction costs. This is achieved by using non-market transactions to bypass imperfect markets.

However, an alternative view can be taken. This is rooted in the analysis of monopoly capitalism (Baran and Sweezy, 1966; Cowling, 1982), which disputes the Coasian assumption of an even distribution of power, going beyond the Coasian superficial obsession with markets and focuses on distributional issues rather than Pareto efficiency (Cowling and Sugden, 1987, 1998a). A transnational is seen as "the means of co-ordinating production from one centre of strategic decision making when this co-ordination takes a firm across national boundaries" (Cowling and Sugden, 1987). This definition emphasises the importance of control, and in particular strategic decision making, rather than market exchange, and sees firms becoming transnationals in order to defend themselves against or attack oligopolistic rivals, in order to maximise returns to owners of capital (Cowling and Sugden, 1987). Moreover transnationals are argued to behave in a manner of divide and rule (Sugden, 1992, drawing on Marglin's analysis (Marglin, 1974) and Peoples and Sugden, 1998). They encourage nations and communities to compete, being in a powerful position since neither can be mobile, unlike the transnational which is free to "roam the world" (Barnet and Cavanagh, 1994). Transnationalism, particularly for the giant firms, gives additional leverage (with this greater *potential* to shift operations) and leads to such problems as monopolisation, deindustrialisation and the undermining of democracy (Cowling and Sugden, 1987, 1993). Although states can have considerable regulatory powers, transnationals possess real economic power with the threat of withdrawal, redundancy or the promise of investment as a counter to government desires to impose some control (Murray, 1981)[2].

Similar concerns have been expressed about transnationals' activities, including their homogenising effects, their insensitivity to local needs, stifling of local initiatives, sovereignty and autonomy (Hood and Young, 1979), as well as their power to erode the state's capacity to control its economic future (Held, 1988; Wilms Wright, 1977). This is of particular importance since transnationals are fundamentally undemocratic organizations, with management being accountable primarily to capital markets. In contrast there is little or no opportunity for stakeholders or those affected by transnationals' activity (e.g. the community) to influence corporate policy other than in the fragmented market for consumer goods or in the electoral ballot (though not the corporate ballot).

The rise of transnationals has also meant that many aspects of economic decision making have been taken out of the hands of government (Labour Party, 1977). This process has accelerated in recent years, following the General Agreement on Tariffs and Trades (GATT), the North American Free Trade Agreement (NAFTA), as well as the recently proposed Multilateral Agreement on Investment (MAI) and ongoing discussions over a multilateral framework on investment (MFI). Yet, despite this increasing loss of sovereignty, states appear to have little information on the operations and impact of transnationals. In contrast a transnational will monitor the performance of its divisions and subsidiaries (Labour Party, 1977) not to mention its employees and rivals and collect information on those countries in which it is located, relies on for supplies and in which it sells.

In the following section we consider the main arguments for regulating transnationals, in particular the case for the setting-up of state monitoring units. In doing so our focus is with the essence of the characteristics and activities of transnationals, regardless of their so-called nationality. In doing so we will draw on research which indicates the interests of Western industrialised countries in transnationals over time (for an argument that the essence of their characteristics is not nation specific see Cowling and Sugden (1998a)).

Arguments for the regulation of transnationals; a transnationals monitoring unit

Clearly transnationals are already regulated to some extent. Like other firms they will be governed by national legislation and local regulation, as well as by other formal and informal contracts with stakeholders. However, the view of transnationals presented here suggests that largely as a result of their pursuit of private profit, their size and their potential for geographical mobility, they pose particular problems for nation states and communities. The asymmetry of power between transnationals and national communities suggests that nations should adopt a coherent economic strategy to counter such power (Cowling, 1990), rather than simply competing to attract investment. This is not to suggest that transnationals do not bring benefits. All forms of economic activity will bring benefits, since consumption inevitably creates employment. In the case of transnationals these may be well paid jobs, with good working conditions, the development of local supplier linkages, contributions to the local exchequer, and exports and reduced imports, which will benefit the balance of payments and local currency. However, although such benefits may exist, they may not represent the best that can be obtained in the circumstances. There might also be the chance to reduce costs imposed on the community by transnationals.

Corporate disclosure

199

AAAJ
13,2

200

The case for regulating transnationals as part of a coherent economic strategy rests largely on their material impact, their manipulation of imperfect markets and the conflict of interests with the community[3]. Otherwise unregulated transnationals are able to impose their strategies on more or less "enslaved" communities (Cowling and Sugden, 1993), where "concentrated decision-making power in a free market economy results in an élite planning for its benefit and without regard to the costs imposed on others" (Cowling and Sugden, 1993). As control over such strategic decisions as investment, output, employment and other issues becomes more firmly enshrined in the hands of a few élite decision makers, the risks of "strategic" failure become more significant, where the objectives of élites conflict with wider interests in society (Cowling and Sugden, 1994). The end result is social inefficiency, with the economic system yielding inappropriate outcomes for the society (or societies) served by that economy.

It is for these reasons that a transnationals monitoring unit has been advocated as a contribution to the development of strategy towards transnationals. A monitoring unit would collect information and inform government policy making, enabling the development of a more active economic strategy in the interests of the community. This policy is advocated not because of some belief that transnationals act in a harmful manner necessarily intentionally, but that consequences harmful to the community arise from their participation in a market system, and the way that system combined with its participants is developing. This is not to deny the possibility of transnationals developing benevolent economic, social and environmental policies which appear to reduce profitability[4]. However, in general we would expect managers to put the welfare of owners of capital before the interests of the community and the workforce, never mind the environment, particularly in the context of recent deregulatory policies. Later, in our discussion of the need for a better developed accounting for transnationals, we draw on this recognition of underlying and irresolvable conflict of interest between labour and capital, in our use of a political economy perspective (Cooper and Sherer, 1984; Ogden and Bougen, 1985).

While transnationals would not willingly accept our advocated regime, and whilst we have argued that transnationals typically possess considerable power, they are not all-powerful. As in any social relationship there would appear to be room for at least some manoeuvre, although presumably transnationals would prefer to have everything their own way. For example, while valuing the freedom given to them by the state, transnationals may be willing to accept greater regulation of accountability (e.g. in disclosure) in return for further deregulation of economic activity, such as proposed in the Multilateral Agreement on Investment and current discussions over a multilateral framework on investment. There is evidence that even those policy makers very resistant to the idea of controlling transnationals, for fear of their reaction, have been willing to contemplate monitoring (for example, the Labour Party leadership in the UK in the late 1980s (*The Guardian*, 2 June 1987).

In fact holding the view that transnationals are too powerful to resist paradoxically strengthens the case for a monitoring unit (see Harte and Sugden, 1990, footnote 7, p. 148). This suggests the need to consider policies which will allow the community to become a more equal partner in industrial development. Clearly an important aspect of any monitoring should be the evaluation of the impact of the unit and its impact on transnationals' activities, in particular whether disclosure results in greater equality of knowledge. In a similar vein the recent history of utility regulation in the UK has revealed a struggle over information, yet the infrastructure of regulation remains in place.

The idea of a monitoring unit has been proposed at various times in the past (e.g. Wilms Wright, 1977; Labour Party, 1977, 1987; Hughes, 1986, 1987; Standing Commission on the Scottish Economy, 1990; European Parliament, 1999[5]) generally to find out more about business plans and to allow better negotiation with (foreign) corporations (Labour Party, 1987). Wilms Wright's proposals follow from the identification of conflicts of interest (e.g. in regard to sovereignty, investment policy, pricing and trading policy, monopoly power, monetary policy, and labour relations). He argued that legislation is needed to develop a framework for the control of transnationals, suggesting that such was already in place in a number of countries, notably Canada, and referred to the development of codes of conduct by UN, ILO and OECD. However, his proposals were substantially more radical and include the development of international trade union co-operation, the encouragement of government economic and industrial policies to benefit domestic firms and specific measures to deal with transnationals (planning agreements between firms and government, greater supervision of inward investment, greater scrutiny of outward investments where these exploit workers abroad, and legislation to deal with restrictive business practices, tax evasion and the impact of transnationals on monetary and trade policy). Greater disclosure of financial and other information was also advocated.

The proposals of the Labour Party (1977) are contained in a 135-page report which described the rise of the transnational and the problems caused for communities (particularly the loss of economic power, the effects of company pricing strategies, transfer pricing, impact on balance of payments and trade, technology, and the impact on trade unions). In particular the report emphasised the need to have a great deal more information on the activities and consequences of transnationals. Although it was recognised that there are occasions when government departments are entitled to information from transnationals (e.g. through the then Exchange Control Act, 1947, the Monopolies and Mergers Commission, etc.) it was suggested that governments did not know whether undertakings given by firms provided with financial and other assistance had been delivered. In addition it was suggested that a substantial number of foreign owned establishments in the UK (just over half) were branches, which did not need to supply information to Companies House[6]. The conclusion was that new government powers were needed, including greater rights to information and the introduction of planning

Corporate disclosure

201

agreements. A Foreign Investment Unit was proposed, which would examine all transactions with transnationals. The Unit was intended to gather information so as to facilitate policy making, to enable government to behave much more like a conglomerate. In this sense transnationals were being viewed as subsidiaries of the state, and so expected to disclose information to allow the state to manage the economy. Following a long list of information which it was felt needed to be disclosed the report recognised that the methods of accounting were a concern, suggesting that "accountants wield so much power that they cannot be left as they are".

However, a unit's potential is much greater and, we would argue, of greater significance with the deregulation of industrial development. It could provide a pool of knowledge influencing government policy, provide a means for wider public accountability of the performance and impact of transnationals, challenging the language of traditional accounts of business performance, be an important institutional catalyst, and possibly affect the policies of transnationals directly. The role of a monitoring unit would therefore be to collect information, prepare accounts of the performance and impact of transnationals and use these to influence (government policy, community attitudes and even corporations themselves). In this a monitoring unit would be performing a task similar to equity analysts, who monitor the performance of actual and potential investments using a variety of sources including the corporate report, so as to construct their own understanding or account of the past and future performance of firms. The monitoring bodies we envisage might thus prepare "economic and social accounts" of transnational firms' activities, drawing on approaches in the social auditing literature to investigate their wider economic and social impact. The exact format of such accounts would be decided in conjunction with community players, but might cover issues such as: ownership and control, competition, research and development, employment and industrial relations, balance of payments impact – all matters of concern to some Western governments in recent years (see below).

We might also envisage a monitoring body catalysing wider community groups; consumers, workers, smaller firms and so on. Some action in monitoring transnationals has already begun in Europe by organisations such as the Centre for Research on Multinational Corporations (SOMO) based in The Netherlands, and in the UK with Ethical Consumer and New Consumer, as well as by ethical investment services such as EIRIS (Ethical Investment Research Services) and PIRC (Pensions Investment Resource Centre). Complementing this, there has also been a growth in interest in social auditing by organisations connected with the "new economics" movement. This is seen both in publication of actual social audits, and in the recently developed SA 8000, a standard on social accountability (CEPAA, 1997), and the development of human rights principles for companies (Amnesty International, 1998). Such activity could be further encouraged through creating monitoring bodies across, say, Europe, which would network with such community groups.

Finally this might also encourage new forms of internationalism, such as "multinational webs", particular types of production networks, as a potential alternative to the internationalism of transnationals (Sugden, 1997)[7].

We should, however, note that competition between nation states (as seen in respect of subsidies, taxes, wages, employment and legislation, etc.) is also possible in respect of the idea of a monitoring unit. It may well be that countries would compete to drive down the terms of any monitoring. Transnationals might decide not to invest where there is monitoring, so long as there is an alternative with less demanding or no monitoring. This suggests that monitoring is best conducted in a co-operative manner, across states (Harte and Sugden, 1992), although the idea of setting up some international monitoring body as a first step seems daunting in comparison to the formation of national bodies, with some agreement to share information[8].

While the detailed workings of a monitoring unit are beyond the scope of this paper, a potential framework has been seen in attitudes to transnationals expressed by governments in the UK, France, Germany, Japan and the USA[9]. This has indicated a wide range of interests, with those appearing in Table I to be most frequently identified.

Overall, UK policy makers in particular appear to have shown a comparative lack of interest over the last 30 or so years, in contrast to the concerns of their counterparts in France, Germany, Japan and the USA. Although we will not address comparative responses in detail here, elsewhere we have documented the similarity in the interests of Western industrialised countries over time (Bailey *et al.*, 1994a). More recently, for example, the growing concern in Japan with the "hollowing out" of Japanese industry as Japanese-based transnationals move production overseas, raises issues similar to those concerning deindustrialisation and transnationals in the UK in the 1980s (see Nagata (1995) and Takenaka (1991), reported in Ramstetter (1997), MITI (1997), Bailey (1999b) and Tomlinson and Cowling (1999)).

In the following section we consider the most recent attempt to "deregulate" industrial development, in the form of the MAI and subsequent discussions. Although our overall concerns are with the impact on democracy and development, and in particular the balance of power between communities and transnationals, we will be concentrating here on the implications of such an agreement for corporate accountability. In doing so we will be emphasising the importance of accounting to accountability, not simply in terms of providing information but also in its facilitating action (Stewart, 1984). In particular, we question the appropriateness of voluntary developments in reporting.

Towards a multilateral framework on investment
The Multilateral Agreement on Investment (MAI) was recently proposed by the members of the Organisation for Economic Co-operation and Development (OECD). Originally due to be signed in 1997, and then more recently in April 1998, it now appears that commentators are unwilling to predict when any form of framework will be reached (*Financial Times*, 1998). The proposed MAI

Corporate
disclosure

203

Ownership and control	Concern regarding takeovers; changes in ownership; structure of the enterprise; local participation as shareholders; local management/directors; importing managerial techniques; concern to protect key sectors (not technological); loss of decision-making power.
Competitive implications	Concentration/market share/industrial structure; marketing; pricing; marketing policies/strategies; distributional impact; "pressure" on small and medium-sized local businesses; concern over licensing/technical agreements, e.g. restrictions on price; no access to most "lucrative" (highly profitable) sectors; levels of concentration of foreign ownership in the industry; prevention of a competitive challenge in a particular sector.
Research and development/ technology	Concern to protect key sectors; R&D/technological processes the firm can bring or take abroad ("technological impact"); ownership/transfer of technology and dependence; product innovation/variety/quality; training; whether encourages or discourages national research; "accelerating modernisation"; concern that the most profitable or advanced production activity would be saved for the foreign parent.
Employment and industrial relations	Rate of "exploitation"; conditions of work and life; job quality; job security; employment; equality of opportunity and treatment; impact on industrial relations/trade unions; competition for scarce labour.
Balance of payments/ international trade	Currency stability (including financing); currency convertibility; size of capital outflows/repatriation of profits; balance of payments.
Compliance/co-operation with wider industrial policy	Whether "indifferent to national interests"; impact on the "smooth running" of the economy or its rehabilitation; maintenance of order in native firms/whether adversely affects domestic firms; whether supplements domestic investment activity; scale relative to national investment levels; compliance with monetary policy; impact on economic independence; contribute to "self-support and sound development of the economy"; inflationary impact; impact on national income/production.
Political issues	Political involvement/donations; to/from which country (foreign policy issues); whether from a foreign government; whether has "harmful" political consequences; impact of foreign legislation

Table I.
Examples of Western governments' interest in transnationals over the last 30 years

and subsequent discussions over a multilateral framework on investment are the latest in a series of policy developments intended to liberalise international trade, following, most notably the General Agreement on Tariffs and Trades (GATT) and the North American Free Trade Agreement (NAFTA).

The draft MAI proposed to remove all national controls on foreign investors, and was seen by advocates as an important step in the development of the global economy, "We are writing the constitution of a single global economy" claimed Renato Ruggerio, director-general of the World Trade Organization, as reported in Rowan (1998).

The primary aim appears to have been the protection of international investment, with all foreign investors in member countries to be treated in the same way as domestic firms. As a consequence transnationals, which are increasingly dominating world trade and investment (United Nations, 1993 and 1997), would face fewer restrictions on their movement of funds. There would be no restrictions on the repatriation of profits, which advocates argued would increase capital flows around the world. The MAI was also expected to attract more Foreign Direct Investment (FDI) to developing countries, reducing the need to provide competitive incentives to transnationals, although it should be borne in mind that developing countries were not party to the development of the draft agreement. It was also proposed that where restrictions were imposed which harmed the rights of investors (except most probably in sectors such as defence, though not in other potentially significant sectors such as land, minerals and forests (Das, 1997)), transnationals were to be able to sue national and local governments at an international tribunal. Governments were not to have a right of appeal.

The agreement was drafted with the intention of applying to OECD countries only in the first instance, although the remaining nations of the world were to be invited to sign, and be bound by the agreement. It was proposed that signing-up involved an initial commitment of 15 years and a notice period of five years on withdrawal (Rowan, 1998).

In some respects the MAI and ongoing discussions can be seen as a logical development from the enormous growth in FDI in recent years. It was essentially concerned with the "protection of investment, investment liberalisation and dispute settlement" (Shelton, 1997), based on three basic principles; non-discrimination, no entry restrictions and an absence of special conditions. It sought to ensure a "uniform, stable and predictable environment in which (transnational) enterprises can conduct their activities" (Kang, 1997).

However, following our earlier discussion, and drawing on the transnational monopoly capitalism perspective we have adopted (Cowling and Sugden, 1987), we would suggest that such deregulation and increase in the freedom of transnationals and capital would probably result in costs for workers and communities. Nations and communities would lose democratic control over their economy, no longer being able to set specific conditions (performance requirements) on inward investment (e.g. in relation to ceilings on equity, restrictions on ownership, employment, the environment, local supplies and technology transfer). They would, however, have been free to continue to "subsidise" transnationals and so it was likely that competition between nation states would have continued. In addition governments would have been unable to restrict investment within their borders from firms located in any particular country even where the firm had a poor record on environmental and social performance (e.g. human rights violations) (Chalmers, 1997).

The proposed MAI involved subordinating "the rights of elected governments to set national economic policy to the right of transnational corporations and investors to conduct business" (Bleifuss, 1998). As a

Corporate disclosure

205

consequence countries may have been forced to bid down in order to attract investment, yet would not have been able to impose sanctions on firms which behave in an economically, socially, politically or environmentally undesirable manner. Countries would have been unable to guide foreign investment to particular sectors and away from others, and would not have been able to provide incentives solely to domestic corporations (for example, it was expected that preferential treatment for small businesses would have been challenged, and it may not have been possible to subsidise local cultural industries, such as French literary and artistic work (Bleifuss, 1998)). As a consequence governments would have been less able to protect their economies, local businesses, workers and the environment. In addition the MAI's focus on investment ignored the importance of exporting labour services for some developing countries (Mukherjee, 1996). Since developing countries were not party to the negotiations, their interests were not represented directly in any negotiations (for example, see Ramaiah (1997) on concern in India over the possible effects of the MAI).

As we have indicated, the proposed MAI and current framework dicussions followed previous liberalisation of trade, including the GATT (which sought to remove all non-tariff trade barriers in order to maximise world trade and create a global economy (Goldsmith, 1997), thus threatening enlightened social and environmental legislation in the name of protectionism), and the NAFTA (which has seen the Canadian and Mexican governments being sued by transnationals as a consequence of their national environmental protection measures (Rowan, 1998)). Together such agreements are developing new rights for transnationals without specifying any additional responsibilities. Yet responsibilities could be incorporated, particularly in regard to improving the accountability of transnationals. Hirst and Thompson (1996) have suggested that a multilateral agreement could draw on previous efforts by the UN to draw up a Code of Conduct for transnationals, and so cover matters such as the rights of labour and conditions of work, the rights of governments to determine certain economic policies, develop a proper disputes mechanism open to governments, and incorporate protocols on environmental protection. In contrast the proposed MAI was more of an incomplete contract between transnationals and communities, where the former have negotiated greater freedom/power without additional responsibilities. At no stage was there any indication of attempts to democratise transnationals, or to improve their accountability.

Of particular importance to us here was the absence of any specific provisions in the MAI regarding corporate accountability and disclosure. Clearly such would be inconsistent with the deregulating ideology, yet we would argue that "deregulation" necessitates an improvement in corporate accountability, and reporting in particular. The overriding desire to promote the negative freedom (i.e. freedom from control or intervention) of transnationals, preserving their choice and reducing the scope for democratically elected government to regulate their affairs, undermines the positive freedom (i.e. freedom or right to do certain things, e.g. contributing to strategic decision making) of the majority (Bailey, 1999a), in a manner similar to attempts to promote free trade through GATT, NAFTA, etc. (Cowling and Sugden, 1998b). Such market freedoms leave communities even more vulnerable to the unelected, and so necessitate the acceptance of greater responsibility and consequent accountability by transnationals. It also requires us to consider whether further accountability, and specifically reporting, can be satisfactorily developed on a voluntary basis.

This focus on deregulation and greater freedom for transnationals, with consequent failure to address issues of sovereignty, minimum standards (concerning the environment and labour), accountability and disclosure, may go some way to explaining the resistance of many countries, particularly France, as well as non-governmental organizations, to the latest draft of the MAI (*Financial Times*, 1998). The opposition of the French government, in particular, stalled the MAI in December 1998 (OECD, 1998). Its concerns were not isolated. The European Parliament condemned the MAI's inherent imbalance of power between firms and governments and also its lack of transparency (United Nations, 1998). Similarly, the UK's House of Commons criticised the MAI's lack of consideration of environmental and social issues, its lack of transparency, and its exclusion of developing countries (House of Commons, 1999). Yet despite such criticisms, discussions on the substance of the MAI will continue at the World Trade Organisation's Working Group on Trade and Investment. The European Commission, in particular, sees the shift to the WTO as a real opportunity to continue the MAI at a new forum, its "ideal result" being almost exactly the basic provisions of the MAI (European Commission, 1998). The name and venue may have changed, but the game remains the same: the USA, the European Commission and transnational corporations continue to aim for an MAI-style multilateral framework on investment.

The need for greater accountability: a political economy approach
The primary accountability of transnationals' economic activity is generally to providers of financial capital. In Britain, and most industrialised market economies, this is governed largely by one or more of the law, the accounting profession and the Stock Exchange. For example the lodging of information with the Registrar of Companies, and for public companies the wide dissemination of annual reports, affords a degree of public accountability in the UK.

In general very little has changed this century regarding the nature of such financial accountability. The volume of information reported has grown, yet the basic system remains largely the same historic cost model of the last century[10]. The traditional view is that external financial accounting statements should capture only those costs and revenues that are internal to an organisation (Solomons, 1991) in order to measure and communicate economic information which will be relevant to decision makers (primarily providers of

Corporate disclosure

207

AAAJ
13,2

208

financial capital and their advisers). As a consequence current accounting practice deals only with a subset of all economic exchange transactions (Tinker, 1985), relying on market exchanges, and in particular the concepts of money measurement and entity. Although there are serious doubts as to the consistency between accounting practice and the demands of the market system, the entity and money measurement concepts can be seen as justification of the need to focus on only those transactions entered into by the firm (rather than its impact), accounted for in financial terms (Tinker, 1985).

This traditional view of accounting can be criticised as partial and one-sided (Morgan, 1988). In some respects one could argue that accounting and accountants are aware of the deficiencies and are attempting to develop accountings which broaden the focus. We have seen criticisms of traditional accounting for failing to reflect new managerial concerns with quality, etc. (e.g. Kaplan, 1984), developments in public sector accounting such as value for money (eg. McSweeney and Sherer, 1990), and concern for the environmental impact of business (Gray, 1990; Gray *et al.*, 1993). Yet the emphasis in accounting practice as illustrated by the annual report and accounts remains largely the same. In many respects the direction of change in external reporting practice appears to be more concerned with refining a picture of so-called economic reality (e.g. ICAS, 1988; Accounting Standards Board, 1995), and continues to be explored very much within the neo-classical/marginalist paradigm.

Of particular interest to us here is that little attention is paid to market imperfections or aberrations in the analysis of multinational and monopoly business (Tinker, 1980). Multinational and international accounting are suggested to offer opportunities for radical and dramatic changes in accounting (Tinker *et al.*, 1982), yet there are few signs that scholars or practitioners have taken this opportunity. Most accounting research appears to ignore the fact that the economy is dominated by such large transnational corporations, often operating in oligopolistic or monopolistic markets (Cooper and Sherer, 1984), and consequently fails to reflect general social and human consequences as well as the wider strategic impact of such organisations (Morgan, 1988). Following our earlier discussion of transnationals, which followed a transnationals monopoly capitalism perspective (Cowling and Sugden, 1987), our critique of transnationals' corporate reporting practices follows a political economy approach, which recognises the underlying and irresolvable conflict of interest between labour and capital (Cooper and Sherer, 1984; Ogden and Bougen, 1985). In doing so we offer an analysis which is explicitly normative, descriptive and critical (Cooper and Sherer, 1984). Specifically in regard to accounting, a political economy of accounting (PEA) approach considers the functions of accounting within the economic, social and political context in which it operates (Cooper and Sherer, 1984), where an accounting system can only be understood in the context of the wider social system in which it is to be found (Puxty, 1986). In a society characterised by class conflict, communication will be systematically distorted. Following political economy theory, accounting reports are seen as a tool for "constructing, sustaining and legitimising political and economic arrangements, institutions and ideological themes which contribute to corporations' private interests" (Guthrie and Parker, 1990).

Annual reports and accounts can therefore be seen as a partisan writing of history, through which individuals and institutions define themselves and are defined by others (Tinker and Neimark, 1988). Corporate reports may therefore reduce the emphasis on any particular matter, must interpret events and construct a history of social and economic events (Tinker and Neimark, 1988). In doing so traditional accounting reports tell one less about the impact of a transnational corporation than about its financial performance, although, as Hoogvelt and Tinker (1978) show, they can still be used to illustrate, among other things, investment, exploitation, and changes in the distribution of value added. In respect of the previously identified issues of concern to Western governments in recent years, it is unlikely that one would find many details, for example, of pricing and marketing policies and practices, training, productivity, transfer pricing, job quality, "rate of exploitation", imports and exports, spending in local economies, consumption of resources, political involvement and environmental impact[11].

While it may be argued that recent developments such as the MAI, GATT and NAFTA emphasise the ideas of marginalism and can be seen as another brick in the house of monopoly capitalism, this emphasis on the market ironically requires us to consider the role of accounting information and the possibility that regulation is needed. The limiting of regulation and specific requirements for FDI can be argued to require a more complete picture of corporate activity. Since the MAI and similar agreements rely on an assumption that additional conditions should not be imposed on transnationals, it implies that the wider social and environmental impact of transnationals can be ignored, yet without information on individual corporate performance and impact how can we be sure that this is acceptable to the community? How can the community decide whether to support elected representatives and their policies towards transnationals? How can communities continue to support the independence and rights attributable to capital (e.g. legal persona and limited liability)? Accepting that the MAI and similar agreements seek to ensure governments do not impose political conditions on transnationals, the absence of reporting on the wider economic, social and environmental consequences of transnationals will also limit the freedom of the community (e.g. in its purchasing or employment decisions). If governments cannot act to implement the will of society then surely communities must be informed of corporate impact so that individuals or groups can decide how to invest their labour or consumption, and whether to allow agreements such as the MAI to exist. Without this information liberalisation cannot be seen as a rational economic strategy but rather an ideology. The absence of wider accountability and reporting means that the opportunities to challenge the ideas of the economic system will be limited.

Corporate
disclosure

209

AAAJ
13,2

210

Our position, therefore, recognises that accounting reports play an important part in forming world views or social ideology (Tinker and Neimark, 1988), in this case giving management an opportunity to present its view of the world, particularly in regard to the performance and impact of transnationals, and, where appropriate, choosing what to comment on and what to ignore. Non-disclosure of economic, social or environmental information may be seen as a means of protecting business self-interest and as an effective means of intervention (preventing participation of other interests) and confusion in itself. Management, as we have stressed, may seek to "confuse, mystify or convince" in its accounting (Cooper, 1984, p. 128), and, we would argue, may have more incentive to do so where there are few regulations governing industrial development.

Following a PEA approach encourages us to focus on accounting's contribution to the distribution of wealth and power in society (Cooper and Sherer, 1984). Accounting techniques enable élite groups and their agents to concentrate on private wealth (Tinker, 1985), yet tell us very little about the impact of corporations. We are also encouraged to recognise the historical and institutional environment in which accounting operates (in this case we argue for a development in reporting practice because of the increased liberalisation of industrial development and the growing power of transnationals). Finally we also recognise the role of interests and the potential for change in accounting (e.g. we are particularly concerned with the consequences of accounting which fails to address the wider economic, social and environmental impact of transnationals, particularly in the light of the well articulated concerns of Western governments in recent years, not to mention our own more radical agenda).

Lessons from using publicly available information to monitor transnationals

Our earlier consideration of proposals for monitoring transnationals revealed a consistent concern with both the quality and quantity of disclosure. Information (accounting) was seen to be an essential element of accountability, so as to allow the community and its representatives to see whether they are satisfied with their relationship with transnationals and its consequences. The central importance of information is illustrated in Barrat Brown's (1986) suggestion that the first point of action by trade unions and local authorities, in a strategy to combat the power of transnationals, would need to be the establishment of a continuous flow of information. This would seem most important if, as Cowling suggests, there is at the moment "no accurate record of their (transnationals') global activities" (Cowling, 1990). Certainly our earlier critique suggests that traditional corporate annual reports are incomplete. This view is supported by the transnationals debate in the USA, where it was recognised that policy was being hampered by the absence of information (Bailey *et al.*, 1992).

An important aspect of any regulation involves taking a systematic approach which involves monitoring, checking or controlling activities. A critical commodity used by any regulator is information and a central feature would be a continuous or regular record of events (Bullock *et al.*, 1988). Such monitoring activity is widely practised in our economy and society, for example: government departments monitor business[12], parent companies monitor subsidiaries, companies monitor rivals, companies monitor their markets/customers, and investors monitor investment opportunities. In each case information is collected in order to inform and/or allow regular control or action in some form. In some respects this focus on the availability of information for regulation is similar to the traditional emphasis on information for investment purposes. In that case information is seen as a commodity, needed to expand the number of trading opportunities, to improve real production decisions, and to eliminate or reduce social costs associated with asymmetric information (Walker, 1988). The objectives of a monitoring unit would seem to be not too dissimilar, in that it would be seeking to consider the consequences of transnationals' activities (returns to the community) in order to inform economic policy.

However, accounting for the wider economic and social consequences of corporate performance is at best a marginal activity (Gray *et al.*, 1995). Despite extensive publicity and advocacy, most recently particularly in regard to the environment, there is little evidence of widespread, comprehensive and reliable reporting. What reporting does occur is substantially voluntary, and so depends for its existence, never mind its nature and form, on managerial discretion. Of course such discretion is subject to influences, such as the market for finance, the market for managerial services and audit (Benston, 1982), but in the main these are narrow financial incentives to report. Yet voluntary disclosure, in a society characterised by unequal distributions of power and influence and conflicts of interest, is likely to reflect the values of dominant groups, and so be used as a means to inform in a way which seeks to "mislead, mystify and legitimate" certain interests and action (Cooper, 1984).

In addition, previous voluntary reporting on the wider social and environmental consequences of corporate performance has differed substantially from actual performance (see Ingram and Frazier, 1980; Wiseman, 1982; Rockness, 1985). More recently studies have shown that voluntary corporate reporting has excluded information on the negative aspects of environmental performance (Deegan and Rankin, 1996; Deegan and Gordon, 1996) and equal opportunities impact (Adams and Harte, 1999).

We might expect something similar in the case of an MAI-type agreement. The MAI is premised on the need to limit restrictions on transnationals and their investment. The preference for market based solutions assumes that sufficient information will be made available to allow participants to make informed decisions. This too will be left to the market. Yet our characterisation of transnationals as powerful agents (becoming even more so) suggests that the community and its representatives will be in a weaker position should an MAI-type agreement be introduced, made worse by the absence of adequate disclosure. The indications from previous attempts to monitor a transnational,

AAAJ
13,2

using a framework of potential relevance to governments, suggested that a reliance on what firms are willing to reveal would severely curtail the potential of a monitoring unit[13].

Conclusion

Optimistically we could conclude that "every social order carries the seeds of its own destruction" (Ascherson, 1998). If, as Ascherson suggests, the global free market is the "most powerful and arrogant world order in human history", then attempts to develop an MAI-style multilateral framework on investment may see transnationals overplay their hand, and force communities to respond to the further loss of sovereignty. This may go some way to explaining the rejection of the latest draft of the MAI agreement.

We have argued that giving even freer reign to transnationals will have adverse consequences for the community. Leaving industrial development to the market means that as a social structure it will support the interests of the most powerful participants. Markets need to be controlled, preferably by democratically elected and accountable organisations, rather than undemocratic transnationals pursuing private interests. Such control is proposed here in the form of a transnationals monitoring unit, with the power to regulate disclosure.

While a number of important issues appear to remain unresolved regarding the development of a multilateral framework on investment (e.g. cultural factors, subnational government action, and labour and environmental standards) (Ley, 1997; Atkinson, 1998), the creation of greater freedom for transnationals through the institution of the market forces us to address the question of control and in particular the role and responsibilities of the state. "(B)ringing global economic institutions under the authority of political institutions is essential to protect the environment, human rights and job possibilities around the world. Making both accountable to the people is essential if the new world economic order is to be democratic, and if it is not democratic it will enjoy neither legitimacy nor stability" (Barnet and Cavanagh, 1994). Perhaps Ascherson's optimism is well placed after all.

Notes

1. Details of the interests shown by governments in the UK, France, Germany, Japan, and the USA over the last 30 years are outlined in Bailey *et al.* (1994a). This paper draws on their findings, and discusses the proposed development of a transnationals monitoring unit in the context of recent policies such as the Multilateral Agreement on Investment.

2. Although it can be argued that few transnationals are truly international, being nationally based and home oriented (Hirst and Thompson, 1996), we should emphasise that it is the *potential* to relocate which is essential here. However, this national attachment does, as we will see, offer some encouragement to national governments in their dealings with transnationals.

3. Intervention is thought justified to serve the public interest (since the alternative, a radical change in the economic and social system, addressing matters of economic democracy, representation, control etc. seems less likely to succeed in the shorter term).

4. We would emphasise "appear to" here and suggest that socially responsible behaviour is most likely to be determined by long-term financial considerations, and not immediate profitability.

5. See Roddick (1999). In January 1999 the European Parliament passed a report calling for a code of conduct for European transnationals operating in the developing world, backed up by a European Monitoring Platform to ensure compliance by such transnationals.

6. Corporate accountability is largely determined by legal definitions rather than economic definitions of the firm.

7. A multinational web would be a large scale production process comprising myriads of smaller firms in a nexus of criss-crossing relationships which span international borders, a multinational (rather than transnationals controlled) production process. If an important longer-run goal of industrial policy is to foster such webs, policy makers need to think beyond webs of firms, and to think of "community webs", particular forms of network which span all interest groups affected by production activity. Yet there does appear to be some desire by European politicians to move in this direction; witness the recent report of the European Parliament calling for a code of conduct for European transnationals, backed up by a European monitoring platform (see Roddick, 1999).

8. The development of an international interest in the regulation of financial reporting, with the International Accounting Standards Committee, followed long histories on national standard setting.

9. See Bailey *et al.* (1994a) for a review of interests over the last 30 or so years.

10. In parallel, mainstream financial reporting research and financial accounting practice concentrates on the behaviour of shareholders and creditors, implicitly accepting the values of a market society (Hines, 1989).

11. Accounting can be seen then as a language which, like any other, names, bounds and separates (Hines, 1991a), and in this respect the real significance of accounting can be said to be in what it denies (Lehman and Tinker, 1987) or excludes. Social costs are seen as values (to be excluded) whereas market costs are fact (Hines, 1991b).

12. Although the registrar of companies simply collects annual reports, some industries (e.g. banking and insurance) are more closely monitored in respect of their financial position and performance.

13. See Bailey *et al.*'s (1994b) analysis of Glaxo, which revealed that very little information is provided regarding the economic and social impact of the firm. While these findings might not be a great surprise, they do alert us to the risks of relying on corporate voluntary disclosure as a means of satisfying demands for corporate accountability. A transnationals monitoring unit would barely function without the ability to regulate corporate disclosure.

Corporate disclosure

213

References

Accounting Standards Board (1995), *Statement of Principles for Financial Reporting*, Exposure Draft, Accounting Standards Board, London.

Adams, C. and Harte, G. (1999), *Towards Corporate Accountability for Equal Opportunities Performance*, Association of Chartered Certified Accountants, London.

Amnesty International (1998), *Human Rights Principles for Companies*, Amnesty International, London.

Ascherson, N. (1998), "We live under the most arrogant of all world orders, but it will not last", *The Independent on Sunday*, 25 January.

Atkinson, M. (1998), "Rich nations retreat", *The Guardian*, 24 April.

AAAJ
13,2

214

Bailey, D. (1999a), "Freedom, markets and industrial policy", *Industrial Development Policy Discussion Paper*, No. 4, Universities of Birmingham and Ferrara, Institute for Industrial Development Policy.

Bailey, D. (1999b), "Japan's embrace of the 'Free Market': heightening the risks of strategic failure?", *Kansai University Review of Business and Commerce*, Vol. 1 No. 1, pp. 49-62.

Bailey, D., Harte, G. and Sugden, R. (1992), "US policy debate towards inward investment", *Journal of World Trade*, Vol. 26 No. 4, pp. 66-93.

Bailey, D., Harte, G. and Sugden, R. (1994a), *Transnationals and Governments*, Routledge, London.

Bailey, D., Harte, G. and Sugden, R. (1994b), *Making Transnationals Accountable*, Routledge, London.

Baran, P.A. and Sweezy, P.M. (1966), *Monopoly Capital*, Penguin, Harmondsworth.

Barnet, R.J. and Cavanagh, J. (1994), *Global Dreams: Imperial Corporations and the New World Order*, Simon & Schuster, New York, NY.

Barrat Brown, M. (1986), "Can European workers cope with transnational capital?", in Coates, K. (Ed.), *Joint Action for Jobs*, Spokesman, Nottingham.

Benston, G.J. (1982), "Accounting and corporate accountability", *Accounting, Organizations and Society*, Vol. 7 No. 2, pp. 87-105.

Bleifuss, J. (1998), "Building the global economy", *In These Times*, 11 January, pp. 13-15.

Buckley, P.J. and Casson, M. (1976), *The Future of the Multinational Enterprise*, Macmillan, London.

Bullock, A., Stallybrass, D. and Trombley, S. (1988), *The Fontana Dictionary of Modern Thought*, 2nd edition, Fontana, London.

Cantwell, J. (1991), "A survey of theories of international production", in Pitelis, C. and Sugden, R. (Eds), *The Nature of the Transnational Firm*, Routledge, London.

Chalmers, D. (1997), "The MAI: a wrong type of globalisation", *Scottish Trade Union Review*, No. 84, September/October, pp. 24-5.

Coase, R.H. (1937), "The nature of the firm", *Economica*, Vol. 4.

Cooper, D. (1984), "Information for Labour" in Carsberg, B.V. and Hope, T. (Eds), *Current Issues in Accounting*, 2nd edition, Philip Allan, Deddington.

Cooper, D.J. and Sherer, M. (1984), "The value of corporate accounting reports: arguments for a political economy of accounting", *Accounting, Organizations and Society*, Vol. 9 No. 3/4, pp. 207-32.

Council on Economic Priorities Accreditation Agency (1997), *Social Accountability 8000*, CEPAA, London.

Cowling, K. (1982), *Monopoly Capitalism*, Macmillan, London.

Cowling, K. (1990), "A strategic approach to economic and industrial policy", in Cowling, K. and Sugden, R. (Eds), *A New Economic Policy for Britain – Essays on the Development of Industry*, Manchester University Press, Manchester.

Cowling, K. and Sugden, R. (1987), *Transnational Monopoly Capitalism*, Wheatsheaf, Brighton.

Cowling, K. and Sugden, R. (1993), "A strategy for industrial development as a basis for regulation" in Sugden, R. (Ed.), *Industrial Economic Regulation – A Framework and Exploration*, Routledge, London.

Cowling, K. and Sugden, R. (1994), *Beyond Capitalism, towards a New World Economic Order*, Pinter, London.

Cowling, K. and Sugden, R. (1998a), "The essence of the modern corporation: markets, strategic decision making and the theory of the firm", *The Manchester School*, Vol. 66 No. 1, pp 59-86.

Cowling, K. and Sugden, R. (1998b), "Strategic trade policy reconsidered: national rivalry vs. free trade vs. international co-operation", *Kyklos*, Vol. 51, pp. 339-5.

Das, B.L. (1997), "A critical analysis of the proposed investment treaty in WTO", @http://www.panasia.org.sg/souths/twn/title/ana-ch.htm

Deegan, C. and Gordon, B. (1996), "A study of the environmental disclosure practices of Australian corporations", *Accounting and Business Research*, Vol. 26 No. 3, pp. 187-99.

Deegan, C. and Rankin, M. (1996), "Do Australian companies report environmental news objectively?", *Accounting, Auditing & Accountability Journal*, Vol. 9 No. 2, pp. 50-67.

Dicken, P. (1998), *Global Shift. Transforming the World Economy*, Paul Chapman, London.

Dunning, J.H. (1977), "Trade location of economic activity and the multinational enterprise: a search for an eclectic approach", in Ohlin, B., Hesselborn, P. and Wijkman, P.M. (Eds), *The International Allocation of Economic Activity*, Macmillan, London.

Dunning, J.H. (1979), "Explaining changing patterns of international production: in defence of the eclectic theory", *Oxford Bulletin of Economics and Statistics*, Vol. 41.

Dunning, J.H. (1980), "Towards an eclectic theory of international production: some empirical tests", *Journal of International Business Studies*, Vol. 11.

Dunning, J.H. (1981), "Explaining the international direct investment position of countries: towards a dynamic or developmental approach", *Weltwirtschaftliches Archiv*, Vol. 117.

Dunning, J.H. (1993), *Multinational Enterprises and the Global Economy*, Addison-Wesley, Wokingham.

European Commission (1998), *DG1A Note to Art. 113 Committee Discussion Paper: Trade and Investment*, M. D. 642/98, 15 December, European Commission, Brussels.

Financial Times (1998), 21 October.

Goldsmith, E. (1997), "Can the environment survive the global economy?", *The Ecologist*, Vol. 27 No. 6, November/December.

Gray, R.H. (1990), *The Greening of Accountancy: The Profession after Pearce*, Chartered Association of Certified Accountants, London.

Gray, R.H., Bebbington, J. and Walters, D. (1993), *Accounting for the Environment*, Paul Chapman Publishing, London.

Gray, R.H., Kuohy, R. and Lavers, S. (1995), "Corporate social and environmental reporting: a review of the literature and a longitudinal study of UK disclosure", *Accounting, Auditing & Accountability Journal*, Vol. 8 No. 2, pp. 47-77.

Guthrie, J. and Parker, L (1990), "Corporate social disclosure practice: a comparative international analysis", *Advances in Public Interest Accounting*, Vol. 3, pp. 159-75.

Harte, G. and Sugden, R. (1990), "A proposal for monitoring transnational corporations", in Cowling, K. and Sugden, R. (Eds), *A New Economic Policy for Britain – Essays on the Development of Industry*, Manchester University Press, Manchester.

Harte, G. and Sugden, R. (1992), "Co-operation in the European community to regulate transnational corporations", in Koubek, N., Gester, H. and Wiedemeyer, G.R. (Eds), *Richtlinien für das Personal-Management in Internationalen Unternehmungen*, Nomos Verlagsgesellschaft, Baden-Baden.

Held, D. (1988), "Farewell, nation state", *Marxism Today*, December, pp. 12, 13, 15-17.

Hennart, S. F. (1991), "The transaction cost theory of the multinational enterprise", in Pitelis, C. and Sugden, R. (Eds), *The Nature of the Transnational Firm*, Routledge, London.

Corporate
disclosure

215

Hines, R.D. (1989), "The socio-political paradigm in financial accounting research", *Accounting, Auditing & Accountability Journal*, Vol. 2 No. 1, pp. 52-76.

Hines, R.D. (1991a), "On valuing nature", *Accounting, Auditing & Accountability Journal*, Vol. 4 No. 3, pp. 27-9.

Hines, R.D. (1991b), "The FASB's conceptual framework, financial accounting and the maintenance of the social world", *Accounting, Organizations & Society*, Vol. 16 No. 4, pp. 313-31.

Hirst, P. and Thompson, G. (1996), *Globalization in Question: The International Economy and the Possibilities of Governance*, Polity Press, Cambridge.

Hood, N. and Young, S. (1979), *The Economics of Multinational Enterprise*, Longman, London.

Hoogvelt, A.M.M. and Tinker, A.M. (1978), "The role of colonial and post-colonial states in imperialism – a case study of the Sierra Leone Development Company", *Journal of Modern African Studies*, Vol. 16 No. 1, pp. 67-79.

House of Commons (1999), *Environmental Audit Committee First Report on the MAI*, 8 February. House of Commons Paper No. HC58-1 (1998-99), HMSO, London.

Hughes, J. (1986), "Industrial democracy and socialist priorities", in Coates, K. (Ed.), *Freedom and Fairness*, Spokesman, Nottingham.

Hymer, S.H. (1960), *The International Operations of National Firms*, (1976), MIT Press, Cambridge, MA.

Ingram, R. and Frazier, K. (1980), "Environmental performance and corporate disclosure", *Journal of Accounting Research*, Vol. 18 No. 2, pp. 614-22.

Institute of Chartered Accountants of Scotland (1988), *Making Corporate Reports Valuable*, Kogan Page, London.

Kang, K-S. (1997), "Opening address", in OECD, *Multilateral Agreement on Investment; State of Play April, 1997*, OECD, Paris.

Kaplan, R. (1984), "Yesterday's accounting undermines production", *Harvard Business Review*, July/August, pp. 95-101.

Kindleberger, C.P. (1969), *American Business Abroad*, Yale University Press, New Haven, CT.

Labour Party (1977), *International Big Business: Labour's Policy on the Multinationals*, Labour Party, London.

Labour Party (1987), *New Industrial Strength for Britain*, Labour Party, London.

Lehman, C. and Tinker, T. (1987), "The real cultural significance of accounts", *Accounting, Organizations and Society*, Vol. 12 No. 5, pp. 503-22.

Ley, R. (1997), "The scope of the MAI", in OECD, *Multilateral Agreement on Investment State of Play in April, 1997*, OECD, Paris.

McSweeney, B. and Sherer, M. (1990), "Value for money auditing: some observations on its origin and theory", in Cooper, D.J. and Hopper, T.M. (Eds), *Critical Accounts*, Macmillan, Basingstoke.

Marglin, S.A. (1974), "What do bosses do? Part 1", *Review of Radical Political Economics*.

MITI (Ministry of International Trade and Industry) (1997), *Structural Reform of the Japanese Economy*, http://www.jef.or.jp/news/97.nov.html

Morgan, G. (1988), "Accounting as reality construction: towards a new epistemology for accounting practice", *Accounting, Organizations and Society*, Vol. 13 No. 5, pp. 477-85.

Mukherjee, N. (1996), "Multilateral investment agreement and poor countries", *Economic and Political Weekly*, 23 November, pp. 3045-6.

Murray, R. (1981), *Multinationals beyond the Market – Intra-Firm Trade and the Control of Transfer Pricing*, Harvester, Brighton.

Nagata, M. (1995), "The Asia-Pacific region in the 21st century: future relations among the United States, Japan and Asia", in Adams, F.G., Katsuhara, T. and Nogami, K. (Eds), *Interdependence and New Directions for Development Policy in East and Southeast Asia*, International Centre for the Study of East Asian Development, Kitakyushu.

OECD (1998), *Informal Consultations on International Investment*, (OECD Press Release 3 December), http://www.oecd.org/daf/cmis/mai/mainindex.htm

Ogden, S. and Bougen, P. (1985), "A radical perspective on the disclosure of information to trade unions", *Accounting, Organizations and Society*, Vol. 10 No. 2, pp. 211-24.

Peoples, J. and Sugden, R. (1999), "Divide and rule by transnational corporations", in Pitelis, C. and Sugden, R. (Eds), *The Nature of the Transnational Firm*, 2nd edition, Routledge, London.

Puxty, A.G. (1986), "Social accounting as imminent legitimation: a critique of technist ideology", *Advances in Public Interest Accounting*, Vol. 1, pp. 95-112.

Ramaiah, B.B. (1997), "Towards a multilateral framework on investment", *Transnational Corporations*, Vol. 6 No. 1, pp. 117-21.

Ramstetter, E.D. (1997), "Export performance and foreign affiliate activity in Japan's large machinery firms", *Transnational Corporations*, Vol. 6 No. 3, December, pp. 113-33.

Rockness, J.W. (1985) "An assessment of the relationship between US corporate environmental performance and disclosure", *Journal of Business Finance and Accounting*, Vol. 12 No. 3, pp. 339-54.

Roddick, A. (1999), "Transnationals must face responsibilities", *Financial Times*, 16 January, p. 8.

Rowan, D. (1998), "Meet the new world government", *The Guardian*, 13 February, p. 15.

Shelton, J.R. (1997), "Opening address", in OECD, *The Multilateral Agreement on Investment: State of Play as of February*, OECD, Paris.

Sklair, L. (1991), *Sociology of the Global System*, Wheatsheaf, Hemel Hempstead.

Solomons, D. (1991), "Accounting and social change: a neutralist view", *Accounting, Organizations and Society*, Vol. 16 No. 3, pp. 287-95.

Standing Commission on the Scottish Economy (1990), *Final Report*, Standing Commission on the Scottish Economy, Glasgow.

Stewart, J.D. (1984), "The role of information in public accountability", in Hopwood, A. and Tompkins, C. (Eds), *Issues in Public Sector Accounting*, Philip Allen, Oxford.

Sugden, R. (1992), "Why transnationals? The significance of divide and rule", in Krishnamarthy, G.R. (Ed.), *Personnel Practices in Multinational Corporations in Different Cultures*.

Sugden, R. (1997), "Economias multinacionales y la ley del desarrolle sin equidad", (Multinational economies and the law of uneven development), *FACES*, Vol. 3 No. 4, pp. 87-116.

Takenaka, H. (1991), *Contemporary Japanese Economy and Economic Policy*, University of Michigan Press, Ann Arbor, MI.

The Guardian (1987), 2 June.

Tinker, A.M. (1980), "Towards a political economy of accounting: an empirical illustration of the Cambridge controversies", *Accounting, Organizations and Society*, Vol. 5, pp. 147-60.

Tinker, A.W., Merino, B.D. and Neimark, M.D. (1982), "The normative origins of positive theories: ideology and accounting thought", *Accounting, Organizations and Society*, Vol. 7 No. 2, pp. 167-200.

Tinker, T. (1985), *Paper Prophets: A Social Critique of Accounting*, Holt, Rinehart and Winston, Eastbourne.

Corporate
disclosure

217

Tinker, T. and Neimark, M. (1988), "The struggle over meaning in accounting and corporate research: a comparative evaluation and critical historiography", *Accounting, Auditing & Accountability*, Vol. 1 No. 1, pp. 55-74.

Tomlinson, P. and Cowling, K. (1999), *The Japanese Crisis – A Case of Strategic Failure?*, mimeo, Department of Economics, University of Warwick, UK.

United Nations (1993), *World Investment Report – 1993*, United Nations, New York, NY.

United Nations (1997), *World Investment Report – 1997*, United Nations, New York, NY.

United Nations (1998), *World Investment Report – 1998*, United Nations, New York, NY and Geneva.

Walker, M. (1988), "Information economics and agency theory: elements for a theory of corporate reporting", in Lee, T.A. (Ed.), *Making Corporate Reports Valuable – The Literature Surveys*, Institute of Chartered Accountants of Scotland, Edinburgh.

Wilms Wright, C. (1977), *Transnational Corporations: A Strategy for Control*, Fabian Society, London.

Wiseman, J. (1982), "An evaluation of environmental disclosures made in corporate annual reports", *Accounting, Organizations and Society*, Vol. 7 No. 1, pp. 53-63.

Further reading

Briston, R. (1984), "Accounting standards and host country control of multinationals", *British Accounting Review*, Vol. 16 No. 1, pp. 12-26.

Gray, S.J., Shaw, J.C. and McSweeney, L.B. (1981), "Accounting standards and multinational corporations", *Journal of International Business Studies*, Spring/Summer, pp. 121-35.

Hamilton, G. (1984), *The Control of Multinationals: What Future for International Codes of Conduct in the 1980s?*, IRM Multinational Reports, Geneva.

Steward, F. (1989), "New times, green times", *Marxism Today*, March, pp. 14, 15, 17.

Sugden, R. (1990), "A warm welcome for foreign-owned transnationals from recent British governments", in Chick, M. (Ed.), *Governments, Industries and Markets – Aspects of Government-industry Relations in the UK, Japan, West Germany and the USA since 1945*, Edward Elgar, Aldershot.

[22]

The current issue and full text archive of this journal is available at
http://www.emeraldinsight.com/0951-3574.htm

AAAJ
15,3

312

Received July 2000
Revised January 2002
Accepted January 2002

An examination of the corporate social and environmental disclosures of BHP from 1983-1997

A test of legitimacy theory

Craig Deegan, Michaela Rankin and John Tobin

School of Accounting and Law, RMIT University, Melbourne, Australia

Keywords Disclosure, Environment, Management, Business policy, Perception, Annual reports

Abstract *This study examines the social and environmental disclosures of BHP Ltd (one of the largest Australian companies) from 1983 to 1997 to ascertain the extent and type of annual report social and environmental disclosures over the period, and whether such disclosures can be explained by the concepts of a social contract and legitimacy theory. This research is also motivated by the opportunity to compare and contrast results with those of Guthrie and Parker, in whose study the social and environmental disclosures made by BHP Ltd were also the focus of analysis. In testing the relationship between community concern for particular social and environmental issues (as measured by the extent of media attention), and BHP's annual report disclosures on the same issues, significant positive correlations were obtained for the general themes of environment and human resources as well as for various sub-issues within these, and other, themes. Additional testing also supported the view that management release positive social and environmental information in response to unfavourable media attention. Such results lend support to legitimation motives for a company's social and environmental disclosures. A trend in providing greater social and environmental information in the annual report of BHP in recent years, and its variable pattern, was also evidenced.*

1. Introduction

This study examines whether an organisation, specifically BHP Ltd (one of Australia's largest diversified public companies), discloses social and environmental information in response to particular social expectations, expectations which typically change across time[1]. The research updates the work undertaken by Guthrie and Parker (1989) which studied the annual reports of BHP Ltd for the 100 years to 1985 and which has become a highly cited and respected paper in the area of social and environmental reporting. The current study examines the extent and type of corporate social and environmental reporting by BHP Ltd over a 15-year period from 1983-1997. As with Guthrie and Parker (1989), this study correlates social disclosure to a measure of public concern. However, this study uses a different measure of public concern than that used by Guthrie and Parker (1989). Specifically, this study uses the extent of media attention devoted to the activities of BHP Ltd

Accounting, Auditing &
Accountability Journal
Vol. 15 No. 3, 2002, pp. 312-343.
© MCB UP Limited, 0951-3574
DOI 10.1108/09513570210435861

The authors would like to acknowledge the helpful comments made by Rob Gray, Lee Parker, James Guthrie, Markus Milne and the anonymous referees.

over the period of the study. It does this on the basis of a belief that media attention reflects (or perhaps shapes) community concerns (see Smith, 1987; Zucker, 1978; Ader, 1993). In undertaking this study, we seek to establish if there have been changes in BHP Ltd's social and environmental disclosures over the period of the study and to investigate whether, consistent with legitimacy theory, specific social and environmental disclosures can be associated with specific societal concerns (as reflected by the media attention).

In contrast to the method used in this paper, Guthrie and Parker (1989, p. 347) used a "data bank of all major events and issues relating to BHP". This "data bank" came from the contents of 11 publications addressing BHP's, and its industry's history. One of the publications was compiled by BHP, whilst the other publications were produced by independent researchers. Guthrie and Parker sought to match peaks and troughs in corporate annual report disclosure with social events and issues identified by the various publications. As they state (Guthrie and Parker, 1989, p. 347):

> For each major category of disclosure (environment, energy, human resources and community involvement), the timing of observed peaks of disclosure was compared with any apparently related BHP activities or socio-economic environmental conditions occurring immediately before or during peak periods. A majority of peak disclosures associated with relevant events is considered evidence of a legitimising explanation for BHP corporate social reporting.

In the Guthrie and Parker (1989) study the authors were unable to confirm legitimacy theory. However, as we would argue, and as they concede, this may have been due, at least in part, to deficiencies in the way they constructed their measure for community concern. As Guthrie and Parker (1989, p. 348) acknowledge, their measure of community concern may exclude some important events or activities in BHP's history. They also acknowledge the possibility that their testing procedures may have failed to detect disclosure reactions if those disclosure reactions lagged behind the various social and environmental events.

Whilst Guthrie and Parker failed to provide results to support legitimacy theory, many other papers have tended to support the theory (for example, Dowling and Pfeffer, 1975; Patten, 1992; Gray *et al.*, 1995a; Deegan and Rankin, 1996; Deegan and Gordon, 1996; O'Donovan, 1999; Brown and Deegan, 1998). We are left to wonder whether there is something different about BHP, or whether Guthrie and Parker's measure for community concern was mis-specified. As we show in this paper, using our method of defining community concern, there does appear to be a strong association between BHP's disclosure policies and community concern – a result consistent with legitimacy theory, but inconsistent with Guthrie and Parker (1989).

The balance of the paper proceeds as follows: the next section investigates the role of the media in either shaping or reflecting community concerns. Reference will be made to media agenda setting theory. Section 3 reviews literature which suggests that corporate social and environmental disclosures are reactive to community concerns. The development of hypotheses are

A test of
legitimacy
theory

313

AAAJ
15,3

314

outlined in section 4, followed by details of the research method in section 5. Section 6 discusses the results of hypotheses testing, with some concluding comments presented in section 7.

2. The role of the media in shaping community concerns

As Brown and Deegan (1998) explain, media agenda setting theory posits a relationship between the relative emphasis given by the media to various topics (referred to as the "media agenda"), and the degree of salience these topics have for the general public (as reflected by the "public agenda")[2]. In terms of causality, increased media attention is believed to lead to increased community concern for a particular issue. The media are not seen as mirroring public priorities; rather, they are seen as shaping them, and in turn, shaping the public agenda. In further exploring the notion of the "public agenda", McCombs *et al.* (1995, p. 282) state:

> Walter Lippmann (1965) defined the public agenda as that array of issues concerning which the well-being of numerous individuals is dependent upon mutual action, cooperation, or, at least, tacit consent. He also noted that this array of issues is largely beyond direct experience:
>
> For the real environment is altogether too big, too complex, and too fleeting for direct acquaintance. We are not equipped to deal with so much subtlety, so much variety, so many permutations and combinations. And although we have to act in that environment, we have to reconstruct it on a simpler model before we can manage it. To traverse the world, men must have maps of the world (p. 16).
>
> It is the news media, noted Lippmann, that provides these maps of the world. Through their selection and display of the daily news, journalists provide major cues about what are the important topics of the day. Over time, many of the issues receiving major emphasis in the news become the major issues on the public agenda. Although this agenda-setting role of the news media is a secondary and unintentional by-product of the necessity to select a few issues for attention, it is one of the most significant effects of mass communication.

McCombs *et al.* (1995) stress that public awareness is the first step in the formulation of public opinion and that the media clearly shapes this awareness. There have been numerous studies of media agenda-setting effects, many of which have adopted media agenda setting theory. Research indicates that the media influences the public's perceived salience for issues (Smith, 1987; Brosius and Kepplinger, 1990; Ader, 1993), and that the media agenda typically precedes public concern for particular issues (McCombs and Shaw, 1972; Funkhouser, 1973; Trumbo, 1995; Neuman, 1990). Research also shows that public concerns and the media agenda are not necessarily reflective of "real world" conditions (Funkhouser, 1973; Ader, 1993). For example, in a review of newspaper articles, a "real-world" pollution indicator[3], and opinion polls from 1970-1990, Ader (1993) found that the amount of media attention devoted to pollution influenced the degree of public salience for the issue, but the "real-world" pollution indicator was negatively correlated with the amount of media coverage. According to Ader (1993, p. 310), "the public needs the media to tell them how important an issue the environment is. Individuals do not learn this from real world cues."

A review of the literature suggests that a number of variables mediate the relationship between media activity and public salience of an issue. These variables include: the obtrusiveness of issues; how the issue is framed (as positive or negative); and associated time lags. Zucker (1978) defined the concepts of obtrusiveness (people's direct experience of an issue) and unobtrusiveness (people may not have direct experience of an issue). Studying six issues, he concluded that the less direct experience the public has with a given issue area, the more it will have to depend on the news media for information about that area. News media coverage preceded the rise of importance of an issue in public opinion polls for the unobtrusive issues, while for the obtrusive issues media coverage and importance to the public seemed to increase together. In a number of studies the environment has been deemed to be an unobtrusive issue, an issue about which the media appears very capable of influencing public concern (Blood, 1981; Eyal *et al.*, 1981; Zucker, 1978). Other issues, such as the ongoing activities of politicians, are also deemed to be unobtrusive. According to Lippmann (1965, p. 18), the world people have to deal with politically is out of reach, out of sight and out of mind. It has to be explored, reported and imagined. He argued that "the pictures in our heads . . . of things we have not experienced personally are shaped by the mass media"[4].

The intensity of the media coverage has also been found to affect the likelihood that particular media coverage will impact the public agenda, although it is not clear what extent of coverage is required before an agenda-setting effect is created (Brosius and Kepplinger, 1990). The way in which the media covers the issue can also affect the likelihood of whether it impacts public attitudes. Dearing and Rogers (1996, p. 64) found that an issue presented in a negative light is more likely to be regarded by the community as an important concern. That is, negative media attention is more likely to have an effect on the public's salience for a particular issue relative to positive, or favourable, attention.

According to McCombs and Shaw (1994, p. 380) any acceptance of the "agenda setting hypothesis" requires that a matching public agenda lags behind the media coverage of the issue. Such a lag has been found in many studies (including some of those referred to above). In relation to the issue of time lags, Stone and McCombs (1981) took the results of two public opinion surveys and compared them with a content analysis of the US national news magazines *Time* and *Newsweek*. As well as supporting the cumulative effect of mass communication on public perception, they demonstrated "a time lag in the movement of issues' salience from the media agenda to the public agenda" (Stone and McCombs, 1981, p. 53) of two to six months. In a similar vein, a content analysis of environmental news stories appearing in the three largest circulation newspapers in the Lansing Michigan area over a 239-day period, and measures of the public agenda from a number of surveys, led Salwen (1988, p. 100) to suggest that the public begin to adopt the media agenda from the five to seven week mark of a particular issue's coverage. This is also consistent with a review of the literature undertaken by McCombs *et al.* (1995). Other

A test of
legitimacy
theory

315

AAAJ
15,3

studies indicate that an issue's salience for the public can commence from within four weeks of the media coverage (see for example, Winter and Eyal (1981) who studied the relationship between public concern about civil rights between 1954-1976 and related media coverage). Of course, it would be reasonable to expect that time lags will vary depending upon the issues in focus, but the evidence does suggest that lags do exist thereby suggesting that media coverage shapes community perceptions.

There are various forms of news-media, including newspapers, television and radio. Research supports the view that newspapers tend to have a greater ability to set the public agenda (McCombs, 1981). A survey undertaken by Bogart (1984) to establish the relative impact of daily newspapers and television on public perceptions documented that:

- half the public is exposed daily to both newspapers and television news;
- newspapers are part of the life of nearly nine out of ten Americans;
- newspapers touch two out of three on a typical day; and
- nearly four out of five readers report looking at any given page.

According to Bogart (1984, p. 719), "for a majority of the audience, the two media complement each other, and newspapers' ability to cover the news of the area in detail and in depth remains a major advantage". In a study of voting behaviour, Stempel and Hargrove (1996, p. 557) indicated that "it is newspaper reading, not TV news use, which relates most to voting". Such a result is also confirmed by McCombs and Shaw (1994, p. 382) who explain that by framing a story within a larger context, the print media is better able to point out its significance to a reader (as opposed to television news which is deemed to be more in the nature of a "headline service").

Related to some of the above studies, convergence in public opinion has also been attributed to media coverage. For example, Shaw and Martin (1992) studied the opinions of people with different demographic characteristics, namely men and women, young and old, educated and uneducated, and Caucasian and non-Caucasian. They found convergence on issues associated with education, pollution, housing and poverty as the exposure to related news items increased.

From the discussion above, and a review of other literature, it does appear that the media attention directed towards particular issues (particularly coverage included within newspapers) can shape and change community concern for many issues. Obviously, for corporate managers to react to media publicity (and in this study we are interested in corporate disclosures) they must perceive that the media publicity will impact community concerns and that the media is simply not a "passive transmitter of a reality that has an existence of its own" (Severin and Tankard, 1992). Managers are obviously not expected to be cognisant of the research undertaken within the context of media agenda setting theory. Nevertheless, consistent with the view that corporate managers do perceive that newspapers can impact public attitudes (which is consistent with the findings of researchers working within the theoretical perspective of media agenda setting theory) it is common for corporations to subscribe to information services which provide daily information about how or whether the corporation has received media coverage in nominated national newspapers. Further, research by O'Donovan (1999), which we will consider in more depth later in the paper (which is embedded within the theoretical perspective provided by legitimacy theory), also shows that corporate managers consider previous newspaper coverage when determining the disclosures they will make in their subsequent corporate annual reports. This evidence is consistent with a view that not only is management aware of media coverage pertaining to their organisation, but that they feel a necessity to respond to it from a disclosure perspective. The next section will briefly consider the possible relationship between community concern and corporate disclosures[5]. Legitimacy theory will be utilised to explain how corporate disclosures might be used by management to change community perceptions about the disclosing corporations. Hence, whilst media agenda setting theory argues that the mass media can shape community perceptions about certain issues, legitimacy theory provides arguments consistent with the view that corporations can also impact community perceptions through their disclosure practices.

3. Corporate social disclosures as a reaction to community expectations

Studies which have examined social and environmental disclosure within annual reports indicate that it has been increasing across time, both in number of companies making disclosures and in the amount of information being reported (Ernst & Ernst, 1978; Harte and Owen, 1991; Gray *et al.*, 1995a; Deegan and Gordon, 1996). Reporting has been generally qualitative in nature and favourable to the company concerned, even to the point of increasing positive disclosures around the time of negative events (Deegan and Rankin, 1996; Deegan *et al.*, 2000).

In research specifically related to the current study, Hogner (1982, p. 249) accorded the growth, decline, and evolution of US Steel's social reporting over an 80-year period to a "concentration on the reporting of activities that society is perceived as valuing most at the time". While concluding that the matrix of forces affecting corporate reporting practice arose from a legitimation motive, he did not empirically test the proposition.

Guthrie and Parker (1989) undertook a study of the social and environmental disclosure practices of BHP Ltd between the years 1885-1985 and compared their observations to Hogner's (1982) examination of US Steel annual reports for a similar period. They observe a history of growth, decline and change in social disclosure over the period studied, rather than a period of growth and development. Human resource disclosures were found to be BHP's primary form of social disclosure, although it was quite inconsistent. The authors also observed a total absence of environmental disclosures until around 1950, with a recurrence in the early 1970s and 1980s, although they remained at a relatively low level.

Guthrie and Parker sought to determine if disclosures were consistent with legitimacy theory and in doing so they compared the disclosure practices of BHP with major events and issues which affected BHP throughout its history as documented within the various publications they reviewed. The authors concluded that the peak in environmental disclosures in the 1970s was associated with a time when mining, steel and oil industries became targets for criticism by conservationists. However, legitimacy theory in relation to environmental activities was not supported in earlier periods when disclosures were rare and not a reaction to public pressure or other external events. The authors also concluded their evidence failed to support a legitimacy perspective for other categories of social disclosure. They acknowledged, however, that they may not have accurately captured the "events" in BHP's history which they were attempting to match with the company's reporting, and that the study may have also suffered from unidentified time lags.

In another study which sought to test legitimacy theory, Brown and Deegan (1998) adopted media coverage as a proxy for community concern. They found support for legitimacy theory in relation to their review of corporate environmental disclosures. In some industries the environmental disclosure strategies of management appeared to be tied to the extent of media attention devoted to environmental issues. Further, changes in media attention, not the level of media coverage *per se*, appeared to explain variations in corporate environmental disclosure strategies[6].

In a further study which considered the role of the media and its impact on corporate disclosures, O'Donovan (1999) conducted interviews with senior management of three major Australian corporations, including BHP, and found that the managers consider that they use the annual report to respond to perceived public concerns, with reports in news media affecting what information they disclosed. The corporate managers' responses were linked to a perception that media attention devoted to particular issues impacts the community's concern about such issues. Management perceived that media reports of a continuing nature, particularly negative or unfavourable reports, were most likely to result in a response in the annual report. O'Donovan's (1999, p. 82) data analysis suggested that "corporate management believe, to some extent, that the annual report is an effective way for informing and educating the public of the corporation's view about certain environmental issues".

As indicated above, in explaining the practice of corporate social reporting, many authors have adopted legitimacy theory (for example, Patten, 1992; Guthrie and Parker, 1989; Deegan and Gordon, 1996; Deegan and Rankin, 1996; Neu *et al.*, 1998; Buhr, 1998; O'Donovan, 1999). Legitimacy theory is a theory that, as applied in the social and environmental reporting literature, is rather simplistic but nevertheless appears to be the theoretical basis most frequently used in attempts to explain corporate social and environmental disclosure policies[7]. Legitimacy theory relies upon the notion of a social contract and on the maintained assumption that managers will adopt strategies, inclusive of disclosure strategies, that show society that the organisation is attempting to comply with society's expectations (as incorporated within the social contract).

Pursuant to legitimacy theory, managers' choices of legitimising strategies are based on the perceptions of the particular managers involved, and different managers will be likely to have different ideas about what society expects (that is, what the terms of the social contract are), and whether the organisation is perceived by community members as complying with these expectations. Nevertheless, when significant events such as a major environmental disaster occur, or when there is sustained mass media interest, then it is reasonable to assume that most managers would perceive that the organisation's ongoing legitimacy is threatened. Conceivably, there will also be different views about appropriate strategies to adopt when legitimacy is threatened (and of course, some managers might perceive a problem when in fact none might exist, and vice versa). Working out the effects of all the various judgements and perceptions with any precision is a difficult if not impossible task. Consequently, researchers have used simplifying assumptions: for example, that evens such as the *Exxon Valdez* disaster (Patten, 1992) or proven environmental prosecutions (Deegan and Rankin, 1996) are assumed to create legitimacy problems for an industry, and that the managers will use disclosure strategies to reinstate damaged legitimacy (as inferred by increasing disclosures around the time of the events).

In this paper we also make assumptions, grounded in media agenda setting theory, that media attention directed at corporations can impact society's views of such corporations. Also, we make the explicit assumption, based on previous research such as O'Donovan (1999), that managers also perceive that the media can impact community perceptions, and that the annual report is perceived by managers to be one means to shift community perceptions back in favour of the organisation. Hence, we predict that if the mass media is focusing upon particular attributes of the organisation's operations then this is potentially legitimacy threatening and therefore likely to provoke a reaction by management – specifically, a disclosure reaction.

As noted above, legitimacy theory posits that organisations seek to ensure that they act, or at least appear to act, within the boundaries and norms of the societies in which they operate. The "social contract" (also frequently referred to as the "community licence to operate") is an implicit agreement between an organisation and society (Shocker and Sethi, 1974)[8]. Failure to act in accordance with the social contract is construed as being detrimental to the ongoing operations of the entity. Community expectations are not considered static, but rather, change across time thereby requiring organisations to be responsive to the environment in which they operate. An organisation could, accepting this view, lose its legitimacy even if it has not changed its activities from activities which were previously deemed acceptable (legitimate). Because community expectations will change across time it is argued that the organisation must also make disclosures to show that it is also changing (or

A test of
legitimacy
theory

319

AAAJ
15,3

320

perhaps to justify why it is not changing). Changing activities without communicating such changes is considered to be insufficient. In relation to the dynamics associated with changing community expectations, Lindblom (1994, p. 3) states:

> Legitimacy is dynamic in that the relevant publics continuously evaluate corporate output, methods, and goals against an ever-evolving expectation. The legitimacy gap will fluctuate without any changes in action on the part of the corporation. Indeed, as expectations of the relevant publics change the corporation must make changes or the legitimacy gap will grow as the level of conflict increases and the levels of positive and passive support decreases.

Again, organisational legitimacy (a perceived state) is deemed to occur when there is congruence between what the community expects of an organisation, and whether they believe the organisation is basically complying with those expectations[9].

Using the report *Tomorrow's Company* as a reference, Solomon and Lewis (2001, p. 7) identify eight "forces" which impact community perceptions about whether an organisation is complying with its social contract. Whilst not emanating from the mass media literature, one such "force" is considered to be the media[10]. Given a perspective that business organisations exist as a result of compliance with their social contract, the argument is that they must establish congruence between "the social values associated with or implied by their activities and the norms of acceptable behavior in the larger social system of which they are a part" (Dowling and Pfeffer, 1975, p. 122). Legitimacy, which is deemed to exist when the entity's value system appears to be congruent with the value system of the larger social system of which the entity is a part (Lindblom, 1994) is, in a sense, treated like a resource provided by parties outside the organisation, much like financial capital or labour (Dowling and Pfeffer, 1975). Pursuant to legitimacy theory, management are deemed to use disclosure media, such as the annual report, to allay community concerns, or more particularly, what they perceive to be the community concerns (Lindblom, 1994). Indeed, Hurst (1970) argues that one of the functions of accounting and related reports is to legitimise the existence of the organisation. Further, the annual report has been deemed to be an important document for an organisation seeking to shape its own "social imagery" (Gray *et al.*, 1995b).

According to legitimacy theory, the disclosures might be made to show that the organisation is conforming with community expectations, or alternatively, they might be made to alter societal expectations. Of course, studies which argue that disclosures can change, or perhaps are perceived to change, community perceptions (many such studies being grounded in legitimacy theory) are based upon an assumption that corporate disclosures, such as those in annual reports, do actually impact community concerns. This assumption is consistent with the views held by senior managers interviewed by O'Donovan (1999) who, when interviewed, responded that annual report disclosures are used as a strategy to change perceptions about the organisation[11].

In summary, to this point we have argued that the media agenda impacts society's level of concerns for particular issues (from media agenda setting theory) and we have provided evidence that managers believe that the mass media has the ability to shape community expectations. We have also argued that the extent and type of corporate social disclosure, in the annual report, is likely to be directly related to management's perceptions about the concerns of the community (from legitimacy theory). The next section of the paper develops the hypotheses of this study.

4. Hypotheses development

The importance that the public ascribe to an issue is influenced by the amount of media attention it receives (for example, see McCombs and Shaw, 1972; Funkhouser, 1973; Ader, 1993). Public salience for an issue increases with the number of media articles between "takeoff" and "tapering" thresholds (Neuman, 1990). A certain "critical" number of articles are required to move an issue to one of public concern, and the pattern of evolving public awareness varies for different types of issues (Neuman, 1990, p. 159). The response function varies according to the issue covered, but there is consistent evidence of a relationship between the volume of media coverage and the level of public concern.

To this point, a varying pattern of social disclosures across both companies, and time, has been displayed (for example, see Pang, 1982; Guthrie, 1982; Guthrie and Parker, 1990; Deegan and Gordon, 1996). If management perceive that in the opinion of the "relevant publics" the organisation is not meeting its "social contract" with society, it is likely that the organisation will take steps to demonstrate its legitimacy and relevance to society and so avoid potential constraints and sanctions. Research has shown that management consider that the media can influence community concern, and that management will use the annual report to counter unfavourable media coverage (O'Donovan, 1999).

The discussion above has focused on establishing that disclosures, inclusive of social and environmental disclosures, are likely to be made to legitimise corporate behaviour in response to public concern, and that public concern is impacted by the media agenda, as expressed by the print media. The underlying proposition is that changes in society concerns, reflected by changes in the themes of print media articles, will be mirrored by changes in the social and environmental themes disclosed, and to the extent of the disclosure made. Applying this specifically to BHP leads to the development of the following hypothesis.

H1. Higher (lower) levels of the print media coverage given to specific attributes of BHP's social and environmental performance will be associated with higher (lower) levels of specific social and environmental disclosures made by BHP in its annual reports.

The above hypothesis does not address whether the media coverage and annual report disclosures are favourable or unfavourable in nature. As noted previously, the framing of an issue in the media as positive or negative influences its salience for the public (Schoenbach and Semetko, 1992; Dearing and Rogers, 1996). The managers in O'Donovan's study indicated that they were most likely to respond to media coverage that depicted their companies in an unfavourable light. Other studies indicated an increase in positive or self-laudatory disclosures around the time of events that depicted the organisation in an unfavourable light (Patten, 1992; Deegan and Rankin, 1996).

In circumstances where media attention is of a negative or unfavourable nature, organisations have a greater incentive to provide more positive disclosure (Brown and Deegan, 1998) to affirm or re-establish their legitimacy. This is consistent with the disclosure strategies described by Lindblom (1994). One way to convince society that the organisation is meeting its social contract is to furnish positive perspectives of its activities. Accordingly:

H2. Higher (lower) levels of unfavourable print media coverage given to specific attributes of BHP's social and environmental performance will be associated with higher (lower) levels of specific positive social and environmental disclosures made by BHP in its annual reports.

5. Research method
Content analysis is used in this study to measure both media attention and corporate social disclosure. Krippendorff (1980) defines content analysis as "a research technique for making replicable and valid inferences from data to their context". The success of the process depends on the reliability and validity of the procedures employed. While there are a number of measures of reliability, Krippendorff's (1980) alpha[12] will be used to assess the replicability of the results. The coding rules are developed in detail to yield standard classifications over each of the 15 annual time-periods of this study.

Ingram and Frazier (1980) state that categories used in content analysis should result from a systematic application of a set of rules to identify exhaustive and mutually exclusive categories. Accordingly, in order to draw valid and reliable inferences from the measurement process, the method suggested by Weber (1985) to create and test a coding scheme has been followed.

First, the recording units are defined. The reliability of different measures of social disclosure has received much attention in the literature. Ingram and Frazier (1980) suggest the sentence as the unit of analysis, as it is easily identified and is less subject to intercoder variation than other measures, such as words and pages. The advantages of sentences are in not needing to standardise words, in obtaining more reliable intra- and inter-rater coding, and in allowing more detailed analysis of specific issues and themes. "Sentences are to be preferred if one is seeking to infer meaning" (Gray *et al.*, 1995b, p. 84). Whilst we use sentences in this study to measure the amount of annual report disclosure it should be noted that many other studies use measures such as words, or proportion of pages. These different measures have been found to be highly correlated (Hackston and Milne, 1996), hence the results should not be greatly influenced by the choice of sentences instead of words, or proportion of pages.

Second, the categories to be classified are defined to allow an item to be allocated to a particular category. They are intended to be mutually exclusive to avoid confounding of the subsequent statistical analysis. This study primarily employs the content classifications of Hackston and Milne (1996), which are based on earlier schemes developed by Ernst & Ernst (1978), Guthrie (1982), and Gray *et al.* (1995b). Accordingly, the dimensions of the content analysis for both media articles and BHP's annual reports broadly embrace the classifications of environment, energy, human resources, community involvement and other.

Third, test coding is undertaken on a sample of the texts by one team member. This reveals some ambiguities in the proposed coding rules, and suggests some minor, but helpful, revisions of the classifications. Fourth, the accuracy or reliability of the coding is assessed by a test-retest, by the same team member, of a sample of the data at different times, and by supplying the coding rules and data samples to a second reviewer for analysis. Fifth, the coding rules are revised to increase the expected reliability of the coding of all texts, and sixth, all relevant text is coded.

Finally, the second reviewer again codes samples of the data to assess achieved reliability and accuracy, using Krippendorff's (1980) alpha. The results of our testing indicate that our coding procedures appear reliable (using the guidance provided by Krippendorff (1980)).

Societal pressure/community concern is measured by the number of relevant articles in the print media. Previous discussion has suggested that coverage of issues in the print media parallels exposure in the overall communication media. Summaries of all articles in the CD-ROM index, the Australian Business Index database (ABIX), mentioning BHP for the period 1983 to 1997, are obtained[13]. The index provides an up-to-date and accurate guide to published information from a wide cross-section of business, finance and trade resources by indexing approximately 85 newspapers and journals (Brown and Deegan, 1998). The number of those newspapers and journals in the ABIX database has steadily increased during the 15-year period. To enable a consistent comparison across the years 1983-1997, only print media services present in the database for those years, and which are available for review in the authors' home university library, are selected. The papers used had the largest circulations of major newspapers in Australia and included *The Age*, *The Australian*, *The Australian Financial Review*, *Westralian*, *The Bulletin*, *Business Review Weekly*, *Courier Mail* and *The Sydney Morning Herald*. It is proposed that this selection includes an adequate number of national and regional papers in Australia to reflect adequately media attention to, and public concern with, the issues of this study.

Following selection of the articles mentioning BHP in the Corporate Name/ Subject area of the ABIX search menu, the abstract of each article is examined for information concerning any of the themes outlined in the previous section. Relevant articles are then examined from microfilm records of the publications, and where relevant, are coded according to the categories or themes provided in the Appendix.

AAAJ
15,3

324

This classification is sufficient to test *H1*, but additionally, to test the *H2*, and following the definitions of Hogner (1982) and Brown and Deegan (1998), each print media article is categorised as:

- unfavourable: where the content indicates that the operations/strategies/performance of BHP are detrimental to, or not in harmony with, the social environment;

- favourable: where the content indicates that the operations/strategies/performance of BHP are beneficial to, or in harmony with, the social environment;

- other: where the content does not indicate that operations/strategies/performance of BHP are beneficial or detrimental to the social environment.

Each media article is then given a score of 1, and allocated to the specific issue within each general theme, with an attendant favourable, unfavourable, or "other" classification[14].

As noted in a previous section, measurement of corporate social disclosure has largely focused on information provided in companies' annual reports. This medium is considered the preferred information source for a number of stakeholder groups (Tilt, 1994; Deegan and Rankin, 1997). Use of the annual report enables comparisons to previous studies (Hogner, 1982; Guthrie and Parker, 1989; Brown and Deegan, 1998), and allows examination of whether managements' perceptions (O'Donovan, 1999) of using information in the annual report to respond to public concerns is supported.

The annual reports of BHP are examined for the years 1983-1997. The content themes and issues, and reasons for the selection of sentences as the recording unit, have already been presented. Positive and negative disclosures are defined similar to Hogner (1982) and Brown and Deegan (1998) as:

- positive: referring to information about corporate social activities which have a positive or beneficial impact on society;

- negative: referring to information about corporate social activities which have a negative or deleterious impact on society;

- neutral: referring to information about corporate social activities whose impact on society cannot be determined as either positive or negative.

The positive/negative measurement is central to the testing of *H2*.

6. Results and interpretation
6.1 Print media coverage and levels of corporate social disclosure
In examining this association, media articles were collated by year for each of the 49 issues shown in the Appendix, and compared to the corresponding annual report sentences on the same issues in the same years[15]. The data are now described for all of the categories of the study.

Summary aggregated totals over the 15-year period from 1983-1997 are displayed in Table I for each theme. Human resources, environment and

Developments in Financial Reporting by Multinationals

Theme	Total annual report sentemces	Total media articles	Positive annual report sentences	Unfavourable media articles
Environment	347	87	276	48
Energy	11	8	11	0
Human resources	403	460	382	400
Community involvement	95	31	79	16
Other	36	2	36	0
Total	892	588	783	464

A test of
legitimacy
theory

325

Notes: Spearman's rank-order correlation between total annual report sentences and total media articles = 0.9000 (p = 0.019); Spearman's rank-order correlation between positive annual report sentences and unfavourable media articles = 0.9747 (p = 0.002); Spearman's rank-order correlation coefficient (one-tailed) expresses the correlation of the number of annual report sentences on the five general themes, with the number of media articles on the same five themes, for 15 years

Table I.
Total social and
environmental
disclosure by general
themes – 1983-1997

community involvement rank in that order in both the print media and the annual reports, with the categories of "energy" and "other" receiving minimal attention in both media. At this aggregated level the results are consistent with the hypotheses in this paper. The two issues attracting the most media attention (human resources and environment which together account for 93 percent of the media coverage) account for 84 percent of the total corporate social and environmental disclosures.

The results in Table I are generally consistent with Guthrie and Parker (1989). They found limited disclosures in relation to community involvement. They also found that human resource disclosures accounted for the highest proportion of total disclosures across the period of their study (1885-1985).

In considering the trends in the disclosure of different categories of social and environmental information, we found that environment related disclosures made by BHP were fairly minimal (one or two sentences) until 1989. This is consistent with Guthrie and Parker who found fairly minimal disclosures across the period of their study (with the period of their study ending in 1985). In 1989, environmental disclosures increased to 11 sentences and then tended to increase in each year to 1997, wherein total environmental disclosures amounted to 140 sentences (in only two years during this period was there any downturn in environmental disclosures, but even then, disclosure did not return to 1989 levels). The disclosures in relation to energy were fairly minimal throughout the period of observation, which again was consistent with Guthrie and Parker. Disclosures pertaining to human resources, community involvement and "other" tended to increase and decrease from period to period with no discernible trends (of continued growth, or otherwise) being apparent. Again, this is generally consistent with the results provided by Guthrie and Parker.

Table I demonstrates the association between public concern (as measured by the proxy of media attention) and annual report social and environmental disclosures, by five themes over the 15 years from 1983-1997. This correlation of total media attention and corporate disclosures produces a correlation coefficient of 0.900, $p < 0.05$, while positive annual report disclosures and unfavourable media articles provides a correlation coefficient of 0.9747, $p < 0.01$.

A view of the overall pattern of attention, in both the media and the annual report, to the sum of the social and environmental issues of this study, is presented in Table II.

For the annual report, there is a general trend of increasing total social and environmental disclosure over time, with comparatively few such disclosures in the 1980s, followed by pronounced upward shifts in 1989 and 1996. Whilst Table II aggregates various social and environmental disclosures and media coverage of different issues it does show that total social and environmental disclosures, which have remained predominantly voluntary within Australia, are generally increasing across time. In noting the general increase in the extent of media coverage (with various peaks and troughs across time), 1989, 1995 and 1997 represented major peaks. In 1989 and 1995 the media concerns are primarily related to employee health and safety issues. In 1995, particular attention was directed to the Moura mine disaster in which a number of BHP employees were killed. The higher level of media attention in 1997 arises primarily from attention directed at the Newcastle plant closure. The Newcastle plant was a major employer of people from the Newcastle area and had been in operation for many years. Overall, the associations between total annual report sentences and total

Year	Total annual report sentences	Total media articles	Positive annual report sentences	Unfavourable media articles
1983	16	20	11	18
1984	36	15	36	15
1985	41	11	40	8
1986	27	0	25	0
1987	21	5	18	5
1988	20	1	20	1
1989	51	47	51	47
1990	43	7	39	6
1991	49	1	49	1
1992	74	3	74	2
1993	54	19	52	6
1994	39	29	37	26
1995	69	139	61	123
1996	148	57	142	35
1997	204	234	128	171
Total	892	588	783	464
Minimum	16	0	11	0
Maximum	204	234	142	171
Mean	59	39	52	31

Table II.
Aggregated social and environmental disclosure and media attention by year

Notes: Spearman's rank-order correlation between total annual report sentences and total media articles = 0.5201 (p = 0.023); Spearman's rank-order correlation between positive annual report sentences and unfavourable media articles = 0.4508 (p = 0.046); Spearman's rank-order correlation coefficient (one-tailed) expresses the correlation of the number of annual report sentences by year, with the number of media articles in the same years

media articles; and positive annual report sentences and unfavourable media articles, is strong, with correlation coefficients of 0.520, $p < 0.05$, and 0.450, $p < 0.05$, respectively. While this year-by-year correlation is interesting, it may be that specific issues in the media generate a greater corporate annual report response than other issues covered by the media. This issue will be investigated shortly.

6.2 Results of testing H1

The first hypothesis posits a relationship between the total print media coverage given to attributes of BHP's social and environmental performance and the total levels of corporate social disclosure in their annual reports. Table III provides the results of the testing of the hypothesis for each of the five major themes.

The above table presents results of tests for the correlation across each of the 15 years for each general theme. *H1* is supported in the themes of environment (correlation coefficient 0.644), and human resources (correlation coefficient 0.578), both with $p < 0.05$. These are the two issues with the greatest level of media attention and annual report disclosures.

A measure of correlation was also obtained for 15 of the 49 specific issues under examination (see the Appendix for details of each of the issues identified under each of the five major themes). These 15 issues recorded 694 of the total annual report sentences (78 percent of all sentences), and 570 media articles (97 percent of the total). With hindsight, the application of 49 categories to this one company was excessive, and as a result, a number of issues could not correlate. Perusal of the 34 issues which attracted no, or very minimal, media attention indicated that, with only three exceptions[16], they received no, or minimal annual report disclosure. This is what would be expected in terms of the hypothesis – with limited concern (as proxied by media attention) there is an expectation that there is limited incentive to provide disclosures. Table IV presents the relationship and level of significance for each of the specific issues for which a correlation statistic was calculated.

Environment. There was a modest rise in media attention and annual report disclosures in the years 1989-1995, and a pronounced rise in both occurring from 1996. A correlation of 0.6441, significance 0.005, is found for the environment category.

	Spearman rank-order correlation coefficient	Significance (one-tailed test)
Total	+0.9000	0.019
Environment	+0.6441	0.005
Energy	+0.3236	0.120
Human resources	+0.5786	0.012
Community involvement	+0.0481	0.432
Others	–0.3270	0.117

Table III.
Correlation by theme between annual report sentences and media articles – *H1*

Note: This table correlates the number of annual report sentences over the 15 years of the study, with the number of media articles in the same years, for each of the five themes

AAAJ
15,3

328

Individual issues	Spearman rank-order correlation coefficient	Significance (one-tailed test)
Environment		
Pollution (issue no. 1)	+0.3850	0.078
Standards and regulations (issue no. 2)	+0.7787	0.000
Prevent/repair damage (issue no. 4)	+0.6235	0.006
Awards (issue no. 9)	+0.1722	0.270
Review/impact studies (issue no. 14)	+0.3660	0.090
Energy		
Conservation awards (issue no. 24)	+1.0000	0.000
Human resources:		
Employee health and safety (issue no. 27)	+0.5786	0.012
Employment of minorities (issue no. 28)	−0.2709	0.164
Employee training (issue no. 29)	+0.3484	0.102
Employee remuneration (issue no. 31)	+0.0628	0.412
Employee morale (issue no. 34)	−0.3347	0.111
Industrial relations (issue no. 35)	+0.2752	0.160
Other (issue no. 36)	+0.0576	0.419
Community involvement		
Donations (issue no. 37)	−0.3359	0.096
Aid or compensation (issue no. 47)	+0.9898	0.001

Table IV.
Correlations between annual report sentences and number of media articles for individual issues – *H1*

Note: This table correlates the number of annual report sentences over the 15 years of the study, with the number of media articles in the same years, for each individual issue that recorded a correlation in testing

Within the environment theme, Table IV shows that four specific sub-issues correlate with values of $p < 0.10$, these relating to pollution, standards and regulations, prevention or repair of damage, and review or impact studies. In considering the respective levels of media attention it is interesting to note that issues associated with the prevention or repair of damage, pollution, and review or impact studies attracted the greatest level of media attention from among the 16 environment sub-issue disclosure categories. The fourth issue with a significant correlation, standards and regulations, ranked as number six in terms of media attention. These four sub-issues within the general theme of environment were also the four issues that attracted the highest level of annual report disclosure (issues associated with repair or damage to the environment attracted the highest level of media attention as well as representing the environmental issue with the greatest amount of annual report disclosure).

These results, for the environment theme in total, and for four of its issues, support *H1* in that these categories record positive correlations ranging from 0.366 to 0.778, with values of $p < 0.10$. Those environmental issues not directly supporting the hypothesis are those with minimal media coverage and minimal annual report disclosures. Interestingly, whilst the company dedicated some space in the annual report to environmental awards, the awards attracted little media attention, perhaps reflecting a view that the media tends to focus on negative attributes of corporate performance (or perhaps, that the media considered the awards to be trivial).

Energy. The theme of energy attracts minimal attention, with media articles appearing only from 1995 and an annual report response in 1996 alone. The Spearman's Rank-order correlation coefficient of 0.3236 (significance 0.12), results entirely from the information on energy conservation awards in 1996. While the general lack of attention to the overall energy theme is interesting, the general absence of data over the years for the theme does not allow a conclusion which supports the first hypothesis.

Human resources. The data for human resources resulted in a Spearman's rank-order correlation coefficient between total media articles and total annual report sentences of 0.5786 at a significance level of 0.012. The sub-issue associated with employee health and safety also produced an association significant at the 10 percent level. The analysis of the total result offers evidence to support *H1*, with further confirmation supplied by health and safety issues. Employee health and safety attracted the greatest level of media attention within the human resources theme as well as representing the human resources issue with the greatest amount of annual report disclosure.

Community involvement. Media articles mentioning BHP's involvement with the community are infrequent, with the majority of the 1995 and 1996 articles arising from compensation and support considerations for the people of the Fly River who were severely affected by the mining operations of Ok Tedi, an organisation in which BHP has an ownership interest. The sporadic pattern of media attention and annual report disclosure led to an absence of an overall association (correlation coefficient 0.048, $p = 0.432$). However, disclosure of aid and compensation issues to communities affected by corporate activities correlated strongly (coefficient 0.989, $p < 0.001$) in the years when the Ok Tedi operations were receiving adverse media exposure. A conclusion supporting *H1* cannot be drawn from the results obtained in this theme, although there is a significant association for the disclosures relating to the aid and compensation issues – the issues attracting the greatest level of media attention within the theme of community involvement.

Other. Under the "other" theme, two media articles on the subject of corporate governance, and an average of 3.5 sentences for ten of the 15 annual reports on BHP's general social responsibility were recorded. Testing did not reveal an association between media articles and annual report disclosures for this theme.

As a concluding comment in relation to *H1* the results show that the specific issues attracting the greatest level of media attention were also generally the issues which had the greatest amount of annual report disclosure.

6.3 Results of testing H2

H2 predicts that higher levels of unfavourable media attention given to BHP's social and environmental implications will result in higher levels of positive social and environmental disclosure in the annual reports. Of the total 892 annual report sentences collated for the study, 783 were positive in nature, as compared to 464 of 588 media articles portraying an unfavourable impact on society or the environment (or both)[17]. Table V presents the results of the aggregate testing of the two variables across the five general themes, where the overall relationship resulted in a Spearman's rank-order correlation coefficient of 0.4508, significance 0.046.

The results for the total, and the environment and human resources themes, are significant ($p < 0.05$). Additionally, nine of the individual issues produced an association, of which five were significant ($p < 0.10$), as shown by Table VI. These nine issues recorded 401 (51 percent) of the positive annual report sentences and 457 (98 percent) of the unfavourable media articles.

	Spearman rank-order correlation coefficient	Significance (one-tailed test)
All themes	+0.9898	0.046
Environment	+0.6640	0.003
Energy	–	–
Human resources	+0.4604	0.042
Community involvement	–0.4901	0.032
Others	–	–

Table V.
Correlation by theme between positive annual report sentences and unfavourable media articles – *H2*

Note: This table correlates the number of annual report sentences over the 15 years of the study, with the number of media articles in the same year, for each theme; Sufficient data were not available to produce a correlation for the themes of energy (zero unfavourable media articles) and others (zero unfavourable media articles)

Individual issues	Spearman rank-order correlation coefficient	Significance (one-tailed test)
Environment		
Pollution (issue no. 1)	+0.3684	0.088
Standards and regulations (issue no. 2)	+0.8126	0.000
Prevent/repair damage (issue no. 4)	+0.5179	0.024
Review/impact studies (issue no. 14)	0.3167	0.125
Energy		
Human resources:		
Employee health and safety (issue no. 27)	+0.4188	0.060
Employment of minorities (issue no. 28)	–0.1590	0.286
Industrial relations (issue no. 35)	+0.3367	0.110
Other (issue no. 36)	+0.0577	0.419
Community involvement		
Aid or compensation (issue no. 47)	0.6274	0.006

Table VI.
Correlations between positive annual report sentences and number of unfavourable media articles for individual issues – *H2*

Note: This table correlates the number of annual report sentences over the 15 years of the study, with the number of unfavourable media articles in the same years, for each individual issue

Environment. At the general level of environment a Spearman's rank-order correlation coefficient 0.6640 is produced, significance $p = 0.003$. Three specific sub-issues are also strongly correlated ($p < 0.10$), namely:

(1) pollution (Spearman's rank-order coefficient of 0.3684, significance 0.088);

(2) standards and regulations (Spearman's rank-order coefficient of 0.8126, significance 0.000);

(3) prevention or repair of damage (Spearman's rank-order coefficient of 0.5179, significance 0.024).

The above three issues attracted the greatest amount of negative media attention and were also the issues within the theme of environment that recorded the greatest amount of positive annual report disclosure. The theme's results, and those of three major categories, offer support for *H2*.

Energy. Only 11 annual report sentences were provided in total across all years (all positive). Consistent with the hypothesis (and the minimal corporate disclosures) there were no negative media articles on the theme of energy for BHP, and consequently no association was derived. Hence, for this theme, there was no statistical support for *H2*.

Human resources. Prominent over the period were safety issues in the oil industry (1989), the Moura disaster (1995), and the proposed Newcastle plant closure (1997). Significant results were obtained for the overall total of the human resources theme (correlation 0.4604, significance 0.042) and health and safety issues (correlation 0.4188, significance 0.060). Health and safety issues attracted the greatest amount of negative media attention within the human resources theme as well as providing the greatest amount of positive annual report disclosures within the theme. The aggregate result for the human resources theme and the result for the sub-issue of health and safety support *H2*.

Community involvement. Similar to the overall total for this theme, unfavourable media articles and positive annual report responses are very infrequent, only occurring in a limited number of years. For eight of the 11 sub-issues within the community involvement theme there was no unfavourable media attention recorded in any of the years, with these same eight issues each attracting a maximum of one sentence of positive annual report disclosure across all the years of the study. The resulting association between the unfavourable media attention and the positive annual report disclosures is negative and hence not in accordance with *H2*. Despite the total theme result, the issue associated with aid or compensation to local communities affected by operations (e.g. Ok Tedi), produced a Spearman's rank-order correlation coefficient of 0.6274, significance 0.006. Issues associated with aid or compensation attracted the greatest amount of negative media attention within the community involvement theme. Hence while the results pertaining to the sub-issue of aid or compensation issues provides results consistent with *H2*, the results of the theme in total do not support *H2*.

6.4 *Time lags*

As prefaced earlier, one objective of this study is to examine the possible existence of time lag effects in social and environmental disclosure. Both Brown and Deegan (1998) and O'Donovan (1999) suggest that there could be time lags from media attention to eventual annual report disclosure, and this is explained on the basis that managers react to media attention. This is also consistent with media agenda setting theory which proposes that media attention precedes shifts in the "public agenda". Accordingly, testing was conducted again, relating media attention in time t, to annual report disclosure in time $t + 1$. The statistical results are presented in Tables VII and VIII[18].

For both hypotheses, the statistical relationship for human resources declined markedly, while the environment theme retained a comparatively stable relationship. However, the absence of significant relationships, and declines in the levels of association for the individual sub-issues of the environment, would suggest that, as for the human resource theme and issues, time lag effects are not in operation.

The community involvement theme now records associations in the expected direction for both hypotheses, with the $H1$ correlation of 0.364 significant, $p < 0.100$. However, this is entirely due to the aid and compensation issues reported in the 1997 annual report, relating to the (1996) Ok Tedi situation.

The finding that time lags did not operate appears quite reasonable. As indicated earlier in this paper, the annual reports of Australian companies

	Spearman rank-order correlation coefficient	Significance (one-tailed test)
Total	+0.3652	0.100
Environment	+0.6089	0.010
Human resources	+0.1881	0.260
Community involvement	+0.3642	0.100

Table VII.
Test results by theme
for time lags – *H1*

Note: This table correlates the number of annual report sentences over the 15 years of the study at time $t + 1$, with the number of media articles in the same years for time t, for each of the above themes

	Spearman rank-order correlation coefficient	Significance (one-tailed test)
Total	+0.3458	0.113
Environment	+0.5929	0.013
Human resources	+0.2616	0.183
Community involvement	+0.2129	0.232

Table VIII.
Test results by theme
for time lags – *H2*

Note: This table correlates the number of annual report sentences over the 15 years of the study at time $t + 1$, with the number of unfavourable media articles in the same years for time t, for each of the above themes

typically are not released for approximately ten weeks after balance date. As this study has recorded the media articles by financial year, this gives the companies at least ten weeks (and up to 62 weeks) to make social and environmental disclosures within the annual report in relation to the media attention.

7. Conclusions and implications

The results presented in the preceding section display the variable pattern of BHP's social disclosure over the period 1983 to 1997, the trend to providing greater levels of social and environmental information in recent years, and the disposition to provide mainly positive information. These results are in line with findings of previous research, as is the finding of a predominance of disclosure on the themes of human resources and environment. Marked increases in social disclosure occurred from 1989, and again from 1996.

The empirical testing supported the first hypothesis. The second hypothesis, proposing that management would release positive information in response to unfavourable media attention, was also confirmed. Support for both hypotheses was also found for many sub-issues within the various disclosure themes[19] (seven of the individual issues supported *H1*, and five supported *H2*). Generally speaking, those sub-issues which attracted the largest amount of media attention were also the issues which provided the greatest amount of annual report disclosures. These results, then, lend support to legitimation motives for a company's social disclosure and also support O'Donovan's (1999) conclusions that management make annual report disclosures in response to newspaper coverage[20].

The results appear to support the theorising of Hogner (1982) on US Steel's reporting, and also suggest that the limiting comments by Guthrie and Parker (1989) on the results of their study of BHP have foundation. In addition, results of the current study support conclusions of other recent studies of the relationship between community concern and corporate social disclosure (for example, Brown and Deegan, 1998), and offers evidence that the findings of O'Donovan (1999) on the perceived responses of management to media attention, is translated into actual social disclosure by the corporate management of BHP.

The findings described above, allied with those of O'Donovan (1999) and Brown and Deegan (1998) suggest some companies provide social disclosure information in their annual reports in response to perceived community concerns, as measured by media attention. Further studies, using similar variables to this one, would provide understanding of the extent to which these results are generalisable across other companies and industries. Research which investigated the impact of all forms of media on corporate social disclosure, would also be a contribution to the literature. Associated with that, it may be possible to examine corporate responses in communications other than the annual report.

In concluding the paper we can perhaps reflect on the implications of the findings. This paper, and a number of others, have provided evidence that managers disclose information to legitimise their organisations' place within society. This paper also provides evidence consistent with a view that greater media attention stimulates greater corporate disclosure. More specifically, when there is perceived to be adverse public opinion, reporting media such as the annual report are used in an endeavour to bring public opinion back in support of the company. Whether this strategy actually works is not something that we directly consider. There is a vast body of literature which shows that the media can shape community perceptions but there is a general absence of literature on how annual report disclosures, especially those relating to social and environmental issues, impact community concerns. This is an avenue for future research. Further research might consider whether particular disclosures are more successful in altering the opinions of some groups relative to others. Clearly, corporate management must believe that the disclosures make a difference (as O'Donovan's 1999 interviews indicate). Another avenue for research is to determine whether management considers that some stakeholder groups are more readily influenced by corporate disclosures. Are these groups the ones with which managers are seeking, through annual report disclosures, to establish legitimacy? Further, do managers tend to consider that some groups are more readily impacted by the mass media?

Whilst the paper to this point has been of a positive nature, seeking to provide explanation of particular disclosure practices, we can conclude the discussion by considering a normative issue. A broader point we can consider is whether legitimising activities, such as those relating to annual report disclosures, are beneficial to the community. Legitimising disclosures mean that the organisation is responding to particular concerns that have arisen in relation to their operations. The implication is that unless concerns are aroused (and importantly, the managers perceive the existence of such concerns) then unregulated disclosures could be quite minimal. Disclosure decisions driven by the desire to be legitimate are not the same as disclosure policies driven by a management view that the community has a right-to-know about certain aspects of an organisation's operations. One motivation relates to survival, whereas the other motivation relates to responsibility.

Arguably, companies that simply react to community concerns are not truly embracing a notion of accountability. Studies providing results consistent with legitimacy theory (and there are many of them) leave us with a view that unless specific concerns are raised then no accountability appears to be due. Unless community concern happens to be raised (perhaps as a result of a major social or environmental incident which attracts media attention), there will be little or no corporate disclosure.

We can return to the earlier point about the lack of evidence to show whether corporate disclosures actually impact or shape public perceptions. If they do, perhaps we can reflect upon whether that would necessarily be a good thing? Cooper and Sherer (1984) argue that legitimising disclosures simply act to sustain corporate operations which are of concern to some individuals within society. To the extent that the corporate social and environmental disclosures reflect or portray management concern as well as corporate moves towards actual change, the corporate disclosures may be merely forestalling any real changes in corporate activities. Some researchers see legitimising behaviour as potentially quite harmful, particularly if it legitimises activities that are not in the interests of particular groups within society. For example, Puxty (1991, p. 39) states:

A test of legitimacy theory

> I do not accept that I see legitimation as innocuous. It seems to me that the legitimation can be very harmful indeed, insofar as it acts as a barrier to enlightenment and hence progress.

335

Legitimising disclosures are linked to corporate survival. In jurisdictions such as Australia, where there are limited regulatory requirements to provide social and environmental information, management appear to provide information when they are coerced into doing so. Conversely, where there is limited concern, there will be limited disclosures. The evidence in this paper, and elsewhere, suggests that higher levels of disclosure will only occur when community concerns are aroused, or alternatively, until such time that specific regulation is introduced to eliminate managements' disclosure discretion. However, if corporate legitimising activities are successful then perhaps public pressure for government to introduce disclosure legislation will be low and managers will be able to retain control of their social and environmental reporting practices.

Notes

1. To put BHP Ltd in its broader context, as at 31 May 1997 BHP Ltd had total reported assets of A\$36,735 million and employed in excess of 61,000 employees (BHP Ltd 1997 Annual Report). In 2001, BHP was party to a merger and became BHP Billiton.

2. According to McCombs and Shaw (1994, p. 378) the dominant view in the mass communication literature prior to media agenda setting theory being embraced in the 1970s and thereafter, was that the media merely reinforces pre-existing attitudes. Since that time, however, agenda setting studies numbering in the hundreds (Shaw and Martin, 1992) have been undertaken and media agenda setting theory still remains a dominant theory in the mass communication literature.

3. This indicator was constructed by Ader (1993) from measures of air pollution, oil spills and solid waste disposals per year and was derived by reference to the publications *Environmental Quality* and *Characterization of Municipal Waste in the United States 1960-2000*.

4. Arguably, one might expect that many of the activities of large corporate entities, and the implications thereof, would be unobtrusive to the majority of people within a particular country (although this might not be the case in smaller "company towns") thereby enabling the media to shape opinions about large corporations.

5. Whilst we have explained the proposed linkage between the media agenda and the public agenda we have not explored the important issue of what actually drives the media agenda in the first place (for example, who are the "gatekeepers"?). This interesting issue is deemed to be outside the scope of this paper.

6. A major limitation of the Brown and Deegan (1998) study, and one that we attempt to overcome in this study, was that rather than considering specific environmental issues the authors identified all organisation-related environmental media articles and all annual report environmental disclosures of the sample companies and thereafter examined the association between the two. Specific environmental issues (such as pollution, and environmental awards) were not separately considered.

AAAJ
15,3

336

7. But of course, all theories of human behaviour can be expected to represent simplifications of reality given the complexity that is typically associated with human decision making processes.

8. Whilst the social contract is considered to be an implicit agreement, some of the expectations held by society, and therefore embodied within the "contract", will be codified in law and therefore explicit. As indicated previously, different managers will have different perceptions about what is embodied within the "social contract" and this different perception might, at least in part, explain why different policies are adopted by different organisations.

9. Consistent with the previous discussion in this paper, it should be acknowledged that legitimacy theory, as applied in the social and environmental reporting literature, generally suffers from an underdeveloped degree of resolution. Discussions of the relationship between societal values and perceptions of corporate operations implicitly assume that there is some form of unified public or societal opinion. This is a simplifying theoretical assumption, given that it is reasonable to accept that society is made up of different groups (or stakeholders) with different views and different abilities or powers to have their views "heard". Whilst we effectively maintain this simplifying assumption in this paper, we make a further assumption (untested) that the media will have an impact on people from different groups (consistent with Shaw and Martin, 1992), or perhaps more to the point, that managers believe that the media can impact a variety of audiences (towards the conclusion of this paper we raise this issue as one worthy of further research).

10. The other forces were: legal/regulatory requirements; industry and market standards; industry reputation; political opinion; pressure group attention; attitudes of customers, consumers, employees, investors, and the community.

11. Like a number of studies which have preceded this work, we also focus on the disclosures being made by the organisation and not the reactions of the readers of the information. Whilst we are not directly concerned with whether the disclosures have any actual impacts on community concerns it is nevertheless believed that this is an important area of research which has received relatively scant attention. As Ashforth and Gibbs (1990, p. 177) correctly state, "despite the problematic nature of legitimacy, most research on the construct has been confined to the means of legitimation and has overlooked the conditions under which such means are or are not successful. Previous work has implicitly assumed that the means indeed produce the desired effects."

12. For a discussion of this, see Krippendorff (1980, pp. 129-53). This measure expresses the level of agreement achieved among coders regarding the assignment of units to categories.

13. Choosing 1983 as the starting point of the analysis was fairly arbitrary and was dictated by the fact that we wanted to collect data across a reasonable number of years. We decided to collect data for 15 years, hence we started in 1983. As it turned out, the ABIX data was only available electronically for periods from 1982, hence for practical purposes we have used all the media data that was available, other than for 1982.

14. That is, a score of one was given to each media article that related to a specific issue regardless of the location or prominence of the article. No explicit consideration was given to whether the respective articles were on the front page, the back page, or in the middle of the paper/magazine, and further, no explicit consideration was given to the size of the headline, or the size of the article. It has also been assumed that all the papers/magazines used in the analysis have the same ability to impact community expectations. Whilst the above assumptions might be considered to be simplistic there is little available guidance from the mass media literature upon which to develop a weighting scheme. Future research might consider this issue.

15. The "years" referred to the financial years of BHP Ltd, which run from 1 June to 31 May. As annual reports are generally released up to ten weeks after balance date this gives the organisation up to ten weeks to determine what they will include in the annual report. For issues that are raised by the media early in the financial year the company has more time to determine how it will respond. This does raise the point that where particular issues

have been raised by the media early in the financial year then the company may wish to make a more timely response in media other than the annual report. However, in this study we have restricted our focus to annual reports. Nevertheless, further research might consider this issue.

16. Employee profiles recorded 55 annual report sentences (average 3.6 per year), employee share schemes 43 (average three per year), and other social responsibility disclosures 36, primarily from occasional mission statements.

17. This again supports the view that the media is more likely to write a story that is critical of the company, rather than one that is positive in attitude. If this is the case and represents an actual bias then this is somewhat of a pity because just as bad performance should be criticised, good performance should arguably be praised.

18. Energy and "Other" were not considered given the low amount of media attention and disclosure.

19. Of the total 49 issues being examined, 15 provided a measure of correlation. The remaining 34 issues only attracted 18 media articles over the 15-year period for BHP, and in line with the hypotheses of this study, a correlation with annual report sentences was therefore not expected.

20. This in itself potentially shows that individuals or groups seeking greater corporate disclosure should, as one strategy, explore the possibility of trying to influence the media agenda. As noted previously, however, how the media agenda is "controlled" is not an issue we investigate in this paper.

References

Ader, C.R. (1993), "A longitudinal study of agenda setting for the issue of environmental pollution", *Journalism and Mass Communication Quarterly*, Vol. 72 No. 2, Summer, pp. 300-11.

Ashforth, B.E. and Gibbs, B.W. (1990), "The double-edge of organisational legitimation", *Organization Science*, Vol. 1 No. 2, pp. 177-94.

Blood, R.W. (1981), "Unobtrusive issues and the agenda-setting role of the press", unpublished doctoral dissertation, Syracuse University, New York, NY.

Bogart, L. (1984), "The public's use and perception of newspapers", *Public Opinion Quarterly*, Vol. 48, Winter, pp. 709-19.

Brosius, H. and Kepplinger, H. (1990), "The agenda setting function of television news: static and dynamic views", *Communication Research*, Vol. 17 No. 2, pp. 183-211.

Brown, N. and Deegan, C.M. (1998), "The public disclosure of environmental performance information – a dual test of media agenda setting theory and legitimacy theory", *Accounting and Business Research*, Vol. 29 No. 1, pp. 21-41.

Buhr, N. (1998), "Environmental performance, legislation and annual report disclosure: the case of acid rain and Falconbridge", *Accounting, Auditing & Accountability Journal*, Vol. 11 No. 2, pp. 163-90.

Cooper, D. and Sherer, M. (1984), "The value of corporate accounting reports – arguments for a political economy of accounting", *Accounting, Organizations and Society*, Vol. 9 Nos 3/4, pp. 207-32.

Dearing, J.W. and Rogers, E.M. (1996), *Agenda Setting*, Sage Publications, Thousand Oaks, CA.

Deegan, C.M. and Gordon, B. (1996), "A study of the environmental disclosure practices of Australian corporations", *Accounting and Business Research*, Vol. 26 No. 3, pp. 187-99.

Deegan, C.M. and Rankin, M. (1996), "Do Australian companies report environmental news objectively? An analysis of environmental disclosures by firms prosecuted successfully by the environmental protection authority", *Accounting, Auditing & Accountability Journal*, Vol. 9 No. 2, pp. 50-67.

Deegan, C. and Rankin, M. (1997), "The materiality of environmental information to users of accounting reports", *Accounting, Auditing & Accountability Journal*, Vol. 10 No. 4, pp. 562-83.

Deegan, C., Rankin, M. and Voght, P. (2000) "Firms' disclosure reactions to major social incidents: Australian evidence", *Accounting Forum*, Vol. 24 No. 1, March, pp. 101-30.

Dowling, J. and Pfeffer, J. (1975), "Organisational legitimacy: social values and organisational behaviour", *Pacific Sociological Review*, Vol. 18 No. 1, pp. 122-36.

Ernst & Ernst (1978), *Social Responsibility Disclosure: Surveys of Fortune 500 Annual Reports*, Ernst & Ernst, Cleveland, OH.

Eyal, C.H., Winter, J.P. and DeGeorge, W.F. (1981), "The concept of time frame in agenda setting", Wilhoit, G.C. (Ed.), *Mass Communication Yearbook*, Vol. 2, Sage, Beverly Hills, CA.

Funkhouser, G.R. (1973), "The issues of the sixties: an exploratory study in the dynamics of public opinion", *Public Opinion Quarterly*, Vol. 37 No. 1, pp. 62-75.

Gray, R., Kouhy, R. and Lavers, S. (1995a), "Corporate social and environmental reporting: a review of the literature and a longitudinal study of UK disclosure", *Accounting, Auditing & Accountability Journal*, Vol. 8 No. 2, pp. 47-77.

Gray, R., Kouhy, R. and Lavers, S. (1995b), "Methodological themes: constructing a research database of social and environmental reporting by UK companies", *Accounting, Auditing & Accountability Journal*, Vol. 8 No. 2, pp. 78-101.

Guthrie, J. (1982), "Social accounting in Australia: social responsibility disclosure in the top 150 listed Australian vompanies' 1980 Annual Reports", unpublished Masters dissertation, West Australian Institute of Technology, Perth.

Guthrie, J. and Parker, L. (1989), "Corporate social reporting: a rebuttal of legitimacy theory", *Accounting and Business Research*, Vol. 19 No. 76, pp. 343-52.

Guthrie, J. and Parker, L.D. (1990), "Corporate social disclosure practice: a comparative international analysis", *Advances in Public Interest Accounting*, Vol. 3, pp. 159-76.

Hackston, D. and Milne, J.M. (1996), "Some determinants of social and environmental disclosures in New Zealand companies", *Accounting, Auditing & Accountability Journal*, Vol. 9 No. 1, pp. 77-108.

Harte, G. and Owen, D. (1991), "Environmental disclosure in the annual reports of British companies: a research note", *Accounting, Auditing & Accountability Journal*, Vol. 4 No. 3, pp. 51-61.

Hogner, R.H. (1982), "Corporate social reporting: eight decades of development at US Steel", *Research in Corporate Performance and Policy*, Vol. 4, pp. 243-50.

Hurst, J.W. (1970), *The Legitimacy of the Business Corporation in the Law of the United States 1780-1970*, The University Press of Virginia, Charlottesville, VI.

Ingram, R.W. and Frazier, K.B. (1980), "Environmental performance and corporate disclosure", *Journal of Accounting Research*, Vol. 18 No. 2, Autumn, pp. 614-22.

Krippendorff, K. (1980), *Content Analysis: An Introduction to Its Methodology*, Sage, Beverly Hills, CA.

Lindblom, C.K. (1994), "The implications of organizational legitimacy for corporate social performance and disclosure", *Critical Perspectives on Accounting Conference*, New York, NY.

Lippmann, W. (1965), *Public Opinion*, Collier-Macmillan Canada, Toronto.

McCombs, M. (1981), The Agenda-Setting Approach, in Nimmo, D. and Sanders, K. (Eds), *Handbook of Political Communication*, Sage Publications, Beverly Hills, CA, pp. 121-40.

McCombs, M. and Shaw, D. (1972), "The agenda setting function of the mass media", *Public Opinion Quarterly*, Vol. 36, pp. 176-87.

McCombs, M. and Shaw, D. (1994), "Agenda-setting function", in Griffin, E.M. (Ed.), *A First Look at Communication Theory*, 2nd ed., McGraw-Hill, New York, NY.

McCombs, M., Danielian, L. and Wanta, W. (1995), "Issues in the news and the public agenda: the agenda-setting tradition", in Glasser, T.L. and Salmon, C.T. (Eds), *Public Opinion and the Communication of Consent*, Guildford Press, New York, NY, pp. 281-300.

Neu, D., Warsame, H. and Pedwell, K. (1998), "Managing public impressions: environmental disclosures in annual reports", *Accounting, Organizations & Society*, Vol. 23 No. 3, pp. 265-82.

Neuman, W.R. (1990), "The threshold of public attention", *Public Opinion Quarterly*, Vol. 54, pp. 159-76.

O'Donovan, G. (1999), "Managing legitimacy through increased corporate environmental reporting: an exploratory study", *Interdisciplinary Environmental Review*, Vol. 1 No. 1, pp. 63-99.

Pang, Y.H. (1982), "Disclosures of corporate social responsibility", *The Chartered Accountant in Australia*, July, pp. 32-4.

Patten, D.M. (1992), "Intra-industry environmental disclosures in response to the Alaskan oil spill: a note on legitimacy theory", *Accounting, Organisations and Society*, Vol. 17, July, pp. 471-75.

Puxty, A. (1991), "Social accountability and universal pragmatics", *Advances in Public Interest Accounting*, Vol. 4, pp. 35-46.

Salwen, M.B. (1988), "Effect of accumulation of coverage on issue salience in agenda setting", *Journalism Quarterly*, Vol. 65, pp. 101-6.

Schoenbach, K. and Semetko, H. A. (1992), "Agenda-setting, agenda-reinforcing or agenda-deflating? A study of the 1990 national election", *Journalism Quarterly*, Vol. 69 No. 4, Winter, pp. 837-46.

Severin, W.J. and Tankard, J.W. (1992), *Communication Theories: Origins, Methods, Uses in the Mass Media*, 3rd ed., Longman, New York, NY.

Shaw, D.L. and Martin, S.E. (1992), "The function of mass media communication", *Journalism Quarterly*, Vol. 69 No. 4, pp. 902-20.

Shocker, A.D. and Sethi, S.P. (1974), "An approach to incorporating social preferences in developing corporate action strategies", in Sethi, S.P. (Ed.), *The Unstable Ground: Corporate Social Policy in a Dynamic Society*, Melville, Los Angeles, CA.

Smith, K.A. (1987), "Newspaper coverage and public concern about community issues: a time-series analysis", *Journalism Monographs*, No. 101, February.

Solomon, A. and Lewis, L. (2001), "Incentives and disincentives for corporate environmental reporting", *Asian Pacific Interdisciplinary Research in Accounting Conference*, Adelaide, July.

Stempel, G.H. III and Hargrove, T (1996), "Mass media audiences in a changing media environment", *J&MC Quarterly*, Vol. 73 No. 3, Autumn, pp. 549-58.

Stone, G. and McCombs, M. (1981), "Tracing the time lag in agenda-setting", *Journalism Quarterly*, Vol. 58 No. 1, pp. 51-5.

Tilt, C.A. (1994), "The influence of external pressure groups on corporate social disclosure: some empirical evidence", *Accounting, Auditing & Accountability Journal*, Vol. 7 No. 4, pp. 47-72.

Trumbo, C. (1995), "Longitudinal modeling of public issues: an application of the agenda-setting process to the issue of global warming", *J&MC Monographs*, No. 152, August.

Weber, R.P. (1985), *Basic Content Analysis*, Sage Publications, Beverly Hills, CA.

Winter, J. and Eyal, C. (1981), "Agenda-setting for the civil rights issue", *Public Opinion Quarterly*, Vol. 45, pp. 376-83.

Zucker, H.G. (1978), "The variable nature of news media influence", in Ruben, B.D. (Ed.), *Communication Yearbook 2*, New Brunswick, NJ, pp. 235-46.

AAAJ
15,3

340

Appendix. Categories of social and environmental disclosure used in this study (49 in total)

  A. Environment

  Environmental pollution

1. pollution control in the conduct of the business operations; capital, operating and research and development expenditures for pollution abatement;

2. statements indicating that the company's operations are in compliance with environmental laws and regulations; *recognition of the need to comply with society standards and regulations;*

3. statements indicating that pollution from operations has been or will be reduced;

4. prevention or repair of damage to the environment resulting from processing or natural resources, e.g. land reclamation or reforestation, *e.g. OK Tedi and its results;*

5. conservation or natural resources, e.g. recycling glass, metals, oil, water and paper;

6. using, *or researching,* recycled materials;

7. efficiently using materials resources in the manufacturing process;

8. supporting anti-litter campaigns;

9. receiving an award relating to the company's environmental programmes or policies;

10. preventing waste.

  Aesthetics

11. designing facilities harmonious with the environment;

12. contributions in terms of cash or art/sculptures to beautify the environment;

13. restoring historical buildings/structures.

  Other

14. undertaking environmental impact studies to monitor the company's impact on the environment; *conducting reviews of performance, employing specialist consultants;*

15. wildlife conservation;

16. training employees in environmental issues.

  B. Energy

17. conservation of energy in the conduct of business operations;

18. using energy more efficiently during the manufacturing process;

19. utilising waste materials for energy production;

20. disclosing energy savings resulting from product recycling;

21. discussing the company's efforts to reduce energy consumption;

22. disclosing increased energy efficiency of products;

23. research aimed at improving energy efficiency of products;

24. receiving an award for an energy conservation programme;

25. voicing the company's concern about the energy shortage;

26. disclosing the company's energy policies.

  C. Human resources

27. Employee health and safety. This broad category includes issues associated with:

- reducing or eliminating pollutants, irritants, or hazards in the work environment;
- promoting employee safety and physical or mental health;
- disclosing accident statistics;
- complying with health and safety standards and regulations;
- receiving a safety award;
- establishing a safety department/committee/policy;
- conducting research to improve work safety;
- providing low cost health care for employees;
- *compensation, litigation or enquiries, related to safety;*
- *providing information on industrial action related to health and safety.*

28. Employment of minorities or women. This broad category includes issues associated with:
   - recruiting or employing racial minorities and/or women;
   - disclosing percentage or number of minority and/or women employees in the workforce and/or in the various managerial levels;
   - *employment of youth or local community personnel;*
   - *information on apprenticeship schemes;*
   - establishing goals for minority representation in the workforce;
   - programme for the advancement of minorities in the workplace;
   - employment of other special interest groups, e.g. the handicapped, ex-convicts or former drug addicts;
   - disclosures about internal advancement statistics.

29. Employee training. This broad category includes issues associated with:
   - training employees through in-house programmes;
   - giving financial assistance to employees in educational institutions or continuing education courses;
   - establishment of trainee centres.

30. Employee assistance/benefits. This broad category includes issues associated with:
   - providing assistance or guidance to employees who are in the process of retiring or who have been made redundant;
   - providing staff accommodation/staff home ownership schemes;
   - *providing scholarships for employees' children;*
   - providing recreational activities/facilities.

31. Employee remuneration. This broad category includes issues associated with:
   - providing amount and/or percentage figures for salaries, wages, PAYE taxes, superannuation;
   - *disclosing workers compensation arrangements;*
   - any policies/objectives/reasons for the company's remuneration package/ schemes.

32. Employee profiles. This broad category includes issues associated with:

AAAJ
15,3

342

- providing the number of employees in the company and/or at each branch/subsidiary;
- providing the occupations/managerial levels involved;
- providing the disposition of staff – where the staff are stationed and the number involved;
- providing statistics on the number of staff, the length of service in the company and their age groups;
- providing per employee statistics, e.g. assets per employee and sales per employee;
- providing information on the qualifications of employees recruited.

33. Employee share purchase schemes. This broad category includes issues associated with:

- providing information on the existence of or amount and value of shares offered to employees under a share purchase scheme or pension programme;
- providing any other profit sharing schemes.

34. Employee morale. This broad category includes issues associated with:

- providing information on the company/management's relationships with the employees in an effort to improve job satisfaction and employee motivation;
- *expressing appreciation or recognition of the employees;*
- *seeking employees' opinions and input to planning;*
- providing information on the stability of the workers' jobs and the company's future;
- providing information on the availability of a separate employee report;
- providing information about any awards for effective communication with employees;
- providing information about communication with employees on management styles and management programmes which may directly affect the employees.

35. Industrial relations. This broad category includes issues associated with:

- reporting on the company's relationship with trade unions and/or workers;
- *reporting on agreements reached for pay and other conditions;*
- reporting on any strikes, industrial actions/activities and the resultant losses in terms of time and productivity;
- providing information on how industrial action was reduced/negotiated.

36. Other. This broad category includes issues associated with:

- improvements to the general working conditions – both in the factories and for the office staff;
- information on the re-organisation of the company/discussions/branches which affect the staff in any way;
- the closing down of any part of the organisation, the resultant redundancies created, and any relocation/retraining efforts made by the company to retain staff;
- *reporting industrial action associated with a reduction in employees;*
- information and statistics on employee turnover;
- information about support for day-care, maternity and paternity leave.

D.   Community involvement

37.   Donations of cash, products or employee services to support established community activities, events, organisations, education and the arts.

38.   Summer or part-time employment of students.

39.   Sponsoring public health projects.

40.   Aiding medical research.

41.   Sponsoring educational conferences, seminars or art exhibits.

42.   Funding scholarship programmes or activities.

43.   Other special community related activities, e.g. *providing civic amenities, supporting town planning.*

44.   Supporting national pride/government sponsored campaigns.

45.   Supporting the development of local industries or community programmes and activities.

46.   *Recognising local and indigenous communities.*

47.   *Providing aid or compensation to communities around their operations.*

E.   Others

48.   Corporate objectives/policies: general disclosure of corporate objectives/policies relating to the social responsibility of the company to the various segments of society; *disclosing corporate governance practices.*

49.   Other disclosing/reporting to groups in society other than shareholders and employees, e.g. consumers, any other information that relates to the social responsibility of the company.

(Adapted from Hackston and Milne (1996), with changes in italics).

A test of
legitimacy
theory

343

[23]

© 1996 American Accounting Association
Accounting Horizons
Vol. 10 No. 1
March 1996
pp. 38–57

Interdependencies in the Global Markets for Capital and Information: The Case of Smithkline Beecham plc

Carol A. Frost and Grace Pownall

Carol A. Frost is Associate Professor at Washington University (St. Louis) and Grace Pownall is Professor at Emory University.

SYNOPSIS: This study analyzes SmithKline Beecham plc's equity characteristics and accounting disclosures in the U.S. and the U.K. We examine non-accounting and accounting explanations for the price differences among SmithKline Beecham's (SK's) equities traded in the U.S. and the U.K., and investigate the claim that U.S. and U.K. accounting principle differences impair the ability of U.S. investors to assess the information contained in SK's earnings disclosures.

Several non-accounting factors are consistent with the observed price differences between SK's A Shares and Equity Units, including differential dividend cash flows, liquidity differences, and what financial analysts call "investor sentiment." In contrast, we find little support for the argument that U.S./U.K. accounting differences cause the price differences, or that U.S. investors are confused by SK's U.K. GAAP disclosures. It is true that SK's earnings based on U.K. GAAP have been greater than SK's U.S. GAAP earnings in every year since the merger, and that information about SK's U.K. GAAP earnings does not appear to be useful for predicting what SK's U.S. GAAP earnings will be. However, our stock price analyses indicate that U.S. investors use information about SK's U.K. GAAP earnings in valuing SK, and that the U.S. market response to SK's disclosures of U.K. GAAP earnings is similar to the U.K. market response. Thus, U.S. investors do not appear to be confused by U.S./U.K. GAAP differences, and in fact use information about U.K. GAAP earnings in their valuations of SK.

Data Availability: Data used in this paper are from publicly available sources.

I. INTRODUCTION

The purpose of this paper is to explore information dissemination and price discovery in global capital markets by investigating the relations among equity characteristics (such as prices, trading activity, liquidity and shareholder clienteles) and firms' accounting disclosures. The investigation is conducted in the context of a single global firm, SmithKline Beecham plc (SK). SK is one of the world's largest health-care corporations, with equity listed in the U.K., the U.S. and Japan.

Several recent articles have noted large price and return differences between SK's equity traded on the New York Stock Exchange (NYSE) and the International Stock Exchange

in London (ISE) (e.g., *Accountancy* 1992; *Management Today* 1989). For example, *The Economist* (1991) reports: "SmithKline

We are grateful for the generous financial support of the John M. Olin School of Business at Washington University (St. Louis) and the Roberto C. Goizueta Business School at Emory University and for comments and suggestions from Linda Bamber, Christine Czekai, Nick Dopuch, Feng Gu, Pat McQueen, Terry Warfield, John Wild and participants in accounting research workshops at Washington University (St. Louis), the Universities of Alabama, Illinois and Wisconsin–Madison, and the AAA/ KPMG Peat Marwick Foundation International Accounting Research Conference. We also thank Greg DeNinno for research assistance, Ron Harris for programming assistance, and SmithKline Beecham staff in Philadelphia and London for many helpful discussions.

Submitted September 1995
Accepted December 1995

Beecham …has just announced its third quarter results. The price of its shares increased by 2.5 percent in London; on Wall Street, by 6 percent. Despite the leap, SK still sells for far less in America than in Britain, and its managers are increasingly unhappy about it."

SK's Finance Director argues that a "communication difficulty" and "contradictory accounting standards" cause the discrepancy between U.S. and U.K. share prices (*Accountancy* 1992; Collum 1991). *The Economist* (1991) points out that because SK's earnings based on U.S. generally accepted accounting principles (GAAP) are lower than U.K. GAAP earnings, the U.K. shares may trade at higher prices than the U.S. shares.

Accounting explanations for SK's share price differences seem inconsistent with the notion that world capital markets are informationally efficient and globally integrated. Commentators assert (e.g. Scarlata 1993, Greenspan 1988) that global capital markets rapidly impound new information, that news affecting a company's equity in one location will be promptly reflected in that firm's share prices everywhere, and that the valuation implications of public information do not depend on where the information is released or where the equities trade.[1] However, there is scant evidence on characteristics of SK's equities and how the firm's disclosures become reflected in its equity prices worldwide.

We therefore focus on two questions. First, do non-accounting factors (such as dividend cash flows) rather than U.S./U.K. GAAP differences explain SK's share price differences? Second, do U.S. investors promptly use information in SK's disclosures, whether based on U.S. or U.K. GAAP, in their valuation decisions? We expect that non-accounting factors do explain SK's share price differences, and that U.S. shareholders do not behave as if they are confused by GAAP differences, but in fact use information about U.K. GAAP earnings in their valuation of SK.

Valid hypotheses tests concerning causes of observed price differences are difficult to design, since many interrelated factors influence SK's share prices, and isolating the causal effect of any one factor is difficult. We therefore present relevant information for assessing whether selected explanations are plausible, but do not attempt to formally test hypotheses about those explanations.

The evidence in this study is relevant for evaluating timely disclosure and conformity of disclosure rules in international equity markets. Conformity of disclosure rules in the U.S., the U.K. and Japan require foreign-listed firms to immediately disclose locally what they disclose in their home market and other markets where their equities are traded.[2] However, foreign firms are not required to provide additional information in their timely disclosures that would help local investors interpret their announcements.

This study begins by documenting the prices, returns and trading volume of SK's equity securities to provide evidence on the nature of the company's so-called equity problems. We then investigate both non-accounting and accounting explanations for the observed price differences. Non-accounting explanations are related to dividend cash flows, share liquidity and investor sentiment. Accounting explanations are related to differences between U.S. and U.K. GAAP, differences between SK's U.S. and U.K. accounting disclosures, and differences in how U.S. and U.K. investors interpret those disclosures.

---

[1] Barriers to global financial market integration have also been discussed and analyzed extensively. See, for example, Aggarwal and Schirm (1995), Frankel (1994), Alexander et al. (1987), Gultekin et al. (1989) and Jorion and Schwartz (1986).

[2] The SEC requires foreign issuers in the U.S. to promptly furnish whatever information the issuer (1) is required to make public in its home country, (2) has filed with foreign stock exchanges on which its securities are traded, or (3) has distributed to its security holders (SEC 1984). The ISE requires foreign issuers to promptly furnish the Company Announcements Office all information publicly released to other stock exchanges (ISE 1993a, sec. 17.30), and the Tokyo Stock Exchange (TSE) requires foreign issuers to announce business results without delay after announcement in the issuer's home country (TSE 1991). The conformity of disclosure rules suggest that securities regulators assume that local investors do not have immediate or low-cost access (either directly or indirectly) to information disclosed overseas. Frost and Pownall (1995) provide evidence relevant for assessing this assumption.

In a final set of analyses we examine the U.S. and U.K. market responses to SK's accounting disclosures made in the two markets. The evidence is relevant for assessing the claim that U.S. investors have difficulty interpreting SK's accounting numbers, and for assessing whether U.S. investors use different information in making valuation decisions at the time of earnings announcements than do U.K. investors.

The rest of this paper is organized as follows. Section II presents evidence on SK's equities traded in the U.S. and the U.K.[3] Non-accounting and accounting explanations for the observed price differences among SK's different types of equity are examined in sections III and IV, respectively. Section V presents evidence on the U.S. and U.K. market responses to SK's earnings disclosures, and a summary and conclusions are in section VI.

II. EQUITY CHARACTERISTICS
A. Description of A Shares and Equity Units

SmithKline Beecham plc incorporated in the U.K. in July 1989 to combine the businesses of SmithKline Beckman Corp. in the U.S. and Beecham Group plc in the U.K. The company devised a complex share structure so that U.S. shareholders, who initially owned about 50 percent of the merged firm, would receive dollar dividends which would not be subject to withholding of U.K. Advanced Corporation Tax. "A Shares" were issued to U.K. shareholders, and "Equity Units" were issued to U.S. shareholders. Holders of A Shares and Equity Units have the same voting rights, and SK's Articles of Association contain special provisions to equalize the dividend rights of one A Share and one Equity Unit (e.g., see SK's 1993 Form 20-F, page 70).[4] Since A Shares and Equity Units are distinct equity types, conversion of an equity ownership claim from one type to another is not possible.

SK's A Shares and Equity Units began trading on the ISE and on the NYSE (as ADRs) on July 27, 1989, the merger date. Currently, A Shares, A Share ADRs, Equity Units, and Equity Unit ADRs are traded in London. Both types of ADR are listed on the NYSE, and A

Shares and Equity Units are traded OTC in the U.S. The company listed its A Shares on the Tokyo Stock Exchange (TSE) on December 4, 1991.

B. Equity Prices and Returns

We obtained U.S. and U.K. market data for July 1989 to August 1994 from Tradeline for SK A Shares, Equity Units, A Share ADRs and Equity Unit ADRs. For each of the four equity types, we collected U.S. and U.K. daily transaction prices, bid-ask quotes and trading volume. Daily return vectors were calculated for each of the eight series using transaction prices for days during which the security traded in the market associated with that vector, and the midpoint of the bid-ask quote on non-trading days, all amounts expressed in U.S. dollars. We obtained daily prices for the FTSE 100 index (the primary ISE market index) from Tradeline, and for the Value Weighted NYSE/ASE index from CRSP.[5] The

---

[3] We analyzed SK's A Shares traded in Japan, its media disclosures released in Japan, and financial documents SK filed with Japan's Ministry of Finance (MOF). TSE daily prices and volume were obtained from Nikkei Telecom I for the period December 1991 to August 1994. However, A Shares trade so infrequently in Japan that several of the stock price analyses would not be meaningful. For example, from May 1, 1992 to May 1, 1993, A Shares traded in Japan on only 34 days. We therefore do not include evidence from Japan in discussion of our primary tests.

[4] For more information about SK's complex share arrangement, see *Management Today* (1989), *Accountancy* (1992), *The Economist* (1989, 1991), *European Chemical News* (1989), and SK's Forms 20-F filed with the SEC. At the merger date, an Equity Unit (EU) consisted of five B shares plus a preference share, which together were "equivalent" to five A shares. The shares were split and the EUs restructured in 1992 so that one A Share is now equivalent to one EU (in terms of ownership claim and shareholder rights).

[5] We use the Financial Times Stock Exchange (FTSE) 100 index as the U.K. market index because it accounts for about 70 percent of the total market value of all U.K. equities, and shows a very close correlation with the most broad index of the market (Lederman and Park 1991). Also, SK is a component of the FTSE 100 index. A comparable U.S. index is the Standard and Poor's 500 Index, which represents about 80 percent of the total market value on the NYSE, and is commonly considered the benchmark against which the performance of individual stocks is measured (Downes and Goodman 1990). However, because SK is not a component of the S&P 500, we chose the closely comparable NYSE/ASE CRSP value-weighted index, since it does have SK as one of its component stocks.

A Share and Equity Unit price vectors generated by OTC trading in the U.S. have numerous observations with bids only. These bid quotes were used as prices, but we report results from analyses of these equity types selectively, since the vectors probably contain substantial measurement error. Weekly returns for use in some analyses were constructed from the Wednesday observations each week, and monthly returns were constructed from observations at the last day of each month.

Table 1 presents evidence on price differences among several SK equity types, both within and across the U.K. and U.S. markets, for the full sample period (panel A) and for two subperiods, July 1989 to December 1991 and January 1992 to August 1994 (panel B). Our goal is to identify whether price differences exist between A Shares and EUs irrespective of the trading markets, and whether price differences exist between trading mar-

kets irrespective of the equity type. Analyzing price differences in two subperiods provides evidence on whether SK's equity prices are converging or diverging across time.

Rows 1–3 of table 1 show that A Share prices exceeded EU and EU ADR prices for all days in the sample period, in both cross-country and within-country comparisons. The mean price differences are all above U.S. $5.00, or over 15 percent of the mean A Share price in the U.K. of U.S. $32.84. Rows 4–7 of table 1 show that, in contrast, mean price differences between U.S. and U.K. A Shares (or ADRs) are close to zero, as are mean price differences between U.S. and U.K. EUs (or EU ADRs).[6] Thus, the systematic price differences are not between SK's U.S. and U.K. equities (when comparisons involve similar types of equity in the two markets), but rather between

[6] For parsimony, we do not present all possible comparisons in table 1. However, comparisons presented in table 1 are representative of those not shown.

TABLE 1
Share Price Differences Among SmithKline Beecham's Equity Securities[1]

Panel A: Full Sample Period
July 1989 to August 1994
(All Amounts are in $U.S.)

	N	Mean	Median	Min.	Max.	Std. Dev.
A Shares and Equity Units						
1. UK A Share minus US EU ADR	1334	5.34	4.69	1.29	11.36	2.34
2. US A Share minus US EU ADR	1066	5.56	4.92	0.92	11.59	2.47
3. UK A Share minus UK EU	1334	5.20	4.52	2.06	10.16	2.11
A Shares						
4. UK A Share minus US A ADR	1334	0.05	0.08	−3.00	2.36	0.53
5. UK A ADR minus US A ADR	1331	−0.02	0.00	−9.50	4.25	0.75
Equity Units						
6. UK EU minus US EU ADR	1334	0.14	0.12	−3.85	3.75	0.57
7. UK EU ADR minus US EU ADR	1331	0.06	0.00	−4.99	4.50	0.72

(Continued on next page)

TABLE 1 (Continued)

Panel B: Two Subperiods
Subperiod 1: July 1989 to December 1991
Subperiod 2: January 1992 to August 1994
(All Amounts are in $U.S.)

A Shares and Equity Units		N	Mean	Median	Min.	Max.	Std. Dev.
1. UK A Share minus US EU ADR	period 1	635	6.28	6.31	1.41	10.94	2.36
	period 2	699	4.49	4.01	1.29	11.36	1.97
2. US A Share minus US EU ADR	period 1	367	7.74	8.12	0.92	11.59	1.78
	period 2	699	4.41	3.92	1.32	11.09	1.95
3. UK A Share minus UK EU	period 1	635	6.11	6.03	2.30	10.16	2.09
	period 2	699	4.38	3.97	2.06	9.26	1.76
A Shares							
4. UK A Share minus US A ADR	period 1	635	0.01	0.06	−3.00	2.29	0.59
	period 2	699	0.08	0.09	−2.50	2.36	0.46
5. UK A ADR minus US A ADR	period 1	632	−0.04	0.00	−3.50	2.50	0.70
	period 2	699	0.00	0.00	−9.50	4.25	0.80
Equity Units							
6. UK EU minus US EU ADR	period 1	635	0.17	0.21	−3.85	3.28	0.64
	period 2	699	0.11	0.09	−1.57	3.75	0.49
7. UK EU ADR minus US EU ADR	period 1	632	0.04	0.00	−3.62	3.38	0.73
	period 2	699	0.09	0.05	−4.99	4.50	0.70

UK A Share	=	A Shares traded on the ISE in the U.K.
UK EU	=	Equity Units traded on the ISE in the U.K.
UK A ADR	=	A Share ADRs traded on the ISE in the U.K.
UK EU ADR	=	Equity Unit ADRs traded on the ISE in the U.K.
US A ADR	=	A Share ADRs traded on the NYSE in the U.S.
US EU ADR	=	Equity Unit ADRs traded on the NYSE in the U.S.
US A Share	=	A Shares traded OTC in the U.S.

[1] Prices are close prices or midpoints of bid/ask spreads. Prices for A Shares traded OTC in the U.S. are bids. In comparisons of share and ADR prices, share prices are multiplied by 5 in order to make them comparable to ADRs. Data for the two week period surrounding the share split, July 13, 1992 through July 28, 1992 are deleted. Mean (median) prices of A Shares and EUs traded in the U.K. were U.S. $32.84 (31.99) and $28.47 (28.31), respectively.

A Shares and EUs, both between and within the U.S. and the U.K.[7] Note, however, that maximum price differences during this period (even for the same instrument across the two countries) are at least U.S. $2.36.

Evidence in rows 1–3 of panel B suggests that A Share/EU prices converged during the sample period. For all three comparisons presented, mean and median subperiod 2 A Share/EU price differences (January 1992 to August 1994) are smaller than mean and median subperiod 1 A Share/EU price differences

[7] In a related analysis, Rosenthal and Young (1992) present evidence on "anomalous" price behavior of shares of the parents of Royal Dutch/Shell and Unilever NV/PLC. Both groups' corporate charters specify the division of distributable cash flows, implying an expected ratio for the market prices for their securities. The authors document persistent differences from the expected price ratios on both the NYSE and ISE. Also see Froot and Dabora (1995).

(July 1989 to December 1991). Mean price differences are significantly smaller in subperiod 2 than in subperiod 1, with all three subperiod differences (rows 1–3) significant at p-values of 0.0001, two-sided tests. This observed convergence in prices is discussed in section III.

Table 2 presents daily, weekly and monthly Spearman pairwise return correlations of SK's most actively traded equity types (A Shares and EUs in the U.K., and A Share ADRs and EU ADRs in the U.S.), and the U.S. and U.K.

market indices. All correlations are positive and significant at the 0.0001 level or better, two-sided tests. Panel A shows that the within-country daily return correlations of A Shares and EUs in the U.K., and A Share ADRs and EU ADRs in the U.S. are 0.90 and 0.81, respectively. The four pairwise cross-country correlations are lower, ranging from 0.58 to 0.67. Panel B of table 2 shows that the two within-country and four cross-country weekly return correlations are each larger

TABLE 2
Spearman Correlations of SmithKline Beecham plc's Stock Returns[1]
December 1991 to August 1994
(Significance levels for all correlations are at .0001 or better)

Panel A: Daily Returns

	UK A Share	UK EU	US A ADR	US EU ADR	FTSE 100	NYSE Index
UK A Share	1.00					
UK EU	0.90	1.00				
US A ADR	0.67	0.62	1.00			
US EU ADR	0.58	0.60	0.81	1.00		
FTSE 100	0.46	0.42	0.36	0.31	1.00	
NYSE Index	0.20	0.20	0.37	0.41	0.33	1.00

Panel B: Weekly Returns

	UK A Share	UK EU	US A ADR	US EU ADR	FTSE 100	NYSE Index
UK A Share	1.00					
UK EU	0.95	1.00				
US A ADR	0.92	0.89	1.00			
US EU ADR	0.86	0.90	0.92	1.00		
FTSE 100	0.43	0.38	0.37	0.32	1.00	
NYSE Index	0.33	0.36	0.34	0.37	0.52	1.00

Panel C: Monthly Returns

	UK A Share	UK EU	US A ADR	US EU ADR	FTSE 100	NYSE Index
UK A Share	1.00					
US EU	0.97	1.00				
US A ADR	0.98	0.96	1.00			
US EU ADR	0.96	0.98	0.97	1.00		
FTSE 100	0.44	0.42	0.46	0.46	1.00	
NYSE Index	0.35	0.34	0.38	0.37	0.69	1.00

UK A Share	=	A Shares traded on the ISE in the U.K.
UK EU	=	Equity Units traded on the ISE in the U.K.
US A ADR	=	A Share ADRs traded on the NYSE in the U.S.
US EU ADR	=	Equity Unit ADRs traded on the NYSE in the U.S.
FTSE 100	=	Financial Times Stock Exchange 100 Index in the U.K.
NYSE Index	=	CRSP NYSE/ASE value-weighted index in the U.S.

[1] Returns computations are based on equity prices and bid-ask quote midpoints expressed in U.S. dollars.

than the corresponding daily return correlation. The within-U.K. and within-U.S. weekly correlations of 0.95 and 0.92, respectively, and the cross-country correlations range from 0.86 to 0.92. The monthly correlations are higher still, ranging from 0.96 to 0.98.[8]

The correlations in table 2 are consistent with the view that the valuation of SK's equities may be similar in the U.S. and the U.K. In section V, we compare SK's U.S. and U.K. equity price responses to earnings disclosures in the two countries to provide further evidence on this issue.[9]

C. Outstanding Shares and Trade Volume

Table 3 presents the number of outstanding A Shares, A Share ADRs, EUs, and EU ADRs in the U.S. (panel A) and the U.K. (panel B).[10] The table shows that the number of EUs traded in the U.S. as ADRs has declined steadily, falling from 1,210.5 million shares (or almost 50 percent of SK's total equity on the merger date in 1989) to only 703.0 million shares (or about 25 percent) as of February 26, 1993. One explanation for the flowback of SK shares to the U.K. is that the number of U.S. investors willing to hold the shares is so small that when a U.S. investor wants to sell SK shares, that investor is more likely to find a U.K. purchaser than a U.S. purchaser.[11]

Table 4 presents average daily trading volume of SK's equity in the U.S. and the U.K., and shows steady declines in trading volume in the U.S. (but not the U.K.). The table shows that average daily trading volume of A Share ADRs reported on the NYSE fell from 1,110 to 70 thousand shares between 1989 and 1993, and average daily trading volume of EUs traded as ADRs fell from 7,470 to 1,606 thousand shares during the same period.[12]

Numerous explanations have been proposed for the declining SK share activity in the U.S. and the flowback of shares to the U.K.[13] First, U.K. institutional investors may be more likely to hold SK shares because SK is included in the FTSE 100 index in London. If an institution's portfolio must match the FTSE 100 index, that institution will buy SK shares in proportion to SK's weighting in the

index. In contrast, SK's ADRs are not part of the Standard & Poor's 500 index or other major indexes in the U.S., so institutions may be less inclined to hold the ADRs. A further consideration is that U.S. investors interested in owning equity of pharmaceutical companies can choose among many U.S. pharmaceutical companies. In the U.K., there are far fewer domestic pharmaceutical companies.

Other explanations are related to investor sentiment. Some commentators propose that British investors are more positive about SK and more interested in holding SK stock than U.S. investors because, prior to the 1989 merger, Beecham Group plc was financially

---

[8] Frost and Pownall (1994) report that the mean and median weekly return correlations for 26 U.K. cross-listed firms are 0.84 and 0.90, respectively, with firm-specific correlations ranging from 0.28 to 0.94.

[9] In a diagnostic analysis, we computed daily, weekly and monthly pairwise return correlations shown in table 2 in two subperiods (as defined in table 1, panel B) to assess whether the correlations were stable during the sample period. We observed no systematic change in the inter-equity correlations between the subperiods, although the correlations of SK's equity instruments with the market indexes are lower in subperiod 2.

[10] SK does not disclose the number of A Shares owned by Japanese beneficial shareholders (which are held by Japan Securities Houses' U.K. custodians), and the amounts are therefore included in the U.K. figures reported in panel B of table 3.

[11] See Clements and Lim (1988) and Velli (1994) for further discussion of the flowback of shares issued in foreign markets, which occurred frequently during the 1980s but has been less common in recent years.

[12] We also analyzed trading volume of A Shares on the Tokyo Stock Exchange (TSE) using daily trade volume from Nikkei Telecom. In Japan, average A Share daily trading volume declined from 39,000 shares during the first month SK was listed on the TSE (December 1991) to 3,800 shares per day during calendar 1992, and down still further to 660 shares per day during 1993. Several commentators note that foreign shares are unpopular in Japan, and the average holdings and turnover of foreign shares are relatively low (see The Economist 1993 and ISE 1993b). See Evans (1994) and The Economist (1994) for discussion of factors such as high cost relative to the volume of shares traded that have caused an exodus of foreign listed firms from the TSE in recent years. The fact that only one Japanese analyst follows SK (from the London Office of Nomura Securities, based on data in Nelson's Publications 1993) is consistent with Japanese investors lacking interest in SK shares.

[13] For example, see Management Today (1989), Accountancy (1992), The Economist (1989, 1991) and European Chemical News (1989).

TABLE 3
Number of SmithKline Beecham Outstanding A Shares, Equity Units, A Share ADRs and
Equity Unit ADRs (in millions)[1]
(Share Amounts are adjusted for the 1992 share split and Equity Unit restructuring)

	A Shares Traded As A Shares	Equity Units Traded as Equity Units	A Shares Traded as ADRs (5 A Shares per ADR)	Equity Units Traded as ADRs (5 Equity Units per ADR)
A. In the U.S.				
1989				
(Mar 12, 1990)	0.4	——	11.5	1,210.5
1990				
(Mar 5, 1991)	0.4	0.08	9.5	1,063.0
1991				
(Mar 27, 1992)	0.3	0.09	10.0	835.5
1992				
(Feb 26, 1993)	0.4	0.06	10.0	703.0
1993				
(Mar 1, 1994)	2.6	0.1	NR	NR
B. In the U.K.				
1989				
(Mar 12, 1990)	1,329.4	192.5	0	2.5
1990				
(Mar 5, 1991)	1,341.8	488.4	0	2.0
1991				
(Mar 27, 1992)	1,345.2	939.1	0	4.5
1992				
(Feb 26, 1993)	1,360.9	1,309.4	0	2.0
1993				
(Mar 1, 1994)	1,368.5	1,309.9	NR	NR

[1] Reported in SK's 1989–1993 Forms 20-F. SK did not disclose ADR data for 1993.
NR = SK did not disclose ADR data for 1993.

TABLE 4
Average Daily Trading Volume of SmithKline Beecham Equities (in thousands)[1]
(Share amounts are adjusted for the 1992 share split and Equity Unit restructuring)

	LONDON		NYSE	
	A Shares Trading as A Shares	Equity Units Trading as Equity Units	A Shares Trading as A Shares (5 Shrs/ADR)	Equity Units Trading as ADRs (5 EUs/ADR)
1989	7,160	1,905	1,110	7,470
1990	5,074	1,268	340	4,955
1991	2,610	1,465	125	3,060
1992	4,448	2,457	95	2,230
1993	4,405	3,296	70	1,606

[1] ISE and NYSE data from SK's 1989–1993 Forms 20-F. 1989 data are for July 27 (the SK merger date) through December 31, 1989.

stronger and had a more favorable reputation than SmithKline Beckman Corp. in the U.S. (e.g., *The Economist* 1991). Also, even in the 1990s, U.S. investors' portfolios have remained strongly biased towards domestic securities (Tesar and Werner 1994). This home bias in portfolio decisions might further explain reduced interest in SK in the U.S.

III. NON-ACCOUNTING EXPLANATIONS FOR EQUITY PRICE DIFFERENCES
A. Cash Dividends

As noted in section II, SK's Articles of Association contain provisions to ensure that gross dividends paid on one A Share will be equivalent, with limited exceptions, to dividends paid on one Equity Unit. However, payment dates, currency, amounts of dividends withheld and tax liabilities vary according to type of issue (share vs. ADR), location (U.K. vs. U.S.) and tax status of the shareholder, so that an equivalent dividends assumption may not be appropriate. This raises the possibility that the consistently higher price of A Shares relative to EUs reflects greater dividend cash flows for at least some A Share holders than for EU holders.

SK declares and pays quarterly dividends on A Shares in pounds sterling net of the U.K. Advanced Corporation Tax (ACT).[14] U.K. entities not subject to tax can reclaim the withheld amounts from Inland Revenue in the U.K. Dividends on the Preference Shares contained in Equity Units are paid by a U.S. subsidiary of SK in U.S. dollars.[15] U.K. taxes are not withheld from the Preference Share dividends.

A Share ADR holders who are qualifying U.S. residents are generally eligible to receive the "ACT Related Tax Credit," but are subject to a U.K. withholding tax of 15 percent of the gross dividend amount (SK 1993 Annual Report). Withheld amounts can be offset by reduced income taxes paid to the U.S. government. However, dividend cash flows to tax-exempt entities in the U.S. are larger for EUs (ADRs or shares) than for A Shares (ADRs or shares), since a tax credit or deduction in the U.S. is not available for the 15 percent with-

held from A Share dividends. In addition, qualifying U.S. holders of EUs or EU ADRs may be able to use the 70 percent dividends received deduction, but similar deductions may not be claimed by U.S. holders of A Shares or A Share ADRs. Consideration of these factors might suggest a higher price for EUs than for A Shares in the U.S., which is opposite to the observed difference.

For U.K. shareholders, tax effects suggest an opposite effect—a higher price for A Shares than for EUs. Cash dividends on A Shares are paid net of ACT, as noted above, but entities not subject to tax can reclaim the ACT from the government (Alexander and Archer 1991), and U.K. taxpayers have no further income tax liability for the dividend. Dividends paid by SK's U.S. subsidiary to EU holders do not have ACT withheld, but are subject to a 15 percent withholding rate (Coopers & Lybrand 1994). U.K. tax-exempt entities are not able to offset the amounts withheld with a lower income tax liability.

In summary, although SK EU and A Share cash dividends are intended to be equivalent, tax-exempt entities in the U.S. probably favor EUs and EU ADRs, and tax-exempt entities in the U.K. probably favor A Shares and A Share ADRs. The extent to which trading activity by these investor classes influences the prices of SK's equities is unknown, but consideration of the tax aspects of SK cash dividends suggests that A Share and EU after-tax dividend cash flows vary among different investor groups in the U.S. and the U.K., and these cash flow differences might result in equilibrium prices that vary between A Shares (which are held and traded primarily in the U.K.) and EUs (which are held and traded in both the U.K. and the U.S.).

---

[14] The ACT rate was 25 percent in 1993. See Alexander and Archer (1991) for discussion of the ACT.
[15] SK's Forms 20-F describe tax consequences and other information about cash dividends which may be paid on the A Shares, and on each of the two components of Equity Units (B Shares and Preference Shares). Since the 1989 merger, SK has paid cash dividends on A Shares, SK Corp. (a U.S. subsidiary) has paid dividends on Preference Shares, but SK has *not* paid any dividends on B Shares.

B. Share Liquidity and Execution Costs

Differences between A Share and EU liquidity and execution costs might also explain the price difference between the two equity types. Liquidity refers to the ability to trade quickly at prices that are reasonable in light of underlying demand/supply conditions (Schwartz 1991). Empirical measures of liquidity include an asset's average bid-ask spread, the frequency with which an asset trades, average trade size, trade volume and number of investors (e.g., Schwartz 1991; NYSE 1994; Wells 1991, 1993). Amihud and Mendelson (1986) develop a theoretical model linking expected returns and liquidity, and provide empirical support for the view that more liquid assets earn lower expected returns (also see Amihud and Mendelson 1989; Diamond and Verrecchia 1991; Reinganum 1990). Thus, we expect to observe a lower price for a share type that is less liquid, but otherwise similar to some other type of share.

Table 5 presents ISE trade data for SK's A Shares and EUs for the two years ending June 30, 1992 and 1993, and shows that A Shares exhibit greater liquidity than EUs as measured by number of trades, number of shares traded, number of shareholders and inside bid-ask spread in both years. For example, table 5 shows that there are over 40 times as many A Share holders as EU holders (e.g., 108,628 and 2,508 shareholders respectively in 1992), and between five and seven times as many trades for A Shares than for EUs, depending on the year. The inside bid-ask spread, which is a measure of execution costs as well as liquidity (since the spread is the execution cost of a round trip), ranges from two to five times as large for EUs than for A Shares, depending on the year. Although many

---

TABLE 5
SmithKline Beecham plc Equities Traded in London:
Market Value, Trade Volume, Shareholders and Inside Bid-Ask Spread[1]

TOTAL TRADE VOLUME

	Equity Market Value at Year-End (*f* Mill.)	Value[2] (*f* Mill)	Number of Trades[3]	Number of Shares Traded Milled[4]	Average Shares Per Trade	Number of Shareholders at Year-End	Inside Bid-Ask Spread (%) at Year-End[5]
A. For Year Ending June 30, 1992							
A Shares	6,065	5,319	64,065	635.11	9,913	108,628	0.2
Equity Units	5,365	2,602	8,821	347.39	39,382	2,508	1.1
B. For Year Ending June 30, 1993							
A Shares	6,003	5,398	72,130	1,101.25	15,268	111,936	0.5
Equity Units	5,120	2,940	14,482	686.33	47,392	2,772	1.0

---

[1] Data are from the 1992 and 1993 editions of the *Quality of Markets Companies Book,* ISE (1992, 1993b). The 1991 edition of the *Companies Book* does not contain separate data for Equity Units, and publication of the *Companies Book* series ended with the 1993 edition.

[2] Value is the total money value of securities traded (i.e., price multiplied by the number of shares bought and sold).

[3] Number of trades is the total number of trades transacted in a period.

[4] Number of shares traded is the total number of shares traded in a period.

[5] Inside Bid-Ask spread is the difference between the best (highest) bid price and the best (lowest) offer price among all market makers quoting a security. In this table, the spread is expressed as a percentage of the mid-price.

trades on the ISE occur inside the spread (Schwartz 1991), differences in the published quotes should indicate differences in execution costs for at least some of the transactions.[16]

C. Investor Sentiment

As noted above, SK equity appears to be more highly valued by U.K. investors than by U.S. investors, and U.S. investors' interest in SK has been steadily declining since SK was formed in 1989. Since almost all SK equity held in the U.S. is in the form of EU ADRs, investor sentiment in the U.S. primarily affects EU prices, and we expect depressed EU prices in the U.S. to depress EU prices in the U.K. Thus, the lower price of EUs and EU ADRs relative to A Shares and A Share ADRs is consistent with the weaker interest in SK in the U.S. than in the U.K.[17]

IV. ACCOUNTING EXPLANATIONS FOR EQUITY PRICE DIFFERENCES

Commentators argue that U.K. investors value SK shares more highly than U.S. investors because of differences between U.S. and U.K. accounting principles, differences in the accounting disclosures made by SK in the U.S. and U.K., and U.S. investors' difficulty interpreting what is actually disclosed by SK.[18] For example, Hugh Collum, SK's finance director, has suggested that non-U.K. investors have difficulty valuing SK shares due to U.S./U.K. accounting principle differences, and that SK needs to "keep talking to (shareholders about the (accounting) differences" and that "these accounting anomalies will one day sort themselves out, but probably not in our lifetime" (*Accountancy* 1991; Collum 1991).

Consistent with Mr. Collum's claims, U.S./ U.K. GAAP differences have caused SK's U.S. GAAP-based earnings to be lower than SK's U.K. GAAP-based earnings for every fiscal year since the 1989 merger. For instance, the initial merger was accounted for under U.K. GAAP using a method similar to pooling of interests, but did not qualify as a pooling under U.S. GAAP. As a result, over 2.5 billion

pounds sterling of goodwill was recognized and is being amortized under U.S. GAAP from the initial merger, but no goodwill resulted from the transaction under U.K. GAAP. In addition, U.S. GAAP requires the amortization of goodwill from SK's subsequent acquisitions over several years, but in the U.K. SK immediately wrote off the goodwill from each subsequent transaction against shareholders' equity. As a result of these and other differences, SK's 1993 net income according to U.K. GAAP was 295 million pounds sterling greater than under U.S. GAAP, or about 36 percent of SK's U.K. GAAP net income of 813 million pounds sterling.[19]

Table 6 summarizes the differences between SK's U.S. and U.K. GAAP-based annual net income for 1989–1993, from SK's Form 20-F reconciliation footnote disclosures. The table shows that accounting differences related to goodwill amortization and use of purchase (versus pooling) accounting for the 1989 merger reduce U.S. GAAP-based earnings relative to U.K. GAAP-based earnings in all five years. The table shows other significant differences which vary in amount and direc-

---

[16] Assessing the liquidity supplied by the U.S. market to trading in EUs is difficult because SK provides little information about trade activity of SK's equity in the U.S. However, SK's 1992 Form 20-F indicates that as of early 1993 there were far fewer EU and EU ADR holders in total (18,136 holders) than A Share and A Share ADR holders in total (114,160). Also, transaction costs for EU trading are higher than for A Shares to the extent that trades are cross-country or across equity types (Shares vs. ADRs).

[17] Investor sentiment and several other factors might explain the convergence in prices shown in table 1, panel B. For example, the steady decline in trade volume of SK shares in the U.S. might lessen the influence of differences in investor sentiment in the U.S. relative to the U.K. Also, investor sentiment in the U.S. might be gradually shifting to a more positive view about SK. Differences in A Share/EU equity characteristics, and relative proportions of different types of shareholder groups might also be changing.

[18] As noted earlier, lower valuation of SK shares by U.S. investors would cause downward price pressure on EU ADRs, the primary equity type outstanding in the U.S. (see table 4). Downward pressure on EU ADR prices in the U.S. would, in turn, be expected to result in lower prices of EUs and EU ADRs in both the U.S. and the U.K., relative to A Shares, whose price primarily reflects valuation in the U.K.

[19] See Weetman and Gray (1991) for related evidence.

TABLE 6
SmithKline Beecham plc
Summary of Differences Between U.S. and U.K. GAAP-Based Net Income[1]
(All Amounts in Millions of Pounds Sterling)

	1993	1992	1991	1990	1989
Net Income per U.K. GAAP	813	728	638	847	130
US GAAP Adjustments (net of tax):					
Elimination of SmithKline results prior to combination	0	0	0	0	−144
Combination transaction and SmithKline restructuring costs	0	0	0	0	281
Goodwill	−13	−11	−12	−88	−26
Intangible Assets	−50	0	0	0	0
Deferred Taxes	−3	35	26	−3	−30
Purchase accounting:					
Amortization of intangible assets	−101	−86	−85	−85	−60
Amortization of goodwill	−67	−67	−67	−67	−28
Depreciation and other	−4	−5	−10	−7	−42
Foreign currency hedging	146	−185	0	0	0
Post-retirement benefits.	−203	0	0	0	0
Other, net	0	−24	−16	32	6
Net Income per U.S. GAAP	518	385	474	629	87

[1] Information is from reconciliation footnote disclosures in SK's 1989–1993 Forms 20-F filed with the SEC.

tion of effect from year to year, related to foreign currency hedging, post-retirement benefits, treatment of intangible assets and deferred taxes.

The argument that differences between SK's U.K. GAAP net income and U.S. GAAP net income lead to pricing differences between the U.K. and U.S. (and hence lower prices for EUs than for A Shares) seems implausible, since it implies that investors' valuation of SK depends more on accounting numbers than on assessed economic value. Two other accounting- and disclosure-related explanations for lower share valuations in the U.S. are more plausible. First, SK might disclose less information in the U.S., or its U.S. disclosures might be less timely relative to U.K. disclosures. As a result, U.S. investors might believe they are disadvantaged relative to U.K. investors in terms of access to timely information about SK. Second, U.S. investors might have difficulty in interpreting SK's financial infor-

mation due to unfamiliarity with U.K. accounting principles.

To determine what SK actually disclosed in the U.S. and the U.K., we analyzed its media disclosures and documents filed with securities regulators in the two countries from July 1989 to May 1993. U.K. disclosures include the complete set of SK filings made with the ISE Company Announcements Office (CAO) and media disclosures.[20] U.S. disclosures include SK's SEC filings and disclosures from full text searches of Dow Jones News

[20] CAO filings include: (1) disclosures made to comply with the ISE timely disclosure and conformity of disclosure rules; (2) interim and annual financial reports; and (3) company announcements. We obtained media disclosures from a full text search of *The Financial Times,* Reuters News Service, and the Press Releases database available on Reuters Textline. *The Financial Times* is the U.K.'s major daily business newspaper, and Reuters News Service is widely regarded as the most comprehensive, most widely used news source in the U.K.

Service (DJNS) and PR Newswire (PRN).[21] We searched the U.S. and U.K. disclosures for earnings announcements (EAs) and management forecasts, and noted disclosure date, fiscal period referenced, accounting principles used, currency and reconciliations of accounting results based on U.K. GAAP to U.S. GAAP. In both the U.S. and the U.K., quarterly and annual earnings were first disclosed in press releases. U.S. and U.K. EAs were similar in content, based on U.K. GAAP, and published on the same day for all fiscal periods. SK reported current period earnings in both pounds sterling and U.S. dollars (but earnings for the prior period were reported only in pounds) in all but one of the EAs.[22]

SK disclosed U.S. GAAP-based earnings in SEC filings, but not in any media announcements. SK disclosed quarterly U.S. GAAP earnings in Forms 6-K for six of the 11 quarters in the sample period, with a mean reporting lag (days between fiscal period end and filing date) of 58 days (reporting lag for U.K. GAAP quarterly earnings disclosed in press releases averaged 33 days in both the U.S. and the U.K.). Annual U.S. GAAP earnings were disclosed in Forms 20-F filed with the SEC on average 100 days after fiscal year-end, compared with a mean reporting lag of 62 days (in both the U.S. and the U.K.) for initial disclosure of annual earnings based on U.K. GAAP in press releases. Thus, SK's U.S. GAAP-based earnings disclosures (quarterly and annual) were made on average several weeks later than disclosures of U.K. GAAP-based numbers, its U.S. GAAP-based quarterly earnings disclosures were less frequent than U.K. GAAP disclosures, and were not widely disseminated in the form of press releases.[23]

Evidence in table 6 indicates that a number of accounting principle differences cause SK's U.S. GAAP annual earnings to be less than its U.K. GAAP earnings, and the nature of these differences and their magnitude vary substantially from year to year. This evidence suggests that predicting what SK's U.S. GAAP earnings will be for a given year, using U.K. GAAP-based earnings for that same year, is difficult. To provide further evidence on

whether U.S. investors might be able to predict U.S. GAAP numbers based on SK's U.K. GAAP press releases, we compared SK's U.K. GAAP and U.S. GAAP annual and interim earnings changes. If U.K. and U.S. GAAP earnings are different but changes in earnings are similar, U.S. investors might be able to estimate the change in U.S. GAAP earnings at the time U.K. GAAP earnings are disclosed. Table 7 presents U.K. GAAP earnings per share (EPS) and percentage earnings change (PEC), computed as this period's EPS minus EPS one year ago divided by EPS one year ago, for fiscal quarters for which SK disclosed earnings. Similar figures are presented for EPS and PEC based on U.S. GAAP earnings.

---

[21] DJNS carries articles published on the "Broad Tape," *The Wall Street Journal* and *Barron's*, and is a comprehensive corporate news source in the U.S. PRN is a media relations wire service that publishes press releases submitted by its members for a fee based on number of words in the release and requested distribution (regional, national, international, etc.).

[22] We also analyzed SK's media disclosures and documents filed with the Ministry of Finance (MOF) in Japan. We were unable to obtain a complete set of MOF filings, even after an exhaustive search which included correspondence with the Mitsui Trust and Banking Co., Ltd., SK's stock transfer agent in Japan, and discussions with staff at SK, the MOF, the TSE and several document vendors. We obtained media disclosures by searching (1) News Telecom, (2) Reuters Textline Far East; (3) Jiji News Wire; (4) Japan Economic Newswire; and (5) the Japan Economic Daily. News Telecom is a Japanese language historic text search database published by Nihon Keizai Shimbun ("Nikkei"), and is the most comprehensive database of news published in Japan. Analysis of disclosures obtained through these sources indicates that SK did not release any EAs in Japan, although Nikkei reporters did file three stories about SK's earnings from London. The absence of media accounting disclosures in Japan suggests a low investor and analyst demand for information about SK, and is consistent with the infrequent trading of SK shares on the Tokyo Stock Exchange.

[23] SK disclosed earnings and sales forecasts in the U.S. and the U.K. but not in Japan. SK's U.S. quantitative forecasts differed from the U.K. forecasts in content and frequency. SK staff explained to us that corporate policy is to not release quantitative forecasts on a regular basis. However, if analysts' earnings forecasts are out of line, SK issues a forecast to correct market expectations. SK also made numerous qualitative forecasts (seven in the U.S. and ten in the U.K.), and the forecasts released in both countries were generally released on the same day in the U.S. and the U.K. and were similar in content.

Table 7 shows that SK's annual and interim U.K. GAAP PECs vary substantially during fiscal 1990, ranging from −12.2% to 59.4%, but are less variable during 1991 and 1992, ranging from 11.6% to 22.2%. In contrast, U.S. GAAP PECs are highly variable throughout the sample period, ranging from −76.4% to 420.9%. U.K. GAAP and U.S. GAAP earnings do not appear to move together. For example, for each quarter in 1991 U.K. GAAP earnings were higher than the one-year-ago amounts, as evidenced by positive PECs. In contrast, U.S. GAAP quarterly earnings in 1991 were lower than in 1990, so that U.S. investors might not be able to predict SK's earnings based on U.K. GAAP earnings.

V. ANALYSIS OF SMITHKLINE BEECHAM'S EQUITY RETURNS ON EA DATES

If U.S. investors have difficulty interpreting U.K. GAAP-based financial information, and if they do not infer changes in SK value by observing share price changes of SK's equity in the U.K., then we expect to observe weak U.S. share price responses to SK's announcements of U.K. GAAP earnings. On the other hand, if U.S. investors are not confused by U.K. GAAP EAs, and if they can interpret SK's disclosures quickly and at low cost (or if they infer SK's value by observing SK's equity price changes in the U.K.), then we expect to observe significant U.S. market responses to SK's U.K. GAAP EAs.

TABLE 7
SmithKline Beecham Earnings Per Share
According to U.K. and U.S. GAAP

Fiscal Period End	U.K. GAAP EPS (in pounds)	Percentage Earnings Change[1]	U.S. GAAP EPS (in pounds)	Percentage Earnings Change[1]
3/31/93 (Q1)	0.150	12.0%	•[2]	•[2]
12/31/92 (An.)	0.546	14.0	0.288	−19.1%
12/31/92 (Q4)	0.152	18.8	•	•
9/30/92 (Q3)	0.136	13.3	0.264	14.8
6/30/92 (Q2)	0.124	11.7	0.214	59.7
3/31/92 (Q1)	0.135	11.6	0.093	27.4
12/31/91 (An.)	0.480	17.1	0.357	−24.7
12/31/91 (Q4)	0.128	16.4	•	•
9/30/91 (Q3)	0.121	22.2	0.230	−38.5
6/30/91 (Q2)	0.110	18.3	•	•
3/31/91 (Q1)	0.121	12.0	0.073	−40.7
12/31/90 (An.)	0.410	12.0	0.474	420.9
12/31/90 (Q4)	0.110	59.4	•	•
9/30/90 (Q3)	0.099	20.7	•	•
6/30/90 (Q2)	0.093	2.2	•	•
3/31/90 (Q1)	0.108	−12.2	0.123	−2.4
12/31/89 (An.)	0.365	0.0[3]	0.091	−76.4[3]
12/31/89 (Q4)	•	•	•	•
9/30/89 (Q3)	•	•	•	•

[1] Percentage Earnings Change is this period's earnings per share (EPS) minus EPS one year ago, divided by EPS one year ago.

[2] Dots denote missing values. We believe these observations were neither announced in the financial press nor filed with the SEC in the U.S.

[3] These percentage earnings changes are calculated using restated EPS values from 12/31/88 (before the merger) which were contained in the 12/31/89 annual earnings announcements and the 20-F filed with the SEC in the U.S.

To examine this issue, we compared abnormal returns to benchmark returns during short windows around EA dates to determine the significance of stock price responses to EA events in each country. We measured abnormal returns using a squared, standardized residual method similar to that used by Chari et al. (1988). We used two-factor market models in the U.S. and the U.K. as models of each of SK's equities' normal returns, and estimated each model over the period July 1989 to August 1994. The two market returns included in each model are the FTSE 100 and the Value Weighted NYSE/ASE index from CRSP.[24]

We computed residual variance over the sample period for each equity return series (denoted by subscript i) and, for each three-day EA interval (k), we computed a squared residual deflated by residual variance. We standardized this measure by the number of days in the announcement period to yield an abnormal return variable for each event, AR_{ikA}. We used a non-announcement period benchmark, computed as the squared, standardized residual (AR_{ikNA}), against which to compare the announcement period abnormal return statistic. We averaged these statistics across the k EAs for equity i during the period to get AR_{iA} and AR_{iNA}. The difference between AR_{ia} and AR_{iNA}, DIF_i, measures the average stock price response of return series (i) to SK's EAs. The expected of DIF_i is zero under the null of no information content (see Frost and Pownall 1994 and Chari et al. 1988 for further discussion of this approach and computational formulas).

Table 8 presents results of this analysis, and shows that the stock price response to SK's U.K. GAAP earnings disclosures is significantly different from zero at the .01 level or better (two-sided tests) based on both parametric t-tests and non-parametric Wilcoxon Signed Rank tests for all SK equities. Table 8 also presents results from several cross-equity statistical comparisons, which do not support the hypothesis that the U.S. A Share ADR price response to EAs is less than the U.K. A Share response, or that the U.S. EU ADR price response to EAs is less than the U.K. EU price

response. The evidence in table 8 thus supports the view that U.S. investors are not confused, and that SK's U.S. equity prices rapidly respond to new information disclosed by SK in its media earnings disclosures.[25]

In a final analysis we estimated two-factor market models conditional on the release of SK's U.K. EAs made simultaneously in the U.S. and the U.K., and U.S. GAAP reconciliations contained in Forms 20-F filed with the SEC. In each model, the U.K. GAAP earnings information variable takes on the value of the U.K. GAAP PEC on the EA dates, zero otherwise, and the U.S. GAAP earnings variable takes on the value of the U.S. GAAP PEC on SEC filing dates, zero otherwise. We estimated separate models for A Share and EU ADRs in the U.S., and for A Shares, A Share ADRs, EUs and EU ADRs in the U.K. jointly using Generalized Least Squares to control for the heteroscedasticity and cross-correlation in the residuals from the two-factor conditional market model (see Frost and Pownall 1995 for a similar application).

This analysis is presented in table 9, with results using one-day and three-day event

---

[24] We estimated single-factor market models (using EU and A Share ADRs in the U.S. and A Shares in the U.K.) in several diagnostic analyses designed to assess the extent to which estimated betas are sensitive to the U.S. market index used (NYSE/ASE CRSP index versus the S&P 500), return interval (daily, weekly, monthly) and subperiod (subperiod 1 is July 1989 to December 1991; subperiod 2 is January 1992 to August 1994. For daily and weekly return intervals, estimated betas using the S&P 500 index (which range from 0.654 to 0.894) are less than comparable betas estimated using the NYSE/ASE index (which range from 0.802 to 1.164). Betas estimated using monthly returns do not differ between the two U.S. market indexes, in both U.S. EU ADR and A Share ADR market models. Estimated U.S. betas are generally the largest (and closest to 1.0 on average) when monthly return intervals are used. Estimated betas using U.S. data are stable across the two subperiods, but when estimated using U.K. data are about twice as large in subperiod 1 as in subperiod 2 (the difference varies in magnitude depending on the return interval).

[25] We repeated the analyses presented in table 8 using one-day and five-day return windows. Results using five-day windows are similar to results using three-day windows presented in table 8, but significance levels are slightly stronger or slightly weaker, depending on type of equity. Results using one-day windows were weaker for all six equities analyzed.

TABLE 8
Stock Price Responses to SmithKline Beecham plc's
Earnings Announcements in the U.S. and the U.K.

	AR_A [1] Mean (Median)	AR_{NA} [2] Mean (Median)	DIF[3] Mean (Median)	Parametric t-test Statistic[4]	Wilcoxon Signed Rank Statistic[5]
A. In the U.S.					
1. A Share ADR	2.77 (1.51)	0.59 (0.41)	2.18 (0.99)	2.88***	22***
2. EU ADR	3.88 (2.60)	0.82 (0.40)	3.06 (2.13)	3.07***	17***
B. In the U.K.					
3. A Share	2.68 (1.86)	0.79 (0.56)	1.88 (0.66)	2.95***	20***
4. EU	2.75 (1.54)	0.80 (0.62)	1.95 (0.655)	3.00***	17***
5. A Share ADR	1.39 (0.96)	0.44 (0.22)	0.94 (0.60)	2.72***	21***
6. EU ADR	2.14 (1.18)	0.66 (0.52)	1.48 (0.73)	3.05***	24***
C. Cross-Equity-Comparisons					
7. U.S. A Share ADR minus U.K. A Share				0.70	83
8. U.S. EU ADR – U.K. EU				1.55*	54**
9. U.S. A Share ADR – U.S. EU ADR				–1.73**	44**
10. U.K. A Share – U.K. EU				–0.28	79

*,**,*** indicate significant at the .10, .05, and .01 level, respectively, one-sided tests.

[1] AR_A is the announcement period abnormal return measure as the squared, standardized two-factor market model residual computed over the three-day period days –1, 0, and +1 relative to the EA date. The two factors are the return on the FTSE 100 Index in the U.K. and the return on the Value Weighted CRSP NYSE/ASE Index in the U.S. Return computations are based on equity prices expressed in U.S. dollars.

[2] AR_{NA} is the non-announcement period benchmark return, measured as the squared, standardized market model residual computed over the three-day period days, –8, –9, and –10 relative to the EA date.

[3] DIF is an EA-specific measure of the difference between announcement period abnormal returns and non-announcement period benchmark returns ($AR_A - AR_{NA}$).

[4] For each equity type, the t-statistic tests the null hypothesis that the mean DIF equals zero. It is computed by dividing the mean DIF by 1/n times its standard deviation. The t-statistic in row 7 tests the null hypothesis that mean U.S. A Share ADR DIF equals mean U.K. A Share DIF. The statistic is computed by dividing the sample mean of the difference in DIF's by its standard deviation divided by the sample size (18).

[5] The Wilcoxon signed rank statistics test the same hypotheses as those described in note 4 above. Refer to Siegel (1956, 81–83) for computational details. The statistic in row 7 is based on the Wilcoxon Matched-Pairs Signed-Ranks Test described in Siegel (1956).

windows in panels A and B respectively. The estimated regression models are all significant at the .0001 level or better, with adjusted R-squares ranging from 0.02 for A Share ADRs trading in the U.K. (three-day window) to 0.19 for EU ADRs trading in the U.S. (both one-day and three-day windows). All estimated coefficients (in both panels) for the U.S. and U.K. market returns are significant at the .05 level or better (one-sided tests throughout). The estimated U.K. GAAP earnings response coefficients are all positive, but significance levels vary depending on whether a one-day or three-day return window is used in the analysis. Results for SK equities trading in the U.K. are stronger in panel A (one-day return window) where significance levels for the estimated earnings response coefficient are all at .05 or better. The U.S. equity results are stronger in panel B (three-day return window), where significance levels are .01. Therefore, evidence in table 9 is consistent with the view that both U.K. and U.S. investors use information about SK's U.K. GAAP earnings to value SK shares.[26]

Evidence in table 9 also indicates that SK's equity returns are positively correlated with SK's U.S. GAAP earnings changes on the SEC filing dates. Panel A of table 9 shows that for three of the six SK equities analyzed, the estimated U.S. GAAP coefficient is significant at the .10 level, even though the estimation is based on only five U.S. GAAP SEC filing dates (for related evidence, see McQueen 1993).

VI. SUMMARY AND CONCLUSIONS

In this study we explored international information dissemination and price discovery by analyzing SmithKline Beecham plc's equity characteristics and accounting disclosures in the U.S. and the U.K. We examined non-accounting and accounting explanations for the price differences among SK's equities traded in the U.S. and the U.K.

A summary of our results is as follows. First, although there are substantial price differences (some negative, some positive) on at least some days between U.S. and U.K. A Shares and between U.S. and U.K. EU ADRs, we observe significant and systematic differ-

ences between A Shares and Equity Units (without respect to the market), both of which trade in the U.K. (primarily as shares) and in the U.S. (primarily as ADRs). We find that A Share prices exceeded EU prices for all days in the sample period in both within-country and cross-country comparisons, and that the mean price differences for all A Share/EU comparisons are above U.S. $5.00, or over 15 percent of the mean A Share price in the U.K. In addition, maximum share price differences between U.S. and U.K. A Shares, and between U.S. and U.K. EUs all exceeded $2 (U.S.) for the full sample period and both subperiods.

Our analysis suggests that several non-accounting factors may explain the large price difference between SK's A Shares and Equity Units. First, although SK EU and A Share cash dividends are intended to be equivalent, tax-exempt entities in the U.S. receive greater dividend cash flows from EUs and EU ADRs than from A Shares and A Share ADRs, and tax-exempt entities in the U.K. receive greater dividend cash flows from A Shares and A Share ADRs than from EUs and EU ADRs. These and other dividend cash flow differences for different investor classes and SK equity types might explain at least some of the A Share and EU price difference. Second, A Shares traded in the U.K. are substantially more liquid than EUs traded in the U.K. based on a number of measures. For example, in 1992 and 1993 there were about 40 times as many A Share holders as EU holders in the U.K., and trade frequency was more than five times greater for A Shares than for EUs. Thus, to the extent that liquidity is positively correlated with share price, a larger price for A Shares relative to EUs is to be expected. More favorable investor sentiment towards SK in the U.K. than in the U.S. is a third non-accounting explanation for A Share price relative to EU prices. Since U.S. investors hold primarily EU ADRs, a weaker interest in SK equities in the U.S. will depress EU prices in aggregate.

---

[26] A second possibility is that U.S. investors infer changes in the value of SK's equity by observing U.K. share price response to EAs.

TABLE 9
Conditional Market Models for SmithKline Beecham's
A Shares, Equity Units, and ADRs in the U.S. and the U.K.[1]

Model: $R_{it} = \alpha_i + \beta_{i1}R_{mtUK} + \beta_{i2}R_{mtUS} + \delta_i PEC_{UK} + \alpha_i PEC_{us} + \varepsilon_{it}$ [2]

Panel A: One-day Return

Time Series	Intercept	U.S. Market Beta	U.K. Market Beta	U.K. GAAP Earnings Response Coefficient	U.S. GAAP Earnings Response Coefficient
US Equity Unit ADR	−0.000 (−0.18)	1.014 (12.62***)	0.270 (5.50***)	0.019 (0.95)	0.003 (0.77)
UK Equity Unit ADR	0.000 (0.03)	0.196 (2.09**)	0.332 (5.81***)	0.065 (2.82***)	0.007 (1.47*)
US A-Share ADR	−0.000 (−0.24)	0.761 (10.28***)	0.319 (7.08***)	0.025 (1.38*)	0.004 (1.34*)
UK A-Share ADR	0.000 (0.18)	0.237 (2.19**)	0.266 (4.02***)	0.054 (2.04**)	0.007 (1.34*)
UK A-Share	−0.000 (−0.18)	0.347 (4.66***)	0.458 (10.08***)	0.049 (2.69***)	0.003 (0.94)
UK Equity Unit	−0.000 (−0.14)	0.372 (4.64***)	0.454 (9.27***)	0.046 (2.31***)	0.003 (0.96)

Panel B: Three-day Return

Time Series	Intercept	U.S. Market Beta	U.K. Market Beta	U.K. GAAP Earnings Response Coefficient	U.S. GAAP Earnings Response Coefficient
US Equity Unit ADR	−0.000 (−0.65)	1.001 (12.49***)	0.265 (5.43***)	0.036 (3.15***)	0.001 (0.60)
UK Equity Unit ADR	0.000 (0.02)	0.186 (1.98**)	0.326 (5.71***)	0.025 (1.83**)	0.001 (0.47)
US A-Shares ADR	−0.000 (−0.58)	0.748 (10.13***)	0.313 (6.98***)	0.030 (2.85***)	0.001 (0.359)
UK A-Share ADR	0.000 (.241)	0.229 (2.11**)	0.260 (3.94***)	0.016 (1.02)	0.000 (0.16)
UK A-Share	−0.000 (−0.30)	0.338 (4.53***)	0.454 (10.02***)	0.025 (2.36***)	0.000 (0.052)
UK Equity Unit	−0.000 (−0.38)	0.361 (4.50***)	0.449 (9.21***)	0.031 (2.72***)	0.000 (0.31)

*,**,*** indicate significant at the .10, .05, and .01 level, respectively, one-sided tests.

[1] T-statistics to test whether the OLS coefficients are equal to zero are given in parentheses under the coefficients.

[2] This model is a two factor market model conditional on: (1) the release of UK GAAP earnings announcements simultaneously in the U.S. and the U.K. and (2) U.S. GAAP reconciliations, where the two factors are the return on the Financial Times Stock Exchange 500 Index in the U.K. and the return on the Value Weighted CRSP NYSE/ASE Index in the U.S. The six returns series (A-Shares and Equity Units, A-Share ADRS and Equity Unit ADRs, each trading in the U.S. and the U.K.) are indexed by i and trading days are indexed by t. PEC is the percentage earnings change calculated as this period's earnings minus earnings one year ago divided by earnings one year ago where PEC_{UK} is calculated from the amount disclosed in UK GAAP in pounds and PEC_{US} is calculated from US GAAP in pounds as disclosed in the reconciliations contained in the four Form 20-Fs filed during the period.

Further analysis indicates that accounting-related factors probably do not explain SK's A Share/EU price differences. SK's earnings based on U.K. GAAP have been greater than SK's U.S. GAAP earnings in every year since the merger, and information about SK's U.K. GAAP earnings does not appear to be useful for predicting what SK's U.S. GAAP earnings will be. However, our stock price analyses indicate that U.S. investors use information about SK's U.K. GAAP earnings (on EA dates) in valuing, SK, and that the U.S. market response to SK's disclosures of U.K. GAAP earnings is similar to the U.K. market response. Thus, U.S. investors do not appear to be confused by U.S./U.K. GAAP differences, and in fact use information about U.K. GAAP earnings in their valuations of SK.

REFERENCES

Accountancy. 1992. Looking towards a healthy future. (February): 20–22.

Aggarwal, R. and D. C. Schirm. 1995. *Global Portfolio Diversification: Risk Management, Market Microstructure, and Implementation Issues.* San Diego: Academic Press.

Alexander, D., and S. Archer. 1991. *HBJ Miller Comprehensive European Accounting Guide—U.S. Edition.* San Diego: HBJ Professional Publishing.

Alexander, G., C. Eun, and S. Janakiramanan. 1987. Asset pricing and dual listing on foreign capital markets: A note. *The Journal of Finance* (March): 151–158.

Amihud, Y., and H. Mendelson. 1986. Asset pricing and the bid-ask spread. *Journal of Financial Economics* 17: 223–249.

———, and ———. 1989. The effects of Beta, bid-ask spread, residual risk, and size on stock returns. *The Journal of Finance* 44 (June): 479–486.

Chari, B., R. Jagannathan, and A. Ofer. 1988. Seasonalities in security returns: The case of earnings announcements. *Journal of Financial Economics:* 101–121.

Clements, J., and Q. Lim. 1988. Syndicated equities, block deals and private placements. In *Stock Answers: A Guide to the International Equities Market,* edited by J. Clements. New York: Nichols Publishing.

Collum, H. 1991. Condemned to confusion. *International Accounting Standards Committee News* (April 18).

Coopers & Lybrand International Tax Network. 1994. *1994 International Tax Summaries: A Guide for Planning and Decisions.* New York: John Wiley & Sons.

Diamond, D. W., and R. E. Verrecchia. 1991. Disclosure, liquidity, and the cost of capital. *The Journal of Finance* 46: 1325–1359.

Downes, J., and J. E. Goodman. 1990. *Barron's Finance and Investment Handbook, Third Edition.* New York: Barron's.

Economist, The. 1989. Eeny meeny miny mo... (November 4): 90.

———. 1991. Doctoring shares. (November 2): 76.

———. 1993. Foreign shares in Japan: Sayonara. (September 25): 88–89.

———. 1994. Hollowing out Japan's financial markets. (August 13): 67–69.

European Chemical News. 1989. SmithKline and Beecham create drugs giant. (April 17): 4.

Evans. G. 1994. Stick-in-the-mud financial center. *Euromoney* (December): 35–37.

Frankel, J.A ., ed. 1994. *The Internationalization of Equity Markets.* Chicago: The University of Chicago Press.

Froot, K. A., and E. Dabora. 1995. How are stock prices affected by the location of trade? Working paper, Harvard University.

Frost, C., and G. Pownall. 1994. A comparison of the stock price response to earnings disclosures in the U.S. and the U.K. *Contemporary Accounting Research* (Summer): 59–83.

———, and ———. 1995. Equal access to information: Do crosslisted firms' stock prices respond to earnings disclosed in overseas and local jurisdictions? Working paper, Washington University (St. Louis) and Emory University.

Greenspan, A. 1988. Remarks by Alan Greenspan, Chairman, Board of Governors of the Federal Reserve System, Before the Annual Convention of the Securities Industry Association. Boca Raton, Florida (November 30).

Gultekin, M., N. Gultekin and A. Penati. 1989. Capital controls and international capital market segmentation: Evidence from the Japanese and American stock markets. *Journal of Finance* (September): 849–869.

International Stock Exchange (ISE). 1992. *Quality of Markets Companies Book 1992*. London: The International Stock Exchange of the United Kingdom and the Republic of Ireland Limited.

———. 1993a. *The Listing Rules*. London: The International Stock Exchange of the United Kingdom and the Republic of Ireland Limited.

———. 1993b. *Quality of Markets Companies Book 1993*. London: The International Stock Exchange of the United Kingdom and the Republic of Ireland Limited.

Jorion, P., and E. Schwartz. 1986. Integration vs. segmentation in the Canadian stock market. *The Journal of Finance* 41 (July): 603-616.

Lederman, J., and K. K. H. Park, eds. 1991. *The Global Equity Markets*. Chicago: Probus Publishing Company.

Management Today. 1989. SmithKline Beecham's early trials. (November): 99–104.

McQueen, P. D. 1993. The information content of foreign and U.S. GAAP earnings in SEC Form 20-F. Working paper, Association for Investment Management and Research.

Nelson Publications. 1993. *Nelson's Directory of Investment Research 1993, Volume II—International Companies*. New York: Nelson Publications.

New York Stock Exchange. 1994. *NYSE Fact Book 1993 Data*. New York: Haines Lundberg Waehler.

Reinganum, M. R. 1990. Market microstructure and asset pricing: An empirical investigation of NYSE and NASDAQ securities. *Journal of Financial Economics* 28: 127–147.

Rosenthal, L., and C. Young. 1992. The seemingly anomalous price behavior of Royal Dutch/Shell and Unilever N.V./PLC. *Journal of Financial Economics* 26 (February): 123–141.

Scarlata, J. 1993. Institutional developments in the globalization of securities and futures markets. In *The International Finance Reader*, Second Edition, edited by R. W. Kolb. Miami: Kolb Publishing Company.

Schwartz, R. 1991. *Reshaping the Equity Markets: A Guide for the 1990's*. Harper Business.

Siegel, S. 1956. *Nonparametric Statistics for the Behavioral Sciences*. New York: McGraw-Hill Book Company.

Tesar, L., and I. Werner. 1994. International equity transactions and U.S. portfolio choice. In *The Internationalization of Equity Markets*, edited by J. A. Frankel. Chicago: The University of Chicago Press.

Tokyo Stock Exchange. 1991. *A Listing Guide for Foreign Companies*, 2nd Ed. Tokyo.

United States Securities and Exchange Commission (SEC). 1984. *Memorandum of the Office of International Corporate Finance, Division of Finance, Securities and Exchange Commission on the Application of the Securities and Exchange Act of 1934 to Foreign Private Issuers*. Washington, D.C. (January).

Velli, J. 1994. American depositary receipts: An overview. *Fordham International Law Journal* (Symposium): 38–57.

Weetman, P., and S. Gray. 1991. A comparative international analysis of the impact of accounting principles on profits: The USA versus the U.K., Sweden and the Netherlands. *Accounting and Business Research* 21 (Autumn): 363–379.

Wells, S. 1991. Less-liquid market. In *Stock Exchange Quarterly with Quality of Markets Review—Autumn Edition (1991)*. London: The International Stock Exchange of the United Kingdom and the Republic of Ireland Limited.

———. 1993. Transparency in the equity market—The publication of last trades. In *Stock Exchange Quarterly with Quality of Markets Review—Spring Edition (1993)*. London: The International Stock Exchange of the United Kingdom and the Republic of Ireland Limited.

[24]

 Pergamon

Scand. J. Mgmt, Vol. 13, No. 1, pp. 95–112, 1997
© 1997 Elsevier Science Ltd
Printed in Great Britain. All rights reserved
0956–5221/97 $17.00 + 0.00

S0956–5221(96)00030–9

NORSK HYDRO'S COMMUNICATION TO INTERNATIONAL CAPITAL MARKETS: A BLEND OF ACCOUNTING PRINCIPLES

NORVALD MONSEN* and WANDA A. WALLACE†

*Norwegian School of Economics and Business Administration, Norway and
†College of William and Mary, U.S.A.

(First received January 1995; accepted in revised form May 1996)

Abstract — Companies operating internationally are faced with the dilemma of how to attract investors from multiple exchanges to provide capital. While each investor may prefer a report tailored to his or her country's generally accepted accounting and auditing framework, such an approach can be prohibitively expensive. The selection of International Accounting Standards Committee (IASC) guidance for reporting suffers from its lack of acceptance to date by the International Organization of Securities Commissions (IOSCO). The choice of the United States Generally Accepted Accounting Principles (U.S.GAAP) and Generally Accepted Auditing Standards (U.S. GAAS) facilitate access to large capital markets on the New York Stock Exchange, AMEX or NASDAQ but may not communicate effectively to the European or other markets. Norsk Hydro, the subject of this paper, chose to blend its domestic and U.S. accounting principles, with some episodic integration of European audit report language. The potential communication and regulatory challenges that resulted are described, as are the plethora of topics for future research, given such experimentation in financial reporting. © 1997 Elsevier Science Ltd. All rights reserved

Key words: International capital markets, civil law and common law countries, accounting disclosures, international accounting standards.

INTRODUCTION

ACCOUNTING magic produced a profit
Actually, Norsk Hydro had a loss of NOK 200 million last year. However, the accounts show a profit of NOK 1800 million. Hydro "earned" NOK 2000 million as a result of playing with the accounting figures and new accounting rules in the U.S. without producing anything. General director Egil Myklebust does not even try to boast of the profit in the accounts. On the contrary: "The correct result is probably a loss", Myklebust admits. New accounting rules in the U.S. are the reason why Hydro reports a profit in the accounts. Hydro is an international company, which is listed on the New York Stock Exchange. It has to follow U.S. accounting principles. And when the U.S. changes the rules, Hydro is also forced to change its routines". (*Verdens Gang*, 23 February 1993; translated by N. Monsen.)

Norsk Hydro is the biggest company listed at the Stock Exchange in Norway. It is generally considered to be the company which gives us an idea of the development of the economy in the business sector in this country, and therefore it is followed closely by the authorities, the investor community, the press, and everybody interested in the economic development in Norway. The excerpt above, which was presented in one of the biggest general newspapers in Norway, attracted our interest.

After reading this brief excerpt, we were left with more questions than answers. What had been the financial performance of this leading Norwegian company in 1992? Did its financial situation improve or worsen? In the excerpt, the two income figures referred to are both based upon U.S. Generally Accepted Accounting Principles (U.S. GAAP): net income for 1992 before and after the cumulative effect of accounting changes; NOK −200 million and NOK 1800 million — a difference of as much as NOK 2000 million. However, if we focus upon Norwegian accounting principles, we will find the following net income figure for 1992: NOK 167 million. The following question therefore attracted our attention: did Norsk Hydro report a profit or a loss for 1992? Given the observation that the general director himself is not sure ("The correct result is probably a loss"), what should we, the press or international capital markets believe?

This situation is not unique to Norsk Hydro. We know that different countries use different and often conflicting accounting principles. But what do companies interested in international exchanges do as international harmonization lumbers around as a future goal, not yet realized? For example, if an entity seeks listings on half-a dozen exchanges, the choices include: six separate reports under respective accounting standards, one report hoping for reciprocity, the International Accounting Standards Committee (IASC) hoping for acceptability, the U.S.A. hoping for acceptability, or combinations thereof. When the IASC has been requested by the International Organization of Securities Commissions (IOSCO) to achieve a set of accounting standards that they can embrace before the turn of the century, the implicit message is that IASC is not yet there.

Our questions then, are how are real companies responding in the interim, how are these steps perceived, are communication problems likely, and what are the trade-offs with which real decision makers and regulators are having to deal? The Norsk Hydro case is an excellent real-world case to use for discussing these problems. Based upon such a discussion of this particular company, suggestions for further research that will enhance our understanding of diverse financial reporting practices are suggested.

The paper is structured as follows: first, the international reporting environment is described, then background on Norsk Hydro is provided. Longitudinal consideration of Norsk Hydro's financial reports permits the evolution of accounting and auditing practices to be detailed, recognizing joint effects of Norwegian, U.S. and U.K. standards on choices both by the company and its auditors and regulators. The summary highlights key implications and issues for further research.

LEVELS OF ANALYSIS

Table 1 outlines the preconditions influencing accounting system selection and associated harmonization efforts (adapted from Monsen and Wallace, 1995). It suggests a number of preconditions for accounting and reporting practices, as well as a number of possible consequences of the applied reporting practices. The preconditions include current infrastructure for standard-setting, relationship to the IASC promulgations, nature of the accounting profession, as well as the state of the economy, the societal goals, and the legal system. Possible consequences of the applied reporting practices include social consequences, economic consequences, accounting consequences, and apprehensions regarding accounting consequences (see Table 1 for further details). In order to limit the focus of this paper, only some of these possible preconditions and consequences of the efforts to harmonize accounting internationally are discussed. This limitation permits discussion of a few interesting aspects of international accounting harmonization

A BLEND OF ACCOUNTING PRINCIPLES   97

Table 1. Preconditions affecting accounting harmonization and possible consequences

Preconditions

	State of economy	*Societal goals*	*Legal system*
● Current laws	● International trade	● Level of education	● History
● Current infrastructure for standard-setting	● Basis of economy	● Nature of enterprise, e.g. encouragement	● Regulatory atmosphere
	— Agriculture	of capital formation	● Political system
● Relationship to IASC promulgations	— Natural resources	through hidden	● Tax system
	— Manufacturing	reserves	● Nature of contracts
● Nature of the accounting profession	● Stability of currency	● Culture	● Ownership structure
— Status	● Growth pattern	● Language	
— Economic resources	● Primary provider of capital		
— Professional experience	— Stockholders		
— Relation to government	— Bankers		

Influence accounting and reporting practices and the degree of harmonization

Required practices	Permitted practices	Recommended practices

Consequences of these practices if harmonized

Social consequences	*Economic consequences*	*Accounting consequences*	*Apprehensions regarding accounting consequences*
● Lifts barriers to entry by professionals, expanding mobility	● Enhancement of capital markets	● Ability to distort or mislead is circumvented	● Lowest common denominator will prevail
	● More efficiency in allocating economic resources	● Common yardstick is formulated — more comparability	● Domination feared by "leaders", potentially inappropriate for developing countries
	● Reduction of information production costs, training costs and regulatory costs	● Expands demand for accounting services in developing countries	

Source: Monsen and Wallace (1995: Exhibit 1).

thoroughly, realizing that this perspective must be viewed in the context of an ongoing stream of international accounting research.

One important accounting precondition is the particular legal system in question. With regard to legal systems, countries can be dichotomized as common law or civil law countries. Most Western countries are civil law, while Anglo–Saxon are common law countries (see, e.g., Nobes, 1992; Lüder, 1988). In common law countries, unwritten law dominates. Detailed accounting requirements are not prescribed in the laws, resulting in a situation which is reasonably flexible in relation to a changing environment. In a civil law country, however, the situation is different. Here the legal system is primarily based on statute law, and the law plays a much more important role than in a common law country. For example, the accounting law usually contains a number of specific accounting requirements that a company has to follow when preparing its financial statements. As a result, a company in a civil law country faces a less flexible situation than its counterpart in a common law country.

However, it is not sufficient to focus upon this general distinction between civil law and common law countries when discussing the accounting flexibility in a country. Even though a country belongs to the group of common law countries, it can issue many accounting requirements (outside the law framework) which the companies have to follow. A better dimension on which to focus, is therefore on the distinctions between required, permitted and recommended reporting practices (see Table 1). For example, in the U.S.A. listed companies have to report in accordance with many detailed required accounting practices (U.S. GAAP) even though these requirements do not belong to the legal framework itself.

To the extent that an international company has to face different and conflicting accounting requirements in order to be listed on stock exchanges in different countries, communication problems are likely to occur. Because these communication problems are the focus of this paper, detailed analyses of the differences between the particular accounting requirements in various countries, for example, between Norwegian and U.S. accounting principles, will not be undertaken here. However, our focus on the likely communication problems, due to different accounting requirements, can form a platform for further detailed analyses in subsequent international accounting research.

REQUIRED, PERMITTED AND RECOMMENDED PRACTICES

The present Norwegian accounting legislation builds upon a Nordic proposal for new Companies Acts, issued in 1969 (see, e.g., Monsen and Wallace, 1995). This proposal was based upon the civil law tradition. However, it is not possible for a law to cover every possible valuation, measurement and disclosure aspect. Nor is this desirable, because this would have hindered the development of accounting practices within a changing environment. Therefore, in most countries which have accounting legislation, we find references to generally accepted accounting principles. Such a reference ("god regnskapsskikk") is also found in the Nordic proposal, and it was later introduced in the Norwegian accounting legislation.

Because of the legalistic accounting framework in Norway, "god regnskapsskikk" has to be developed within the boundaries of required and permitted practices. This means that "god regnskapsskikk" within the Norwegian accounting framework will differ from generally accepted accounting principles within other legalistic frameworks. In particular, the development of "god regnskapsskikk" within the Norwegian legalistic framework will be more inflexible than the development of generally accepted accounting principles within a common law country, such as the U.S.A.

The present Norwegian Companies Act (1976) contains the following general reference:

> Årsoppgjøret skal settes opp i samsvar med god regnskapsskikk. (The financial statements are to be presented in accordance with generally accepted accounting principles within the general framework of the law. (§11-4; translated by N. Monsen.)

This general reference warrants some comments. Given the fact that the Companies Act is based upon a legalistic approach and that it contains a number of specific requirements (for example, how to present the income statement and the balance sheet), it is doubtful if the general reference to "god regnskapsskikk" can override the specific requirements in the law (see also Monsen and Wallace, 1995). On the other hand, the content of "god regnskapsskikk" is intended to be developed within the general framework of the law in accordance with a changing environment. In other words, as a new particular accounting problem arises, it is supposed to be dealt with in accordance with "god regnskapsskikk", which is within the general framework of the law.

This means that there is no straightforward procedure to apply if one wants to translate "god regnskapsskikk" into a foreign language, such as English. One has to appreciate that "god regnskapsskikk" is bounded by the legalistic accounting framework on which the Norwegian Companies Act is based. Because this legal framework differs from the accounting rules found in the U.S.A., "god regnskapsskikk" differs from U.S. GAAP. As a result of this, different expressions have been used when translating "god regnskapsskikk" into English, including "generally accepted accounting principles" (Monsen and Wallace, 1995), "good accounting practice" (Flower, 1994), and "Norwegian GAAP" (the annual reports of Norsk Hydro). In this paper, we chose the expression "Norwegian GAAP" as the English translation of "god regnskapsskikk" as it is used in the Norwegian Companies Act. Moreover, the term "Norwegian accounting principles" is used when referring to accounting principles that are in conformity with the Norwegian Companies Act, incorporating Norwegian GAAP. Because the translation of specific Norwegian terms into English may create added disclosure problems, we have deliberately chosen to present Norwegian and English texts when the translation problem is important. This practice makes the following possible: (1) the readers may check our English translation, and apply their own if they disagree with us; and (2) we can discuss the added disclosure problems due to the translation process.

A further discussion of the Norwegian Companies Act may be found in Johnsen (1993), Kinserdal (1994) and Monsen and Wallace (1995). For the purpose of the present study, however, it is sufficient to focus upon the fact that a Norwegian company listed on the stock exchange in Norway (the Oslo Stock Exchange) has to prepare its financial statements in accordance with the Norwegian Companies Act and Norwegian GAAP, or in other words: in accordance with required, permitted and recommended accounting practices in Norway. Moreover, it is one of the main tasks of the company's auditors to express their opinion on whether or not the company has done so (Companies Act §10-9).

NORSK HYDRO

Norsk Hydro was founded in 1905 to utilize Norway's large hydro-electric energy resources for the world's first industrial production of nitrogen fertilizers. Through the further development of Norwegian energy and natural resources, Hydro has become the country's largest publicly-owned industrial concern. Energy, both in the form of hydro-electric power and petroleum, has been the basis for Hydro's growth and represents a common link between its business activities.

In 1951, Hydro broadened its activities by going into magnesium production, and in 1967 expanded further in the energy-intensive light metal sector by establishing aluminium production. When the search for oil and gas began in the North Sea, Hydro became involved from the allocation of the very first concessions on Norway's continental shelf in 1965. Hydro and its partners discovered oil and gas in the Ekofisk field in 1969 and the Frigg field in 1971. It was these discoveries which laid the basis for Hydro's development as a producer of oil and gas. As an operator for major offshore projects, in particular the Oseberg field, Hydro has subsequently developed into a full-fledged oil company.

North Sea oil production gave Hydro long-term supplies of natural gas liquids, which formed the foundation for further expansion into the petrochemical industry. In 1975, Hydro commenced oil refinery operations, and gradually built up a retail marketing organization for oil products in Norway, Sweden and Denmark.

The various divisions and subsidiaries form Hydro's key operating units which are grouped together in four industry segments. The segments reflect the company's core businesses. These segments are: Agriculture, Oil and Gas, Light Metals, and Petrochemicals. Hydro's portfolio of business activities can be divided into two main categories: (1) the production of energy, both hydro-electric power and hydrocarbons; and (2) the utilization of energy, often together with other natural resources, in the manufacture of mineral fertilizers, metals and petrochemicals.

Starting from its base as a Norwegian producer with Scandinavia as its home market, Hydro has gone through a period of strong international growth, primarily in Europe, during the last 20 years. New operations have been established and existing businesses acquired in many countries in the fertilizer, petrochemicals and light metal segments.

Norway is still the main base for the Group's varied production, with large facilities in different parts of the country. Almost all of Hydro's oil and gas production takes place on the Norwegian continental shelf. However, the most important markets for Hydro's products lie outside Norway; between 55 and 62% of Hydro's total sales have gone to the European Community during the previous 5-year period. Moreover, between 13 and 17% of the sales has gone to other European countries during the same time period.

Norsk Hydro's shares are listed on stock exchanges in seven countries in Europe and on the New York Stock Exchange (see Table 2). The Norwegian State owns 51% of the shares of Norsk Hydro, while the remainder are owned by a large number of private shareholders in Norway, Europe and the U.S.A. In Figs 1 and 2, it appears that the New York Stock exchange has become the most important stock exchange for listing of Norsk Hydro's shares that are not owned by the Norwegian state, followed by the Oslo Stock Exchange.

INTERNATIONAL DISCLOSURE PRACTICES

This section traces the development of Norsk Hydro's attempts to incorporate international accounting principles in its annual report.

The first attempt

Under the heading "International accounting" we find the following excerpt in the annual report for 1982:

> As a result of the increased internationalisation of the company's activities and financing it was felt necessary to present Norsk Hydro's accounts in a form which complies with international accounting principles, more particularly those practised in the U.S.A. This is not fully permitted under Norwegian company law. In the 1982 accounts, therefore, the principles laid down by Norwegian legislation and Norwegian accounting standards have been followed for Norwegian companies. For companies abroad international accounting principles have been employed. (English version of Norsk Hydro's Annual Report for 1982, p. 44.)

Table 2. Exchanges with Norsk Hydro listing

Exchange	Year of listing
Oslo	1905
Paris	1909
Geneva	1909
London	1972
Frankfurt	1975
Zürich	1976
Stockholm	1983
Amsterdam	1986
New York	1986

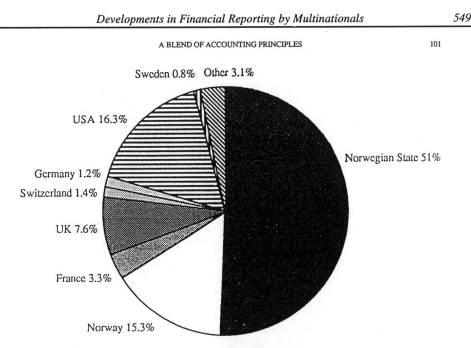

Fig. 1. Distribution of share capital (1983).

As a result of its growing internationalization, the company felt a real need to present its financial statements in accordance with international, mainly U.S., accounting principles. At the same time it realized that it was not possible to do this to its full extent within the boundaries of the Norwegian Companies Act. Therefore, it chose a strategy of presenting a mixture of Norwegian and U.S. accounting principles.

The following attempts

In the succeeding annual report (for 1983), Hydro continued its practice of applying Norwegian accounting principles for Norwegian companies and U.S. accounting principles for foreign subsidiaries. In fact, it devoted two pages of the annual report to promote the use of international (U.S.) accounting principles, and to explain the differences between Norwegian and U.S. accounting principles.

In the annual report for 1984, the focus on U.S. accounting principles increased even more, as evidenced by the fact that the Board of Directors' report refers to Hydro's results based upon international accounting principles. Furthermore, a longer paragraph promoting the focus on U.S. GAAP is now presented in the Board of Directors' report, as opposed to a more distant location as in the previous annual report. In addition, in a note to the financial statements for 1984 we find the following excerpt:

> Hydro wishes to present its accounts as much as possible in a format which complies with international accounting principles. Norwegian company law and accounting practices deviate in certain respects from these principles. The amounts shown below comply with U.S. "Generally Accepted Accounting Principles." (English version of Norsk Hydro's Annual Report for 1984, from Note 26, p. 28.)

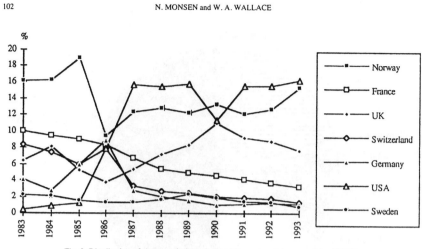

Fig. 2. Distribution of share capital (excluding Norwegian state ownership of 51%).

The financial statements present a summary of the consolidated income statement and balance sheet in conformity with U.S. GAAP, three notes, and an explanation of the difference between the official Norwegian result and equity, and their U.S. counterparts. Thus, for the first time Norsk Hydro has presented its consolidated income statement and balance sheet entirely in accordance with U.S. GAAP. But this presentation is clearly supplemental to the official Norwegian financial statements.

Increased focus on U.S. GAAP

When presenting its annual report for 1985, Norsk Hydro took new steps towards increased "accounting internationalization". It is of particular interest to the present study to observe the increased focus on U.S. GAAP in the annual report: the consolidated income statement now ends by focusing on net income in accordance with U.S. GAAP. Furthermore, net earnings per share is reported in accordance with U.S. GAAP, and in connection with the balance sheet, the company presents the shareholders' equity in accordance with U.S. GAAP.

The focus on U.S. GAAP is maintained in the subsequent annual report for 1986. The consolidated income statement and balance sheet are presented similarly to the corresponding financial statements in the annual report for 1985. Moreover, the Operating and Financial Highlights presented at the forefront of the annual reports for 1985 and 1986, are based upon U.S. GAAP.

U.S. GAAP takes precedence

In 1987's annual report Norsk Hydro proceeded with presenting its consolidated income statement and balance sheet as it did in its two previous reports. However, the following excerpt is found at the forefront of this report:

> With the exception of note 26, the financial statements presented on pages 11 to 29 are prepared in accordance with generally accepted accounting principles in Norway. All other financial data presented in this annual report, unless otherwise stated, is prepared in accordance with generally accepted accounting principles in the United States. (English version of Norsk Hydro's Annual Report for 1987, p. 2.)

The following year's annual report (for 1988) also presented a similar excerpt. Now, however, the excerpt is presented even more prominently, i.e. on page 1 directly after the contents of the annual report. The income statement and balance sheet continued to be presented as they were in the annual report for 1985. The annual reports for 1989 and 1990 are presented in a similar manner.

The precedence of U.S. GAAP over Norwegian accounting principles is signalled very clearly with the excerpt mentioned above, as well as the focus on U.S. GAAP both in the income statement and the balance sheet. Norsk Hydro is clearly trying to draw the attention more and more towards U.S. GAAP and away from Norwegian accounting principles. But as long as the Norwegian Companies Act is in force, Hydro also has to present its financial statements in accordance with Norwegian accounting principles.

Application of U.S. GAAP — a turning point
In the annual report for 1991, Norsk Hydro went even further towards focusing on U.S. GAAP as opposed to the Norwegian Companies Act and Norwegian GAAP. In the previous annual reports, the financial statements started with applying Norwegian accounting principles, and then continued by focusing on U.S. GAAP. Now, however, the consolidated income statement and balance sheet are presented entirely in accordance with U.S. GAAP, and this presentation is given before, rather than after, the presentation of these financial statements in accordance with Norwegian accounting principles. In fact, a number of notes to the financial statements are also presented before the financial statements in accordance with Norwegian accounting principles. Consequently, Norsk Hydro signals very clearly that it focuses on U.S. GAAP as opposed to Norwegian accounting principles.

Reactions to the U.S. GAAP focus
The Oslo Stock Exchange issues each year an accounting circular based upon a study of the annual reports of companies listed on the exchange. Norsk Hydro's focus on U.S. GAAP in its annual report for 1991 attracted the attention of the Oslo Stock Exchange, resulting in a separate section in the circular focusing on the location of the financial statements in accordance with Norwegian accounting principles:

> *5. Location of the Norwegian financial statements in the annual report*
> As mentioned in point 4, the Oslo Stock Exchange is positive to the increased focus on supplementary information presented in accordance with international accounting standards. However, Norwegian investors must be able to expect that financial statements presented in accordance with Norwegian laws and rules have priority. Moreover, the Norwegian financial statements must also be easily accessible, avoiding the procedure of first going through notes following financial statements based upon foreign accounting principles.
> Some companies have experimented with the form of presenting the information in the annual report in order to improve the presentation of the financial information. This development may, however, in some instances be at the expense of the value of the information to Norwegian users. In one particular instance, the Stock Exchange has noted that the main part of the financial statements have been presented in accordance with foreign accounting principles, while the Norwegian financial statements have been allocated a more distant location and is also strongly integrated in the notes to the financial statements presented in accordance with foreign accounting principles. The Oslo Stock Exchange considers this to be an unfortunate development. (The Oslo Stock Exchange, 1992, p. 6; translated by N. Monsen.)

Thus, the Oslo Stock Exchange expressed very clearly that it did not like the focus on U.S. GAAP at the expense of Norwegian accounting principles, even though it did not require Norsk Hydro to reissue its financial statements for 1991, focusing on Norwegian accounting principles. It is true that the Oslo Stock Exchange did not use the name of Norsk Hydro in the excerpt above. But because it explicitly underlined that it is one, and not two or more companies, that it criticized for focusing on U.S. GAAP at the expense of Norwegian accounting principles, there is no doubt that this particular company is Norsk Hydro.

Still U.S. GAAP focus

Apparently, as a result of the very clear critique from the Oslo Stock Exchange, Norsk Hydro increased its focus on Norwegian accounting principles in its annual report for 1992. That is, financial statements presented in accordance with Norwegian accounting principles were presented immediately after the U.S. GAAP financial statements, and before the notes to the financial statements. Also, the Norwegian financial statements were clearly marked as presented in accordance with Norwegian accounting principles, avoiding the appearance of being subject to the U.S. GAAP statements or as a part of the notes to the U.S. financial statements. But the focus is still on U.S. GAAP accounting principles, illustrated, among other things, by the fact that U.S. financial statements are presented before the Norwegian statements, and by the fact that the key financial figures are based upon U.S. GAAP.

In the following annual report (for 1993), Norsk Hydro presents the following excerpt:

> Hydro prepares financial statements both in accordance with the accounting principles generally accepted in Norway and those generally accepted in the United States (U.S. GAAP). For information on the results in accordance with accounting principles generally accepted in Norway please refer to the Director's report on pages 6–11, the consolidated financial statements and notes on pages 39–61 and the financial statements for Norsk Hydro a.s. on pages 62–65.
>
> Other financial information in this annual report is presented in accordance with U.S. GAAP, unless otherwise stated. (English version of Norsk Hydro's Annual Report for 1993, p. 2.)

As it appears from this excerpt, Norsk Hydro makes it very clear — on page 2 — that it prepares its financial statements both in accordance with Norwegian and U.S. accounting principles. Interestingly, the company starts in the extract by focusing on Norwegian accounting principles in front of U.S. accounting principles. However, after this focus on Norwegian accounting principles in the particular excerpt, Hydro changes the focus on U.S. GAAP. In particular, U.S. GAAP financial statements are still presented in front of Norwegian financial statements. By stating very clearly on page 2 that Norwegian financial statements also have been prepared, Hydro clearly informs that it also follows Norwegian accounting principles, and not only U.S. GAAP. But the focus in the annual report is still on U.S. GAAP.

Evolution of the cash flow statement

The cash flow statement has been presented as a financial statement of minor importance in Norsk Hydro's annual reports. The company has used the indirect method of presenting cash flows from operating activities. It has started with net income (before minority interests, appropriations and taxes) as it appeared in the income statement based upon Norwegian accounting principles, has made adjustment for non-cash expenses and revenues, and has then deduced net cash flow from operating activities.

Given use of the indirect method, this was a natural starting point, as long as the income statement was based upon Norwegian accounting principles, and U.S. GAAP supplemented these principles. However, when Norsk Hydro in its 1991 annual report presented its income statement in accordance with U.S. GAAP before Norwegian accounting principles, it presented its indirect cash flow statement starting from net income according to U.S. GAAP. This cash flow statement was clearly marked as prepared in accordance with U.S. GAAP. No consolidated cash flow statement was complementing the consolidated income statement and balance sheet presented in accordance with Norwegian accounting principles.

According to the Norwegian Companies Act (§11-13, point 8), however, it is required that a consolidated cash flow statement is to be presented in addition to a consolidated income statement and a consolidated balance sheet according to Norwegian accounting principles. This requirement, as well as the criticism from the Oslo Stock Exchange, are probably the main reasons why Norsk Hydro in its annual reports for 1992 and 1993 presented two different indirect cash flow statements: one starting from net income according to U.S. GAAP and the other starting from net income according to Norwegian accounting principles. Nonetheless, of considerable interest is the acceptance by regulators of the 1991 report, ostensibly not complying with the law.

As a result of the particular cash flow statement chosen (indirect method), Norsk Hydro faced a problem: should it present one or two different cash flow statements, starting from net income according to U.S. GAAP and/or Norwegian accounting principles? As shown above, it chose one statement in its 1991 annual report, and two statements in the succeeding reports. If, however, the company had chosen the direct method of presenting the cash flow statement, it would have avoided this dilemma. One cash flow statement would have been enough, and it would also have been more informative (see, e.g., Monsen and Olson, 1996). This example demonstrates the complexity spawned by multiple reporting frameworks available to companies interested in attracting capital beyond their national boundaries.

Summary

It appears from the description above, that Norsk Hydro has focused more and more on U.S. GAAP as opposed to Norwegian accounting principles in its annual report (see Fig. 3). At the start, it clearly stated that U.S. GAAP was not in conformity with the Norwegian Companies Act, and therefore it presented U.S. GAAP information as supplementary to Norwegian accounting principles. Norwegian accounting principles were applied for Norwegian companies and U.S. GAAP were applied for foreign subsidiaries, resulting in a mixture of accounting principles. The focus on U.S. GAAP increased steadily, however, until U.S. GAAP financial statements clearly dominated financial statements presented in accordance with Norwegian accounting principles. Due to criticism from the Oslo Stock Exchange, however, financial statements based upon Norwegian accounting principles increased in their focus in the 1992 report, although U.S. GAAP continued to dominate the annual report of Norsk Hydro. In the 1993 report, Hydro takes another small step towards focusing on Norwegian accounting principles, by clearly drawing the reader's attention to these principles on page 2 in the annual report. But the focus in the annual report is still on U.S. GAAP at the expense of Norwegian accounting principles.

Given this evolution of Norsk Hydro's financial reporting practices, it is of particular interest to study how the auditors have reacted to the increased application of U.S. GAAP at the expense of Norwegian accounting principles. The criticism by the Oslo Stock Exchange, and the subsequent development in the 1992 and 1993 reports, including the reference to the evolution of the cash flow statement, may indicate that the auditors also have expressed their opinion on the development. In other words, in the auditors' opinion, has Norsk Hydro presented its financial statements in accordance with Norwegian accounting principles, U.S. GAAP or both? This is the topic of the following section.

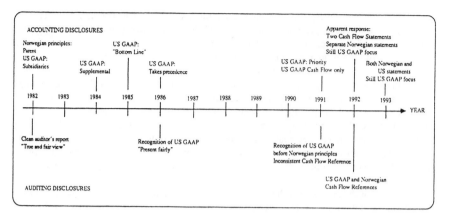

Fig. 3. Overview of accounting and auditing disclosures.

THE AUDITORS' REACTION

The evolution towards the application of U.S. GAAP started in Norsk Hydro's annual report for 1982. As reported earlier, Hydro used Norwegian accounting principles for Norwegian companies and U.S. accounting principles for foreign subsidiaries, resulting in a mixture of different accounting principles. Did this mixture result in a comment being made by the auditor? Did he state that different accounting principles had been used, and that some of the principles (U.S. GAAP) were not in conformity with the Norwegian Companies Act and Norwegian GAAP?

First: no reaction

The following excerpt is from the auditor's report to the financial statements for 1982:

> Jeg har utført revisjonen . . . i henhold til god revisjonsskikk. . . . Selskapets årsoppgjør og konsernopgjøret er avgitt i samsvar med aksjelovens bestemmelser, og de gir etter min mening et uttrykk for selskapets og konsernets årsresultat og stilling, som stemmer med god regnskapsskikk. (The auditor's report in the Norwegian version of Norsk Hydro's Annual Report for 1982, p. 11.)

> I have conducted the audit . . . in accordance with generally accepted auditing standards. . . . Both the company's annual accounts and the consolidated accounts have been prepared in accordance with the Norwegian Companies Act and with generally accepted accounting principles. In my opinion they give a true and fair view of the financial position of the company and the group, and of the results of their operations. (The auditor's report in the English version of Norsk Hydro's Annual Report for 1982, p. 11.)

Thus, the auditor states that the audit is carried out in accordance with generally accepted auditing standards, and that the financial statements have been prepared in accordance with the Companies Act, and in accordance with "god regnskapsskikk". In other words, he did not comment upon, or react to, Norsk Hydro's application of U.S. accounting principles for foreign subsidiaries. This means that the information content of the auditor's report as it relates to providing assurance with generally accepted accounting principles in Norway — a requirement of the law — may be questioned.

Still no reaction

As outlined earlier, Norsk Hydro continued its practice of using a mixture of Norwegian and U.S. accounting principles in its two succeeding annual reports. At the same time, the auditor continued his practice, stating that the financial statements were prepared in accordance with the Norwegian Companies Act and "god regnskapsskikk". Still, he did not comment upon the company's use of U.S. accounting principles.

A communication problem

Because Norsk Hydro issued an English version of its annul report in addition to the Norwegian version, the auditor had to face the language question regarding how to communicate the content of the term "god regnskapsskikk" in English. The following excerpts of the auditor's report are found in the Norwegian and English annual reports for 1985 for Norsk Hydro, respectively:

> Jeg har utført revisjonen . . . i henhold til god revisjonsskikk. . . . Selskapets årsoppgjør og konsernoppgjøret er avgitt i samsvar med aksjelovens bestemmelser, og gir etter min mening et forsvarlig uttrykk for selskapets og konsernets årsresultat og finansielle stilling som stemmer med *god regnskapsskikk*. (The auditor's report in the Norwegian version of Norsk Hydro's Annual Report for 1985, p. 10; our italicization).

> I have audited the financial statements . . . in accordance with generally accepted auditing standards. . . . Both the company's financial statements and the consolidated financial statements have been prepared in accordance with the Norwegian Companies Act and with accounting principles generally accepted in Norway. In my opinion they give a *true and fair view* of the financial position of the company and the group, and of the results of their operations. (The auditor's report in the English version of Norsk Hydro's Annual Report for 1985, p. 10; our italicization).

The auditor clearly stated that the financial statements have been prepared in accordance with the Norwegian Companies Act. Moreover, he also underlined that Norwegian, as opposed to some other country's accounting principles, have been used. Then he faced the problem of communicating the content of the term "god regnskapsskikk" in English, and he chose the English expression "true and fair view". This expression was also used in the auditor's reports for 1982–1984.

In the authors' opinion, this auditor's report does not help the reader very much when interpreting the financial statements of Norsk Hydro. On the other hand, it may increase uncertainty regarding the particular accounting principles used. As outlined above, Norsk Hydro increasingly focused on U.S. GAAP as opposed to Norwegian accounting principles. But the auditor stressed that Norwegian accounting principles have been used. It has been argued earlier, that the general reference to "god regnskapsskikk" cannot overrule the particular requirements of the various sections of the Companies Act. However, the auditor's use of the expression "true and fair view" may lead a foreign reader who is familiar with U.K. financial reporting to believe that British principles have been applied. And finally, the U.K. term "true and fair view" has been used, in spite of the company's explicit reference to U.S. and not U.K. accounting principles. Hence, we are left with a blend of three countries' reporting practices: Norway, the U.S. and the U.K.

The first reference to U.S. GAAP

Norsk Hydro continued to present its financial statements in a similar way with a U.S. focus in is annual report for 1986. However, we observe some differences in the auditor's report. First, it changed from a personal report ("In my opinion") to a company report ("In our opinion"). While the auditor's report for 1985 was signed by a state authorized auditor, as a representative of an auditing firm, the report for 1986 is only signed by the name of the auditing company, and not by an auditor belonging to the company. The following are excerpts from the auditors' reports:

> ... Vår revisjon er utført i henhold til *gjeldende lov* og god revisjonsskikk. ... Etter vår mening er selskapets årsoppgjør og konsernoppgjøret avgitt i samsvar med aksjelovens bestemmelser og gir et forsvarlig uttrykk for selskapets og konsernets årsresultat og finansielle stilling som stemmer med god revisjonsskikk. ... Som det framgår av note 27, avviker norske regnskapsprinsipper fra regn-skapsprinsipper som anvendes i USA (US GAAP). Vi har revidert sammendraget av konsernets resul-tatregnskap for 1986 og 1985 samt sammendraget av konsernbalansen pr. 31. desember 1986 og 1985 slik det fremgar i note 27. Etter vår mening gir sammendraget et forsvarlig uttrykk for konsernets årsresultat og finansielle stilling som stemmer med god regnskapsskikk i USA. (The auditors' report in the Norwegian version of Norsk Hydro's Annual Report for 1986, p. 10; our italicization).

> We have performed the audit ... in accordance with generally accepted auditing standards. ... In our opinion, the financial statements are in conformity with the Companies Act and present fairly the result for the year and current financial position of the company and the Group in accordance with generally accepted accounting principles. ... As described more fully in Note 27 to the consolidated financial statements, Norwegian accounting principles differ from generally accepted accounting principles in the United States. We have also audited, in accordance with generally accepted audit-ing standards, the condensed consolidated balance sheets at December 31st, 1986 and 1985, and the related condensed statements of income for the year then ended.

> In our opinion, the information set forth in the condensed financial statements in Note 27, when read in conjunction with the related consolidated financial statements, is fairly stated in conformity with generally accepted accounting principles in the United States applied on a consistent basis. (The auditors' report in the English version of Norsk Hydro's Annual Report for 1986, p. 10.)

A number of interesting observations can be drawn from this auditors' report: First, the Norwegian version of the report states that the audit is carried out both in accordance with "gjeldende lov" (the present law) and "god revisjonsskikk" (generally accepted auditing stan-dards). In the previous Norwegian versions of the auditor's reports, no reference was found to the law, only to generally accepted auditing standards. Thus, a reference to the law is introduced in the Norwegian version. However, it appears from the English excerpt presented above, that no reference is given to the law here, only to generally accepted auditing standards.

Second, the expression "true and fair view" has now been replaced with "present fairly ... in accordance with generally accepted accounting principles". Third, an explicit reference to gen-erally accepted accounting principles in the U.S.A. is made. It is true that this reference explic-itly addresses a note to the financial statements, and not the financial statements themselves. But as pointed out earlier, the financial statements are presented similarly to the previous statements, mixing Norwegian and U.S. accounting principles, and focusing on net income in accordance with U.S. accounting principles.

Increased reference to U.S. GAAP

As pointed out earlier, U.S. GAAP takes precedence in Norsk Hydro's annual report for 1987. The auditor continued to refer both to the law and generally accepted auditing standards in the Norwegian report, but only to the latter in the English report. It also states that the financial state-ments are in conformity with the Companies Act and fairly present the results of the year and cur-rent financial position in accordance with generally accepted accounting principles.

However, the auditor also takes a step towards focusing more on U.S. GAAP. In the Norwegian version of the auditors' report, the U.S. GAAP focus in the financial statements is explicitly addressed. However, in the English version, it still refers to the use of U.S. GAAP principles in a note (similar to the reference in the previous report), and it does not explicitly address the U.S. GAAP focus in the financial statements themselves. However, a change in the reference to U.S. GAAP is observed:

> In our opinion, the information set forth in the condensed consolidated financial statements in Note 26, when read in conjunction with the related consolidated financial statements, is fairly stated in conformity with generally accepted accounting principles in the United States consistently applied during the period except for the change, with which we concur, in the method of accounting for pension costs as described in Note 26. (The auditors' report in the English version of Norsk Hydro's Annual Report for 1987, p. 9.)

As it appears from the excerpt, the auditors' report states that there is one change from U.S. GAAP, and it is related to the method of accounting for pension costs. However, the auditor concurs with this change.

Continued reference to U.S. GAAP

The auditors' report in the annual reports for 1988, 1989 and 1990 was presented in a similar manner to the report for 1987, with one change: the exception for the method of accounting for pension costs no longer appears. On the other hand, the following phrase is used: "In our opinion, the information . . . is fairly stated, in all material respects, in conformity with generally accepted accounting principles in the United States".

Reference to U.S. GAAP — a turning point

The auditors' report changes to some extent in the annual report for 1991. This is partly due to a proposal for a new recommendation on how to present the auditors' report (NSRF, 1991), and partly due to Norsk Hydro's focus on U.S. GAAP as the dominating accounting principles. In particular, the auditors' report becomes much longer than previously presented. Furthermore, following the new proposal, a reference to the cash flow statement is now incorporated in the auditors' report. Moreover, the auditors' report now refers to U.S. GAAP before it refers to Norwegian accounting principles.

Reactions to the cash flow statement

We have pointed out earlier that the evolution of the cash flow statement in the annual report may have created a reaction from the auditor. It is therefore of particular interest to study the auditors' reaction to this evolution. In the auditors' report, no reference to the cash flow statement is found until the annual report for 1991. However, following the new proposal from the NSRF in 1991, the auditor started to refer to the cash flow statement in addition to the income statement and balance sheet.

In its annual report for 1991, Norsk Hydro presents one version of its consolidated cash flow statement. The cash flow statement is presented in accordance with the indirect method, departing from net income in accordance with U.S. GAAP, as opposed to Norwegian accounting principles. The following excerpts are found in the auditors' report:

> In our opinion, the financial statements on pages 44–46 . . . present fairly, in all material respects, the financial position . . . and the results . . . and . . . cash flows . . . in conformity with accounting principles generally accepted in the United States. (The auditors' report in the English version of Norsk Hydro's Annual Report for 1991, p. 72; Excerpt 1.)

> The . . . statements of cash flows on page 46 and financial statements on pages 66–68 . . . have been

prepared in accordance with the requirements of the Norwegian Companies Act and with accounting principles generally accepted in Norway. (The auditors' report in the English version of Norsk Hydro's Annual Report for 1991, p. 72, Excerpt 2.)

Pages 44–46 show the consolidated income statements, balance sheets, and statements of cash flows under the heading "U.S. GAAP". However, pages 66–68 show the consolidated income statements and balance sheets, as well as the income statements and balance sheets for the mother (parent) company. These financial statements are presented under the following heading: "In Accordance with Generally Accepted Accounting Principles in Norway".

Given these headings in the annual report, the auditors' report leads to some interesting observations. First, it states that the cash flow statement on page 46 is presented in accordance with accounting principles in the U.S.A. (Excerpt 1). Then it states that the cash flow statement on page 46 has been prepared in accordance with the requirements of the Norwegian Companies Act and with accounting principles generally accepted in Norway (Excerpt 2).

Both of these statements would have been appropriate if the direct method had been used when presenting the cash flows from operating activities: net cash flow from operating activities is the net difference between cash inflows and cash outflows from operating activities. However, as pointed out earlier, the indirect method departs from net income in the income statement, and this figure is definitely dependent on the particular accounting principles applied.

In the subsequent annual report (for 1992), Norsk Hydro presents two versions of its cash flow statement (indirect method). One is presented under the heading "U.S. GAAP" and begins with net income (loss) in accordance with U.S. GAAP. The other is presented under the heading "In Accordance with Accounting Principles Generally Accepted in Norway", and is starts with net income (loss) in accordance with Norwegian accounting principles. The auditors now stated that the former cash flow statement is based upon U.S. GAAP and the latter is based upon Norwegian accounting principles, clearly avoiding the inconsistency in their previous report. In the annual report for 1993, Hydro has continued its practice of presenting two versions of the indirect cash flow statement.

Summary

When Norsk Hydro first started to apply U.S. accounting principles, the auditor did not comment upon this development (see Fig. 3). However, because Norsk Hydro issued an English version of its annual report, the auditor faced a communication problem, in particular with regard to communicating the content of the Norwegian term "god regnskapsskikk". It is also of interest to observe that the auditor refers to the auditing law in addition to "god revisjonsskikk" (generally accepted auditing standards in Norway) in the Norwegian version of his report, but only to generally accepted auditing standards in the English version.

As a result of the increased focus on U.S. GAAP in Hydro's annual report, the auditors have also increased their focus on U.S. GAAP. The particular model of the cash flow statement applied (indirect method) caused some problems for the auditors in 1991. However, for 1992 and 1993, the company presented two versions of the cash flow statement — one in accordance with U.S. GAAP and the other in accordance with Norwegian accounting principles.

Beginning in 1991, U.S. GAAP is presented as the main accounting principles both by the company itself and by its auditors. This development, however, was criticized by the Oslo Stock Exchange, resulting in a minor change towards increased focus on Norwegian accounting principles in the 1992 and 1993 reports and the duplication of the cash flow statements, explicitly based on Norwegian income. But U.S. GAAP still dominates. Thus, given the present legalistic accounting framework in force in Norway, supplemented by Norwegian GAAP within the boundaries of the laws, the development observed raises a number of interesting questions to be discussed. It is to these questions to which we now turn our attention.

DISCUSSION AND CONCLUDING REMARKS

The struggle of companies interested in capital sources beyond their domestic boundaries to prepare useful financial presentations that comply with law and regulations of various countries' accounting professions can produce paradoxical and contradictory representations. The question we posed early on is: what can companies interested in international exchanges do currently, given the fact that IASC has not yet been embraced by IASCO, meaning that listings on the New York Stock Exchange must reconcile to U.S. GAAP? The "answer" apparently identified by Norsk Hydro was to combine Norwegian and U.S. presentations. The interplay between accounting numbers that resulted and auditors' attestations on hybrid presentations, pose an added complication from such a strategy. In this case setting, a company belonging to a particular accounting context, i.e. a context with a particular relationship between required, permitted and recommended accounting practices (Norway), desired a growing stockholder presence of investors in another accounting context (the U.S.A.) and after first blending U.S. GAAP numbers with Norwegian accounting principles, evolved toward total U.S. GAAP-based numbers that preceded Norwegian presentations. In some cases, the U.S. numbers even supplanted the Norwegian computations: specifically, the cash flow presentation was U.S.-based.

While speculative, two explanations have been discussed in the literature as to why U.S. GAAP is emphasized in such settings: (1) U.S. GAAP statements seem to suffice in the international arena (Choi and Mueller, 1993, p. 51); and (2) a uniform measurement yardstick for management of foreign operations is needed for control and performance evaluation (Choi and Mueller, 1993, p. 47). In other words, rather than having to generate three or four versions of the annual report, the U.S. GAAP-based disclosure is often acceptable to a plethora of other markets. Of particular interest in the case of Norsk Hydro, is the verbal representation by managers that their joint control-related concerns over international operations prompted a U.S. GAAP focus (the authors appreciate this information provided by a colleague at NHH, Frøystein Gjesdal).

As articulated earlier in this paper, the question of perception arises. Are these steps perceived as positive by market participants? In particular, are communication problems likely? Are regulators receptive to experimentation? What trade-offs are evidenced in this particular setting? The action by domestic regulators in Norway is a telling display of the dangers of experimentation. While accepting the 1991 report with the U.S.-based dominance as a public filing, the stock exchange commented on the importance of Norwegian users of financial statements. The exchange cited the impropriety of relegating Norwegian presentations as secondary to any foreign presentations. This admonishment was clearly less costly than forced reissuance of 1991 financials or delisting which are, of course, among the sanctions available to regulators. There is little doubt that the displeasure of the regulators was clearly perceived as necessitating a substantive reaction by Norsk Hydro. Indeed, it led to a duplication of cash flow presentations using both Norwegian and U.S.-based income figures, and to a clear statement that both Norwegian and U.S. accounting principles had been followed.

Interestingly, the auditors seem to have accepted blends of U.S. GAAP subsidiary numbers and presentations in accordance with Norwegian accounting principles, with no direct highlighting of the mixture. As English versions of reporting evolved, the auditors' report used the "true and fair" language, despite directed attention to U.S. GAAP rather than U.K. GAAP. Eventually, the U.S. phrasing of the auditors' report displaced former phrasing. Of consequence is the lack of qualifying language when hybrid accounting and presentation in apparent contradiction of the law were included in the annual report. Discussion is needed among researchers and auditors of companies participating in international capital markets on how to phrase useful auditors' reports in the presence of multiple accounting reports applying diverse measurement rules. In the absence of such dialogue, the sort of conflicting and perhaps misleading communications as those detailed herein may proliferate. It appears that the auditors judged the steps by Norsk Hydro to globalize its financial presentations as acceptable within a GAAP and GAAS context, rather than imposing the legalistic benchmark of needing a cash flow statement which, if indirect, began with Norwegian income.

Another issue suggested by the case of Norsk Hydros is that of domestic versus international regulatory perspectives. As domestic regulators struggle for relative power in dominating disclosure practices, both legal and political fallout can be anticipated. Perhaps IOSCO and similar initiatives hold promise to avoid such costs. As international capital markets grow in importance, research is needed on how to satisfy diverse stockholder groups' information demands, bearing in mind the different accounting traditions of various countries and the sizeable costs of multiple presentations.

REFERENCES

Choi, F. D. S. and Mueller, G. (1993) *Globalization of Financial Accounting and Reporting*. Management Reporting Monograph, Financial Executive Research Foundation, Morristown, NJ.

Flower, J., (ed.) (1994) *The Regulation of Financial Reporting in the Nordic Countries*. (Fritzes, Centre for Research in European Accounting).

Johnsen, A. (1993) Accounting regulation in Norway. *The European Accounting Review* 3, 617–626.

Kinserdal, A. (1994) Norway. In *The Regulation of Financial Reporting in the Nordic Countries*, ed. J. Flower, pp. 149–180. Fritzes, Centre for Research in European Accounting.

Lüder, K. (1988) Governmental accounting in west European countries: with special reference to the Federal Republic of Germany. In *Governmental Accounting and Auditing, International Comparisons* eds J. L. Chan and R. H. Jones, pp. 82–104. Routledge, London.

Monsen, N. and Olson, O. (1996) Silent accounting harmonisation — towards the presentation of cash flow models in the local governmental and business fields in Norway. *Scandinavian Journal of Management*, 12, 411–423.

Monsen, N. and Wallace, W. A. (1995) Evolving financial reporting practices: the dilemma of conflicting standards in the Nordic Countries. *Contemporary Accounting Research* 11, 973–997.

Nobes, C. (1992) *International Classification of Financial Reporting*, 2nd edn. Routledge, London.

Norges Statsautoriserte Revisorers Forening (NSRF) (1991) Anbefaling vedrørende form og inn-hold i revisors beretning av 26. september 1991 (Proposal for a new recommendation on how to present the auditors' report of 26 September 1991).

Norsk Hydro Annual Reports (Norwegian and English versions) for 1967/68–1979/80; 1 July–31 December, 1980; 1981–1993.

Norwegian Companies Act (1976) Lov om aksjeselskaper av 4. juni 1976 nr. 59, med senere endringer (The Companies Act of 1976, including later changes).

Oslo Børs (The Oslo Stock Exchange) (1992) Regnskapssirkulære for 1991 (Utgitt i 1992) (Accounting circular for 1991, issued in 1992).

[25]

The International
Journal of
Accounting

Problems in Comparing Financial Performance Across International Boundaries: A Case Study Approach

Mark Whittington
Warwick Business School, Coventry, UK

Key Words: International accounting practices; Financial reporting issues; Dual listed companies

Abstract: In increasingly global markets for finance, goods, and services, a variety of decision makers need to assess companies from numerous countries on a common basis. Differences between national and international accounting principles and practices make such a task difficult, if not impossible.

This article considers the contribution of previous research to resolving this problem. Much of the earlier work in this area has used metrics based on a broad database of companies from many different industries and worked out conservatism indices based on a comparison of profit levels of companies reporting in two generally agreed accounting principles and practices (GAAPs). While useful, this does not address the problems of conversion for any one industry or company. In order to examine the implications of GAAP differences for international comparisons, a case study approach is adopted, considering two of the major players in the European steel industry. Accounting information is produced for both companies under their domestic GAAPs and under United States (US) GAAP, thus allowing for an analysis based on a common, US, GAAP. As a part of this analysis, a time series approach is taken.

The article concludes that there are additional factors that may affect the evaluation of relative conservatism and the financial comparison of individual companies even when carried out on a common GAAP basis.

The use of financial analysis, based on published accounts, is both commonplace and fraught with difficulties. Even within one country, company directors may choose accounting policies that differ from those of their competitors making the validity of any comparison questionable. The level of difficulty is increased if the analysis requires comparison of companies from different countries as the set of available policy choices may be different for each one. The existence of differing GAAPs (generally agreed accounting principles and practices), the reasons for this and the problems caused, has given rise to an extensive literature that has attempted to

Direct all correspondence to: Mark Whittington, Warwick Business School, Coventry CV4 7AL UK; E-mail: m.whittington@warwick.ac.uk.

The International Journal of Accounting, Vol. 35, No. 3, pp. 399–413   ISSN: 0020-7063.

400   THE INTERNATIONAL JOURNAL OF ACCOUNTING   Vol. 35, No. 3, 2000

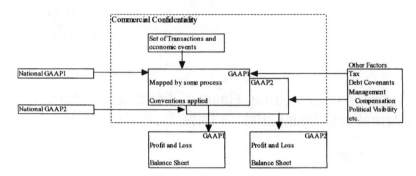

Figure 1. International Accounting Differences.

catalogue and describe differences and develop taxonomies; for example, Nobes and Parker (1998).

In parallel with this literature has been one that has considered the effects on reported performance of alternative GAAPs. A number of adjustment indices, that measure the relative conservatism in the level of published profit, have been developed and these provide a conversion multiplier metric for translation from one GAAP to another (for example, Gray, 1980; Simonds and Azieres, 1989; French and Poterba, 1991; Economist, 1992; Weetman et al., 1998). It is worth noting that all these studies have examined the effect of GAAP conversion on profit rather than that on other measures such as return on equity.

Companies that produce more than one set of accounts, each governed by different GAAPs, have provided one means of comparing the out-turn effect of one set of accounting principles with another. However, these results can only be indicative, as the available companies for such studies are limited in number and unlikely to be an unbiased sample of companies from an accounting regime. Analysis of such companies shows that the degree of disparity in GAAP translation from company to another can be large and impossible to predict from a linear conversion metric. For example, Pareira et al. (1994) calculate that on converting RTZ's net income from UK to United States (US) GAAP, the metric falls by 59 percent in 1993, but the same adjustment to Midland Bank's figures produces an increase of 20 percent. Hence, while conservatism studies are of interest, they would have to be used with caution when applying a conversion ratio to a particular company.

To a great extent, the cause of differences, and any understanding of real underlying performance, is hidden to the external user. Samuels et al. (1995) examined the possibility of translating the accounts from six different European countries as an outsider. They concluded that not enough information was available to the external analyst to make the necessary adjustment (p. 371). Hawkins (1990) is more pragmatic in setting out the Merrill Lynch method of translation, but observes that the method lacked accuracy despite being the best that could be done. The process of mapping raw accounting data to each GAAP that might be published takes place inside the company and is confidential with only the legally required information being made public. This process is shown in Figure 1, taken from Whittington and Steele (1998).

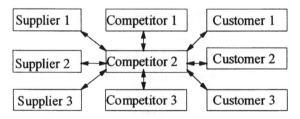

Figure 2.   Supply Chains and Comparative Analysis.

While recognizing this problem of the "black box," the article investigates whether a comparison between two competitor companies, which are based in different countries, might be said to be more meaningful when based on a common GAAP than when carried out based on the companies' domestic GAAPs. In addressing this issue, it also considers the relative stability of translation for one company.

THE NEED FOR COMPANY APPRAISAL

Many companies and individuals need to make economic choices and decisions based on the information available to them. An important subset of decisions faced by companies and individuals require analysis of individual companies and, in many cases, the comparative analysis of competitor companies. For example, an investor concerned to spread risk will attempt to diversify a portfolio over a number of industry sectors. The question that arises is which company in a sector should be chosen and which rejected. Also, companies that trade with others need to assess whether they have chosen the most appropriate trading partner. Figure 2 shows three competing supply chains and the arrows indicate the companies that "competitor 2" would need to analyze. In order to decide whether they have the best trading partners, customers, and suppliers, the company needs to analyze each of the available alternatives and to assess its own performance, comparison with competitors is required.

Some of the pieces of the decision jigsaw will be formed from analysis of the accounts of the companies concerned. Indeed, comparative ratio analysis of companies in one industry sector reduces some of the problems inherent in analyzing a company without having considered the context and the particular features of the industry. A company from an industry where cash payment for sales is the norm, for example, may well have a current ratio considerably lower than a second company in another sector whose customers generally pay after six weeks. Such a comparison would not, in itself, reveal whether either company had a liquidity problem.

Despite the advantages of analysis by competitor comparison, put forward by Moon and Bates (1993), two otherwise identical companies may publish differing accounts due to different accounting policy choices. These differences may be due to a number of reasons. Each company may have a different view of the commercial and economic environment, which may lead to differing assumptions of likely asset life. One company may decide to value intangible assets, another may not do so. The problem becomes one of a higher order

402   THE INTERNATIONAL JOURNAL OF ACCOUNTING   Vol. 35, No. 3, 2000

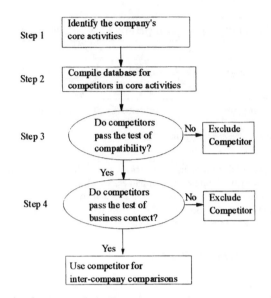

Figure 3. Choosing Companies for the Purpose of Intercompany Comparisons (from Ellis and William, 1993).

when the companies concerned are based in different countries with dissimilar culture, relationship between tax (see Lamb et al., 1998) and financial reporting, legal system, and GAAP. Some textbooks, for example Ellis and Williams (1993), advocate a selection process, as in Figure 3, where companies with incompatible accounting policies are weeded out and excluded from analysis. The desire for such a process is understandable, but will not stop senior managers requesting and needing comparison with key competitors, who may be few in number and based in different countries.

This article seeks to provide insight to these issues by adopting a case study approach, considering two key players in the European steel industry.

THE CASE STUDY: BACKGROUND

Competition in the European steel industry is international, but, mostly, still within the continent; the concept of the global steel company is still in the future, but perhaps the near future. Table 1 shows the world's leading steel companies and their sales in million of tons for 1995. It can be seen that, by this definition of size, British Steel and Usinor were the two leading European companies at the time. Both companies produce a wide range of steel products and are alternative suppliers for companies in a variety of industries including construction and vehicles. This implies that a meaningful comparison of their relative performance and financial strength will be important to investors, suppliers, customers, and other steel companies as well as to each other.

In addition to producing accounts in accordance with their domestic GAAPs, UK in the case of British Steel and French in the case of Usinor, both companies also restate their

Table 1. Largest Steelmakers

| Company | Country | 1995 | |
		Rank	Output
Nippon Steel	Japan	1	26.84
Posco	South Korea	2	23.43
British Steel	UK	3	15.74
Usinor	France	4	15.50
Riva	Italy	5	14.40
Arbed Group	Luxembourg	6	11.50
NKK	Japan	7	11.26
US Steel	USA	8	11.03
Kawasaki	Japan	9	10.44
Sumitomo Metals	Japan	10	10.44

Note: Million tons of steel sales in calendar year. Source: International Iron and Steel Institute.

Table 2. Accounting Adjustment Indices

Country	Smithers et al. (1992)	Simonds and Azieres (1989)	Gray (1980)
USA	97	NA	NA
UK	100	100	100
France	89	78	71

financial numbers in line with US GAAP. It might be assumed that such restatement to one common GAAP would improve the quality of analysis that can be undertaken and the quality of any decisions based on the results of such analysis. A time series analysis questions whether using different GAAPs produces systematic differences in the results of the analysis.

Three of the conservatism studies mentioned earlier (Gray, 1980; Simonds and Azieres, 1989; Economist, 1992) provide adjustment metrics for conversion between UK and French GAAP, our interest here. The relevant restated portion of their findings is shown in Table 2. Each of the three statistics implies that French GAAP is more conservative than UK GAAP, but differs in the degree of relative conservatism. A US comparison is also shown because both British Steel and Usinor restate their results for their US investors in accordance with US GAAP. The result shown in the table implies little difference between US and UK GAAP. Other research that has compared US and UK GAAP has concluded that US GAAP is generally more conservative (see Weetman and Gray, 1990, 1991; Weetman et al., 1998).

DATA SOURCES

The information required for the analysis is taken from the public domain. British Steel shares are traded on the International Stock Exchange in London and American Depository Receipts, equivalent to 10 shares, are traded on the New York Stock Exchange. This dual listing requires the company to produce a UK set of annual report and accounts and also a document for the Securities and Exchange Commission, form 20-F. Dual listing

Developments in Financial Reporting by Multinationals

404   THE INTERNATIONAL JOURNAL OF ACCOUNTING   Vol. 35, No. 3, 2000

Table 3. Adjustments Stated as Required in the Conversion to US GAAP

	British Steel (US$)	Usinor (US$)
Profit adjustments		
Profit attributable to shareholders: domestic GAAP	372	351
Amortization of goodwill	−23	−1
Interest costs capitalized (net of depreciation)	31	9
Investment write-down	0	15
Pension costs	−30	0
Stock-based employee compensation awards	−10	0
Treasury stock	0	1
Rationalization costs	23	0
Deferred taxation	15	−12
Accounting change	0	−23
Profit attributable to shareholders' US GAAP	379	340
Shareholders' equity adjustments		
Shareholders' equity: domestic GAAP	7,779	4,478
Goodwill	348	355
Interest costs capitalized (net of depreciation)	231	47
Pension costs	173	0
Stock-based employee compensation awards	−19	0
QUEST shares held in trust	−30	0
Treasury stock	0	−49
Rationalization costs/Restructuring provisions	24	16
Deferred taxation	−835	121
Investments in equity securities	52	0
Proposed dividend	231	0
Minority interests	0	0
Accounting change	0	61
Investments	0	48
Shareholders' equity: US GAAP	7,954	5,078

in the US has become an increasingly common practice for UK companies with some 90 companies likely to have to file a 20-F for the accounting period covering the end of 1997. The latter contains a wealth of information, including the adjustments required to convert British Steel's profit for shareholders from UK to US GAAP. The changes to convert shareholder's equity from one GAAP to the other are also included. Both the UK and US documents are independently audited.

The data for Usinor is taken from the company's annual report and accounts. Usinor is quoted on the Paris exchange, but unlike British Steel, it does not have a full listing in the US. Investment is possible in the US, however, through private placements. This method does not usually require the filing of a 20-F document, but Usinor provides information on French and US GAAP differences for both profit and shareholders' equity as a note to the English language version of their annual accounts. The company produces its main set of accounts in accordance with both International Accounting Standards (IAS) and French GAAP. The auditor comments that there is a material transaction that is not in accordance with French GAAP (or IAS) in 1993 and 1994. Each year until 1997, the auditor also comments on the translation to US GAAP as being shown "on a consistent basis," but does not state whether the revised figures also conform to US GAAP. This phrase was not used by the auditors of any of the other French companies filing 20-Fs. For the year ending December 1998 the comment is more straight forward, stating that "a complete reconciliation...is set forth in note 26" (page F2 in the 20-F for that year).

Table 3 shows the adjustments required for translation of domestic GAAP to US GAAP for both British Steel and Usinor for the years ending March 1998 and December 1997. Note the number of adjustments and that some counter each other out. Hence, there is a greater degree of underlying disharmony between the GAAPs than the net movement in profit or equity suggests.

The two companies do not have the same financial year-ends. British Steel has a financial year-end of March 31 and Usinor, December 31. Despite the 3-month difference, it was decided not to adjust the results, but to compare, for example British Steel's year ending on March 31st 1996 with Usinor's ending on December 31st 1995. Two reasons for this were, firstly, to limit the impact of one-off adjustments to one time period and, secondly, a realization that the UK and French economies did not have identical growth paths. Given a longer time series of data for both companies, the second point might be addressed by considering relative performance at similar stages of each company's domestic economic cycle. The importance of the economic cycle cannot be overstated for companies such as these (Financial Times, 1996).

CONSERVATISM INDICES

British Steel has had a quote in New York and produced a 20-F since privatization in 1988. The prospectus also included a previous year, so there are 11 data points available for the translation. Weetman et al. (1998) examine the trend in GAAP translation for UK companies with US listings from 1988 to 1994. Using the conservatism index first introduced by Gray (1980), they examine whether UK GAAP has moved closer to US GAAP over the period. They find that the distance between the two accounting approaches has widened rather than diminished as the number of companies with a material increase in reported profit when converting from UK to US GAAP has increased. Profit is a residual arising from the gap between revenue and cost, hence materiality of difference is dependent on the size of the gap. Basing materiality on a percentage of turnover would be an alternative, but, as in the case study here, assuming a materiality level of perhaps 3 percent of turnover could easily lead to the disappearance or doubling of profit that would be deemed immaterial.

The British Steel conservatism index tells an interesting, but unclear story over the 11 years (Table 4). In 5 out of the 11 years the increase in profit when converting to US GAAP is material as defined in Weetman et al. (1998), that is a gain of over 10 percent, in four there is no material adjustment and in two a material decline. Taking just the movement between 1988 and 1994, as in the aforementioned article, there is a large increase in the relative liberalism of the UK figure. However, over the 11 years as a whole, there is no discernible time trend, a regression returning an R^2 of just 0.02. The second column in the table excludes 1992 and 1993, as in these years British Steel was loss making and Whittington and Steele (1998) point out that the conservatism index has a discontinuity at zero; there remains 5 years of material

406   THE INTERNATIONAL JOURNAL OF ACCOUNTING Vol. 35, No. 3, 2000

Table 4. British Steel Conservatism Index

Year	Index value	Ignoring years with losses
1988	0.949	0.949
1989	1.391	1.391
1990	1.234	1.234
1991	1.376	1.376
1992	1.079	
1993	0.539	
1994	2.059	2.059
1995	1.365	1.365
1996	1.079	1.079
1997	0.727	0.727
1998	0.983	0.983
Index < 0.9	2	1
1.1 > Index > 0.9	3	2
Index > 1.1	5	5

Table 5. Usinor Conservatism Index

Year	Index value	Ignoring years with losses
1993	0.769	
1994	1.032	1.032
1995	0.882	0.882
1996	1.521	1.521
1997	1.097	1.097
Index < 0.9	2	1
1.1 > Index > 0.9	2	2
Index > 1.1	1	1

increase on translation, three of no significant change, and one material fall. The only noticeable trend is that of the last 3 years, two are not significant, and the other is a fall. Hence, for the way in which GAAP translation affects British Steel at least, UK GAAP has become relatively less conservative over the last 3 years than before.

As Usinor was privatized by the French government rather later than British Steel in the UK, there are less years of translation available. All three of the adjustment indices in Table 2 would lead to the expectation that the US GAAP profit reported would be higher than the French one. Table 5 shows that of the 5 years of conservatism indices, two show a material fall on translation from French to US GAAP, two no significant change, and one material rise. When rejecting the loss making 1993, there remains only one significant fall.

The variability in index is high year by year and this might be caused by a number of factors. Changing GAAPs due to introduction of new standards will mean that each year's translation is not necessarily comparable for the one before or the one after. Changing activities of the companies concerned may give rise to more significant positive or negative factors on conversion than before. For example, the movement in the index for British Steel from 1990 to 1991 could be said to be due to the

Table 6. British Steel

(US$ million)

	March 1994		March 1995		March 1996		March 1997		March 1998	
GAAP	UK	US	UK	US	UK	US	UK	US	UK	US
Net income	105	51	736	539	1,290	1,318	491	675	384	367
Equity	5,551	5,660	6,641	6,682	7,882	7,972	8,362	8,653	8,370	8,575
Return on equity (%)	2	1	11	8	16	17	6	8	5	4

Usinor

	December 1993		December 1994		December 1995		December 1996		December 1997	
GAAP	France	US	France	US	France	US	France	US	France	US
Net income	−1,199	−1,559	410	397	1,109	1,258	339	223	372	339
Equity	3,377	3,577	4,136	4,493	5,902	6,297	5,727	6,067	4,691	5,315
Return on equity (%)	−35	−43	10	9	19	20	6	4	8	6

acquisition and goodwill write-off that British Steel carried out in that year. Indeed, if it had been accounted for in the US manner in the UK accounts, then the conservatism index for 1991 would have been lower than 1990 rather than higher. Both companies have a high level of volatility in their profit levels over the periods under examination and this might also cause a distortion on the translation.

RATIO ANALYSIS

The conservatism index addressed the question of change in profit level on GAAP translation. Investors, and indeed others concerned for assessing company success, are interested in comparing profit to the level of investment made in order to generate the return. This assessment requires the use of ratios such as return on capital employed, return on net assets or return on equity.

The relative conservatism of profit calculation may be undermined by the relative conservatism of the equity stake. As not all changes in reserves are effected through the profit and loss account under some GAAPs, the likely relative change is not clear. However, it is also possible to analyze the effect of GAAP translation on some balance sheet and return based measures as well as profit because the 20-F requires a restating of the equity stake on conversion as well as the profit for the year. A breakdown of the material reasons for difference in both these figures is given by most companies, the alternative being the preparation of complete financial statements to US norms. The key measure analyzed is return on equity, this compares the profit available for shareholders to the level of shareholder investment. The ratio, and movement of it, may be taken to give an indication of relative success or failure.

408   THE INTERNATIONAL JOURNAL OF ACCOUNTING   Vol. 35, No. 3, 2000

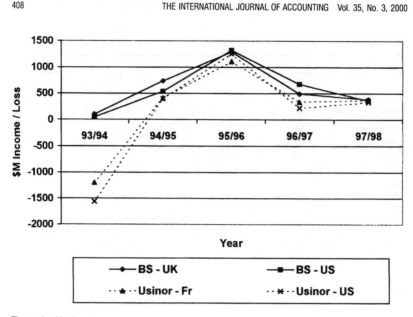

Figure 4. Net Income.

RETURN ON EQUITY

Table 6 gives the key figures for both British Steel and Usinor for the last 5 years. The accounting information has been translated into US dollars in order for direct comparison, using average rates for profit and loss account items and closing rates for balance sheet figures.

The relative movement of the domestic and US GAAP lines in Figure 4 indicates that over this limited period there is no linear pattern of adjustment in translating either company's profits from their domestic to US GAAP; this concurs with the conservatism index findings in Tables 4 and 5. Both the UK and US GAAP British Steel figures are higher than Usinor's in every year except 1997/1998, when the French GAAP profit for Usinor is greater than the US profit for British Steel despite still being below the UK GAAP profit. Figure 4 also highlights the similar trend behind each company's result showing how both companies are subject to similar competitive and economic pressures.

Figure 5 shows the size of the equity stake in each company under both domestic and US GAAP. There is a small, but repeated increase in equity when restating both companies' domestic GAAP figures to US GAAP. This appears particularly stable for Usinor. The level of British Steel's equity investment is considerably larger than that of Usinor, hence it is not clear whether the higher profit level of the UK company will translate into a higher return on equity.

Arguably, British Steel's equity stake is overstated as it includes the sizeable, £2,338 million (approximately US$3,935 million), statutory reserve that was set aside on

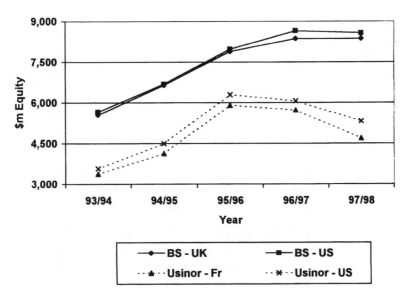

Figure 5. Equity.

privatization to equate the balance sheet size with the value of the issued shares. In effect there is no duty of care due to any stakeholder for this sum as the funds represented by it were not provided by the current shareholders. For the purpose of comparison, however, it needs to be included as it does represent investment made at an earlier stage in the company's life. British Steel's equity stake is also likely to higher than Usinor's due to adopting a different, longer, view of likely asset life. This policy of slower depreciation should lead to higher profits, as seen above, and higher equity stake as long as both companies keep investing in fixed assets.

The return on equity figures, from Table 6, are plotted on Figure 6. Usinor's return for 1993 is not shown as the large negative percentage distorts the *y* axis range unduly. Again, Figure 6 shows the two companies moving in tandem and that the industry is a volatile one. There is no obvious pattern behind the relative performance of one company against the other or, indeed, between either basis for reporting. It would seem that British Steel outperformed on both a domestic and common GAAP basis in 1993/1994, but that Usinor did the same in 1995/1996 and 1997/1998. The results for 1994/1995 and 1996/1997 are more confused. In 1994/1995, British Steel outperforms on a domestic comparison and Usinor does so under US GAAP. In 1996/1997, British Steel outperforms on the US GAAP figures, but Usinor does so on the domestic ones. Without considering the remaining differences in accounting policy choice and application, the figures suggest that since 1993/1994 performance has been fairly similar and certainly that neither company is consistently outperforming the other.

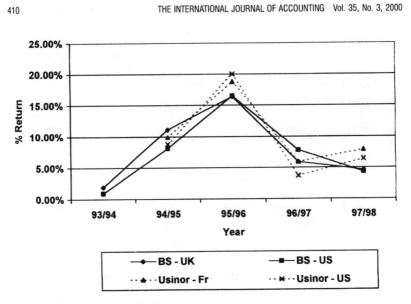

Figure 6.   Return of Equity (US$ million).

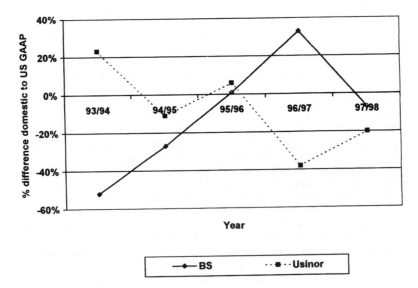

Figure 7.   Percentage Difference on Return of Equity.

Figure 7 shows the percentage difference in translating the return on equity from domestic to US GAAP. There appears no common pattern of adjustment here, the particularly large swings in 1996/1997 occurred when return on equity was low. Hence, a difference of 2.2 percent represents a swing of some 60 percent.

CONCLUSION

The degree in improvement in the quality of analysis of using a common GAAP is difficult to quantify. If one of the companies is outperforming the other consistently, then the consistent GAAP analysis does no more to reveal this than the domestic comparison. The seeming lack of predictability, at least from past conversion factors, of the overall effect of conversion to US GAAP, especially for British Steel, as shown in both Table 4 and Figure 7, potentially undermines any attempt to address the problem of future trends and likely relative success of each company. However, some progress towards predicting converted profit or return may be possible because component parts of the conversion could be forecast with some accuracy.

The high level of cyclical variation in the industry may distort consistent differences that might have been found if performance were more stable. The cyclical impact on profit and return for both companies is clearly seen whichever GAAP is adopted.

An analyst is interested in investigating both static and dynamic performance using a variety of analytical techniques and should be concerned about how differences in accounting might potentially undermine any conclusions that might otherwise be reached. Year-on-year changes in relative performance might be caused by a combination of four factors:

a. change in company performance,
b. change in performance of key markets and economies;
c. change in corporate accounting policy choice; and
d. change in either domestic or US GAAP.

The assessment of underlying corporate performance would be the objective of customer, supplier or competitor appraisal, the other three factors are likely to distort the interpretation of financial results in such an analysis. The differing relative importance of individual markets to each company would need to be understood. In this instance, the French domestic steel market is of greater importance to Usinor and the UK market similarly to British Steel. Both are players in each, but the effect of boom or slump in either will not cause equal joy or pain.

A decision to change accounting policies may not be apparent to the casual reader of a set of accounts, but the impact on profit could be significant, particularly if profit levels are not high. It needs to remembered that US GAAP still allows a degree of accounting policy choice for a company and so, for example, British Steel and Usinor use very different asset lives for similar categories of asset when US GAAP is adopted. Domestic cultural and legal frameworks for each company remain unaltered and the application of US GAAP under these differing circumstances is unlikely to produce completely comparable accounts. If one were to introduce a US company into the comparison, it would be

412   THE INTERNATIONAL JOURNAL OF ACCOUNTING   Vol. 35, No. 3, 2000

materially affected by the nature of pension funds in the US and how US companies are instructed to account for pension and post-retirement liabilities. Any time series analysis would be affected by the related changes in US GAAP over the last few years.

GAAPs only remain "generally accepted" within a short time frame, and in many years, one could argue that introduction of new standards implies a discontinuity from previous results for the same company.

The need to produce comparative company analysis spanning international boundaries is likely to increase rather than diminish as many markets continue their trend to globalization. Analysis of published accounts is not the only tool available; use of stock market data, undercover investigations, conversations with mutual trading partners, for example, are also useful. It would be anticipated, at least by non-accountants, that ratio analysis could play a part in building up a complete picture. Hence, the quality of such analyses remains a serious issue. A line-by-line approach to accounting statement adjustment can be attempted, reworking each company to a common base, but lack of information will force the analyst to rely on their own judgment as well as published information. The additional US GAAP data may assist in this lengthy process. The individual undertaking the task needs to be well informed regarding all relevant GAAPs.

Further Research

The examination of other pairings of companies that report in multiple GAAPs would shed further light on the advantages of common GAAP assessment; choosing an industrial sector with a more stable environment might enable the benefits of using a common GAAP to appear more obvious. Further longitudinal studies of companies to seek out any common adjustment factor for a single firm may also be of interest. The volatility in the conservatism index over time for one company suggests that there may be further work to be done in this area focusing on the underlying causes of the measurement disparity between GAAPs. This article has highlighted the need to assess the effect of GAAP selection on the balance sheet as well as the profit and loss account. There is further work here, too, assessing GAAP impact on issues such as leverage and provisions.

REFERENCES

Economist. 1992. "Market Focus: All the World's a Ratio—The Boom in International Portfolio Investment is Stimulating New Ways of Comparing Stockmarkets." *Economist,* (February) *22.*

Ellis, J. and D. Williams. 1993. *Corporate Strategy and Financial Analysis.* London: Pitman Publishing.

Financial Times. 1996. "The Lex Column: Cyclical Stocks." *Financial Times,* September 2: 20.

French, K. R. and J. M. Poterba. 1991. "Were Japanese Stock Prices Too High?" *Journal of Financial Economics, 29:* 337–363.

Gray, S. J. 1980. "The Impact of International Accounting Differences From a Security-Analysis Perspective: Some European Evidence." *Journal of Accounting Research, 18*(1): 65–76.

Hawkins, D. F. 1990. *"Direct Transnational Financial Statement Analysis: Converting IAS to US GAAP."* Accounting Bulletin, (September). A publication of Merrill Lynch Capital

Markets. Reprinted in Zeff and Dharan (1994). *Readings and Notes on Financial Accounting.* McGraw-Hill 2: 1–13.

Lamb, M., C. Nobes, and A. Roberts. 1998. "International Variations in the Connection Between Tax and Financial Reporting." *Accounting and Business Research, 26*(3): 173–188.

Moon, P. and K. Bates. 1993. "Core Analysis in Strategic Performance Appraisal." *Management Accounting Research,* June*(4)*: 139–152.

Nobes, C. and R. Parker. 1998. *Comparative International Accounting,* 5th edn. UK: Prentice-Hall.

Pereira, V., R. Paterson, and A. Wilson. 1994. *UK/US GAAP Comparison.* London: Kogan Page.

Samuels, J. M., R. E. Brayshaw, and J. M. Craner. 1995. *Financial Statement Analysis in Europe.* London: Chapman and Hall.

Simonds, A. and O. Azieres. 1989. *Accounting for Europe—Success by 2000 AD?* Touche Ross.

Weetman, P. and S. J. Gray. 1990. International Financial Analysis and Comparative Performance: The Impact of UK versus US Accounting Principles on Earnings. *Journal of International Financial Management and Accounting, 2* (2 and 3): 111–130.

Weetman, P. and S. J. Gray. 1991. "A Comparative International Analysis of the Impact of Accounting Principles on Profits: the USA versus the UK, Sweden and the Netherlands." *Accounting and Business Research, 21*(84): 363–379.

Weetman, P., E. A. E. Jones, C. Adams, and S. J. Gray. 1998. "Profit Measurement and UK Accounting Standards: A Case of Increasing Disharmony in Relation to US GAAP and IAS's." *Accounting and Business Research, 28*(3): 189–208.

Whittington, M. and A. Steele. 1998. "Still Searching for Excellence? International Accounting and the World's Most Outstanding Companies." *British Journal of Management, 9*(3): 233–247.

Name Index